Research Guide
to Philosophy

Research Guide to Philosophy

Terrence N. Tice and Thomas P. Slavens

SOURCES OF INFORMATION
IN THE HUMANITIES
NO. 3

CHICAGO

American Library Association

1983

312 944-6780

Sources of Information in the Humanities
Thomas P. Slavens, series editor

Research Guide to Religious Studies by John Wilson
and Thomas P. Slavens

Research Guide to the History of Western Art by W. Eugene
Kleinbauer and Thomas P. Slavens

Designed by Harvey Retzloff

Composed by Automated Office Systems Inc.
  in Sabon on a Text Ed/VIP
  phototypesetting system

Printed on 60-pound Glatfelter, a pH-
  neutral stock, and bound in
  C-grade Holliston Roxite cloth
  by Braun-Brumfield, Inc.

Library of Congress Cataloging in Publication Data

Tice, Terrence N., 1931– .
  Research guide to philosophy.

  (Sources of information in the humanities ; no. 3)
  Includes bibliographies and indexes.
    1. Philosophy—Study and teaching—History.
  2. Philosophy—Historiography.   I. Slavens, Thomas P.,
  1928- . II. Title. III. Series.
  B52.T5   1983   107   83-11834
  ISBN 0-8389-0333-9

CONTENTS

Preface   ix

Preface to the Series   xi

Part I.   THE HISTORY OF PHILOSOPHY

1. *Philosophy Past and Present*   3
   A Historical Approach to Philosophy   3
   General Histories   7

2. *Ancient Philosophy*   11
   The Presocratics and After   11
   Socrates (470–399 B.C.)   18
   Plato (427–347), Aristotle, and the Academy   21
   Aristotle (384–322)   33
   Hellenistic Philosophy and Its Aftermath   46

3. *Medieval, Renaissance, and Reformation Philosophy*   51
   Medieval Philosophy   51
   Renaissance and Reformation Philosophy   69

4. *Seventeenth-Century Philosophy*   74
   Overview   74
   René Descartes (1596–1650)   80
   Blaise Pascal (1623–1662)   83
   Benedict (Baruch) Spinoza (1632–1677)   85
   Gottfried Wilhelm Leibniz (1646–1716)   88
   Thomas Hobbes (1588–1679)   91
   John Locke (1632–1704)   94

5. *Eighteenth-Century Philosophy* 97
Overview 97
George Berkeley (1685–1753) 102
David Hume (1711–1776) 107
Jean-Jacques Rousseau (1712–1778) 110
Immanuel Kant (1724–1804) 113

6. *Nineteenth-Century Philosophy* 123
Continental European Philosophy 123
Georg Wilhelm Friedrich Hegel (1770–1831) 135
British Philosophy 143

7. *Twentieth-Century Philosophy* 150
Analysis: Logic and Language 150
Diversity of Methods, Approaches, and Positions 156
Philosophy Around the World 158

8. *Twentieth-Century British Philosophy* 161
Analytic Philosophy 161
Bertrand Russell (1872–1970) 172
G. E. Moore (1873–1958) 181
R. G. Collingwood (1889–1943) 188
Karl Popper (1902–) 198
Ludwig Wittgenstein (1889–1951) 203
Alfred North Whitehead (1861–1947) 210

9. *Twentieth-Century American Philosophy* 216
Early History 216
Scholarship and Tasks 220
Further Developments and Themes 223

10. *Pragmatism* 231
Themes and Developments 231
William James (1842–1910) 235
Charles Sanders Peirce (1839–1914) 237
John Dewey (1859–1952) 241
George Herbert Mead (1863–1931) 246

11. *Marx and Marxism* 248
Karl Marx (1818–1883) 248
Marxism 256

12. *Existentialism* 262
Overview 262

Søren Kierkegaard (1813–1855)   265
Friedrich Nietzsche (1844–1900)   267
Martin Buber (1878–1965)   271
Karl Jaspers (1883–1969)   272
Gabriel Marcel (1889–1973)   274
Jean-Paul Sartre (1905–1980)   275
Martin Heidegger (1889–1976)   278

13. *Phenomenology, Hermeneutics, and Critical
    Theory   285*
    Overview of Phenomenology   285
    Edmund Husserl (1859–1938)   287
    Maurice Merleau-Ponty (1908–1961)   291
    Hermeneutics and Critical Theory   293

Part II. AREAS OF PHILOSOPHY

14. *Contemporary Philosophical Inquiry   305*
    Contemporary Study of Philosophy   305
    The Areas of Philosophy   306
    Relations to Other Disciplines   307
    Rising Themes   310

15. *Epistemology: Theory of Knowledge   313*

16. *Logic   328*

17. *Philosophy of Language and Linguistic
    Philosophy   339*

18. *Metaphysics   348*

19. *Philosophy of Mind   361*

20. *Philosophy of Action   372*

21. *Axiology: Values Inquiry   379*

22. *Ethics: Moral Philosophy   385*

23. *Philosophy of Science   410*

24. *Philosophy of History   428*

25. *Social-Political Philosophy   436*

26. *Philosophy of Law   452*

27. *Aesthetics: Philosophy of Art   460*

28. *Philosophy of Religion*   471

29. *Philosophy of Psychology and Psychoanalysis*   483

30. *Philosophy of Education*   490

Part III. REFERENCE WORKS

Bibliography   503
Dictionaries and Encyclopedias   508
Digests and Handbooks   511
Directories   512
Dissertation Index   513
Series   513

Author-Title Index   517

Subject Index   587

PREFACE

Philosophy has ancient beginnings, yet most of its significant literature has appeared in the last 100 years, a major revolution has occurred since 1945, and a still sharper rise in quality and scope of effort has become manifest during the past twenty years in virtually every area. This work depicts the principal changes since the late nineteenth century in the main areas of philosophy and the history of philosophy, and registers the more representative and exemplary literature in each subfield. It is the first survey of its kind. The timing is most propitious because the field has burgeoned to such an extent that even philosophers are often not in touch with more than a few areas; because the bibliographic resources in philosophy are comparatively poor; and because a great deal of the material from recent years is of interest to readers from other fields.

In modern tradition, the "humanities" has comprised essentially the triad philosophy, literature, and history, accompanied by various hybrids and extensions into history and criticism of the arts, including music, into religion, and into other concerns with language. Philosophy significantly deals with the specific subject matter of all these fields as well as its own, and with subject matter from the sciences as well. Thus there was a great deal to examine; but the more important work in practically every area can be accessed through the resources cited here.

Further, the work is designed so that it can either be read through as an introduction to philosophy and its developing historical-critical literature, or be read by sections according to interest. Readers are encouraged to use the indexes for further garnering of themes, bibliographies, and cross-references.

I must emphasize that, with rare exceptions, a piece of genuine philosophical work cannot be summarized. What is offered here is mostly background and characterization. Without this, most of the references would be meaningless or misleading to the nonexpert. At the same time, in providing significant order, clarity, perspective, and critique, this book is something of a philosophical work in its own right.

Several acknowledgments are in order. First are the dozens of other philosophers over the past thirty years who have influenced the understanding, methods, and perspectives I have brought to this work. Apart from numerous contemporaries, I especially think of teacher-colleagues Robert Bretall and Charles Wallraff from Tucson; Martin Buber, Emile Cailliet, Walter Kaufmann, Gregory Vlastos, and Ledger Wood from Princeton; from my Basel sojourn the brothers Heinrich and Karl Barth and Karl Jaspers; and from the University of Michigan Henry David Aiken, Richard Brandt, Irving Copi, William Frankena, Abraham Kaplan, Arnold Kaufman, George Mavrodes, Julius Moravcsik, and J. O. Urmson. I also think gratefully upon my parents, who first taught me both to inquire critically and to explore widely but not to shirk affirmation—and who insisted that I learn to type. All these were necessary conditions for the production of this work. Heaven knows where my willingness to do the indexing came from; but I do believe such work is an author's responsibility.

Thanks also to my colleagues in the School of Education, who awarded me a resources grant and other invaluable supports, and in the Urban, Technological and Environmental Planning doctoral program, who tolerated a two-year diminution of involvement there. I am equally appreciative of the help given by the University of Michigan's library staff and by Marilyn Gross, who ably assisted me in the stacks.

TERRENCE N. TICE

PREFACE TO THE SERIES

The purpose of this series is to help humanists, librarians, students of library science, and other interested persons in the use of resources in the humanities. The series encompasses art, linguistics, literature, music, philosophy, and religion. These fields share an interest in the creative, aesthetic, and imaginative impulses of human beings and the cultures in which they live. Individuals find joy in music, art, and literature; others thoroughly enjoy discussing linguistics and philosophy; and a basic religious impulse has prompted the quest for emotional and intellectual fulfillment. Scholarship in the humanities has been produced with the goal of enhancing the quality of human life while seeking to understand it more adequately, and those who seek information about the humanities make use of libraries; often, however, they become confused by the large quantities of available materials.

This series, then, is intended as a guide in the search for information in the humanities. The series, as previously noted, consists of six titles covering art, linguistics, literature, music, philosophy, and religion. The plan calls for each volume to be divided into two parts. The first (in the present volume the first two parts) features a survey of the field by a specialist, and the second (here the third) is an annotated list of major reference works. The survey in this volume was prepared by Terrence N. Tice of the University of Michigan. It includes a history of the field, a description of methodology, and current issues and research. The descriptions of issues and research summarize critical assessments of significant monographs, with an emphasis on modern scholarship. Ordinarily they do not cite primary sources, such as the Bible, Shakespeare's plays, music, or art, with the exception that works in philosophy are generally primary sources, even works about philosophers. Rather, the essays focus on the concepts presented in key secondary works. They stress Western subjects and titles; in the case of literature, because of the mass of materials available, the essays emphasize Engish literature. Citations are given in full following each section.

The second part of each volume (here the third part) lists and annotates major reference works. The list, prepared by the series editor, relates subject scholarship to bibliography, thus expediting information retrieval.

Many people have assisted in the preparation of this series. They include the Publishing Services staff of the American Library Association, without whose encouragement the series would not have been produced. The collaborators are also grateful for financial assistance from the University of Michigan which granted us the first Warner G. Rice Faculty Award in the Humanities for the purpose of assisting in the preparation of this book. These funds were used to employ Marjorie Corey, Anne Deason, Richard Heritage, Margaret Hillmer, Patricia Kirschner, Karen O'Donnell, Robert Krupp, Gail Davis, Nancy Green, Rex Miller, Mary Beth Sasso, and Barbara Vaccaro as research assistants in this project; their endeavors are very much appreciated. Shirley A. Culliton, the faculty secretary of the School of Library Science at the University of Michigan, has been invaluable in the preparation of these books.

We also take pleasure in thanking the professors who wrote the essays. They represent the best of humanistic scholarship in the United States and have made a major contribution to the organization of information in their disciplines.

THOMAS P. SLAVENS

PART I

THE HISTORY
OF
PHILOSOPHY

1

Philosophy
Past and Present

A historical approach dominates both of the first two parts of this book, governing both exposition and bibliographic selection. For brevity's sake, I offer six tightly packed theses, regrettably without argument, so as to show where I stand in general terms. The expositions themselves should make fairly clear what primary arguments could be offered in their support.

1. *Problem Orientation.* The discourse that is of philosophical interest among the thoughts philosophers have presented consists of responses to questions that have truly arisen for them, out of their own personal, historical, and intellectual circumstances (all three, probably for the most part inseparably). To a great extent, these questions will also have led to formulations of specific problems for further inquiry. (In contrast, the vision of constructing a cohesive philosophical system—an "ism"—ordinarily lies more in the eye of the pedantic beholder than in the minds of philosophers themselves, particularly in our day. Moreover, it is the various types of problems that keep cropping up, not the same problems; and this recurrence is not always or necessarily because the old problems failed of solution. Actually, in philosophy, as in science and art, sometimes the most effective "solutions," though faulty, have alone made the discovery of important new problems possible.)

2. *Attention to Argument.* Philosophers have tended to be strongly influenced by argument and to present arguments for their own positions with a rigor that exceeds the canons of rhetoric and is often in opposition to them. (See chapter 2 for discussion of philosophical disagreement.)

3

3. *Pluralistic Tradition.* Cultural and biographical factors, direct and indirect (and including factors of temperament or character), though rarely made explicit, bear an extremely important influence on the methods and positions philosophers take. So far, philosophical historians have seldom sought out such information. That they have nonetheless succeeded in interesting other philosophical readers bears witness to the powerful presence of philosophical tradition, within which many of these factors are simply presupposed. Ordinarily philosophical tradition is manifested in several divergent strains within each period.

4. *Meaningful Development.* Meaningful continuity and development of thoughts can be demonstrated when extracted from the variegated display found in philosophically minded discourse. In the strict sense, such development is perhaps never to be seen as representing a perennial repetition or sheer identity of thoughts. Nor is it wholly appropriate to interpret the development according to preordained dialectical rules (Hegel; see Walsh in Passmore, 1965), prefabricated component "ideas" (Lovejoy, 1936) or a supposed "spirit" of the age (Cassirer; see Klibansky, 1936). (This is not to proscribe all interpretative schemes or to deny that there is any such thing as "philosophic tradition," but rather to point out excesses often found in histories of ideas.)

5. *Historical Mindedness.* Historical studies and surveys are valuable to philosophical thinkers not only to stimulate current inquiry, for which we need do neither accurate nor very culturally informed reading, but especially to inform our understanding and estimate of past efforts, to enable us to appreciate where our own presuppositions have come from, and to strengthen our grasp both of the nature of philosophical controversy and of what constitutes genuine advance in philosophical inquiry.

6. *Joint Inquiry.* The history of philosophy is studied with greatest success if one learns how to listen to modes of speaking from several traditions of interpretation, a secondary but essential means to critical, interactive, and comparative analysis of the texts themselves. Moreover, the ultimate aims of learning such attentiveness are greater understanding of problems and possibilities and facility for further joint inquiry and dispute, not prowess in combat.

In some fashion philosophers have reflected systematically on their uses of the past at least since Augustine. Not until the onset of formal, comprehensive histories of philosophy in the eighteenth century did a few begin to form an argued position on the matter. With

Friedrich Schleiermacher in the early nineteenth century, thorough-going engagement of interpretive issues, which he called "hermeneutic," began in earnest. This discipline was firmly grounded in a combination of logical, metaphysical, epistemological, and historical inquiry that he called "dialectic," a term that had gained new currency since Kant. Only some of Schleiermacher's relevant work has been translated from the German (e.g., 1966; and *Hermeneutics*, 1977, cited on p. 301); more is in process. Hermeneutical interests came to be accompanied, and for a long time surpassed, by Georg W. F. Hegel's own version of dialectic, which attempted to capture the dynamic processes of human history in terms of a logical structure of advancing ideas. The kind of inquiry advocated by Hegel, though not his alone, has influenced twentieth-century efforts to do intellectual history, especially the history of ideas (Boas et al., 1953; Lovejoy, 1936) and to a lesser extent both cultural history with a philosophical center (Klibansky, 1936) and culturally oriented history of philosophy (Dewey, 1948; Randall, 1963). In viewing philosophy as social expression, Albert Levi (1974) utilizes all three approaches.

Three motifs govern current activity in this area, which I will call the hermeneutical, the dialectical, and the analytical. Hermeneutics, as inaugurated by Schleiermacher, is a deep-set examination of intellectual assumptions, psychological orientations, and linguistic usages bent toward understanding distinctive patterns of thought. It has only begun to come into its own over the past three decades (see Palmer, *Hermeneutics*, 1969, cited on p. 301). Echoes are to be found, however, in R. G. Collingwood's question-and-answer method (1939; see also chapter 8) and in existential and other humanistic investigations of language and its social contexts, as in James Collins's extraordinary survey (1972) of philosophical scholarship. Echoes resound in psychoanalytically oriented studies, as in essays on philosophical method by linguistic philosopher Morris Lazerowitz (e.g., *The Language of Philosophy*, 1977) and in Ben-Ami Scharfstein's unparalleled comprehensive study, *The Philosophers* (1980); in Walter Kaufmann's numerous studies (e.g., *Discovering the Mind*, 1980) geared toward "discovering the mind"; and in radical critiques of its own recent traditions within analytic philosophy itself, most recently in an eminently stimulating challenge by Richard Rorty (1979). In all these examples dialectical and analytic strands are also evident. I take "hermeneutics" to be the more encompassing category, though by this I do not mean to identify specifically with contemporary European schools of hermeneutical philosophy. Dialectical features are especially evident where comparisons are made on the basis of a formal, not merely metaphorical, scheme of concepts; sometimes, as in Hegel, these are presented in a synoptic or historically developmental framework, or both. Analysis goes to the fine details of language and logic. Over the past decade or so, each year an increasing number of interpretive works by analytic philosophers have deliberately folded hermeneutical and dialectical elements into their predominately analytical approach.

In short, a new area of philosophy is emerging, currently called by some "philosophy of the history of philosophy," for example by Lewis White Beck et al. (1969). Accordingly, the field has begun to form its own historiography, already significantly marked by Harold Clark (1962) and more recently treated in essays by Jonathan Ree et al. (1978), preeminently by Maurice Mandelbaum (1976). Most notably, this has begun to occur within analytic philosophy itself, spurred especially by John Passmore (1964, 1965). For several decades only a few analytic philosophers would have anything to do with historical studies that incorporated the hermeneutical or the dialectical strands, which are today much stronger in Europe. In North America and Britain those two strands are more evident in intellectual history, now mostly practiced by scholars in other fields, or in history of ideas, which some philosophers pursue. In fact, most of the significant work both in the history of philosophy and in the philosophy of the history of philosophy is being done by analytic philosophers. Although there are some signs of a broadening of interest beyond analysis of language and arguments, analysis is currently the predominant mode among Anglo-American studies in this area.

Beck, Lewis White, et al. "Philosophy of the History of Philosophy." *Monist* 53, no. 4: 523–670 (Oct. 1969).

Boas, George, Harold Cherniss, et al. *Studies in Intellectual History*. Baltimore, Md.: Johns Hopkins Univ. Pr., 1953.

Clark, Harold R. *Philosophy and Its History*. La Salle, Ill.: Open Court, 1962.

Collingwood, Robin G. *Autobiography*. Oxford and New York: Oxford Univ. Pr., 1939.

Collins, James. *Interpreting Modern Philosophy*. Princeton, N.J.: Princeton Univ. Pr., 1972.

Dewey, John. *Reconstruction in Philosophy*. Enl. ed. Boston: Beacon Pr., 1948. (1st ed., 1920.)

Kaufmann, Walter. *Discovering the Mind*. 3v. New York: McGraw-Hill, 1980. (Goethe, Kant, Nietzsche, Heidegger, Buber, and Freud versus Adler and Jung.)

Klibansky, Raymond, and Herbert James Paton, eds. *Philosophy and History: Essays Presented to Ernst Cassirer.* Oxford: Clarendon Pr., 1936.

Lazerowitz, Morris. *The Language of Philosophy: Freud and Wittgenstein.* Dordrecht and Boston: Reidel, 1977.

Levi, Albert William. *Philosophy as Social Expression.* Chicago and London: Univ. of Chicago Pr., 1974.

Lovejoy, Arthur O. *The Great Chain of Being: A Study of the History of an Idea.* Cambridge, Mass.: Harvard Univ. Pr., 1936.

Mandelbaum, Maurice. "On the Historiography of Philosophy." *Philosophy Research Archives* 2:708–44 (1976).

Passmore, John A. "Philosophical Scholarship in the United States, 1930–1960." In *Philosophy,* pp. 1–124. Ed. by Roderick M. Chisholm et al. Englewood Cliffs, N.J.: Prentice-Hall, 1964.

———, ed. *The Historiography of the History of Philosophy,* Beiheft 5 of *History and Theory.* The Hague: Mouton, 1965. (Essays by Passmore, Maurice Mandelbaum, W. H. Walsh, and Eugene Kamenka.)

Randall, John Herman, Jr. *How Philosophy Uses Its Past.* New York: Columbia Univ. Pr., 1963.

Ree, Jonathan; Michael Ayers; and Adam Westoby. *Philosophy and Its Past.* Hassocks, Sussex: Harvester Pr., 1978.

Rorty, Richard. *Philosophy and the Mirror of Nature.* Princeton, N.J.: Princeton Univ. Pr., 1979. (A review article: Richard J. Bernstein, "Philosophy in the Conversation of Mankind." *Review of Metaphysics* 33, no. 4:745–75 (June 1980).)

Scharfstein, Ben-Ami. *The Philosophers: Their Lives and the Nature of Their Thought.* Oxford: Blackwell; New York: Oxford Univ. Pr., 1980.

Schleiermacher, Friedrich. *Brief Outline on the Study of Theology.* Tr. with introductions and notes by Terrence N. Tice. Richmond, Va.: John Knox Press, 1966. (Application of historical-hermeneutical principles to theological studies.)

GENERAL HISTORIES

Much of the best historical work is, of necessity, in the form of commentaries or critical, reflective encounters. In contrast, general histories better serve to provide orientation and background, if taken with more than a grain of salt, rather than to represent or reenact actual thought. Most of the methodological spectrum of general histories produced since the late nineteenth century is well represented in the following eleven among those available in English. Almost all these histories are primarily what John Passmore has called "elucidatory" histories. As such, each tends to emphasize either a "doxographical" form (a listing of opinions, usually by "systems" or "schools of thought"), a "retrospective" form (a tracing of continuous development to the present) or a "problematic" form (an account of so-called perennial problems or of types of problems that change with new understanding), though elements of the "polemical" (in opposition or defense) and the "cultural" motifs are also present.

J. E. Erdmann (1890) was a conservative, right-wing Hegelian, and the last two volumes of his work are good surveys of German philosophy as seen from that vantage point. In a masterfully tolerant and percipient way, Frederick Copleston (1963–66) envisions what he takes to be the truth from the perspective of a modern-day Thomas Aquinas, in his nine volumes attempting to distinguish what serves understanding of that truth from what diverges from it. In contrast to both, the survey by Wilhelm Windelband (1901), a neo-Kantian classicist, attempts to offer a "historical interweaving of various lines of thought, out of which our theory of the world and life has grown." Most of his book is devoted to premodern philosophy, especially that of the Greeks and Romans. This plan is based on the belief that "for a historical understanding of our intellectual existence, the forging out of the conceptions which the Greek mind wrested from the concrete reality found in Nature and human life, is more important than all that has since been thought—the Kantian philosophy excepted." All three works are primarily doxographical and polemical.

The history by Frank Thilly, twice revised by Ledger Wood (1957), is perhaps the most solid short survey ever made. Adding more features of the retrospective and problematic type to the mixture just described, they sought to expose important ideas as these arose within specific movements and within still larger historical patterns. Their accounts are informed by a comparatively open rationalistic and critical idealism. The work focuses broadly on philosophies as "systems of thought." Perhaps its greatest value lies in its firm and clear reminder that every substantial effort in philosophy is indebted to critically informed study of past efforts and could always benefit from still more such study. Here I take "critical" to mean especially (1) being aware of assumptions, including tacit or implicit ones, of the principal determinants of method or personal approach, and of sociocultural influences; and (2) uncovering inconsistencies, omissions, and other difficulties once the thought is understood on its own terms. This view has become something of a norm among philosophers using primary texts in instruction, though it is countered by a strong current against first understanding texts historically.

Bertrand Russell's history (1945) is an impressionistic, entertaining romp in seventy-six brisk chapters. The main purpose is "to exhibit philosophy as an integral part of social and political life." The book is more notable for its ready wit than for the rigorous logical-empirical analyses that have made him one of the premier philosophers of this century. He does look at some problems in a philosophically interesting way, but the discourse is chiefly polemical and cultural, although also elucidatory in a broad sense.

Analytic philosopher John Passmore has become something of a dean of analytic historians of philosophy. His superb problem-oriented work (1957) is restricted to logic, epistemology, and metaphysics since the mid-nineteenth century, and the main criterion of choice is: "To what extent have the ideas of this writer entered into the public domain of philosophical discussion in England?" D. J. O'Connor's collection (1964) presents essays by twenty-four British and three American scholars, mainly depicting doctrines and arguments of major philosophers, critically and in the analytic mode. These bear a distinct, though not exclusive, preoccupation with epistemology. (See chapter 15 for an explanation.) The authors primarily draw out what interests them, given concerns of our own period. Only seven chapters are devoted to premodern thought. Antony Flew (1971) is also a prominent analytic philosopher, looking especially to past ideas that are of interest for current inquiry.

W. T. Jones (1952) for the most part serves up "representative thinkers," each mostly through key passages, adding linking comment and criticism. He also strives to place each thinker within his local cultural milieu. The "modern mind," for Jones, is distinguished by its regrettable failure to achieve anything like the great syntheses of Plato, Aristotle, and Aquinas in the light of its own predominant world view based on science. This is not a worry that the analytic colleagues just cited would share, though they do tend to share elements of a "scientific" world view. Stimulated by John Dewey, whose philosophical program centers on what it means to think and act with scientific intelligence in contemporary culture, John Herman Randall (1962–65) imbeds the "career" of philosophy within cultural history. Neither man sees philosophical problems to be so distinctly separable from sociocultural determinants or consequences as analytic interpreters have usually viewed them.

Intellectual historians who use a history of ideas approach often border on what Randall was doing, as in Crane Brinton's much-read *Ideas and Men* (1962) and in the multivolume popular histories of Will Durant (not cited here). Their work tends to be about philosophy, not in or of it. Such studies may contain important philosophical elements or may contribute to the historical understanding of philosophy, and in these ways may serve philosophical study well. Ordinarily, however, they do not analyze specific puzzles, problems, and arguments, together with their conceptual interrelations, or subject them to critical scrutiny, tasks emphasized in recent historical studies in philosophy.

Brinton, Crane. *Ideas and Men: The Story of Western Thought.* 2nd ed. New York: Prentice-Hall, 1962. (1st ed., 1950.)

Copleston, Frederick C. *A History of Philosophy.* New rev. ed. 8v. Ramsey, N.J.: Newman Pr., 1963–66. Vol. 9, *Maine de Biran to Sartre.* Ramsey, N.J.: Paulist/Newman Pr., 1975. (A tenth volume is to appear.)

Erdmann, Johann Eduard. *History of Philosophy.* 3v. New York: Macmillan, London: Sonnenscheim, 1890. (German ed., 1866.)

Flew, Antony. *An Introduction to Western Philosophy: Ideas and Argument from Plato to Sartre.* Indianapolis, Ind.: Bobbs-Merrill, 1971.

Jones, William T. *A History of Western Philosophy.* New York: Harcourt, Brace, 1952.

O'Connor, Daniel J., ed. *A Critical History of Western Philosophy.* London: Free Pr., 1964.

Passmore, John A. *A Hundred Years of Philosophy.* London: Duckworth, 1957.

Randall, John Herman, Jr. *The Career of Philosophy.* 2v. New York: Columbia Univ. Pr., 1962–65. (Middle Ages through the age of Darwin.)

Russell, Bertrand. *A History of Western Philosophy and Its Connection with Political and Social Circumstances from the Earliest Times to Present Day.* New York: Simon & Schuster, 1945.

Thilly, Frank. *A History of Philosophy.* 3rd ed. Rev. by Ledger Wood. New York: Holt, 1957. (Earlier eds., 1914, 1951.)

Windelband, Wilhelm. *A History of Philosophy.* 2nd ed. Tr. by James H. Tufts. New York: Macmillan, 1901. (1st ed. was translated from the 1st German ed. of 1892; the 3rd German ed., 1903.)

2

Ancient Philosophy

Before the sixth century B.C., Greek thought about the world emphasized chaos, sudden immediacy, and a frightful feeling of confusion, what Julian Jaynes (1976) termed a relatively "unconscious," unreflective awareness. Otto Brendel's study (1977) of the sphere as an important symbol in Greek philosophy from that time on nicely illustrates the change. He focuses on a Hellenistic painting that shows Thales, the first Presocratic philosopher, heading the company of the Seven Sages (with Thales the only philosopher) in conversation about a sphere. This symbol came to signify several things the discovery of which was attributed by early Greek thinkers to Thales, namely: that the sphere represents that divine unity and origin which has no beginning or end and which encompasses everything. Brendel notes that the sphere was also to point from physical cosmology, the major preoccupation of the Presocratic philosophers, to magical and mystical speculation, thus representing basic themes retained throughout the Middle Ages and into modern times. Among subsequent Greek thinkers, the firmament was depicted as spherical and the sphere as the most perfect, most beautiful body. In Stoic thought universal mind *(nous)* also came to be so regarded, as was universal necessity or divinely determined law *(ananke)*.

Somewhat fancifully, F. M. Cornford (1912) once characterized the continuity between the earliest rational speculation and the religious perspective that underlay it as "two successive products of the same consciousness," radically separating its "scientific" from its earlier "mystical" strands. The locus of this continuity, he thought, lies in notions of a primary distributive (and thus "moral") world order.

11

Later (1952), however, he explicitly showed opposition to the view, long received and prominently represented by John Burnet (1892) and himself, that the Presocratics brought what we call "science" into the world.

Cornford's late antipositivist position, achieved by the early 1940s, had already been supported by Werner Jaeger (1936 Gifford Lectures, published in 1947), then by William Chase Greene (1944) and by E. R. Dodds (1951), who together produced a solid refutation of the Burnet thesis. (See Gregory Vlastos' review of Cornford in Furley and Allen, 1970.) In fact, Dodds showed in decisive fashion that irrational themes persisted throughout Greek philosophy; they did not stop in the sixth or the fifth century. More detailed studies on the development of science among the Greeks by G. E. R. Lloyd (1979) and others now tend to assume the new interpretation, depicting a mixture of nonscientific motifs with the gradual formation of a basic scientific framework of open-ended critical inquiry, skepticism, and careful examination of assumptions from Thales to Aristotle. Nevertheless, Vlastos (in Furley and Allen, 1970) fittingly objects to Jaeger's (1947) application of the term "theology" to the Presocratics, in that the divinity of which they speak has no direct connection with that of the public cult, whereas that of the early theogonists certainly does. Vlastos holds that only they, among all the people of the Mediterranean world, "dared transpose the name and function of divinity into a realm conceived as a rigorously natural order and, therefore, completely purged of miracle and magic." He continues: "To moralize divinity was not their main and certainly not their unique contribution. They took a word which in common speech was the hallmark of the irrational, unnatural, and unaccountable and made it the name of a power which manifests itself in the operation, not the disturbance, of intelligible law."

By firmly established convention, "Presocratic" means thinkers whose few extant fragments, preserved as quotations in later authors, have been collected by Hermann Diels and Walther Kranz in German (1934), later by Kathleen Freeman (1946, 1977) and by G. S. Kirk and J. E. Raven (1957) in English. They are a new breed, having no predecessors, beginning with Thales in the early sixth century and ending in the late fifth century B.C. To me, it is highly significant that Thales and his followers came from Miletus, a vigorously multicultural Ionian Greek trading center, where the challenge to sort out radically conflicting beliefs must have been strongly felt. Presocractic thought is characterized by a supplanting of traditional mythical ex-

planations of causation with natural, cosmologically oriented perspectives. These, modern scholars have come to see, contained fascinating efforts to understand the nature of things, without which not
only later Greek philosophy but also subsequent development of science would be inconceivable (e.g., see Solmsen, *Intellectual Experiments of the Greek Enlightenment,* 1975). Yet their historic role is
also set apart by the marked opposition to their proposals by Socrates (470–399). Both will be summarized below.

Plato's Universe, by Vlastos (1975), presents a convincing account
of what happened overall, substantially revising Cornford's popular
interpretation (1937). He first shows a basic agreement between
Plato (427–347) and his predecessors, then called the *physiologoi,* as
to the unending regularity of the cosmos, not broken even by the
gods and immanent in nature. Plato's radical difference lies in his
postulation in the *Timaeus* that this cosmos is the artful design of a
god, one driven, moreover, to share his own excellence with others.
Vlastos demonstrates that Plato took this view in order to structure
the considerable advances of observational astronomy into a coherent scheme that conceives the solar, lunar, and planetary orbits as
spirals, thus preparing the way for later discoveries by Eudoxus,
Ptolemy, and others. Although seventeenth-century scientists were to
find the rival Democritean atomism preferable, Vlastos shows to my
satisfaction that there was no empirical way to choose between the
two in their own time. The bifurcated, supernaturally determined
universe Plato depicted in the *Timaeus,* moreover, made it the most
used of his works throughout the Middle Ages. "If you cannot ex-
punge the supernatural," Vlastos explains, "you can rationalize it,
turning it paradoxically into the very source of the natural order,
restricting its operation to a single primordial creative act which
insures that the physical world would be not chaos but cosmos
forever after." Michael Stokes (1971) has described how this theme
of "the one and the many" emerged among the Presocratics. Leo
Sweeney (1972) has emphasized the theme of "infinity."

Most of the huge twentieth-century literature on the Presocratics
attempts to form a historical-developmental line, deep-set in ancient
culture, an interest pursued in many of the articles collected by Allen
and Furley (1970, 1975), Alexander Mourelatos (1974), and Roger
Shiner and John King-Farlow (1976). This approach has continued
to flourish throughout the post-1945 period, notably through the
example of multidisciplinary philosophers such as Werner Jaeger
(1934), Harold Cherniss (*Aristotle's Criticism of Presocratic Philoso-*

phy, 1935, cited on p. 45 and his lecture in Furley and Allen, 1970), Gregory Vlastos (eleven articles in the Allen and Furley collections and others elsewhere; also see Edward Lee, 1973), and W. K. C. Guthrie in his five-volume overview, *A History of Greek Philosophy* (1962–78). A professedly nonhistorical approach is taken by Jonathan Barnes (1979), who charmingly avers that "philosophy lives a supracelestial life, beyond the confines of time and space" but contributes superb, extensive analyses of arguments in the texts based on a detailed grasp of the secondary literature. Among those who have studied single authors or schools, the following may be singled out: on Anaximander, Charles Kahn (1960); on Empedocles, Denis O'Brien (1969); on Heraclitus, G. S. Kirk (1954); on Parmenides, Francis Cornford (1951), Alexander Mourelatos (1970) and Joseph Owens (1979); on Zeno, Wesley Salmon (1970); on the Pythagoreans, Walter Burkert (1972); and on the Atomists, David Furley (1967). What has emerged among these commentators is an exciting picture of profound reflection and discovery among the first philosophers, greatly diverse in perspective, full of interesting problems and puzzles, vast in implications for the further development of both philosophy and science, which in the classic period were not distinguished from each other.

How did the Presocratics differ from their predecessors in the way they reasoned? G. E. R. Lloyd's *Polarity and Analogy* (1966) perhaps best outlines the main differences. The following summary is drawn chiefly from his work. First, we notice that the use of opposites to describe or explain reality was already widespread among ancient societies (opposites such as right and left, male and female, dark and light, up and down, front and back, hot and cold, dry and wet). This simplifying method, with many of the comparative value assignments traditionally given to pair attributes (for example, "male" stronger than "female") continued in fifth-century Greek philosophy and medicine. Aristotle was later to distinguish between uses of paired propositions as contradictories, contraries, and subcontraries, but was also well aware of other kinds of contrasting terms or expressions (for example, complementaries like "word and deed"). What sets apart the opposites generally used by the Presocratic philosophers is their abstract quality and the assumptions either that two compared groups of phenomena are incompatible, exhaustive alternatives, or that they are somehow reciprocal, interdependent, or even the same thing seen from different perspectives.

As to argument, Presocratic philosophers typically set up dual alternatives in order to force a choice, to refute the opposite of a thesis or to show that opposite consequences follow from it, or to refute a thesis by disproving each of the alternatives that must be true if it is true. Often the terms were quite equivocal or the options were treated as though they must be either true or false, and the relations between opposites were misconceived or oversimplified. Although Plato recognized these features to be mistaken by the time he wrote the *Sophist,* a late work, even then he did not seem to have a systematic account of the use of opposites. Aristotle (384–322) later attempted this in his logic, revealing several serious errors one can make in stating problems in this manner. Nonetheless, as Vlastos has indicated (1973), from the *Phaedrus* on (a work from his middle period) Plato regarded his closely allied, purified method of "division" (preferably dichotomous, or at least as parsimonious as possible) as the method of philosophy par excellence. The careful making and logical checking and justifying of distinctions remains a major office of philosophy today.

The use of analogy is another method chronicled by Lloyd that has played a prominent role in philosophy since the Presocratics, in the modern period especially through some modes of induction. As a mode of reasoning, analogy fixes upon similarities and associated differences between one thing or set and another, which is usually taken to be unknown or less well known. Metaphorical imagery is often featured. Analogies of a sort, often magical, are used in all primitive societies, especially in efforts to grasp the mysterious or unknown. For example, the Presocratics drew heavily from biological, social, political, and technological imagery in trying to explain natural process, and not as mere metaphors. Plato may have been the first to separate out the distinctive use of imagery in demonstrative argument, frequently employed in his writings, whereas Aristotle attempts so far as possible to form nonfigurative comparisons. The cosmologies of both Plato and Aristotle, however, further elaborate the following features of Presocratic discourse that sharply divorce their work from earlier thought (Lloyd, 1966): (1) the imagery used points to the world as a whole (the cosmos); (2) the myths are abstract and general, rarely personal or particular in form; and (3) analogies are used to present argued accounts, open to critical scrutiny.

Plato constantly uses analogy, chiefly for heuristic and didactic purposes, and occasionally warning against using resemblance or what seems likely as proofs; but, as Lloyd has shown, in important instances Plato also attempts to prove an analogy true or even to accept one as true without resort to evidence, using analogies as a means for discovering truth. Aristotle explicitly rejects some of these attempts by Plato, most notably Plato's use of Forms as figurative models *(paradeigmata);* to him metaphors are appropriate as stylistic ornaments, exemplifications, inductions, or persuasive means, and to open up inquiry—and he often uses analogy in these ways—but they are not for use in formal demonstrative argument or definitions. Despite the impressive interventions of Plato and Aristotle, uses of analogy familiar from Plato and the Presocratics long continued unabated in Greek philosophy.

Regarding the interpretations by Lloyd and Vlastos as overly restricted to logical and scientific considerations, Raymond Prier (1976) has set forth what I take to be a complementary view of the Presocratics as partaking of a specific religiously informed logic he calls "the archaic mind," one unique to its time. He detects its rise in the late sixth- to early fifth-century lyric poets, elegiac poets, and in Aeschylus but especially in Heraclitus, Parmenides, and Empedocles (all three Presocratic philosophers). The following features are emphasized: dualism, opposition, and apposition; a pictorially symbolic quality; the presence of a mythical, synchronous common order; and, most important to Prier, the transformation of opposites through a third term into an inherent unity or identity. Using these methods, Heraclitus is seen to present an "inner cosmos" (in *psyche*) as a clearing ground for understanding the whole cosmos, enjoining others to "awaken" to consciousness by such means. The subsequent logics of Parmenides and Empedocles are variations on the logic Heraclitus had already established, though more conscious and more precisely explicated. Parmenides' main symbol for the third term is Light (spherical Being, linking *doxa* and Truth). Empedocles' thought is the acme of this archaic logic, for Prier, speaking outright of things being "other" yet "always continuously the same," choosing *philotes* (friendly love) for his third term, used as a way of moving toward the One. Those who are conscious as Empedocles proposes are in a "mixed" realm shared with the immortals.

There will no doubt be many more highly suggestive theses like Prier's before the Presocratic picture is cleared; in fact, it probably never will be cleared, if only because we must rely on mere fragments for evidence. There can now be little doubt, however, that the Presocratics effected a distinctive advance of consciousness in the ancient world.

Allen, Reginald E., and David J. Furley, eds. *Studies in Presocratic Philoso-*

phy. Vol. 2, *The Eleatics and Pluralists*. New York: Humanities Pr., London: Routledge & Paul, 1975. (Vol. 1, see Furley.)

Barnes, Jonathan. *The Presocratic Philosophers*. 2v. London and Boston: Routledge & Paul, 1979.

Brendel, Otto J. *Symbolism of the Sphere: A Contribution to the History of Earlier Greek Philosophy*. Leiden: Brill, 1977.

Burkert, Walter. *Lore and Science in Ancient Pythagoreanism*. Tr. by Edwin L. Minar, Jr. Cambridge, Mass.: Harvard Univ. Pr., 1972. (German ed., 1962.)

Burnet, John. *Early Greek Philosophy*. 4th ed. (1930) Repr.: New York: Meridian, 1957. (1st ed., 1892.)

Cornford, Francis M. *From Religion to Philosophy: A Study in the Origins of Western Speculation*. London: E. Arnold, 1912; New York: Harper & Row, 1957.

————. *Plato and Parmenides*. London: Routledge & Paul, 1930; New York: Humanities Pr., 1951.

————. *Plato's Cosmology: The Timaeus of Plato*. New York: Harcourt, Brace; London: Paul, Trench, Trubner; 1937.

————. *Principium Sapientiae: The Origins of Greek Philosophical Thought*. Ed. by W. K. C. Guthrie. Cambridge: Cambridge Univ. Pr., 1952; New York: Harper & Row, 1965.

Diels, Hermann, and Walther Krans, eds. *Die Fragmente der Vorsokratiker*. 5th ed. 3v. Berlin: Weidmann, 1934. (1st–4th eds., 1903–12, by Diels alone; vol. 3 is an index.)

Dodds, Eric R. *The Greeks and the Irrational*. Berkeley: Univ. of California Pr., 1951.

Freeman, Kathleen. *Ancilla to the Pre-Socratic Philosophers: A Complete Translation of the Fragments in Diels* Fragmente der Vorsokratiker. Cambridge, Mass.: Harvard Univ. Pr., 1977.

————. *The Pre-Socratic Philosophers: A Companion to Diels* Fragmente der Vorsokratiker. Cambridge, Mass.: Harvard Univ. Pr., 1966; Oxford Univ. Pr., 1946. (From the 5th ed.)

Furley, David J. *Two Studies in the Greek Atomists*. Princeton, N.J.: Princeton Univ. Pr., 1967.

————, and R. E. Allen, eds. *Studies in Presocratic Philosophy*. Vol. 1, *The Beginnings of Philosophy*. New York: Humanities Pr.; London: Routledge & Paul, 1970.

Greene, William Chase. *Moira: Fate, Good, and Evil in Greek Thought*. Cambridge, Mass.: Harvard Univ. Pr., 1944. Repr.: Gloucester, Mass.: Peter Smith, 1968.

Guthrie, William K. C. *A History of Greek Philosophy*. 5v. Cambridge and New York: Cambridge Univ. Pr., 1962–78.

Jaeger, Werner. *Paideia*. 2v. Tr. by Gilbert Highet. Oxford: Blackwell, 1939. (2nd ed., Oxford Univ. Pr., 1945; German ed., 1934.)

————. *The Theology of the Early Greek Philosophers*. Tr. by Edward S. Robinson. Oxford: Clarendon Pr., 1947.

Jaynes, Julian. *The Origin of Consciousness in the Breakdown of the Bicameral Mind*. Boston: Houghton Mifflin, 1976.

Kahn, Charles H. *Anaximander and the Origins of Greek Cosmology*. New York: Columbia Univ. Pr., 1960.

Kirk, Geoffrey S. *Heraclitus: The Cosmic Fragments.* Cambridge and New York: Cambridge Univ. Pr., 1954. Repr., 1970.

———, and J. E. Raven. *The Presocratic Philosophers: A Critical History with a Selection of Texts.* Cambridge and New York: Cambridge Univ. Pr., 1957.

Lee, Edward N., Alexander P. D. Mourelatos, and Richard Rorty, eds. *Exegesis and Argument: Studies in Greek Philosophy Presented to Gregory Vlastos.* In *Phronesis.* Supplementary vol. 1. New York: Humanities Pr.; Assen: Van Gorcum, 1973.

Lloyd, Geoffrey E. R. *Magic, Reason, and Experience.* Cambridge and New York: Cambridge Univ. Pr., 1979.

———. *Polarity and Analogy: Two Types of Argumentation in Early Greek Thought.* Cambridge and New York: Cambridge Univ. Pr., 1966.

Mourelatos, Alexander P. D. *The Route of Parmenides: A Study of Word, Image, and Argument in the Fragments.* New Haven, Conn.: Yale Univ. Pr., 1970.

———, ed. *The Pre-Socratics: A Collection of Critical Essays.* Garden City, N.Y.: Anchor Pr., 1974.

O'Brien, Denis. *Empedocles' Cosmic Cycle.* Cambridge and New York: Cambridge Univ. Pr., 1969.

Owens, Joseph, ed. "Parmenides Studies Today." *Monist* 62, no. 1:1–106 (Jan. 1979).

Prier, Raymond A. *Archaic Logic: Symbol and Structure in Heraclitus, Parmenides and Empedocles.* The Hague: Mouton, 1976.

Salmon, Wesley C., ed. *Zeno's Paradoxes.* Indianapolis, Ind.: Bobbs-Merrill, 1970.

Shiner, Roger A., and John King-Farlow, eds. *New Essays on Plato and the Pre-Socratics.* In *Canadian Journal of Philosophy.* Supplementary vol. 2. Guelph, Ontario: Canadian Assn. for Publishing in Philosophy, 1976.

Solmsen, Friedrich. *Intellectual Experiments of the Greek Enlightenment.* Princeton, N.J.: Princeton Univ. Pr., 1975.

Stokes, Michael C. *One and Many in Presocratic Philosophy.* Cambridge, Mass.: Harvard Univ. Pr., 1971.

Sweeney, Leo, S.J. *Infinity in the Presocratics: A Bibliographical and Philosophical Study.* The Hague: Nijhoff, 1972.

Vlastos, Gregory. *Platonic Studies.* Princeton, N.J.: Princeton Univ. Pr., 1973. (Repr., 1981, with addition of three short essays on Socrates.)

———. *Plato's Universe.* Seattle: Univ. of Washington Pr., 1975.

SOCRATES (470–399 B.C.)

Ancient accounts of the great Athenian "lover of wisdom," Socrates, are highly contradictory and untrustworthy. A good case can be made for using chiefly, but not totally, Plato's extensive portrayal of his revered teacher in the early dialogues. This is now the conventional view, though it is also generally supposed that Plato uses Socrates, faithfully but imaginatively, to advance his own views and inquiries even in those dialogues and that it is impossible to disen-

tangle the two completely. Since antiquity, in fact, Plato's portrait
has formed the basis for an almost universal admiration of the living
Socrates as a lofty prototype of the philosopher, for whom "an unexamined life is not worth living" *(Apology)* and of the dying Socrates as a tragic hero. Perhaps he has been largely protected from
criticism until recently because he is said to have offered no doctrine
and founded no school. In his self-appointed midwifing (maieutic)
role, he has been thought simply to have exemplified the life dedicated to rigorous inquiry.

Among interpretations still current, A. E. Taylor's (1932) takes as
historically accurate the heroic figure whose life and thought is given
in Plato's dialogues wherever Socrates is the central figure. In this
view, the famous theory of Forms is unquestionably a Socratic tenet.
In contrast, Richard Robinson (1941, 1953) separates an especially
Socratic mode of argumentation (the *elenchus,* to be described below) and interest in definitions from Plato's own early dialectic. By
the early dialectic he particularly means Plato's theories of hypothesis
and division in the middle dialogues, his profound new interest in
methodology there, as a "great logician," and his corresponding development of the theory of Forms. Santas (1979) and many others
writing since the 1940s (see Vlastos, 1971) have accepted variants of
the Robinson position, taking the Socrates of Plato's early dialogues
to be roughly authentic and subjecting him to critical scrutiny. (Most
of the exposition that follows is richly exemplified in Santas' outstanding (1979) contribution to the Arguments of the Philosophers
series and, like his, relies exclusively on Plato's early "Socratic" dialogues.) An unmistakable odor of philosophical piety arises nonetheless from nearly all this literature, what Friedrich Nietzsche (1872)
sniffed out as "Apollonian" rationality (strict orderliness and attention to reasoned argument) versus "Dionysian" passion and tragedy.
This bittersweet odor emits from nearly all the philosophical kitch-
ens, ancient or modern; and it is almost always the dominant savor,
though perhaps never the only one.

The man we discover in these early "Socratic" dialogues is a great
talker who created a revolution in philosophy, a probing, sly, sarcastic
questioner, and a wise, just man devoted to clear thinking as "the most
important requisite for right living" (Bertrand Russell, quoted in Santas). Socrates viewed his rivals, the Sophists, with contempt because
they used rhetorical tricks to persuade others of their opinions. Plato
agreed and, despite some counter evidence, this has remained the prevailing interpretation. Against such practice and against the poorly
reasoned cosmology-building of others, Socrates pitted his own *elen-*

chus, a deep questioning of assumptions, opinions, and arguments aimed at refutation to the point of destruction and bent to the search for true knowledge. Socrates' use of the *elenchus* was exasperating, sometimes boorish; he had little use for facts; his interlocutors ended up literally not knowing what to think. But, for all its faults, the process itself was, and is, enormously illuminating.

Plato displays Socrates questioning many of the leading figures of the day and others from many walks of life, not one a philosopher. As Santas shows, Socrates raised numerous questions presumably never asked before, almost all of them about what makes for excellence in human life and how we can know what is right to be and do. For Plato, at least, some questions led to difficult paradoxes, notably, "that no one desires evil things and that all who pursue evil things do so involuntarily" and "that virtue is knowledge and that all who do injustice or wrong do so involuntarily" (Santas' restatements). The primary questions Plato has him bring up, moreover, presuppose (as Socrates seems to have been quite aware) a great many propositions of general scope and importance; most of these are "about kinds or universals and about general terms and abstract singulars in the Greek language" (Santas). But Socrates does not seem to have doubted that these underlying presuppositions were true.

According to Aristotle, Socrates was the first to seek definitions as essential to the search for knowledge and to inquire about the nature of definitions; and Socrates offered a few he must have thought adequate for the purpose. It is not possible to know what kinds of definitions he knew about. All those presented in Plato's early dialogues, as Santas shows, were explicit definitions (of several forms: disjunctive, conjunctive, and a few by simple synonym, but not quantitative), none of them contextual, recursive or axiomatic definitions; and he excluded definitions by example. Santas points out that all the definitions Socrates himself offers, and both Plato and Aristotle after him, are achieved by analysis of the definiendum rather than by finding synonyms. All Socrates' definitions are of common attributes, state what those attributes are according to formal rules (mostly implicit), and are taken to have truth-value.

All the features of Socrates' thinking so far mentioned distinctly mark him off from his predecessors and contemporaries (save perhaps his older contemporary, Protagoras, about whom we lack direct evidence); and they represent contributions of permanent importance to philosophy. Socrates was also extraordinarily artful in constructing arguments, which Santas indicates are of nearly every general form recognizable today, and in testing the truth or falsity of claims. Many of these arguments are very strong and valid arguments by modern criteria, often ingenious and sophisticated. Soundness is another matter; for this the premises must be true. Santas concludes that the influential notion that we can test our beliefs, especially moral ones, by such arguments is almost entirely due to Socrates and his skillful examples. Furthermore, the later discovery of logic by Aristotle and the Stoics must have been indebted to the rich hunting grounds provided by Socrates' arguments.

If Socrates' contributions were great, so were his failures. Vlastos (1971) sees Socrates' basic failure to be a "failure of love." This is not because of his pugnacity but because his care for others' souls is limited and conditional. "If men's souls are to be saved, they must be saved his way. And when he sees they cannot, he watches them go down the road to perdition with regret but without anguish. Jesus wept for Jerusalem. Socrates warns Athens, scolds, exhorts it, condemns it. But he has no tears for it. One wonders if Plato, who raged against Athens, did not love it more in his rage and hate than ever did Socrates in his sad and good-tempered rebukes. One feels there is a last zone of frigidity in the soul of the great erotic; had he loved his fellows more, he could hardly have laid on them the burdens of his 'despotic logic' [Nietzsche, sec. 14], impossible to be borne." Over the centuries Socrates' crucial flaw is continually repeated in all academic disciplines, perhaps nowhere more tragically than in philosophy.

Nietzsche, Friedrich. *The Birth of Tragedy* and *The Case of Wagner*. Tr. by Walter Kaufmann. New York: Vintage Books, 1967. (The first work was first published in 1872.)
Robinson, Richard. *Plato's Earlier Dialectic*. 2nd ed. Ithaca, N.Y.: Cornell Univ. Pr.; Oxford: Clarendon Pr., 1953. (1st ed., 1941.)
Santas, Gerasimos Xenophon. *Socrates: Philosophy in Plato's Early Dialogues*. London and Boston: Routledge & Paul, 1979.
Taylor, Alfred E. *Socrates: The Man and His Thought*. London: Peter Davies, 1932. Repr., 1939, 1951 and after.
Vlastos, Gregory, ed. *The Philosophy of Socrates: A Collection of Critical Essays*. Garden City, N.J.: Doubleday Anchor, 1971.

PLATO (427–347 B.C.), ARISTOTLE, AND THE ACADEMY

Philosophical Disagreement

In philosophy the tragedy of distemper resides in the necessity for considerate and probing criticism. Without disagreement there is little or no advance. But to the degree that we are not open to entertain an opposing position, or are inclined simply to pit one set of propositions against another, ignoring the requirements of logical and reflective inquiry, disagreement is philosophically pointless. The same is true of agreement. In this light, Plato's thought has probably suffered more misplaced opinionating, from friend and foe, than that of any other philosopher. Often "Platonism" has been set forth as if it were complete, unrevised, or unrevisable, as if his changing inquiries and arguments were relatively unimportant. To the contrary, in a supremely even-tempered article, "Taking Sides in Philosophy," Gilbert Ryle (1971) has pointed out: "Every 'ism' that can get to the point of acquiring a name is *philosophically* questionable, and is actually questioned by genuine philosophers. And that means that no philosopher has any excuse for cleaving to it."

At the very outset of his own penetrating analysis, "Philosophical Disagreement," Nicholas Rescher (1978) aptly quotes R. G. Collingwood (1933): "No one philosopher's system can be acceptable to another without some modification. That each must reject the thoughts of others, regarded as self-contained philosophies . . . is due not to causes in taste and temperament but to the logical structure of philosophical thought." None of these authors considers taste, temperament, and the like irrelevant to the practice of philosophy. Nor do I. But we would either deny or severely restrict their significance with respect to the probity of arguments. Rescher appropriately observes that argumentation intent upon resolution of philosophical issues fosters rather than removes diversity. Often, as he says, eminently plausible arguments, arguments that may even appear to have equal cogency, can be formed on mutually incompatible sides of issues that are addressed philosophically. In all these respects Plato's work, together with what has been done with it, provides the most classic example.

Disagreement widely persists among Plato experts, especially as to (1) the chronological order of Plato's writings, important with respect to claims about the growth of his thought; (2) the relation of Aristotle's thought to Plato's; and (3) Plato's very elaborate, complicated theory of Forms (his "idealism," sometimes called Platonic "realism"), which comprises or underlies many of his most prominent views. The resolution of many other issues, for example those having to do with his place in Greek thought generally, with developments in his dialectical method, with his views of ethics, politics, art and religion, and with the relation of his thought to succeeding types of "Platonism," chiefly depends upon what is established in these three areas.

1. *Chronological Order of Plato's Writings.* Early twentieth-century analyses of style, historical references, concepts, and modes of argument already revealed an early, middle, and late division of Plato's writings. These analyses were done mostly by German scholars, with Friedrich Schleiermacher's remarkable efforts a century earlier initiating the search. There was fair agreement among the lists as to what writings fit into the three divisions, with notable exceptions, but not as to the actual dating (see Ross, 1951). There is, in fact, still a great deal of disagreement over how Plato's thought changed. Roughly in the order listed (from Ryle, 1966), today almost all commentators would (*a*) place the Socratic, eristic dialogues early: *Lysis, Laches, Euthyphro, Charmides, Hippias Major, Hippias Minor, Ion, Protagoras, Euthydemus, Gorgias, Meno,* and *Republic* Book I; (*b*) list the following as middle dialogues, most of which include aspects of Plato's theory of Forms: *Apology, Crito, Republic, Phaedo, Critias, Symposium, Timaeus* (some maintain that this came later), the unfinished *Philebus, Laws* III–VII, and *Phaedrus;* and (*c*) put later: *Cratylus, Theaetetus, Sophist, Politicus (Statesman), Parmenides,* and the unfinished revision of *Laws* (adding I–II and VIII–XII), some of which include substantial criticisms or modifications of the theory of Forms. The closest thing to an authentic "life" of Plato would have to be an account of the development of his thinking in these writings; little independent evidence exists.

Some scholars place the founding of Plato's Academy as early as 388 B.C., on an estate Plato had bought within or near a public park called Academeca. Alternatively, I think there is even stronger evidence that after he had taught in Athens for many years, at no fee, some unknown circumstances around 372–369 led him to start up the Academy itself, with Theaetetus (inventor of solid geometry), Eudoxus (another great mathematician and astronomer) and others, when he was in his mid-fifties. The institution lasted over 900 years, especially in the first half a model of higher learning and free exchange of ideas, until the Emperor Justinian forbade pagans to teach in the schools of philosophy in 529 A.D. We know most of this history only from fragments. Plato is the only leading academic whose published works are extant. Most of them do not appear to have been issued until after his death at age eighty in 347.

2. *Aristotle's Relation to Plato.* Among the numerous general interpretations of Aristotle's relation to Plato the following five are representative. The differences are important because Aristotle's comments have significantly shaped traditional views of Plato's thought.

Werner Jaeger (*Aristotle: Fundamentals of the History of His Development,* 1923, cited on p. 45), one of the truly great philosophical interpreters of Greek culture, thought that for many years, at least until Plato's death in 347, Aristotle (384–322) was a committed Platonist (in *Eudemus* and *Protrepticus,* ca. 354–347). He was so in both manner and substance, drawing especially from the later, more abstract and critical spirit of Plato encountered when he joined the Academy in the early 360s. After some trips abroad (347–335, age thirty-seven to forty-nine), he developed some alternative views, in particular opposing Plato's theory of Forms. Jaeger, like G. W. F. Hegel and others, believed Aristotle had understood Plato perfectly well, through lectures as well as the dialogues, but had gradually moved to a position of his own.

Through detailed comparative analysis of the texts, Harold Cherniss (1945; 1936 article in Vlastos, 1970; and *Aristotle's Criticism of Plato and the Academy,* 1944, cited on p. 45) discovered the "riddle" that Plato was supposed to have taught in the Academy for twenty years after Aristotle joined it; yet, when compared with the dialogues, Aristotle's references to Plato's thought tend to be quite inaccurate. This enigma, he argued, cannot be settled by positing an unwritten tradition of lectures, the contents of which are not consistent with Plato's writings. Instead he proposed that Plato neither lectured on the doctrines treated by Aristotle nor discussed them with students under thirty, that there was great openness to dispute in the Academy and no official doctrine, not even the theory of Forms, and that Aristotle distorted what little he knew of Plato's views apart from some of the dialogues, especially by refuting inferences he thought were to be drawn from them. Cherniss elsewhere (*Aristotle's Criticism of Presocratic Philosophy,* 1935, cited on p. 45) shows that Aristotle regularly puts forth garbled interpretations of the Presocratics as well.

In *Plato's Theory of Ideas* (1951) David Ross, one of the great interpreters of Aristotle, admits that much of Aristotle's treatment of Platonic doctrine is faulty or captious, but he accepts an unwritten tradition and uses Aristotle extensively to help understand the changing features of Plato's theory of Forms. This theory he sees in the dialogues from first to last; there is no fundamental change of view but only differences in interest or standpoint. According to Ross, in his last period Plato is nonetheless far from making the Forms the be-all and end-all of his philosophy, if he ever did. Like Jaeger, Ross believes that Aristotle was long a faithful Platonist but gradually withdrew during his fifties, no doubt spurred on in this by his experiences abroad (see Ross, *Aristotle,* 1923, cited on p. 46).

The theory of Forms in the middle dialogues issues in what may look like a two-level universe. This dualistic feature has been emphasized in Neoplatonism and in most standard interpretations of Plato. J. N. Findlay (1974) opposes the dualistic interpretation of Plato and claims that in his conception of matter versus mind Aristotle is the dualist, not Plato. In its place Findlay puts an ingenious picture of an unwritten program of thought by Plato, intimated most fully in passages from Aristotle (contra Cherniss). Its intention was to reduce all ideal meanings to number, as opposed to mere particulars. This program, which Aristotle reported but never understood, is only partly revealed in the dialogues. Plato felt "ever varying attitudes of confidence and criticism, of impassioned defense and despairing retreat" about what he was achieving in the project. Therefore, he was unable to publish more than hints as to his more central ideas, which Findlay assumes were vigorously discussed on an ongoing basis by Aristotle and others in the Academy. Ultimately, he sees no great difference between Plato's metaphysical doctrines and Aristotle's, though Aristotle is "a clipped, truncated, dismembered Platonist." Moreover, the Neoplatonist view of Plato, especially Plotinus', is much closer to Plato's doctrines than is ordinarily admitted today, representing as it does a like reference to one or two absolute principles as contrasted with subjective idealism or materialism. Findlay therefore regards the treatment of Plotinus and Plato together, a treatment that prevailed until Schleiermacher separated them in the early nineteenth century, to be completely justified. He believes that although Plotinus did not understand some aspects of Plato's teaching as well as may be possible today, and therefore tended to be more of a dualist, it is only in the light of his kind of interpretation that it assumes its full stature. Hegel, he thinks, is "the supreme modern developer" of Plato's teachings, standing on the shoulders of Plotinus, of the church fathers Clement and Origen (as opposed to Augustine), of Aquinas and Eckhart (versus Duns Scotus and Ockham), and brilliantly succeeded by the early Bertrand Russell, G. E. Moore (versus Ludwig Wittgenstein) and Alfred North Whitehead, all in contrast to the many "empiricists, pluralists, nominalists, sceptics, formal logicians, antimystics and pure scholars" who are not willing to carry Plato's theory to the limits.

Charles Bigger (1968) has called Gilbert Ryle's view of *Plato's Progress* (1966) an amusing parody of traditional metaphysical explanations. To the contrary, I think that Ryle's arguments and evidence comprise a serious, highly plausible explanation, without which much of Plato's thought remains an unnecessary enigma. In a masterful reconstruction based on available evidence of many kinds, Ryle concluded that Plato originally assigned supreme ontological status to concepts and cognitive primacy to the mental faculty by which we apprehend them for "heuristic" purposes. That is, Plato postulated this short-lived theory (ca. 370–364) in order to confer nobility upon dialectical study, which emphasized formal disputation over opposing concepts or theses (especially through eristic matches) as the coping stone of the sciences in the ideal state. Moreover, there is a good reason why Aristotle was ignorant both of the *Republic* and other dialogues and of developments in Plato's thought, despite his joining in the last twenty years of Plato's life as a student and teacher in Plato's Academy: that Plato did not teach dialectic there in the early years (after its founding in about 370), except perhaps to men in their thirties or older, and may never have taught the younger men at all.

As Ryle reconstructs the situation, Plato had likely come to feel that it was politically unwise to teach dialectic, or he had been prohibited from doing so. (It is especially noteworthy that in *Republic* Book VII "Socrates" is made to veto participation in dialectical disputes because of the bad reputation this gives to philosophy.) The earlier *Apology,* then, is to be seen chiefly as Plato's own defense against defamatory attacks by democratic politicians on the use of the Socratic method by Plato and his colleagues, not Socrates' defense. The *Gorgias, Crito,* and *Phaedo* represent the same effort. Ryle thinks that a trial may well have occurred, resulting in suppression of Plato's eristic teaching and a disastrous reduction of his wealth. Accordingly, the *Phaedo* contains not Socrates' farewell but Plato's own farewell before his departure for Sicily in 367, perhaps never to return. If a prosecution took place, Plato might easily have provoked it by his own heretical attacks (via orations as well as teaching) on current democratic politics, on the humble origins of other would-be philosophers, and on Homer and the poets, homiletic attacks such as are found in the *Republic.*

During his fateful 367–366 trip to Syracuse in Sicily, Ryle surmises, Plato wrote the *Timaeus,* his first work intended only for the Academy (see previous references to this work). (Sicily was then the wealthiest, most powerful of the Greek states.) Aristotle, who in 367 had just joined the Academy at eighteen, knew that work rather well, though it was not issued in book form until after Plato's death at about eighty in 347, and he did not know much else from the other dialogues. Meanwhile, Plato had also grown detached from his old theory of Forms and had begun to demolish it, as we can now see from the later dialogues. There is some evidence, Ryle indicates, that the early dialogues had been intended not for study as writings but as dialectical mimes for public presentations, on popular or official lists of topics, and to young audiences, such as at the Olympic Games (in sequences of three, each about the same length). Plato had probably performed the role of Socrates himself on these occasions. All this happened before he founded the Academy in the late 370s or early 360s. Possibly because of some debilitating illness, the aging Plato could no longer speak publicly after the late 350s, so the protagonist's part is usually taken by others thereafter.

Ryle concludes from examination of pertinent evidence that certain of the *Letters* (not the forged Dionist, anti-Dionysius propaganda letters III, VI, VIII, and XII, unfortunately long taken to be authentic) and the two mammoth dialogues, *Republic* and *Laws,* themselves gathered from writings of different times, must have been composed for senior listeners—possibly a select political club, and if so a rather conservative, nondemocratic one. He contends that the unfinished *Critias* and a first draft of *Republic* Books II–V were prepared for a festival at Syracuse in 367–366; both were thinly disguised advisory addresses to the old tyrant, Dionysius, who died while Plato was en route, and were therefore never delivered. *Laws* III–XII were prepared for another festival there in 361–360, a relatively nonutopian code for the younger Dionysius. Aristotle was only acquainted with some parts of *Laws,* an earlier version in Books III–VII (see Glenn Morrow in Düring and Owen, 1960, cited on p. 45). Aristotle may also have gone to that second festival, hearing there Plato's first version of *Laws.* He might then have stayed at Syracuse for a time to study its more advanced science, about which he clearly knew more than is presented in *Timaeus.*

By the mid-350s, Plato was in his mid-seventies. The Academy appears to have become self-supporting through endowment, and dialectic was then reinstated, taught by Aristotle, who had also inaugurated the teaching of rhetoric there in 360.

Staying with Ryle's account: Plato's early dialectic was specifically a means of placing the answerer in an impasse (also see Robinson, *Plato's Earlier Dialectic,* 1953, cited on p. 21). Its form as a staged question-and-answer contest was already familiar in Athens early in the fifth century. It was probably introduced there by Protagoras and only refined by Socrates, requiring the questioner to take either a "pro" or "contra" position on an issue and having the answerer reply only with a "yes" or "no." The eristic, "Socratic" dialogues may well have been formed from notes taken at such matches. Later Plato learned to form solitary dialogue as a substitute for those now-forbidden matches and to use the method as a serious, nonadversarial effort to get out of impasses. By the 350s, then, philosophy had begun to assume these new qualities within the Academy as well. Eristics was henceforth viewed as only a set of exercises preliminary to philosophy.

Aristotle's *Topics* provided the detailed theory for what we see of Plato's later practice. Aristotle, however, tended to reserve the term "philosophy" for bodies of knowledge and their methods (science) and to regard dialectic as separate from these, whereas Plato tended to identify philosophy with dialectic. Both agreed that dialectic was to be concerned with discovery and analysis of general truths and concepts, such as are shared by the various sciences or severally presupposed by them; among these notions are Aristotle's original work in "analytics" (which centuries later came to be called "logic").

On balance, Ryle's 1966 reconstruction is still the most plausible, though it certainly does not exclude everything of substantive interest in interpretations by Findlay and others. The scholarship of recent decades, in any case, has made a simple "unity of Plato's thought" thesis impossible to uphold. Ryle's basic arguments do not, however, impel us to accept his view that Plato held the theory of Forms only temporarily.

3. *The Theory of Forms.* Until 1965 (Vlastos, *Platonic Studies,* 1973, cited on p. 18), R. G. Collingwood (1945) almost alone noted that Plato does not use "is real" as a synonym for "exists," but by "really real" means real as to degree—genuinely, to the highest degree, thus perfectly real. (Sometimes it also means "being in itself" in contrast to "being in another.") Thus, as Gregory Vlastos has argued, "really real" means "reliably F" (where F = a qualifying predicate), both cognitively and in terms of value, in the latter sense as one who ecstatically "loves" the Forms. "Thus in one and the same experience Plato finds happiness, beauty, knowledge, moral sustenance and regeneration, and a mystical sense of kinship with eternal perfection." For Plato to have thought that the Forms are self-predicating (for example, that Beauty is beautiful) and that vision of Form itself carries infallibility (that is, logical certainty) are serious

flaws in the theory, on Vlastos' analysis. Nevertheless, his achievement is great: it was the first exploration of the categorial differences between things like Beauty, Justice, and Triangularity, on the one hand, and individuals, states, events, or processes of which general terms of this kind can be predicated, on the other. He showed that "all, and only, the first had to be nonsensible, incorporeal, incomposite, timeless, spaceless, incapable of causal agency, structured eternally by logical chains of entailment and bars of incompatibility." Plato got all this from a "degrees of reality" theory, Vlastos points out, whereas all he needed was a "kinds of reality" theory.

Twentieth-century scholarship leaves no doubt that in the later writings Plato himself raised numerous objections to his own earlier formulations of the theory of Forms, but that he gave evidence of retaining it just the same. If he did not give up the theory altogether, why not? Vlastos (1973) reminds us that Plato, having seen and failed to solve its logical difficulties, had nonlogical reasons for retaining the theory. Right to the end he continued to think of the actual world as a copy of an ideal model by a divine craftsman, one that can always be improved by human imitators. Correspondingly, the important notion of love in Plato's thought—apparently in his life as well—is not a love for persons; it does not consider individuals as whole persons and does not wish them well for their own sakes, as love is depicted in Aristotle's writings. Rather (Vlastos, 1969 article in *Platonic Studies,* 1973, cited on p. 18), Plato is the first Western thinker to realize with what erotic intensity we may attach ourselves to abstract objects, not only to objects such as art and poetry, but also to academic subjects or social ideas. Like Socrates, Plato has but one reason for moral conduct: the perfection of his soul. In persons one only loves the manifestation of excellence. "Were we free of moral deficiency we would have no reasons to love anyone or anything except the Idea: seen face to face, it would absorb all our love." The same analytic pattern, says Vlastos, operates in every other aspect of Plato's philosophy.

In one of the most illuminating articles yet published on Plato's complex theory of Forms, Julius Moravcsik (in Werkmeister, 1976) sorts out a plurality of tasks in the theory. He first distinguishes ontological and epistemological arguments offered by Plato for the existence of Forms as representing general features of reality (analogous to theoretical constructs in the sciences) and as unchangeable objects of infallible knowledge. Then he indicates characteristics that quite separate arguments by Plato try to show some or all of the

Forms have, and perhaps other entities as well: they are eternal, not subject to perishing and becoming, are not in space, are simple and self-sufficient, are self-exemplifying and have participants from the perceptible world. A third set of arguments is also seen to be distinct from the first set, one in which Plato assigns explanatory roles to the Forms thus characterized: both epistemological ones, presented in the theory that all our knowledge is recollected, and ontological ones, neither entailing the other. A very important role derivative of these two is found in the moral domain, such that moral knowledge is not an imitation of paradigms, as was generally thought in his day, but intuitive awareness of a priori forms (idealistic objects or rules).

Significantly, Moravcsik rejects as irrelevant any application of the metaphorical dichotomy between transcendental and immanent so important in medieval philosophy. Even the "separateness" predicated of the Forms in *Philebus* does not necessarily entail transcendence (compare Gosling, 1975; Shiner, 1974). His analysis also leads him to reject the crude interpretation that Plato thought the Forms were superspecimens of what we observe in artifacts or living organisms. Plato's distinction of "images" versus "originals" could not have led him to hold any such view, he argues. Finally, Moravcsik points out difficulties that do inhere in Plato's views, some of which are still nagging features of sophisticated philosophical inquiry today, notably those concerning the functions of names versus descriptions with reference to abstract singular terms.

Other Areas of Plato's Philosophy

Collections edited by R. E. Allen (1965), Renford Bambrough (1965), Gregory Vlastos (1970–71), Julius Moravcsik (1973), and W. H. Werkmeister (1976) are indispensable pointers to the enormous literature on Plato, especially works published since World War II. A number of works previously cited portray contexts of values and social practice in ancient Greek society and the place of both Plato and Aristotle within them. In addition, A. W. H. Adkins (1960, 1970), Ernest Barker (1918), and K. J. Dover (1974) look especially, though not exclusively, at political and personal morality.

Among the general interpretations not already cited, those by Robert Brumbaugh (1962), I. M. Crombie (1962), J. C. B. Gosling (1973), Nicholas White (1976), and Jerry Clegg (1977) represent several exegetical trends. Richard Robinson (*Plato's Earlier Dialectic*, 1953, cited on p. 21) and R. E. Allen (1970) have contributed whole works to Plato's early dialectic, Kenneth Sayre (1969) to his later methods. Hans-Georg Gadamer's essays on Plato's use of "dialogue and dialectic" (1980) come from a leading European "hermeneutical" philosopher. Norman Gulley (1962) was the first to give a systematic account in English of how Plato's epistemology developed. Both Gulley's analysis and W. G. Runciman's summary of Plato's later epistemology in *Theaetetus* and *Sophist* (also in 1962) must now be qualified in the light of detailed discussion that has occupied much space in the literature since then.

John Gould's 1955 work outlines the development of Plato's ethics. Several of the very recent studies have focused on early dialogues, for instance those by David Bolotin (1979), Ilham Dilman (1979), and R. E. Allen (1980). Terence Irwin's analytic survey (1977) stops short of the late period. The interplay of individual ethics, politics, and education is often discussed in works on Plato, though not fully in any, even in those on the *Republic* by F. M. Cornford (1955) and Thorsten Andersson (1971). Robin Barrow (1975) also treats all three. From outside the analytic mainstream, Leo Strauss (1975) has done a provocative study of *Laws;* Jacob Klein (1977) attempts a jargon-free reading of three late dialogues, paraphrased as a continuous conversation: *Theaetetus, Sophist,* and *Statesman.*

In the meager literature on Plato's aesthetics, Iris Murdoch's small, gemlike contribution (1977) stands out. As has been true for nearly two millennia, the huge interest in Plato's religious thought is almost entirely imbedded in works not strictly devoted to this area or not treating his philosophy alone. Several works previously cited deal with this subject.

There is much room for further study in every area of Plato's thought, a factor not only of his classic greatness, but of the unending change of fashions and of advancing philosophical consciousness as well.

Adkins, Arthur W. H. *From the Many to the One: A Study of Personality and Views of Human Nature in the Context of Ancient Greek Society, Values, and Beliefs.* Ithaca, N.Y.: Cornell Univ. Pr., 1970.

——. *Merit and Responsibility: A Study in Greek Values.* Oxford: Clarendon Pr., 1960.

Allen, Reginald E. *Plato's "Euthyphro" and Earlier Theory of Forms.* New York: Humanities Pr.; London: Routledge & Paul, 1970.

——. *Socrates and Legal Obligation.* Minneapolis: Univ. of Minnesota Pr., 1980.

——, ed. *Studies in Plato's Metaphysics.* New York: Humanities Pr., 1965.

Andersson, Thorsten J. *Polis and Psyche: A Motif in Plato's Republic*. Stockholm: Almqvist & Wiksell, 1971. (Studia graeca et latina gothoburgensia 30.)
Bambrough, Renford, ed. *New Essays on Plato and Aristotle*. New York: Humanities Pr.; London: Routledge & Paul, 1965.
Barker, Ernest. *Greek Political Theory: Plato and His Predecessors*. London: Methuen, 1918; New York: Barnes & Noble, 1957, 1960.
Barrow, Robin. *Plato, Utilitarianism and Education*. London and Boston: Routledge & Paul, 1975.
Bigger, Charles P. *Participation: A Platonic Inquiry*. Baton Rouge: Louisiana State Univ. Pr., 1968.
Bolotin, David. *Plato's Dialogue on Friendship: An Interpretation of the "Lysis," with a New Translation*. Ithaca, N.Y.: Cornell Univ. Pr., 1979.
Brumbaugh, Robert S. *Plato for the Modern Age*. New York and London: Crowell-Collier, 1962.
Cherniss, Harold. *The Riddle of the Early Academy*. Berkeley: Univ. of California Pr.; Cambridge Univ. Pr., 1945. Repr.: London: Russell & Russell, 1962.
Clegg, Jerry S. *The Structure of Plato's Philosophy*. Lewisburg, Pa.: Bucknell Univ. Pr., 1977.
Collingwood, Robin G. *Essay on Philosophical Method*. Oxford: Clarendon Pr., 1933.
———. *The Idea of Nature*. Oxford: Clarendon Pr., 1945.
Cornford, Francis M., ed. and tr. *The Republic of Plato*. Oxford: Clarendon Pr., 1955.
Crombie, Ian M. *An Examination of Plato's Doctrines*. 2v. New York: Humanities Pr.; London: Routledge & Paul, 1962.
Dilman, Ilham. *Morality and the Inner Life: A Study in Plato's "Gorgias."* New York: Macmillan, 1979.
Dover, Kenneth J. *Greek Popular Morality in the Time of Plato and Aristotle*. Berkeley: Univ. of California Pr.; Oxford Univ. Pr., 1974.
Findlay, John N. *Plato: The Written and Unwritten Doctrines*. London: Routledge & Paul, 1974.
Gadamer, Hans-Georg. *Dialogue and Dialectic: Eight Hermeneutical Studies on Plato*. Tr. by P. Christopher Smith. New Haven, Conn. and London: Yale Univ. Pr., 1980.
Gosling, Justin C. B. *Plato*. London and Boston: Routledge & Paul, 1973.
———, ed. *Plato's "Philebus."* Oxford: Clarendon Pr., 1975.
Gould, John. *The Development of Plato's Ethics*. Cambridge and New York: Cambridge Univ. Pr., 1955.
Gulley, Norman. *Plato's Theory of Knowledge*. New York: Barnes & Noble; London: Methuen, 1962.
Irwin, Terence. *Plato's Moral Theory: The Early and Middle Dialogues*. Oxford: Clarendon Pr., 1977.
Klein, Jacob. *Plato's Trilogy*. Chicago and London: Univ. of Chicago Pr., 1977.
Moravcsik, Julius M. E., ed. *Patterns in Plato's Thought: Papers Arising out of the 1971 West Coast Greek Philosophy Conference*. Dordrecht and Boston: Reidel, 1973.

Murdoch, Iris. *The Fire and the Sun: Why Plato Banished the Artists.* Oxford: Clarendon Pr., 1977.

Rescher, Nicholas. "Philosophical Disagreement: An Essay Towards Orientational Pluralism in Metaphilosophy." *Review of Metaphysics* 32, no. 2:217–52 (Dec. 1978).

Ross, William David. *Plato's Theory of Ideas.* Oxford: Clarendon Pr., 1951.

Runciman, Walter G. *Plato's Later Epistemology.* Cambridge and New York: Cambridge Univ. Pr., 1962.

Ryle, Gilbert. *Plato's Progress.* Cambridge and New York: Cambridge Univ. Pr., 1966.

———. "Taking Sides in Philosophy" (1937). In *Collected Papers,* vol. 2, pp. 153–69. New York: Barnes & Noble, 1971.

Sayre, Kenneth M. *Plato's Analytic Method.* Chicago and London: Univ. of Chicago Pr., 1969.

Shiner, Roger A. *Knowledge and Reality in Plato's Philebus.* Assen: Van Gorcum, 1974.

Strauss, Leo. *The Argument and the Action of Plato's Laws.* Chicago and London: Univ. of Chicago Pr., 1975.

Vlastos, Gregory, ed. *Plato: A Collection of Critical Essays.* Vol. 1, *Metaphysics and Epistemology;* vol. 2, *Ethics, Politics, and Philosophy of Art and Religion.* Garden City, N.Y.: Doubleday Anchor, 1970–71. (See first section above for *Plato's Universe,* 1975 and *Platonic Studies,* 1973; second section for *The Philosophy of Socrates,* 1971.)

Werkmeister, Willliam H., ed. *Facets of Plato's Philosophy.* Assen: Van Gorcum, 1976. (*Phronesis,* Supplementary vol. 2.)

White, Nicholas P. *Plato on Knowledge and Reality.* Indianapolis, Ind.: Hackett, 1976.

ARISTOTLE (384–322 B.C.)

Aristotle's School

Before Aristotle's day Athenian education consisted of two major parts—physical and intellectual—separately housed. It extended only through what is called the elementary level today. By the fifth century, the sophists were adding postelementary education for youth and adults. Some teachers, like Socrates, went from place to place; others established schools. Many buildings about the city, public and private, were being used for such purposes by the time Plato founded the Academy in the early fourth century. In 307 Epicurus opened his school in Athens and in about 304 the Stoa (Stoics) was established, both stemming from Presocratic traditions. Chief among the buildings used for educational purposes was the Lyceum. In 335, after a twenty-year association with the Academy and twelve years away from Athens after Plato's death in 347, Aristotle was sent by Alexander of Macedon to found his own quite different school there (Lynch, 1972). He used especially the colonnaded walkway in the gymnasium (Peripatos—hence for centuries people connected with the school or its traditions were called "Peripatetics"). Athens was then under Macedonian control. Aristotle's father had been physician to the Macedonian king Amyntas II during Aristotle's childhood and had died when he was ten. After Plato's death he was closely associated with Philip of Macedon (and married his daughter), then with Philip's son Alexander, who ascended to the throne after Philip's murder.

Aristotle's school had sumptuous backing. It was meant to be a community of friends, dedicated not only to dialectical disputation but even more to common inquiry over an extremely, unprecedentedly wide range of theoretical and practical subjects. For this purpose, it was also characterized by systematic information gathering (establishing a division of subjects still used today), by attention to rhetoric and massive expository writing, by instruction (with accompanying outlines, diagrams and other aids) more than discussion, by use of organized library materials, and by use of public lectures before large audiences. In all these respects the Peripatos differed from the Academy and made its own pioneering contributions, from which schools of higher learning derive many of their practices today. Moreover, most of the known faculty, like Aristotle, were non-Athenians, which gave them little freedom to discuss politics. Aristotle's was the first substantial library in Greek history, and it was to become a model for the great libraries at Alexandria and Pergamum. Large numbers of students attended, perhaps as many as 2,000.

Upon Alexander's death in 323, anti-Macedonian sentiment was high in Athens. Aristotle fled to his mother's estate in Chalkis, where he died the next year, at age sixty-two. For a time the school prospered under Aristotle's successor, Theophrastus. The year 225 B.C. is the last we hear of its presence in Athens. Because of its relative lack of political security, destruction and loss of funds through war, the early removal of its library, many teachers leaving to form new schools and assume other positions elsewhere, and other reasons, its position as a cooperative research institution was never very solid after the early decades. Thus it underwent continual decline in the Hellenistic period (323 to 31 B.C.). Although the school was never designed to foster Aristotle's teachings, as a consequence of the school's decline, his teachings had a much less solid base for transmission than Plato's. Most, perhaps almost all, of the Aristotelian writings are taken from lecture courses delivered by others, some of them well after his lifetime. Evidence that the Athenian school continued into the Imperial period is slim. After Sculla's capture of Athens in 86 B.C., the library of Aristotle and Theophrastus, recently bought and returned to Athens, was taken to Rome as plunder. From the third century A.D. on, most of the important commentators on Aristotelian writings seem to have lived in Alexandria. There is also evidence that by the third century A.D. the Imperial chairs accorded major teachers were held by rhetoricians, not by philosophers as they had been.

In the late first century B.C., Andronicus of Rhodes put together an edition of the Aristotelian corpus. This set of writings is what we rely on for our knowledge of Aristotle, and it is the basis for his subsequent fame. From ancient times through the late nineteenth century these writings were all assumed to be Aristotle's own. Historical and critical study of the texts has since established that much of the material is combined from several sources and from more than one author. In 1912 Werner Jaeger announced, and in 1923 worked up a strong case for, the position that the writings are mostly Aristotle's own but evidence a development from Platonic idealism to his own realism. Since the 1930s this position has been under fire. It is no longer generally accepted, though a smaller number of writings and passages have been established as vintage Aristotle.

As Felix Grayeff (1974) has shown with particular clarity, even the *Metaphysics* (a section of materials placed "after physics"), traditionally the most basic work used for exposition of Aristotle's philosophy, consists of several different positions, variously conjoined and interposed. It can only have been the work of Peripatetic editors. Book Zeta, for example, contains three different approaches to the problem of substance—doxographic-critical, logical, and basic-physical (ontological)—and differing points of view about the meaning of "substance." It was apparently collected by librarians from several versions of standard Peripatetic courses originating at different times, before the mid-first century B.C. Thus it cannot all be from Aristotle. The latest added sections, for example, show signs of Skeptical and Stoic influence. Other books are made up in the same way. Grayeff (who concentrates on *Metaphysics* Zeta, Eta, and Lambda) concludes that they comprise several rival theories already prevalent among the Peripatetics in Aristotle's time but further developed in some passages.

Only in the fifth and sixth centuries A.D., when the Neoplatonic school in Athens busied itself with the *Corpus Aristotelicum,* do

Aristotelian studies seem to have returned there. Lynch (1972), from whom much of the above story is taken, has pointed out that the Justinian decree of 529, normally held to have closed the pagan schools of philosophy, actually only acted to forbid pagans the right to teach in them. He opines that the sixth-century invasions had more to do with their closing than the decree. In any case Aristotelian studies, never very steady after Theophrastus, again subsided. They were to see their first real flowering among Arab translators and scholars in the ninth to eleventh centuries (chapter 3).

All, or a major portion, of each of the following works are widely treated as Aristotle's today: (1) in logic and methodology: *Categories, On Interpretation, On Sophistical Refutations, Prior Analytics* and *Posterior Analytics,* and *Topics;* (2) in philosophy: *The Art of Poetry, Metaphysics, Nicomachean Ethics, Politics* and *Rhetoric,* plus extracts extant from other writings, especially *Eudemian Ethics, Magna Moralia, On the Good, On the Ideas, On Philosophy* and *Protrepticus;* and (3) in science and natural history: several works, including *On the Heavens, On the Soul, Physics,* and four treatises on animals. Aristotle's ways of interpreting his own predecessors have already been discussed, especially in reference to the classic studies by Harold Cherniss (1935, 1944).

General Interpretations and Collections

The present tendency does not discover a coherent world view in the writings attributed to Aristotle, contrary to the medieval scholastics and most modern interpreters. Instead, contemporary philosophical interpreters usually find a stimulating, diverse set of problems, inquiry methods, and attempted solutions. All these features stretch toward the goal of consistency, but are often only loosely connected with each other (Moravcsik, 1967). In my opinion, the interpreter is now freed to view the relevant documents either as Aristotle's own or as collections of Peripatetic thought largely Aristotle's or based on his thinking (which situation calls for form-critical study) but not necessarily identical with it. The inquiries and controversies rule, not the positions, and one need not strive to grasp a unity in all respects. Actually, no single study as yet draws together the excitingly fresh, rich findings of the past two decades of Aristotelian studies.

Among the old summaries, W. D. Ross (1923, 1953) presents his interpretation of Aristotle's system of thought, without much reference to development and without criticism. Werner Jaeger (1923, 1948) presents the thesis that many inconsistencies in and among the texts can be understood by positing three periods in the development of Aristotle's thought, the first a Platonic one, the last oriented more to empirical research. What follows is an advance, rather than a debased form of Platonism as some detractors have thought. Later, more popular overviews by D. J. Allan (1952, 1970) and G. E. R. Lloyd (1968) both reject Jaeger's notion of marked development. Allan holds that Aristotle may never have been a strict Platonist but that within a few years after Plato's death he formed his own philosophy, which remained "fixed" in that form thereafter. Lloyd is a bit closer to Jaeger but emphasizes continuity from beginning to end: a common method, which includes (1) discussing the views of predecessors in order to formulate problems and identify difficulties, (2) resolving difficulties by both dialectical argument and appeal to concrete evidence, and (3) detailed research, and common doctrines, especially regarding (*a*) the antithesis of form and matter, (*b*) the antithesis of actuality and potentiality, and (*c*) final causes—withal a comprehensive, well-ordered whole. American naturalist John Herman Randall (1960) also sees his philosophy as an open but organic system. Randall interprets Aristotle as keeping much that was already present in Plato but working out a much more naturalistic approach. In modern terms, Aristotle was, in his view, a behaviorist, an operationalist, a contextualist, and a thoroughgoing process philosopher.

Among the collections, those edited by J. M. E. Moravcsik (1967) and Amélie Rorty (1980) well represent the current tendency, though a number of viewpoints are included. The fourteen critical essays (from 1953 to 1965) in the Moravcsik volume deal with select topics in logic, categories, metaphysics and ethics. They include early essays by Oxford realists John Cook Wilson (1926) and H. A. Prichard (1935) and new ones by J. L. Austin (from the 1930s), Moravcsik, J. O. Urmson and M. J. Woods. The twenty-one essays on Aristotle's ethics collected by Amélie Rorty are from 1972 to 1980 and include nine new ones by Julia Annas, M. F. Burnyeat, T. H. Irwin (two), L. A. Kosman, Martha Craven Nussbaum, David Pears, Amélie Rorty, and Bernard Williams. The sixteen essays collected by I. Düring and G. E. L. Owen (1960) are mostly from a 1957 Oxford symposium and are still useful but represent stages of discussion that are now either presupposed or left behind. The same is true of some of the essays gathered in the excellent four-volume set of articles edited by Jonathan Barnes et al. (1975), though some quite up-to-date essays are provided as well (including some translated ones). Volume 1 is on logic, methodology, science and issues regarding the development of Aristotle's thought, volume 2 on ethics and politics, volume 3 on metaphysics, and volume 4 on psychology, anthropology, and aesthetics.

Logic, Science, and Metaphysics

Aristotle's term for what has been called "logic" in its narrower sense by the Stoics and modern logicians is "analytics." Since he regarded logic and other methodological disciplines as an instrument *(organon)* of study, rather than fields of knowledge (not philosophy or science) in themselves, works in these areas were later organized under the title *Organon*. Briefly described, *Categories* deals with terms, *On Interpretation* with propositions, *Prior Analytics* with the syllogism, *Posterior Analytics* with conditions of scientific knowledge, *Topics* with Aristotle's new version of dialectic. *Sophistical Refutations* is in effect an appendix to *Topics*.

Until the 1950s very little attention was given to Aristotle's *Topics*. It was thought to be an early work, closely identified with Plato and the Academy. Even then E. Weil (1951, in Jonathan Barnes et al., 1975, and in an important 1959 German work) was one of the few to recognize its basic importance in Aristotelian thought before the excellent critical-synoptic study of J. D. G. Evans (1977). Both interpreters demonstrate its distance from Plato and the Academy, its sparkling originality, and its strategic, propaedeutic role in relation to philosophy and the sciences. Evans attempts not only to show the consistency of Aristotle's views of dialectic in *Topics* with that in *Metaphysics* and elsewhere, but also to indicate how the role of dialectic is grounded, for Aristotle, in his corrections of Plato's theory of Forms and of Plato's theory of definition.

Walter Leszl (1970), out of an informed interest in contemporary analytic debates on logic and methodology, likewise demonstrates that Aristotle's method of definition is more advanced and sophisticated than Plato's and that this method and the metaphysics reflect each other. Both, he argues, contain an appreciation of the essential equivocity of basic philosophical terms such as "being," "one," and "good." Similarly, Julius Moravcsik (in E. N. Lee et al., *Exegesis and Argument*, 1973, cited on p. 18) has argued that for Plato the method of divisions explicates the ontology of natural kinds, is thus applied primarily to the a priori disciplines, and is directed far more to the objects and results of inquiry then to the process itself. Aristotle disagrees with all three aspects of Plato's approach, holding that there can be no uninstantiated species, hence that empirical and conceptual tasks tend to coalesce. In a highly perceptive study Alan Blum (1974) holds that whereas for Plato thinking is internal conversation, for Aristotle it is communicative exchange, an interactive means of bringing one person's thought into contact with other thought. He also helpfully contrasts their views of the sciences, which Aristotle, unlike Plato, separates from metaphysics, and of other areas such as grammar and rhetoric, ethics and aesthetics, with the aim of specifying the distinctive nature of theorizing in each one. Then he similarly uses Emile Durkheim, Max Weber, and Karl Marx to look at modern theorizing, especially in sociology, again with Aristotle emphasizing interactive qualities in relationship versus rationalist isolation or rule by a preconceived, overarching "Being."

In short, Aristotle is not only the great founder of demonstrative, syllogistic logic—of "analytics," later called "Aristotelian logic"—but is a substantial innovator in other areas of logic and methodology as well. Typically among contemporary studies, Richard Bosley (1975) treats only certain "aspects" of it, not the entire program.

What did he accomplish in "topics"? Aristotle may well have begun the study of topics (dialectic) early, but the text as we have it does not offer a primitive position. For one thing, Aristotle there rejects Plato's identification of the philosopher and the dialectician. For Plato dialectic especially involves the search for definition and as such is taken to be the only true science; for Aristotle it does not do this and is not scientific, but is concerned with the foundations of the sciences. For Aristotle dialectic has no empirically definite subject matter of its own. As such, it focuses on what is already given in experience. It offers rules for engaging in a communal search for truth preparatory to doing effective empirical research. It cannot be a science that studies everything; strictly speaking, there is no such science in his view. As J. D. G. Evans (1977) suggests, in Aristotle's account even ontology studies "that which is" only in respect of its being, that is, being as something true of everything that is. Empirically precise accounts are possible only within the bounds set within each particular science. But dialectic is not science and is ontologically neutral; that is, it is concerned with everything that is but not with precisely what it is for anything to be. More specifically, then, what does it do? As a guidebook for dialectic, *Topics* deals with certain features of discourse in general. In particular, it is concerned with methods of extracting truth (or possible truth) from past or current discourse, whereas the *Analytics* books present demonstrative, syllogistic logic, which is also not a part of philosophy and not one of the empirical sciences but is to be applied in both. Dialectics and analytics are purely formal, propaedeutic methods. (Although as we have them the works on analytics use predominately mathematical examples, Aristotle, unlike Plato, has serious reservations about the cognitive value of mathematics. The mathematicizing of logic is a late nineteenth-century innovation.)

As E. Weil (in Barnes et al., 1975) outlines the matter, topics is a set of techniques newly discovered by Aristotle and his colleagues. Working from a historically given state of knowledge, it teaches how to find and formulate problems, to find syllogisms, to assess premises, to acquire appropriate arguments, to anticipate obstacles to effective reasoning (treating sophistic tricks and failures of moral judgment along with logical mistakes), and to grasp the importance of argument rightly carried out. The method of question and answer is a prominent feature of this approach, as is the doxographical-critical method of examining past opinions *(doxa)*. As Aristotle views them, these *doxa* are not mere opinions, as Plato held, but theses or arguments that are set forth by acknowledged specialists and that retain currency. *Topics* is also a teaching manual on types of interaction (for example, tutorial, joint investigation, thesis testing, public presentation) in use of argument between persons engaged in scientific activity. *Topics* II–VII contains (1) a map of the "places" to find general arguments relevant to construction and rejection of syllogistic premises and (2) a catalog of the "predicables" (general points of view—for instance definition, identity, genus and species—that may hold for any judgment and that are distinct from the categories, which have to do with substances and what is said of them), with methods for reducing what is carried by the categories to irreducible first principles.

In addition to dialectic, analytics, and the setting up of categories, intuitive reason must be used for grasping first principles and empirical, investigative reason for making discoveries. These procedures are also discussed in various of the Aristotelian writings. The terms "intuitive" and "empirical, investigative" are not Aristotle's but are modern parlance for what his views come to. The distinction I have employed between "science" and "philosophy" must not be taken in any modern sense, however. Aristotle's predecessors made no clear distinction between them; nor is he to be interpreted as having proffered one. Some fields of knowledge, in his view, did have a directly empirical, investigative character, while what the literature singles out as philosophical and methodological inquiries do not. Identification of true science with purely empirical, investigative methods would in any case be a mistake today (see chapter 23).

With respect to science, Anthony Preus (1975) outlines Aristotle's critical use of a teleological perspective (derived from *Physics* and *Metaphysics*) in explaining biological phenomena, itself a major contribution with enormous influence, good and bad. Using a history of ideas approach, Friedrich Solmsen's (1960) study of the nonbiological works in what is now the domain of physical science wisely eschews synthesis but emphasizes his revised treatment of the theme of "genesis" already announced among the Presocratics, comparing their views and Plato's with Aristotle's. A 1961 conference report, edited by Ernan McMullin (1963), usefully traces the history of the concept of "matter," on which Aristotle has had a strong influence, from Greek philosophy to modern philosophy and science. A new synopsis drawing upon the substantial advances made in the history and philosophy of science over the past twenty years is not yet available.

The scholastics and their successors thought that the *Metaphysics*—what Aristotle sometimes called "first philosophy," sometimes "wisdom" or "theology"—presents a consistently ordered plan of exposition, issuing in a fully developed ontological system, a universal science of being. Until modern times the system was usually thought to be either dependent on or coordinated with the theology set forth (almost exclusively, in fact) in Book Lambda. Jaeger introduced the thesis that the theological conception of ontology was early, Platonic, and dualistic and was given up in favor of an autonomous, nondualistic science of being as such. In recent years many scholars have come to assume instead that it is a more or less loosely connected set of materials, some of which may not be Aristotle's, gathered after his death. At the very least, textual analysis now indicates that parts were written at different periods (difficult or impossible to date), for different purposes, and with quite different results. Even on this basis interpretations still greatly differ, and the tendency now is to discuss the arguments in one or more of the fourteen books separately or to compare them. Walter Leszl (1975) does this effectively in a more speculative Continental style, writers like Jaakko Hintikka (1973), J. M. E. Moravcsik (1967, and a number of articles not cited here) in a more analytic style, Joseph Owens (1951) in a contemporary historical-critical scholastic style. Aristotle's view that there are concrete individual substances, to which genera and species are secondary, sharply differentiates his overall perspective from that of Plato. So do his analyses of causation (that is, of how and why a thing comes to be what it is), his discussions of potentiality and actuality (of how form is achieved in concrete individual substances, or in what their essence consists), and the theology in Book Lambda ("God" as final cause, pure matterless actuality, the unmoved mover, etc.). Speculative views of a dynamic single world order, wherein all things are purposively drawn up to the divine or to ultimate being, and wherein the meanings of things are accessible to reason in and through immediate experience, can easily be derived from these Aristotelian views. No wonder, then, that the *Metaphysics* had such powerful attraction for medieval Islamic scholars, scholastics, and their successors, both religious and secular. Owens's solid treatment shows the religious appeal, as does George Stead's (1977) attempt to demonstrate how "substance" language (essence, existence, nature, substance) in theology early and variously developed from Plato, Aristotle, and the Stoics especially and can still gain salutary clarification through closer study of their writings.

Anthropology, Psychology and Aesthetics

There is little or no necessary connection between Aristotle's ontology and his ethics. The same cannot be said of his psychology or his overall view of human behavior. Recently, considerable new examination of his thinking about things human has been applied to contemporary issues. Analytic philosopher Edwin Hartman (1977), for example, attempts to show how Aristotle's ontological theories regarding the primacy of substance and the identity of substance and essence apply to the person. In doing so Hartman makes him out to be a materialist, in that for him bodily identity is personal identity, but of a particular sort; that is, Aristotle denies that there are any sufficient bodily conditions of thoughts and holds that pains and sense impressions are only accidentally identical with certain physical events. Like most contemporary interpreters, Hartman does not find the texts to be entirely consistent, however. A much broader, looser overview of Aristotle's views of human nature by Stephen Clark (1975) aptly refers to studies by analytic and other philosophers, with scholars in several other fields, for more speculative purposes. This work particularly reveals how very stimulating Aristotelian inquiries into human experience can still be.

Signs point to the probability of a lively debate in Plato's Academy over the relation between emotion and cognition, one in which Aristotle took part. In an excellent brief study on this subject, W. W.

Fortenbaugh (1971) outlines Aristotle's own complex causal view, one that had important consequences for his rhetoric, poetics, ethics, and politics. In the 1970s philosophical scholarship has gone ever deeper into the details of his psychology and anthropology. Usually careful not to transform him into a twentieth-century philosopher, these scholars have produced results immensely fruitful for current inquiry on related issues. One type of effort is magnificently illustrated in Martha Nussbaum's 1978 edition of Aristotle's *De Motu Animalium,* a translation with interpretive essays and the first commentary in 600 years on this brief but significant essay. The connections between his general biological views and his anthropological ones are disputable, but the disputes are themselves illuminating. Another excellent translation with commentary is that on *De Memoria et Reminiscentia* by Richard Sorabji (1972), which he claims is similar to discussions in British empiricist tradition, but fuller. Discussions on the art of mnemonics may be profitably compared with accounts by Francis Yates (1966) of the history of this art from the Greeks, through the Middle Ages, to its recovery in Renaissance Hermetic traditions and its transformation for new scientific purposes by seventeenth-century philosophers.

Studies on Aristotle's aesthetics are cited in chapter 27 on pages 467–69, especially by Monroe Beardsley (*Aesthetics from Ancient Greece to the Present,* 1966), Eva Schaper (*Prelude to Aesthetics,* 1968) and Wladyslaw Tatarkiewicz (*History of Aesthetics,* 1970).

An outstanding analytic and historical-critical study of Aristotle's theory of the will by Anthony Kenny (1979) provides a bridge from a key aspect of Aristotle's anthropology to his ethics. Kenny examines how Aristotle relates human action in an interlocking manner to ability (voluntariness), desires and goals (intentionality) and belief (practical rationality). In doing so, he turns on its head the historical interpretation of Aristotle's ethical writings generally accepted since Jaeger by arguing that the *Eudemian Ethics,* which he uses extensively, is later than the *Nicomachean Ethics* (often mistakenly referred to as "the Ethics") and that the *Magna Moralia,* though sometimes divergent in content, may be a student's notes of the Eudemian course. Against the widespread tradition of viewing the will as a causally indeterminate, introspective, conscious event, Kenny also claims a contrary Aristotelian view of will similar to those of Ludwig Wittgenstein, G. E. M. Anscombe, Donald Davidson and himself (cited on pp. 210, 368, 377, and 369, respectively).

Ethics, Values and Politics

However conceived, Aristotle's ethics remains as richly provocative of philosophical reflection today as in previous centuries. A strong impetus for the recent renewed interest among analytic philosophers, manifest in the indispensable collection of essays on the subject edited by Amélie Rorty (1980), is a sense that ethics has become too narrowly focused and removed from practical concerns. As Rorty has noted, Aristotle emphasizes not so much the conditions motivating rational moral agency (the Kantian tradition) or the evaluation of actions or practices (the utilitarian) as the proper development of character. Thus ethics is firmly rooted in psychology, is dialectical rather than scientifically demonstrative in approach, and necessarily moves to political theory.

The Rorty collection is organized as a running commentary on the *Nicomachean Ethics.* Except for a 1965 article by W. F. R. Hardie, the same focus is present in the four essays included in the Moravcsik volume (1967). In contrast, the *Eudemian Ethics* is often cited in the articles on anthropology, ethics, economics, politics, law and history collected by Jonathan Barnes et al. (vol. 2, 1977). Anthony Kenny's companion study (1978) to that on the will draws heavily from the *Eudemian Ethics,* viewed in its relation to the other work. The differences this makes are displayed in comparing this study with the very different but also effective study by John Cooper (1975), who takes the *Eudemian Ethics* and the *Magna Moralia* to be early works and who, perhaps accordingly, chooses to concentrate on Aristotle's theories of practical reasoning and *eudaimonia* (well-being, living well, flourishing—not "happiness," the usual translation until recent years). Richard Sorabji (1980) represents Aristotle as an indeterminist in his anthropology (against Hintikka and others but with the main drift of current interpretation) and relates Aristotle's sophisticated discussions of "necessity" to issues of culpability in human action, with reference both to personal morality and to politics and law. Politics, for Aristotle, is an extension of ethics as practical wisdom into the affairs of the *polis* (city). The incomplete work *Politics* deals briefly with this extension; most of it surveys types of constitutions, without arguing for a fully developed position.

Value theory is a late modern invention (see chapter 21). But since Aristotle's scope is so wide, how might it be accommodated, if at all, to contemporary axiological interests? A study by the noted classical scholar Whitney Oates (1963), assuming a Platonic perspective in the "unity of Plato's thought" tradition of Paul Elmer More, claims that Aristotle's empiricist metaphysics prevented him from adequately coming to grips with the problem of value and its ontological grounding. In effect, he splits off questions of value from questions of being, in Oates's view. Probably few of the interpreters mentioned above would disagree, for this split has been taken for granted in most twentieth-century logical empirical tradition. The issue, as Oates raised it, has not yet come under much explicit discussion in Aristotle studies. No doubt it will, for there is in Aristotle's thought a breadth of vision that invites such discussion, and modern empiricist presuppositions are themselves not wholly imbedded in his scheme of things.

Allan, Donald J. *The Philosophy of Aristotle.* 2nd ed. London: Oxford Univ. Pr., 1970. (1st ed., 1952.)

Barnes, Jonathan, Malcolm Schofield, and Richard Sorabji, eds. *Articles on Aristotle.* 4v. London: Duckworth, 1975–79. (Previously published articles, most not recent.)

Blum, Alan F. *Theorizing.* London: Heinemann, 1974.

Bosley, Richard. *Aspects of Aristotle's Logic.* Assen: Van Gorcum, 1975.

Cherniss, Harold. *Aristotle's Criticism of Plato and the Academy.* New York: Russell & Russell, 1944. Repr., 1962. (Only vol. 1 of a projected 2v. study was published.)

——. *Aristotle's Criticism of Presocratic Philosophy.* Baltimore, Md.: Johns Hopkins Univ. Pr., 1935. Repr.: New York: Octagon Books, 1964.

Clark, Stephen R. L. *Aristotle's Man: Speculations upon Aristotelian Anthropology.* Oxford: Clarendon Pr., 1975.

Cooper, John M. *Reason and Human Good in Aristotle.* Cambridge, Mass.: Harvard Univ. Pr., 1975.

Düring, Ingemar, and G. E. L. Owen, eds. *Aristotle and Plato in the Mid-Fourth Century.* Goeteborg: Almqvist & Wiksell, 1957. (Studia graeca et latina Gothoburgensia, Vol. 11.)

Evans, John D. G. *Aristotle's Concept of Dialectic.* Cambridge and London: Cambridge Univ. Pr., 1977.

Fortenbaugh, William W. *Aristotle on Emotion.* New York: Barnes & Noble, 1975; London: Duckworth, 1971.

Grayeff, Felix. *Aristotle and His School: An Inquiry into the History of Peripatos with Commentary on Metaphysics Z, H, Λ and Θ.* London: Duckworth, 1974.

Hartman, Edwin. *Substance, Body and Soul: Aristotelian Investigations.* Princeton, N.J.: Princeton Univ. Pr., 1977.

Hintikka, Jaakko. *Time and Necessity: Studies in Aristotle's Theory of Modality.* Oxford: Clarendon Pr., 1973.

Jaeger, Werner. *Aristotle: Fundamentals of the History of His Development.* 2nd ed. Tr. by Richard Robinson. Oxford and New York: Oxford Univ. Pr., 1948. (1st ed., 1934; German eds., 1923 and 2nd rev. ed., 1955.)

Kenny, Anthony. *The Aristotelian Ethics: A Study of the Relationship be-

tween the Eudemian and Nicomachean Ethics of Aristotle. Oxford: Clarendon Pr., 1978.

———. *Aristotle's Theory of the Will.* New Haven, Conn. and London: Yale Univ. Pr., 1979.

Leszl, Walter. *Aristotle's Conception of Ontology.* Padua: Editrice Antenore, 1975. (Studia Aristotelica 7.)

———. *Logic and Metaphysics in Aristotle: Aristotle's Treatment of Types of Equivocity and Its Relevance to His Metaphysical Theories.* Padua: Editrice Antenore, 1970.

Lloyd, Geoffrey E. R. *Aristotle: The Growth and Structure of His Thought.* London: Cambridge Univ. Pr., 1968.

Lynch, John P. *Aristotle's School: A Study of a Greek Educational Institution.* Berkeley: Univ. of California Pr., 1972.

McMullin, Ernan, ed. *The Concept of Matter.* Notre Dame, Ind.: Univ. of Notre Dame Pr., 1963.

Moravcsik, Julius M. E., ed. *Aristotle: A Collection of Critical Essays.* Garden City, N.J.: Doubleday Anchor, 1967.

Nussbaum, Martha Craven. *Aristotle's De Motu Animalium: Text with Translation, Commentary, and Interpretive Essays.* Princeton, N.J.: Princeton Univ. Pr., 1978.

Oates, Whitney J. *Aristotle and the Problem of Value.* Princeton, N.J.: Princeton Univ. Pr., 1963.

Owens, Joseph. *The Doctrine of Being in the Aristotelian Metaphysics: A Study in the Greek Background of Medieval Thought.* 2nd ed., rev. Toronto: Pontifical Institute of Medieval Studies, 1963. (1st ed., 1951.)

Preus, Anthony. *Science and Philosophy in Aristotle's Biological Works.* Hildesheim, N.Y.: Olms, 1975.

Randall, John Herman, Jr. *Aristotle.* New York: Columbia Univ. Pr., 1960.

Rorty, Amélie Oksenberg, ed. *Essays on Aristotle's Ethics.* Berkeley and London: Univ. of California Pr., 1980.

Ross, William David. *Aristotle.* 5th rev. ed. New York: Barnes & Noble, 1953. (Orig. ed., 1923.)

Solmsen, Friedrich. *Aristotle's System of the Physical World: A Comparison with His Predecessors.* Cornell Studies in Classical Philology, vol. 33. Ithaca, N.Y.: Cornell Univ. Pr., 1960.

Sorabji, Richard. *Aristotle on Memory.* Providence, R.I.: Brown Univ. Pr., 1972.

———. *Necessity, Cause and Blame: Perspectives on Aristotle's Theory.* Ithaca, N.Y.: Cornell Univ. Pr.; London: Duckworth, 1980.

Stead, George Christopher. *Divine Substance.* Oxford: Clarendon Pr., 1977.

Yates, Francis A. *The Art of Memory.* Chicago: Univ. of Chicago Pr.; London: Routledge & Paul, 1966.

HELLENISTIC PHILOSOPHY AND ITS AFTERMATH

The achievement of Aristotle and his school was of such magnitude that many have regarded the succeeding Hellenistic period, even the next 1,600 years or more, as largely one of decline in philosophy. Scholarship of the past several decades has shown this view to be mistaken. Throughout the period between the death of Alexander the Great to the end of the Roman Republic (323–31 B.C.), called the Hellenistic Age, Athens remained the supremely hospitable environment for philosophical study, though Alexandria and other cities also came to be known as centers of learning. Greek philosophy ruled intellectual life. In Athens and elsewhere the record shows attention to new questions of philosophical importance, lively dialectical dispute and, with increasing knowledge, further specialization. David Sedley sums up the situation well (Schofield et al., 1980). Physics was a largely speculative discipline, he reports. The empirical and mathematical disciplines, including astronomy, were now left to specialists, as were literary studies to grammarians. Philosophy, too, became a specialty, isolated from other branches of learning. The philosophical systems that survived competition offered a comprehensive ethical vision that could explain the proper relation of human beings to the world and serve as an organizer for all other permitted areas of inquiry.

The Epicureans and Stoics, especially, offered new moral perspectives. Inseparably, they also attempted to form knowledge of all sorts not by contemplation of eternal forms but through observation of particulars; and in doing so they had to face challenges from the Skeptics, the third great constellation of Hellenistic thinkers. In approximately 266 the Skeptic Arcesilaus became head of the Academy itself.

To provide something of the flavor of inquiry, I simply list in quite general form some new issues that emerged among these philosophers. Each one gets unusually clear, perceptive treatment in the essays collected by Malcolm Schofield et al. (1980). (1) Are all perceptions true? (2) Is there any valid or reliable knowledge? If so, how "proved" or by what criteria? Is demonstrative argument either possible or useful? Can the senses provide reliable evidence for belief? (3) How are we to recognize redundancy in explanatory argument, that is, what does not add any logical weight to it? Once we have found what is redundant, is anything very significant left (notably, that would not have been initially evident)? (4) Can one live by radical *skepsis,* by relentless examination of the assumptions and conditions of belief? In particular, if one withholds assent to anything not given in appearance *(epochē),* what can one reasonably assent to for purposes of knowledge or behavior? (5) In philosophy/ science and art, how may thought mirror (or interpret or construct expressions of) what is first presented in experience? (6) In the strict sense, is the term "cause" to be reserved for nonpropositional items that actively bring about effects (Stoics)? How is causal action to be understood, and how does it differ from the functioning of events and propositions (for example, in an explanation or in an ascription of responsibility)? What (other) kinds of causes are there? Further, what physical implications could derive from our understanding of causation? (7) Is every event necessarily linked with exceptionless causal regularity of some sort? (8) Among our preconceptions, those general concepts that we may be said to hold naturally and to use as bases for testing our philosophical ideas, is "God" such a notion or can the existence of God be proved by such notions?

These questions all presuppose skeptical challenges, either of the radical sort that seeks to establish that no knowledge is possible ("Academic skepticism," first formulated in the Platonic Academy, third century B.C.), or of the sort which recommends suspension of judgment in that evidence is not sufficient to establish that knowledge is possible ("Pyrrhonian skepticism," dating from Pyrrho of Elis, ca. 360–275 B.C.).

A. A. Long (1975) provides the most comprehensive account of major developments in the Hellenistic Age. John Dillon (1977) traces what happened to Platonism in the five centuries after Plato's death, especially from Antiochus of Ascalon to the great Neoplatonist, Plotinus (80 B.C. to 220 A.D.). Epicurus' thought has been masterfully outlined by J. M. Rist (1972), whose companion volumes on the Stoics (1969, 1978) and Plotinus (1967) are also important. Fresh material on Stoic logic, metaphysics, epistemology, and ethics has been collected by A. A. Long (1971). Several kinds of epistemological interests among the Skeptics have been carefully distinguished by Charlotte Stough (1969). In view of the almost unparalleled influence of Stoic thought for nearly five centuries and since the Renaissance, both F. H. Sandbach's (1975) more popular treatment and David Haym's (1977) account of Stoic cosmology are useful to know.

The Cambridge History volume edited by A. H. Armstrong (1967) displays something of the transition from ancient to medieval themes, as do his other works (1940, 1979), Philip Merlan's noted historical-critical studies (1960, 1969), and the collection of essays on Neoplatonism edited by R. Baine Harris (1976). James Coulter's study (1976) of literary theory among fifth-sixth century A.D. Neoplatonists who commented on Plato's dialogues is important. It suggests a potential interplay among interests in logic, rhetoric, and hermeneutics (the study of interpretive process) as yet rarely explored among scholars who have ranged within the 1,100-year period between the first Presocratics and the later Neoplatonists.

A history of ideas approach, very different from that just anticipated and from analytic and historical-critical methods used by scholars so far cited, is taken by George Boas in his *Rationalism in Greek Philosophy* (1962). His is a synoptic exposition, based on a reading of the original texts but not entering into scholarly problems. It marks out a thousand-year story from the Presocratics to the Neoplatonists, emphasizing four themes: appearance versus reality, the methods used to establish that distinction, appraisals of life, and ethical theories. He places the high watermark in Plato and Aristotle, by virtue of their effort to attain "logical consistency" and to accept the material world "as an integral part of their philosophic architecture," and sees "degeneration" thereafter. Many standard histories have adopted a similar appraisal, which leaves us with a quandary as to why ancient successors to Platonic and Aristotelian philosophy have been extremely attractive to a broad array of modern thinkers.

Armstrong, Arthur Hilary. *The Architecture of the Intelligible Universe in the Philosophy of Plotinus: An Analytic and Historical Study.* Cambridge and New York: Cambridge Univ. Pr., 1940. Repr., 1967.

———. *Plotinian and Christian Studies.* London: Variorum Reprints, 1979.

———, ed. *The Cambridge History of Later Greek and Early Medieval Philosophy.* Cambridge and New York: Cambridge Univ. Pr., 1967.

Boas, George. *Rationalism in Greek Philosophy.* Baltimore, Md.: Johns Hopkins Univ. Pr.; Oxford: Oxford Univ. Pr., 1962.

Coulter, James A. *The Literary Microcosm: Theories of Interpretation of the Later Neoplatonists.* Leiden: Brill, 1976.

Dillon, John. *The Middle Platonists: 80 B.C. to A.D. 220.* Ithaca, N.Y.: Cornell Univ. Pr., 1977.

Hahm, David E. *The Origins of Stoic Cosmology.* Columbus: Ohio State Univ. Pr., 1977.

Harris, Random Baine, ed. *The Significance of Neoplatonism.* Albany: State Univ. of New York Pr., 1976. (Vol. 1 of Studies in Neoplatonism: Ancient and Modern for the International Society for Neoplatonic Studies.)

Long, A. A. *Hellenistic Philosophy: Stoics, Epicureans, Skeptics.* New York: Scribner's; London: Duckworth, 1975.

———, ed. *Problems in Stoicism.* London: Athlone Pr.; New York: Oxford Univ. Pr., 1971.

Merlan, Philip. *From Platonism to Neoplatonism.* 2nd ed. The Hague: Nijhoff, 1960. (1st ed., 1953.)

———. *Monopsychism, Mysticism, Metaconsciousness: Problems of the Soul in Neoaristotelian and Neoplatonic Tradition.* 2nd ed. The Hague: Nijhoff, 1969. (1st ed., 1963.)

Rist, John M. *Epicurus: An Introduction.* Cambridge and New York: Cambridge Univ. Pr., 1972.

———. *Plotinus: The Road to Reality.* Cambridge and New York: Cambridge Univ. Pr., 1967.

———. *Stoic Philosophy.* Cambridge and New York: Cambridge Univ. Pr., 1969.

———, ed. *The Stoics.* Berkeley: Univ. of California Pr., 1978.

Sandbach, F. H. *The Stoics.* New York: Norton; London: Chatto & Windus, 1975. Repr.: Berkeley: Univ. of California Pr., 1978.

Schofield, Malcolm, Myles Burnyeat, and Jonathan Barnes, eds. *Doubt and Dogmatism: Studies in Hellenistic Epistemology.* Oxford: Clarendon Pr., New York: Oxford Univ. Pr., 1980.

Stough, Charlotte L. *Greek Skepticism: A Study in Epistemology.* Berkeley and London: Univ. of California Pr., 1969.

3

Medieval, Renaissance, and Reformation Philosophy

Themes and Developments

Except in metaphysics and philosophy of religion, medieval thought has not been extensively studied by non-Roman Catholic philosophers in the twentieth century. There are occasional references in specialized studies, notably in logic and epistemology. As we move out of the classical period, five thematic points are to be emphasized at this stage in medieval historical scholarship.

1. First, the notion of a "mind" of the Middle Ages, and of "the medieval outlook," long held popular by intellectual historians Henry Osborne Taylor, Frederick B. Artz, and others, has become too misleading to retain. It tends to divide us more sharply from that part of our heritage than is warranted. As more knowledge about this period is accrued, the more interestingly diverse it becomes and the clearer is its continuing influence in current intellectual life, including philosophy.

2. Although the main outlines to be found in histories of medieval thought are about the same now as they were over fifty years ago, the content is gradually shifting. As yet, no overall account of medieval philosophy as such captures these changes. Apart from the general histories, there is a fine intellectual history (400–1350) by Gordon Leff (1958), a sketch by Julius Weinberg (1964), a brief account of logic and metaphysics by D. P. Henry (1972), the classic survey of "Christian philosophy" in this period by Etienne Gilson (1955), and a more general summary by Armand Maurer (1962)—the latter two from the Pontifical Institute of Medieval Studies in Toronto. The Cambridge history of early (Armstrong, *Cambridge History of Later*

51

Greek and Early Medieval Philosophy, 1967, cited on p. 49) and later medieval philosophy (Kretzmann, 1982) is an indispensable resource. Much of the relevant work remains in German, Italian, Latin, Arabic, Hebrew, Polish, and French. The extensive German writings of Martin Grabmann (1875–1949) and successors, for example, have not been translated, unlike most of Gilson's work. Moreover, twentieth-century historical-critical scholarship has shown many works long attributed to various of the great medieval philosophers to be spurious, with other, authentic works, newly assigned to them. Finally, the extremely technical language of the late medieval scholastics and the complexity of their argumentation often served admirable purposes but make large portions of their writings inaccessible to all but specialists, as is true of the secondary literature itself. Many of the texts and relevant historical literature are still available only in Latin, Arabic, or Greek. Among works helpful to nonspecialists, Lutheran theologian Jaroslav Pelikan's ongoing history of the development of Christian doctrine, which so far extends to 1300 (1971–78) provides indispensable background. Ideally, none of these works should be used independent of scholarship on other aspects of medieval life and thought. However, none substantially reflects that other scholarship, which has made great strides in the post-World War II period. None even begins to look at the rich confluence of cultures and other influences (such as technology, disease) in the rise and development of the so-called West which William H. McNeill's historical studies have especially explored. Leff's (1958) comes closest.

3. While Augustine and Aquinas retain the key roles long imputed to them, Augustine more than ever—as have lesser giants like Anselm, Abelard, and Bonaventure—in recent decades a clearer picture of Jewish and Islamic contributions has been emerging. More is also understood about the more general achievements of late medieval "scholasticism," especially about the importance to philosophy of William of Ockham and of the Oxford Franciscans, particularly John Duns Scotus.

4. Studies have provided a much better grasp on the intertwining history of logic, theory of language, and rhetoric than was true thirty years ago. As this knowledge is more fully developed and assimilated, ways of understanding the entire history of philosophy may well change significantly.

5. The division of philosophy into two major streams, Platonic and Aristotelian, is a widespread error, chiefly perpetrated by nineteenth-century historians as they looked at the Middle Ages and its after-

math. There may be some value in applying the distinction very roughly to, say, twelfth- or twentieth-century interests; and the two philosophers certainly have had a rather divergent influence, as they were interpreted, from their own lifetimes on. For example, some Platonic aspects of Augustinian doctrine and modes of inquiry—far from all—were radically countered by thirteenth-century thinkers like Aquinas who were newly impressed with Aristotle. It is especially pertinent to note that Neoplatonic thought, especially its dualistic metaphysics, had an important bearing on medieval thought through Augustine. But evidence does not support making general use of this myth of two streams.

The Emergence of Christian Thought

From the biblical period on, both theology and theologically oriented philosophy emerged from "apologies," attempts to defend the faith against detractors by a tiny, beleaguered Christian minority. Christian apology had four main features: (1) reflection first on oral, then on written traditions about the extraordinary salvific events they believed God had brought to pass through Jesus' life, death, and resurrection; (2) appropriation of the Jewish scriptures and God's covenant with Israel; (3) in the face of "pagan" attacks, coming to terms with classical thought, using arguments taken from defenses of Judaism and from Greek philosophy and often attempting to show continuity of the divine Logos from beliefs and practices of philosophy to those of faith (from Jewish apology, perhaps the most-used theory to explain such continuity was the claim that Plato and others had read the Old Testament); (4) in that the early Christian communities saw themselves as part of a life-transforming process, one universal in scope, bearing an equal concern with moral issues as with other matters of faith.

Apologetics, both as defense against attack and as a way of commending the faith to cultural outsiders, was an active, philosophically respectable enterprise long after Christendom was safely established. For example, when Thomas Aquinas wrote his *Summa of the True Christian Faith against the Gentiles* (1259–64) few "pagans" were left in the West to read it. The treatise was not really intended for them. In fact, proofs for the existence of God only became part of doctrinal theology when they were no longer necessary for purposes of defense. As Pelikan has averred (Vol. 1, 1971), theologians could afford to give reason its due "when its subordination to revelation had been secured." Doctrinal theology, conceived as an ordered explication and grounding of Christian faith and life, was also supposed to function as the true philosophy or successor to philosophy. Theology was meant to be the way to wisdom that properly fulfills both the messianic hopes of Israel and Gentile needs and aspirations. As Pelikan rightly indicates, problems inherent in this view have never left theology. Nor could they ever have been totally ignored. Once the sociopolitical and ecclesiastical props of orthodoxy began to fall away after the Reformation, these problems were to gain prominence once more; and they remain prominent to this day.

Augustine (354–430) and His Influence

Western medieval theology, with what remained of philosophy, was chiefly a series of footnotes to Augustine. His works, affirming yet often transforming the methods and doctrines of philosophy available to him from the past 900 years, set forth the primary terms and conditions under which even those opposing him were to do theology over the next millenium and more. His *City of God* (413–27) served as the definitive apologia until the modern era. His *Enchiridion* (421–23) established faith, hope, and love as the three theological virtues to accompany the cardinal moral virtues of antiquity. Ambrose had introduced the notion of "cardinal virtues" in the fourth century A.D. (Plato had singled out wisdom, courage, temperance, and justice). In doctrine, his formulations on nature, sin, reason, and grace (an anti-Pelagian view which emphasized the sovereign predestinating—but not damning—grace of God versus redemption through human initiative and merit), the person and work of Christ, the trinitarian framework, church and ministry, and almost everything else, were used by every theologian, even if frequently honored in the breach. More, it was principally he among the church fathers on whom theologically oriented thinkers relied, right through the Reformation and beyond. In the twelfth century, for example, Peter Lombard's *Sentences,* which for two centuries was to be the basic compilation of authorities used in the universities, quotes Augustine more than twice as often as all others combined. In many respects, the theologies of Luther and Calvin were a repristination of Augustine's theology, accompanied by a fresh reading of the Bible made possible through Renaissance scholarship. One cannot read them accurately without knowing his language and arguments, both those that are quite clear and those that are bothersomely ambiguous or faulty. Here we speak of the West only; Augustine had little influence in the East, though some of his works were translated into Greek in his lifetime.

In the areas that were to bear "Western" culture, Christendom became a reality during the fourth century—a cultural crisis of enormous proportions. Augustine lived through this crisis; his life and thought encapsulate it. In the fifth century the University of Constantinople, possibly founded by Constantine himself, became the successor to Athens as the center of Greek learning, so that non-Christian philosophers had almost nowhere to turn for status and support long before Justinian forbade pagans to teach in the schools in 529. Henceforth philosophy had to serve chiefly as the handmaid to theology, as it had already done in Augustine's case. In its defense of free will and divine providence, Boethius' *Consolation of Philosophy* (523–24), nonbiblical and nondoctrinal in content though written by a theologian, did continue to have an effect on medieval literature and devotion. One of the most widely read books for over 500 years, this and his other writings had a great influence on early Scholastic philosophy. From the beginning, much of the language and ideas of doctrinal theology had derived from philosophy. Discussions on the immortality of the soul and on the absoluteness or impassibility of God were heavily philosophical, not biblical. Augustine's philosophy consummately represents these traditions.

His mother a Christian, his father not, Augustine had a classical education, was already a teacher early in his twenties and by age thirty had become public orator of Milan. His *Confessions* (397–401), a self-reflective probing scarcely matched for its unveiling of a course of life until modern times (see Weintraub, *The Value of the Individual,* 1978, cited on p. 113), relates his intense struggle to gain a true view of things, climaxed in his conversion experience of August 386 at age thirty-one but continued in a deep-going "search for understanding" thereafter as a convert, priest, bishop, and theologian. The notion of faith seeking understanding, later taken up and made popular by Anselm, was drawn by Augustine from an early Latin translation of Isaiah 7:9, "Unless you believe, you will not understand." This became an idea of key importance for medieval theology and, in new forms, within much modern theology as well. Despite the exceptional inwardness and individuality of the *Confessions,* it was written to present one man's part in a universal story, a typical, not a distinctively individual, narrative, a testimony to the divine work of creation and redemption. In this light, it seemed perfectly natural to him to present his whole life in an integrated manner, not as one in which the preconversion life, including the philosophy, was split off from what followed.

Augustine used Neoplatonic language extensively. His notion of learning as recollection within (the indwelling Christ as teacher) bears this cast, as does his talk of God as unchangeable essence. Informed scholarship nevertheless places his theological understanding overall as Pauline, not Platonic. The philosophical language used was normally bent to fit that frame.

The best general exposition of Augustine's philosophy is still Etienne Gilson's (1960). R. A. Markus has contributed a seventy-eight page summary in the *Cambridge History* (ed. by A. H. Armstrong, 1967, cited on p. 49) and has edited a collection of critical essays (1972). In an existential style, Robert Meagher (1978) offers a broader introduction, interspersed with readings from Augustine. Robert O'Connell's (1978) work on his aesthetics is cited in chapter 27 on page 469. The *Cambridge History* also has useful chapters by Philip Merlan on Greek philosophy from Plato to Plotinus, by Henry Chadwick on Philo, the beginnings of Christian philosophy and the Alexandrians, by A. H. Armstrong on Plotinus, by A. C. Lloyd on the later Neoplatonists, by I. P. Sheldon-Williams on Christian Platonist tradition in the East, by H. Liebeschütz on Western Christian thought from Boethius to Anselm, and by Richard Walzer on early Islamic philosophy.

Islamic Thought

After the death of Mohammed in 632 A.D., Islam was left with the Koran and increasing pressures to defend the faith. In their assiduous search for support, Islamic scholars began to produce translations from the Greeks, especially Aristotle, in the early ninth century, a tradition already begun in Syria in the fifth century and a century earlier in the Latin West but with relatively few texts. The entire corpus of Aristotelian writings, except the *Politics,* had been translated into Arabic by the mid-eleventh century, when the translation movement stopped.

Quite gradually over the next two centuries the distinctively philosophical phase of Islamic thought began to emerge. Use of syllogistic form and of new modes of analogical argument especially affected the philosophization of traditional Islamic thought through the twelfth century. Between the eleventh and thirteenth centuries a scholastic-Aristotelian natural theology called Kalam (in a narrower sense) became the orthodox Muslim position, as it continues to be today. In his mammoth work *The Philosophy of the Kalam* (1976), a study of this aspect of Islamic religion, Harry Wolfson emphasizes these problem areas: divine attributes, the Koran, creation, atomism, causality, predestination, and free will.

Other philosophical scholarship on the wider history of medieval Arabic philosophy is especially well represented in essays by the influential Oxford philosopher Richard Walzer (1962), a German Jewish emigrant, and in a collection presented to him on his seventieth birthday (Stern et al., 1972). An excellent historical introduction to the formation of Aristotelian tradition in Islam has been given by F. E. Peters (1968). The recent collection of essays on medieval Islamic philosophy and science edited by George Hourani (1975) betokens some fine ongoing work. Two Arabic philosophers had marked influence on Christian scholastic philosophy as prime interpreters of Aristotle: first Avicenna (980–1037), then Averroes (1126–98) even more. Nicholas Rescher (1964, 1967, and other works; also in Hourani, 1975) has demonstrated the outstanding contributions of the Arabic logicians to the late medieval understanding of Aristotelian logic.

Jewish Thought

A thoroughgoing history of Jewish medieval philosophy in English, using the fruits of twentieth-century interpretative scholarship, has yet to be written. Julius Guttmann's *Philosophies of Judaism* (1964) is a helpful start. Guttmann's work also discusses ancient and modern philosophy and is notable for its emphasis on "Judaism" rather than on particular problems or thinkers, as such. Over several decades Harry Wolfson (1979) studied repercussions of their encounters with Arabic philosophy on several themes pursued by Jewish thinkers. Wolfson emphasized the essential rationalism of Jewish philosophy during that period, notably regarding the divine attributes, creation, causality, and free will. Jacob Dienstag's excellent selection (1975) of twenty articles on relationships between the philosophy of Maimonides and that of Aquinas was dedicated to Wolfson (1887–1974), whose influence on such studies has been considerable. The volume opens with a characterization of non-Jewish sources in Greek and Arabic philosophy used by Maimonides—Aristotle above all. Although Maimonides (1135–1204) played an extremely important role in Jewish thought long after the twelfth century, only since the late nineteenth century have historians explored his influence and that of other Jewish thinkers on Christian thinkers. This influence appears to have been minor overall, though it is of special interest in Aquinas. Within the fast-growing literature on medieval Jewish thought David Hartman's summary (1976) of Maimonides's work is representative.

Jewish traditions have never yielded truly systematic works of doctrine and apologetics like those of Augustine and Aquinas, or even like those of Friedrich Schleiermacher, Karl Barth, and Paul Tillich in modern times. This no doubt partly explains why the search for philosophical structure and analysis has not attended Jewish religious thought to nearly the same degree and why most of the studies are historical-critical and philological, not analytic.

Logic, Language, and Rhetoric

The history of medieval logic is still in its elementary stage. D. P. Henry (1972) has used the system of Polish logician Stanislaw Lesniewski to analyze the highly systematized Latin contrived by scholastic logicians from Anselm on for use in metaphysical disputes. Among items of interest to modern logicians are scholastic attempts to distinguish between the meaning of a name *(significatio)* and the ways a name may be related to things *(suppositio),* inclusion, negation and nonbeing, and demonstrations of infinite regress. Of interest to students of metaphysics are the ways in which these later medieval logicians used such tools to discuss "being," changes of being, and the existence of God. Philotheus Boehner's brief historical survey of scholastic logic (1952) is not informed by interests of modern logic but is still illuminating. Ernest Moody's essays (1975) comprise both interests but deal more with substantive issues outside logic. Since 1935 he has published several books on medieval logic.

Robert Ayers (1979) has shown of Tertullian (ca. 160–ca. 240), a prominent early apologist and theologian, that, far from arguing in a paradoxical way, as he has regularly been interpreted by modern writers, he was skillfully using standard forms of rhetoric, semantics, and logic familiar to him from Aristotle and the Stoics. Tertullian, moreover, did not condemn all philosophy—also contrary to the conventional interpretation—but used and praised it as an instrument of reason. What he did strongly oppose was speculative uses of philosophy to lead unwary Christians into heresy and disbelief, a major motif in Christian thought that still continues. Ayers also finds in Augustine, Anselm (eleventh century), and Aquinas (thirteenth century) a sophisticated ability to use philosophical language theory, analysis, and logic to supply a rational and intelligible faith, features of their work long neglected. Augustine, in his view, had a very rich philosophy of language, gained especially from rhetorical tradition, and considered propositional logic, as he had learned it from the Stoics, to be divinely ordained. The general assumption that Thomas Aquinas used only Aristotelian syllogistic logic in his critical work is also held in doubt by Ayers. Rather, he finds strong evidence of Aquinas' having used a sophisticated semiotics derived from Anselm and other earlier scholastic logicians, well understanding features of what would today be called the pragmatics, semantics, and syntactics of language use.

It was Augustine who first formulated a distinct theory of signs. As Marcia Colish (1968) has demonstrated, the influence of Augustine's theory on many Western medieval thinkers from his time to the fourteenth century was strong. Classically, verbal signs had been viewed as only one species among sensible signs. Augustine's theory places emphasis on signs as verbal. On this basis the medieval trio of basic studies (grammar, rhetoric, and dialectic—called the *trivium* after about 600) came to be formed, with its focus on words as intermediaries between subject and object, speaker and audience; and these means were primarily related to issues of religious knowledge. God, according to Augustine, can be known through the creation, chiefly by infusion of grace in the experience of faith, but also in another way, through the book of nature. The knowledge of God is mediated through signs, seen as instrumental, not as identical with the object.

Because of the varying circumstances of their times, Augustine expresses the theory primarily through rhetoric, Anselm through grammar, Aquinas through dialectic, which by the thirteenth century had come to dominate, even quash, the other two in university education. This trio of linguistic studies had been accompanied by what was later called the *quadrivium:* arithmetic, geometry, astronomy, and music. In the sixth century Cassiodorus named them "the seven liberal arts." Later on, natural philosophy and ethics were included in advanced curricula, and when philosophy became a university subject in the thirteenth century metaphysics and logic were added.

In his excellent introduction to the history of rhetoric, George Kennedy (1980) distinguishes three strands in evidence from the fifth century B.C. on: the technical (originally for public speaking, especially in the courts, but also turned to literary use—predominant in the medieval period), the sophistic (in the Middle Ages much stronger in the East but reemergent in the Renaissance), and the philosophical (starting with Socrates and Plato against the sophists—until the seventeenth century chiefly manifest in dialectic or logic, but not strong). It is important to know the history of rhetoric, not only because of its general influence on styles of discovery and communication but more specifically because of its powerful effect on education, on the place of philosophy in curricula, and on methods used by philosophers themselves.

According to Kennedy, until the twentieth century any direct influence of Plato's thought on rhetoric had been minor, despite its intrinsic value. Until the twelfth century the influence of Aristotle's more developed views were also only occasional, and he, too, was not regularly cited by rhetoricians until the twentieth century. Drawing from the Stoics, Augustine treated rhetoric, especially in *De Doctrina Christiana* (397, 427), as a part of logic (along with canonics—the study of criteria for truth—and dialectic). In the West rhetoric was largely accepted on the terms set by Augustine, who in substance was chiefly adapting Cicero, until the twelfth century, though in the early medieval period he did not contribute so much to the survival of classical rhetoric as did Gregory the Great (sixth century) or Isidore of Seville (seventh century). Before his conversion to Christianity at age thirty-one, Augustine had supported himself as a teacher of rhetoric for most of his adult life. Stanley Bonner's (1977) study of rhetorical tradition in Roman education illustrates a great deal of the content and styles he would have adopted. Since his major contributions to the theory are within the context of biblical studies, preaching, and Christian education, the emphasis is on technical rhetoric, style, and consistent development of themes, not on logical argument.

In the Christian East, the sophistic strand has been prominent; there rhetorical tradition has been far more conservative and static over the past 2,000 years. In both the East and the Latin West, nonphilosophical rhetoric was the dominant structuring element in classical education wherever it survived. Since the Renaissance, nonphilosophical rhetoric has remained a powerful influence in education generally, though with fluctuating fortunes, up to the present. Philosophical interests have not fared nearly so well.

Scholasticism

In its clearest sense, "scholasticism" simply refers to the pattern of organization and methods of inquiry and communication used in medieval universities, the earliest of which derived from monastic or cathedral "schools" in the twelfth century (see Anton Pegis, 1963, in an excellent discussion of issues that plague twentieth-century views of scholasticism). The pattern was that of going through a prescribed course of formal study within a corporation of masters and students, first in "arts," then in advanced studies, and receiving a degree at the end. By the end of the twelfth century, nearly all Aristotle's writings tended to be on the prescribed list. Eleventh-century contributions to methods of discourse, especially formed through their own reading of Aristotle by Anselm and Abelard, undergirded the two primary scholastic methods of lectures (readings and explications of prescribed texts) and of disputation (formal examination of "questions"—"the living cell of school teaching," as Gilson has said) in class and in public. Following the church fathers, masters wrote treatises (continuous expositions of a question or set of questions) and commentaries.

These scholastic centers were established in France, Italy, and England in the thirteenth century and in the Germanic areas in the fourteenth. All used Latin. Among the liberal arts only dialectic had much of a place in higher learning. By the thirteenth century the universities were virtually dominated by the mendicant orders, especially the Franciscans and Dominicans—both of whom had their own doctors of theology and their own arts schools—and, with the notable exception of Oxford, were pursuing a very restricted range of interests.

A second meaning of "scholasticism" refers to its full blooming in the thirteenth century. Several other meanings are associated with the view that scholastic doctrine reached its fullest and finest form in Aquinas, one which long tended to ignore, downplay, or discredit other scholastic syntheses (most notably by Bonaventure, Duns Scotus, and Ockham). By the eighteenth century interest in these competing schools of thought had dwindled, even among Roman Catholics. When scholasticism as a concerted enterprise reemerged in the mid-nineteenth century, Thomism was dominant. In a 1879 encyclical Pope Leo XIII called for a return to scholasticism, especially Thomism. He then asked the University of Louvain to establish a chair of Thomistic philosophy, first held by the zealous Desiré Mercier, who in 1882 began promulgating the notion of a "perennial" philosophy best represented by scholasticism in its Thomist form. This position has not died out; it is often what is currently, if falsely, meant when the word "scholasticism" is used.

For over thirty years, from 1895 on, Maurice De Wulf prominently insisted that beginning with Anselm and reaching consummate expression in Aquinas, a "common," coherent scholastic philosophy separate from theology had been attained. Those who accepted his position ranked all philosophers according to their conformity with

Aquinas's great synthesis. Others held that there were two or three main traditions (Augustinian, Averroist, Thomist) but only one authentic philosophy, the Aristotelianism of Aquinas. Then, from the 1920s on, with more thoroughgoing scholarship, Thomist Étienne Gilson laid out a far more variegated map, in which many distinct and competing syntheses appear, all of them chiefly using the new-found possibilities of philosophy to acquire greater theological wisdom. As late as 1937, however, the rationalist Emile Bréhier was trying to write a history reducing medieval philosophy to an appendix of Greek ideas, totally separate from theological encounter with those ideas. Only variants of Gilson's perspective have held up. Medieval philosophy, including that of Aquinas, was created almost completely by theologians and within the framework of their theological interests. Scholasticism itself was a diverse achievement. It includes numerous philosophical developments, some of which can be applied independently of the theological setting, as can be seen in a collection of thirteen essays published between 1947 and 1965 and one original essay by Timothy Potts, edited by James Ross (1971).

Eleventh and Early Twelfth Centuries

Scholastic method began in the eleventh-century controversies over the degree to which reasoned discourse in the Aristotelian manner (then called "dialectic") should be used in theology. The issues of whether universals are real and of whether logic was simply the science of words, of grammar versus dialectic, played a central role in these debates. Stimulated by writings of Porphyry (a teacher of Augustine) and Boethius on Aristotle's *Categories,* the problem of universals was a theologically important issue. For example: are individuals embodiments of universals, they wondered; and, accordingly, what does it mean to speak of three persons in one godhead?

Anselm (1033–1109) applied dialectic, along with the philosophical classics, only to theological topics, in a refreshing but unsystematic way. Even his famed "ontological" argument for the existence of God (as Kant called it) is offered in the framework of a prayer. In his view, faith and scripture are not to be subjected to dialectic, but one uses dialectic in order to understand rationally what one believes. Thus one comes closer to the light, though he does not suppose that the mysteries to which faith points can be grasped by reason alone. Anselm believed that universals—genera and species—have reality.

Abelard (1079–1142), in contrast, was more of a dialectician, developing a logic of terms, propositions, and arguments via commentaries on Boethius's interpretations of Aristotle. Though unsystematic by later standards, Abelard's discussion of 150 theological questions in *Sic et Non* (1122) was the first comprehensive exposition of theology as an ordered discipline versus a contemplative practice. Through it, he sharpened a customary way of reconciling contradictory authorities through methodical doubt and inquiry that was influential for several centuries. Abelard carefully argued for the position that universals are significant words or concepts, and as such they are real in that they are terms that can be predicated of things, but are not things.

These two men and the other precursors of scholasticism tried to deal with the problem of universals with very limited tools, using some logic taken from the classics but lacking a critically supportive metaphysics. Using more advanced means, Aquinas held that universals have being and correspond to ultimate reality. The two Franciscans, Duns Scotus and nominalist Ockham, in arguing against such positions, developed still more sophisticated ways of considering relations between what we observe, what we say, and what is. In this fashion they broadened the scope of inquiry considerably.

Late Twelfth and Thirteenth Centuries

In the twelfth century new translations from Arabic and Greek science, Aristotle, and part of Plato's *Timaeus* stimulated more informed inquiry into relations between nature and God, with emphasis on Platonic and Neoplatonic themes. Other translations, especially from Aristotle and the Arabic thinkers, also enabled new work in logic, metaphysics, and humane letters. The seven liberal arts began to flourish. Some have named the period after the late twelfth century "the century of naturalism." The name fits, in that there was a widespread flowering of interest in nonspiritual nature—in the arts, in ethics and politics, in the greater use of vernacular language in literature, popular religion, historical writing and the law, and in what by the end of that century had come to be called "natural" or "experimental" science. These trends soon led to the rediscovery of the more humanistic, less scholastic Augustine as well. Walter Ullmann's (1966) study has outlined the influence of feudalism and other forces in the rapid upswing of interest in the free, self-standing individual within this period, an interest enhanced and clarified in Aquinas's brilliant Aristotelian account of the natural order.

The Franciscans first came to Oxford, in D. E. Sharp's (1930) account, in 1224, soon bringing it prominence as a center of learning. Among them, Robert Grosseteste (ca. 1175–1253), first chancellor of the university, was its most distinguished teacher. It was he (not the thirty-years younger Albert the Great, as some have supposed) who introduced Aristotle to the West, followed in this philosophical interest by other great Oxford Franciscan scholars treated by Sharp: Thomas of York, Roger Bacon, John Peckham, Richard of Middleton, and Duns Scotus.

Albert the Great (ca. 1206–80) was indeed responsible for bringing Aristotle to prominence among the scholastics (Kovach and Shahan, 1980), though his own thought also had a non-Aristotelian, Neoplatonic cast to it, as did the strongly Augustinian Franciscans'. Thomas Aquinas studied with him during Albert's brief tenure in Paris (1240–48) and followed him to Cologne (1248–52). His more intensive study of Aristotle, however, occurred during his years in Italy (1259–68). His two greatest works were conceived there—the *Summa Contra Gentiles* (1259–64) and the *Summa Theologiae* (1266 on, never completed). Both Albert and Aquinas believed that revealed truth was accessible to faith, not reason, but that reason had much work of its own to do, building knowledge through appeal to experience (being, sensible reality) and through demonstration. Aquinas's own philosophical interest was strictly in reason for purposes of a natural theology that utilizes reason to support faith, not for pursuits of an independent secular philosophy. In 1277, at both Paris and Oxford, where seculars had been battling the clerics for some time, such independence was decisively condemned by the ecclesiastical authorities.

What Thomas Aquinas brought forth did not issue in a period of Thomism, but in more controversy. For a time this was true even within his own order, though by the end of the thirteenth century Thomism was well on its way to becoming the official Dominican position. His greatness resides in his having achieved a monumental synthesis of scholastic learning in an age of synthesis and in a highly consistent Augustinian and Aristotelian frame.

Bonaventure and Thomas Aquinas

Bonaventure (1221–74) and Thomas Aquinas (1226–74) were exact contemporaries. A collection of eight essays edited by Robert Shahan and Francis Kovach (1976) shows the juxtaposition of their philosophical views and approaches. The Pope appointed them, respectively, to the Franciscan (Augustinian) and Dominican chairs at

Paris in 1257. The more entrenched Aristotelianism became among the Dominicans the more set upon critical opposition Bonaventure and his Franciscan followers became, appealing above all to Augustine. Bonaventure, however, went beyond Augustine to assert that all knowledge comes through the illumination of faith and that no independent role is to be attributed to sensory experience, philosophy, or science (Quinn, 1973).

Although Aquinas's overriding concern was also theological, his thinking made room for reasoned investigation of nature independent of doctrinal theology. He prominently added a refurbished use of analogy in his metaphysics and theology (George Klubertanz, 1960, a textual study; the logic of using analogy is further explored by Ralph McInerny, 1961). Moreover, Aquinas regarded the four cardinal virtues of antiquity (see p. 54), which he called "human" or "political" virtues, as sufficient in themselves, not having to be accompanied by Augustine's three theological virtues ("infused" by grace) to be truly virtuous. Others in his century also set in contrast, as he did, the "civic" man, whose actions were based on natural law, versus the man of faith, the "citizen" versus the "subject" (Ullmann, 1966).

Until recent decades, twentieth-century philosophical literature on the scholastics was dominated by that on Aquinas. A tight summary by the noted Thomist historian of philosophy, F. C. Copleston (1975), updates Gilson's lengthy, now classic account (1956). Ralph McInerny (1977) provides a broader overview. From an analytic perspective, D. J. O'Connor (1967) examines the fundamental place of natural law in his ethics. Three collections are especially notable: two sets of critical essays by both Thomist and non-Thomist philosophers—essays chosen for their interest to analytic philosophers, edited by Anthony Kenny (1969), new ones by him, Herbert McCabe and Peter Sheehan on Aquinas's philosophy of mind, and twelve previously published (1954–67) and new essays in *Monist*, edited by Lewis White Beck (1974); also a two-volume commemoration (*St. Thomas*, 1974) from the Pontifical Institute, only partly philosophical.

Fourteenth Century: Duns Scotus and William of Ockham

Like Aquinas, John Duns Scotus (ca. 1266–1308) also had a thorough knowledge and admiration of Aristotle's philosophy. He was a great master to American philosopher Charles Sanders Peirce (see Boler, *Charles Peirce and Scholastic Realism*, 1963, cited on p. 241), who called him "a vast logical genius," and there has been a major revival of his thought since mid-century. Unlike Aquinas, he did not believe an independent philosophy could adequately reveal any part of reality. The "subtle doctor," so named for the difficulty of his thought, drew with unusual effectiveness from Avicenna and very largely in the service of theology. An irenic spirit, he developed his own great synthesis almost entirely in dialogue with unnamed contemporaries—chiefly over against the Augustinian Henry of Ghent, not Aquinas—and in an effort to accommodate Augustinian and Aristotelian themes to each other. Scotist schools and studies of Scotus flourished into the eighteenth century. Allan Wolter's still valuable 1946 study of his metaphysics is prominent among the many fine-tuned studies done by him and others since the late 1930s. The revival is also betokened in two commemorative volumes: a *Monist* issue by Richard McKeon and others (1965) and an indispensable collection of fifteen new advanced studies edited by John Ryan and Bernardine Bonansea (1965).

Even greater interest has arisen among contemporary philosophers in the extraordinary philosophical accomplishments of William of Ockham (ca. 1285–1349). This is already superbly reflected in a synoptic analysis by Gordon Leff (1975) of his thinking about the cognitive-linguistic order (substituting a logical order, in which universals are treated solely as concepts, for a metaphysical order), the theological order (founded exclusively on faith), and the created order (man, nature, society). A *Monist* issue edited by Richard Martin (1978) covers historical influences of nominalist views, first brought fully to light by Ockham, and some contemporary forms.

Ockham entered Oxford a year or two after Scotus's death but had a close knowledge of Scotus's writings. By a decade later he had made his own mark through lectures on Peter Lombard's *Sentences* (Scotus's masterwork had been a commentary on the *Sentences*) and had advanced far toward becoming the most influential philosopher of his century. Trouble with the Avignon popes led to his excommunication in mid-life, and much of his last twenty years were taken up with polemics against absolutism in church or government. Thus, virtually all of his basic philosophical and theological writings come from the 1317–28 decade—in philosophy, especially in metaphysics, logic, and epistemology.

All the great thirteenth-century synthesists through Scotus had been realists. That is, in varying ways they attempted to demonstrate necessary truths about first causes and God based upon an assumed discovery within the details of sense experience of an intelligible order of abstract essences and necessary relations. Ockham roundly, painstakingly rejected this approach, radically restricting knowledge to direct experience of individuals and particular events, which he believed would yield objective, reliable knowledge. Through a bold semantic reconstruction of Aristotelian logic, he also found a way to restrict the acceptable reference of terms to the "naming" (hence "nominalism") of individual substances and singular sensible qualities. In this manner he cut away all realist use of abstract terms to refer to supposed entities ("Ockham's razor") and opened the way for a more richly detailed empirical analysis of relations between individuals or events, with strict appeal to empirical evidence and nonspeculative meanings.

Far from being the extravagant destroyer of scholasticism he was long painted to be, Ockham was a philosophical innovator of the first rank and produced a distinctive, masterful theological synthesis well within the scholastic tradition. Nevertheless, his scintillating breakthroughs did help dissolve many typically medieval perspectives and moved toward more "modern" themes, as Gordon Leff (1976) has aptly shown of a wide spectrum of changes in the fourteenth century.

Ayers, Robert H. *Language, Logic, and Reason in the Church Fathers: A Study of Tertullian, Augustine, and Aquinas.* New York: Olms, 1979.

Beck, Lewis White, ed. "Thomas Aquinas 1274–1974." *Monist* 58, no. 1:1–172 (Jan. 1974).

Boehner, Philotheus, O.F.M. *Medieval Logic: An Outline of Its Development from 1250 to c. 1400.* Manchester: Manchester Univ. Pr., 1952.

Bonner, Stanley F. *Education in Ancient Rome: From the Elder Cato to the Younger Pliny.* Berkeley and London: Univ. of California Pr., 1977.

Colish, Marcia L. *The Mirror of Language: A Study in the Medieval Theory of Knowledge.* New Haven, Conn. and London: Yale Univ. Pr., 1968.

Copleston, Frederick C. *Aquinas.* Baltimore, Md.: Penguin, 1975.

Dienstag, Jacob I., ed. *Studies in Maimonides and St. Thomas Aquinas.* New York: Ktav, 1975.

Gilson, Etienne. *The Christian Philosophy of Saint Augustine.* Tr. by L. E. M. Lynch. New York: Random House; London: Victor Gollanz, 1960. (From 2nd French ed., 1943.)

———. *The Christian Philosophy of Saint Thomas Aquinas.* Tr. by L. K. Shook. New York: Random House, 1956. (6th rev. ed. in French, 1965.)

———. *History of Christian Philosophy in the Middle Ages.* New York: Random House, 1955.

Guttmann, Julius. *Philosophies of Judaism: The History of Jewish Philosophy from Biblical Times to Franz Rosenzweig.* Tr. by David W. Silverman. New York: Holt, Rinehart & Winston, 1964.

Hartman, David. *Maimonides: Torah and Philosophic Quest.* Philadelphia, Pa.: Jewish Publication Society of America, 1976.

Henry, Desmond P. *Medieval Logic and Metaphysics.* London: Hutchinson, 1972.

Hourani, George F., ed. *Essays on Islamic Philosophy and Science.* Albany: State Univ. of New York Pr., 1975.

Kennedy, George A. *Classical Rhetoric and Its Christian and Secular Tradition from Ancient to Modern Times.* Chapel Hill: Univ. of North Carolina Pr., 1980.

Kenny, Anthony, ed. *Aquinas: A Collection of Critical Essays.* Garden City, N.Y.: Doubleday, 1969; London: Macmillan, 1970.

Klubertanz, George P. *St. Thomas on Analogy: A Textual Analysis and Systematic Synthesis.* Chicago: Loyola Univ. Pr., 1960.

Kovach, Francis J., and Robert W. Shahan, eds. *Albert the Great: Commemorative Essays.* Norman: Univ. of Oklahoma Pr., 1980.

Kretzmann, Norman, et al., eds. *The Cambridge History of Later Medieval Philosophy.* Cambridge and New York: Cambridge Univ. Pr., 1982.

Leff, Gordon. *The Dissolution of the Medieval Outlook: An Essay on Intellectual and Spiritual Change in the Fourteenth Century.* New York: Harper & Row, 1976.

———. *Medieval Thought: St. Augustine to Ockham.* Chicago: Quadrangle, 1958.

———. *William of Ockham: The Metamorphosis of Scholastic Discourse.* Totowa, N.J.: Roman & Littlefield, 1975.

McInerny, Ralph M. *The Logic of Analogy: An Interpretation of St. Thomas.* The Hague: Nijhoff, 1961.

———. *St. Thomas Aquinas.* Boston: Twayne, 1977.

McKeon, Richard, et al. "Philosophy of Duns Scotus, in Commemoration of the 700th Anniversary of His Birth." *Monist* 49, no. 4:519–669 (Oct. 1965).

Markus, Robert A., ed. *Augustine: A Collection of Critical Essays.* Garden City, N.Y.: Doubleday Anchor, 1972.

Martin, Richard M., ed. "Nominalism: Past and Present." *Monist* 61, no. 3:351–494 (July 1978).

Maurer, Armand A. *Medieval Philosophy.* Vol. 2 of *A History of Philosophy.* Ed. by Etienne Gilson. New York: Random House, 1962.

Meagher, Robert E. *An Introduction to Augustine.* New York: New York Univ. Pr., 1978.

Moody, Ernest A. *Studies in Medieval Philosophy, Science, and Logic: Collected Papers, 1933–1969.* Berkeley and London: Univ. of California Pr., 1975.

O'Connor, Daniel J. *Aquinas and Natural Law.* London: Macmillan, 1967.

Pegis, Anton C. *The Middle Ages and Philosophy: Some Reflections on the Ambivalence of Modern Scholasticism.* Chicago: Regnery, 1963.

Pelikan, Jaroslav. *The Christian Tradition: A History of the Development of Doctrine.* Vol. 1–3. Chicago and London: Univ. of Chicago Pr., 1971–78. (Two more volumes were to follow.)

Peters, Francis E. *Aristotle and the Arabs: The Aristotelian Tradition in Islam.* New York: New York Univ. Pr., 1968.

Quinn, John F. *The Historical Constitution of St. Bonaventure's Philosophy*. Toronto: Pontifical Institute of Medieval Studies, 1973.

Rescher, Nicholas. *The Development of Arabic Logic*. Pittsburgh, Pa.: Univ. of Pittsburgh Pr., 1964.

————. *Studies in Arabic Philosophy*. Pittsburgh, Pa.: Univ. of Pittsburg Pr., 1967.

Ross, James F., ed. *Inquiries into Medieval Philosophy: A Collection in Honor of Francis P. Clarke*. Westport, Conn.: Greenwood, 1971.

Ryan, John K., and Bernadine M. Bonansea, eds. *John Duns Scotus, 1265–1965*. Studies in Philosophy and the History of Philosophy, vol. 3. Washington, D.C.: Catholic Univ. of America Pr., 1965.

St. Thomas Aquinas, 1274–1974: Commemorative Studies. 2v. Toronto: Pontifical Institute of Medieval Studies, 1974.

Shahan, Robert W., and Francis J. Kovach, eds. *Bonaventure and Aquinas: Enduring Philosophers*. Norman: Univ. of Oklahoma Pr., 1976.

Sharp, Dorothea E. *Franciscan Philosophy at Oxford in the Thirteenth Century*. New York: Russell & Russell, 1930. Repr., 1964.

Stern, S. M., Albert Hourani, and Vivian Brown, eds. *Islamic Philosophy and the Classical Tradition: Essays Presented . . . to Richard Walzer. . . .* Columbia: Univ. of South Carolina Pr., 1972.

Ullmann, Walter. *The Individual and Society in the Middle Ages*. Baltimore, Md.: Johns Hopkins Univ. Pr., 1966.

Walzer, Richard. *Greek into Arabic: Essays on Islamic Philosophy*. Oxford: B. Cassirer, 1962.

Weinberg, Julius R. *A Short History of Medieval Philosophy*. Princeton, N.J.: Princeton Univ. Pr., 1964.

Wolfson, Harry A. *The Philosophy of the Kalam*. Cambridge, Mass. and London: Harvard Univ. Pr., 1976.

————. *Repercussions of the Kalam in Jewish Philosophy*. Cambridge, Mass. and London: Harvard Univ. Pr., 1979.

Wolter, Allan. *Transcendentals and Their Function in the Metaphysics of Duns Scotus*. St. Bonaventure, N.Y.: Franciscan Institute, 1946.

RENAISSANCE AND REFORMATION PHILOSOPHY

An adequate account of philosophical activity during the fifteenth-sixteenth century Renaissance and Reformation periods would have to show intertwinings among at least eight basic strands: (1) the harvesting of medieval scholastic interests for more "modern" purposes; (2) the advent of modern humanism, partly secular and partly not, and allied aesthetic preoccupations in the Italian Renaissance; (3) transformations of classical, biblical, and patristic studies (beyond philology to the analysis and interpretation of texts); (4) new interests in methodology, including logic; (5) new understandings of "the individual" as a self-conscious agent and inquirer in relation to institutions, society, God, and the cosmos; (6) the sparkling recrudescence of rhetoric vis-à-vis philosophy; (7) magical and occult thought; and (8) the role of skepticism later in the period. No such account exists, though the scholarship of recent decades has begun to make one possible.

Twentieth-century philosophers have paid little attention to this era. The main reasons seem to lie in the powerful tendency after the sixteenth century to appreciate its liberating humanism in general terms but to regard the rest as hopelessly irrational and passé. In actuality, the modern emphases on appeal not to authority or magical contrivance but to reason and empirical experience owe as much to the successes of this era as to its failures.

Much of the knowledge about Italian humanistic philosophy now available in English has been recovered or gathered by Paul Oskar Kristeller, long the leading scholar in the field. Recently (1979; also most of his 1980 book) he has issued a collection of some 1944–75 lectures and essays. In an introduction reviewing the half-century of his scholarship he reasserts his early view that in Renaissance Italy the two main currents of humanism and Aristotelian scholasticism were not so much opposed as confluent, the first centering on *studia humanitatis* (grammar, rhetoric, poetry, history), the second on the philosophical disciplines (logic, natural philosophy, metaphysics). Both included moral philosophy among their major concerns. As an intellectual historian and like most philosophical interpreters of the period, Kristeller has often presented the story person by person—as, for example, in his lectures on eight philosophers (1964): Petrarch, Valla, Ficino, Pico, Pomponazzi, Telesio, Patrizi, and Bruno. Kristeller has consistently held to the position that while the Italian humanists were not necessarily anti-Christian, theirs was a chiefly secular movement. In an outstanding set of lectures on "scholarship as a Christian calling," historian E. Harris Harbison (1956) continues part of this story into the Reformation. He discusses Petrarch, Valla, Pico, and John Colet, then presents Erasmus, Luther, and Calvin as special types.

Kristeller also regularly traces the considerable medieval aspects of Renaissance learning (1974), as theological historians have increasingly done for the entire period. As yet, however, neither a systematic analysis of this subject nor one treating the philosophical elements in Reformation theology is readily accessible. Far more is available related to philosophical interests in the arts (for example, see section 3 of Kristeller, 1980) and letters (Kristeller, 1969). In all these respects major forays toward a comprehensive account reside in a large treatise by intellectual historian Charles Trinkaus (1970). There he develops the thesis that interpretations of the biblical notion that man exists in the image and likeness of God provided the central metaphor in Italian humanist thinking about the relation between humanity and divinity.

Neither Kristeller nor Trinkaus finds the Italian humanists so tightly bound to scholastic methods and problems as did Ernst Cassirer (1927), a leading German philosopher who performed some first-rate, now classic analyses of Renaissance thought. Cassirer shows as well as anyone has how faulty are the conventional strict dividing lines between "scholastic," "Renaissance," and early "modern" philosophy. Cassirer also clearly demonstrates that the most significant, far-reaching philosophical work in this period is embedded in theological inquiry and that independent of this context philosophical thinkers were not usually very clear or innovative.

Individual consciousness is a strong motif in all the writings so far cited. This is only altered, not rejected, in the perceptive Marxist interpretation of "Renaissance man" by Agnes Heller (1978), Georg Lukács's best-known student in Hungary. Heller's deep-going, complex synopsis emphasizes efforts to surmount identification with particular communities in the interest of grasping species characteristics.

Trinkaus persuasively traces key influences of magical ("hermetic") elements early in the story, even before the development of Renaissance Platonism—a movement largely distinct from humanism—and sees some of its use as attempts to wrestle with important problems. No systematic analysis of what is of philosophical interest in this strand of thought appears to be available. The writings of Frances Yates (1979, and her earlier books on Giordano Bruno and on the art of memory) are indispensable aids to any effort to understand why "the occult philosophy" attained prominence at this time and what its effects on later thought were.

As Neal Gilbert (1960) demonstrates, an ongoing debate over intellectual methods continued throughout this period, with some development. Jerrold Seigel (1968), in studying the combination of eloquence and philosophical wisdom in early fifteenth-century Italian Renaissance thought, acknowledges that the humanist passion for rhetoric was overriding. This condition did not persist unabated, however. Through the vast influence of Philip Melanchthon (1497–1560) and Peter Ramus (1515–72) and through much other writing in the later fifteenth and the sixteenth centuries, logical, analytical, and dialectical methods also became matters of intense interest. Melanchthon has brief notice but star billing in Gilbert's history. Walter Ong (1958) examines the role and influence of Ramus, a most prolific and orderly scholar who tried to tear down traditional barriers between dialectic, rhetoric, and logic, subsuming all within a properly organized scientific logic, which he also termed "logical analysis." Richard Popkin (1979) has depicted the rise of skepticism as a function of "intellectual crisis" in the Reformation, beginning his story with Desiderius Erasmus (1466–1536). The roots in other theological activity of the period and earlier have yet to be fully explored, however. Eventually, all these features are likely to be seen as overlapping in their significance for later philosophy.

Cassirer, Ernst. *The Individual and the Cosmos in Renaissance Philosophy.* Tr. by Mario Domandi. New York: Harper Torchbooks, 1964. (German ed., 1927.)

Gilbert, Neal W. *Renaissance Concepts of Method.* New York: Columbia Univ. Pr., 1960.

Harbison, E. Harris. *The Christian Scholar in the Age of the Reformation.* New York: Scribner, 1956.

Heller, Agnes. *Renaissance Man.* Tr. by Richard E. Allen. London and Boston: Routledge & Paul, 1978. (Hungarian ed., 1967.)

Kristeller, Paul Oskar. *Eight Philosophers of the Italian Renaissance.* Stanford, Calif.: Stanford Univ. Pr., 1964.

———. *Medieval Aspects of Renaissance Learning: Three Essays.* Ed. and tr. by Edward P. Mahoney. Durham, N.C.: Duke Univ. Pr., 1974.

———. *Renaissance Thought and Its Sources.* Ed. by Michael Mooney. New York: Columbia Univ. Pr., 1979. (Includes two earlier works: *Renaissance Thought: The Classic, Scholastic, and Humanistic Strains* (1955) and *Renaissance Concepts of Man* (1972), with introduction surveying his work and three previously unpublished essays. Also see his essay "Changing Views of the Intellectual History of the Renaissance since Jacob Burckhardt." In *The Renaissance: A Reconsideration of the Theories and Interpretations of the Age,* pp. 27–52. Ed. by Tinsley Helton. Madison: Univ. of Wisconsin Pr., 1969.)

———. *Renaissance Thought and the Arts: Collected Essays.* Princeton, N.J.: Princeton Univ. Pr., 1980. (Original ed., *Renaissance Thought II,* 1965. New four-page preface.)

———. *Studies in Renaissance Thought and Letters.* Roma: Edizioni de storia e letteratura, 1969. (Original ed., 1956.)

Ong, Walter J. *Ramus, Method, and the Decay of Dialogue: From the Art of Discourse to the Art of Reason.* Cambridge, Mass.: Harvard Univ. Pr., 1958.

Popkin, Richard H. *The History of Skepticism from Erasmus to Spinoza.* Rev. ed. Berkeley and London: Univ. of California Pr., 1979. (Original ed., 1960.)

Seigel, Jerrold E. *Rhetoric and Philosophy in Renaissance Humanism: The*

Union of Eloquence and Wisdom, Petrarch to Valla. Princeton, N.J.: Princeton Univ. Pr., 1968.

Trinkaus, Charles. *In Our Image and Likeness: Humanity and Divinity in Italian Humanist Thought.* 2v. Chicago and London: Univ. of Chicago Pr., 1970.

Yates, Frances A. *The Occult Philosophy in the Elizabethan Age.* London and Boston: Routledge & Paul, 1979.

4

Seventeenth-Century
Philosophy

OVERVIEW

Works by E. A. Burtt, Basil Willey, and Paul Hazard from the
1930s still carry the predominant views about seventeenth-century
thought. In one respect this is unfortunate, for they posit a more
radical break between medieval and modern thought than later
scholarship permits. Nonetheless, each valuably points to remarkable uses of newfound powers of "reason" in that period. E. A.
Burtt (1924; 2nd ed., 1932) and Basil Willey (1935) both concentrate on England, though not exclusively. Burtt emphasizes the
religiously metaphysical foundations of the new scientific outlook,
culminating in Isaac Newton. Willey highlights the opposition to
scholasticism, from the Renaissance to John Locke. Paul Hazard's
celebratory account (1935) of this so-called birth of the modern
age views especially the French scene from 1680 to 1715. George
Boas's later book (1957), a classic history of ideas work, centers
on several dozen thinkers from Machiavelli to Sartre, also devoting
special attention to the French and thus defining what are "dominant themes in modern thought."

More recent scholarship suggests six major themes.

1. *The Problem of Scholasticism.* All the major philosophers to be
featured here were in many ways still thinking within terms contributed by the scholastics, at the very least in opposition. Yet they did
so with two purposes in mind: first, of rejecting what they took to be
metaphysical dogma (and often replaced with dogma of their own)
and, second, of discovering new bases for both knowledge and action
in natural phenomena and in reason not aided by faith. Going beyond scholasticism, they favored experiment, self-reflection, and

74

mathematically patterned explanations. All three elements were to undergo considerable change in the following three centuries, however, so that we are not justified in reading twentieth-century ideas into them witout taking significant modifications into account.

2. *The Foundations of Knowledge.* There was also a new quest for certainty, this time so far as possible achieved within the bounds of reason alone. Peter Schouls (1980), however, aptly complains that for a long time philosophical interest in seventeenth-century thought has been too narrowly occupied with the contrasts of empirical and skeptical versus rationalist issues. The unmistakably radical change in thinking that occurred then, he argues, derives above all from the replacement of different approaches to particular subjects by a general method. Though diverse in it formulations, this method uniformly broadened the meaning of "rational" beyond the syllogistic logic of demonstration and, with that, provided a new definition of the human being, though often still using scholastic terms. Schouls marks especially the twin methods of "resolution" (which usually meant reduction to supposedly clear and distinct fundamentals) and "composition." By 1600 *analytica* and *synthetica* were commonly used as synonyms, some precedent for which usage can be found as far back as the twelfth century. For both René Descartes and John Locke, the period's two most influential philosophers, and for most "modern" thinkers in between, both methods were considered necessary constituents of philosophy and the sciences; and they were used as methods of discovery, not only of exposition.

Twentieth-century historians have taken their own interpretive emphasis from the analytic side—appropriately so, in a perverse sense, in that the fragmentation characteristic of much modern thought has flourished in the soil of analysis. What many philosophers find attractive in Locke is put in bold relief in the Preface to his famous treatise, *An Essay on Human Understanding* (1689): " 'tis ambition enough to be employed as an under-labourer in clearing ground a little, and removing some of the rubbish, that lies in the way to knowledge." Locke, as Schouls demonstrates, was not a mere underlaborer; he, like Descartes, was a master builder as well—and just as seriously in theology and medicine as in politics and epistemology. For that building he relied on methods of composition, methods structually the same in all areas of inquiry. It did not occur to either man, or to most of their "modern" contemporaries, to question the reliability of reason so conceived or the utter importance of such reasonable methods for God and humans alike.

3. *Religion and Authority*. With respect to religion, all these thinkers strenuously objected to the imposition of external authority. Each also carried a deep concern for ultimate meaning and wholeness identified with the domain of religious faith. Many pursued extensive biblical and theological studies and did not consider these at odds with their more strictly philosophical interests. Leroy Loemker (1972) sees the greatest accomplishments of systematic thinkers in this century to be an "enlarged version" of Augustine's Christian Neoplatonism, which bears its own internal struggle between freedom in escape from bondage to authority and freedom in loyal conformity to a superior rule or order. John Tulloch's two-volume survey (1872) of rational theology and Christian philosophy in seventeenth-century England and its sixteenth-century background is still unsurpassed. He regarded the thought of the Cambridge Platonists, notably of Benjamin Whichcote, Ralph Cudworth, and Henry More, the highest accomplishment of philosophy in England, though he admitted that their thought was not only historically precritical, as was characteristic of the time, but also fell below the speculative method of their own age. Tulloch especially prized their doctrine of toleration, separating as it does the sphere of religious faith from that of dogmatic opinion, and their special focus on the moral life. In contrast, twentieth-century interpreters have tended to set the religious interests of seventeenth-century philosophers aside. Historical accuracy, however, would seem to ordain that this interest not be ignored; in fact, it looms as a major feature.

4. *Probability*. The notion of probability now in use, and related thinking about induction and statistical inference, came into being in some reflections by Pascal in the 1650s and in numerous investigations by Leibniz and others from the 1660s on. In a highly illuminating, brief account of this development, Ian Hacking (1975) has portrayed the duality of this notion at the time, having to do with degrees of belief and with devices that can produce stable long-run frequencies. As he shows, Hume's later skepticism about induction (1737) could only have arisen within this new climate of expectation. Likewise, discourse about probability, along with the emphasis on achieving a general method already noted, brought about a collapse of the traditional distinction between high and low science, based on "knowledge" versus "opinion."

5. *Skepticism*. The pursuit of all these themes was bound to run up against skeptical questions. In one of the finest studies in philosophical history ever done, Richard Popkin (*The History of Skepti-*

cism . . . , 1979, cited on p. 72) shows exactly how this happened. Particularly instructive is the fact that the major energy was not put either into utter skepticism (Pyrrhonism) or into grandiose schemes of belief but into moderate routes between these two extremes, what he calls "fideism" and "constructive skepticism." Both of these solutions had already arisen before the seventeenth century, in response to the Reformation crisis over reliable criteria for knowledge. Popkin also depicts the latter half of the century as a watershed in the history of skepticism, in that Descartes' refutation of skepticism shifted the object of skeptics' opposition from scholastic and Platonic views to Cartesian views and in that Baruch Spinoza carried Descartes' skeptical method into the religious domain while ardently maintaining opposition to epistemological skepticism.

6. *Logic, Rhetoric, and Philosophical Method.* Methods of logic and rhetoric were more noticeably entangled in seventeenth-century philosophy than at any time since. Wilbur Howell has traced this development in two works (the second, *Eighteenth-Century British Logic and Rhetoric*, 1971, is cited on p. 102). To trace the interaction of logic and rhetoric up to the present remains a major unfulfilled task of philosophical scholarship. Howell's basic work (1956) on English Renaissance theories of discourse—both scholarly and scientific (logic) and popular (rhetoric), poetry excluded—emphasizes changing views of communication during the sixteenth and seventeenth centuries. Aristotelian scholastic logic, he shows, ruled the first seventy years of the sixteenth century; rhetoric was traditional during this same period (Ciceronian, stylistic, and formulary). Howell sees the late sixteenth-century revolt in England to have been influenced chiefly by educational reforms proposed by the Frenchman, Peter Ramus, a convert to Protestantism, reforms that had a sizable following during most of the seventeenth century. A counterreform, systematics, tried to combine Ramist with traditional logic, while the Neo-Ciceronians tried a similar accommodation in rhetoric. Near the end of the seventeenth century, a critique of both was to be found in the *Port-Royal Logic* (English translation, 1685), already known in Latin versions and still used in Britain up to the time of John Stuart Mill's *System of Logic* (1843) and even a generation later.

A new rhetoric also appeared in the seventeenth century, beginning with Francis Bacon's *Advancement of Learning* (1605), the most influential book of the century on English learning. Articles on Bacon's own wide learning have been collected by Brian Vickers (1968).

Lisa Jardine (1975) looks at Bacon's new proposals in both dialectic and logic against the background of widely used sixteenth-century dialectic handbooks, in which universally applicable methods of discovery and communication had become increasingly important topics. This change had occurred mainly through the pioneering efforts of men like Lorenzo Valla, Rudolph Agricola, Philip Melanchthon, and Peter Ramus, who had all brought Platonic dialectic back into the rigidly orthodox Aristotelian framework of their time, though this was not their only medium of reform. Bacon's own type of "induction" was not of the later sort but was intended to guarantee the certainty and natural priority of first principles by eliminating conjecture. This was to be done through appeal to sense experience at each stage of discovery and presentation.

Overall, according to Howell's account (1956), what developed during the English Renaissance was, first, a greater emphasis on concrete descriptions of reality as having scientific status alongside the old deductive sciences of the moralists and theologians; second, assertion of authority among the middle class (a very important theme, that must be marked here though the philosophical literature has given it little treatment); and, third, the Reformation. All three forces pressed for new theories of communication.

We must be careful, however, not to read unquestionable advance into this story. Antidotes to any such wish are presented in a splendid work on English Renaissance discourse by literary historian Russell Fraser (1977). There he terms the widespread influences of nominalism "atrocious nonsense" and deplores the fleshless abridgement, rarefaction, homogenizing trends of the time, the rage for order, the distrust of physicality, the addiction to number, the devitalizing intellectual rituals—in fine, the superseding of conventional language and its attendant richness of concrete meaning, hence the abjuring of "honest commerce with reality." Fraser's is a powerful indictment, reaching far forward to what he would perceive as bloodless linguistics and logic-obsessed philosophy in the present.

Fraser also gives evidence of countering influences, even within those who chiefly purveyed these practices. In philosophical history the conflicts are always of primary interest, not the doctrines alone. Virtually by acclamation, those so far voted the main philosophers of the age are Descartes, Spinoza, Leibniz, Hobbes, and Locke; I add Pascal. All contributed to the trends Fraser deplores; all display deep conflicts regarding all or most of the themes just outlined. None has received biographical treatment sufficient to illuminate these conflicts from within their respective personal and historical contexts. Frank Manuel's unsurpassed portrait (1968) of Isaac Newton (1642–1727) approaches this end in a probing manner rarely achieved in biographies of philosophers. Although Newton's influence was primarily that of a great mathematician and physicist, his name deserves mention among the philosophers, too, in that his thought strikingly represents the basic themes and conflicts of seventeenth-century philosophy. Moreover, it is not by accident that we have learned to speak of "the Newtonian universe" in a fashion that points beyond the domain of physics.

Boas, George. *Dominant Themes of Modern Philosophy: A History*. New York: Ronald, 1957.

Burtt, Edwin Arthur. *The Metaphysical Foundations of Modern Science*. 2nd ed. Repr.: Garden City, N.Y.: Doubleday Anchor, 1954. (1st ed., 1924; 2nd ed., 1932.)

Fraser, Russell. *The Language of Adam: On the Limits and Systems of Discourse*. New York: Columbia Univ. Pr., 1977.

Hacking, Ian. *The Emergence of Probability: A Philosophical Study of Early Ideas about Probability, Induction and Statistical Inference*. Cambridge and London: Cambridge Univ. Pr., 1975.

Hazard, Paul. *The European Mind, 1680–1715*. New Haven, Conn.: Yale Univ. Pr.; London: Hollis & Carter, 1953. (Repr., 1971; French ed., 1935.)

Howell, Wilbur Samuel. *Logic and Rhetoric in England, 1500–1700*. Princeton, N.J.: Princeton Univ. Pr., 1956.

Jardine, Lisa. *Francis Bacon: Discovery and the Art of Discourse*. Cambridge and London: Cambridge Univ. Pr., 1975.

Loemker, Leroy E. *Struggle for Synthesis: The Seventeenth Century Background of Leibniz's Synthesis of Order and Freedom*. Cambridge, Mass.: Harvard Univ. Pr., 1972.

Manuel, Frank E. *A Portrait of Isaac Newton*. Washington, D.C.: New Republic Books, 1979. (Original ed., 1968.)

Schouls, Peter A. *The Imposition of Method: A Study of Descartes and Locke*. Oxford: Clarendon Pr., 1980.

Tulloch, John. *Rational Theology and Christian Philosophy in England in the Seventeenth Century*. 2v. Edinburgh and London: William Blackwood, 1872.

Vickers, Brian, ed. *Essential Articles for the Study of Francis Bacon*. Hamden, Conn.: Archon Books, 1968; London: Sidgwick & Jackson, 1972.

Willey, Basil. *The Seventeenth Century Background: Studies in the Thought of the Age in Relation to Poetry and Religion*. New York: Columbia Univ. Pr., 1935.

RENÉ DESCARTES (1596–1650)

The Search for a Rational Method

In the eighteenth century, historians had already named René Descartes a pioneer of modern philosophy, sometimes its founder. Although aspects of his thought may be perceived as a regression from advanced scholastic methods, there can be no doubt of his originality both as a philosopher and as a mathematician. In my view, Descartes' entire life's work already took its distinctive form in a youthful search for identity, which came to be focused in his intention to bring "an entirely new science" into the world and a rational method appropriate to it. The search came to a climax in a succession of three dreams on St. Martin's Eve, November 10, 1619, in which, to his great relief, he experienced the impression of "the Spirit of Truth" descending upon him in a thunderous event. It was very likely the next day that he put himself into seclusion, went through his famous experiment in radical doubt, and emerged with the basic ideas he was to spend the next thirty years elaborating, in part through gradual dissociation from ideas of contemporaries such as Nicolas Malebranche, Baruch Spinoza, and Gottfried Wilhelm Leibniz. These ideas have come down to us especially in his *Discours de la méthode* (1637), a preface to treatises on geometry, dioptric, and meteors, a book remarkable for its autobiographical flavor, its being written in French for popular consumption, and its succinct statement of his views; in an extensive metaphysical, heuristic work, *Meditationes de Prima Philosophia* (1641), his major opus, published with a set of objections by others and his replies; and a scholastically formal treatise, *Principia Philosophiae* (1644).

The history of "Cartesian" studies, as they are called, seems to be one of increasing precision and refinement, arising from changing critical tools and interests, rather than of radical breaks with past interpretive tradition. Yet there is still no general agreement on what Descartes' fundamental views were or how they were formed. Early twentieth-century studies by Norman Kemp Smith (1902, 1953) show considerable continuity over fifty years, though there was a definite revival of interest in Descartes' thought with publication of the thirteen-volume standard edition of his works (1897–1913), of Étienne Gilson's first Cartesian study in 1913, and of some further translations into English since that time, and though Smith's 1953 studies are unquestionably "new," as he averred. In turn, the overall picture Smith offers is significantly different in both style and interest from the excellent recent analytic work by Bernard Williams (1978), who offers a historical summary of Descartes' thought as a "project of pure enquiry," and by Margaret Wilson (1978), who takes a close look at some of Descartes' arguments, especially in the *Meditations*. Wilson's reconstruction of arguments builds on Anthony Kenny's fine study (1968) and on articles by Harry G. Frankfurt (two of them are reprinted in collections by Doney and by Hooker, noted below) but differs in important details. All of these more recent studies openly view Descartes in the light of mid-twentieth-century language and interests. In contrast, L. J. Beck (1965) had followed a 1952 study on Descartes' early unfinished treatise on "Rules for the Direction of the Mind" (written by 1629 but not published until 1701) with a new investigation of the *Meditations*. There he attempted to restrict himself largely to a historical introduction and an exposition of his metaphysical "doctrines" in Descartes' own terminology.

What Descartes thought he had found was a foundation of certain knowledge in the "clear and distinct" perceptions of consciousness ("I think, therefore I am"—and when I subject my thinking to radical doubt what remains are certainty as to the existence of God and a "real distinction" between mind and body). In a historical-biographical fashion, Hiram Caton (1973) has investigated the explicit "subjectivity" in these largely unexamined assumptions; he positively interprets the Cartesian mind as "consciousness of a specific kind." E. M. Curley (1978) has critically traced how Descartes used skeptical and other arguments against the skeptics.

General Accounts and Collections

S. V. Keeling's 1968 overview of thought by Descartes and his immediate followers is a revision of his 1934 book but without a basic change of position. His own critical views are informed by the thought and expository style of an earlier generation of English philosophers, notably J. Ellis McTaggert, H. W. B. Joseph, and C. D. Broad. Anthony Kenny (1968), who has also published books on ancient and medieval philosophy and on philosophy of mind, wrote his introductory account more in the contemporary analytic mode. He is one of those who have gone especially to the *Meditations* to find the basic texts on issues of metaphysics, epistemology, and philosophy of mind. Jonathan Ree's equally brief introduction (1974) takes more of an intellectual history approach. Those by Bernard Williams (1978) and Margaret Wilson (1978), mentioned above, are

excellent full-fledged monographs; along with that of Peter Schouls
on his method (*The Imposition of Method . . . ,* 1980, cited on p.
79), they are among the finest produced so far. Schouls has argued
that Curley, Williams, and Wilson have all misinterpreted Descartes
by failing to consider the full range of his methodology.

　　In an intellectual history informed by analytic interests, Richard
Watson (1966) aptly explains the "downfall of Cartesianism," during its chief period of influence as a metaphysical and epistemological
position (to about 1712), as due to the inability to handle an ontology of mind and extension as two substances different in essence, or
(later) of two categories, substance and modification of substance. In
particular, the Cartesians could not meet objections as to how a
mind, on their account, could be directly acquainted with ideas, how
mental ideas could represent objects, and how a mind could causally
interact with a body. Looking forty years and more beyond the
bounds of his study, Watson, like many others, further dates the final
breakdown of Cartesian metaphysics with Hume, who abandoned
substance philosophy altogether and thus became "the father of contemporary philosophy."

　　Among the collection, that by Willis Doney (1967) gathers sixteen
important articles, all but two originally written in English, and all
but two—by A. K. Stout (1929) and Émile Brehier (1937)—since
1949. The Bernd Magnus and James Wilbur collection (1969) comprises new essays by six philosopher-humanists, dedicated to Descartes translator Laurence J. LaFleur. That by R. J. Butler (1972)
presents new work, chiefly by Canadian analytic philosophers, from
two 1968 workshops. Michael Hooker's outstanding collection
(1978) of fifteen essays not previously published has a broader scope;
it includes several noted analytic scholars (Danto, Doney, Frankfurt,
Hintikka, Wilson, and others) who have devoted careful attention to
Descartes in recent years. Hooker highlights two sets of issues of
special current interest: whether or how it is appropriate to use
reason to defend the use of reason, if Descartes did; and whether or
how it is possible to defend a mind-body dualism, as Descartes tried
to do, in the interest of understanding the nature of persons.

Beck, Leslie J. *The Metaphysics of Descartes: A Study of the Meditations.*
　　Oxford: Clarendon Pr., 1965.
Butler, Ronald J., ed. *Cartesian Studies.* New York: Barnes & Noble; Ox-
　　ford: Blackwell, 1972.
Caton, Hiram. *The Origin of Subjectivity: An Essay on Descartes.* New
　　Haven, Conn. and London: Yale Univ. Pr., 1973.

Curley, Edwin M. *Descartes against the Skeptics*. Cambridge, Mass.: Harvard Univ. Pr.; Oxford: Blackwell, 1978.

Doney, Willis, ed. *Descartes: A Collection of Critical Essays*. Garden City, N.Y.: Doubleday Anchor, 1967.

Hooker, Michael, ed. *Descartes: Critical and Interpretative Essays*. Baltimore, Md.: Johns Hopkins Univ. Pr., 1978.

Keeling, Stanley V. *Descartes*. 2nd ed. Oxford: Oxford Univ. Pr., 1968. (1st ed., 1934.)

Kenny, Anthony. *Descartes: A Study of His Philosophy*. New York: Random House, 1968.

Magnus, Bernd, and James B. Wilbur, eds. *Cartesian Essays: A Collection of Critical Studies*. The Hague: Nijhoff, 1969.

Ree, Jonathan. *Descartes*. London: Allen Lane, 1974.

Smith, Norman Kemp. *New Studies in the Philosophy of Descartes: Descartes as Pioneer*. New York: Russell & Russell, 1953. (Repr., 1963.)

———. *Studies in the Cartesian Philosophy*. London: Macmillan, 1902. (Repr.: New York: Russell & Russell, 1962.)

Watson, Richard A. *The Downfall of Cartesianism, 1673–1712: A Study of Epistemological Issues in Late 17th-century Cartesianism*. The Hague: Nijhoff, 1966.

Williams, Bernard. *Descartes: The Project of Pure Enquiry*. New York: Penguin Books; Hassocks, Sussex: Harvester Pr., 1978.

Wilson, Margaret Dauler. *Descartes*. London and Boston: Routledge & Paul, 1978.

BLAISE PASCAL (1623–1662)

Knowledge, Faith, and the Human Condition

Blaise Pascal was a mathematical genius, already producing a major work on conic sections at sixteen, others on geometry, probability, and number theory later. He was an important contributor to the new science, especially on theory of the vacuum, one of the clearest articulators of the scientific method in his century, and inventor of the calculating machine. He also invented a large carriage, using it to start the first bus line in Paris so as to make money for the poor. Pascal has nonetheless been best known for his religious and philosophical writings, to which he was chiefly devoted after having an ecstatic religious experience on November 23, 1654.

In "The Spirit of Geometry," first published only in the eighteenth century, Pascal presented the axiomatic method as affording the best approximation to certitude our limited capacities can achieve. Elsewhere he established a falsifiability criterion for checking scientific discoveries. In "The Art of Persuasion" he considered how we come to be convinced of axiomatic first principles, through intuition and divine revelation. In his masterpiece, *Pensées* ("Thoughts"), unfinished fragments on knowledge and the human condition and a Christian apologetics (colorful, passionate, well-reasoned, in magnificent French), he argued that "the heart has its reasons, which reason does not know," reasons which ultimately God alone can make evident. Skepticism was for him the most honorable philosophical position in that it reveals both our wretchedness and finitude and the glory of the human being as a "thinking reed," a reed small and fragile before the infinite vastness and complexity of the universe yet capable of intuition and reflection.

Interpretations

Emile Cailliet's intellectual biography (1961) sympathetically reveals how the post-1654 religioskeptical position came about and what it means. Among the more recent works in English, a study of *Pensées* by Hugh Davidson (1979), a professor of French literature, presents a tight analysis of Pascal's method, brief but comprehensive and amply illustrated. A. W. S. Baird (1975) emphasizes continuity between Pascal's earlier and later thought, eventually expressed in terms of dualistic, Platonic aspects of Augustinian theology, and critically summarizes Pascal's teleological approach to ethics.

Very few works have traced the career of a philosopher's writings and their influence. John Barker (1975) has done this effectively for Pascal, focusing especially on England through the early nineteenth century. Pascal was a celebrity virtually overnight for his *Provincial Letters* (1656–57), a brilliant defense, directed against the Jesuits, of the more spiritual understanding of Christianity among the Jansenists of Port-Royal (who also produced the Port-Royal Logic mentioned above). After his death, in England Royal Society members especially came to discuss and spread the knowledge of his other works as well. There had already been significant interaction between Thomas Hobbes and Pascal within the circle of Père Marin Mersenne in Paris. Hobbes and Locke both knew *Pensées* in the 1670s. Locke was particularly indebted to it. Both philosophers used the very limited, biased selection by Port-Royal, which ruled all subsequent editions until the mid-nineteenth century. This edition emphasized proofs for validity of the Christian religion, not showing so well that sense of human perplexity in the search for meaning and salvation that has attracted readers to today's more accurate, comprehensive versions.

Until publication in English in 1688, *Pensées* were perhaps the least known of his writings, thereafter the best known. Developments toward a less religiously oriented philosophy, well signaled by Locke's

Essay (1689), ushered in some countertrends. After the 1730s the rising tide of deism brought about a decline in Pascal's reputation among British intellectuals, most notably with Hume as with Voltaire in France, but increased it in the area of popular piety and among many Protestant thinkers, especially in Scotland and in the Methodist movement. Interest in Pascal's life arose in part through a biography by his sister and through Pierre Bayle's *Dictionnaire historique et critique* (1697, translated in 1709 and 1710). Although the rich fullness of *Pensées* was made available in the mid-nineteenth century, a comprehensive French edition, in its ordering close to Pascal's expressed intentions, was not produced until 1951 (by Louis Lafuma). Consequently, Pascal has only really come into his own within the post-World War II period, with emphasis on his existential thought, philosophy of religion, and philosophy of science.

Baird, Alexander W. S. *Studies in Pascal's Ethics.* The Hague: Nijhoff, 1975.
Barker, John. *Strange Contrarieties: Pascal in England during the Age of Reason.* Montréal: McGill-Queen's Univ. Pr., 1975.
Cailliet, Emile. *Pascal: The Emergence of Genius.* 2nd ed. New York: Harper Torchbooks, 1961. (1st ed., 1945; repr.: New York: Greenwood Pr., 1969.)
Davidson, Hugh M. *The Origins of Certainty: Means and Meanings in Pascal's Pensées.* Chicago and London: Univ. of Chicago Pr., 1979.

BENEDICT (BARUCH) SPINOZA (1632–1677)

The Pure Philosopher

Spinoza was a pure philosopher who devoted himself almost entirely to the search for understanding and clarity. His philosophy is the very type of a totally integrated intellectual and religious vision. Spinoza lived out his forty-five years in Holland, whence Descartes had fled to have breathing space to think and had spent most of his own last twenty years (to 1649). Although Holland was the safest European haven from religious persecution throughout the seventeenth century, the Jewish community held a precarious position there. At twenty-four, Spinoza was expelled from the synagogue, apparently because of the infavorable light his radically unorthodox views would cast upon that community. This act severed him from the only social group to which he could truly attach himself. As a consequence, he became a virtual recluse, spending his remaining years grinding and polishing lenses, writing philosophy, and discussing and corresponding about philosophy with a few friends.

Every seventeenth-century thinker featured here, except Locke, was greatly taken by the example of Euclidean geometry and tried to emulate it in some fashion. None did this so compactly, with so little leakage, as Spinoza, though Leibniz came close. Every problem was to be formulated and solved in the nonmetaphorical language and the impersonal, lean form of geometry.

Spinoza believed that God and Nature are indistinguishable, that everything is part of a single determined whole, that freedom means becoming more and more identified with that whole, becoming more nearly objective about it and more nearly happy in it, and that socio-political institutions must be studied and fostered by this same rule, not by moral and religious exhortations. So much most interpreters would agree upon today. But to capture the actual meaning and abundance of Spinoza's thought is an unusually difficult task. Almost every major reading of it appears quite different from the others. There are several reasons for this situation. First, Spinoza was an isolate in more ways than one. His thought, though immediately stimulating, is written in a sparse, systematic form extremely demanding of the reader, and it was almost totally ignored until the famous "Pantheism Controversy" in Germany, set off by Friedrich Heinrich Jacobi (1743–1819) in 1785, over a century after his death. Of his major works, the first one was a study of Descartes (1663), not a direct exposition of his own views; the *Tractatus Theologico-politicus* (1670) was published anonymously; his greatest work, the *Ethica,* was too unconventional to publish until after his death; the *Tractatus de Intellectus Emendatione* was not discovered until the late eighteenth century. A second reason is that a thoroughly critical commentary on his writings would require knowledge of the Latin, Hebrew, and Dutch of that period, which fact has contributed to the generally poor quality of the translations. Third, Spinoza has usually been dismissed either as an atheist or as an obscure rationalist, though neither ascription is accurate.

Interpretations

In English, the first systematic study of importance was idealist Harold Joachim's in 1901 (and another in 1940), the next by Harry Wolfson (1934), who traced antecedents from Aristotle and medieval Jewish philosophy. Both still have value, though E. M. Curley (1969) and others have shown that their divergent understandings of Spinoza's key term "substance" are faulty. Curley views Spinoza as a precursor of Bertrand Russell and Ludwig Wittgenstein. Until recently, subsequent interpretations have also dwelt upon his metaphysics and epistemology as the central topics of his "Ethics," though Leo Strauss (1930) examined his critique of religion and almost every collection has one offering on that subject. The brief, highly sympathetic overview by analytic philosopher Stuart Hampshire (1951) is the best to date. He has made very important use of Spinoza's moral philosophy in another work (*Two Theories of Morality*, 1977, cited on p. 407). Curley, who is currently preparing a translation of Spinoza's complete works for Princeton University Press, has also opposed Hampshire's interpretation that "substance" means the totality of things, though he admits that there is some textual warrant. Good full-scale studies on Spinoza's moral and political philosophy are still needed. Gail Belaief (1971) provides the first careful analysis of his philosophy of law.

The most useful of the several collections are two *Inquiry* symposia, by Ruth Saw et al. (1969) and Wallace Matson et al. (1977)—typically, a mixture of analytic and historical-critical studies; Marjorie Grene's edition (1973), which includes six new and seventeen old essays on action, experience, freedom, and imagination and two new ones on his moral and political philosophy; and a collection by Eugene Freeman and Maurice Mandelbaum (1975), mostly from a 1971 *Monist* symposium and with less than usual on metaphysics as such. The volume honoring his 300th anniversary edited by Siegfried Hessing (1977) mirrors how widespread and remarkably diverse European interests in Spinoza have become. A set of eleven new essays, edited by Robert Shahan and J. I. Biro (1978), includes work by several scholars who have published independent studies—notably, Thomas Mark, G. H. R. Parkinson, S. Paul Kashap, E. M. Curley, and Richard Popkin.

Another collection, by Jon Wetlesen (1977), comes especially from Norway, where much work has been done, as has been true especially in the Soviet Union (because of the belief that he was a "materialist") and in Holland and Israel. Emilia Giancotti Boscherini prepared a massive two-volume *Lexicon Spinozanum* ((1970), and new English translations of various works have been appearing in the 1970s. In these areas and in Anglo-American philosophy Spinoza studies have achieved their first great push in the post-World War II period. His reputation is likely to continue improving in the 1980s.

Belaief, Gail. *Spinoza's Philosophy of Law*. The Hague: Mouton, 1971.
Boscherini, Emilia Giancotti, ed. *Lexicon Spinozanum*. 2v. The Hague: Nijhoff, 1970.

Curley, Edwin M. *Spinoza's Metaphysics: An Essay in Interpretation.* Cambridge, Mass.: Harvard Univ. Pr., 1969.

Freeman, Eugene, and Maurice Mandelbaum, eds. *Spinoza: Essays in Interpretation.* La Salle, Ill.: Open Court, 1975. (Includes *Monist* symposium, 55, no. 4:527–685 (Oct. 1971).)

Grene, Marjorie, ed. *Spinoza: A Collection of Critical Essays.* Garden City, N.Y.: Doubleday Anchor, 1973.

Hampshire, Stuart. *Spinoza.* Baltimore, Md.: Penguin, 1952. (British ed., 1951.)

Hessing, Siegfried, ed. *Speculum Spinozanum, 1677–1977.* London and Boston: Routledge & Paul, 1977.

Joachim, Harold H. *Spinoza's Tractatus de Intellectus Emendatione: A Commentary.* Oxford: Clarendon Pr., 1940.

———. *A Study of the Ethics of Spinoza.* Oxford: Oxford Univ. Pr., 1901.

Matson, Wallace, et al. "Spinoza." *Inquiry* 20, no. 4:401–528 (Winter 1977).

Saw, Ruth L., et al. "Spinoza." *Inquiry* 12, no. 1:1–143 (Spring 1969).

Shahan, Robert W., and J. I. Biro, eds. *Spinoza: New Perspectives.* Norman: Univ. of Oklahoma Pr., 1978.

Strauss, Leo. *Spinoza's Critique of Religion.* Tr. by E. M. Sinclair. New York: Schocken, 1965. (German ed., 1930.)

Wetlesen, Jon, ed. *Spinoza's Philosophy of Man: Proceedings of the Scandinavian Spinoza Symposium, 1977.* Oslo: Universitetsforlaget; New York: Columbia Univ. Pr.; London: Global Book Resources, 1977.

Wolfson, Harry Austryn. *The Philosophy of Spinoza: Unfolding the Latent Processes of His Reasoning.* 2v. Cambridge, Mass.: Harvard Univ. Pr., 1934. (Repr.: New York: Schocken, 1969.)

GOTTFRIED WILHELM LEIBNIZ (1646–1716)

The Rediscovery of Leibniz

Gottfried Wilhelm Leibniz was a compulsive writer who left behind an extensive body of unpublished writings and correspondence on a great variety of subjects. Because the setting of his work remains scholastic, he is appropriately placed among the great seventeenth-century philosophers. However, before Kant he was also perhaps the most original philosopher working in the eighteenth century; thus he may be seen as a transition figure. Unfortunately he published little; the only large philosophical work published during his lifetime was the popular *Theodicée* (1710). Despite his lifelong efforts to cultivate cooperative ventures among scholars and among Christian theologians, his thought was generally neglected. The six-volume *Opera Omnia* edited by Louis Dutens (1768) still contains the most material among the sundry collections; but much important work, without which an accurate understanding of how he grounded his most fundamental ideas is impossible, did not appear until the twentieth century, and a complete critical edition is still lacking. Leroy Loemker's standard two-volume English translation of some of his *Philosophical Papers and Letters* only first appeared in 1956 (rev. ed., 1969).

Nevertheless, through Christian Wolff (1679–1754), who purveyed a chiefly Leibnizian position, elements of his philosophy did bear a marked influence on eighteenth-century philosophy. Wolff, at first an influential mathematician and logician, had corresponded with Leibniz from 1704 to 1716. Wolff became the greatest philosophical systematizer of the early phase of the German Enlightenment and was more responsible than any other thinker for the establishment of German philosophical terminology. Although his tightly organized system is largely taken from Leibniz, his influential distinction of a priori (ontological, essentialist) science from a posteriori (empirical) science is Cartesian. Not until Bertrand Russell's detailed analysis of Leibniz's logic and metaphysics in 1900 did his philosophy begin to emerge among interpreters in the form he intended.

A Logical Base for Metaphysics and Science

The basis of Leibniz's metaphysics, thence of his vast encyclopedic program in philosophy and science, is his belief that all truths whatsoever, whether necessary or contingent, are analytic. There is still some dispute over whether he may have come to hold that existential propositions are synthetic. Bertrand Russell argued for this interpretation in his still invaluable 1900 book; but he changed his view, in agreement with Louis Couturat's outstanding account of 1902, derived from newly discovered key texts. Essays by E. M. Curley and others in Harry Frankfurt's collection (1972) show that the issue is still very much alive. What attracted Russell to Leibniz was his resting the entire metaphysical enterprise on a few principles of logic and his corresponding conceptual atomism and search for a universal language.

Other issues that have drawn attention in twentieth-century works on Leibniz include his attempt to account for the relation of individual entities to the universe by positing "monads," a divinely created "preestablished harmony" among all substances, and a grounding of all freedom and possibility in the reasonable government of the world by God. In short, what has intrigued most twentieth-century interpreters has been the close interplay of logical, metaphysical, and even theological issues.

Other Interpretations

In a remarkable work of intellectual history, Leroy Loemker (*Struggle for Synthesis . . .*, 1972, cited on p. 79) has placed Leibniz's synthesis of order and freedom as a culmination of typically seventeenth-century struggles. The strictly analytic summary by R. M. Yost (1954) and the more generally stated 1948–50 lectures by C. D. Broad (posthumously published, 1975) presage the recent brief introduction by logician Nicholas Rescher (1979), whose methodological bent is similar to that of Leibniz. The simpler introduction by Herbert Carr (1929), divided into life and times, doctrine, and influence, is still useful for general orientation but does not refer to other studies and lacks the benefit of later scholarship. Recently, excellent studies have been done by G. H. R. Parkinson on Leibniz's metaphysics (1965), by Hidé Ishiguro on fundamental issues of logic and language (1972), and by John Hostler on his moral philosophy (1975). Parkinson and Ishiguro significantly differ in interpretive details. Parkinson's principal aim was to establish that Leibniz drew upon a conception of logic and ideal languages similar to a program of philosophical analysis that would be formed today. Ishiguro's careful examination of select arguments refers more often to other interpretations.

The fourteen essays collected by Harry Frankfurt (1972) are of high quality and center on logic and metaphysics, though not exclusively; he includes classic essays by Broad, Couturat, and Russell and adds brand new essays by E. M. Curley, Ian Hacking, Jaakko Hintikka, Hidé Ishiguro, and Martha Kneale. The seven essays edited by Mark Kulstad (1977) are exclusively analytic and show that in the 1970s the radical rediscovery of Leibniz, inaugurated by Russell in 1900, has gained new intensity. Many of the first fruits appear in Michael Hooker's collection of essays (1982).

Broad, Charlie D. *Leibniz: An Introduction.* Ed. by C. Lewy. Cambridge and London: Cambridge Univ. Pr., 1975.

Carr, Herbert Wildon. *Leibniz.* New York: Dover, 1960. (Original ed., London: Ernest Benn, 1929.)

Frankfurt, Harry G., ed. *Leibniz: A Collection of Critical Essays.* Garden City, N.Y.: Doubleday Anchor, 1972. (Repr.: Notre Dame, Ind.: Univ. of Notre Dame Pr., 1976.)

Hooker, Michael, ed. *Leibniz: Critical and Interpretive Essays.* Minneapolis: Univ. of Minnesota Pr., 1982.

Hostler, John. *Leibniz's Moral Philosophy.* London: Duckworth, 1975.

Ishiguro, Hidé. *Leibniz's Philosophy of Logic and Language*. Ithaca, N.Y.: Cornell Univ. Pr., 1972.

Kulstad, Mark, ed. *Essays on the Philosophy of Leibniz*. Rice University Studies, vol. 63, no. 4. Houston, Texas: Rice Univ., 1977.

Parkinson, George H. R. *Logic and Reality in Leibniz's Metaphysics*. Oxford: Clarendon Pr., 1965.

Rescher, Nicholas. *Leibniz: An Introduction to His Philosophy*. Totowa, N.J.: Rowman & Littlefield, 1979.

Russell, Bertrand. *A Critical Exposition of the Philosophy of Leibniz, with an Appendix of Leading Passages*. London: Allen & Unwin, 1967. (Original ed., 1900.)

Yost, Robert M., Jr. *Leibniz and Philosophical Analysis*. Berkeley: Univ. of California Pr., 1954.

THOMAS HOBBES (1588–1679)

Political Order and Political Obligation

Michael Oakeshott, a devotee of Thomas Hobbes, has nominated his *Leviathan* (1651) "the greatest, perhaps the sole, masterpiece of political philosophy written in the English language" (1975). Most of the literature of Hobbes has mined this vein, and with good reason, for this great summa of modern rationalism does not isolate politics from other subjects. Rather, it approaches its main task from first principles concerning human nature and human interests, and it ends contrasting the absolutist "Christian Commonwealth" he prefers with barbaric alternatives. Although Hobbes did not see political philosophy as his primary task, it probably was the finest achievement of his long, illustrious life. Until the jurist John Austin made use of his theory of civil law in a noted 1832 volume, the work was not well received in England, partly because of his supposed atheism and partly because of his support of an absolutist monarchy. John Locke's more democratically oriented writings won far greater attention and acclaim. As I see it, the core of Hobbes's analysis of human affairs lay in the notions of self-interest as the basic feature of human psychology, of unbridled anarchy as the state of nature, of the desire for self-preservation as the sole foundation of "natural law" (or perhaps better: natural right), and of the consequent willingness to alienate sovereignty to a ruler as the underlying motive of civil covenant.

In 1941, during the bombardment of London, R. G. Collingwood was to essay a project similarly organized in face of the barbarisms of that time (*The New Leviathan*, 1942, cited on p. 448), a work richly endowed, like his predecessor's with insights and unfinished inquiries but, unlike Hobbes's, passionately opposed to absolutism and curiously ignored. Collingwood's *New Leviathan* may be viewed as an important indirect commentary on Hobbes's main work. In 1936 the refugee German scholar, Leo Strauss, had published what has become one of the leading interpretations. Strauss's study attempted to show how Hobbes founded modern political philosophy by taking strong stands against traditional theory and how Hobbes's mature philosophy gradually developed over several decades. But he took it to be based on a "moral attitude" largely independent of his introduction at middle age to the new mathematics and science, which Strauss thought adversely affected his subsequent theorizing. Howard Warrender (1957) held, against Oakeshott and Strauss, that for Hobbes political obligation is prior to and independent of the fiat of the civil sovereign; but he, too, did not see much meaningful connection of Hobbes's moral and political views with the rest of his thought. On the latter point, J. W. N. Watkins (1965) strongly disagreed with both Strauss and Warrender.

Other Issues of Interpretation

The great upsurge of scholarly interest in Hobbes in the two decades after World War II is well displayed in the collection of thirteen previously published essays edited by K. C. Brown (1965). These are among the key issues treated: (1) is Hobbes's ethical theory logically independent of his egoistic psychology, and is it thereby a strict deontological (duty- or rule-oriented) view, as A. E. Taylor, Warrender, and Oakeshott have held against the traditional interpretation? Stuart Brown thinks not, for Hobbes himself argues otherwise and in fact uses the notion of "covenant" to forge a necessary link between psychological considerations and political obligation. What is dispensable, argues Brown, is Hobbes's references to prudential maxims and divine commands, by other interpreters thought to be indispensable. (2) Is Hobbes clear about what he means by "liberty"? No, argues J. Roland Pennock, who claims that Hobbes's downfall lay in the attempt to force a degree of clarity incompatible with his subject matter, which produced confusion instead. (3) Is Hobbes's reputation for atheism warranted? Willis Glover argues in the negative, as had Warrender and Oakeshott, though he does find use of postmedieval but Christian motifs of nominalism, materialism, and skepticism in Hobbes's thought.

More essays on political obligation and other aspects of his bourgeois economic and political philosophy are featured in the Maurice

Cranston and R. S. Peters collection (1972). It includes W. H. Green-leaf's keen distinction (1969) of three main types of interpretation: the traditional case (as noted above, for instance, R. S. Peters, 1956), the Christian natural-law case (for instance, A. E. Taylor, War-render), and the individualist or nominalist case (for example, Strauss, Oakeshott, Watkins, Glover). Greenleaf also indicates some-thing of the obstacles that must be avoided if one is to reconstruct a synthetic type of philosophical system such as Hobbes tried to build as opposed to one that progresses through examination of dialectical contrasts, as in a comparison of changing social contexts, or one unified more by a distinct method of thinking than by an intercon-necting of topics. Various interpreters of Hobbes have emphasized each of these types of system. These nine essays on Hobbes, accom-panied by nine on Jean-Jacques Rousseau, one on both, show contin-uing developments in critical interpretation. Three were written espe-cially for the volume.

The most recent summary of Hobbes's philosophy, by Charles H. Hinnant (1977, 1980), has not wholly superseded that of R. S. Peters (1956) but draws from these later developments. The strongest case for a borrowing from a new scientific paradigm, based on Hobbes's understanding of "motion," has been put in a history of ideas study by Thomas Spragens (1973).

Brown, Keith C., ed. *Hobbes Studies*. Oxford: Blackwell, 1965.
Cranston, Maurice, and Richard S. Peters, eds. *Hobbes and Rousseau: A Collection of Critical Essays*. Garden City, N.Y.: Doubleday Anchor, 1972.
Hinnant, Charles H. *Thomas Hobbes*. Boston: Twayne, 1977.
———. *Thomas Hobbes: A Reference Guide*. Boston: G. K. Hall, 1980.
Oakeshott, Michael. *Hobbes on Civil Association*. Berkeley: Univ. of Cali-fornia Pr.; Oxford: Blackwell, 1975.
Peters, Richard S. *Hobbes*. Baltimore, Md.: Penguin, 1967. (Original ed., 1956.)
Spragens, Thomas A., Jr. *The Politics of Motion: The World of Thomas Hobbes*. Lexington: Univ. Pr. of Kentucky, 1973.
Strauss, Leo. *The Political Philosophy of Hobbes: Its Basis and Its Genesis*. Tr. by Elsa M. Sinclair. Oxford: Clarendon Pr., 1936. (Repr.: Chicago: Univ. of Chicago Pr., 1952.)
Warrender, Howard. *The Political Philosophy of Hobbes: His Theory of Obligation*. Oxford: Clarendon Pr., 1957. (Repr., 1970.)
Watkins, J. W. N. *Hobbes's System of Ideas: A Study in the Political Signifi-cance of Philosophical Theories*. 2nd ed. London: Hutchinson, 1973. (1st ed., 1965.)

JOHN LOCKE (1632–1704)

Empiricism and Liberal Politics

John Locke grew up in a liberal Puritan family and was chiefly a man of practical affairs throughout his adult life. He turned to philosophical interests in his early thirties, largely through the influence of the first Earl of Shaftesbury (1621–83), a noted Whig political leader with whom he was closely associated over the years. Locke took nearly twenty years to work out his two greatest writings: *An Essay Concerning Human Understanding* (1689) and *Two Treatises on Government* (published anonymously in 1690); the first he saw through several editions. These books, plus numerous writings on religion and a popular work on education (1693), also published late in life, bore enormous influence well into the next century, in France and America as well as in Britain. They established him as the founder of modern British philosophy. The *Two Treatises,* however, did not have a critical edition until that produced by Peter Laslett (1960), whose introduction and notes are also now indispensable. Many papers valuable for interpretation of Locke's ideas have only been available since the 1950s.

Strong rationalist elements resided in Locke's methodology—more than has ordinarily been acknowledged until recently and closer to Descartes' own (Schouls, *The Imposition of Method . . . ,* 1980, cited on p. 79). Nevertheless, he is rightly credited with setting strong roots for the tradition of common sense empiricism in British thought and with contributing a firm rationale both for liberal politics and for religious toleration in the modern mind. Today he is known more for the freshness and drift of his arguments than for their rigor or consistency. Locke, in contrast to Descartes, audaciously reduced the foundations of knowledge to sense perception and denied any valid existence to ideas (thoughts and modes of thinking) said to be innately held, prior to sense experience. On this ground, he has come to be called an "empiricist," Descartes a "rationalist," though this two-party system never existed in the seventeenth century and though something of each element is to be found in both philosophers.

Other Interpretations

Among the general accounts, that by D. J. O'Connor (1952) is still important, coming from one who closely identifies with Locke's "moderate empiricism" and who tries to demonstrate his current relevance, especially for epistemology (political theory gets thirteen pages). The more balanced survey by J. D. Mabbott (1973) reflects accession to the Bodleian Library of the Lovelace collection of Locke's extensive correspondence, now appearing in eight volumes (1976–), and other papers. Although these materials, discovered by R. I. Aaron in 1935 and purchased by the Bodleian in 1947, have enabled a more critical awareness of the development of Locke's ideas, they have yet to be used to their full. Mabbott includes sections on epistemology, on logic and language, on ethics and theology, and forty-two pages on political theory. The collection of new essays edited by John Yolton (1969), who himself has produced many publications on Locke, is similarly broad in scope; most are written by professors of history and political science. Aaron's work (1937; 3rd ed., 1971) remains an indispensable overview, particularly on the development of Locke's *Essay*. To Laslett's work must be added John Dunn's account (1969) of the development of Locke's *Two Treatises*. The latter especially concentrates on analysis of arguments.

Because of the close tie in the early empiricist tradition of successors George Berkeley and David Hume to Locke, studies often link Locke with one or both. Jonathan Bennett (1971), for example, has selected three themes of current interest that are also central in the thinking of all three: meaning, causality, and objectivity. He has then used analysis of passages from their works to reflect upon those themes. A collection of essays by C. B. Martin and D. M. Armstrong (1968) has ten on Locke and nine on Berkeley; most are on their epistemology and metaphysics, though there are three essays on Locke's political theory.

Aaron, Richard I. *John Locke.* 3rd ed. New York: Oxford Univ. Pr., Oxford: Clarendon Pr., 1971. (1st ed., 1937; 2nd ed., 1955.)

Bennett, Jonathan. *Locke, Berkeley, Hume: Central Themes.* Oxford: Clarendon Pr., 1971.

Dunn, John. *The Political Thought of John Locke: An Historical Account of the Argument of the "Two Treatises of Government."* Cambridge and New York: Cambridge Univ. Pr., 1969.

Locke, John. *Two Treatises of Government: A Critical Edition with an Introduction and Apparatus Criticus by Peter Laslett.* 2nd ed. Cambridge and New York: Cambridge Univ. Pr., 1967. (1st ed., 1960.)

Mabbott, John D. *John Locke.* London: Macmillan, 1973.

Martin, Charles B., and D. M. Armstrong, eds. *Locke and Berkeley: A Collection of Critical Essays.* Garden City, N.Y.: Doubleday Anchor, 1968.

O'Connor, Daniel J. *John Locke*. Baltimore, Md. and Harmondsworth: Penguin, 1952.
Yolton, John W., ed. *John Locke: Problems and Perspectives—A Collection of New Essays*. Cambridge and New York: Cambridge Univ. Pr., 1969.

5

Eighteenth-Century Philosophy

Themes and Developments

As the century of the Enlightenment, the eighteenth has been comprehensively surveyed by intellectual historian Peter Gay (1966–69), interpreting its chief representatives as a cosmopolitan, quarrelsome family of highly articulate, urbane intellectuals called "philosophes." In his view, these people, whose capital was Paris, were united by a single style of thinking, one which through critical reason pitted against each other the Christian and classic pagan past and thereby aimed to secure a new secularized autonomy in, and power to shape, every sphere of life. All the thematic areas indicated for the seventeenth century here continued to be important over the next one hundred years and more. However, Gay agrees with Ernst Cassirer (1932) and most interpreters after Cassirer in characterizing the period not as a developing colloquy of systems (as was the previous century, despite Christian Wolff's efforts—see chapter 4) but as a congeries of critiques. Nonetheless, in attempting to sum up the "mind" of the Enlightenment regarding several areas—natural science, psychology and epistemology, religion, history, society and politics, and aesthetics—Cassirer had emphasized the search for unity between rational principles and phenomena in both periods, with a shift of emphasis to the latter concern; and in this process he saw the strong though indirect influence of Leibniz. (Such continuity and development within the two centuries is rarely shown in the detail provided by Ben Lazare Mijuskovic, 1974, who traces a single rationalist argument, much used throughout: the argument that the power of thinking is the essential nature of the soul; thought, being immaterial, is unextended, or simple; and what is simple, as having no parts, is an indestructible unity and identity.)

Though a philosopher of some substance himself, Cassirer did not provide a history of philosophy in the narrower sense, accepting the broader definition of philosophy held by the philosophes themselves. The same is true of Charles Frankel (1948) in his study of the eminently important idea of progress in the French Enlightenment. A synthetic history of ideas approach is used by Lester Crocker (1959, 1963) to outline French Enlightenment themes concerning the place of human beings in the universe, freedom and determinism, human nature and motivation, moral values and moral experience.

Although Leslie Stephen's (1876) two-volume history of English thought in this period is outdated, nothing so extensive has taken its place; it is still useful, particularly as a reminder of the extensive spread of deist views and related controversies. The second volume is devoted to moral and political philosophy. Wilbur Samuel Howell's (1971) work on British logic and rhetoric carries forward his perceptive earlier study of the 1500–1700 period (*Logic and Rhetoric in England, 1500–1700*, 1956, cited on p. 79).

The history of American philosophy will be treated as background to twentieth-century interests, largely because the field did not really come into its own in America until the late nineteenth century. Nevertheless, it should be noted that the Puritan preacher-theologian Jonathan Edwards (1703–58), also probably America's most gifted philosopher until that time, was greatly influenced by Locke and the Cambridge Platonists and flourished during the lifetime of Berkeley and Hume—though very likely without influence from either one.

Much of the history of eighteenth-century philosophy, viewed in a still narrower sense than that represented in the studies so far mentioned, would have to emphasize (1) pre-Kantian thought in Germany, which was usually overshadowed by discussion of the French scene before Lewis White Beck's survey (1969) came along; (2) the Italian, Giambattista Vico, who came to be known only through Johann Gottfried Herder late in the century and thus bore virtually no influence within the period; (3) Jean-Jacques Rousseau, who was generally in ill repute among the philosophes because of his "irrationalist" tendencies; (4) George Berkeley, who is even more decidedly an anti-Enlightenment figure and until recently has held an awkward, improper place as a so-called empiricist between Locke and Hume; (5) David Hume, who was accepted but whose skepticism does not quite belong; (6) Johann George Hamann whose eccentric, jagged style and radically Christian orientation was offensive to the philosophes; and (6) Immanuel Kant, whose own critiques were a culmination of the Enlightenment but also helped mark its end. Because the subsequent influence of Berkeley, Hume, Rousseau, and Kant has been especially great, they are singled out for more lengthy treatment here.

Pre-Kantian German Philosophy

For the roots of Enlightenment philosophy in the German territories, Lewis White Beck reaches back to medieval and Reformation times. Its principal home from 1759 to 1786 was Berlin, which had an unusually large foreign population, mostly Reformed (Calvinist, not Lutheran), and whose citizens were stimulated to adopt Enlightenment interests by the King of Prussia, Frederick II ("the Great"), himself a much-published popular philosopher. Moses Mendelssohn (1729–86) and Gotthold Ephraim Lessing (1729–80) held forth there, both as adherents and as critics of Enlightenment thought. In the early nineteenth century it was to be the workplace of Friedrich Schleiermacher and G. W. F. Hegel (see chapter 6). Beck also highlights German counter-Enlightenment ideas outside Berlin, notably by partial pietists Friedrich Heinrich Jacobi (1743–1819) and Johann Georg Hamann (1730–88) and by the broader-minded Johann Gottfried Herder (1744–1803). He ends with Kant, who shared much of the Enlightenment ethos, though he drew from many other sources and though it was probably his own pietist background, which he rejected to a far greater extent than did Jacobi or Hamann, that led him to oppose the eudaemonistic (happiness) ethics held by almost all the Enlightenment thinkers.

Vico and the Theme of History

Until recently, Giambattista Vico (1668–1744) has rarely been discussed in histories of philosophy outside Italy, though, because of his remarkably new contributions to the understanding of historically oriented thought, he deserves a prominent place. In two independent and complementary works, philosophers Leon Pompa (1975) and Isaiah Berlin (1976) have both rendered interpretations of principal ideas in Vico's philosophy. His own unusual *Autobiography* (translated in 1944) is also important for this purpose. Pompa's study is a more technical analysis, with the aim chiefly of illuminating Vico's masterpiece *Scienza Nuova* (1725), the first of its kind in English. Both diverge from the classic, still valuable interpretation of Vico as an early absolute idealist by his idealist countryman, Benedetto Croce (1911), translated by R. G. Collingwood in 1913. At issue in all these works are the extent to which Vico's proposed historical methods of understanding the social world and of reconstructing the distinct expressive means and phases of its history are "science," as understood either in his day or our own, and what the proper relations are between philosophy and philology, sociology, and history. Berlin's study carries the added value of comparing the ideas of Herder, another encyclopedic thinker of similar bent. Although such themes were of considerable interest to others in this period, they were perhaps never so probingly examined as by Vico. His rising reputation of late is well betokened in the tercentenary collection edited by Giorgio Tagliacozzo and Hayden White (1969), to which Berlin, Max Fisch, Stuart Hampshire, and other philosopher-historians contribute along with scholars from other fields. More recently, Donald Verene (1981) has highlighted the central role of "imagination" in his view of science. Between them, he and Tagliacozzo have also edited three further collections (1976–81).

Hamann

How far could the critiques of the critiques go? Highly appreciative of Hume yet presenting himself forthright as a Christian thinker, Johann Georg Hamann (1730–88) roamed the boundaries of language and reason, doubt and faith—in loyal opposition to much Enlightenment thought, frequently reporting what he saw by sarcastic or satirical means. His style is often extremely indirect and puzzling, and his writings are usually occasional; but he repays patient reading, as the many thinkers who have felt his impact then and since have testified. Although Hamann was a key figure in his own time, and an important influence on Herder and Goethe and on Romantic and existential thought later on, an edition of his works only appeared in the 1810s and complete editions of his writings and letters only in 1949–75. Only one of his numerous major works has been translated into English, his quite early *Socratic Memorabilia* (1759). Two excellent studies of his entire production have appeared in English, by W. M. Alexander (1966) and James O'Flaherty (1979). Both emphasize unifying themes and methods, the first showing in greater detail the ways Hamann related philosophy to faith; both display the pertinence, especially of his critique of language for current inquiry.

Who's Who in Continental Metaphysics

James Collins (*Interpreting Modern Philosophy*, 1972, cited on p. 6) has usefully termed Hamann, with Pascal and Søren Kierkegaard, a "paraphilosopher"—one whose chief orientation and activities lie elsewhere but who has notably reshaped some "methods and questions, concepts and living springs of evidence" in modern philosophy. In contrast, nineteenth-century philosophers Arthur Schopenhauer and Ludwig Feuerbach he terms "middle-range philosophers" in that their significance for current thought has come to be recognized as something independent of their intermediate influence. Among eighteenth-century figures, Vico fits the latter category. Among seventeenth-century philosophers, the status of Nicolas Malebranche (1638–1715) is going to be in dispute for a while. Louis Loeb (1981) persuasively argues that the most important historical succession for over a century before Kant is Descartes, Spinoza, Malebranche, Berkeley, and Leibniz—all representatives of what he calls "Continental Metaphysics." Thus Loeb rehabilitates Malebranche as at least a major philosopher in his time. In his terms, Malebranche would probably make the cut as a middle-range philosopher today. On the other hand, the philosophical temperaments of Locke and Hume place them outside the historical list, but not because they presented a clear "empiricist" alternative at the time (the standard interpretation, which normally includes Berkeley). The differences, for Loeb, lie in how they understood causation—in Locke's case, as a Cartesian rationalist, not an empiricist. The core of Hume's critique of causation—which Loeb thinks was directed especially to Malebranche—was that the only way we could possibly determine causation would be by observed or experienced constant conjunctions between objects, but that by this means we cannot determine either that there are any objects which are the causes of any other or that there are not. This argument, I should think, leads to skepticism, not necessarily to empirical doctrine, at least in this one crucial area.

Alexander, William M. *Johann Georg Hamann: Philosophy and Faith.* The Hague: Nijhoff, 1966.

✓ Beck, Lewis White. *Early German Philosophy: Kant and His Predecessors.* Cambridge, Mass.: Belknap Pr. of Harvard Univ. Pr., 1969.

Berlin, Isaiah. *Vico and Herder: Two Studies in the History of Ideas.* London: Hogarth, 1976.

Cassirer, Ernst. *The Philosophy of the Enlightenment.* Tr. by Fritz C. A. Koelln and James P. Pettegrove. Princeton, N.J.: Princeton Univ. Pr., 1951. (German ed., 1932.)

Croce, Benedetto. *The Philosophy of Giambattista Vico.* Tr. by R. G. Collingwood. New York: Russell & Russell, 1913. (Repr., 1964. Italian ed., 1911.)

Crocker, Lester G. *An Age of Crisis: Man and World in Eighteenth Century French Thought.* Baltimore, Md.: Johns Hopkins Univ. Pr., 1959.

———. *Nature and Culture: Ethical Thought in the French Enlightenment.* Baltimore, Md.: Johns Hopkins Univ. Pr., 1963.

Frankel, Charles. *The Faith of Reason: The Idea of Progress in the French Enlightenment.* New York: King's Crown Pr., 1948.

Gay, Peter. *The Enlightenment: An Interpretation.* 2v. New York: Knopf, 1966–69.

Howell, Wilbur Samuel. *Eighteenth-Century British Logic and Rhetoric.* Princeton, N.J.: Princeton Univ. Pr., 1971.

Loeb, Louis E. *From Descartes to Hume: Continental Metaphysics and the Development of Modern Philosophy.* Ithaca, N.Y. and London: Cornell Univ. Pr., 1981.

Mijuskovic, Ben Lazare. *The Achilles of Rationalist Arguments: The Simplicity, Unity, and Identity of Thought and Soul from the Cambridge Platonists to Kant.* The Hague: Nijhoff, 1974.

O'Flaherty, James C. *Johann Georg Hamann.* Boston: Twayne, 1979.

Pompa, Leon. *Vico: A Study of the New Science.* Cambridge and New York: Cambridge Univ. Pr., 1975.

Stephen, Leslie. *History of English Thought in the Eighteenth Century.* 3rd ed. 2v. New York: P. Smith, 1949. (1st ed., London, 1876.)

Tagliacozzo, Giorio, and Hayden V. White, eds. *Giambattista Vico: An International Symposium.* Baltimore, Md.: Johns Hopkins Univ. Pr., 1969.

Verene, Donald Phillip. *Vico's Science of Imagination.* Ithaca, N.Y. and London: Cornell Univ. Pr., 1981.

GEORGE BERKELEY (1685–1753)

Metaphysics

George Berkeley's chief lifelong concern was to oppose positions likely to undermine theistic belief, especially deistic, mechanistic, and skeptical positions. Although in later life he became an Anglican clergyman, then a bishop (1734–53), he was far from being a mere apologist. His discourse, at once exceptionally eloquent and down-to-earth, is also notable for its serious consideration of objections and its evolving refinement of arguments and positions. Without adequate examination, in his view, Locke and others had simply assumed the metaphysics of matter as a substratum hidden under appearances, the metaphysics of seventeenth-century mathematical physics. Himself an able mathematician, Berkeley attempted to reclaim the common sense view that the world is as it appears. He wished to show that such concepts as "matter" in the new physics are phantoms, that the abstractions used by mathematicians and scientists are at best operationally useful but unreal, artificial constructs that do not in themselves show us reality. He was appalled at the splitting of mind from matter, believing that the ultimate result is utter skepticism and nihilism. Was he, then, a substantialist, an empiricist, or a phenomenalist? Did his own metaphysics come down to solipsism, pure subjective idealism, or a form of objective idealism?

Which labels are appropriate? Great confusion is still present in the literature. To a considerable extent, I think, this stems from the constant failure to accommodate to Berkeley's particular style. The style often features getting inside the opponents' views first (as if he accepted their own language and assumptions), then gradually, dialectically revealing their futility and providing his own remedies. The traditional identification of Berkeley as one who was building an empiricist idealism on premises supplied by Locke especially derives from such a misreading of *An Essay towards a New Theory of Vision* (1709) and *A Treatise Concerning the Principles of Human Knowledge* (1710), his two main philosophical works. It would also have helped if Berkeley had given us a much fuller statement of his philosophy of mind.

Another reason for the confusion probably resides in a strong, partly unconscious conflict in Berkeley himself as to what he actually wanted to say. The latter claim has been penetratingly argued by philosopher John O. Wisdom (1953), who uses chiefly a sideline psychoanalytic theory from Melanie Klein to set forth fifty-six interpretations about how Berkeley dealt with the belief that he had a poison inside him, clogging and destroying him, notably by denying the existence of matter. It is unfortunate that Wisdom was not more guarded in his speculations and more broadly psychoanalytic in his knowledge, as commentators have tended to be put off by the attempt. Thus they have not been able to use his account, so far the sole full-scale attempt to get at the unconscious motivations of a philosopher. Wisdom thinks Berkeley was consciously a theocentric phenomenologist in the early works, holding that the world is externally known by God but through creation made perceptible to finite minds, in this doctrine of "immaterialism" (as Berkeley called it) denying the existence of matter without mind. By 1710 he was already showing signs of an unconscious and inconsistent solipsism. Like most more recent interpreters, Wisdom opposes the traditional view that Berkeley's metaphysics, which presumably denied the existence of the external world altogether, was Locke's made consistent or misapplied, or that it was an anticipatory but incomplete version of Kant's, and that in *Siris* (1744), his last philosophical work, he changed his mind and became a Platonist. Wisdom also gives us a way of understanding how a philosopher of Berkeley's acuity could have pushed tar water as a cleansing, purgating cure-all in *Siris*, a very odd moment in an otherwise brilliant career.

Changing Interpretations

The traditional view, though still tenacious, was already being critically undermined by the early 1930s, first in a now-famous article by J. D. Mabbott (1931) on "The Place of God in Berkeley's Philosophy," then through work by A. A. Luce on his newly discovered 1707–8 notebooks (*Philosophical Commentaries*—critical ed., 1944), and other fresh work and editing by Luce and T. E. Jessop. Luce (1934) was able to show decisively that Berkeley's chief early stimulus was from the attack on abstractions by the Cartesian Malebranche, specifically in his first and most important work *De la recherche de la vérité* ("On the Search for Truth," 1674–75). Later (see the 1967 preface to the reissued 1934 study), Luce was to modify this thesis somewhat, seeing an even more subtle dialectic in the strong impetus provided by Malebranche and by skeptic Pierre Bayle (1647–1706) through his *Dictionnaire historique et critique* (1692–1707; translated 1734–41 in ten volumes). Only with completion of the Luce-Jessop nine-volume set of Berkeley's works (1948–57) has their full range been accessible.

Following Luce and Jessop, Gavin Ardley (1968) rightly warns against the serious inaccuracies that regularly accrue to analytic studies of Berkeley (for example those by G. E. Moore, J. L. Austin, and G. J. Warnock) because they pounce on isolated passages and fail to take a synoptic view. (In 1950, Ardley had issued a valuable work comparing Aquinas's and Kant's views of science). At the same time, he denies that Berkeley had a full-orbed metaphysical or moral system, though he holds that his philosophy is in the main remarkably clear and consistent, a unity from youth to death. Berkeley's position centers on an investigation of the ontological foundations of the exact sciences. He holds, against his opponents, that to be is to be perceived by the divine mind or to have the possibility of perception by human minds (*esse* is *percipi* and *esse* is *posse percipi*, respectively). He added a nonmechanistic, teleological concept of motion. Berkeley's approach opposes overly introspective, fine-spun metaphysics, too far removed from practical affairs. He is himself essentially a practical reformer—a participant, not a mere spectator.

Ardley's more holistic approach thus emphasizes Berkeley's effort to make good on an enlightened "common sense" perspective. At a deeper level than Berkeley ordinarily shows until *Siris,* to Ardley this effort reflects the *philosophia perennis* ("the perennial philosophy," by Ardley formed on an Aristotelian-Thomist base, as usual, but including Plato). He admits, however, that by throwing away all matter and all causation between unthinking beings, along with autonomous matter and autonomous secondary causation as these were conceived in seventeenth-century physics, Berkeley went too far; he drifted from common sense, working too strictly with the current narrowly static concepts of both causation and matter, such as were found in deism. Moreover, the properly deepening sense of mystery in his later works marks a change of balance, not of principle.

In a 1953 article, Karl Popper called Berkeley's view of science and mathematics nonessentialist, because—unlike most theories after Newton—it eliminates all essentialist explanations from these disciplines. All entities are ruled out except those that are perceived. At the same time, Berkeley had a profound appreciation of the operational functioning of fictive concepts in these same disciplines. In both respects, Popper sees striking similarities to positivist, instrumentalist positions reintroduced by Ernst Mach, Albert Einstein, and others nearly two hundred years later.

Direct observation, however, bears problems of its own. In examining Berkeley's theory of vision from beginning to end—or what Colin Murray Turbayne has named "the metaphor of vision"—George Stack (1970) examines these problems with care and then distinguishes Berkeley's protopragmatic, experiential phenomenalism, that posits a hierarchy of knowledge from sense perception to apprehension of the divine mind, from Kantian and other forms, that restrict knowledge to phenomena alone. Although Stack finds inconsistencies and confusions among Berkeley's arguments, much of this, in his view, comes from complexities in the perceptual process itself. These cannot be reduced to a generation of pseudoproblems that contemporary philosophers must abolish.

Other aspects of Berkeley's philosophy have been treated primarily in articles. An exception is Paul Olscamp's (1970) extensive study of his ethics, placed in historical context.

General Accounts and Collections

The latest overall interpretation, by George Pitcher (1977), a fine analytic study of arguments, stays with the Locke-plus tradition regarding Berkeley's theory of perception. It does not register the dialectical structure of his writings, does not cover his entire philosophy, and does not manifest any use of Ardley and Luce or of the recent works by Bracken and Stack. The analytic study by I. C. Tipton (1974) does incorporate something from these studies and is perhaps the most judicious of the recent summaries, though Tipton restricts his efforts to an examination—from philosophical, ordinary language, and psychological angles—of Berkeley's case for immaterialism. Gavin Ardley's work (1968), on the other hand, rests largely with general characterization; it does not reconstruct actual developments of arguments in the texts. Harry Bracken (1974) presents Berkeley as a Cartesian via Malebranche, in the Luce manner, but he too ignores Ardley. The 1953 analytic account by G. J. Warnock makes of Berkeley an extreme exponent of subjective idealism, mostly achieved in response to Locke; his self-criticisms in a 1969 reissue are instructive reminders of how tangled and changeable the interpretations of Berkeley have been.

There are only two overlaps—the much-noted articles by J. D Mabbott (1931) and Karl Popper (1953) just referred to—between the collections of critical articles edited by Colin Murray Turbayne (1970) and by C. B. Martin and D. M. Armstrong (*Locke and Berkeley . . .*, 1968, cited on p. 95). Three of the eleven essays are new in Turbayne, accompanied by a text of the *Principles* (pp. 223–331). Martin and Armstrong present twelve essays published from 1931 to 1966. The thirteen studies edited by Warren Steinkraus (1966) are all new; Luce, Turbayne, Tipton, Bracken, and Jessop are among the authors. Together, these writings well display the improving, though still confused, fortunes of Berkeley; and they broaden the normal scope of interests considered.

✓ Ardley, Gavin. *Berkeley's Renovation of Philosophy*. The Hague: Nijhoff, 1968.

Berkeley, George. *A Treatise Concerning the Principles of Human Knowledge, with Critical Essays*. Ed. by Colin Murray Turbayne. Indianapolis, Ind.: Bobbs-Merrill, 1970.

Bracken, Harry M. *Berkeley*. New York and London: Macmillan, 1974.

Luce, Arthur A. *Berkeley and Malebranche: A Study in the Origins of Berke-*

ley's Thought. Oxford and New York: Oxford Univ. Pr., 1934. (Repr., 1967 with new preface.)

Olscamp, Paul J. *The Moral Philosophy of George Berkeley.* The Hague: Nijhoff, 1970.

Pitcher, George. *Berkeley.* London and Boston: Routledge & Paul, 1977.

Stack, George J. *Berkeley's Analysis of Perception.* The Hague: Mouton, 1970.

Steinkraus, Warren E., ed. *New Studies in Berkeley's Philosophy.* New York and London: Holt, Rinehart & Winston, 1966.

Tipton, I. C. *Berkeley: The Philosophy of Immaterialism.* London: Methuen, 1974.

Warnock Geoffrey J. *Berkeley.* Baltimore, Md. and Harmondsworth: Penguin, 1969. (Original ed., 1953.)

Wisdom, John Oulton. *The Unconscious Sources of Berkeley's Philosophy.* London: Hogarth, 1953.

DAVID HUME (1711–1776)

The Many-sided Skeptic

The radically skeptical arguments of Scottish philosopher and historian David Hume awakened Immanuel Kant from his "dogmatic slumbers." For a century and a half after Hume's death, this was the best to be said of him. Most of the slight recognition of his thought, which we now know even Kant misread, was non-English, especially German. Today Hume texts are among those most read among students of philosophy, texts taken especially from *A Treatise of Human Nature* (1739), *Dialogues Concerning Natural Religion* (probably from the 1750s, published posthumously), *Enquiry Concerning Human Understanding* (1748), and *Enquiry Concerning the Principles of Morals* (1751). A major new interpretive work by David Morton (1982) well represents the underlying current interest in his skeptical approach especially to religion but also, in order to clear the way, to metaphysics and epistemology, and in his common-sense approach to morality, whereby sentiment and experience, not reason alone, is seen to be the appropriate ground of moral decision, and sentiment points to what is either pleasant or useful. Alongside morals, the empirical, experimental sciences, which he modeled after Newton, and mathematics both emerged from Hume's analyses relatively unscathed. In all these respects, Hume's views closely accord with those held by a great many empiricist philosophers in the twentieth century.

Hume studies in English emerged after Charles Hendel's treatise (1925). They still often manifest the inappropriate tendency to concentrate on Book I of his three-part *Treatise* (1739), the authorship of which he did not acknowledge until many years later (as is true of his 1740 *Abstract* of it) and on select parts of his *Enquiries* (1748, 1751), despite Norman Kemp Smith's brilliant analysis to the contrary (1941). His only other significant contribution to philosophy thereafter was the *Dialogues Concerning Natural Religion,* which on the whole gave him an extremely negative reputation. Until very recently, Hume's "many-sided genius" (Merrill and Shahan, 1976) as a philosophical historian, man of letters, and political economist, already depicted in Ernest Campbell Mossner's sagacious *Life* (1954; rev. 1980), was virtually ignored. In the eighteenth century, he was especially known for his best selling, prophetic *History of England* (see Norton and Popkin's excellent collection, 1965) but was reviled then and thereafter for his empiricist critique of religious belief, a major lifelong occupation of this eminent nonbeliever.

Despite the widespread interest in Hume's views on religion, there was no full-length treatment until John Gaskin's small book (1978). Among earlier studies, Antony Flew's analysis of Hume's antireligious epistemology and metaphysics (1961) is exemplary. Robert Hurlbutt (1965) had surveyed relations of his thinking to eighteenth-century theology, especially the popular Newtonian design argument for the existence of God.

Hume's greatness as an economic and political theorist awaits an adequate account, though J. B. Stewart (1963) has made a good beginning. His view of human nature in the *Treatise* (Árdal, 1966) and epistemological concerns as related to his ethics (first McNabb, 1951; then, mirroring current analytic interests, Harrison, 1976) have fared somewhat better. Recently Nicholas Capaldi (1975) has reviewed his Newtonian background, Stanley Tweyman (1974) his relation to rationalist predecessors, and John Bricke (1980) his philosophy of mind, all providing solid critical treatment. Other specialized studies like David Stove's on Hume's skepticism about induction (1973) will no doubt follow.

Puzzlement over what Hume's intentions actually were, especially in epistemology, an issue sharpened by John Passmore (1952), seems to account in large part for Hume's continual eclipse of his more famous predecessor, John Locke, in the periodical literature since the 1930s. So opines Roland Hall (1978) in his rare systematic bibliographical study. If so, the analytic depth and lucidity of Hume's inquiries may in themselves make the task worth pursuing.

Other Accounts and Collections

The collections, V. C. Chappell's (1966) especially notable among them, have typically featured his epistemology and ethics, as have several excellent analytic synopses of his thought and its development, notably by James Noxon (1973), Terrence Penelhum (1975), and Barry Stroud (1977)—each fine-tuned but distinct as to interpretation. The more recent collections have broadened their scope, first the Mossner Festschrift edited by William Todd (1974), then the bicentenary collections by Donald Livingston and James King (1976) and George Morice (1977).

Árdal, Páll S. *Passion and Value in Hume's Treatise.* Edinburgh: Edinburgh Univ. Pr., 1966.

Bricke, John. *Hume's Philosophy of Mind.* Princeton, N.J.: Princeton Univ. Pr., 1980.

Capaldi, Nicholas. *David Hume: The Newtonian Philosopher.* Boston: Twayne, 1975.

Chappell, Vere C., ed. *Hume: A Collection of Critical Essays.* Garden City, N.Y.: Doubleday Anchor, 1966.

Flew Antony. *Hume's Philosophy of Belief: A Study of His First Inquiry.* New York: Humanities Pr.; London: Routledge & Paul, 1961.

Gaskin, John C. A. *Hume's Philosophy of Religion.* London: Macmillan, 1978.

Hall, Roland. *Fifty Years of Hume Scholarship: A Bibliographic Guide.* New York: Columbia Univ. Pr.; Edinburgh: Edinburgh Univ. Pr., 1978.

Harrison, Jonathan. *Hume's Moral Epistemology.* Oxford: Clarendon Pr., 1976.

Hendel, Charles W. *Studies in the Philosophy of David Hume.* Princeton, N.J.: Princeton Univ. Pr., 1925. (Repr.: Indianapolis, Ind.: Bobbs-Merrill, 1963.)

Hurlbutt, Robert E. *Hume, Newton, and the Design Argument.* Lincoln: Univ. of Nebraska Pr., 1965.

Livingston, Donald W., and James T. King, eds. *Hume: A Re-evaluation.* New York: Fordham Univ. Pr., 1976.

McNabb, D. G. C. *David Hume: His Theory of Knowledge and Morality.* 2nd ed. Hamden, Conn.: Archon Books, 1966. (1st ed., Oxford Univ. Pr., 1951.)

Merrill, Kenneth R., and Robert W. Shahan, eds. *David Hume: Many-Sided Genius.* Norman: Univ. of Oklahoma Pr., 1976.

Morice, George P., ed. *David Hume: Bicentenary Papers.* Edinburgh: Edinburgh Univ. Pr., 1977.

Morton, David Fate. *David Hume: Common-Sense Moralist, Skeptical Metaphysician.* Princeton, N.J.: Princeton Univ. Pr., 1982.

Mossner, Ernest Campbell. *The Life of David Hume.* 2nd ed. Oxford: Clarendon Pr., 1980. (1st ed., 1954.)

Norton, David F., and Richard H. Popkin, eds. *David Hume: Philosophical Historian.* Indianapolis, Ind.: Bobbs-Merrill, 1965.

Noxon, James H. *Hume's Philosophical Development: A Study of His Methods.* Oxford: Clarendon Pr., 1973.

Passmore, John A. *Hume's Intentions.* Cambridge and New York: Cambridge Univ. Pr., 1952.

Penelhum, Terence. *Hume.* New York: St. Martin's Pr.; London: Macmillan, 1975.

Smith, Norman Kemp. *The Philosophy of David Hume: A Critical Study of Its Origins and Central Doctrines.* London: Macmillan, 1941.

Stewart, John B. *The Moral and Political Philosophy of David Hume.* New York: Columbia Univ. Pr., 1963.

Stove, David C. *Probability and Hume's Inductive Scepticism.* Oxford: Clarendon Pr., 1973.

Stroud, Barry. *Hume.* London and Boston: Routledge & Paul, 1977.

Todd, William B., ed. *Hume and the Enlightenment: Essays Presented to Ernest Campbell Mossner.* Austin: Univ. of Texas, Humanities Research Center; Edinburgh: Edinburgh Univ. Pr., 1974.

Tweyman, Stanley. *Reason and Conduct in Hume and His Predecessors.* The Hague: Nijhoff, 1974.

JEAN-JACQUES ROUSSEAU (1712–1778)

Education and Personal Growth

Although Jean-Jacques Rousseau wished to be considered an essayist rather than a philosopher, he now has the latter standing. Moreover, he represents a special interest in the interplay of personal and social life that leads to Romantic philosophy later in the eighteenth century and to both existentialist and liberal social philosophy beyond that era. Ernst Cassirer (1945) has also beautifully summarized Rousseau's influence on Immanuel Kant. Kant said he learned from Rousseau to respect human nature. He also learned from him to recognize the sharp distinction between mores and morality, still further: that between the vain Enlightenment hope that cultivation of the mind, as such, would bring steady progress to humankind and a far more difficult task, reasoned response to the moral law. The passionate, sentimental spirit of Rousseau was worlds away from the stern, orderly spirit of Kant. Yet he repeatedly went back to his predecessor's writings in appreciation of the motifs of autonomy and independence he found there. He liked, too, Rousseau's placing the true source of religion in moral conscience, his pure sense of justice, and his lofty goals for civilized society.

Intellectual historian Karl Weintraub (1978) especially features two philosophers, Augustine and Rousseau, in his outstanding historical essay on individuality and autobiography. (Abelard and Vico are also considered, with nonphilosophers such as Petrarch, Cellini, Montaigne, and Goethe.) Read in the context of the entire study, Weintraub's interpretation of Rousseau's *Confessions* (1781) is indispensable for an understanding of Rousseau's place in intellectual history. In particular, he emphasizes Rousseau's dilemma of dependency versus individuality and his being the first among the great autobiographers to take the formative influence of the early years seriously, hence to form a considered view of personal development and self-building creativity.

The standard interpretation of his educational theory is still that of William Boyd (1911). Boyd has perhaps overvalued the didactic work *Emile* (1762). A new critical synopsis is needed. Meanwhile Allan Bloom's 1979 translation and introduction is helpful. *Emile*, which includes a famous defense of natural religion, can only be adequately grasped as part of the fabric of Rousseau's thinking about human nature and society, especially as setting forth the thesis that humans are naturally undespoiled but are corrupted by evil social practices. Numerous adjacent studies like that by Marc Plattner (1979) on his notion of the "state of nature" would now have to be drawn upon to achieve a fuller account of his philosophy of education and personal growth. The severe complaint Russell Fraser lodged against seventeenth-century thinkers (*The Language of Adam . . .* , 1977, cited on p. 79) would not fit Rousseau, who abjured subtle, high-flown systems of abstraction. Instead, he recommended a reasoned examination of the whole of human experience, warts and all, beginning with one's own inner feelings. His own primary purpose in philosophizing was to understand his own nature and end. An appreciation of this perspective rules Ronald Grimsley's introduction to Rousseau's philosophy (1973), the best brief overview so far.

Sociopolitical Theory

Rousseau's political ideas were meant to be an integral part of his philosophy. His works on other subjects, however, were of far greater interest to eighteenth-century readers until the French Revolution. Since then, they have if anything overshadowed the others, except the *Confessions;* the *Social Contract* (1762) has been ranked among the classics of sociopolitical thought. In her critical review of his social theory, using an intellectual history approach, Judith Shklar (1969) detects two unreconciled "journeys to utopia"—the Spartan city and the tranquil household. A major conflict has centered on how or whether this and other similar contrasts could be made consistent with each other. David Cameron (1973) places historical perspective on this kind of issue in his comparison of Rousseau's social thought with that of conservative Edmund Burke (1729–97). A more modest study by John Charvet (1974) reconstructs what he takes to be a unified argument about the individual's relations to others in society in three works, *Discourse on the Origins of Inequality* (1755), *Emile* and *Social Contract* (both 1762). He does not refer to other secondary studies. These and other works had already been critically analyzed at length by Roger Masters (1968), a Rousseau translator, who had tried to reconstruct a system, chiefly by commentary on successive texts, and then to show the grounds of its failure, as many others have done in briefer compass. Masters' intended focus was on politics, but social and political theory are, in any case, not readily separable in Rousseau's writings taken as a whole.

Though brief, John Hall's introduction (1973) to aspects of his political philosophy gives us a more analytic account of the arguments than any of the above works tended to do. A more recent, substantial work by Stephen Ellenburg (1976) has not only attended to the major literature and to Rousseau's own dialectical relation to earlier thinkers but has also built an impressive argument on issues concerning Rousseau's unified, basically "nonindividualist" position and his radical egalitarianism. Ellenburg discovers no shift of direction in the political writings.

As a liberal theorist, did Rousseau favor participatory democracy, as was claimed by some of the New Left in the 1960s? Or does he advocate representative government? And are repressive elements to be found? In his insightful work on the development of Rousseau's concept of political institutions, Richard Fralin (1978) argues that he was ambivalent on these issues. Unlike Masters, Ellenburg, and Fralin, Ramon Lemos (1977) does not refer to the literature in his critical exposition of *Social Contract* and the two discourses (the other was *Discourse on the Science and the Arts*, 1750); and he does not try to put them in historical perspective, except occasionally to place Rousseau's views in dialectical relation to those of Hobbes, Locke, Kant, and a few others. Like Hall's, this work purports to restrict itself to the timeless philosophical significance of his position and arguments.

Four of the nine critical essays collected by Cranston and Peters (*Hobbes and Rousseau*, 1972, cited on p. 93) were contributed by Shklar, Masters, Grimsley, and Charvet. The latter two authors and William Pickles contributed new essays. This choice betokens that Rousseau has so far won only a small circle of philosophical interpreters. Some of his ideas are nonetheless widely referred to outside the field, and he is now counted among the premier political theorists.

Boyd, William. *The Educational Theory of Jean Jacques Rousseau.* New York: Russell & Russell, 1911. (Repr.,1963.)

Cameron, David. *The Social Thought of Rousseau and Burke: A Comparative Study.* London: Weidenfeld & Nicolson, 1973.

Cassirer, Ernst. *Rousseau, Kant, Goethe: Two Essays.* Tr. by James Gutmann et al. Princeton, N.J.: Princeton Univ. Pr., 1945. (Repr.: Hamden, Conn.: Archon Books, 1961.)

Charvet, John. *The Social Problem in the Philosophy of Rousseau.* Cambridge and New York: Cambridge Univ. Pr., 1974.

Ellenburg, Stephen. *Rousseau's Political Philosophy: An Interpretation from Within.* Ithaca, N.Y.: Cornell Univ. Pr., 1976.

Fralin, Richard. *Rousseau and Representation: A Study of the Development of His Concept of Political Institutions.* New York: Columbia Univ. Pr., 1978.

Grimsley, Ronald. *The Philosophy of Rousseau.* Oxford and New York: Oxford Univ. Pr., 1973.

Hall, John C. *Rousseau: An Introduction to His Political Philosophy.* London: Macmillan, 1973.

Lemos, Ramon M. *Rousseau's Political Philosophy: An Exposition and Interpretation.* Athens: Univ. of Georgia Pr., 1977.

Masters, Roger D. *The Political Philosophy of Rousseau.* Princeton, N.J.: Princeton Univ. Pr., 1968.

Plattner, Marc F. *Rousseau's State of Nature: An Interpretation of the Discourse on Inequality.* DeKalb: Northern Illinois Univ. Pr., 1979.

Shklar, Judith N. *Men and Citizens: A Study of Rousseau's Social Theory.* Cambridge and New York: Cambridge Univ. Pr., 1969.

Weintraub, Karl Joachim. *The Value of the Individual: Self and Circumstance in Autobiography.* Chicago and London: Univ. of Chicago Pr., 1978.

IMMANUEL KANT (1724–1804)

The Standard Approach

Ordinarily the interpreters of Immanuel Kant have concentrated on the chief works of his "critical" philosophy, which is a critical examination of the powers of intellect operating on its own. Primary interest has been directed to logical and epistemological issues in his first and greatest book, the *Critique of Pure Reason* (1781, 2nd ed.,

1787). There he tries to demonstrate, among other things, that although all knowledge indeed begins with experience, so that there are no innate ideas, some knowledge is not derived from experience (that is, is a priori, as in the intuitions of space and time). The book has been translated by Norman Kemp Smith (1929) in a composite edition. Smith's commentary (1923) is still a major aid to understanding this extremely difficult treatise. Kant's *Prolegomena to Any Future Metaphysics* (1783) is a simpler work, issued out of concern for the numerous criticisms and misconceptions that greeted the first book. His "second critique," *Critique of Practical Reason* (1788) was preceded by another short discussion, *Foundations of the Metaphysics of Morals* (1785, 2nd ed., 1786), the most popular of his writings. Lewis White Beck's (1960) commentary is still useful. The *Critique of Judgment* (1790) was produced more quickly and so more loosely, of necessity has a different ordering than the one used in the first two critiques, and thus has a somewhat unfamiliar ring to it. For these reasons, and because it deals with "aesthetic" and "teleological" judgment, this third critique has also been influential but has won much less analytic attention until recently (see chapter 27). In contrast, *Religion within the Limits of Reason Alone* (1792–93) has been an object of great interest from the beginning, since here Kant refutes the traditional arguments for the existence of God, replaces them with a moral argument, and is thought to have reduced religion to a form of morality.

The standard interpretation has been that in these works Kant is attempting to destroy all or most traditional metaphysics, ethics, aesthetics, and theology, and that, primarily in response to Hume's skepticism (in a critical analysis of reason in its "pure" state, that is, not as such derived from sense experience), he is laying the groundwork for a thoroughly empirical, scientific outlook. This he does by purporting to reveal a priori forms of intellectual functioning, for instance in the intuitions of space and time and various basic categories such as unity and plurality, without which we cannot be aware of or know phenomena. God, freedom, and immortality are postulates underlying such transcendentally derived forms. Things in themselves—the noumenal, nonphenomenal world, including the physical world, God, the self and other minds—cannot be known. Their existence is not doubted, however; thus Kant not only uses so-called transcendental arguments, as opposed to dogmatic ones, but also subscribes to what he calls "transcendental idealism."

Commentators have generally affirmed that Kant's affected rigor does not hold up under scrutiny: that he is irritatingly confused, conflicting, and inconsistent in his use of language and in his argumentation, and that many of his attempts simply failed. Thus, Jonathan Bennett (1966, 1974), who sticks with the first critique, says Kant is "wrong on nearly every page." Nevertheless, Kant's relentless efforts to deal with the problems of knowledge raised by skepticism not only had an immense impact on philosophy during his later years but has remained an ever-present influence.

Among the standard interpreters of the first critique, Bennett, like many others, ignores the final section on "Methods." Much that is important in this section had been alluded to in earlier sections; but it also displays Kant's serious effort to construct an "architectonic" of pure reason, showing in rather Leibnizian fashion what he took the elements of a proper philosophical system to be, both internally and in relation to mathematics and historical-empirical scholarship. P. F. Strawson (1966) does the same, bending his own efforts to show that Kant's transcendental arguments were useful but that he would have done better without his extravagant transcendental idealism. For him, Kant's conception of a priori judgments (necessary but not known by experience of an object) that are synthetic (having a sufficient ground in experience but not derivable from analysis of logical properties) is unclear and has value only in support of transcendental idealism. This is a devastating conclusion, in that Kant's main problem in the first critique was to establish that synthetic a priori knowledge is possible. (Recently Beck—in W. H. Werkmeister, 1975—has helpfully disentangled Kant's highly specialized use of the analytic/synthetic distinction from those of his predecessors. This clears up some of the confusion Strawson found.) Strawson changes the basic question to: What are the necessary conditions of a possible experience? Ralph Walker (1978) takes a position just the opposite of Strawson's and appends brief chapters on aesthetics, the moral law, and God. W. H. Walsh's (1975) analysis has a more measured, historically oriented character. He agrees with Strawson that Kant does not have a clear and general conception of synthetic a priori judgments, though his arguments for restricting them to pure mathematics and pure natural science are still interesting, quite apart from any appeal in support of transcendental idealism. T. E. Wilkerson's (1976) commentary is within the same analytic tradition, though he uses Strawson's, not Kant's, question. His is the most clearly presented brief introduction, though he makes very little reference to the rest of Kant's philosophy.

Among writers on Kant's ethics who take the standard approach, Bruce Aune (1979) goes beyond the second critique and presents an account accessible to those who do not know other parts of Kant's philosophy. However, he refers very little to those other parts or to the Kant literature. Keith Ward's (1972) introductory work on the development of Kant's views of ethics refers to many other writings by Kant so far as they bear on his ethical theory. He takes the unusual position that it is a teleological one.

Other Approaches

Most of the first critique was what Kant called a "transcendental logic," which consists of a basic "analytic" part followed by a "dialectical" part which was supposed to be addressed to metaphysical errors that can be made by reason but, in effect, further expounds his own brand of idealism. This logic Thomas Kaehao Swing (1969) appropriately terms a "material logic," as a logic of the contents of knowledge (versus a formal logic). In his study, Swing disentangles what he takes to be two programs for constructing such a logic in Kant's first critique, the axiomatic and the postulational. The first issues from Kant's material view of pure reason and is Kant's own innovation. The second is a formal view of pure reason and is a legacy from the Leibnizians. Kant, he claims, never clearly recognized this split in his own thinking. The two views are interposed to fulfill his dream of enabling the Cartesian subject to transcend mere subjectivity and gain objective knowledge.

There can be no question that Kant was imbued with Leibnizian ideas from early on and that, in modified forms, Leibnizian language persisted to the very end, with some carry-over of the ideas. The literature Kant himself heavily drew upon is so dense and profuse that scholars have understandably tended to shy away from it. A nice example of its impact is Kant's examination of the "antinomies" of pure reason, which pit dogmatic metaphysical claims about the nature of reality against each other. Sadik al-Azm (1972) shows how Kant's discussion of four antinomies directly reflects the 1715–16 controversy between Leibniz and Newtonian Samuel Clarke (1675–1729). Kant counts his consideration of the antinomies a chief influence, with Hume, that aroused him from dogmatic slumber and set him on the path of critically examining reason itself.

Henry Allison (1974) has discussed the continuance of Kant's endeavor to define and defend his position vis-à-vis Leibnizian rationalism in an excellent study of a 1790 polemical work, *On a Discovery*

According to Which Any New Critique of Pure Reason Has Been Made Superfluous by an Earlier One. This fifty-three-page essay, translated by Allison along with some other related documents, was in response to an attack by the popular philosopher Johann August Eberhard (1739–1809), who claimed that what was of value in the first critique had already been said by Leibniz.

Such accounts have established that the Anglo-American tendency to relate the critical philosophy chiefly to Hume is a mistake. Kant's thought world was far more influenced by his engagement with Wolffian-Leibnizian philosophy.

Almost systematically overlooked by these interpreters until recently is the simple fact that Kant had in mind a much larger philosophical system, one that he never fully articulated, but the lineaments of which significantly affected what he was able to put in writing. Frederick van de Pitte (1971) has demonstrated that the nature of this system is reflected in Kant's broad concept of "anthropology." This concept goes beyond strictly empirical or practical studies (and thus is not identified with what we call anthropology today) to include metaphysics, morals, and religion—these, respectively, in answer to the questions "What can I know? What ought I to do? What may I hope?" and ultimately "What is man?" Broadly anthropological interests had already stirred Kant during his precritical period (from the mid-1750s to 1769), especially under Rousseau's influence after 1762 (see above); and he taught the subject annually from 1772–73 to 1796–97. The last sizable work published by Kant (1798) sketched out some aspects of his *Anthropology,* a mishmash of often indistinguishably descriptive and normative material on the intellect, aesthetic experience, appetitive faculties, personal (especially moral) character, and the social-cultural nature of the species. Other, better written evidence of this overarching teleological interest in the nature and destiny of man is present in his occasional writings and other short works. (On his educational views, see p. 492.)

Pitte's is one of the few overall treatments of Kant's philosophy. I believe he has demonstrated his thesis well. The distraction of interpreters from Kant's thoroughgoing teleological interest—which for me does not involve adhering to a teleological ethics—is no doubt partly contributed by Kant, in that he does not permit teleological arguments within the system. Instead, he regards teleology as a rule of our judgment, one that regulates systematizing reason, but not a rule of nature. Newtonian though he was in his mechanistic approach to physics, he did not regard conceptions of mechanisms as sufficient to enable understanding of even the simplest natural event.

Along a similar line, though not referring to Pitte, Michel Despland (1973) has valuably interpreted Kant's several important writings on history—from *What Is Enlightenment?* (1784) to *The Strife of the Faculties* (law versus philosophy, 1798)—as a working out of the problem of a "moral teleology." Both these and the writings on religion—also mostly late—Despland sees to be characterized by a natural and historical teleology, as ways of dealing with the ideas of progress and of the development of humanity (holding a reasonable hope for it via adherence to the moral law). They set forth conditions for moral freedom and for growth of the moral commonwealth, each of these a legal and moral progress, not a natural one; and they do so on a theistic base. Despland regards Kant as a religious man and credits him with setting forth some key conditions for a turn from traditional metaphysical interests in the rational theology of his century to the modern interest in the nature of religion itself. This turn was to be inaugurated by Friedrich Schleiermacher in his famous 1799 addresses *On Religion* (see chapter 28). William Galston (1975) has also highlighted Kant's approach to the problem of history but in narrower scope.

Another important study on the anthropological-teleological nature of Kant's entire system, by J. D. McFarland (1970), places special but not exclusive reference on problems in natural science. Although Allen Wood (1978) does not refer to the teleological issue and does not cite these recent predecessors, his careful analyses of Kant's notion of God and of his strategy for examining theistic proofs support the openness to positive uses of theology indicated by Pitte and Despland; and they are not generally inconsistent with the other interpretations. All take seriously Kant's claim to be making room for faith, in Kant's case a faith less denuded for Despland than for the others. It was this quality in his critical philosophy that especially endeared Kant to many nineteenth-century Protestant theologians.

A very different tack has been taken by Susan Shell (1980), who cleverly applies the moral-legal-political concept of "right," which plays a primary role in Kant's entire thought after his discovery of Rousseau in 1762, to the entire critical philosophy. There is already clear warrant for this connection in the first critique. Shell also takes the broader anthropological approach of Kant seriously and here emphasizes its Rousseauian cast.

Kant the Man and the Professional

Kant was the first major modern philosopher to spend his entire adult life teaching and writing philosophy. He rarely left Königsberg, his birthplace, had no place whatsoever in his personal life for the arts (including modern literature), studiously avoided emotive and sensuous experience, and continually fought off hypochondria by plunging himself into his work and holding to fixed daily rituals. Although he was a polite, friendly man, was a faithful friend (he never married), taught, and took his turn as rector of the university, he was not an intimate friend, could not bear opposition, and engaged very little with the world outside his study. The extremely orderly routines of his life had grown to the point of extreme compulsion and fastidiousness by mid-life. The two things he once said filled him with greatest awe—the starry heavens above and the moral law within—refer to very important experiences he reported having with his mother, who died when he was thirteen. They also represent the two major successive emphases in his life as a thinker. His father, a harness maker, died when he was twenty-one. Both parents were of deeply pietist persuasion, though not of the more familiar enthusiastic and fundamentalist sort, insisting on moral uprightness, sometimes in a harsh manner. Kant grew up poor and remained poor, first doing private tutoring and then, after age thirty-one, lecturing at the university for a living until he got his professorship at age forty-six. He was by then already reputed for his essays on natural science and on philosophy of natural science, working primarily within the Leibnizian mode though further stimulated first by Newton, then by Rousseau. For eleven years after becoming a professor he published almost nothing, though several times he thought he was about to finish his first ambitious project. The *Critique of Pure Reason* (1781), the first major philosophical work in German, was initially rejected or ignored by the leading philosophers but within a few years was heralded as a turning point in German intellectual history. This was followed by an astounding production of "critical" works over the next decade, from ages fifty-six to sixty-six, issued, as he said, partly in fear that he would die before he got his main ideas out; and he continued to publish essays and treatises on a variety of philosophical subjects until his death at seventy-nine.

The more external biography of a philosopher does not always necessarily tell us much about what determined his thought. In

Kant's case, even such information is indeed revealing. Not least, it enables us to enter the reading of this most difficult thinker patiently, with an expectation that we will meet with rigidity and significant conflict as to both themes and methods, and that we will find emphases ultimately explicable only on internal, personal grounds.

General Accounts and Collections

We still lack a truly comprehensive, relatively accurate account of Kant's philosophy in English. In addition to the accounts already mentioned, that of Marxist Lucien Goldmann (*Immanuel Kant,* 1945, cited on p. 260) is especially interesting in that it is his first work, was written under the direct influence of György Lukács, and was a historical inquiry intentionally performed as part of his effort to build a dialectical philosophy of his own, one steeped in sociological considerations. The idea of "totality" in Kant's critical philosophy is taken to be central, together with what Goldmann terms "the identity of subject and object." What especially interests him—as was true earlier of Hegel and Marx—were the opposition between universal form and particular content, the distinction between knowledge based on experience and synthetic a priori judgments, and the notion that we human beings in part create the world we perceive and come to know. In 1945 Goldmann thought Kant was the first to have made these points clearly; by 1967 he was saying that Pascal was the first, though acknowledging that Kant did his work independently of Pascal. Yirmiahu Yovel (1980) argues, against the grain of conventional Kant studies, that the notion of a history of reason is important in Kant's thought, thus placing him closer to Hegel than is ordinarily thought. Whether or not Yovel's case holds up, it may well be true that the first nonchronology, nonsectarian histories of philosophy, notably by Dieterich Tiedemann (1791–97) and G. W. Tennemann (1798–1819), were inspired by the sense of a turning point in the history of thought noted by early readers of Kant. Hegel's later view of history as the self-development of spirit was very different from theirs and from almost all history of philosophy today (see Mandelbaum, "On the Historiography of Philosophy," 1976, cited on p. 7). W. H. Werkmeister (1980), a long-time Kant scholar, has investigated the "architectonic" and development of his philosophy. All three works are introductions in a quite specialized sense. The same is true of a collection of thirteen of his own essays by Lewis White Beck (1965).

Beck (1969) has also edited a fine collection of twenty-one essays by others, including sixteen previously published in *Monist* (1967), two previously published elsewhere, and three new ones. These do not overlap with the twenty edited by Robert Paul Wolff (1967), which include two by Beck, two by Walsh, several on the categorical imperative (a principal concept in Kant's ethics), and two on his aesthetics. As is the tradition, most entries in both collections treat issues in the first critique almost exclusively. The Beck volume includes a new essay by H. J. Paton on "Kant on the Errors of Leibniz" and a 1955 article by Colin Murray Turbayne on "Kant's Relation to Berkeley."The eight essays edited by W. H. Werkmeister (1975) are by Kant experts, gathered in commemoration of Kant's 250th birthday on April 22, 1974.

al-Azm, Sadik J. *The Origins of Kant's Arguments in the Antinomies.* Oxford: Clarendon Pr., 1972.
Allison, Henry E. *The Kant-Eberhard Controversy.* Baltimore, Md.: Johns Hopkins Univ. Pr., 1974.
Aune, Bruce. *Kant's Theory of Morals.* Princeton, N.J.: Princeton Univ. Pr., 1979.
Beck, Lewis White. *A Commentary on Kant's Critique of Practical Reason.* Chicago and London: Univ. of Chicago Pr., 1960.
————. *Studies in the Philosophy of Kant.* Indianapolis, Ind.: Bobbs-Merrill, 1965.
————, ed. *Kant Studies Today.* La Salle, Ill.: Open Court, 1969. (Includes essays from *Monist* 51, no. 3–4:317–639 (July, Oct. 1967), plus others.)
Bennett, Jonathan. *Kant's Analytic.* Cambridge and New York: Cambridge Univ. Pr., 1966.
————. *Kant's Dialectic.* Cambridge and New York: Cambridge Univ. Pr., 1974.
Despland, Michel. *Kant on History and Religion, with a Translation of Kant's "On the Failure of All Attempted Philosophical Theodicies."* Montreal: McGill-Queen's Univ. Pr., 1973.
Galston, William A. *Kant and the Problems of History.* Chicago and London: Univ. of Chicago Pr., 1975.
McFarland, John D. *Kant's Concept of Teleology.* Edinburgh: Edinburgh Univ. Pr., 1970.
Pitte, Frederick P. van de. *Kant as Philosophical Anthropologist.* The Hague: Nijhoff, 1971.
Shell, Susan Meld. *The Rights of Reason: A Study of Kant's Philosophy and Politics.* Toronto, Buffalo, and London: Univ. of Toronto Pr., 1980.
Smith, Norman Kemp. *A Commentary to Kant's 'Critique of Pure Reason'.* 2nd ed. London: Macmillan, 1923. (Repr.: Atlantic Highlands, N.J.: Humanities Pr., 1962. 1st ed., 1918.)
Strawson, P. F. *The Bounds of Sense: An Essay on Kant's Critique of Pure Reason.* New York: Barnes & Noble; London: Methuen, 1966.
Swing, Thomas Kaehao. *Kant's Transcendental Logic.* New Haven, Conn.: Yale Univ. Pr., 1969.

122   *The History of Philosophy*

Walker, Ralph C. S. *Kant*. London and Boston: Routledge & Paul, 1978.
Walsh, William H. *Kant's Criticism of Metaphysics*. Edinburgh: Edinburgh Univ. Pr., 1975.
Ward, Keith. *The Development of Kant's Ethics*. New York: Humanities Pr.; Oxford: Blackwell, 1972.
Werkmeister, William H. *Kant: The Architectonic and Development of His Philosophy*. Cambridge, Mass.: MIT Pr., 1980.
———, ed. *Reflections on Kant's Philosophy*. Gainesville: Univ. Presses of Florida, 1975.
Wilkerson, Terence E. *Kant's Critique of Pure Reason: A Commentary for Students*. Oxford: Clarendon Pr., 1976.
Wolff, Robert Paul, ed. *Kant: A Collection of Critical Essays*. Garden City, N.Y.: Doubleday Anchor, 1967.
Wood, Allen W. *Kant's Rational Theology*. Ithaca, N.Y.: Cornell Univ. Pr., 1978.
Yovel, Yirmiahu. *Kant and the Philosophy of History*. Princeton, N.J.: Princeton Univ. Pr., 1980.

6

Nineteenth-Century
Philosophy

The entire nineteenth century was a heyday for philosophy in European universities, especially in Germany. No general account yet does it justice either in a comprehensive sense or in the light of twentieth-century interests. Among the most noted philosophers, G. W. F. Hegel is to be discussed separately, chiefly because he lived early in the century and influenced much subsequent effort. Edmund Husserl belongs with the story of phenomenology, Karl Marx with Marxism, and both Søren Kierkegaard and Friedrich Nietzsche with existential philosophy, and so all four will be presented in those contexts later on.

Other nineteenth-century philosophers will be cited at this point in order to illustrate several major themes that have retained importance a century later: the hermeneutic perspectives of Friedrich Schleiermacher and Wilhelm Dilthey; the protests of the Young Hegelians, especially in Ludwig Feuerbach's radical humanism; the dynamic world views of Arthur Schopenhauer and Henri Bergson; positivism and realism, especially in Ernst Mach, Franz Brentano, Alexius Meinong, and Gottlob Frege; neo-Kantian thought after mid-century; and the values-sensitive outlook of Max Scheler. The post-Kantian idealism of early nineteenth-century philosophers like Johann Gottlieb Fichte (1762–1814) (Tom Rockmore, 1980, in a comparison of individualist themes in Marx) and Friedrich Wilhelm Joseph Schelling (1775–1854) (Esposito, 1977) still retains interest for some philosophers today; but most ideas that would be of interest are already found in contemporaries, such as Schleiermacher or Hegel, or successors, such as existentialist philosopher-theologian Paul Tillich, whose

123

early treatises on Schelling were basic for his thought and have recently been translated.

Throughout the nineteenth century, developments on the European continent largely determined developments in philosophy elsewhere. To some extent, British philosophy pursued its themes independently. Since such independence occurred to a far lesser extent on the North American continent, the overall history of American philosophy will be noted only in the twentieth-century context.

Overviews

Because of vast differences in style, interest, and approach, analytic philosophy has largely ignored Continental European philosophy since Kant. To a fair degree, this explains why no truly comprehensive history of this philosophy has appeared in English, though several attempts have been made in other languages. A few quite partial surveys are available in English translation, notably those by Karl Barth and Karl Löwith. One of the more discerning overviews, by the great Swiss theologian Karl Barth (1947), focuses on interactions between philosophy and Christian theology. This was still a major theme through much of the century, even where (as with all the thinkers to be noted here) dogma-invested religion was vigorously opposed.

Half of the highly reputed intellectual history by Karl Löwith (1941) also discusses issues in the history of the nineteenth-century "bourgeois-Christian world"; the other half specializes in the thinking of Johann Wolfgang Goethe and Hegel and its aftermath in Germany. Löwith wished to portray something of the developing "spirit" of European thought, especially in Germany, rather than to essay a complete account. He took Hegel's to be the first philosophy distinctively of his era and ends with Nietzsche's philosophy, with its call for the transcendence of modern man and with his sense of eternal recurrence in human affairs, as the first of our own era. Only slight critical reference is made to National Socialism, but much of the enduring power of this book resides in its having been completed in 1939. Unlike the Nazis, he took Nietzsche's thought to be radically alien to the Third Reich, though he admitted that Nietzsche and others were forerunners in ways they would not have anticipated or approved.

Also reflective upon that demonic time, nine essays edited by Nathan Rotenstreich (1968) widen the curtain a bit more in analyzing main currents of Jewish philosophy from Kant's time to the early twentieth century, emphasizing its ethical core and the need to preserve the distinct character of Judaism as this was understood by Jewish thinkers.

No doubt some years of specialized scholarship will be required before an adequate account of this period can be formed. Richard Schacht's studies (1975), for example, done in a critical, expository style like that of Walter Kaufmann, treat only a few philosophers: Hegel, Marx, Schopenhauer, Kierkegaard, Nietzsche, Husserl, and Martin Heidegger—an overview only in a most minimal sense. In contrast, Maurice Mandelbaum's history of philosophical trends (1971), emphasizing what he takes to be the two basic and continuing forms, idealism and positivism, serves up many more thinkers but viewed as carriers of themes related to issues regarding historicism, human malleability, and the limits of reason.

Hermeneutic Perspectives

Another fruitful way to view this history would be to start with hermeneutical concerns—that is, with ways in which various expressions of human experience, notably but not exclusively in written texts, are interpreted—and then to view the wide array both of idealist and antiidealist thought primarily in this light. Friedrich Schleiermacher (1768–1834), himself one of the early idealists, would provide the proper place to begin. The classic translator of Plato into German, a first-rate philosopher, and the father of modern theology and study of religion, Schleiermacher drew much of his own distinctive contribution from the close study of texts. These he viewed as presentations of language that are socially, culturally, and psychologically informed. He understood the act of interpretation in the same way, thus reflecting a dialectic of inward and outward tending experience that runs through all his thought. Little of his extensive philosophical work is yet available in English; much of it was not released until decades after his death; and a critical German edition is only now slowly emerging in the 1980s, in the midst of a Schleiermacher renascence. Schleiermacher scholarship (Tice, 1966) has advanced considerably since the systematic interpretation by Richard Brandt (1941), for the present still useful as a general orientation.

Wilhelm Dilthey (1833–1911) was the first Schleiermacher biographer of note (1870—after Daniel Schenkel, 1858) and the primary traducer of his hermeneutical interests into later philosophy. He also sparked later antipositivist, historical-humanist extensions of those interests into psychology, history, and social science, which have flourished especially since the early 1970s (Ermarth, 1978).

The Young Hegelians

Schleiermacher, a founder of the University of Berlin in 1810, brought in Georg Wilhelm Friedrich Hegel (1770–1831) in 1818. In Berlin, Hegel, who got along poorly with Schleiermacher and vehemently opposed his "Romantic" view of religion, truly came into prominence and gained numerous disciples. His subsequent influence has been so great that he must be given special treatment. An intellectual history by William Brazill (1970) traces ways in which philosophy came to transcend religion in German intellectual life through the Young Hegelians—notably, in the *Hallische Jahrbücher* and through David Friedrich Strauss, Ludwig Feuerbach, and Arnold Ruge. A more extensive study has been done since by John Toews (1980).

Because of his radically humanistic critique of religion and of Hegelian philosophy, Ludwig Feuerbach (1804–72) had a high reputation in the 1840s. His thought impressed Karl Marx and Friedrich Engels as taking one as far as one can go toward liberation from bourgeois constraints without turning to economics and politics. Interest in his thought revived again in the 1920s and has continued to increase. Usually this has occurred in connection with Marxian studies, but recently he has been studied more in his own right, especially in two excellent works by Eugene Kamenka (1970) and Marx Wartofsky (1977). Kamenka's briefer account sees Feuerbach struggling through his critical encounter with Hegel toward a naturalist, positivist outlook. Wartofsky emphasizes his development as itself representing a new materialist dialectic of consciousness, alternative to Hegel's. Neither considers the influence of Schleiermacher, whose lectures he attended alongside Hegel's in 1823–26, especially regarding his critique of religion and his all-important notion of "species-consciousness," later passed on to Marx.

Dynamic World Views

In the first generation after Kant, many philosophers began to form comprehensive, secular world views, all influenced in some fashion, as was Hegel's, by his critiques of traditional metaphysics, epistemology, and ethics. The thought of Arthur Schopenhauer (1788–1860), first interpreted for an analytically minded audience by Patrick Gardiner (1963) and then by D. W. Hamlyn (1980), has a prominent place among these. Schopenhauer attended lectures by Schleiermacher and Fichte at Berlin in 1811–13. Thereafter he expressed unbroken contempt for academic philosophy, and from 1818 on worked for the most part in solitude, living on private income. Although his major work, *The World as Will and Idea,* was published in 1818, his reputation did not grow until the 1850s. For the next fifty years he was among the most read of the Continental philosophers. This is chiefly because of his attempt to build a total, dynamic, nonreligious world view. This world view was deeply pessimistic, ultimately life-denying, mystical, and ascetic. To those who did not care for these features it could still be attractive as one based on a rigorous critique of experience, centered in individual perception, sensitive to the roles of art, and placing the kernel of human nature in the capacity to will. Except for the stark individualism and the repudiation of religious consciousness, much of his thought is far more reminiscent of Schleiermacher than of Hegel. Gardiner's book is still an indispensable introduction. Hamlyn's analysis of arguments relates chiefly to his major opus of 1818 but on the basis of his *Fourfold Root of the Principle of Sufficient Reason* (1813, rev. 1847), which sets up his life-long encounter with Kant. It is an excellent guide to reading Schopenhauer.

Like Schopenhauer, Henri Bergson (1859–1941) drew special attention to nonrational, unconscious components of human functioning and to a posited involvement of human beings in the dynamic processes of nature. Neither of his two greatest books, *Creative Evolution* (1907) and *The Two Sources of Morality and Religion* (1932) was published in the nineteenth century; yet his thought represents a major problematic of that period, especially in French philosophy: the limitations of a materialistic and mechanistic interpretation of the world and human experience, as seen through the new lenses of evolutionary biology. Imageful, even rhapsodic, and in the end mystical, Bergson's world view emphasized the intuition of duration in the lived moment, a metaphysics of creative evolution and pure change. A major interpretation by Jacques Maritain (1913, 1955) views these contributions as Thomism manqué. As Milič Čapek (1971) has shown, however, there is reason even now to take Bergson's reflections seriously in the philosophy of physics.

Positivism

The name "positivism" has come to be used in both a broader and a narrower sense. As an interpretation of the narrower sense, associated with the Comteans, John Stuart Mill's *Auguste Comte and Positivism* (1865) is still essential. In the 1820s attempts by Comte

(1798–1857) to view sociopolitical reality scientifically and according to laws of development had helped Mill break with Jeremy Bentham's simpler utilitarianism. He was nonetheless sharply opposed to the sect-building efforts of the Comteans and other socialists of the time. Mill later expressed indebtedness to Comte's six-volume *Cour de philosophie positive* (1830–42), especially his philosophy of the "moral" (social) sciences. Perhaps the greatest methodological difference with Comte lies in Mill's beliefs that the sociological content of these sciences must derive from data provided by scientific psychology and that positive science itself is not nearly ready to constitute a sociorevolutionary school. His own *System of Logic* (1843) also makes logical demands on inductive inquiry that Comte had not worked out.

As its course is traced by W. M. Simon (1963), nineteenth-century Comtean-style positivism had by far its greatest impact in France. It found a quite guarded but sympathetic response in England, notably through Mill's championing. Among the few outside the labor movement who might have been attracted to positivism because of its antimetaphysical and secularist premises, many like Mill were repelled by its attempts to become a secular religion. In Germany philosophers were too occupied with their own somewhat similar neo-Kantian and anti-Hegelian movements to pay much attention, and there was already a strong tendency among German scientists, philologists, aestheticians, and historians to turn away from philosophy, particularly in any metaphysical or teleological form, in favor of "objective" empirical observation. Simon avers that probably the only direct links, though very weak ones, between Comtean positivism and the widespread logical positivism of the twentieth century are the idealist-positivist "as if" philosophy of Hans Vaihinger (1852–1933), which claimed the necessity of using fictions known to be false, and the empiriocritical position of Ernst Mach (1838–1916).

In his noted critique, Leszek Kolakowski (1968) aptly represents the broader sense of positivism in terms of four assumptions: (1) phenomenalism, of the sort that denies any real difference between "essence" and "phenomenon"; (2) nominalism, that views the world we know as a collection of individual observable facts and does not accept any real referent of general terms other than to specific concrete objects; (3) the denial of cognitive worth to value judgments and normative statements; and (4) belief in the essential unity of the scientific method. (He personally opposes all four assumptions.)

Kolakowski emphasizes the positivists' constant rejection of all reflection, whether materialist or spiritualist, that is not based on or disallows contradiction of its judgments by empirical data. He sees continuity, with variations in style, among many modern positivist thinkers and finds aspects of these four major themes in the Stoics and some other ancient philosophers, in medieval nominalist thought as it began to be reinterpreted in the light of scientific programs in the thirteenth century (Roger Bacon) and in the fourteenth century (Ockham and even more radically among some Paris nominalists like Jean de Mirecourt and Nicholas d'Autrecourt, whose thought excluded natural theology and placed faith beyond the scope of reason). These nominalists, however, won very little notice until similar ideas began to emerge again in the twentieth century. In contrast, strands of seventeenth-century positivist thought bore great influence, as Kolakowski reconstructs the story, notably that of Galilei Galileo, Marin Mersenne, and Pierre Gassendi. Descartes, Leibniz, and Berkeley, for example, assimilated some of these lines of thought but were positivists only in a very limited way.

Hume, for Kolakowski and others who have adopted the broader definition, was the first unreservedly positivist thinker. In dramatic fashion, Hume's philosophy not only sought to destroy the rational ideals of the Enlightenment but served to diminish the cognitive value of all knowledge not given in discrete empirical descriptions. Hume left all modern epistemology with clearly formulated questions about whether it is possible to obtain knowledge that is both absolutely reliable and not devoid of content. Comte, on the other hand, was not wholly a positivist on Kolakowski's reading, especially in his social theory, though he invented the term and is heir to Hume in his totally antisubjectivist theory of science.

Several great works contributed to the eventual triumph of positivism in the late nineteenth century—works by Mill, Charles Darwin, Claude Bernard, Herbert Spencer, and Karl Marx; in different ways, each also illustrates trends away from Comte's utopianism. Richard Avenarius (1843–96) and especially Ernst Mach both added an empiriocritical interpretation of knowledge that abolished scientific claims to objective, factual knowledge and gave rise to the notion of a scientific philosophy, the goal of which would be to construct a unified scientific view of the world. These latter views won trenchant criticism from Edmund Husserl, Henri Bergson, and Lenin (in 1909), though all three agreed with their naturalistic abhorrence of metaphysical speculation. Kolakowski holds that conventionalist and pragmatist views also derive some of their fueling from positivism. He sees logical positivism to be its fullest twentieth-century heir, a product of technocratic ideology and culture that has played an important role in intellectual culture, notably in counteracting ideological misuses of science, but one that is now in decline as a distinct philosophical school.

Most philosophical interpreters would now tend to agree with Kolakowski as to the general background, contributions, and decline of logical positivism. They would not uniformly agree with his general definition or with his fundamental opposition to its assumptions.

Realism

Idealist views have emphasized the role of consciousness in constructing "the world" and, usually with some religious accompaniment, have regarded the spiritual or mental as the ultimate or basically determining reality. In contrast, Schopenhauer tended to reify will, Bergson to reify vital impulse. These are all metaphysical positions. Customarily the choice of such a position greatly affects positions one may hold in other areas of philosophical inquiry. In its purest forms, realism is, first of all (against nominalism), the view that there are nonmental properties or relations or both; second (against idealism), it is the view that abstract (mental) entities do not exist—that is, that nothing is mental in the strict sense (materialist realism) or that abstract entities can be used only as empirically based constructs to explain what is in the world (constructivist realism). Most idealists and realists have presented a modified rather than a pure view.

The first type of realism does not imply the second, while the second may imply the first. Likewise, not every form of idealism implies the purely phenomenological or subjectivist view that everything is mental. Moreover, some positions called "phenomenological" have assumed a nonnominalist view of reality (for example, by Husserl), and some realists of the second type (for example, Gustav Bergmann since the early 1950s) are phenomenologists in a modified sense. Further, Hegel's "phenomenology" emphasizes causal and genetic explanation, whereas Husserl plumps for sheer description. It might be easier to sort out these distinctions were they merely semantic ones, but they are not. Rather, they point to two traditions of adherence—more, when one gets down to the detailed arguments— that have related to each other in many different ways. In his superb introduction to some texts on versions of realism and phenomenology (Brentano, Meinong, Husserl, H. A. Prichard, E. B. Holt et al., Samuel Alexander, Russell, Arthur C. Lovejoy, and Moore), Roderick Chisholm (1960) shows how very complicated even the basic issues can get.

In these various forms, realism gained great importance in the late nineteenth century. Though a realist only in the first (nonnominalist) sense, physicist Ernst Mach (1836–1916) contributed significantly to its development, especially through his *Analysis of Sensations* (1886). Mach tried to clarify the troublesome lack of distinction between the sensory, perceptual, and reflective or linguistic aspects of "presentation" *(Vorstellung)* on the part of Schopenhauer and most other thinkers to that time. He did so by asserting that all knowledge is to be reduced to sensation, to sense data. Mach was a pure phenomenologist, in that to him the world is the sum of sense data. Philosophy, moreover, was itself to be reduced to science, no other objects being available to it than are within the provenance of science— namely, studies of the connections of sensations (psychology), of the laws for these (physics), and the clear establishment of these laws (psychophysics). Mach's program was to simplify our understanding of ordinary experience through description. Efforts by physical theorists Heinrich Hertz and Ludwig Boltzmann and other contemporaries to do this through mathematical models eventually won out and were more influential in the thinking of the logical positivists, of Russell and of Wittgenstein (see Janik and Toulmin, *Wittgenstein's Vienna*, 1973, cited on p. 210); but their aims were similar.

Later realism also stems from the work of Franz Brentano and his students Alexius Meinong and Edmund Husserl. English translations of their extensive writings have been appearing especially since the early 1970s, a few earlier.

Franz Brentano (1838–1917), for a time a Roman Catholic priest (1864–73), left the church but retained many of his former religious beliefs, unlike a great many modern realists. (No book on Brentano alone has appeared in English.) At the core of his extensive writings is the view that all philosophy is grounded in an exact science he called descriptive psychology or phenomenology, understood as the study of "intentional" phenomena—that is, of mental activities directed toward objects. This notion became the most distinctive feature of the philosophy of his student Edmund Husserl and of phenomenology as a school. Of the three classes of such activity, presentations (*Vorstellungen,* here meaning ideas or thoughts) are basic (and cannot be called either correct or incorrect), judging and emotion presuppose the first (and are presented in nonpropositional pairs, one member of which must be correct and the other incorrect). The distinct "realism" of his position resides especially in his claim that only concrete (versus abstract) particular things exist.

Alexius Meinong (1853–1920) was a student of Brentano, under whom he did his noted *Hume Studies* (1877, 1882), and he adopted many of his predecessor's views; but he called his position "objectivism" to distinguish it from Brentano's. Meinong greatly expanded the classes and analyses of objects beyond what his teacher allowed—for example, to say that some objects do not exist—and he differed considerably on the functions of propositions and suppositions. He also developed an important emotive theory of value (versus desire, interest, or utilitarian theories). The continuing interest in Meinong, especially among Anglo-American philosophers, has stretched from Russell, Moore, and Wittgenstein to others like C. D. Broad, Gilbert Ryle, and more recently Roderick Chisholm. For many years the chief overall interpretation was that of J. N. Findlay (1933). In presenting his own realist metaphysics, Gustav Bergmann (1967) devotes a long section each to Brentano and Meinong. A fresh analytic account of Meinong's relation to Husserl's phenomenology, often quite different from Findlay's and not referring to Bergmann's at all, has been given by Marie-Luise Schubert Kalsi (1978), with translations of some Meinong texts and critical notes. Another major study comes from realist Reinhardt Grossmann (1974).

Although Gottlob Frege (1848–1925) was perhaps the most profound contributor to philosophical logic and mathematical logic in the nineteenth century, and a major contributor to the philosophy of mathematics, his work was known only to Husserl, Russell, Whitehead, and Wittgenstein among the philosophers and to a few mathematicians. Since World War II, a number of translations have appeared, and there has been a resurgence of interest in his thought. Some controversy has arisen as to whether Frege was a nonnominalist type of realist and, if so, a Platonist as well. E. D. Klemke has argued "yes" to both questions. Klemke is one of the more exacting interpreters of Frege and has edited a collection of essays on his ontology, semantics, logic, and philosophy of mathematics (1968). In his book on Frege's ontology, Reinhardt Grossmann (1969) holds that he is a realist in both senses I have noted above and that he also thought logical signs represent real concepts and relations, thus not mere conventions, agreeing with him on all these points. Grossmann, unlike Michael Dummett (1973), sees several stages of development.

The two also differ on other basic issues of interpretation. Dummett has devoted a 700-page volume to a detailed analysis of Frege's philosophy of language, treating his doctrine as a unity and interpreting its evolution only as a six-part series of emendations and minor adjustments. David Bell (1979) has singled out his philosophy of judgment for special analysis, with frequent reference to Kant and Wittgenstein. Bell holds that all three philosophers reject the view, with which he also disagrees, that formation of concepts may precede or occur independently of judgment, though Bell regards the realist underpinnings of Frege's position to be unnecessary, adopting a constructivist position instead. J. N. Mohanty (1982) has argued that Husserl and Frege inhabit nearly the same neo-Kantian thought-world.

Neo-Kantian Thought

Apart from the general histories, there is no general survey of the remarkable revival of Kant-inspired philosophy from about 1860 to 1914, the date many scholars mark as the true end of the nineteenth century in Europe. However, historian Thomas Willey (1978) appropriately places that revival within its political and intellectual setting, then outlines aspects of the thinking of Rudolf Hermann Lotze, Kuno Fischer, and Eduard Zeller, of Friedrich Albert Lange, of Wilhelm Windelband and Heinrich Rickert, and of neo-Kantian brands of socialism, finally examining some significant consequences of these neo-Kantian philosophies for German social and historical thought.

Emphasis on Value

Even now, general value theory is a grossly underdeveloped area of philosophy. With few exceptions, twentieth-century philosophers have preferred to work on one value domain at a time, mostly ethics or aesthetics. Attempts to renew attention to this endeavor will surely benefit from the seminal efforts of Max Scheler (1874–1928), who brought a chiefly phenomenological method to bear on this problem. He is included here because the ambience of his thought carries mostly late nineteenth-century qualities. He cannot be comfortably fitted into any school, however, in either century. Scheler's major work on values is his *Formalism in Ethics and Non-Formal Ethics of Values* (1913–16, translated 1973). Values, on his unusual and complex analysis, are always felt. Feelings are cognitive, intentional acts, directed toward objects. The feelings in acts of valuing can be hierarchically ordered as to depth—for example, the spiritual feeling of beatitude is deeper than the sensual feeling of pleasure or, progressively, the vital feeling of good health or the pure ego feeling of cheerfulness. The function of preference in value activity is similarly analyzed, and both the feeling and the preference functions are grounded in love (as the fundamental form of having an object) versus hate. And there is much else, as Eugene Kelly (1977) has helpfully indicated. A commemorative volume edited by phenomenologist Manfred Frings (1974), who has served as editor of Scheler's collected works in German (1954–, still in progress) and who in 1965 published the first introduction to Scheler in English, contains four interpretive essays plus two late essays by Scheler on "Metaphysics and Art" and "Suffering."

Barth, Karl. *Protestant Theology in the Nineteenth Century: Its Background and History.* Tr. by Brian Cozens and John Bowden. London: SCM Pr., 1972. (German ed., 1947.)

Bell, David A. *Frege's Theory of Judgement.* Oxford and New York: Oxford Univ. Pr., 1979.

Bergmann, Gustav. *Realism: A Critique of Brentano and Meinong.* Madison and London: Univ. of Wisconsin Pr., 1967.

Brandt, Richard B. *The Philosophy of Schleiermacher.* New York: Harper, 1941.

Brazill, William J. *The Young Hegelians.* New Haven, Conn.: Yale Univ. Pr., 1970.

Čapek, Milič. *Bergson and Modern Physics: A Reinterpretation and Reevaluation.* Dordrecht and Boston: Reidel, 1971.

Chisholm, Roderick M., ed. *Realism and the Background of Phenomenology.* Glencoe, Ill.: Free Pr., 1960.

Dummett, Michael A. E. *Frege: Philosophy of Language.* New York: Harper & Row; London: Duckworth, 1973.

Ermarth, Michael. *Wilhelm Dilthey: The Critique of Historical Reason.* Chicago and London: Univ. of Chicago Pr., 1978.

Esposito, Joseph L. *Schelling's Idealism and Philosophy of Nature.* Cranbury, N.J.: Bucknell Univ. Pr., 1977.

Findlay, John N. *Meinong's Theory of Objects and Value.* 2nd ed. Oxford: Clarendon Pr., 1963. (1st ed., *Meinong's Theory of Objects,* Oxford Univ. Pr., 1933.)

Frings, Manfred S. *Max Scheler: A Concise Introduction into the World of a Great Thinker.* Pittsburgh, Pa.: Duquesne Univ. Pr., 1965.

———, ed. *Max Scheler (1874–1928): Centennial Essays.* The Hague: Nijhoff, 1974.

Gardiner, Patrick. *Schopenhauer.* Baltimore, Md. and Harmondsworth: Penguin, 1963.

Grossmann, Reinhardt. *Meinong.* London and Boston: Routledge & Paul, 1974.

———. *Reflections on Frege's Philosophy.* Evanston, Ill.: Northwestern Univ. Pr., 1969.

Hamlyn, D. W. *Schopenhauer*. London and Boston: Routledge & Paul, 1980.

Kamenka, Eugene. *The Philosophy of Ludwig Feuerbach*. New York: Praeger; London: Routledge & Paul, 1970.

Kelly, Eugene. *Max Scheler*. Boston: Twayne, 1977.

Klemke, E. D., ed. *Essays on Frege*. Urbana and London: Univ. of Illinois Pr., 1968.

Kolakowski, Leszek. *The Alienation of Reason: A History of Positivist Thought*. Garden City, N.Y.: Doubleday, 1968.

Löwith, Karl. *From Hegel to Nietzsche: The Revolution in Nineteenth Century Thought*. Tr. by David E. Green. New York: Holt, Rinehart & Winston, 1964. (2nd German ed., 1949; original ed., 1941.)

Mandelbaum, Maurice. *History, Man, and Reason: A Study in Nineteenth-Century Thought*. Baltimore, Md.: Johns Hopkins Univ. Pr., 1971.

Maritain, Jacques. *Bergsonian Philosophy and Thomism*. Tr. by Matelle L. Anderson. New York: Philosophical Library, 1955. (2nd French ed., 1929; 1st ed., 1913.)

Mill, John Stuart. *Auguste Comte and Positivism*. Ann Arbor: Univ. of Michigan Pr., 1961. (Original ed., London, 1865; Boston: William V. Spencer, 1866.)

Mohanty, Jitendranath N. *Husserl and Frege*. Bloomington: Indiana Univ. Pr., 1982.

Rockmore, Tom. *Fichte, Marx and the German Philosophical Tradition*. Carbondale: Southern Illinois Univ. Pr.; London: Feffer & Simons, 1980.

Rotenstreich, Nathan, ed. *Jewish Philosophy in Modern Time: From Mendelssohn to Rosenzweig*. New York: Holt, Rinehart & Winston, 1968.

Schacht, Richard. *Hegel and After: Studies in Continental Philosophy between Kant and Sartre*. Pittsburgh, Pa.: Univ. of Pittsburgh Pr., 1975.

Schubert Kalsi, Marie-Luise. *Alexius Meinong on Objects of Higher Order and Husserl's Phenomenology*. The Hague and Boston: Nijhoff, 1978.

Simon, Walter M. *European Positivism in the Nineteenth Century: An Essay in Intellectual History*. Ithaca, N.Y.: Cornell Univ. Pr., 1963.

Tice, Terrence N. *Schleiermacher Bibliography*. Princeton, N.J.: Princeton Theological Seminary, 1966.

Toews, John Edward. *Hegelianism: The Path toward Dialectical Humanism, 1805–1841*. Cambridge and New York: Cambridge Univ. Pr., 1980.

Wartofsky, Marx W. *Feuerbach*. Cambridge and New York: Cambridge Univ. Pr., 1977.

Willey, Thomas E. *Back to Kant: The Revival of Kantianism in German Social and Historical Thought, 1860–1914*. Detroit, Mich.: Wayne State Univ. Pr., 1978.

GEORG WILHELM FRIEDRICH HEGEL (1770–1831)

Hegel and Hegelianism

Hegel's philosophy purported to find a place for all ideas within an all-encompassing, historical-dialectical system, offered an idealist perspective from which to criticize relatively undeveloped ideas, and enabled religious believers and nonbelievers, social-cultural-political conservatives and revolutionaries alike to claim a firm understanding of their destiny within the total scheme of things. His remarkably widespread influence from the 1820s to at least a century afterwards was due as much to the enthusiasm of early disciples as to his own writings. For the Hegelians, his refulgent, dynamic (if often heady and confused) account of reality had come along at just the right time, for European thought and society were undergoing vast and rapid change.

From 1832 to 1840 associates brought out an eighteen-volume edition of his works, many of which were lectures and student notes not previously published. In 1844 Karl Rosenkranz issued an intellectual biography, using manuscripts from 1795 to 1806 to establish a picture of his early philosophy, before publication of his first major work, *The Phenomenology of Spirit* (1807). Soon after Friedrich Schleiermacher had Hegel brought to Berlin in 1818, a devoted circle of colleagues and disciples gathered around him. Then and after his death of cholera in 1831, several of these men were to develop influential Hegelian approaches not only to philosophy—for example, conservative academicians Karl Michelet (1801–93), Karl Rosenkranz (1805–79), Johann Erdmann (1805–92), Eduard Zeller (1814–1908), Rudolf Haym (1821–1901), and Kuno Fischer (1824–1907), but also to theology—for example, Karl Daub (1765–1836), Philipp Karl Markeineke (1780–1846), Bruno Bauer (1809–82), D. F. Strauss (1808–74) and Ludwig Feuerbach (1804–72), to law—for example, Eduard Gans (1798–1839), and to other fields. These approaches made vigorous use of Hegel's dialectical method, which emphasized historical movement of the "Absolute Spirit" through changing and opposing tendencies, each pair of which was seen first to be held in tension, then in some fashion overcome and advanced in new syntheses. The system of thought that had emerged from Hegel's own bold historical reconstructions was from 1826 defended in the *Jahrbücher für wissenschaftliche Kritik*. This system was initially comprised of a rationalist, "right wing" accommodation of idealism, of toned-down versions of Christian thought, of bourgeois culture and of monarchical politics. From about 1839 to the political revolution of 1848, a "left wing," revolutionary group (the antiacademic "younger Hegelians") was strongy attacking all four aspects of this accommodation in a series of periodicals and books. Most notable among this second group were D. F. Strauss (1808–74), Arnold Ruge (1803–80), Ludwig

Feuerbach (1804–72), Max Stirner (1806–56), and Karl Marx (1818–83). To this group should be added the Danish existentialist anti-Hegelian Søren Kierkegaard (1813–55). Since the early twentieth century, much existentialist thought, after the manner of Kierkegaard, has been directed to or against conditions set forth in Hegelian philosophy.

Through their systematic histories of philosophy, Michelet, Erdmann, Zeller, Fischer and others markedly affected the prevailing views of philosophical development through much of the nineteenth century and, in some respects, to the present. Although other versions of post-Kantian idealist thought were current throughout the nineteenth century, Hegelian forms were dominant, largely because of their considerable historical bent; Hegel himself was usually thought to be the successor of contemporary idealists such as Johann Gottlieb Fichte (1762–1814), Friedrich Schleiermacher (1768–1834), and Friedrich Schelling (1775–1854), even though the latter two outlived him. The movement, as strong in the nineteenth century as analytic philosophy has been in the twentieth (though not in Britain or North America), rapidly spread to the rest of Europe, Britain (but only from about 1865 into the early 1900s), and North America. Since the 1920s the primary interest in Hegel and Hegelian thought has been directed to views of historicity and historical development and to understandings of dialectical tension and alienation in human experience. There has also been some residue of interest in Hegelian idealism. Frequently, sometimes quite mistakenly, an identification of idealism and Hegelian thought has also been made. Even George Berkeley may not have been a strict subjective idealist, who would not only regard the world as an essentially mental or spiritual expression but would also restrict its knowability to the individual mind. Hegel and his followers have taken a great interest in the mental or spiritual constitution of the world and in the knowing subject, but they have done so as objective idealists. That is, they have tended to assume that an objectively knowable reality is revealed through intersubjectively verifiable investigation and discourse. (See p. 130 for a contrast between idealism and some nineteenth-century forms of realism.) In any case, there are other versions of objective idealism than those associated with Hegel; some of both sets regularly come under fire for appearing to be overly speculative; and the practical meaningfulness of the distinction has become questionable to those who do not strictly hold to positions at either extreme on the realist-idealist continuum.

Hegel's Development

H. S. Harris (1972) holds that although many of Hegel's later ideas are present in his early writings, they represent a religious-aesthetic quest, which Hegel came to believe must be superseded by a rational, philosophical one. On balance, I think his reading is correct. Even though Hegel early opposed numerous methods and dogmas of Christian theology, his critiques were not strictly "antitheological" as Walter Kaufmann (1965) claims; nor is their expressive feature altogether "anti-Romantic," as he also supposes.

Marxist György Lukács (1938, 1976) also mistakenly has Hegel's political interests early eclipsing all concern for religious issues; however, he does appropriately highlight Hegel's early participation in the surmounting of subjectivism and irrationalism, in his time especially represented for him by his one-time friend Schelling but also by Schleiermacher and other Romantics. Lukács also shows how Hegel forged a rational, dialectical position that melds individual consciousness with the "objective" problems of society. More specifically, Lukács believes that from his earliest inquiries on, Hegel held social praxis to be the fundament of all thought. In this light, the notion of "externalization" *(Entäusserung)* is seen to be the central philosophical concept of *The Phenomenology of Spirit* (1807), Hegel's first major work. Lukács admits that a nontheological, humanized religious motif remains in his later thought.

In his study of the religious dimension in Hegel's thought, Emil Fackenheim (1968) skirts the controversy about his earlier perspectives and simply outlines the religious basis of the later Absolute philosophy and Hegel's later transfiguration of faith into philosophy. Stephen Crites (1972), to the contrary, terms Hegelian Christianity "the religion of Christendom," maps out a development in Hegel's understanding of "faith" to a final unity of the human and the divine, then compares these with Søren Kierkegaard's faith "against Christendom."

Hegel's long *Phenomenology of Spirit* (1807) is perhaps the most rapt, uncontrolled, enigmatic prolegomenon in the history of philosophy, though much of his own development of self-consciousness—his principal theme—is here clearly revealed and though it presents the seedbed of his subsequent philosophy. An extensive commentary by Jean Hyppolite (1946) has brought much essential information to light, but the work will doubtless always remain somewhat obscure, albeit exciting and philosophically challenging. The latest and best translation of the entire text is dated 1977. A quite readable account of it by Merold Westphal (1979) is sensitive both to Hegel's dialogue with others and to themes in contemporary Hegel literature. Westphal argues that a single coherent argument runs through the entire work, moving from sense certainty to absolute knowledge. A more difficult and extensive reading by phenomenologist Quentin Lauer (1976), to which Westphal does not refer, closely follows the text and rarely notes his disputes with other interpreters. Lauer takes the Preface as epilogue, in that it was written some months after the rest; Westphal regards it as prologue, explaining all that is to follow. Both rightly take it very seriously. Walter Kaufmann (1965), like only a few earlier interpreters, had placed great stock in the Preface as the key to understanding Hegel's philosophy; thus he included a translation of it, with commentary, in his important survey of Hegel's development. Charles Taylor (1975) devotes a fifth of his long exposition to this work, viewed as "interpretive dialectic."

In contrast, political philosopher Judith Shklar (1976) lifts out one theme from the book, the identity of personal goals and public ends, and does not consider the development of Hegel's thought. The political theme was unquestionably a major one from the start. In view of fascism, Herbert Marcuse (1941, 1955) defends what he takes to be Hegel's dialectical, progressive, rationalist, proto-Marxian social theory. This theory, for him, is primarily a critique of prevailing social reality versus the positivist position that came after, giving modern social theory its greatest impetus, and versus the antiliberal beliefs of some later right-wing British and Italian idealists who claimed to follow Hegel. Two collections that mirror the renewed interest in his social-political thought are edited by Z. A. Pelczynski (1971) and Donald Verene (1980). George Armstrong Kelly (1978) collects eight of his own fine essays on Hegel's new departures in political thought, placing them within the social-poitical context as Hegel saw it.

Dialectic and Logic

Today most interpreters agree that the Hegelian synthesis, dominant in the German intellectual world of the 1820s and 1830s and still a prominent factor during the rebellions of the Young Hegelians, Feuerbach, Marx, Kierkegaard, and others in the 1840s, and in many forms revivified there and elsewhere after the late nineteenth century, has dissolved. That is, his specific ontology, and the so-called logic, as the demonstrable unfolding of ideas by which he thought to capture the dynamic structures of social reality, is no longer usable. Not only has the post-Enlightenment situation, as he saw it, largely disappeared; his mode of seeing, his philosophical style, has also fallen under massive critical bombardments. Nonetheless, the historically reflective projects he opened up still attract many philosophers. In the prime years of British idealism and in their aftermath, the functioning of his "logic" within an idealist, dialectical system was the primary focus of interest (McTaggart, 1896, 1922; Mure, 1950). An exposition of the entire system, as by W. T. Stace (1924), is not something contemporary writers would aspire to, although the "reexamination" by J. N. Findlay (1958) comes close in his exposition of central ideas in the system and his presentation of the dialectical structure of Hegel's main works. Neither takes his development seriously. In contrast, phenomenologist Quentin Lauer (1977) is more interested in Hegel's philosophy as quest and as invitation to dialogue on select themes. The German Heideggerian, hermeneutical philosopher, Hans-Georg Gadamer (1976), emphasizes those anticipations of philosophical truth to be found embedded in ordinary language and thought. Another phenomenologically oriented scholar, Malcolm Clark (1971), carefully traces Hegel's notion of a transition from sense, intuition, or feeling through the mediation of phenomenal language or perception *(Vorstellung)* to philosophical thought *(Denken);* in this way he attempts to show the central if unsteady, metaphysically ambiguous role played by the logic in forming the system.

Accounts and Collections

    Hegel scholarship has been hampered by the lack of a critical edition of his works, a great many of which are in the form of lecture notes. Such an edition was only barely begun in the 1970s. Nevertheless, good fresh studies continue to appear. For example, recently Murray Greene (1972) has focused especially on "anthropology" as the first of Hegel's three sciences of subjective spirit (the others are phenomenology and psychology). W. H. Walsh (1969) has prepared a brief, careful exposition of his ethics. Burleigh Taylor Wilkins (1974) has explored the place of his philosophy of history within the overall system, examining his claim that the question "What is the ultimate purpose of the world?" can be answered by this means.

Two of the more recent general accounts have already been mentioned, those by Walter Kaufmann (1965) and Charles Taylor (1975). Taylor's, the most systematic and complete to date, comes from one who closely identifies with Hegelian thought. Kaufmann's scintillating critical commentary is also sympathetic but goes for the capsule comment and is less evenhanded. Both his account and the succinct exposition of Hegel's system by Stanley Rosen (1974) are geared to the reader who has little or no knowledge of Hegel. Rosen also looks at Hegel's relation to predecessors, especially the Greeks, as Kaufmann does not, and centers his account on the logic.

Among the collections of essays, Alasdair MacIntyre's (1966) gathers seven recent previously published critical essays and adds new ones by Klaus Hartmann, Charles Taylor, Richard Schacht, and himself. Warren Steinkraus (1971) includes new or newly translated material from Findlay, Hyppolite, Harris, Kaufmann, and ten other Hegel scholars. Frederick Weiss (1974) compiles nine new essays on Hegel's views of knowledge and truth over a wide range of areas (religion, history, natural science, phenomenology, hermeneutics, etc.). Joseph J. O'Malley et al. (1974) have twelve new essays on Hegel's conception of the history of philosophy and relations of Hegel to thinkers before and after him. An outstanding first comprehensive bibliography has been issued by Kurt Steinhauer (1980).

Clark, Malcolm. *Logic and System: A Study of the Transition from 'Vorstellung' to Thought in the Philosophy of Hegel.* The Hague: Nijhoff, 1971.

Crites, Stephen. *In the Twilight of Christendom: Hegel vs. Kierkegaard on Faith and History.* Chambersburg, Pa.: American Academy of Religion, 1972.

Fackenheim, Emil L. *The Religious Dimension in Hegel's Thought.* Bloomington and London: Indiana Univ. Pr., 1968.

Findlay, John N. *Hegel: A Re-examination.* New York: Macmillan; London: Allen & Unwin, 1958.

Gadamer, Hans-Georg. *Hegel's Dialectic: Five Hermeneutical Studies.* Tr. by P. Christopher Smith. New Haven, Conn. and London: Yale Univ. Pr., 1976. (The original German essays were published between 1961 and 1973.)

Greene, Murray. *Hegel on the Soul: A Speculative Anthropology.* The Hague: Nijhoff, 1972.

Harris, Henry S. *Hegel's Development toward the Sunlight (1770–1801).* Oxford: Clarendon Pr., 1972.

Hyppolite, Jean. *Genesis and Structure of Hegel's Phenomenology of Spirit.* Tr. by Samuel Cherniak and John Heckman. Evanston, Ill.: Northwestern Univ. Pr., 1974. (French ed., 1946.)

Kaufmann, Walter A. *Hegel: Reinterpretation, Texts and Commentary.* Garden City, N.Y.: Doubleday, 1965.

Kelly, George Armstrong. *Hegel's Retreat from Eleusis.* Princeton, N.J.: Princeton Univ. Pr., 1978.

Lauer, Quentin, S.J. *Essays in Hegelian Dialectic.* New York: Fordham Univ. Pr., 1977. (Eleven previously published essays, some revised.)

———. *A Reading of Hegel's "Phenomenology of Spirit."* New York: Fordham Univ. Pr., 1976.

Lukács, György. *The Young Hegel: Studies in the Relations between Dialectics and Economics.* Tr. by Rodney Livingstone. Cambridge, Mass.: MIT Pr., 1976. (German ed., 1954.) (Originally written in 1938, then revised for its first publication, in German, in 1948.)

MacIntyre, Alasdair, ed. *Hegel: A Collection of Critical Essays.* Notre Dame, Ind.: Univ. of Notre Dame Pr., 1966.

McTaggart, John M. E. *Studies in the Hegelian Dialectic.* 2nd ed. New York: Russell & Russell, 1922. (1st ed., 1896; reprinted, 1964.)

Marcuse, Herbert. *Reason and Revolution: Hegel and the Rise of Social Theory.* 2nd ed. New York: Humanities Pr., 1954; London: Routledge & Paul, 1955. (1st ed., 1941; the 2nd ed. adds only an 8-page epilogue.)

Mure, Geoffrey R. G. *A Study of Hegel's Logic.* Oxford: Clarendon Pr., 1950.

O'Malley, Joseph J., K. W. Algozin, and Frederick G. Weiss, eds. *Hegel and the History of Philosophy: Proceedings of the 1972 Hegel Society of America Conference.* The Hague: Nijhoff, 1974.

Pelczynski, Z. A., ed. *Hegel's Political Philosophy—Problems and Perspectives: A Collection of New Essays.* Cambridge and New York: Cambridge Univ. Pr., 1971.

Rosen, Stanley. *G. W. F. Hegel: An Introduction to the Science of Wisdom.* New Haven, Conn. and London: Yale Univ. Pr., 1974.

Shklar, Judith N. *Freedom and Independence: A Study of the Political Ideas of Hegel's Phenomenology of Mind.* Cambridge and New York: Cambridge Univ. Pr., 1976.

Stace, Walter T. *The Philosophy of Hegel: A Systematic Exposition.* London: Macmillan, 1924. Repr., 1955.

Steinhauer, Kurt, ed. *Hegel Bibliography.* New York and Munich: K. G. Sauer, 1980.

Steinkraus, Warren E., ed. *New Studies in Hegel's Philosophy.* New York: Holt, Rinehart & Winston, 1971.

Taylor, Charles. *Hegel.* Cambridge and New York: Cambridge Univ. Pr., 1975.

Verene, Donald P., ed. *Hegel's Social and Political Thought.* Atlantic Highlands, N.J.: Humanities Pr.; Brighton, Sussex: Harvester Pr., 1980.

Walsh, William H. *Hegelian Ethics.* New York: St. Martin's Pr.; London: Macmillan, 1969.

Weiss, Frederick G., ed. *Beyond Epistemology: New Studies in the Philosophy of Hegel.* The Hague: Nijhoff, 1974.

Westphal, Merold. *History and Truth in Hegel's "Phenomenology."* Atlantic Highlands, N.J.: Humanities Pr., 1979.

Wilkins, Burleigh T. *Hegel's Philosophy of History.* Ithaca, N.Y.: Cornell Univ. Pr., 1974.

Background and Overview

Although important, long-lasting philosophical work was done in the British Isles during the Middle Ages—most notably by Erigena in the ninth century and by late medieval nominalists Duns Scotus and Ockham—all of this belonged within the larger orbit of the Roman Catholic Church. In contrast to these men, Anselm was not even English, though he was Archbishop of Canterbury from 1093 to 1109, and his marked influence on both Augustinian and dialectical modes of thought in England began to show up only in the thirteenth and fourteenth centuries. None of the British philosophy that followed was particularly distinguished, except perhaps for aspects of religious thought, until well into the English Renaissance. Francis Bacon's *Advancement of Learning* (1605) was the first major philosophical work to be published in the English language.

Trends and figures from the seventeenth and eighteenth centuries have been traced in earlier sections. These make up most of the intellectual history by Meyrick Carré (1949), who surveys much beyond the nominalist and empirical strains in their history that have chiefly interested British philosophers since 1900. The same is true of W. R. Sorley (1920), whose briefer account up to 1900 is now something of a period piece. Sorley chiefly presents individual thinkers, viewed from the perspective of his own theistic idealism, while Carré outlines the major movements—which he broadly categorizes as Augustinian, Aristotelian, and Newtonian—epoch by epoch. Carré's work includes notice of the eighteenth-nineteenth century Scottish philosophers, already valuably gathered in James McCosh's classic work (1875) and often overlooked today. His interpretation is also illuminating in many other ways. However, no truly philosophical synopsis of this story has yet appeared and no intellectual history based on recent scholarship. The closest for the century after John Stuart Mill's *System of Logic* (1843) is John Passmore's unparalleled concoction of themes in epistemology, logic, and metaphysics (*A Hundred Years of Philosophy*, 1957, cited on p. 10), an object lesson in English analytic cuisine.

The principal motifs in nineteenth-century British philosophy are associated either with the quite different utilitarian views of Jeremy Bentham (1748–1833) and John Stuart Mill (1806–73) or with versions of idealism. The literature on Thomas Reid (1710–96) and the

Scottish philosophers is not sufficiently developed to represent here, though their "common sense" approach dominated both British and American philosophy well into the nineteenth century. Richard Olson (1975) has outlined some aspects of its development, especially of its marked influence on the simplified, analogically based building of dynamic models characteristic of nineteenth-century British physics, culminating in the work of James Clerk Maxwell. Such models had to fulfill the common sense condition that terms applicable to the material world must have a clearly determined sensory referent. The subsequent preferences among British scientists for geometry and pictorial schemes, as in vector analysis, are grounded in the Scottish philosophy. The Kantian influence usually assigned to methods of forming theoretical constructs in British physics must be reassessed in the light of this history, including their bearing on the development of field theory.

Utilitarianism

   Like much of the Scottish philosophy, the utilitarian approach of Bentham and his followers draws significantly from Hume, in this case not only from aspects of his empirical epistemology and associationist psychology but also from his identification of value with utility. Bentham's is an "act utiliarian" view, one held in common with J. S. Mill, Henry Sidgwick, and many successors. Their position is that the good or bad consequences of a particular action alone determine what moral judgment is to be made of it. In contrast, "rule utilitarian" views look toward the consequences of adopting some actual or possible rule. Bentham, unlike Mill, stuck to a purely hedonistic analysis of moral quality, according to which "goodness" means pleasant consequences and "badness" the opposite. Mill admitted further qualifying characteristics so as to distinguish between higher and lower pleasures and claimed that the higher pleasures are especially to be sought after. In contrast to both Bentham and Mill, G. E. Moore and other "ideal utilitarians" included other indexes than modes of pleasure, notably such as may issue from intellectual or aesthetic contemplation. Some utilitarians, like Bentham, have defended or have tended toward a theory that attempts simply to describe what people do. Most, beginning with Mill and Sidgwick, have presented a normative position, an account of what people in general ought to do. Finally, some utilitarians have adopted a chiefly individual-oriented, egoistic theory; most, like Sidgwick and Moore, have presented a universalistic one. Most of these diverse views, and the many still more sophisticated versions that followed, are not reducible to the popular aim, "the greatest good for the greatest number," as this was advanced by Bentham. Issues about what kind of happiness and how it is to be distributed remain once this principle has been enunciated.

In a provocative new interpretation, David Lyons (1973) has analyzed Bentham's notion of utility, especially as it relates to politics and law. A collection edited by Bhikhu Parekh (1974) rounds out the picture of Bentham's ethical and political views, including a long essay by J. S. Mill (1838), others by William Whewell (1862) and John Watson (1895), several from the 1950s and 1960s, and two new essays by Parekh. The collection edited by John Robson and Michael Laine (1976) manifests the line from Bentham's disciple James Mill (1773–1836) to his son, J. S. Mill (with emphasis on the son's views of religion, economics, society, and politics), as does the fine intellectual psychobiography by Bruce Mazlich (1975). The older three-volume survey of the utilitarians by Leslie Stephen (1900) is still valuable for its coverage but suspect in its scholarship.

Most accounts of John Stuart Mill (works, 1963–) have not seen him as a systematic thinker. In contrast, an overview of his thought by Alan Ryan (1970) presents Mill as the author of a self-styled philosophical system that Ryan terms "inductivism." The intellectual-historical introduction to his political thinking by political theorist R. J. Halliday (1976) characterizes it not only as a new variant of utilitarianism, as usual, but also as a cautious, grumbling, romantic pessimism. There is as yet no comprehensive study of Mill's philosophy, which would require extending far beyond the ordinary interests in his logic or politics and examining significant changes and inconsistencies. Historian Gertrude Himmelfarb (1974) has persuasively argued that some central positions in his deservedly most noted essay, *On Liberty* (1859), knowingly contradict positions in all his other writings except those on women. She explains this by ascribing joint authorship to Mill and his wife, who died in 1859. The "other" Mill, she shows, belonged to an older liberal tradition than that represented in this essay, one that accorded to each individal equal voice and equal power. Dennis Thompson's study (1976) looks chiefly at his *Considerations on Representative Government* (1861), only one of several political works by Mill (1963–) but one Himmelfarb assigns to the "other" Mill even though it followed *On Liberty*. Although the ambivalence about the foundations of representative democracy that Himmelfarb detects in his political thinking surely existed, there can be no doubt of his support of educational institutions for the liberation of individuality and the improvement of mankind. For the first time, Francis Garforth (1979) cleverly lays out the main elements of his educational philosophy, placing them in social and historical context. Other areas of his philosophy—logic, mathematics, epistemology, and aesthetics, as well as ethics and politics—are also observed in the collection of critical essays on Mill edited by J. B Schneewind (1969), three of them new.

Schneewind (1974) has also edited some essays on the ethics of a leading follower of Mill, Henry Sidgwick (1838–1900), and has added a fulsome study (1977) on Sidgwick's most important book, *The Methods of Ethics* (1874), set within the Victorian context and against the background of eighteenth-nineteenth century moral philosophy in England and Scotland. Later subjected to much well-founded criticism, that book was nonetheless the most thorough, lucid, systematic work on ethics ever written to that time and bore great influence; this description also holds of his *Outlines of the History of Ethics for English Readers* (1886). Schneewind's study is itself a premier contribution to the history of ethics over the entire nineteenth century.

Idealism

Idealism has been so firmly trounced and repudiated over the past half-century and more that it is now difficult to realize what a powerful hold it had on British philosophy from the 1870s until the 1920s. As always, British trends had a marked effect on American philosophy as well. A classic history of this quite diverse movement by a leading idealist, J. H. Muirhead (1931), highlights its Platonic character and includes Hegelian themes. A critical summary of doctrine with historical references by A. C. Ewing (1934) deliberately omits Hegelian factors altogether. *Idealist Epilogue* (1978) by a long-time idealist, G. R. G. Mure, expresses special affinity to both Plato and Hegel and evidences that idealism has not completely disappeared, though it has long been overshadowed by other trends. Ewing (1957) has also gathered a selection of writings by prominent idealists in order to depict it as a long tradition from Berkeley through Kant, Hegel, T. H. Green, and others to the American Brand Blanshard, adding some typical early twentieth-century critiques by Cook Wilson, G. E. Moore, Bertrand Russell, and the American Ernest Nagel.

In his brief lifetime T. H. Green (1836–82) is said to have made as strong a contribution to the secularization of Oxford as did Henry Sidgwick at Cambridge. Green was a towering figure in the idealist tradition, despite the Victorian stiffness of his style. He was influential not least because of his thoroughgoing use of Kant to criticize empiricism, his temperate, undogmatic interest in religion, his antimaterialist metaphysics, his wide-ranging, systematically organized conception of the human mind both as a developing part of divine reality and as capable of grasping the ideal system of relations by which reality is constituted, his liberal individualist social views, and his teleological but nonutilitarian interpretation of education and the state as agents of moral improvement. Overall, such perspectives among the idealists were strongly influenced by Hegel, Green's considerably less than most. His close friend, the Scotsman Edward Caird (1835–1908), Master of Balliol College in Oxford from 1893 to 1908, also adopted much from Kant but added an evolutionary feature from Hegel, emphasizing attainment of spiritual harmony through reconciliation of apparent opposites in mental life. His philosophy was theologically informed. Two of Caird's more distinguished students, Henry Jones and J. H. Muirhead, have written about his life and philosophy (1921).

Melvin Richter (1964) assembles the marked political interests of T. H. Green and his cohort. Peter Gordon and John White (1979) look at their activities in educational reform. Using methods borrowed from R. G. Collingwood, himself something of an idealist, A. J. M. Milne (1962) examines the broader moral and social philosophy of idealists T. H. Green, F. H. Bradley, Bernard Bosanquet, and the American Josiah Royce. Milne holds that the central notion was that of the concrete universal, taken from Hegel and bound up with a like theory of rationality but having no necessary connection with a theory of the Absolute as eternal consciousness. Absolute idealism had been held first by Fichte, then by Schelling and Hegel, all of whom variously referred to ego, mind, or ideas as absolute versus things, which are merely finite and determined. In England, Absolute idealism had been mediated especially by Samuel Taylor Coleridge (1772–1834) and Thomas Carlyle (1795–1881). Both Bradley and Bosanquet were called Absolute idealists. Others would argue, in keeping with this history, that the free activity of mind in interpreting, even altering, the world was not only crucial for them, as for all the others just mentioned, but that some view of an Absolute was also essential to each view.

For some forty years after Green's death in 1882, British philoso-

phy was dominated by F. H. Bradley (1846–1924) and Bernard Bosanquet (1848–1923)—both of Oxford and decided contrasts in
temperament, political views, and intellectual style—and to a lesser
extent by John McTaggart Ellis McTaggart (1866–1925) of Cambridge. Bosanquet remained more of a Hegelian than did Bradley and
supported social reform. He covered most areas of philosophy in his
writing but is little noted today. A Tory in his political affinities,
Bradley concentrated mostly on metaphysics, logic, and ethics. His
detailed argumentation and sharp polemical style plus the empiricist
elements in his thought and the nearly epoch-making demands of his
Appearance and Reality (1893) no doubt all attracted Moore, Russell, and others to him as the chief object of their antiidealist attacks.
An overview of his philosophy by Richard Wollheim (1959) and a
specialized study of his metaphysics, including his distinctive doctrines on relations and on degrees of reality, and his understanding of
the self by Garrett Vander Veer (1970) both reflect a continuing
interest in his work.

McTaggart was at least as influential in his critical readings of
Hegel and in his friendly ways of aiding clarity as in his own philosophy, which denied the existence of God and posited that ultimate
reality consists solely of individual minds, who are immortal and
who are essentially related by bonds of love. For a long time, the
lengthy two-volume impressionistic commentary by the successor to
his chair, C. D. Broad (1933–38), was the standard work on his
philosophy. This has been successfully critiqued and in part supplanted by Peter Geach's introduction (1979).

Carré, Meyrick H. *Phases of Thought in England.* Oxford: Clarendon Pr.,
1949.
Ewing, Alfred C. *Idealism: A Critical Survey.* 3rd ed. London: Methuen,
1961. (1st ed., 1934.)
———, ed. *The Idealist Tradition from Berkeley to Blanshard.* New York:
Free Pr., 1957.
Garforth, Francis William. *John Stuart Mill's Theory of Education.* New
York: Barnes & Noble; Oxford: Martin Robertson, 1979.
Geach, Peter T. *Truth, Love, and Immortality: An Introduction to McTag-
gart's Philosophy.* Berkeley: Univ. of California Pr.; London: Hutchinson,
1979.
Gordon, Peter, and John White. *Philosophers as Educational Reformers: The
Influence of Idealism on British Educational Thought and Practice.* Lon-
don and Boston: Routledge & Paul, 1979.
Halliday, Richard J. *John Stuart Mill.* London: Allen & Unwin, 1976.
Himmelfarb, Gertrude. *On Liberty and Liberalism: The Case of John Stuart
Mill.* New York: Knopf, 1974.

Jones, Henry, and J. H. Muirhead. *The Life and Philosophy of Edward Caird.* Glasgow: Maelehose, Jackson, 1921.

Lyons, David. *In the Interest of the Governed: A Study in Bentham's Philosophy of Utility and Law.* Oxford: Clarendon Pr., 1973.

McCosh, James. *Scottish Philosophy: Biographical, Expository, Critical, from Hutcheson to Hamilton.* New York: Robert Carter; Cambridge: John Wilson, 1875.

Mazlich, Bruce. *James and John Stuart Mill: Father and Son in the Nineteenth Century.* New York: Basic Books, 1975.

Mill, John Stuart. *Collected Works.* Ed. by E. F. L. Priestley. Toronto: Univ. of Toronto Pr., 1963– . (18 volumes published so far; vol. 1 includes two drafts of his *Autobiography.*)

Milne, Alan J. M. *The Social Philosophy of English Idealism.* London: Allen & Unwin, 1962.

Muirhead, John H. *The Platonic Tradition in Anglo-Saxon Philosophy: Studies in the History of Idealism in England and America.* New York: Macmillan; London: Allen & Unwin, 1931. Repr.: New York: Humanities Pr., 1965.

Mure, Geoffrey R. G. *Idealist Epilogue.* Oxford: Clarendon Pr., 1978.

Olson, Richard. *Scottish Philosophy and British Physics, 1750–1880: A Study in the Foundations of the Victorian Scientific Style.* Princeton, N.J.: Princeton Univ. Pr., 1975.

Parekh, Bhikhu, ed. *Jeremy Bentham: Ten Critical Essays.* London: Cass, 1974.

Richter, Melvin. *The Politics of Conscience: T. H. Green and His Age.* Cambridge, Mass.: Harvard Univ. Pr.; London: Weidenfeld & Nicholson, 1964.

Robson, John M., and Michael Laine, eds. *James and John Stuart Mill: Papers of the Centenary Conference.* Toronto, Buffalo, and London: Univ. of Toronto Pr., 1976.

Ryan, Alan. *John Stuart Mill.* New York: Pantheon, 1970.

Schneewind, Julius B. *Sidgwick's Ethics and Victorian Moral Philosophy.* Oxford and New York: Oxford Univ. Pr., 1977.

————, ed. *Mill: A Collection of Critical Essays.* Garden City, N.Y.: Doubleday Anchor, 1968; London: Macmillan, 1969.

————, ed. "Sidgwick and Moral Philosophy." *Monist* 58, no. 3:349–517 (July 1974).

Sorley, W. R. *A History of English Philosophy to 1900.* Cambridge and New York: Cambridge Univ. Pr., 1920. Repr., 1965.

Stephen, Leslie. *The English Utilitarians.* 3v. New York: Peter Smith, 1950. (Original ed., 1900.)

Thompson, Dennis F. *John Stuart Mill and Representative Government.* Princeton, N.J.: Princeton Univ. Pr., 1976.

Vander Veer, Garrett L. *Bradley's Metaphysics and the Self.* New Haven, Conn. and London: Yale Univ. Pr., 1970.

Wollheim, Richard. *F. H. Bradley.* 2nd ed. Baltimore, Md. and Harmondsworth: Penguin, 1969. (1st ed., 1959.)

7

Twentieth-Century
Philosophy

In effect, this entire book traces the course of twentieth-century philosophy. At this point, therefore, I need only pull together the several basic trends, with emphasis on Anglo-American thought. Although philosophy has become a worldwide interest for the first time in this century, the sheer numbers of philosophers in Britain and North America and the immigration of a large proportion of European philosophers to those countries in the 1930s have brought the preponderance of activity there. Because of their prominence, additional accounts must be added on pragmatism, Marx and Marxism, existentialism, phenomenology, hermeneutics, and critical theory, all but the first of which have an initially European base. These will be treated in chapters 10–13.

To begin, I underscore (1) the heavy occupation with analytic issues with respect to logic and language, (2) the unprecedented diversity of methods, approaches, and positions, and (3) the fast spread of philosophy around the world, especially since World War II, including the interesting case of Scandinavian philosophy.

ANALYSIS: LOGIC AND LANGUAGE

The chief problematic orientation running through twentieth-century philosophy may be outlined, in rough brush strokes, as follows. Finding fault with the seemingly overquick, vague, overgeneralized, empirically unsupportable doctrines of Hegelian idealism and other systems of thought believed to possess these qualities, philosophers were driven to wonder whether it might be possible to clarify propositions by breaking them into their basic elements through logical, truth-functional analysis and then, also by such analysis, to see

150

whether empirical observation statements can be similarly reduced, so that we can tell which propositions to keep and which to let go. Philosophy would become scientific and science would be thoroughly grounded—as Russell and Whitehead argued is true for mathematics—in logic. Perhaps it would even be possible, as the early Wittgenstein proposed, to produce elementary (that is, simple, mutually exclusive, but not necessarily independent) atomic propositions, truths that are nonfactual and independent of the contingent facts of the world. Enormous effort went into this program. Since the early methods of analysis were suitable only for investigating the grammar and syntax of language, not discovery, for clarifying concepts and not theory-building, and since ordinary language did not directly yield the information needed, much emphasis had to be placed on translation of ordinary language into symbols or even into artificial languages. Initially all these efforts were especially stimulated by the logical positivists and by Bertrand Russell.

But from the 1930s to the 1950s it became clear to many positivists and other empiricists that serious limitations are placed on our ability to make such translations, and that the translations are not strictly reliable. Even to some of the strongest adherents of this program, there appeared to be neither support in actual language for the existence of elementary propositions nor any firm grounding for the radically empirical venture. With respect to the latter, those who represented a change of view held that if a proposition of science were a truth-function of observation statements, strict verification or falsification would be possible, and it is not. Thus the ultimate logical forms being sought through analysis do not mirror reality as it had been hoped they would. We must learn to live with uncertainty. (For a similar account, see that of an early logical positivist, Friedrich Waismann, 1977.) This conclusion did not in itself obviate analysis; it only pointed to failures in the program and the need for complementary methods of imaginative construction, explanatory and persuasive critique and synthesis, which in various ways were being used anyway. However, the deconstructive effect on analysis as a method led some toward psychologistic, mystical, subjectivist, or radically constructivist solutions. It led others to shift analytic attention, still within the same formalist tradition, to ordinary language structures (see chapter 8) and to semantics (inquiry into meanings and into factual matters in relation to logical truth; see chapter 17). Others, of course, have not left the program.

The dreams of certainty and order die hard. Their dissolution may lead to other similar but apparently safer dreams. I think this is what has happened to many philosophers in the two decades after World War II and is still happening to some. The resultant accomplishments are not small, though critics opine that they might have been greater given other basic assumptions. With particular sensitivity, clarity, and historical care, Stanley Rosen (1980) has examined the dream of analysis and its alleged breakdown, holding that conceptual analysis is highly important but not sufficient as a philosophical method, and that in fact it can be damaging and distorting. It must be accompanied by reasonable and lucid imagination ("intuition") and by modes of rhetoric bent to the requirements of honest dialogue, not to system-building. His historical thesis is that, by and large, in its conceptualizing of the world analytic philosophy is an unself-conscious, deteriorated version of Hegelianism, and that if its adherents are Kantians they are so only without Kant's essential transcendental ego, thus in effect believing in concepts but not in the conceiving subject.

Perhaps this last part of Rosen's excellent critique is a bit overdrawn. Russell, for example, always started with the observing subject but sought an anchor in logical and empirical analysis. Others have moved in ways reminiscent of the critical-psychological-rationalist reconstruction of Kant that the German philosopher Leonard Nelson (1882–1927) performed in the manner of Jacob Friedrich Fries (1773–1843). Only in the past thirty years has Nelson's impressive systematic work (e.g., *Socratic Method and Critical Philosophy,* 1949) begun to get notice among Anglo-American philosophers. Also steeped in mathematics, like many of the early analytic philosophers, Nelson rejected metaphysical logicism, mysticism, and empiricism in favor of an interplay between logical, conceptual analysis and a Kantian-style critical metaphysics conceived as a synthetic discipline, based on nonintuitive immediate cognition—both disciplines ever provisional in their basically problem-solving content. Ernst Cassirer's neo-Kantian interests in nonlogical as well as logical symbols, in myth and wider aspects of culture (1979), has received much greater notice (Schilpp, 1949; Itzkoff, 1977), though not by logical empiricists. In the 1930s Cassirer (1874–1945) was an immigrant first to Oxford, then to Sweden, then to the United States.

Logical Positivism

Rudolf Carnap (1891–1970) is a paradigm case for the influence of logical positivism on analysis and some of its later vicissitudes.

Before World War I Carnap studied mathematics (including seminars with Frege) and physics; after the war he became a philosopher. At that time, stimulated by his reading of Frege and of *Principia Mathematica* by Whitehead and Russell, he began to apply symbolic notation in his philosophical thinking and in his construction of axiom systems in physics. Thereafter his main interests were in logic, epistemology, and philosophy of science. Inspired above all by Russell, he developed a logical-empirical approach of his own, first systematically articulated under the prescient title, *The Logical Structure of the World* (1928, tr. 1969). In 1924, through his close associate, Hans Reichenbach (1891–1953) of Berlin, he met Vienna Circle founder Moritz Schlick (1882–1936), who invited him to teach philosophy at the University of Vienna, which he did (1925–31). There he became both a member of the Vienna Circle and its leading exponent. He joined circle member Philipp Frank in Prague (1931–35), where he taught philosophy of science and worked on syntactical analysis of scientific language, subsequently presented (1935) as the circle's way of doing philosophy. Then, under the Nazi threat, he came to the United States in 1935, where he taught first at the University of Chicago (1936–54), then after Reichenbach's death in 1953 as his successor at U.C.L.A.

Other members of the circle who came to America include Hans Reichenbach (U.C.L.A), Alfred Tarski (from Warsaw to Berkeley), Philipp Frank (Harvard, d. 1966), Carl Hempel (Princeton), Herbert Feigl (Minnesota), Gustav Bergmann (Iowa), and mathematician Kurt Gödel (Institute of Advanced Studies, Princeton; in 1931 Gödel had proven that no formal system of arithmetic is completable, a turning point in the philosophy of mathematics). Otto Neurath (d. 1945) went to Holland, Friedrich Waismann to Cambridge, then Oxford (d. 1959). American philosophers who were closely associated with the "logical positivists" (as Feigl and A. E. Blumberg first called them in 1931) included Ernest Nagel, Vienna Circle member W. V. O. Quine, and pragmatist Charles Morris; in Britain, Vienna Circle member A. J. Ayer and Gilbert Ryle at Oxford, Susan Stebbing and John Wisdom at Cambridge.

For many years A. J. Ayer's *Language, Truth and Logic* (1936) principally represented the logical positivist position to English readers. Ayer emphasized the early beliefs that the meaning of a proposition is identical with the method of verifying it, that transcendental metaphysics is nonsense in that it does not admit of scientific, empirical verification, and that values have emotive but not cognitive meaning. The recommended surgery was so drastic as to put the legitimacy of almost all previous philosophy in doubt. A collection edited by Ayer (1959) indicates its continuing tenacity and attractiveness through the 1950s. An early history by a Scandinavian logical positivist, Joergen Joergensen (1951) and that by Hans Reichenbach (*The Rise of Scientific Philosophy*, 1951, cited on p. 426) have been updated by Herbert Hochberg (1978). A fine critical study of logical positivism's attack on Christian belief by Kenneth Klein (1974) represents some kinds of concerns that have arisen among philosophers whose primary topical interests are different.

Later Shifts and Turns

Changes from their initially radical empiricism and the attendant verifiability principle began to appear within the Vienna Circle in the 1930s. Neurath had always rejected empirical realism. Reichenbach had always held a probability theory not a verifiability theory of meaning. Popper's *Logik der Forschung* (*The Logic of Scientific Discovery*, 1934, cited on p. 426) helped change the direction of belief to a varied emphasis on rules and hypothetical constructs, degrees of confirmation or testability, and the like. This was followed by a new interest in semantics, thence in modal logic, in altered conceptions of probability and induction, in exploring the noncognitive (emotive) character of value statements, and in arguing for the legitimacy of abstract entities in mathematics, science, and semantics (Schilpp, 1963). Some effects on the more general conception of "analytic philosophy" have been summarized by Michael Corrado (1975). An indispensable set of essays on the foundations of analytic philosophy has been edited by Peter French et al. (1981). Effects on the philosophy of science are detailed in an important set of essays edited by Peter Achinstein and Stephen Barker (*The Legacy of Logical Positivism . . .*, 1969, cited on p. 423). Broader influences in philosophy are exemplified in a Festschrift for Jaakko Hintikka edited by Esa Saarinen et al. (1979). Among later American empirical-naturalist interest in relations between logic and language these shifts were predominant, as is well shown in the careers of Gustav Bergmann (e.g., *Realism*, 1967, cited on p. 134) and W. V. O. Quine (e.g., *Ontological Relativity . . .*, 1969).

The shift to linguistic philosophy in Britain, which also affected a fair number of American philosophers in the 1950s and 1960s, is represented by the work of P. F. Strawson (e.g., *Freedom and Resentment . . .*, 1974). In *The Linguistic Turn* (1967) Richard Rorty presents a still quite useful set of thirty-seven selections, mostly from that period, with an important introductory essay, to display issues that have been most significant in the development of Anglo-American linguistic philosophy. He begins with classic positions holding that philosophical questions are questions of language, by Schlick, Carnap, Bergmann, Ryle, Wisdom, and Norman Malcolm (the latter on "Moore and Ordinary Language"), then moving to ideal-language and ordinary-language oriented metaphilosophical problems, and finally to some retrospective and prospective contributions. Rorty himself (*Philosophy and the Mirror of Nature*, 1979, cited on p. 7; and 1982), has offered a powerful critique of the logical-empirical tradition from within. In part this critique is a later manifestation of the linguistic turn; in part it represents the still further widening of the mainstream in the late 1960s and 1970s. Particularly remarkable in Rorty's "pragmatist" moves beyond the logical-empirical, foundationalist tradition during the 1970s is his positive borrowing from John Dewey, Martin Heidegger, and contemporary European philosophers as well as American analytic philosophers (chiefly Wilfrid Sellars and W. V. O. Quine).

Ayer, Alfred J. *Language, Truth and Logic.* London: Gollancz, 1936. Repr.: New York: Dover, 1952.

———, ed. *Logical Positivism.* New York: Free Pr., 1959.

Carnap, Rudolf. *The Logical Structure of the World and Pseudoproblems in Philosophy.* Tr. by Rolf A. George. Berkeley: Univ. of California Pr., 1969. (German ed., 1928.)

———. *Philosophy and Logical Syntax.* London: Paul, Trench, Trubner, 1935.

Cassirer, Ernst. *Symbol, Myth and Culture: Essays and Lectures of Ernst Cassirer, 1935–1945.* Ed. by Donald Phillip Verene. New Haven, Conn. and London: Yale Univ. Pr., 1979. (Selection of 12 previously published essays.)

Corrado, Michael. *The Analytic Tradition in Philosophy: Background and Issues.* Chicago: American Library Assn., 1975.

French, Peter A., Theodore E. Uehling, Jr., and Howard K. Wettstein, eds. *Midwest Studies in Philosophy.* Vol. 6, *The Foundations of Analytic Philosophy.* Minneapolis: Univ. of Minnesota Pr., 1981.

Hochberg, Herbert I. *Thought, Fact, and Reference: The Origins and Ontology of Logical Atomism.* Minneapolis: Univ. of Minnesota Pr., 1978.

Itzkoff, Seymour. *Ernst Cassirer: Philosopher of Culture.* Boston: Twayne, 1977.

Joergensen, Joergen. *The Development of Logical Empiricism.* In *International Encyclopedia of Unified Science.* Vol. 2, no. 9. Chicago: Univ. of Chicago Pr., 1951.

Klein, Kenneth H. *Positivism and Christianity: A Study of Theism and Verifiability*. The Hague: Nijhoff, 1974.

Nelson, Leonard. *Socratic Method and Critical Philosophy: Selected Essays*. Tr. by Thomas K. Brown III. New York: Dover, 1949.

Quine, Willard Van Orman. *Ontological Relativity and Other Essays*. New York and London: Columbia Univ. Pr., 1969.

Rorty, Richard. *Consequences of Pragmatism: Essays 1972–1980*. Minneapolis: Univ. of Minnesota Pr., 1982.

✓ ———, ed. *The Linguistic Turn: Recent Essays in Philosophical Method*. Chicago: Univ. of Chicago Pr., 1967.

✓ Rosen, Stanley. *The Limits of Analysis*. New York: Basic Books, 1980.

Saarinen, Esa, et al., eds. *Essays in Honour of Jaakko Hintikka on the Occasion of His Fiftieth Birthday on January 2, 1979*. Dordrecht and Boston: Reidel, 1979.

Schilpp, Paul Arthur, ed. *The Philosophy of Ernst Cassirer*. Evanston, Ill.: Northwestern Univ. Pr., 1949.

———, ed. *The Philosophy of Rudolf Carnap*. La Salle, Ill.: Open Court; London: Cambridge Univ. Pr., 1963.

Strawson, P. F. *Freedom and Resentment and Other Essays*. New York: Harper & Row; London: Methuen, 1974.

Waismann, Friedrich. *Philosophical Papers*. Ed. by Brian McGuiness. Dordrecht and Boston: Reidel, 1977.

DIVERSITY OF METHODS, APPROACHES, AND POSITIONS

The already wide spectrum of analytic views that has dominated twentieth-century philosophy is accompanied by a still greater diversity of other methods, approaches, and positions. A clever overview of analytic philosophy edited by Ted Honderich and Myles Burnyeat (1979), for example, presents overlaps between eight areas of philosophy by using seventeen representative articles on special problems, all recently published. (More works in this vein are referred to in other parts of this section.) These are quite diverse in character. In his popular lectures on the "new world of philosophy," Abraham Kaplan (1961) witnesses to the extraanalytic diversity by adding chapters on perspectives from psychoanalysis, Marxism, and Eastern philosophies to those on analytic philosophy and pragmatism. In a later synoptic account of twelve areas in philosophy, Kaplan (1977) gives still further testimony, impressive even though the literature he recommends rarely goes beyond the early 1960s. American-born, but living in Israel since 1970, in both books Kaplan combines his earlier logical-empirical interests with pragmatic ones, this is in a style fetchingly admixed with rabbinic anecdotal wit, itself a peculiarly mid-twentieth-century accomplishment. Although Kaplan is one of the few mainstream philosophers influenced by Eastern thought, this interest has also caught on here and there—as, for example, in work by Ben-Ami Scharfstein (1978) and other Israeli colleagues. So far, thinkers like Sarvepalli Radhakrishnan (1888–1975; Schilpp, 1952), who are more than merely conversant with both Eastern and Western thought on a philosophical plane, have not come to the fore. Even philosophy of religion remains almost entirely Western in venue. Most of the literature cited in the philosophy of religion chapter, in fact, reflects interests deriving primarily from Christian traditions. Of broader scope, yet still religious in orientation, is Eliezer Berkovits's study (1974) of modern philosophies of Judaism (neo-Kantian Hermann Cohen, existentialists Franz Rosenzweig and Martin Buber, naturalist-reconstructionist theologian Mordekai Kaplan, and mainline theologian Abraham Heschel).

Some of the diversity has come from practical interests. An ingenious work by Richard Bernstein (*Praxis and Action . . . ,* 1971, cited on p. 377) selects a few examples (Hegel, Marx, Kierkegaard, Sartre, Peirce, Dewey, and some analytic philosophers) to show how an interest in "action" has itself become a major theme. A recent treatise by analytic philosopher Robert Nozick (1981) argues for philosophy as an art form that intends to probe "the meaning of life." His associated claim that philosophy should seek explanation, not proof or refutation, is not new, but it is illustrated here in fine detail. It is perhaps a sign of the complex, hidden circulation system of contemporary philosophy that logical positivist Friedrich Waismann, for example, had already taken this position in the 1950s (see H. D. Lewis, *Contemporary British Philosophy,* 1956, cited on p. 171) and that the existentialist Karl Jaspers before him had emphasized explanation or illumination as the primary end of philosophy.

The belief that philosophy is relevant to the rest of life, especially in its clarifying role, would be shared by most philosophers. Some emphasize this more than most. I. M. Bochenski (1956) wrote his survey of the origins and emphases of contemporary philosophy with this end in view. He divided his treatment into philosophy of matter (Bertrand Russell, neopositivism, dialectical materialism), philosophy of the idea (Henri Bergson, pragmatism, historicism, Wilhelm Dilthey, German philosophy of life), philosophy of essence (Edmund Husserl, Max Scheler), philosophy of existence (Martin Heidegger, Jean-Paul Sartre, Gabriel Marcel, and Karl Jaspers), and philosophy of being (Nicholai Hartmann, Alfred North Whitehead, Thomism), with an appendix on mathematical logic. Convinced that the logical empiricist program was impotent, Marjorie Grene (1976) associated herself first with the existentialists and with Michael Polanyi, then with Merleau-Ponty and the phenomenologists. A comparative encounter with European and Anglo-American philosophy has resulted in a book of instructive essays (1938–74), mostly on existentialism and logical positivism, by Thomist Frederick Copleston (1956). Influenced by the great Spanish philosopher, José Ortega y Gasset (1883–1955), whose aristocratic sociocultural philosophy centered on the tasks reasoning individuals have the mission to do with their historical circumstances, José Ferrater Mora (1960) especially views the influence of Marxism, existentialism, and phenomenology, logical positivism and analytic philosophy.

Berkovits, Eliezer. *Major Themes in Modern Philosophies of Judaism*. New York: Ktav, 1974.

Bochenski, I. M. *Contemporary European Philosophy*. Tr. from the 2nd rev. ed. by Donald Nicholl and Karl Aschenbrenner. Berkeley: Univ. of California Pr., 1956.

Copleston, Frederick C. *Contemporary Philosophy: Studies of Logical Positivism and Existentialism*. London: Burns & Oates, 1956.

Ferrater Mora, José. *Philosophy Today: Conflicting Tendencies in Contemporary Thought*. New York: Columbia Univ. Pr.; Oxford: Oxford Univ. Pr., 1960.

Grene, Marjorie. *Philosophy In and Out of Europe*. Berkeley and London: Univ. of California Pr., 1976.

Honderich, Ted, and Myles Burnyeat, eds. *Philosophy as It Is*. New York and Harmondsworth, Middlesex: Penguin, 1979.

Kaplan, Abraham. *In Pursuit of Wisdom: The Scope of Philosophy*. Beverly Hills, Calif.: Glencoe Pr.; London: Collier Macmillan, 1977.

———. *The New World of Philosophy*. New York: Vintage, 1961.

Nozick, Robert. *Philosophical Explanations*. Cambridge, Mass.: Belknap Pr. of Harvard Univ. Pr., 1981.

Scharfstein, Ben-Ami, ed. *Philosophy East/Philosophy West: A Critical Comparison of Indian, Chinese, Islamic, and European Philosophy*. Oxford and New York: Oxford Univ. Pr., 1978.

Schilpp, Paul Arthur, ed. *The Philosophy of Sarvepalli Radhakrishnan*. New York: Tudor, 1952.

PHILOSOPHY AROUND THE WORLD

A remarkable featuree of twentieth-century philosophy is its spread around the world, especially since World War II. The six-volume *Encyclopedia of Philosophy,* edited by Paul Edwards (1967) covers the history of philosophy in numerous countries and its twentieth-century developments. John Burr's *Handbook of World Phi-*

losophy (1980) emphasizes the revival of philosophical studies since World War II. The best handbook for quick, all-round information is W. L. Reese's *Dictionary of Philosophy and Religion: Eastern and Western Thought* (1980). (All three are cited in Part III.) Four important works are not included in the Burr volume's bibliographies: Henryk Skolimowski's study of Polish versus British analytic philosophy (1967), dealing with the period from 1895 to the early 1960s, Rüdiger Bubner's work on modern German philosophy (1981), Vincent Descombes's on modern French philosophy (1980), and Kwasi Wiredu's essays on African philosophy (1980). The once standard survey of contemporary European philosophy by I. M. Bochenski (1956, outlined above) is seriously out of date but still useful for historical purposes, as is Colin Smith's on French philosophy (1964).

Raymond Klibansky has edited two four-volume sets of studies surveying contemporary philosophy, each of which refers to literature from many areas. His *Philosophy in the Mid-Century* (1958–59) deals with the period 1848–1955; his *Contemporary Philosophy: A Survey* (1968–71) surveys 1956–67 (both are cited in Part III). Klibansky's aims are to highlight the main problems under discussion, to trace the course of their discussion, and to point out new trends.

Scandinavian Philosophy

A special note on the Scandinavians is fitting, since their contributions have usually required translation if they were to be used by others and since their interactions with other Europeans are of interest. From the mid-nineteenth century to the early twentieth century Swedish philosophy was dominated by the idealism of Christopher Jacob Boström, then countered on virtually all essentials by Uppsala philosophy, notably by Axel Hagerström, Adolf Phalén, and their successors. Most of these thinkers have not been translated.

Idealism was never strong in Finland during this period. Psychological studies were in the ascendency from the late nineteenth century on. However, British (though not Oxfordian) influence became strong in the twentieth century. Two distinguished Finnish philosophers taught in England, Edward Westermarck (University of London, 1907–30) and Georg Henrik von Wright (Cambridge, 1948–51) and have published in English. Von Wright is a widely discussed logician and analytic philosopher, as are his slightly older contemporaries, Erik Stenius and Jaakko Hintikka.

Although by far the greatest genius of Danish philosophers was Søren Kierkegaard, founder of existentialism, he has had very little influence on Danish philosophy. For nearly a century, from the mid-nineteenth century on, the most influential figure there was Harald Høffding, known best abroad for his two-volume *History of Modern Philosophy* (London, 1900).

Since Arne Naess became professor at Oslo in 1939, his interest in empirical semantics has brought about a renascence in Norwegian philosophy, following about seventy years of Hegelianism, during which nothing was published. Some of his work, like that of other Scandinavian contemporaries and successors, has appeared in English.

Bubner, Rüdiger. *Modern German Philosophy.* Tr. by Eric Matthews. Cambridge and New York: Cambridge Univ. Pr., 1981.
√ Descombes, Vincent. *Modern French Philosophy.* Cambridge: Cambridge Univ. Pr., 1980.
Skolimowski, Henryk. *Polish Analytical Philosophy: A Survey and a Comparison with British Philosophy.* New York: Humanities Pr.; London: Routledge & Paul, 1967.
Smith, Colin. *Contemporary French Philosophy: A Study in Norms and Values.* New York: Barnes & Noble; London: Methuen, 1964.
Wiredu, Kwasi. *Philosophy and an African Culture.* Cambridge and New York: Cambridge Univ. Pr., 1980.

8

Twentieth-Century
British Philosophy

Since Russell's and Moore's pioneering efforts around the turn of the century, British philosophers have continued to create most of the methodological features now to be identified as "analytic philosophy," although significant learning from philosophers in other English-speaking areas and elsewhere has increased. Here we view the story in three thematically separable parts—the early years, the years between the wars, and the post-World War II period, mostly to about 1960. Later trends are reflected more directly in all the other sections.

The Early Years

When G. E. Moore was at Cambridge in 1892 "metaphysics" tended to include all philosophy but ethics. Absolute idealism was in the ascendency. By the 1930s, all metaphysics in this sense, not only the narrower area, had come under widespread attack in Britain, and ethics was viewed in a manner in keeping with the newer "analytic" interests. Moore's philosophy teachers were Henry Sidgwick, James Ward, John McTaggart—three members of the Apostles, a secret intellectual club at Cambridge which, in its changing membership, was to have a marked effect on the future of philosophy (Levy, *Moore . . .* , 1979, cited on p. 188)—and G. F. Stout. Moore was for a time most affected by McTaggart, especially by his insistence on clarity, but has acknowledged that Sidgwick (1883–1900) greatly influenced his own *Principia Ethica* in both style and content. The influence of Ward (1843–1925) and his pupil Stout (1860–1944) is less noticeable, but both are distinctive less for their idealist, specula-

161

tive bent than for their considerable contributions to philosophy of mind and toward the establishment of psychology as a field separate from philosophy. Both Moore and Bertrand Russell were idealists in their early days; neither ever found it necessary to give up metaphysics altogether; both had also followed Sidgwick in advancing the tradition of Mill. So much for continuity. Both also used McTaggart's idealist philosophy in particular as a foil—actually beginning with Moore's critique of a passage from the *Logic* of McTaggart's idealist counterpart at Oxford, F. H. Bradley—while in later years Alfred North Whitehead drew from it to form his own process philosophy.

The change took remarkable effort. For one thing, nearly all the leading early twentieth-century British philosophers, including both Moore and Russell, were at some time modified Hegelians; and neither of these great instigators seems ever to have given up the metaphysical search to describe the whole of things. Even in the mid-1920s it was possible for such a noted observer as J. H. Muirhead (1924, 1925) to produce two volumes of contributions, representing "contemporary British philosophy," that were primarily suffused with the holistic spirit of Bradley and Bernard Bosanquet and that scarcely noticed the changes underway. G. J. Warnock (1969) has made the significant point, however, that despite the dominance of Absolute idealism in the late nineteenth and early twentieth centuries, such Continental-style thinking had never been in the mainstream tradition of British thought and was even then accompanied by other trends. One of these was the piecemeal realism of John Cook Wilson (1849–1915) and followers like H. A. Prichard (1871–1947) and H. W. B. Joseph (1867–1943)—a view that was to give historically minded R. G. Collingwood great difficulty during his entire tenure there from the 1910s through 1941.

How did the change come about? Around 1897–98, through numerous discussions together, G. E. Moore, while writing his dissertation on Kant, was beginning to take Russell with him down the path from idealism to realism. Moore's 1899 *Mind* article, "The Nature of Judgment," marked the way ahead for both philosophers. The decisive moment, however, came with publication of Moore's *Principia Ethica* in 1903, and in the same year the publication of his famous *Mind* article "The Refutation of Idealism." Russell's own extraordinary feat, *Principles of Mathematics,* also appeared in 1903. Unfortunately, Moore came heartily to dislike Russell. As a result, he would not include Russell in the annual Easter reading parties he organized from 1898 to 1914, parties that were important steps in the development of British philosophy. These events included many

Apostles (Russell was also a member) and most of those who would become members of the Bloomsbury Group, a company of influential intellectuals and artists who adopted him as their philosopher (Levy, 1979, cited above). However, the separate contributions of these two men to the new traditions of philosophical analysis probably derive far more from their primary backgrounds—Moore's in the classics, Russell's in mathematics—than in their relationship. In those days, Russell was making prodigiously concentrated inquiry into the foundations of mathematics and epistemology.

With Russell's publication of *Our Knowledge of the External World* (1914), logical atomism was available as a full-fledged metaphysics and method of philosophical analysis. Although Moore and Russell had had differences, their efforts were similar at base and mutually supportive until Ludwig Wittgenstein came to Cambridge in 1912. This book especially marks the result of that stimulus on Russell, who thereafter busied himself with a wide range of new problems related to philosophical logic, making large circles, while Moore stayed within the arena of epistemology and moral problems long customary in British philosophy, making very small circles. The two were to remain the major figures in British philosophy until well into the 1930s.

Particularly helpful accounts of this early period are those of A. J. Ayer (1971) and of ordinary language philosopher G. J. Warnock (1958). Other influential Cambridge philosophers were logician John Maynard Keynes (1883–1946), later a famous economist; the somewhat analytic, critical philosopher C. D. Broad (1887–1971; Schilpp, 1959); philosophical psychologist C. A. Mace (1894–1971); idealist A. C. Ewing (1899–1973); and the wide-ranging analytic philosophers Susan Stebbing (1885–1943), R. B. Braithwaite (1900–), and John Wisdom (1904–). A Cambridge symposium on British philosophy at mid-century, edited by Mace (1957, 1966), includes an account of Cambridge philosophy by C. D. Broad.

Between the Wars

As J. O. Urmson (1956) relates, within the decade after 1914 atomism as a metaphysics—that is, as a view of reality—was widely adopted among those sympathetic as a rationale for the method called logical analysis. The analytic method it referred to had already been formed, largely through application to epistemology of Russell's previous theories of description and logical construction. Problems inherent in the earlier approach—too technical and complex to depict here—led at the same time to metaphysical atomism and to the devising of another level of analytic method. Therein the strictly logical constructions contained in propositions are replaced, through use of extensional language, by names of possible objects of acquaintance in experience (versus inferred entities). The term "extensional" (versus intensional) referred to the beliefs that all atomic propositions are logically independent of each other and that all complex propositions are truth-functions of atomic propositions. Accordingly, "atomism," now conceived as a metaphysics as well as a logical doctrine, was concerned with acquiring new knowledge of the structure of facts, though not knowledge of new facts.

But how is the relation between analytically identified sentences and facts to be understood? Wittgenstein ventured a theory that conceived of such sentences as pictures of facts. Most other atomists tried other tactics, but the overall enterprise was short-lived both because defects were found—also too technical and complex to note here—and because by the mid-1930s metaphysics itself came to be rejected under new influence from Wittgenstein together with that from the Vienna Circle. To Ayer and the other positivists at that time philosophy must be restricted to a particular kind of analysis, namely the logical analysis of necessary truths, following the model of mathematics. Its subject matter is the language of science, which philosophy seeks to clarify by revealing the structure of that language and by reducing its expression to empirically based elements, often called "protocol sentences." Thereby the metaphysics of logical atomism was not only found to be seriously defective but was also held to be an improper element of genuinely analytic philosophy.

If the props are knocked out from under its rationale, what becomes of reductive analysis? The historical answer is that by the 1930s it began to come under attack, but it continued to be practiced, often in rather different forms and for different reasons. Moreover, analysis is still the prevailing attitude today, though its rubrics have greatly expanded beyond the generally agreed limits of reductive analysis to include, for example: (1) various forms of definition (especially definition in use, as in Russell's theory of descriptions); (2) clarification of common-sense statements by putting them into longer synonymous verbal paraphrases and examining the parts (Moore); (3) arguments on justification of belief (especially over whether indirect knowledge of something is inferred deductively or inductively and, if the latter, whether validly or not); (4) constructive reformulation of concepts (to sharpen them and make them more useful, such as examination of what necessary and sufficient conditions must or should be fulfilled for a concept to have clear meaning or to be useful for certain purposes—sometimes first by way of clearing up related puzzles, dilemmas, or paradoxes); (5) problem (re)formulation; (6) putting arguments, assumptions, theories or conjectures into forms that admit of precise, critical refutation or revision (as Karl Popper argued, basic to scientific practice); (7) unveiling systematically misleading expressions and category mistakes (Ryle); (8) descriptive metaphysics (a Kantian program, Strawson); (9) tightly formulated explanation; (10) comparative analysis (for any of the above purposes); and (11) careful study of ordinary language usage (Austin). In all, the emphasis is on logically clear analysis of thought, not of the psychological process of thinking, and the chosen method is analysis of language.

In the late 1930s some philosophers, at Oxford above all, were moving especially toward ordinary language analysis of the Austinian sort, which erupted on the scene after the war. All the forms of analysis just mentioned came to be used and further developed in the postwar period, however. Wittgenstein's work, which was heavily directed to language uses (not all of them in ordinary language, as was in principle also true of Austin) but was concerned with a wide range of philosophical problems (for example, memory, perception) that are not strictly about language, stimulated several of them (most notably numbers 4, 5, 7, 8, and 11). At that time, only a few British philosophers joined Carnap in continuing the old program through analysis of artificial languages.

At this juncture, A. J. Ayer's story (1977) becomes important—at first indicative of the growing trend, then focal in it, then in some respects divergent from it. (Other works by him are cited below and in chapters 10 and 15.) When Ayer (1910–) went up to Oxford in 1929 the three philosophy professors—Hegelian idealist Harold Joachim (1868–1938), Italian idealist J. A. Smith (1863–1930), and Cook-realist H. A. Prichard—were near the end of their careers. All three were hostile to the analytic movement that had by then gained great strength at Cambridge. His principal tutor was the twenty-nine-year-old Gilbert Ryle (1900–76) who, with other dons of the time later to become professors—H. H. Price (1899–) and R. G. Collingwood—had independence from that rather stifling atmosphere and attitude and were developing positions of their own. (Ryle succeeded Collingwood in the Chair of Metaphysics upon his death in 1943. Ryle's collected papers, 1971, are cited here as is a posthumous book on "thinking," 1979. Others of his works are cited in chapters 2 and 19.)

From early on, Ayer, like many of his British confrères, was especially interested in epistemology, having neither background nor inclination toward mathematics and philosophy of science. The budding philosopher learned of Wittgenstein's *Tractatus* (1921) from Ryle in 1931 and met him in Cambridge the following summer. This encounter made an overwhelming impression on him, he reports, and disposed him toward his later advocacy of logical analysis; but he had taken the principle of verifiability from Hume before he knew of Wittgenstein or of Viennese positivism. In 1932–33, on Ryle's advice, he went to Vienna. W. V. O. Quine was also there, having just obtained his Harvard doctorate, and the two visitors became members of the Vienna Circle (Ayer thinks they were the only visitors ever to become members). Then he returned to teach at Oxford. The journal *Analysis* was founded in 1933, arising from common logical-empirical interests discovered among a number of philosophers attending joint sessions of the Mind Association and the Aristotelian Society held at various universities. Moore was then quite in evidence at those meetings and held special seminars each time on Sunday mornings, exciting occasions for the analytically minded.

The immediate post-World War I period was also highly productive of metaphysical systems—for example, neorealist Samuel Alexander's *Space, Time and Deity* (1920), McTaggart's neo-Hegelian *The Nature of Existence* (1921), and Whitehead's *Process and Reality* (1929, cited on p. 215). More extensive interaction than in any previous period commenced with American philosophers, who were among other things working out new versions of metaphysical and epistemological realism, idealism, and Kantian views. Collingwood's *Speculum Mentis* (1924, cited later in this chapter) announced the major task of philosophy to be a historically oriented critical review of the chief forms of human experience (especially knowledge of the aesthetic, religion, science, history, and philosophy). Like Popper (until the 1950s), Collingwood got scarce notice within the mainstream of British philosophy; today he is among the few philosophers from that period to retain currency.

After World War II

Just before World War II, two activities among Oxford philosophers prepared the way for a radical change that occurred there after the war. This change caused the somewhat misleadingly called "Oxford philosophy" to be de rigueur in Britain from the late 1940s to the late 1960s. The first activity was of a quiet, ordinary sort—a discussion group led by J. L. Austin (1911–60). Austin had come up to Oxford in 1929, the same year as Ayer, and was elected to a fellowship in 1933. There Wilson and Prichard, like Moore but without his grand flair, had been noted for their predilection to plain language and slow, painstaking examination of minute points. These qualities the austere Austin was to raise to a fine art, all in the service of clarity. As an undergraduate he was especially stimulated by Prichard's epistemological interests and manner. Trained in the classics, during the 1930s Austin was occupied with textual studies of several great philosophers, especially Plato, Aristotle, Leibniz, and Kant, whereas in the postwar years historical references were rare. From 1936 to 1939 Austin led topical discussions on Thursday evenings in Isaiah Berlin's rooms, with Ayer, Stuart Hampshire, and two or three other philosophers, all in their twenties. The main topics were perception, a priori truths, counterfactuals, personal identity, and other minds, all to become major topics in the postwar period. As Berlin relates this story, Ayer and Austin were constantly at odds. It is no doubt fateful that in 1946 Ayer obtained a professorship at University College, London, where he remained for thirteen years before returning to Oxford (1959–78).

During the war Austin attained high distinction for his management of intelligence preparatory to the Normandy invasion. His experience of management through cooperative division of labor led to the Saturday morning sessions he held for many years after the war. Working in the same fashion on one topic each term—by invitation and at first quite formal, assigning tasks to each participant, then less so. This kind of process had a profound effect on the conduct of philosophy at Oxford, though the original plan was not replicated.

The second activity was a political revolt, led by Ryle, Ayer, and Austin against Joseph and Prichard. The new group had won by war's end, capturing almost all the philosophy posts—first Berlin, Hampshire, H. L. A. Hart (philosopher of law), J. O. Urmson, Friedrich Waismann, then many others—then lost cohesion within a few years' time (see Michael Dummett's account, *Truth and Other Enigmas,* 1978, cited on p. 325). Both the victory and the subsequent divergences are important factors in the history of philosophy over the next thirty years.

The strongest influence in the 1940s was Ryle's. One of his accomplishments was to promote addition of a doctoral degree, which attracted large numbers of students from abroad. His masterwork, *The Concept of Mind* (1949, cited on p. 370)—the first substantial application of the newer analytic style to a major traditional problem—was an epitome of the effort to base philosophy primarily in conceptual analysis, with special appeal (contrary to Wittgenstein) to psychological and semantic concepts, and (against Carnap, or rather something of a caricature of Carnap, at that time many American philosophers' friend but Ryle's sworn enemy) without any close tie to mathematics and science. These were the main characteristics of the newly dominant "ordinary language" philosophy for some years. At this time Wittgenstein's later work was coming to be more widely known as well.

Austin's famous "Other Minds" paper of 1946 also distinctly marked the change, as did his 1947 lectures on perception, published posthumously as *Sense and Sensibilia* (1962, cited on p. 325). (No book by Austin was published during his lifetime; his papers were collected in 1961 by Urmson and Warnock.) Austin's work was done without the growing fealty to Wittgenstein, or even much influence from this man, whose productions seemed to him to possess that very hastiness, inaccuracy, and oversimplification that he now decided had been disastrous in most previous philosophy. Unlike Wittgenstein, Austin also intended to gain new knowledge from analysis of ordinary language, a work to be approached without doctrinal or methodological preconceptions, and to reach definite solutions. Only attention to particular problems counted for Austin, bringing whatever help one could get from outside of philosophy. The aim was to advance discussion of the problem, not to attain a general doctrine, though in order to advance discussion about language he did try to form a general theory of speech-acts, first outlined in his 1955 Harvard lectures *How to Do Things with Words* (1962, cited on p. 344). Thereby his analyses of language were directed not only to statements, previously the preoccupation of philosophers, but to "performative" utterances as well—that is, to utterances by which something is done (for example, promises).

The first successor to J. H. Muirhead's 1924–25 volumes, edited by H. D. Lewis (1956), shows how very far the changes had come, though the approaches were numerous and several of the twenty contributors were not analytic philosophers. In the next volume (Lewis, 1976) almost all the eighteen contributors had adopted chiefly analytic methods in their work. Lewis's own papers (1962, from 1947 on) are somewhat outside the trend in that they do not follow the prevailing linguistic interests; five are critiques of nineteenth-century idealist T. H. Green, and several are on theological discourse.

By 1960 about sixty tenured philosophers were teaching at Oxford, enjoying about twenty-eight weeks a year out of term and, compared with many of their colleagues elsewhere, relatively free from administrative responsibilities and official pressure to publish. Students were taught to seek logical rigor and clarity above all else, and chiefly in terms of their own language. Although Oxford then set the general tone for British philosophy, and for much of it elsewhere in the English-speaking world, it was said to be not so much a school of philosophy as a school for philosophers.

Three collections of essays chosen by Antony Flew (1951, 1953, 1956, cited on p. 345) probably did as much as the critics of linguistic philosophy to bring analytic philosophy to the attention of philosophers elsewhere and to foster a narrow identification of "ordinary language philosophy" with "Oxford philosophy" and "analytic philosophy." Almost all the authors Flew chose were people whose work Russell disapproved of. Other collections of that period redress the imbalance, especially those edited by C. A. Mace (1957, 1966), by New Zealand (later American and Canadian) philosopher R. J. Butler (1962, 1965), and by Bernard Williams and Alan Montefiore (1966). So do the brief retrospective essays by Ayer et al. (1956), introduced by Ryle, under the title *The Revolution in Philosophy,* and P. F. Strawson's 1968 collection of British Academy lectures (1958–66).

In the mid-1950s Strawson, himself an Oxford fellow and a leading advocate of ordinary language analysis, had shifted to descriptive metaphysics (*Individuals . . . ,* 1959, cited on p. 359). By the mid-1970s a younger Oxonian, Michael Dummett (1978, cited earlier), could aptly and approvingly remark that nearly everyone there was doing metaphysics. This could readily have been said in 1960, though it would usually have been called logic then and was radically skeptical. Not all metaphysical discourse purported to be merely descriptive of the structures of our thought about the world, though little was pursued in the grand manner of their idealist predecessors.

Excellent symposia on a few of the main actors in the postwar drama have appeared: on Ryle (Konstantin Kolenda, 1972; and critical essays edited by Oscar Wood and George Pitcher, 1970), on Austin (K. T. Fann, 1969), and on Ayer (G. F. Macdonald, 1979).

Critiques of Linguistic Philosophy

Two works devoted to criticism of linguistic philosophy must be mentioned here because of their influence. Although they are full of inaccuracies, they do reflect important features of what had become a hot debate over the nature and proper functions of philosophy. The most noted work is that by Ernest Gellner (1959), favorably introduced by Russell. Gellner continued this open opposition in later writings. Both this work and one by C. W. K. Mundle (1970) were reissued in 1979. Typical among these and other critiques are arguments to the effect that linguistic philosophy simply purveys biased or unfounded cultural assumptions, is not logically rigorous, begs serious questions by simply referring to language usage, oversteps the proper analytic bounds of philosophy by moving into empirical areas, is empirically inaccurate, ignores better linguistic theory, or confuses truth with "ordinary" opinion. A collection of nineteen previously published essays on specific topics, edited by H. D. Lewis (1963), is intended to offer a working critique from several quarters, including those inhabited by A. J. Ayer, A. C. Ewing, J. N. Findlay, and Stuart Hampshire. From the Thomist domain is a critical study by Maxwell Charlesworth (1959). Wolfe Mays and S. C. Brown (1971) have edited contributions on phenomenological methodology and on several themes (freedom and determinism, the person, aesthetics, mind and body, good and evil) by a range of philosophers, including some phenomenologists and some analytic philosophers. The conference report contains elements of a dialogue between British and Continental thinkers on matters of common interest.

A workmanlike study by Keith Graham (1977), which perhaps overemphasizes Austin's role in the postwar analytic movement, uses criticisms of Austin's approach to several problems to support the view that study of ordinary usage is a stultifying, wrongly conservative approach to philosophical problems. The collection from the 1975 Oxford International Symposium, edited by Gilbert Ryle (1977), is a fitting contrast to this study both in its analytic variety and in its witness to the spread of analytic and not just ordinary language philosophy to the Continent. Bryan Magee's (1971) illuminating B.B.C. conversations with thirteen leading British philosophers also evidences the growing diversity, as does his follow-up series (1978). These are both autobiographical and expository in form.

In a critical-historical examination of themes in linguistic philosophy from a Marxist, Maurice Cornforth (1965) attempts to show its social role as an "establishment" philosophy and argues that philosophical theories like Marxism need not depend on a muddled use of language. A section of the book is devoted to presenting his own

Marxist philosophy (metaphysics, dialectics, axiology, moral and so-cial philosophy, etc.), using concepts learned about language and logic from linguistic philosophy.

In the 1970s one form of protest was the gathering of ten or so volumes in the Harvester Press "Philosophy Now" monograph series, edited by Roy Edgley (not cited here). Its aim was to move beyond ivory tower specialism and to establish connections with the practical problems facing philosophy and with Continental thought. Although a modest effort, the intent was met and it was indicative of allied pressures within the field.

Austin, John L. *Philosophical Papers.* Ed. by J. O. Urmson and G. J. War-nock. Oxford: Clarendon Pr., 1961.

Ayer, Alfred J. *Part of My Life: The Memoirs of a Philosopher.* New York and London: Harcourt, Brace, 1977.

———. *Russell and Moore: The Analytic Heritage.* Cambridge, Mass.: Har-vard Univ. Pr., 1971.

———, et al. *The Revolution in Philosophy.* New York: St. Martin's Pr.; London: Macmillan, 1956.

Butler, Ronald J., ed. *Analytical Philosophy.* 1st and 2nd series. Oxford: Blackwell, 1962, 1965.

Charlesworth, Maxwell John. *Philosophy and Linguistic Analysis.* Pitts-burgh, Pa.: Duquesne Univ. Pr., 1959.

Cornforth, Maurice C. *Marxism and the Linguistic Philosophy.* New York: International; London: Lawrence & Wishart, 1965.

Fann, K. T., ed. *Symposium on J. L. Austin.* New York: Humanities Pr.; London: Routledge & Paul, 1969.

Gellner, Ernest. *Words and Things: A Critical Account of Linguistic Philoso-phy and a Study in Ideology.* Rev. ed. Boston: Beacon Pr.; London: Gol-lancz, 1979. (1st ed., 1959.)

Graham, Keith. *J. L. Austin: A Critique of Ordinary Language Philosophy.* Hassocks, Sussex: Harvester Pr., 1977.

Kolenda, Konstantin, ed. *Studies in Philosophy: A Symposium on Gilbert Ryle.* Houston, Tex.: William Marsh Rice Univ., 1972.

Lewis, Hywel D. *Freedom and History.* New York: Humanities Pr.; London: Allen & Unwin, 1962.

———, ed. *Clarity Is Not Enough: Essays in Criticism of Linguistic Philoso-phy.* London: Allen & Unwin, 1963.

———, ed. *Contemporary British Philosophy: Personal Statements.* 3rd and 4th series. New York: Macmillan; London: Allen & Unwin, 1956. Repr.: Atlantic Highlands, N.J.: Humanities Pr.; London: Allen & Unwin, 1976.

Macdonald, G. F., ed. *Perception and Identity: Essays Presented to A. J. Ayer with His Replies.* Ithaca, N.Y.: Cornell Univ. Pr.; London: Macmil-lan, 1979.

Mace, Cecil A., ed. *British Philosophy in Mid-Century: A Cambridge Sym-posium.* 2nd ed. New York: Humanities Pr.; London: Allen & Unwin, 1966. (1st ed., 1957.)

Magee, Bryan, et al. *Men of Ideas: Some Creators of Contemporary Philosophy.* London: British Broadcasting Corp., 1978.
———, ed. *Modern British Philosophy.* London: Secker & Warburg, 1971.
Mays, Wolfe, and S. C. Brown, eds. *Linguistic Analysis and Phenomenology.* Lewisburg, Pa.: Bucknell Univ. Pr., 1971; London: Macmillan, 1972.
Muirhead, John H., ed. *Contemporary British Philosophy: Personal Statements.* 1st and 2nd series. New York: Macmillan; London: Allen & Unwin, 1924, 1925.
Mundle, C. W. K. *A Critique of Linguistic Philosophy.* Oxford: Clarendon Pr., 1970. Repr.: London: Glover & Blair, 1979.
Ryle, Gilbert. *Collected Papers.* 2v. Vol. 1: *Critical Essays;* Vol. 2: *Collected Essays, 1929–1968.* London: Hutchinson, 1971. (Vol. 1 is on other philosophers.)
———. *On Thinking.* Ed. by Konstantin Kolenda. Oxford: Blackwell, 1979.
———, ed. *Contemporary Aspects of Philosophy.* Boston: Oriel Pr., 1977. (Oxford International Symposium, Christ Church College, 1975.)
Schilpp, Paul Arthur, ed. *The Philosophy of C. D. Broad.* New York: Tudor, 1959.
Strawson, P. F., ed. *Studies in the Philosophy of Thought and Action.* Oxford and New York: Oxford Univ. Pr., 1968. (A selection of British Academy lectures from 1958 to 1966.)
Urmson, J. O. *Philosophical Analysis: Its Development between the Two World Wars.* Oxford: Clarendon Pr., 1956.
Warnock, Geoffrey J. *English Philosophy since 1900.* 2nd ed. Oxford and New York: Oxford Univ. Pr., 1969. (1st ed., 1958.)
Williams, Bernard A. O., and Alan Montefiore, eds. *British Analytic Philosophy.* New York: Humanities Pr.; London: Routledge & Paul, 1966.
Wood, Oscar P., and George Pitcher, eds. *Ryle: A Collection of Critical Essays.* Garden City, N.Y.: Doubleday Anchor; London: Macmillan, 1970.

BERTRAND RUSSELL (1872–1970)

The Long Career

Bertrand Russell's publications in technical and popular philosophy stretch for seventy-three of his ninety-seven years, overall a collection marked by unusual verve, clarity, and originality. Moreover, in his case more obviously than most, the more personal aspects of the story are luminescent features of the philosophy itself.

Russell was brought up by his father's aristocratic parents. On their country estate he spent a great deal of his time alone in their garden. His mother had died when he was two and his father about a year and a half later, and he knew little about their lives until he was twenty-one. Their absence seemed to have haunted him his entire life. Russell's formal training in mathematics began at age eleven, with the study of Euclid. As he approached puberty, he became a misera-

ly lonely child. Mathematics then saved him, as he reports, from
elf-doubt and suicide, as did intense scholarly work, love of nature,
nd numerous passionate attachments to women throughout his
dult life.

From his college days until at least into his fifties, the Whiteheads
vere Russell's surrogate family. Alfred Whitehead was his mentor,
ong-time sponsor for academic positions, friend, and collaborator.
,velyn Whitehead was probably one of the three deepest loves of his
fe (in this case an unconsummated one)—the others being Lady
)ttoline Morrell and Lady Constance (Colette) Malleson; and she
'as also his close confidante, steady guide, and supporter. In 1901,
rhen observing her in intense pain, apparently from a heart attack,
,ussell underwent a sudden, life-changing "conversion." Within
1inutes, through identification with what he thought was her un-
peakable and tragic loneliness from her husband's neglect, and expe-
iencing thoughts of the evil inherent in the use of force to solve
uman problems (as Whitehead was not a man of force, the connec-
on is not clear), Russell was overcome with feelings of love and
entleness. Thoughts of the Boer war in South Africa suddenly led
im to become a pacifist and anti-imperialist, and he found within
imself an intense love of children, indeed of all humanity, and a
ecognition that children loved him. At that moment he also felt that
 public school education, allied in his mind with the use of force
ather than love, was "abominable," and that "in human relations
ne should penetrate to the core of loneliness in each person and
peak to that." Although the mood faded, the changes that particular
xperience wrought never left him. The analytic mode remained
trong but accompanied and suffused by all these interests.

In effect, Bertrand Russell was a virtuoso of depression, by such
1eans fighting it continually, for long periods on a daily basis. What-
ver merits his philosophical work may have in its own right, and
1ese are considerable, neither its motives, its contents, nor its form
an, I think, be separated from this central reality.

On his eightieth birthday Russell spoke of three strong passions
1at had governed his life: "the longing for love, the search for
nowledge, and unbearable pity for the suffering of mankind"—the
1tter, he said, out of his own continual and profound inner pain.
)uring his twenties and thirties he especially searched for a certain
ase for the sciences in the impersonal truth of mathematics. At forty
e wrote to Colette Malleson: "The centre of me is always and
ternally a terrible pain—a curious wild pain—a searching for some-

thing beyond what the world contains, something transfigured and infinite—the beautific vision—God—I do not find it, I do not think it is to be found—but the love of it is my life—like a passionate love for a ghost. At times it fills me with rage, at times with wild despair, it is the source of gentleness and cruelty and work, it fills every passion that I have—it is the actual spring of life within me." As with other atomists (Buddhists, Muslim Mitakallimun, Hume, Mach, James, and the early Wittgenstein), as Ben-Ami Scharfstein (*The Philosophers*, 1980, cited on p. 7) has outlined the approach, experience became an atomic construction; a coherent, substantial self is not seen to exist; human beings are viewed only as assemblages; "mind" and "matter" are thought to be constructions out of something prior to both; and a metaphysical sense of causality is denied. Russell added a belief in the fundamental independence of both things and persons from each other.

As Ronald Jager (1972) argues, Russell's entire philosophical output can be seen as expressing the relentless exploration of one specific hypothesis, namely (in Jager's words) that "philosophical scrutiny begins at the subjective pole, where certainty lies, and works outward in criticism, reconstruction, tentative hypothesizing, toward the public world, and then beyond to the structure of systematized science"—that is, from immediate perception to scientific objectivity, viewed as an escape from subjectivity. He appropriately distinguishes three phases, in which Russell in effect lives through the classical systems of the seventeenth and eighteenth centuries: a realist (Cartesian) phase, from 1898 to 1912; an atomistic, antiskeptical (Leibnizian) phase, to roughly 1920; and a relatively neutral (Humean) phase, for the remainder, in which mind and matter are interpreted as what Russell (drawing from Whitehead) called "logical constructions" from metaphysically neutral stuff. "Wherever possible," Russell had already said before 1920, "logical constructions are to be substituted for inferred entities" (*Mysticism and Logic*, 1918, p. 156). In this last phase Russell was quite skeptical about whether philosophy, contrary to science, can achieve firm results. Two main themes run through all three phases: the use of logical analysis, especially to eliminate surplus meaning and in piecemeal fashion to work toward logical synthesis, and efforts to show reciprocity between the technical and the more general aspects of philosophy.

Russell started out a Hegelian, under the influence of John McTaggart. In 1895, his first year after undergraduate study, and a fellow at Cambridge, he decided to devote his life to philosophy. Especially under the stimulus of G. E. Moore, he began to emerge from idealism, abandoning Kant and Hegel in 1898. Intensely excited after meeting the great Italian logician Giuseppe Peano in 1900, he wrote a first draft of one of his finest works, *The Principles of Mathematics,* that year. The decade 1900–10 became the most intellectually fertile period of his entire life. By 1910 he had also become very active in politics and had already lost in a race for Parliament. Like many mathematicians and scientists at his age (now nearly forty), he also then felt unable to concentrate on abstractions with the intensity on which he had long relied.

Unlike his university mentor, Whitehead, whose life and thought was intricately intertwined with his own during his most philosophically productive years, Russell started writing voluminously almost as soon as he began to form views of his own, and he never stopped writing. Over the some ʈ nty years of close collaboration in philosophy and logic at a b, ,ic level, Whitehead was by far the more careful an ˙ exacting thinker, and perhaps the more creative question-finder, whereas Russell was the quick-witted leaper and the more driven pursuer of an idea. Hence it is somewhat ironic that Whitehead went on to more speculative, reconstructive activity after their joint masterpiece, *Principia Mathematica* (1910–13), was completed (except for a projected fourth volume on geometry, which they started but never finished) and that Russell continued his search for reductive simplicity through painstaking analysis. In these later works, moreover, Russell's extraordinary swift, eloquent way of working out a problem sharply contrasts with Whitehead's thicker, sometimes vaguer, more deliberate style. Nor is the style separable from the content in either case.

Whereas in the 1895–1905 period Whitehead was led to give up the quest for certainty, confronted by the overthrow of Newtonian physics and new developments in mathematics, Russell was unceasingly driven by this quest, though not without numerous bouts of despair. The strong contribution of G. E. Moore to his conception of analysis and of the young Wittgenstein to his atomism—with his philosophy of mathematics and his later extensive work in what he called "popular philosophy," two of his four major legacies to subsequent philosophy—have already been noted. Immensely original, among his contemporaries Russell had an unsurpassed ability to take partially formed ideas—most notably from Leibniz, Frege, Meinong, and Whitehead, from mathematicians Dedekind, Cantor, and Peano, and from Moore and Wittgenstein—and to work them out in instructive, occasionally epoch-making new configurations, bent on the anvil of skeptical argument. The systematic impulse was also very strong in him. Like Whitehead, he brought an unusually fine historical culture into this work. Although neither man was noted for dogged accuracy of historical interpretation, both used engagemen with their predecessors very effectively. In the end, this motif contributed, alongside his "service to moral civilization," to his being awarded the Nobel Prize for literature in 1950. (Like Whitehead before him, Russell was given the Order of Merit in 1949.)

By the World War I period Russell, then in his forties, had done almost all the philosophical work for which he is famous among philosophers. His main concerns, he said, lay in the epistemologica domain. He expressed some sympathy for logical positivism and aspects of phenomenology, among the other movements of his time and for the early Wittgenstein. He had none for existentialism, the later Wittgenstein or other "ordinary language" trends in Britain after World War II, and very little for pragmatism. The motifs of Humean empiricism, naturalism, realism, and logical analysis in hi philosophy, plus his longevity as a productive thinker and his fre quent stays in the United States, yielded him sufficient allies to make him the most reputed philosopher of the twentieth century.

Publications and Concerns

Russell's first book was *German Social Democracy* (1896), lec tures given at the London School of Economics. This was accompa nied by four articles in mathematics that year and *An Essay on the Foundations of Geometry* in 1897. Five more articles on mathematics and science led up to his Leibniz treatise (1900), seven more to *The Principles of Mathematics* (1903)—a pattern of writing he was to follow over the next sixty years, almost annually from 1914 to 1960. In 1903 Russell was thirty-one years old. During the years of very close cooperation with Whitehead (from the 1890s to 1913), he published some forty-five articles on a variety of topics, including his great ones "On Denoting" (1905), presenting a theory of descrip tions partly worked out through critical analysis of Meinong' thought; "Mathematical Logic as Based on the Theory of Type' (1908); and "Knowledge by Acquaintance and Knowledge by De scription" (1911). He also issued *Philosophical Essays* (1910) an *The Problems of Philosophy* (1912), followed by his major epistemo logical work, *Our Knowledge of the External World as a Field fo Scientific Method in Philosophy* (1914). (In some significant parts of the latter work Whitehead complained to Russell that he had not acknowledged Whitehead's detailed contributions.) He was soon to change some key ideas worked out in this book.

As David Pears (1967) has indicated in his (misnamed) book on the subject, *Bertrand Russell and the British Tradition in Philosophy*, the main theme during the 1905–19 period is Russell's reconstruction of empirical knowledge. He asks: What does it mean to say something exists? To what extent can ordinary proper names occurring in sentences affirming or denying existence be replaced by descriptions? What kinds of knowledge are there (for example, knowledge by acquaintance versus knowledge by description, and factual knowledge versus a priori knowledge)? And what is their proper logical construction? Whereas Hume had given knowledge a psychological framework, Russell's was logical. To him sense-data are not located in the nervous system but are physical entities, and his philosophy dealt not with words and phrases but with propositions.

Russell lost his lectureship in 1915 because of his antiwar activities. Near war's end came *Mysticism and Logic and Other Essays* (1918). Meanwhile there had been three social-political works: *Principles of Social Reconstruction* (1916), *Political Ideals* (1917), and *Roads to Freedom: Socialism, Anarchism and Syndicalism* (1918).

A brief new period of philosophical activity first yielded an essay "On Propositions: What They Are and How They Mean" (1919) and lectures on "Philosophy of Logical Atomism" (1918–19), published in *Monist*. Although he had been presupposing elements of logical atomism since 1900, it was only completely worked out here, very largely, as he said, in order to explain certain ideas learned from Wittgenstein, of whom he had heard virtually nothing since 1914. Wittgenstein's critiques and the war agonies had undermined his confidence about what philosophy could do. Receiving in mid-1919 the manuscript of Wittgenstein's *Tractatus,* which Wittgenstein thought would solve all the problems they had worked on, did not change this perspective. Although Russell thought the work remarkable and helped see to its publication, he did not understand it and the two did not resume a working relationship as Wittgenstein had hoped. Two other works were begun during a six-month imprisonment for political writing associated with his ardent pacifist efforts, which took up much of the war years: *Introduction to Mathematical Philosophy* (1919) and *The Analysis of Mind* (1921). In the latter work he returned to some thoughts in *Problems of Philosophy* (1912), arguing for a kind of behaviorist position. That is, no radical distinction is to be made between mind and matter; psychological concepts can be reduced to nonpsychological ones. Thereafter Russell issued very little basic philosophical work, apart from some essays, the introduction and notes (from which Whitehead disassociated himself) to a reissuing of *Principia Mathematica* (1925), *The Analysis of Matter* (1927), and two very late works produced during his long sojourn in the United States (1938–43): *An Inquiry into Meaning and Truth* (1940), the William James Lectures at Harvard, formed especially vis-à-vis the logical positivists, and *A History of Western Philosophy* (1945). The history was written to show that "every important system is equally . . . an effect and . . . a cause of social relations" (Schilpp, 1944, p. 19). From about 1916 on, his chief ambition was to give people what philosophical guidance he could for life and politics. The next eighteen years after the war he devoted principally to money-making through journalism, lecture tours, and popular books. He made several lecture tours in America from 1921 to the mid-1930s.

In popular philosophy, between the wars he first wrote (excluding pamphlets) *The Practice and Theory of Bolshevism* (1920), an anticommunist analysis, and *The Problem of China* (1922), based respectively on visits to Russia and China in 1920, and *The Prospects of Industrial Civilization* (1923), written with his second wife, Dora Black, whom he married in 1921. In 1927 he and Dora opened the very progressive Beacon Hill School (which she kept open until the mid-1940s; he left it in 1932). She was mother of the first two of his three children. He also wrote on topics related to science: *The ABC of Atoms* (1923), *Icarus or the Future of Science* (1924), and *The ABC of Relativity* (1925). Further, *What I Believe* (1925) and *On Education Especially in Early Childhood* (1926), also entitled *Education and the Good Life* and written when his children were young, were accompanied by the popular summary, *An Outline of Philosophy* (1927), *Selected Papers of Bertrand Russell* (1927), and *Sceptical Essays* (1928).

This period came to a close with *Marriage and Morals* (1929), a bold and controversial discussion, *The Conquest of Happiness* (1930), *The Scientific Outlook* (1931), *Education and the Social Order* (1932), offering about the same position as in 1926 but wiser and not so optimistic in his psychology, *Freedom and Organization 1814–1916* (1934), *In Praise of Idleness and Other Essays* (1935), *Religion and Science* (1935), and *Which Way to Peace?* (1936). With his third wife, wed in 1936, he produced *The Amberly Papers*

(1937), an edited collection from his family archives. In 1931 he succeeded to the earldom upon the death of his brother. In that same year he renewed the relationship with Wittgenstein, who was not, however, to have much further influence on his thinking.

During Russell's stay in the United States he issued *Power: A New Social Analysis* (1938), followed by a year at the University of Chicago, and *Let the People Think: A Selection of Essays* (1940), after a year at the University of California at Santa Barbara, in addition to the two philosophical works already mentioned. He then suffered a scandalous revocation of his appointment at City College of New York because of his moral views. After a bitter public controversy over this event, he was rescued by being given a lectureship at the Barnes Foundation (1940–42), which provided him support to write his history of philosophy. In 1943, now seventy-two, he was granted a Fellowship at Cambridge; this was made a lifetime appointment in 1949.

After the war came his last book in the basic philosophical vein, *Human Knowledge: Its Scope and Limits* (1948), which includes his only extended discussion of the problem of induction, at age seventy-six, a twin book featuring nondemonstrative inference with *Human Society in Ethics and Politics* (1954). Then came *Authority and the Individual* (1949), *Unpopular Essays* (1950), *New Hopes for a Changing World* (1951), *The Impact of Science on Society* (1951), and *Why I am Not a Christian* (1957). Most of his books are still in print. In 1952 he had married a fourth and final wife, reportedly an ideal companion to life's end and a great support to him in his public efforts.

Through the B.B.C., Russell became a national figure after the war. From 1945 to his death in 1970 he was also a prominent fighter for control of atomic energy and after 1957 for nuclear disarmament, on which he spent a great deal of his energies. In the 1950s he was also noted for his attacks on the new linguistic philosophy.

Russell's extensive use of philosophical reflection for practical purposes has not been even distantly matched in either amount or influence in this century. In quality the closest approximations would perhaps be those of John Dewey and Lewis Mumford, a philosophical thinker who, like them, has enjoyed a long life but who early chose not to identify himself with academic philosophy. Appropriately, Russell's own story was the main occupation of his final works: *My Philosophical Development* (1959), *Bertrand Russell Speaks His Mind* (1960), and the three-volume climax, *The Autobi-*

ography of Bertrand Russell (1967–69), in itself a major work, written in his nineties.

Interpretations

In this century particularly, it is unusual to have extensive autobiographical material from a philosopher. Its availability has made possible an excellent biography by Ronald Clark (1976), which is rare in the field but curiously omits his bout with linguistic philosophy; a study of his philosophical development by Ronald Jager (1972), the first comprehensive analysis of his philosophy; a collection of fourteen essays on a wide range of Russell's work, basic and popular, edited by George Nakhnikian (1974); and an analytic work on his philosophy from 1905 to 1919 by David Pears (1967). In contrast, the analysis of particularly significant philosophical arguments by R. M. Sainsbury (1979) is nondevelopmental. Like Pears, he concentrates on Russell's contributions in epistemology and mathematical logic and his thinking on meaning, names, and reference. Elizabeth Eames (1969) focuses on his epistemology and related logical matters alone, as do most philosophers referring to Russell.

Several collections show developments in the discussion of Russell's philosophy. That edited by Paul Arthur Schilpp (1944) is not generally well thought of, but aspects of it are still of value. Those edited by E. D. Klemke (1970), David Pears (1972), J. E. Thomas and Kenneth Blackwell (1976), and George W. Roberts (1979) are of better quality. Klemke's contains sixteen old essays that have appeared since 1944 and ten new ones on his ontology, his theories of reference and descriptions, and his philosophy of logic and mathematics. These are the subjects chiefly treated in the twenty-six new essays edited for the Muirhead Library of Philosophy by Roberts. All but five of the sixteen essays included in Pears's volume were new, each treating some area of Russell's basic philosophy. About half of the Thomas and Blackwell collection of fourteen new essays cover other areas.

Apart from Russell's own works, two collections of his essays edited by others together comprise important resources on his basic philosophy. That edited by Robert Marsh (1956) contains ten major essays, eight of them from 1901 to 1924. The other two are "On Order in Time" (1936) and "Logical Positivism" (1950). Only "On Denoting" is repeated by Douglas Lackey (1973). All but two of these are from the 1904 to 1911 period: "Mr. Strawson on Refer-

ring" (1957) and "Is Mathematics Purely Linguistic?" (1950–52).
Other Russell books are cited in chapters 1, 15, 16, and 30.

Clark, Ronald W. *The Life of Bertrand Russell*. New York: Knopf, 1976.
Eames, Elizabeth Ramsden. *Bertrand Russell's Theory of Knowledge*. New York: Braziller, 1969.
Jager, Ronald. *The Development of Bertrand Russell's Philosophy*. New York: Humanities Pr.; London: Allen & Unwin, 1972.
Klemke, E. D., ed. *Essays on Bertrand Russell*. Urbana: Univ. of Illinois Pr., 1970.
Nakhnikian, George, ed. *Bertrand Russell's Philosophy*. London: Duckworth, 1974.
Pears, David. *Bertrand Russell and the British Tradition in Philosophy*. 2nd ed. London: Fontana, 1972. (1st ed., New York: Random House, 1967.)
———, ed. *Bertrand Russell: A Collection of Critical Essays*. Garden City, N.Y.: Doubleday Anchor, 1972.
Roberts, George W., ed. *Bertrand Russell Memorial Volume*. New York: Humanities Pr.; London: Allen & Unwin, 1979.
Russell, Bertrand. *The Autobiography of Bertrand Russell*. 3v. Vol. 1, *The Early Years: 1872–World War I*; vol. 2, *The Middle Years: 1914–1944*; vol. 3, *The Final Years: 1944–1969*. Vols. 1–3: New York and London: Bantam Books, 1968–70; London: Allen & Unwin, 1967–69. Vols. 1–2: Boston: Little, Brown, 1967–68. Vol. 3: New York: Simon & Schuster, 1969; London: Allen & Unwin, 1967–69.
———. *Essays in Analysis*. Ed. by Douglas Lackey. London: Allen & Unwin, 1973.
———. *Logic and Knowledge: Essays, 1901–1950*. Ed. by Robert Charles Marsh. London: Allen & Unwin, 1956.
———. *My Philosophical Development*. New York: Simon & Schuster; London: Allen & Unwin, 1959.
Sainsbury, Richard M. *Russell*. London: Routledge & Paul, 1979.
Schilpp, Paul Arthur, ed. *The Philosophy of Bertrand Russell*. 3rd ed. New York: Tudor, 1951. (1st ed., 1944.)
Thomas, J. E., and Kenneth Blackwell, eds. *Russell in Review: The Bertrand Russell Centenary Celebrations at McMaster University, Oct. 12, 1972*. Toronto: Samuel Stevens, 1976.

G. E. MOORE (1873–1958)

The Life in Cambridge

Something of the nature and influence of G. E. Moore's philosophy has already been depicted in this chapter, as it is integral to the early history of analytic philosophy. Commentators close to Moore agree that his impact came chiefly from his personal character and his style as a philosopher. Nevertheless, his realist, "common-sense" oriented beliefs would appear to be inseparable either from his character or his method. From his early years on, Moore had an unusual passion for clarity and a capacity to electrify people, which with other remarkable traits are said to have accounted more than any particular doctrines for his unexcelled influence at Cambridge and beyond for half a century.

Although Moore himself was unclear even in later years as to what his famed "method" had been—perhaps because he took it so much for granted—it is possible to detect consistent evidence of it throughout his works. Briefly, on a consistently realist base (after the very early years), he analyzed "concepts" (in his earlier works, "facts") into the purportedly plainer components of other identical concepts, cutting off excrescent meanings or dismissing them altogether as nonsense. (Almost all of what interested him for such purposes, he said, came from other philosophers, not science or other external sources.) He then constructed a clarification of some issues to which they refer, or an account of the meaning or truth of propositions in which they appear, according to the best evidence and most plausible arguments available to him. In doing so, Moore trusted implicitly in his own perceptions and in the possibility of communicating, on a "common-sense" basis, with others about these perceptions, getting as close to ordinary beliefs (not necessarily to ordinary usage) as he could. To discredit a view he normally tried to reduce it to absurdity or used an example to show that it cannot achieve what it says it does. In all of this, Moore maintained a strict separation and independence of the known or perceived object from the knowing or perceiving subject. As the years went by his unrelenting skepticism led to his increasing puzzlement and pessimism over beliefs he had once held as certain.

As to the externals, in marked contrast to Russell he was so ensconced in his own customary pursuits, and so comfortably accepting of its cultural terms, that only once did he break away to participate in any of the major aesthetic, scientific, moral, or political controversies of his time. This was on the occasion of World War I. On January 20, 1915, Moore finally made up his mind about the war and came out against it (as had most of the Apostles, whose part in his life will be noted below, although McTaggart, Ward, and Whitehead were vigorously in favor of it). He went so far as to distribute leaflets at the train station. By April 1916, after great agonizing, he had nonetheless reconciled himself to military service; but he was never called up.

In most of these respects, including the almost exclusive attention to the narrower pursuits of philosophy, Moore ran within the main-stream of analytic philosophy and helped to form it. In other respects he ran against the stream. He had no penchant for mathematics or symbolic logic; he imbibed neither scientific nor historical culture; he held nonnaturalist views in ethics; he believed in the synthetic a priori; and he had neither reformist nor system-building inclinations.

Moore grew up in a suburb near London, within an affluent, middle class, devoutly Baptist family. He was born fifth among four girls and four boys. From ages eight to eighteen he attended Dulwich College, a mile's walk from his home, working almost entirely in the classics. It was a lonely but enjoyable time, he said. Among all the events of his childhood and youth, he singled out one for special mention (Schilpp, 1942): for several years, from age eleven or twelve on, he faithfully participated in an "ultraevangelical" group of young men during summer holidays at the beach, distributing tracts and witnessing to people about "the love of Jesus." This he did with great embarrassment but also with a feeling that his eager and dutiful efforts were never sufficient. For several years afterward he contin-ued daily to read the Bible and take part in after-breakfast family devotions, but by his late teens his beliefs had faded away into "com-plete agnosticism." This later position he attained especially through conversations with his three-year-older brother, Thomas Sturges Moore, then an art student, later a well-known poet and critic. This deeply conflictual experience at the turn into adolescence may well betoken his later reluctance to take up causes of any kind or to purvey settled answers, even in philosophy. It may also have helped to funnel into adult life the singular combination of traits in Moore that others saw, many of which often led them to become his enthu-siastic followers: the bold probing; the passionate confutation of error and confusion; the obsessive, patient pursuit of details; the utter seriousness and unassumingness; the exquisitely pure, inspiring appearance; the occasional titanic wrath together with his amazing childlike innocence, simplicity, and naiveté.

When Moore entered Trinity College, Cambridge, in 1892, he be-came enormously excited at the opportunity for intelligent conversa-tion. Among those he met early was Bertrand Russell (two years ahead of him), whose urging brought him to study philosophy, then a subject virtually unknown to him. Later he was to point out that what Russell owed to him was mostly early mistakes, which both came to reject, but that he owed a great deal to Russell's lectures; that he had spent more time studying Russell's writings than those of any other philosopher; and that he had gained much from conversations with Russell first from 1893 to 1901, then from 1911 to 1915, when both had rooms in Trinity. Thus, he had been "more influenced by him than by any other single philosopher," followed in degree by Wittgenstein and C. D. Broad. All three were also Fellows of Trinity. (Moore further acknowledged a special debt to A. N. Whitehead, also of Trinity, but without signifying its nature.) In 1903, Russell (in the preface to his *Principles of Mathematics)* had listed the following among his own philosophical positions at the time as specifically derived from Moore: (1) the nonexistential nature of propositions (except such as happen to assert existence) and their independence of any knowing mind; (2) pluralism of the sort that regards the world of existents and entities as composed of an infinite number of mutually independent entities, with relations that are ultimate and not reducible to adjectives of their terms or of the whole which these compose. Without these beliefs, Russell said, he had been unable to construct any philosophy of arithmetic; their effect was to liberate him from a large number of insuperable difficulties. No small praise.

In a book on Moore's life to 1914, unparalleled in its account of a philosopher's influences on those around him, Paul Levy (1979) has shown the astounding effectiveness of Moore within a small, secret club of Cambridge intellectuals called the Apostles, founded in 1820. Almost all the philosophers Moore knew in his twenties were Apostles, including all but G. F. Stout among his teachers; several of his friends were Apostles. Moore became Apostle No. 229 in February, 1894. As an infant philosopher Moore not only cut his teeth on the questions discussed with unusual openness, critical edge, and humor in this group. From his very first appearance he made the same electrifying impact that was later reputed of him. That evening, with great smoothness, earnestness, and intensity he defended the waggish proposition that news of the skepticism gained from the gloriously impractical education of Cambridge men should be spread abroad, until at last everyone is persuaded that the Cambridge-educated can know absolutely nothing. His first paper, delivered on May 12, was a defense of psychological and (against Sidgwick) ethical hedonism, which he had apparently been discussing with Russell.

Moore's social life burgeoned through these relationships, his loneliness ended. He became the Apostles' forty-ninth secretary in 1895, a position he held until 1901, by which time he had become its acknowledged spiritual leader. In all but two years, from 1898 through 1913, Moore organized annual reading parties. Those present chiefly comprised an inner group of Apostles, including most among them who were to become members of the Bloomsbury Group of artists and literati—Leonard Woolf, Lytton and James Strachey, J. M. Keynes, Harry Norton, Roger Fry, and Moore's close friend Desmond McCarthy—plus other Apostles (like Robert Trevelyan and Rupert Brooke) who were only on the fringes of Bloomsbury. (Only Roger Fry, Vanessa Bell, and very few others among the group did not come to regard themselves as disciples of Moore.) These people chiefly took from Moore's 1903 *Principia Ethica*, which made him famous and was a bible to them, its emphasis on rigorous, honest self-examination and on aesthetic, contemplative and intimately friendly pleasures. They do not appear to have dwelt much on his ideal utilitarianism (see the discussion in chapter 6, p. 144 on), though that too had a considerable influence on others in his lifetime, not all of them philosophers by any means.

Alfred Ainsworth, a brilliant young classics scholar, was for a decade after his election to the Apostles in 1899 the most important person in Moore's life. Although neither had or apparently expressed any overtly homosexual interest, in 1899–1900 Moore was infatuated with his new friend. (Russell told Virginia Woolf in 1924 that he then believed that the relationship ruined Moore as a philosopher, in that his *Principia Ethica* was not nearly so good as his remarkable 1899 *Mind* article on "The Nature of Judgment." The relation between Russell and Moore remained quite strained after this time.) In 1904 Moore joined Ainsworth in Edinburgh, where his friend taught Greek from 1903 to 1907. They lived there together over three years, then Moore set up household in Richmond, Surrey (the county of his boyhood) with two of his sisters. In 1908 Ainsworth married Moore's youngest sister. He did not himself marry until 1916, at age forty-three. His wife, Dorothy Ely, was a student twenty years his junior, whom he met in October 1915 just as he was being dropped by his first really close woman friend, Mary Fletcher. Two sons were born to this late but happy union, in 1918 and 1922.

Works and Interpretations

During most of the 1897 to 1903 period Moore's philosophy especially showed the influence of idealist F. H. Bradley. He published articles in *Mind,* in the *Proceedings of the Aristotelian Society* (for which society most of his subsequent writings were produced), and Baldwin's *Dictionary of Philosophy and Psychology.* By dint of two years' work, mostly on Kant's ethics, he was awarded a coveted six-year research fellowship at Trinity (1898–1904). He spent most of this period writing *Principia Ethica* (1903), which with his "Refutation of Idealism" article of the same year made his reputation. During the years out of a job (1904–11) he had sufficient inherited income to live on, left by his parents, who had recently died—and never really had to work thereafter. A few other essays were capped by the 1910–11 lectures *Some Main Problems of Philosophy,* not published until 1953, and *Ethics* (1912). In 1911 Moore was twenty-eight years old. In the remainder of his life only some essays and two collections of these appeared, no books.

Friends lured Moore back to Cambridge in 1911 by securing a lectureship, which he held until 1925. He was then a professor—succeeding James Ward, with McTaggart one of his two most favored professors—from 1925 to 1939, when he reached the mandatory age of retirement.

During this entire twenty-eight-year period Moore's life and work bore the signs of unusual fixedness and regularity, qualities consistent with details recorded in his earlier diaries (he had the ones after 1914 destroyed). For example, from 1911 to 1925 he gave three lectures a week on psychology; from 1918 to 1925 he added two lectures a week on philosophy of nature (as a part of metaphysics); from 1925 to 1939 he gave three lectures a week, nominally on metaphysics. During the entire twenty-eight years he also held a "conversation class" one hour a week, patterned after McTaggart's. These lectures were prepared in the days preceding each one, in the form of extensive notes, from which he did not read but talked, a habit that he said left him little time for any other scholarly work during term (at most a total of some twenty-two weeks a year). The rest of the time he was at home, in the company of friends, attending philosophical meetings in the area, or editing, but traveling and writing very little. In 1918 he was elected a fellow of the British Academy. From 1921 to 1947 he was editor of *Mind,* succeeding Stout (the centenary volume, January 1976, has articles on work done under its five editors to that time), during his lifetime one of the most prestigious journals in the field.

After his retirement in 1939, for one term he lectured weekly to large audiences at Oxford. He then spent 1940–44 in the United States, his only trip there, lecturing for a term each at several colleges and universities and giving single lectures at numerous other institutions. Having continued his customary life as the "philosopher's philosopher" in subsequent years, Moore was appointed to the Order of Merit in 1951, in his late seventies still active in many of the same old ways and highly reputed for it.

Since Moore's philosophical work is very far from being consistent or systematic, essays on particular points or areas of exploration are the best form for presenting his ideas. Thus, three collections of essays must head the list of the Moore literature. That edited by Paul Arthur Schilpp (1942) is of lasting value. It includes nineteen essays, chiefly on ethics, sense perception, and method and most by leading philosophers, a brief autobiography, and a 144-page "Reply." Among the sixteen essays presented by E. D. Klemke (1969), all appeared since 1939, most from 1962 on; four of them—one each by Herbert Hochberg and M. S. Gram and two by Klemke—are new. These are on his ethics, ontology, methodology, and epistemology, with some memories of the 1942 period by Morton White. A very different set of nineteen essays, some of them on less widely treated aspects of his philosophy, are edited by Alice Ambrose and Morris Lazerowitz (1970); nine of these are new, by Gilbert Ryle, Morris Lazerowitz, A. C. Ewing, W. E. Kennick, A. J. Ayer, William and Martha Kneale, Gordon Greig, Theodore Redpath, and J. O. Urmson. Klemke (1969) also published a careful examination of Moore's epistemology.

In addition to the two collections of Moore's own essays (1922, 1959) listed here and the 1910–11 lectures (1953), Casimir Lewy has also edited *The Common Place Books, 1919–1953* (Edinburgh University Press, 1962). The two works on ethics (1903, 1912, cited on p. 408) are the only others by Moore's hand to appear. As he said in 1942, he always wrote "slowly and with great difficulty," and he was typically "very lazy" about getting down to work, preferring to converse, to pursue aesthetic enjoyments (especially music—he could accompany himself on the piano while singing lieder) and to read stories of all kinds. What he did produce, however, constituted a story distinctly its own—persistently structured upon his realist assumptions, a story of a convivial philosopher who maintained an influence of over fifty years through arresting, sometimes trenchant analyses and proposals, many of which he himself came to reject, of a philosophical iconoclast who nonetheless took aesthetic, moral, and social reality pretty much as he found it, and of a plain-spoken man who demanded clarity of others (on his very special but increasingly popular terms), who took great pains to achieve what little he could for himself, and who encouraged others to do the same.

Ambrose, Alice, and Morris Lazerowitz, eds. *G. E. Moore: Essays in Retrospect.* New York: Humanities Pr.; London: Allen & Unwin, 1970.
Klemke, E. D. *The Epistemology of G. E. Moore.* Evanston, Ill.: Northwestern Univ. Pr., 1969.
————, ed. *Studies in the Philosophy of G. E. Moore.* Chicago: Quadrangle, 1969.
Levy, Paul. *Moore: G. E. Moore and the Cambridge Apostles.* London: Weidenfeld & Nicholson, 1979.
Moore, George E. *Philosophical Papers.* New York: Colliers, 1962; London: Allen & Unwin, 1959.
————. *Philosophical Studies.* London: Routledge & Paul, 1922. Repr., 1960.
————. *Some Main Problems of Philosophy.* London: Allen & Unwin, 1953. (His 1910–11 lectures, given at Morley College, London.)
Schilpp, Paul Arthur, ed. *The Philosophy of G. E. Moore.* Evanston, Ill.: Northwestern Univ. Pr., 1942.

R. G. COLLINGWOOD (1889–1943)

Achievement

R. G. Collingwood became Waynflete Professor of Metaphysical Philosophy at Oxford in 1935. He had been a fellow and tutor in philosophy at Pembroke College there since 1912, when he was graduated with a first in *Literae Humaniores* (historical and philosophical study of Greek and Latin texts), and had served as university lecturer in philosophy and Roman history since 1927. Since he had previously been forced to scratch out a living from teaching fees, only then did he obtain the relative calm necessary for writing out his more mature philosophical ideas somewhat systematically. Of his philosophical books only *Religion and Philosophy* (1916), *Speculum Mentis* (1924), *Outlines of a Philosophy of Art* (1925), and *An Essay on Philosophical Method* (1933) had so far appeared.

His last books were issued under the increasing pressure of failing health and in dismay over what he prophetically saw was happening to Western civilization in the 1930s. First came *The Principles of Art* (1938), *An Autobiography* (1939), and *An Essay on Metaphysics* (1940). The 1940 treatise was written in response to the antimetaphysical crisis that the influence of positivist A. J. Ayer's *Language, Truth and Logic* (1936) represented to him. His final book, *The New Leviathan* (1942), focused on political issues against the backdrop of a rather fully developed philosophy of mind. It was produced in response to the failure of Western governments and intellectuals, including his Oxford colleagues, to understand the significance of Nazism and fascism.

Illness forced Collingwood to resign his professorship in 1941, in which year he was appointed to the British Academy. He died on January 9, 1943, at the age of fifty-three. *The Idea of Nature* (1945) and *The Idea of History* (1946) were gathered from recent manuscripts and appeared posthumously. Twenty years later most of his philosophical essays were also collected in three volumes on his philosophy of art, history, and religion. Some of his writings remain unpublished or uncollected.

Collingwood's philosophy sharply contrasts with that of all the other noted British philosophers featured here. The distinctive greatness of his philosophy lies in his having found ways to explore the interrelatedness and historicity of human experience without sustaining the chief faults of speculative idealism, on the one hand, or succumbing to historicism or to any of the less palatable forms of relativism, on the other. (Although some of his critics have not granted these points, more recent studies would seem to require them.) At the same time, he was determined to escape what he took to be the disintegrative, often noncivilizing effects of much contemporary realism. That is, its piecemeal attention to details and refusal to consider the larger human picture or matters of historical development were linked, for him, to moral and political failure—eventually, most tragically to the inability to foresee or protest Nazi barbarism but also to the persistent miseducation of youth. Although his own methods and positions can be termed historical realism, as contrasted with positivist, logical-empiricist, and phenomenological realism, he early gave up the ascription "realism" because of the serious damage he believed these other forms were doing. The "minute" activities of Cook Wilson and company at Oxford and their harsh inhospitality to his own alternative ventures were a particularly bitter pill to swallow. Nor could he join forces with the idealists, though he could more nearly identify his thought as in succession to aspects of theirs and though he respected the more historically oriented work of contemporary Italian idealists.

Despite his short life and his isolation from the main strands of philosophy in his day, Collingwood's influence in several areas of philosophy continues to increase. His books are still in print forty years after his death, attractive not only because of their penetrating thought and their sparkling clear style but also because they contain one of the few truly fresh systematic efforts in this century, to some interpreters possibly the most promising one of all.

Collingwood worked especially in philosophy of art, history, language, science, religion, metaphysics, and action (including ethics, politics, and economics inseparably in annual lectures from 1918 to 1935, when he left Pembroke). Much of his work can now be re-termed philosophy of mind. Herman Stanage (in Michael Krausz, 1972) has claimed that "almost everything he ever wrote presents at least an implicit philosophy of education." Implications for logic and epistemology, which he pursued very differently from his contemporaries, are also present throughout. Among these dozen or so areas he contributed more to philosophy of art and philosophy of history than any other British philosopher of his time. His books on metaphysics and philosphical method are also major contributions. Collingwood attracted a great many students to his ethics lectures in the 1930s (like those on cosmology, still unpublished) and issued a major work on political philosophy near the end of his life. His short philosophical autobiography is a significant contribution to the genre in its own right, and it is possible through the succession of articles and incomplete larger works to see the developments of his intense forays of thought on each major area over a thirty-year period. (Collingwood was openly appreciative of Russell's willingness not to stick with formal anaysis but to share the struggles of his own thinking in some of these areas.)

Background and Development

Collingwood's background is little known but perhaps even more important to grasp than those of his other illustrious contemporaries, since his work as a philosopher contrasts so greatly with theirs. The following reconstruction of his early years draws from numerous sources and somewhat supplements the fine study on the 1889–1925 period by William Johnston (1967).

His grandfather, William Collingwood (1819–1903), was a landscape painter, as was his father William G. Collingwood (1854–1932), who had already exhibited before he joined the drawing school of the noted art critic and passionate social reformer John Ruskin (1819–1900) as an Oxford undergraduate in 1872. His mother was also a painter, mostly of miniatures and flowers, and a trained pianist who in her frequent playing for the family favored Chopin and Beethoven (he was to prefer Bach). As a boy Robin often accompanied his parents as they worked out-of-doors, perched between them with his own sketching pad. As a man he used highly developed drawing skills both for pleasure and to record archaeological artifacts. This life-long immersion in art—not only as recording but as seeing, feeling, understanding, and expression—became an essential feature in his philosophizing.

Other major features were contributed by the relationships with his father and with John Ruskin. As the ascendance of photography diminished the call for engravures, on which most landscape artists had made their living, Collingwood's father turned to studies of Scandinavian Britain, producing several well-written books and articles (especially from 1899 to 1927) and becoming acknowledged as a leading scholar on the subject. Collingwood's father kept in close touch with Ruskin in the 1870s, came to Ruskin's Brantwood estate in the Lake Country to be an assistant in 1881, his traveling companion in 1882 and thereafter, and then his aide and close friend until Ruskin's death in 1900, an artistic and literary executor thereafter. In 1883 he married Edith Mary Isaac (1857–1928) and settled into a nearby cottage. From there the couple moved with their two-year-old son and three daughters to Lanehead, Coniston, half a mile across Coniston Waters from Brantwood by boat, some two-and-a-half miles away by road. This is where Collingwood grew up. His family was of paltry means, and later a wealthy friend put him through Rugby and Oxford; but it was one of considerable culture. Along with modern history and the arts, geology and natural history were major topics in the family, illuminated on ramblings and drawing tours through the mountainous environs.

Until age thirteen Collingwood was taught by his father at home; after two or three hours of lessons each morning he was free to read (which he did, very widely), to roam this Wordsworthian countryside, to sail, or to write stories (as he did incessantly). His mind was filled with his father's precise, admiring talk about Ruskin, and he lived within a short distance of the old sage, who was of precarious (depressive) mental health and unable to travel or work after 1889, but who was much loved by the children of the area and was at times available to Collingwood in person.

At Ruskin's centennial in 1919 Collingwood stated that Ruskin, though not a philosopher in the strict sense, was "in philosophy the best-equipped mind of his generation." Such an intimacy with two older thinkers, combined with the considerable freedom he was granted to form his own thoughts, skills, and appreciations (with specific help when needed)—in short, such an education—is rare. The content was rarer still. In 1903, when Collingwood was fourteen, his father described the versatile Ruskin as "the last of the sages, lingering into an age of specialists. I do not rate him as an infallible authority, neither in taste, nor in ethics, nor in anything. But he was a great teacher, because he took you by the hand as he went on his voyage of discovery through the world; he made you see what he saw, and taught you to look for yourself." This was true of the father too, and of the son as Oxford don, almost all of whose teaching activities from 1912 to 1934 were spent in showing students how to interpret philosophical texts and to reflect upon the main forms of experience through the texts. Careful observation and accurate reconstruction were, moreover, always imbedded in the modes of seeing; and the objects were not so much separate atomic elements (as for Russell and Moore) but relations, processes, and wholes (as for Whitehead in his later years). Accordingly, Collingwood dedicated the most important of his early books, *Speculum Mentis* (1924, cited on p. 468), to his father, his "first and best teacher of Art, Religion, Science, History and Philosophy."

The father summarized Ruskin's art teaching (1891), from which numerous themes are recognizable in the son's aesthetics later on; he also wrote several other books on Ruskin, especially during Collingwood's early boyhood. The son could follow these works closely because he was a fluent reader at four. He began Latin at that age, Greek at six, and became expert in both. Later he added French, German, Italian, and Spanish. At eight he came across Kant's *Foundations of the Metaphysics of Morals,* which he was astonished to realize he could not understand but which excited him in its attention to "things of the highest importance." He felt then "as if a veil had been lifted and my destiny revealed."

In his 1919 centennial address on Ruskin, Collingwood recognized that the man was outright hostile to philosophy and avoided its study—except Plato, whom he repeatedly reread to the end of his life, but for anything but his metaphysics. Ruskin wrote no formal philosophy. Yet his mind had a remarkable philosophical nucleus, much of it held in an underlying manner and not examined. (In the *Essay on Metaphysics* Collingwood was to give a much-noted extension of this thought through an account of the "presuppositions" that underlie the thinking of a person or an age; these, too, are often unconscious and unexamined.) As a kind of "historical idealism" its characteristics were: (1) a belief in the unity and indivisibility of the human spirit (versus the compartmentalism of mental faculties, forms, or functions); (2) a quite modern historical-dialectical perspective on changing human reality (versus rationalist logic or mathematics); (3) extreme tolerance of others' systems, even those he rejected; (4) a sense for the many-sidedness, even contradictoriness of truth and respect for the struggles required to attain it (versus scholastic distinctions and the expectation that there is a right and a wrong side to every issue); and (5) accordingly, for all its analytic exactness, a breadth, imaginativeness, and intensely synthetic nature.

All these characteristics, though placed in a more realist frame, were highlighted in Collingwood's philosophy as well. The difference lay in his having undertaken the tasks of examination and expression. Moreover, he had opened the address by saying that we must now look at the encyclopedic Ruskin "as a whole or not at all." The same, ultimately, could be said of him. The problem that remained in this address to nonphilosophers was to show his place within the history of thought. Not to do so is to stay at the level of half-truth, as he complained once it was published.

In the following year, 1920, Collingwood finished translating Guido de Ruggiero's *Modern Philosophy* (1921). In a letter to this Italian philosopher he said, somewhat expansively: "In you I for the first time find and possess myself." This was also an extremely creative period in the development of his own philosophy, issuing in his first and only fully systematic work, *Speculum Mentis* (1924), on which he was already working. Collingwood had formed enormous respect for the new, historically sensitive approaches of Italian idealists Benedetto Croce, the leading figure, and especially de Ruggiero. He translated several of their writings, including the second English edition of Croce's *Aesthetics* (1922), although this was never acknowledged because of a copyright problem, Croce's book on Giambattista Vico (1913) and his autobiography (1915), and one other of de Ruggiero's major works, *A History of European Liberalism* (1927). This relationship has been little explored in the Collingwood literature, despite its importance to him.

I have emphasized, as he did, the historical spirit in his thought, especially the process of self-discovery and self-creation that comes through expression of the various forms of experience and eventually through philosophical reflection upon each one. As Lionel Rubinoff (1970) has shown particularly well, the main elements of this outlook were established in *Speculum Mentis* and, though significantly modified, were never dropped. Constant involvement in archaeological digs had much to do with this, for it was chiefly through the stimulus of these inquiries that he was led to discover his now famous "question and answer" logic and his understanding that the core of historical reconstruction is the history of what the actors must or may have thought in order to act the way they did.

Collingwood came to many decisive insights in this regard during his service in Admiralty Intelligence (1915–19), where his father also worked. This interest he received first through his father and then through the leading archaeologist of Roman Britain, F. J. Haverfield. But there was more. First, he saw an almost complete neglect of historiography in England; and while Haverfield's work was transforming the study of the Roman Empire, Greek history was left high and dry. He thought that by concentrating on such problems—thus helping to strengthen the revolution in historical studies, which he anticipated growing to the same stature as that in scientific studies in the seventeenth century—he might also hit upon some epistemological truths the realists were missing. Second, the war left him with the belief that the loss of control over human events had reached such proportions and with such potential for destruction, because of the triumphs of natural science, that there was only one way to avoid converting the civilized world into "a wilderness of Yahoos." "What was needed was not more goodwill and human affection, but more understanding of human affairs and more knowledge of how to handle them," he said in 1939, looking back but now anticipating a near and still more terrible war. And by this he did not mean a supposedly scientific psychology.

Pressed by these interests and concerns, Collingwood decided in about 1919 to spend the rest of his life on this task, with a special focus on understanding the relations between philosophy and history. He had already rejected the historicism of Croce by this time, so was forced to search out his own questions and answers. In several changing editions, this intense search was indeed the essence of his work.

Like Ruskin's before him, however, his special efforts were to meet with strong resistance and indifference. In 1931 he wrote de Ruggiero: "My own attempts to introduce a slender thread of historical thought into English philosophy are met everywhere with a blank refusal." But he kept working, agonizingly, at his central problem, using his historical and archaeological studies as both material for his philosophy and practical uses of it.

When Haverfield died in 1919, Collingwood was the only person fully trained in the subject of Roman Britain left in Oxford. The obligation that he felt, he said, made him refuse "all offers of professorships and other employments elsewhere." He also held it to be a basic obligation of "scientific morality" to publish the results, which many investigators were not doing. Consequently much of his time off term was spent on these studies. From 1913 to 1939 he published some 114 articles and field reports (excluding reviews) on Roman Britain, 55 of them from 1923 to 1929, and 56 from 1930 to 1939. With Miss M. V. Taylor, former secretary to Haverfield, he prepared the annual report on Roman Britain in the *Journal of Roman Studies* from 1921 to 1938. Even more of his effort went into collections for the Corpus of Inscriptions, which Haverfield had begun, asking Collingwood to serve as draughtsman. For this purpose he spent much time each year traveling about the country and drawing Roman inscriptions (published by his successor, R. P. Wright, in 1965), even though he found that they threw very little light on the questions that most interested him. These questions found partial attention in his three major historical-archaeological works, *Roman Britain* (1923, rev. ed. 1934), *The Archeology of Roman Britain* (1930), and volume one in *The Oxford History of England: Roman Britain and the English Settlements* (1936, with J. N. L. Myres; 2nd ed., 1937), plus a "goodbye" to these studies written in 1934, a long section in volume three of Tenney Frank's *An Economic Survey of Ancient Rome* (1937)—and in his philosophy.

In 1918 Collingwood married; his son and daughter were born in the next two years. For about two years after the war he continued work for Admiralty Intelligence and for the Royal Geographical Society in London. On the weekends thereafter he was always at his country home at North Moreton in Berkshire, thirteen miles from Oxford, and he was hard at work as a teacher four days a week in term. Although he attended philosophical meetings, he was thus cut off from much Oxford sociability, which contributed to his reputation of being apart. Nor was he at all involved in university politics. But he was a busy delegate of Oxford University Press, as a reader specializing in continental European works, from 1928 to 1941, when he retired to Coniston. He was constantly unwell after a serious illness in 1932, the year his father died, and another in 1937, which climaxed with a serious stroke in 1938. His British Academy obituary by R. B. McCallum stated that "he had a natural command of elegant and literate English and his wide knowledge made him conversant with a wider range of subjects than almost anyone at Oxford."

Collingwood's apparent shift to radically Marxist-sounding, liberal political views in the 1930s was shocking to both friends and oppo-

nents then, but it was not actually a shift and seems critically insightful and prophetic today. Because of his stroke, by the time he was
penning *The New Leviathan* he was able to speak, move, and write
only with great difficulty.

Interpretations

Quite independently, Louis Mink (1970) and Lionel Rubinoff
(1970) have produced superb and, I think, largely accurate interpretations of Collingwood's philosophy. Both view it as on an
essentially continuous track of inquiry from at least *Speculum
Mentis* (1924) on. Mink emphasizes its dialectical form and its
significant affinities with pragmatic, existentialist, and hermeneutical philosophy. In his view, the method was formally worked out
in *The Essay on Philosophical Method* (1933) and is manifest in
all his other works. Rubinoff emphasizes Collingwood's own characterization of his life's work in *Autobiography* (1939) as "in the
main an attempt to bring about a rapprochement between philosophy and history." From early on Collingwood had viewed this as,
for both cultural and political purposes, the most important task
of contemporary philosophy. In Rubinoff's account numerous
changes are recorded in the way Collingwood thought about the
relations between science, history, and philosophy from 1912 to
his death, but with an interpretation of strong continuity. Both
Mink and Rubinoff detect several levels of activity in his theory
and practice of philosophy since he began to formulate his distinctive dialectical approach between 1916 and 1924. Both lay out
developments in his logic of question and answer, which he had
basically worked out by 1917, and in his doctrine of overlapping
scales of forms, outlined by 1924—as alternatives to traditional
propositional logic. Both try to show how these two features,
along with his theory of absolute presuppositions, are manifest in
the formation of his own thinking. Rubinoff's unusually probing
account is a first in the history of philosophy, in that he uses
Collingwood's own detailed approach to historical inquiry to reca-
pitulate the core of his thought. Both deny that he was ever a
radical historicist, as has often been claimed.

Perhaps the best set of examples of how his theory of philosophy
developed over time are collected in Rubinoff's edition of his essays
in philosophy of religion (1968). Examples are also found in the
other essay collections edited by Alan Donagan (1964) and William
Debbins (1965). The latest study on his philosophy of history, by

W. J. Van Der Dussen (1982) deals with issues about the scientific nature of history not treated in detail by Mink or Rubinoff.

Mink's study vigorously challenges two theories of radical change in Collingwood's philosophy that have permeated almost all the Collingwood literature; Rubinoff's overturns them. The first theory, set forth by his literary executor T. M. Knox in the introduction to *The Idea of History* (1946), is that he converted from an early idealist skepticism (1916 on) to views about rapprochement between history and philosophy (by 1933) to radical historicism (after 1938) in a period of mental decline. The second theory, in a tightly argued study of his later philosophy by Alan Donagan (1962), agrees that between 1936 and 1938 there was a radical break in favor of historicism but that he overcame this temporary position in *The New Leviathan* (1942), his greatest book. On a very different basis of analysis, he dates the three periods as 1912–27, 1927–37, and 1937–43. Both of these theories presuppose that Collingwood embraced idealism for a long time, then struggled toward rejection of it. Knox thinks he lost his philosophical vocation in the later years. Donagan believes he brought it to consummation.

So far the only volume of critical essays is that edited by Michael Krausz (1972). There Donagan's discussion of philosophical method acknowledges influence from Mink, and both Mink and Rubinoff contribute essays. By and large, however, the latter two men had not borne an effect. Among the fourteen essayists Mink's study is cited only by Donagan and W. H. Walsh, Rubinoff's only by himself. Nevertheless they are a fresh, valuable set, touching upon most areas covered by Collingwood, whom Mink aptly called "the best known neglected thinker of our time."

Several books by Collingwood are cited in chapters 1, 18, 19, 24, 25, and 27.

Collingwood, Robin G. *An Essay on Philosophical Method.* Oxford: Clarendon Pr., 1933.

———. *Essays in the Philosophy of Art.* Ed. by Alan Donagan. Bloomington: Indiana Univ. Pr., 1964.

———. *Essays in the Philosophy of History.* Ed. by William Debbins. Austin and London: Univ. of Texas Pr., 1965.

———. *Faith and Reason: Essays in the Philosophy of Religion.* Ed. by Lionel Rubinoff. Chicago: Quadrangle, 1968.

———, and R. P. Wright. *The Roman Inscriptions of Britain,* vol. 1. Oxford: Clarendon Pr., 1965.

Donagan, Alan. *The Later Philosophy of R. G. Collingwood.* Oxford: Clarendon Pr., 1962.

Johnston, William M. *The Formative Years of R. G. Collingwood.* The Hague: Nijhoff, 1967.

Krausz, Michael, ed. *Critical Essays on the Philosophy of R. G. Collingwood.* The Hague: Nijhoff, 1972.

✓ Mink, Louis O. *Mind, History, and Dialectic: The Philosophy of R. G. Collingwood.* Toronto and Buffalo: Univ. of Toronto Pr., 1970.

✓ Rubinoff, Lionel. *Collingwood and the Reform of Metaphysics: A Study in the Philosophy of Mind.* Toronto and Buffalo: Univ. of Toronto Pr., 1970.

Van Der Dussen, W. J. *History as a Science: The Philosophy of R. G. Collingwood.* The Hague: Nijhoff, 1982.

KARL POPPER (1902–)

Against the Stream

Vienna-born Karl Popper was largely ignored in Britain until after World War II. In 1945, partly because of a book that registered a scathing critique of philosophical traditions he believed had contributed to totalitarian inroads against "the open society," he suddenly began a rise to fame. Popper remained odd man out among British philosophers, as he had earlier been among the Viennese. By the 1960s, however, he had become the most popularly influential philosopher in England and an acknowledged leader in philosophy of science. He was knighted in 1965. No doubt his charm largely derives from his constantly moving against the philosophical mainstream and his providing a graspable philosophy of practical action in both science and society. His principled emphasis on the open-endedness of philosophy, as of science, must also appeal to many.

As a philosopher, Popper's reputation rests chiefly on four major works: *The Logic of Scientific Discovery* (1934, tr. 1959, cited on p. 426); *The Open Society and Its Enemies* (1945, cited on p. 450) and *The Poverty of Historicism* (1957, cited on p. 434)—speculative, historically inaccurate but powerfully argued works, both begun upon receiving the news in March, 1938, of Hitler's occupation of Austria; and essays collected in *Conjectures and Refutations: The Growth of Scientific Knowledge* (1963, cited on p. 426). His *Objective Knowledge: An Evolutionary Approach* (1972) is a collection of essays. At least half of his production has not been published. In 1982 books by Popper were still coming out, as did a volume honoring his eightieth birthday, edited by Paul Levinson.

Popper was reared in the cultured, bookish home of a prominent Viennese jurist, who was greatly interested in philosophy. Through his mother, who came from a family of musicians and was a fine pianist, music became a dominant theme in his life, especially his appreciation for the classical composers. His early reflections on music led to a number of his philosophical concerns. Already intrigued by philosophical puzzles and problems as a child, attracted especially to problems of meaning and truth in mathematics and physics, these three areas became his major subjects at the University of Vienna. Like his Mill-liberal father, he was also interested in social problems from his youth onward. After a very brief Marxist phase in 1919, he immediately became an anti-Marxist but remained a socialist for some years. From 1922 to 1924 he apprenticed himself to a cabinet-maker, in order to work with his hands since no teaching posts were available; he then spent a year doing social work with neglected children. Five more years were spent as a student and teaching assistant at the Pedagogic Institute, founded in 1925 to support progressive school reform in Vienna. An influential teacher at that time was Karl Bühler, one of the first Gestalt psychologists. Popper was married in 1930, to a woman he met at the Institute. Her involvement in his work, he said, was to be as "strenuous as my own" throughout his career.

Popper spent five more years as a schoolteacher, having once dreamed of founding a school wherein "young people could learn without boredom." In 1928 he received his Ph.D., culminating his principal engagement of several years in the psychology of thought and discovery. After this he gave up psychology for good and turned against psychologism in both logic and epistemology. Publication of his now-famous *Logik der Forschung* in 1934, extracts from a much larger work conceived chiefly as a critique of Vienna Circle doctrines, set his course. Both this book and his discussions with Vienna Circle members in the 1920s and 1930s helped in many ways to bring about the eventual demise of logical positivism, though the logical, critical, scientific view of philosophy they shared with Bertrand Russell—to him "perhaps the greatest philosopher since Kant"—made him feel very much at one with them. In his view it was not their mistakes that dissolved logical positivism but their attention to minutiae in place of the great problems. This was also his main criticism of ordinary language philosophy in the 1950s and 1960s.

The great success of Popper's 1934 book brought two long lecture tours in England and opened an opportunity to teach philosophy at Canterbury University College in Christchurch, New Zealand, in 1937. There he worked until his appointment, arranged by Friedrich Hayek, to a readership at the London School of Economics, which he began in January of 1946. From 1949 until his retirement in 1969 he was Professor of Logic and Scientific Method there. He also made his first visit to the United States in 1949–50, when he gave the William James Lectures at Harvard. Until age thirty-five a philosopher outside academia, Popper developed his basic ideas without the academic pressures and distractions under which most twentieth-century philosophers have worked in their early years. This situation doubtless contributed to his striking independence of mind. Like Wittgenstein, however, he is very much a scion of Viennese philosophy and culture.

Principal Concerns

Popper's main philosophical concerns have been cosmological ones. That is, they have centered on understanding the world as opposed to the isolated elucidating of concepts. In this respect and through numerous proposals he continually advanced from the 1920s and 1930s on, considerable systematic unity can be attributed to his thought, though any tendency to overemphasize this unity must come up against his own characteristic attempts in later writings to learn from his mistakes. Thus in his case we can effectively indicate his place as a philosopher by clustering several of his major claims. (1) Already impressed in 1920 by Einstein's statement that he would consider his relativity theory untenable if it failed certain tests, Popper adopted falsifiability (and the view that the most strictly falsifiable hypotheses are the simplest and therefore have the most empirical content but may be logically the least probable) rather than verifiability as a point of demarcation between science and metaphysics. This set his approach radically apart from those of the logical positivists. Moreover, he never used this principle as a criterion of meaning, as the positivists used their principle of verifiability, contrary to what many of his interpreters have supposed. Accordingly, he opposed claims of psychoanalytic theory, the Marxian theory of history, and many others to be either scientific or very useful, as he understood them, on the ground that they are not falsifiable. (2) He has thought that metaphysics, on the other hand, can be a fruitful venture, not least because of its critical and synoptic functions. He was himself consistently a metaphysical realist. Metaphysical research programs (such as Darwinism), moreover, are not testable but are nonetheless invaluable spurs to the practice of science.

Further: (3) Nothing is first known through the senses. We start with conjectures, interpreted data; there is no such thing as passive experience. Scientific induction (with Hume) is a myth; nor are there any sensible rules of inductive inference. Induction is simply one of many psychological processes by which one may arrive at a theory, but it is not a logical one; accordingly, scientific theories are hypo-thetico-deductive systems and, strictly speaking, empirical justification of them is not possible. (4) Critical method is the chief instrument by which knowledge develops. In science every critical phase in theory formation is preceded by a dogmatic phase. (In his later thought Popper lay still greater stress on the view that all knowledge is evolving and provisional—that is, against the more nearly static metascientific view of Rudolf Carnap—and so is best advanced by critical argument—using the powers of imagination and conjecture—and by refutation. All scientific observation is theory-soaked. Yet Popper does not recommend a nominalist-conventionalist approach. Rather, we must do everything we can to let nature decide. After 1958 his greatest concern was to fight for rationality and objectivity in science—this against dangers he thought he saw in Thomas Kuhn, Michael Polanyi, and others.)

From his early period on, moreover, Popper professed the following two sets of propositions: (5) Compared to questions of fact and the problems they raise or solve, problems about words and their meanings are not to be taken very seriously. Accordingly, logic is directed principally to problem solving and discovery. The quest for a precise language, like the quest for certainty, is a wild goose chase and should be abandoned, except as it serves specific problem-solving, pragmatic ends. (6) In matters of the intellect the only things worth striving for are theories that come closer to the truth than older ones.

(7) A late notion of his is that in addition to the world of physical objects and subjective experiences (such as thought processes) there is a "world 3," just as real as the other two, that is essentially a product of the development of human language, a world whose nucleus is comprised of problems, theories, and critical arguments, which has its own history, and which is dominated by the values of objective truth and of its growth. (8) Popper was always an indeterminist regarding science, history, and politics. Accordingly, in his later writings he strongly opposed "historicism," viewed as a claim to prediction via laws, and blueprint politics (that is, the past-looking kind of Plato or the future-looking kind of Marx).

Interpretations

The most important interpretive volumes on Popper's philosophy are the two edited by Paul Arthur Schilpp (1974). These include thirty-three critical essays (mostly by noted philosophers), a long autobiography (in 1976 separately published in revised form), and extensive "Replies" by Popper to his critics. Robert Ackermann (1976) presents a largely favorable account of his "strongest positions." Anthony O'Hear (1980), on the other hand, focuses on his epistemological arguments, adding chapters on closely related aspects of his philosophy of science and social philosophy. He argues against Popper's rejection of certainty, attempts to refute his theory of falsification, and argues that his philosophy is not strong enough to withstand relativism.

In a translation of his 1973 Gothenburg dissertation on Popper's methodology Ingvar Johansson (1975) takes *The Logic of Scientific Discovery* as his point of departure but considers Imre Lakatos's arguments for the position that Popper later took a more sophisticated falsificationist view identical with his own. (Lakatos, who died in 1974, was once a student of Popper at the London School of Economics, then a professor there.) He also contrasts Popper's methodological proposals with those of Thomas Kuhn and Paul Feyerabend (see chapter 23). True to his lights, Popper often presented his ideas in an attempt to refute others'. Another significant discussion, by Alex Michalos (1971), analyzes one such controversy, started in 1954 by an article in whch Popper claimed that Rudolf Carnap and others had failed to distinguish between degree of confirmation and degree of probability. This work includes a comparative analysis of views by Lakatos and Jaakko Hintikka.

Still another controversy instigated by Popper is highlighted in a collection of fifteen articles edited by Renford Bambrough (1967). These previously published articles look at his social-political contentions with special reference to his interpretation of Plato in *The Open Society and its Enemies* (1945). Marxist Maurice Cornforth's (1968) strong opposition to his interpretation of Marxism there makes a fascinating companion volume. Both must be corrected and supplemented by the later works already indicated. Finally, Popper's philosophy of history, essentially outlined in the last chapter of his 1945 work but further argued in *The Poverty of Historicism* (1957), is critically examined by Burleigh Wilkins (1978).

Ackermann, Robert J. *The Philosophy of Karl Popper.* Amherst: Univ. of Massachusetts Pr., 1976.

Bambrough, Renford, ed. *Plato, Popper and Politics: Some Contributions to a Modern Controversy.* New York: Barnes & Noble; Cambridge: Heffer, 1967.

Cornforth, Maurice C. *The Open Philosophy and the Open Society: A Reply to Dr. Karl Popper's Refutations of Marxism.* London: Lawrence & Wishart, 1968.

Johansson, Ingvar. *A Critique of Karl Popper's Methodology.* Göteborg: Esselte Studium, Akademiförlaget, 1975.

Levinson, Paul, ed. *In Pursuit of Truth: Essays on the Philosophy of Karl Popper on the Occasion of his 80th Birthday.* Atlantic Highlands, N.J.: Humanities Pr., 1982.

Michalos, Alex C. *The Popper-Carnap Controversy.* The Hague: Nijhoff, 1971.

O'Hear, Anthony. *Karl Popper.* London and Boston: Routledge & Paul, 1980.

Popper, Karl. *Objective Knowledge: An Evolutionary Approach.* Oxford: Clarendon Pr., 1972.

Schilpp, Paul Arthur, ed. *The Philosophy of Karl Popper.* 2v. La Salle, Ill.: Open Court, 1974.

Wilkins, Burleigh T. *Has History Any Meaning? A Critique of Popper's Philosophy of History.* Hassocks, Sussex: Harvester Pr., 1978.

LUDWIG WITTGENSTEIN (1889–1951)

Life and Thought

Born the same year as R. G. Collingwood and already influential in Britain during his later years, Ludwig Wittgenstein has since been placed among the great philosophers of the century. Over the past twenty-five years a sizable portion of the philosophical literature has referred to his work. He was one of the age's preeminent puzzlers, fertile and provocative. He crafted two remarkable systems of thought, the second virtually opposite to the first. The one was thought to be a boost to logical positivism; the other has had a huge impact on linguistic philosophy.

Wittgenstein was an intense and captivating talker. From his unhappy childhood to his death, he was also a constantly tormented soul. A solitary ascetic, he depended greatly on others but almost entirely on his own terms. He was, furthermore, a highly cultured Viennese thinker, whose mind had been formed in a neo-Kantian environment, later working in a neo-Humean, empiricist Cambridge environment alien to his roots and style. Nevertheless, by virtue of its special hospitality, tolerance, and supply of bright, ductile scholars,

Cambridge was perhaps one of the few places in which he could have survived as a philosopher.

If ever a man's thought was a triumphant, if eccentric, product of almost unmitigated internal struggle, Wittgenstein's was. Although the bases for understanding how this feat was possible have been gradually coming to light over the past fifteen years, through publication of correspondence, drafts, typescripts, notebooks, memoirs (by Norman Malcolm, G. H. von Wright, Fania Pascal, and others), and student lecture notes, the links between his life and thought are yet to be reconstructed. (Most of these resources are referred to in C. G. Luckhardt, 1979, and important new ones added. The major portion of Wittgenstein's own material is noted here.) What we are chiefly faced with now is an unusual set of documents, mostly presented in terse, unelaborated remarks, and their vast, even exorbitant, influence.

Wittgenstein was educated at home until age fourteen in one of the most wealthy, cultivated households of Vienna and during the greatest flowering of culture in that city's history (Carl Schorske, 1980). When he was not living there he annually returned for vacations throughout most of the remaining forty-eight years. Nor can he be properly understood apart from that background (Janik and Toulmin, 1973). His adult life may be divided into five periods.

1. *1908–11* (ages nineteen to twenty-two), chiefly in Manchester, England. First we see a gradual shift from his industrialist father's wish that he be an engineer, through more self-determined interests in aeronautical research, then pure mathematics, then philosophical foundations of mathematics.

2. *1912–18* (ages twenty-three to twenty-nine), in Cambridge, Norway (late 1913–14), and the Austrian army. On his visit to Jena, to show Gottlob Frege a plan for a philosophical work he wanted to write, Frege advised him to go to Cambridge to study with Bertrand Russell. This he did in early 1912, having already read Russell's *Principles of Mathematics* with great excitement. His seventy-five-page *Tractatus Logico-philosophicus* (a title suggested by G. E. Moore, which Wittgenstein liked because of its Spinozistic ring) began to be worked out (a title suggested by G. E. Moore, which Wittgenstein liked because of its Spinozistic ring) began to be worked out during his five terms there, but mostly during several months of seclusion in Norway and a four-year stint in the Austrian army. Its preface announces that the book contains all that is necessary to solve the problems of philosophy. The book was finished in August

1918 but only first published in 1921 (in German, then in a German-English edition, 1922). Only this book and one 1929 article on "logical form" were published during his lifetime.

Wittgenstein's father died in January 1913, leaving him a large fortune, which he dispersed to members of his family and to a number of writers and artists. His largely metaphysical *Notebooks* from 1914–16 (1961) have accidentally survived the burning of his other writings from this period that he ordered in 1950, plus a draft, called *Prototractatus* by its editor (1971).

3. *1919–29* (ages thirty to forty), in Austria. After a year as an Italian prisoner of war, he tried in vain to get his book published, experiencing both Frege's disinterest and Russell's serious misunderstanding of what he had done. (Russell's enthusiastic Introduction eventually enabled its publication.) Thereafter he spent six years as a village schoolteacher. In 1926, perhaps not coincidentally the year of his mother's death, he sought to enter a monastery but was dissuaded by its head. After that he worked with some monks as a gardener's assistant, then devoted two years to helping design and supervise the building of a mansion for a sister in Vienna.

4. *1929–47,* spent in Cambridge, except for a year writing in Norway (1936–37) and three years as a hospital worker during World War II. Apparently, hearing a paper on the foundations of mathematics read before the Vienna Circle by Dutch philosopher L. E. J. Brouwer in 1928 helped him decide to resume philosophical work. In 1929 he returned to Cambridge, where he received a Ph.D. for the *Tractatus* and a research fellowship. He lectured nearly every term, with the exceptions noted, from 1930 to 1947 and in 1939 was made Professor of Philosophy, succeeding Moore.

Some say there was a distinctly different period from 1929 to 1935. G. H. von Wright, for example, finds the *Blue Book*, dictated in 1933–34, hard to fit into the development of his thought, whereas others consider it the best short introduction to his later philosophy. Morris Lazerowitz regards it a fundamentally new breakthrough toward understanding, in a style reminiscent of psychoanalysis, why philosophy has conventionally come to no uncontested results. The *Blue and Brown Books* (1958) were his only writings first done in English (the latter dictated in 1934–35); they were widely circulated in typescript from that time on. I think they represent a distinct and crucial stage on the way to the *Philosophical Investigations* (1953), which he was writing from 1936 on but did not complete in its present form until 1950. *Zettel* (1967) comprises remarks Wittgenstein cut from his typescript for Part I of that work. *Remarks on the Philosophy of Psychology* (1980) contains further such material. Already in the early 1930s he presented arguments rejecting basic theses in the *Tractatus,* displayed greater interest in philosophy of mathematics than in logic, and turned to issues in philosophy of mind. Another inbetween period is from 1937 to 1944, when he was primarily occupied with philosophy of mathematics. *Remarks on the Foundations of Mathematics* (1956) collects relevant, roughhewn material from his post-1937 notebooks on that subject.

5. *1947–51, away from Cambridge.* In the fall of 1947 Wittgenstein resigned his chair, finding academic life less satisfying since the war; thereafter he led a mostly secluded existence until his death of cancer in April 1951. *On Certainty* (1978), a collection of first-draft notes and remarks on epistemology, remains from the final year and a half. Some other material from this post-Cambridge period is included in a small companion volume, *Culture and Value* (1980).

Interpretations

Timothy Binkley (1973) aptly characterizes the major shift in Wittgenstein's philosophy as follows. The *Tractatus* is a unitary vision of the logical mystic, wherein the picture is confused with reality, while the *Philosophical Investigations* is an album of greatly varied artistic sketches made on a journey, an open-ended, constructivist view of language and reality. Those who would prefer the earlier logical-reductive enterprise, and its rigorous boundary-setting, would probably eschew the suggestion of either a mystical or a metaphysical quality. Assuredly, that was not what made his thought seem profoundly original to Russell or Moore in the early years. In any case, the *Tractatus* set forth a boldly stated "picture" theory of propositions. The theory, which he was eventually to repudiate in all respects noted here and many more, assumed a universal form of language such that any proposition presupposes the whole of language. The ultimate elements of language are names that designate simple objects; sentences combine names; every proposition can be anticipated as a different combination of elements. "Use" or context, as he later understood them, have nothing to do with their meanings. Now it is easier to see that in thus reducing the rules of logic to syntactic (versus semantic) rules, that is rules about the manipulation (versus the meaning) of symbols, Wittgenstein was actually dismantling *Principia Mathematica,* rejecting the very possibility of a philosophy of logic as Russell and Whitehead, and Frege before them, had conceived it. Moreover, although in conversations Wittgenstein had contributed substantially to the logical positivists' notion of "verification" (Gordon Baker in Luckhardt, 1979), no trace of such empirical doctrine appears in the *Tractatus*. As Allen Janik and Stephen Toulmin have amply illustrated (1973), Wittgenstein's thought seemed strikingly new not only then but all through the years in Cambridge because he was heard through empiricist ears, whereas his search for a unitary account of the forms of knowledge and experience and especially for an understanding of the limits of what we can reasonably say, quite apart from what may independently exist, puts him closer to Kant than to Hume or Locke. This is a Viennese philosopher speaking, through and through.

All general accounts of Wittgenstein's philosophy start with the *Tractatus*. Among books devoted to that work, G. E. M. Anscombe's has remained a useful introduction since 1959 (4th ed., 1971); Max Black's (1964) is the most comprehensive interpretation. A comparison of the fine critical expositions by Erik Stenius (1960) and Henry Finch (1971) reveals how the discussion was advancing. The large collection by Irving Copi and Robert Beard (1966) is indispensable.

Already in the *Blue Book* (1933–34), S. Morris Engel (1972) discerns both the linguistic and the psychological strains that came to dominate much of Anglo-American philosophy from that time, especially under Wittgenstein's influence. As two extremes, the former includes A. J. Ayer's rejection of metaphysics as "nonsense" and the latter includes the more psychoanalytically informed approach of Morris Lazerowitz, which probes for concealed, unconscious motives underlying philosophical activity. Wittgenstein seems never to have taken either extreme. Engel emphasizes his indebtedness to Kant and Schopenhauer and views him as contributing a new chapter within a mainline Western tradition that also stems from Plato, Spinoza, and the existentialists, one that examines ways in which our conceptual systems determine what sort of world we are able to experience.

In a brief introductory work, and following a lead in P. M. S. Hacker's excellent study (1972) on the relation of Wittgenstein's metaphysics of experience to his approaches to philosophy, John Richardson (1976) indicates the influence of Brouwer (mentioned above) on his later theory of language. This theory may be termed constructivist, as opposed to realist. The general reconstruction of the theory had already begun to be fleshed out, however, in the late 1950s. Hacker had also indicated something of how Wittgenstein tried to overcome the deep early influence of Schopenhauer's idealism and solipsism on him; he also explored the Kantian affinities of Wittgenstein's earlier and later philosophy, especially with regard to the problems of self-consciousness, knowledge of other minds, and knowledge of objects. Binkley (1973) has laid out an impressive number of parallels with Augustine in style, interests, themes, and purpose, to which must be added explicit opposition to some key views in Augustine, such as of the role of ostensive definitions in learning (Robert Arrington in Luckhardt, 1979).

Garth Hallett (1977) has produced a mammoth "companion" to *Philosophical Investigations,* and the first volume of an equally first-rate commentary by Gordon Baker and P. M. S. Hacker (1980) already runs to nearly 700 pages: testimony enough that there is something to comment about. Of continuing importance among earlier treatments are the collection edited by George Pitcher (1966) and the brief introduction by German philosopher Ernest Specht (1969). A second work by Henry Finch (1977) offers a somewhat fuller exposition of this book. As with the *Tractatus* literature, all of this is heavily analytic, with some few dialectical and hermeneutical elements.

In 1972 James Bogen plausibly argued that it was not yet possible to form a clear picture of Wittgenstein's philosophical development, especially of his critique of language. Sources recently published may ease the task now. It is already evident, however, that he never restricted his attention to "ordinary language," as is sometimes supposed. Nor do there seem to be good grounds for the view by Russell, C. D. Broad, and others that his later thought was both radically different and wrong-headed. The exact nature of the contrasts and continuities between the two major works is still in dispute, partly because Wittgenstein spoke to so many issues, often cryptically.

In an introductory work that emphasizes continuity, Anthony Kenny (1973) has briefly examined some of the interpretive options. Kenny helpfully devotes each of nine chapters to a presentation of a single problem within a single work. This is a welcome change from the necessarily almost exclusive presentation of two works in the 1960s. In a still more elementary introduction, David Pears (1970) had moved but little from that norm, and in his more advanced examination of arguments Robert Fogelin (1976) not much farther, though both are expositions of high quality. A superb revelation of how one philosopher, no doubt among many who have not so spoken, has lived with *Philosophical Investigations* over twenty-five years is Stanley Cavell's large work (1979).

Special thematic areas treated include: some problems of logic by Ilham Dilman (1973); reflections on epistemology in *On Certainty* by Thomas Morawetz (1978); the foundations of mathematics by Crispin Wright (1980); social-political philosophy by Hanna Pitkin (1972, cited on p. 450); and sociology by Derek Phillips (1977). Many or all of these areas regularly appear in the major collections, which mostly offer new essays, notably those edited by Peter Winch (1969), E. D. Klemke (1971), Alice Ambrose and Morris Lazerowitz (1972), the Royal Institute of Philosophy (1974), Jaakko Hintikka (1976), and Elizabeth Leinfellner et al. (1978).

Ambrose, Alice, and Morris Lazerowitz, eds. *Ludwig Wittgenstein: Philosophy and Language.* London: Allen & Unwin, 1972.

Anscombe, Gertrude E. M. *An Introduction to Wittgenstein's Tractatus.* 4th ed. London: Hutchinson, 1971. (2nd ed., New York: Harper Torchbooks, 1963; 1st ed., 1959.)

Baker, Gordon P., and P. M. S. Hacker. *An Analytical Commentary on the Philosophical Investigations.* Vol. 1, *Wittgenstein—Understanding and Meaning.* Chicago: Univ. of Chicago Pr.; Oxford: Blackwell, 1980.

Binkley, Timothy. *Wittgenstein's Language.* The Hague: Nijhoff, 1973.

Black, Max. *A Companion to Wittgenstein's Tractatus.* Ithaca, N.Y.: Cornell Univ. Pr.; Cambridge: Cambridge Univ. Pr., 1964.

Bogen, James. *Wittgenstein's Philosophy of Language.* London: Routledge & Paul, 1972.

Cavell, Stanley. *The Claim of Reason: Wittgenstein, Skepticism, Morality, and Tragedy.* New York: Oxford Univ. Pr.; Oxford: Clarendon Pr., 1979.

Copi, Irving M., and Robert W. Beard, eds. *Essays on Wittgenstein's Tractatus.* London: Routledge & Paul, 1966.

Dilman, Ilham. *Induction and Deduction: A Study in Wittgenstein.* New York: Harper & Row; Oxford: Blackwell & Mott, 1973.

Engel, S. Morris. *Wittgenstein's Doctrine of the Tyranny of Language.* The Hague: Nijhoff, 1972. (Study of the *Blue Book.*)

Finch, Henry Leroy. *Wittgenstein: The Early Philosophy—An Exposition of the 'Tractatus'.* New York: Humanities Pr., 1971.

———. *Wittgenstein: The Later Philosophy—An Exposition of the 'Philosophical Investigations'.* Atlantic Highlands, N.J.: Humanities Pr., 1977.

Fogelin, Robert J. *Wittgenstein.* London and Boston: Routledge & Paul, 1976.

Hacker, Peter M. S. *Insight and Illusion: Wittgenstein on Philosophy and the Metaphysics of Experience.* Oxford: Clarendon Pr., 1972.

Hallett, Garth. *A Companion to Wittgenstein's Philosophical Investigations.* Ithaca, N.Y.: Cornell Univ. Pr., 1977.

Hintikka, Jaakko, ed. *Essays on Wittgenstein in Honour of G. H. von Wright, Acta Philosophica Fennica.* Vol. 28, nos. 1–3. Amsterdam: North-Holland, 1976.

Janik, Allan, and Stephen Toulmin. *Wittgenstein's Vienna.* New York: Simon & Schuster, 1973.

Kenny, Anthony. *Wittgenstein.* Cambridge, Mass.: Harvard Univ. Pr.; London: Allen Lane, 1973.
Klemke, E. D., ed. *Essays on Wittgenstein.* Urbana and London: Univ. of Illinois Pr., 1971.
Leinfellner, Elizabeth, et al., eds. *Wittgenstein and His Impact on Contemporary Thought: Proceedings of the Second International Wittgenstein Symposium.* Vienna: Hölder-Pichler-Temsky, 1978.
Luckhardt, C. G., ed. *Wittgenstein: Sources and Perspectives.* Ithaca, N.Y.: Cornell Univ. Pr.; Hassocks, Sussex: Harvester Pr., 1979.
Morawetz, Thomas. *Wittgenstein and Knowledge.* Amherst: Univ. of Massachusetts Pr., 1978. (On *On Certainty.*)
Pears, David. *Ludwig Wittgenstein.* New York: Viking Pr.; London: Fontana, 1970. Repr.: Penguin Modern Masters series, 1977.
Phillips, Derek L. *Wittgenstein and Scientific Knowledge: A Sociological Perspective.* Totowa, N.J.: Rowman & Littlefield; London: Macmillan, 1977.
Pitcher, George, ed. *Wittgenstein, the Philosophical Investigations: A Collection of Critical Essays.* Garden City, N.Y.: Doubleday Anchor, 1966; London: Macmillan, 1968.
Richardson, John T. E. *The Grammar of Justification: An Interpretation of Wittgenstein's Philosophy of Language.* New York: St. Martin's Pr.; London: Chatto & Windus, 1976.
Royal Institute of Philosophy Lectures. Vol. 7 (1972–73), *Understanding Wittgenstein.* New York: St. Martin's Pr., 1974.
Schorske, Carl E. *Fin-de-Siècle Vienna: Politics and Culture.* New York: Knopf, 1980.
Specht, Ernest Konrad. *The Foundations of Wittgenstein's Late Philosophy.* Tr. by D. E. Walford. New York: Barnes & Noble; Manchester: Manchester Univ. Pr., 1969. (German ed., 1963.)
Stenius, Erik. *Wittgenstein's Tractatus: A Critical Exposition of Its Main Lines of Thought.* Ithaca, N.Y.: Cornell Univ. Pr.; Oxford: Blackwell, 1960.
Winch, Peter, ed. *Studies in the Philosophy of Wittgenstein.* New York: Humanities Pr.; London: Routledge & Paul, 1969.
Wittgenstein, Ludwig. *Philosophical Investigations.* Tr. by G. E. M. Anscombe. New York: Macmillan; Oxford: Blackwell, 1953. (In both German and English.)
———. *Tractatus Logico-Philosophicus.* New York: Harcourt, Brace; London: Kegan Paul, Trench, Trubner, 1922.
Wright, Crispin. *Wittgenstein on the Foundations of Mathematics.* Cambridge, Mass.: Harvard Univ. Pr., 1980.

ALFRED NORTH WHITEHEAD (1861–1947)

The Mathematician-Philosopher

For at least three generations, including his own, the men in Alfred North Whitehead's family had been engaged in educational, religious, and local administrative activities. Thoroughly trained in the classics, Whitehead grew up on the Isle of Thanet in Kent, where his grandfather and father had been heads of a private school in Rams- gate. By 1867 his father had become a full-time Anglican clergyman. Although Whitehead seems to have given up any interest in specific doctrine quite early, the interest in religion never left him. Nor did education or the broader issues of civilization and social change. At the university it was mathematics that absorbed his attention. He never attended any other lectures during his undergraduate years in Cambridge but developed the habit of advancing his thought in a very wide range of other areas through reading and conversation. Whitehead attributed to his wife Evelyn (1890 until his death in 1947), of military and diplomatic background, the awareness "that beauty, moral and aesthetic, is the aim of existence; and that kind- ness, and love, and artistic satisfaction are among its modes of attain- ment." The more systematic attainments of logic and science disclose relevant patterns and aid in avoiding irrelevances, he thought, but the culminating experiences of civilization do not wait for this work to be accomplished. This collocation of values explains as well as any- thing why the personal influence of the Whiteheads on Russell and many others was so substantial and why Whitehead's philosophical influence for most of his life came chiefly through lectures and con- versation, rather than writing.

Until about 1911, when he was fifty-two, Whitehead was chiefly a mathematician, interested in the logical foundations of mathematics and in the application of mathematics to problems in physics and cosmology. Even the latter concerns did not get much notice until he began issuing books on them from 1917 on. His most famous philo- sophical works did not appear until his final years, spent at Harvard University (1924–47), when he flourished as one of the most noted and influential American philosophers of that period. These are the reasons why he is placed last among the British philosophers featured here, even though he is the oldest among them.

Having published only two 1888 articles on the mathematics of viscous fluid motion, Whitehead issued the 612-page first volume of his projected two-volume work, *A Treatise on Universal Algebra,* in 1898. He had devoted seven years' labor to this treatise, a truly important contribution in its own right but not very influential ex- cept on his own subsequent efforts, probably because it presented a mixture of conceptual levels that neither mathematicians nor philoso- phers were used to. The second volume was set aside in favor of

Principia Mathematica, which took almost all his time from 1900 to 1910. Symbolic logic attracted him especially as a powerful tool by which to show how mathematical physics and other disciplines can explore new entities and relations in the natural world. In 1898, however, neither he, his eleven-year-younger student Bertrand Russell, nor anyone else (except Gottlob Frege, who had not yet been discovered) had thought of mathematics as the discipline concerned with logical deduction from the general premises of all reason. This possibility was not to be fully demonstrated until Russell's 1903 book.

In contrast to Russell, the Leibnizian notion of logic as the essence of philosophy never captured Whitehead's mind. Victor Lowe (Schilpp, 1941) has summed up the difference in the following way. First, Whitehead viewed mathematics, in the 1890s and later, as a facilitation of reasoning, not as a systematic abridgment of rational investigation in all fields. Second, based especially on recent mathematical advances in algebra and in non-Euclidean and projective geometry, he also consistently countered the classical idea that mathematics is concerned with number and quantity alone. This critique is not only basic to the *Principia Mathematica* project, on which he and Russell worked as equal partners for ten years. It is also basic to his later advocacy of process cosmology, as opposed to classical materialism, and to his rejection of the Humean epistemological tradition, which rests its conceptions of experience on relatively narrow definitions of sense perception. Both positions draw special attention to relations, to dynamic processes, to complex systems, and to a sense of the wholeness of things as opposed to purportedly discrete, isolated entities ("misplaced concreteness"); neither assumes that the foundations of our knowledge can be discovered at a simple level of perception or held with certainty. Allied influences on his cosmology and epistemology came from vector physics, theories of molecular and submolecular energic vibration, and the notion of a field. Whitehead's procedure from the 1880s to the World War I period, as in his subsequent speculative philosophy, was to gather characteristic ideas from diverse fields, to reconstruct them into a unity on a different level with its own concepts, then to deduce applications in the form of both new and familiar propositions to show the possible fruitfulness of the reconstruction.

It is perhaps difficult for us, nearly a century later, to realize what a shock the overthrow of Newtonian physics was even to the most advanced scientists of the 1890s. When Whitehead went up to Cambridge in 1880 it appeared that in mathematical physics only a few discrepancies remained to be looked after; but in the attempt to do this, the whole Newtonian conception was upset. As Whitehead (1954, p. 193) put the matter in 1943: "There is not a single concept of the Newtonian physics that has not now been displaced. The Newtonian ideas are still useful, as useful as they ever were, but they are no longer true in the sense in which I was taught that they were true. This experience has profoundly affected my thinking," he said. "To have supposed you had certitude once, and certitude about the solidest-looking thing in the universe, and then to have had it blow up on your hands into inconceivable infinities has affected everything else in the universe for me."

Works and Interpretation

The 1898 work was followed by several articles and monographs on algebra, geometry, and symbolic logic (1899–1907), then the massive three-volume *Principia Mathematica* and his seminal (but uninfluential) essay "On Mathematical Concepts of the Material World" (1906), a logical critique of classical materialism. From 1910, when he moved to the University of London, thence to the professorship of applied mathematics at the Imperial College of Science and Technology in London (1914–24), he directed his efforts to philosophy of science and education, including essays reprinted in *Aims of Education and Other Essays* (1969, cited on p. 500) and culminating in his best-known work, *Science and the Modern World* (1925).

Throughout his life, a great part of Whitehead's thought was addressed to educational issues and closely related problems regarding processes of thinking. His principal 1912–17 essays were gathered in *The Organization of Thought, Education and Scientific* (1917). This was followed by three works in philosophy of science: *An Enquiry Concerning the Principles of Natural Knowledge* (1919), *The Concept of Nature* (1919), and *The Principle of Relativity* (1922). During his Harvard years, from ages sixty-three to eighty-six, he published *Religion in the Making* (1926), *Symbolism, Its Meaning and Effect* (1927), his great metaphysical treatise *Process and Reality* (1929), *The Function of Reason* (1929), *Adventures of Ideas* (1933), *Nature and Life* (1934), *Modes of Thought* (1938), and *Essays in Science and Philosophy* (1947). The titles alone display both the range and the primary foci of Whitehead's philosophical thinking. They also suggest why he was one of the eminent philosophers of

America's "Golden Age." Despite the fact that analytic philosophy was already taking other methodological directions during his residence in America, in many respects overshadowing his contributions, Whitehead's influence has remained current.

The emphasis of interpreters has been on his metaphysics, which provides a way of summing up everything else. Although there were much earlier books by Dorothy Emmet and others, signals of the renascence of interest during the 1950s and 1960s came especially through a study of the background of *Process and Reality* by Nathaniel Lawrence (1956), an extensive analysis by William Christian (1959), an introduction by Ivor Leclerc (1958), and an overview of his entire philosophy by Victor Lowe (1962). One of the more noted American philosophers, Charles Hartshorne (1972), has to a large degree patterned his work after Whitehead's. Recently Ann Plamondon (1979) reconstructed the development of Whitehead's organic philosophy of science, emphasizing its continuity with metaphysics; Elizabeth Kraus (1979) issued a "companion" to *Process and Reality*. The indispensable volume on his philosophy edited by Paul Arthur Schilpp (1941) inlcudes new material by Whitehead and is supplemented by a centenary commemorative volume edited by Ivor Leclerc (1961).

Whitehead's conversational style is beautifully exemplified in the *Dialogues* volume prepared by Lucien Price (1954). Three of his major books were meant to supplement each other in presenting both the structure of his thought, his ways of thinking, and historical perspectives he brought to bear on each: *Science and the Modern World* (1925), *Process and Reality* (1929), and *Adventures of Ideas* (1933). Among his later books, *Modes of Thought* (1938) catches up especially well his notions about relations of philosophy to other ways of thinking.

Christian, William A. *An Interpretation of Whitehead's Metaphysics*. New Haven, Conn.: Yale Univ. Pr., 1969.

Hartshorne, Charles. *Whitehead's Philosophy: Selected Essays, 1935–1970*. Lincoln: Univ. of Nebraska Pr., 1972.

Kraus, Elizabeth M. *The Metaphysics of Experience: A Companion to Whitehead's Process and Reality*. New York: Fordham Univ. Pr., 1979.

Lawrence, Nathaniel M. *Whitehead's Philosophical Development: A Critical History of the Background of Process and Reality*. New York: Greenwood, 1956. Repr., 1968.

Leclerc, Ivor. *Whitehead's Metaphysics: An Introductory Exposition*. New

York: Macmillan; London: Allen & Unwin, 1958. Repr.: Bloomington: Indiana Univ. Pr., 1975.

———, ed. *The Relevance of Whitehead: Philosophical Essays in Commemoration of the Centenary of the Birth of Alfred North Whitehead.* New York: Macmillan; London: Allen & Unwin, 1961.

Lowe, Victor. *Understanding Whitehead.* Baltimore, Md.: Johns Hopkins Univ. Pr.; Oxford Univ. Pr., 1962. Repr., 1966.

Plamondon, Ann L. *Whitehead's Organic Philosophy of Science.* Albany: State Univ. of New York Pr., 1979.

Schilpp, Paul Arthur, ed. *The Philosophy of Alfred North Whitehead.* Evanston, Ill.: Northwestern Univ. Pr., 1941.

Whitehead, Alfred North. *Adventures of Ideas.* New York: Macmillan; Cambridge Univ. Pr., 1933. Repr., 1955.

———. *Dialogues of Alfred North Whitehead.* Recorded by Lucien Price. Boston: Little, Brown, 1954. Repr.: New York: Mentor, 1956.

———. *Modes of Thought.* New York: Macmillan, 1938. Repr., 1958.

———. *Process and Reality: An Essay in Cosmology.* New York: Macmillan, 1929. Repr., 1957, 1969. (Corrected ed., New York: Free Pr., 1978.) (Gifford Lectures, 1927–28.)

———. *Science and the Modern World.* New York: Macmillan, 1925. Repr., 1956. (Lowell Lectures, 1925.)

9

Twentieth-Century
American Philosophy

Historical Overview

Before the late nineteenth century America had produced a number
of men distinguished for their thought and action in other fields who
bore some philosophical interests. The Calvinist preacher, Jonathan
Edwards (1703–58), is generally acknowledged to be chief among
them, perhaps the only philosopher of substance. Ironically, while
Edwards was an excellent philosopher he contributed mightily to the
very annihilation of intellectual liberalism in vast areas of the country, wrought by the several waves of evangelical revivalism. Where
freedom of inquiry is stifled, philosophy cannot thrive. Religious
interests helped to stifle free inquiry even in the new land, a major
cause of the fact that few philosophers of any significance appeared
there. In a penetrating analysis of "Later Philosophy," Morris Cohen
(1921) wrote that "American philosophy before the Civil War produced not a single original philosophic work of commanding importance." In my view, to search for hidden greats or try to rescue this
dismal situation by celebrating minor triumphs would be a mistaken
approach. Rather, the authentic task for the period would be to ask
what were the influences of philosophically informed reflection upon
American thought and life, and vice versa. This task is yet to be
performed in any systematic way.

Pragmatism, America's most homegrown philosophy, emerged as a
result of over four centuries of adventure in the "new world," in
which problem solving in the face of ever-changing experience tended
more than rigorous reflection to mold beliefs (see John McDermott
in Caws, 1980). Pragmatism still has some influence in contemporary

216

philosophy but within an extremely pluralistic environment, which is itself a consequence of great diversity in social experimentation and educational practice from the colonial period on; and current pragmatic thinking is strongly influenced by other major trends. Between the two world wars pragmatism had a powerful effect upon movements toward social reconstruction and in the rise of the social sciences, especially through the influence of John Dewey. (See chapter 10 on pragmatism.)

The "Golden Age" of American philosophy (roughly 1880–1914 at its core, 1860–1930 in broader perspective) preeminently included part-time pragmatist William James, nonpragmatists Josiah Royce, George Santayana, and (after 1924) Alfred North Whitehead, all of Harvard, and pragmatists Charles Sanders Peirce and John Dewey elsewhere. These thinkers were all distinctively American in style and purpose, as were the naturalists and new brands of realists during the period between the world wars, and as are the latter-day pragmatists and successors to Whitehead, notably the speculative philosopher Charles Hartshorne, in the contemporary period. Before the Golden Age, however, an authentic history of philosophy would have to emphasize the interactions between philosophical reflection and its American milieu. Not only have these relations not so far been thoroughly explored in any general historical account; even treatments of the Golden Age are fragmentary.

Some themes that could be used in forming a good general account of the earlier history have been struck by John McDermott (1976). His historical references, however, like those of almost all American philosophers, are chiefly from the early twentieth century on. The standard history by Herbert Schneider (1946) would scarcely be recognizable as a work of philosophical history today. Schneider was John Dewey's assistant at Columbia from 1920 to 1935, founded the *Review of Religion* (1936–58), and was later a cofounder of the *Journal of the History of Philosophy* (1963–). His book chiefly surveys typical doctrines, divided by schools. Nonetheless it is probably correct in depicting most of American philosophical activity until 1945 as heavily speculative and as grounded in religious interests or formed in response to them. Yet as these burdens were lifted, a new shift in the modern tension between relevance and technical competence gradually formed. Morris Cohen, one of the great leaders in the field, once observed upon looking back at 1931, the year his first book, *Reason and Nature,* was published: "In few earlier ages has the general craving for philosophic light seemed so vast and the offerings of professed philosophers, preoccupied with problems of technique, so unsubstantial." Appropriately such statements have been reiterated by internal critics since the mid-1960s, though none could reasonably claim that very little work is substantial in quality. Much of it, furthermore, has certainly become relevant for a great variety of purposes.

The first great turn in American philosophy occurred in the late nineteenth-century controversy over evolution. Valuable summaries of this development have been made by Cohen (1921) and Schneider (1946), with special reference to early efforts to form an evolutionary philosophy by polymath Chauncey Wright (1830–75), who profoundly influenced Peirce and James, by cosmic theist John Fiske (1842–1901), and by Hegelian William T. Harris (1835–1909). From about 1867 to his death Harris was one of the most influential educationists in the United States. In 1867 he founded the first English language periodical devoted strictly to philosophy, *The Journal of Speculative Philosophy,* which he edited until 1893. The first philosophy papers of Peirce, Royce, James, and Dewey all appeared there. By the 1890s philosophers established in several graduate departments had adopted an evolutionary perspective, many of them also holding nontheistic, naturalist views. The separation of philosophy from theology, greatly aided by the controversy, as by the greater interest in science and scientific method at that time, had enabled philosophy to have a place in American universities as a field in its own right.

Harvard and the Emergence of the Profession

Harvard University under President Charles Eliot led the way. In fact, as Bruce Kuklick (1977) has shown in his mostly institutional history of American philosophy as it was typified and dominated by Harvard from 1860 to 1930, Harvard set the pace for most of the first seven decades of the modern phase. This was done notably through Peirce (associated with Harvard, though not a professor there), James, Royce, Santayana, and Whitehead. Another way of bounding this formative period is to note two books: Darwin's *Origin of Species* (1859), which opened up the interest in evolutionary thought, and C. I. Lewis's *Mind and the World Order* (1929, cited on p. 326), which marked the coming of age of academic philosophy (professional, specialized, and for the most part nonpopular). Kuklick discusses decisive challenges to the long-dominant Scottish, "common-sense" realism during the evolution controversy (especially by Wright, Fiske, and Peirce); the Golden Age in the narrower sense, beginning with James's appointment to the philosophy department in 1880 and Royce's in 1882 (Santayana came as an instructor in 1889); the heyday of the neorealists after 1910 (Ralph Barton Perry, at Harvard 1902–46, and others) and of the critical realists after 1916 (Santayana, Arthur O. Lovejoy, Roy Wood Sellars et al.); then the postwar years, when the leading American idealist Ernest Hocking (1914–43), the superbly talented logician and epistemologist C. I. Lewis (1921–53) and Whitehead (1924–37) came aboard; and a few later developments. "Neorealism" and "critical realism" were refinements of the general empiricist effort to secure an objective and reliable basis for knowledge of the external world. Each was announced and upheld with some fervor in its time, but neither is much referred to today. Between 1878 (when the great psychologist and educationist G. Stanley Hall got his Ph.D.) and 1914 the Harvard department, including a few lesser knowns not mentioned here, trained almost the entire first generation of professional philosophers in the United States. Many of the first leading psychologists also came from that department.

Kuklick makes the point that, with the exception of a few generalists like Harvard-trained Yale philosophers Brand Blanshard, F. S. C. Northrop, and Paul Weiss, almost all the better-known philosophers after World War I were specialists. This has remained true of the profession generally. It must be added, however, that only after World War II did American philosophy for the first time organize in a thoroughly professional pattern, claiming its own subject matter and rigorous techniques, encouraging subfield specialization, and achieving autonomy from other fields, especially theology, history, and psychology. Many of its traditional functions are now carried by social commentators, consciousness-raisers, aesthetes, theologians, cultural historians, psychologists, literary critics, journalists, ecologists, futurists, planners, and theorists of all kinds. Although John Smith (in Caws, 1980) has aptly singled out receptivity to varying opinions, openness to temporality and change, and the demand for relevance to important human purposes as hallmarks of philosophy in America since about 1880, these characteristics do not seem quite so prevalent within the analytic mainstream as they generally were thirty years ago. If the American scholarly environment is to be compared with that of continental European and British philosophy, however, the three hallmarks are still accurate.

Historical Scholarship

From a British analytic viewpoint, one of the foremost philosophical historiographers, John Passmore (in Chisholm et al., 1964) has set forth an indispensable account of main tendencies in American historical scholarship regarding philosophy produced in the 1930–60 period. This detailed, 124-page essay on the literature deals chiefly with scholarship about philosophy and historical studies, excluding aesthetics and political philosophy and saying little about several others. Other essays in this volume on American philosophy in recent decades cover metaphysics (Manley Thompson), epistemology (Roderick Chisholm), ethics (William Frankena), and philosophy of science (Herbert Feigl).

By and large, Passmore did not find studies in the history of American philosophy very impressive. He found that much of the historical literature was produced by scholars writing about philosophy rather than doing it, and that very few of the relatively small number of important works of philosophical scholarship of a historical nature were done by persons who had made an independent mark in any branch of pure philosophy.

Only about thirty quite positively regarded works have been gleaned from his entire survey, of which the chief ones seem to be these: articles on the Presocratics and Plato by Gregory Vlastos (1940s and 1950s); Benson Mates, *Stoic Logic* (1953); Harry A. Wolfson's medieval studies; Ernest A. Moody, *The Logic of William of Ockham* (1935) and his subsequent Carnapian studies in medieval logic; A. B. Wolter, *The Transcendentals and Their Function in the Metaphysics of Duns Scotus* (1946); Paul Oskar Kristeller's writings on Renaissance philosophy; Harry A. Wolfson's outstanding *Spinoza* (1934); Lewis White Beck, *Commentary on Kant's Critique of Practical Reason* (1960); Richard H. Popkin, *The History of Scepticism from Erasmus to Descartes* (1960); G. W. Cunningham's survey on *The Idealistic Argument in Recent British and American Philosophy* (1933); R. B. Perry's biography of William James (1935); Philip Paul Wiener, *Evolution and the Founders of Pragmatism* (1949); Herbert Spiegelberg, *The Phenomenological Movement* (1960); and J. R. Weinberg's pioneering effort, *An Examination of Logical Positivism* (1936). These works do indeed tend to set high standards, though not unsurmountable ones. It is a remarkable characteristic of the period since 1960 that the standards are well met in numerous instances, especially in studies of major philosophers and philosophical movements. Until the 1970s, however, the overwhelming bulk of the more noteworthy philosophical scholarship in America went into highly specialized, nonhistorical studies.

General Histories

Among recent general histories, no single work has both scholarly thoroughness and philosophical depth. The nearest fulfillment of these aims is Morton White's (1972) brief, philosophically informed intellectual history of the response of American philosophy to challenges from modern science. This stimulating overview is directed especially to "middle range" thinkers (poised between pundits and sages, on the one hand, and workers in epistemological detail, on the other), especially the six most influential philosophers in Dewey's lifetime (1859–1952): Edwards, Ralph Waldo Emerson and the Transcendentalists, James, Royce, Santayana, and Dewey (with special recognition to Wright and Peirce). A bicentennial collection of essays, edited by Peter Caws (1980), is also of good quality. Andrew Reck (1964) has provided systematic accounts of ten representative twentieth-century philosophers up to World War II: Perry, Hocking, pragmatist George Herbert Mead, pragmatic metaphysician John Elof Boodin, value theorists Wilbur Marshall Urban and DeWitt H. Parker, critical realist Roy Wood Sellars, temporalistic realist Arthur O. Lovejoy (founding father of the history of ideas), corporatist Elijah Jordan, and personalist Edgar Sheffield Brightman. He followed this up with a similar volume (1968) featuring post-World War II thinkers: logical empiricist C. I. Lewis, value theorist Stephen C. Pepper, idealist-rationalist Brand Blanshard, Columbia naturalists Ernest Nagel, John Herman Randall, and Justus Buchler, pragmatist Sidney Hook, ideology critic F. S. C. Northrop, axiological realist James K. Feibleman, realist and existentialist John Wild, Whiteheadean process philosopher Charles Hartshorne, and ontologist Paul Weiss. These accounts portray the interests of their author in speculative philosophy, emphasizing theories and systematics. The approach lost ground during the 1960s and 1970s, giving way to more strict attention to logical and linguistic analysis.

Collections

As in British philosophy, there is an important succession of collections that present the current views of American philosophers. These begin with a two-volume set of thirty-four personal statements gathered by George Adams and William Montague (1930). A second series of fifteen statements is edited by John Smith (1970), who also published his own interpretation that year. In the latter volume, two-thirds of those included were over sixty years of age; it provides a wide sampling of styles, mostly nonanalytic. Waterfront coverage is also given in twenty-five statements collected by Horace Kallen and Sidney Hook (1935). Some thirty representative articles on specific topics in logic and scientific method, in metaphysics and epistemology, and in ethics and social philosophy, edited by Sidney Hook (1956), more accurately display the new developments, many of them analytic, than does the later Smith volume. Like Smith's, however, the latest collection of fourteen statements by senior philosophers, edited by personalist Peter Bertocci (1974), shows the great diversity of approaches alternative to analytic ones still operative. Evidence of the excellent new analytic work that was being done by the 1960s is given in fourteen original essays edited by Max Black (1965), all by younger philosophers. Brief overviews of current efforts in nine areas of philosophy, edited by Franklin Donnell (1965), likewise manifests the decided change of emphasis.

From the pre-1960 period it has not been possible to refer in the present work to more than a few among the dozens of philosophers once prominent. For example, only ten of the thirty-four included in the 1930 Adams and Montague collection are referred to, only six from the Kallen and Hook collection of 1935. Most of those not cited are rarely, if ever, referred to today. In contrast, eighteen of twenty-nine in Hook's 1956 volume are mentioned. The proportion from more recent collections is not greatly different, not because the contributions are necessarily less important but because the work is being done by hundreds more people of competence today, people far more reliant on each other's efforts than was true in the past.

Conceptions of Tasks

General stock-taking has been a prominent feature of American philosophy since at least 1945. In that year Brand Blanshard and four associates presented a lengthy report to the American Philosophical Association on the state of the field and its relation to American life and education. It was well conceived and is still timely. Among the characterizations of the major tasks of philosophy, service toward social reconstruction had already found a strong advocate in John Dewey, notably in his *Reconstruction in Philosophy* (1937, cited on p. 6). This idea has had enormous appeal in countries such as China and Japan, which Dewey visited, and in the many others where his books have been widely used in translation. In a similar vein, Albert Levi (1974) has proposed a history of ideas approach that carefully investigates the interrelationships between ideas, agents, and social contexts. In a "pilot study" he illustrates this approach to the history of philosophy by focusing especially on the thinking of Plato, Aquinas, Descartes, and G. E. Moore within their social settings. His chief aim is to show "how social necessity and personal identity interact in producing notable philosophic achievement."

Morton White (1956), cognizant of warring factions, asked for their "reunion" through a reflective method that does not distinguish radically between different methods of discovering what is, what must be, and what should be. This call does not seem to have been much heeded, though White's arguments remain pertinent. The tasks of philosophy today are rather differently proposed among the eighteen philosophers invited by Charles Bontemps and Jack Odell (1975) to comment, eight of them from outside the United States. These range all the way from logician Willard Van Orman Quine to Marxist Herbert Marcuse. In a Festschrift for Paul Arthur Schilpp (edited by Eugene Freeman, 1976), himself editor of a distinguished series of volumes on outstanding living philosophers, another company of twenty-one philosophers, mostly American, competently direct philosophy toward solution of social problems in an age of world crisis. On the heels of these challenging works came a masterful argument by Richard Rorty (1979, cited on p. 7) for the "deconstruction" of modern pretensions among philosophers, including most of his own analytic comrades, to mirror nature (notably through empiricism), to provide foundations for the sciences that are timeless and certain, and to oversee culture. He claims that Wittgenstein, Heidegger, and Dewey have already effectively argued that philosophy must give up these intentions. Wilfred Sellars's attacks on "the myth of the given" and allied efforts by Quine had led the way for this extraordinarily provocative critique by one of the leading contemporary analytic philosophers. That he is far from alone is exemplified in a set of previously published challenges to the still widely presupposed foundations of empiricism, edited by Harold Morick (1972).

FURTHER DEVELOPMENTS AND THEMES

Three major thematic areas receive treatment in other chapters: pragmatism in chapter 10, existentialism in chapter 12, phenomenology, hermeneutics and critical theory in chapter 13, and Marxism in chapter 11. Until recently, at least, these have been of descending order of importance in American philosophy, respectively. British philosophers, in contrast, have paid little notice to any of these trends. Nonetheless, by the 1950s all the themes previously indicated for British philosophy were prominent in the United States and Canada as well, but within a far more pluralistic environment, in which almost every current approach to philosophy has its adherents.

The Ideal, the Real, and the Rational

The realist turn from idealism, like the pragmatist, took several forms, some directed against pragmatism and phenomenology as well. Probably because they comprised much of the turbulent mainstream, an overall account is not yet available; it would have to be pieced together from a great many sources. Realism, in general terms, is the view that what we call material objects exist independent of sense perception and external to any mental operation. Differences of view refer especially to ways in which various mental operations are seen to relate to the external world, for example, the nature of sense perception and its role in attaining reliable knowledge. Most realists have held an empiricist, naturalist (versus supernaturalist) and humanistic (versus traditionally religious) orientation, and they have tended to adopt some version of behaviorism in the psychological and social domains.

In contrast, George Herbert Palmer (1842–1933) and Josiah Royce (1855–1916), both at Harvard for many years, represented continuity with German idealist traditions. Thomas Powell (1967) has provided a good overview of Royce's work and influence. Later Brand Blanshard (1892–) of Yale represented an idealist, rationalist alternative (Schilpp, 1979). From 1910 to 1921 (with four years off in Europe, Mesopotamia, and India) Blanshard studied at Michigan, Columbia, and Harvard and with H. H. Joachim and other idealists at Oxford. He taught at Michigan (1921–25), Swarthmore (1925–44), and Yale (1944–61) and was very active in the profession nationally. His autobiography as a near-nonagenarian and his replies to critics in the 1979 Schilpp volume present a fascinating commentary on the career of philosophy during his lifetime. Another reminiscence (1969), presented in a charmingly sparse, clipped style, comes from Roy Wood Sellars (1880–1973) of Michigan, written at age eighty-seven. Sellars was a critical realist and evolutionary naturalist. In 1910 he taught the first philosophy of science course in the country. Although his work did not win nearly the attention Blanshard's did, despite its being nearer the norm, Sellars provides an intimate picture of what has constituted a large part of the American philosopher's world in this century. With slight adjustments for specialized interests and generally untold tales of departmental and professional politics, it could be taken as typical. Perhaps more than most, however, Sellars was always interested in whatever was happening, if only to see whether it conformed with or corrected his own line of thought; and, as Blanshard's discourse also shows, a great deal was happening—more than ever before in this field. Sellars's recollections also help one understand how a philosopher during this period could have been preoccupied with the mind-body problem and a narrow range of issues in epistemology, circling round and round the same issues. A great many philosophers did this as new scientific information forced open new investigations; getting a clear grasp on these matters was necessary in order to comprehend the foundations of either science or ordinary experience.

At Columbia University Ernest Nagel (1901–), a naturalist and logical empiricist best known for his work in philosophy of science, held forth strongly for the role of "sovereign reason" (the title essay in a collection, 1954) in every domain of human life. The defense of reason has been a strong theme in twentieth-century American philosophy, against perceived irrationalist and antiintellectual currents in the culture.

Idealism, realism, and the defense of reason (in which rationalists and nonrationalists alike participate) all persist in the contemporary period. A volume edited by John Howie and Thomas Buford (1975) includes current representatives of Absolute idealism (which identifies reality with a mental or spiritual totality called the "Absolute"), panpsychistic idealism (which holds that all things consist of or are imbued with mind), and personalistic idealism (which takes reality to be constituted by finite persons, ultimately by God for most adherents). Personalism has been most notably advocated by Bordon Parker Bowne (1845–1910) at Boston University and by his successor there, Peter A. Bertocci. The volume includes a survey of idealism in American philosophy since 1900. Realism in various forms is widely presupposed today.

Naturalism

The development of naturalist perspectives has been another imposing trend. Naturalism is the view that every single thing or event is natural; it is continuously, systematically, and consistently so with respect to every other thing or event and is susceptible to scientific explanation. The movement called naturalism flourished in the 1930s and 1940s. Like realism, the position is widely presupposed among philosophers today, though problems of interest are not often phrased in these terms. From the 1940s the collection of essays edited by Yervant Krikorian (1944) well represents the movement. A study by C. F. Delaney (1969) views it through the work of three leaders: Morris R. Cohen, Frederick J. E. Woodbridge (1867–1940) of Columbia University, and Roy Wood Sellars. Santayana, Dewey, C. I. Lewis, and Nagel were also influential naturalists. David Hollinger (1975) has retraced important themes of the times through the career of Cohen, viewed both as a powerful contributor to the expansion of scientific culture in the United States and as the foremost critic from within the naturalist tradition of more formalist methodologies (for instance, in logical positivism).

Publication of the papers of the great logical empiricist, C. I. Lewis (1970), and of the critical volume on his thought edited by Paul Arthur Schilpp (1968) have helped keep his influence alive. He is still much cited, especially as epistemologist and logical analyst, more than almost any American philosopher of his period. In his later years Lewis devoted special attention to ethics and valuation. Roger Saydah's (1969) study examines this part of his thought, including use of unpublished manuscripts.

Satayana and Materialism

George Santayana (1863–1952) is regarded by some interpreters to be a major philosopher today, as he was widely held to be in his middle years. A poet, novelist, literary and social critic, and popularizer of philosophical themes, as well as a philosopher in the more exact sense, Santayana held forth at Harvard from 1889 until he retired in 1912 on income from a small inheritance. Thereafter he lived in England, Paris, and Rome, still publishing. His earliest philosophical work was primarily in aesthetics and literary criticism. His five-volume work, *The Life of Reason* (1905–6) had great influence, especially on the development of naturalism. Though systematically argued, it bore an introspective, psychological cast later repudiated by him. A third and final period is especially represented by *Scepticism and Animal Faith* (1923), a then highly regarded book, and the four-volume *Realms of Being* (1927–40), largely neglected until recently. In it he distinguished four realms: essences (universal, self-identical entities, infinite in number, which need not be exemplified materially), matter, truth, and pure intuitive, transcendental consciousness. Santayana wrote in a sharply reasoned style, his positions stated with unusual clarity; but he saw argumentation only as preparatory to the visionary and poetic, which also abound.

To no small degree it was presumably Santayana's sometimes Olympian disdain for the typical attachments to science and logical analysis that led John Smith (1963) to state that "the American mind . . . has been everything but what Santayana was and stood for." I do not think this judgment is accurate, however. The "American mind," even when viewed strictly in terms of philosophical culture, is multifaceted. For some decades Santayana's thought belonged significantly to it, and indeed seems still to belong. In particular the materialism for which he stood and the attempts to distinguish between various types of entity on a purely naturalist base are quite current (see chapter 19).

Timothy Sprigge (1974) offers an excellent, highly respectful analysis of Santayana's arguments for his mature epistemology and ontology. Broader coverage, including a brief autobiography and a 110-page reply to his interpreters, is available in the volume edited by Paul Arthur Schilpp (1940). Beth Singer (1970) critically examines his social thought. A chapter in White (1972) and three essays in Caws (1980) are also useful.

New Amalgams of Analysis

Currently something of a new synthesis and reorientation, featuring the dimensions and made-in-America qualities that pragmatism once had, appears to have been forming within American philosophy (for example, see A. C. Genova in Caws, 1980). This is happening through an interpretation of language as intentional rule-governed activity, wherein formal rules are seen to function as organizing principles (though not necessarily as categorical ones) within natural discourse—a merging of modifications of logical positivism with ordinary language analysis on a new plane. At any rate, a great deal of energy is being put into this effort. (See especially chapter 17.)

Self-Criticism

Two examples of a vigorous tendency within American philosophy toward criticism of its own nearer traditions have already been singled out: Wilfrid Sellars (1912–), son of Roy Wood Sellars, and Willard Van Orman Quine (1908–). A collection of eighteen disparate essays by Sellars (1974)—another large collection was published in 1967—is especially notable in that his occupation with current themes has been nourished by careful historical study, notably of Plato and Kant. Recently six essays on his epistemology, ontology, philosophy of science, philosophy of mind and ethics have been issued by C. F. Delaney et al. (1977). Alex Orenstein (1977) contributes a brief account of the philosophy of Quine, whose first book, *A System of Logistic* (1934), like most of his other books, was on logic. Donald Davidson and Jaakko Hintikka (1975) have edited a set of more technical essays on his work. A second important collection is edited by Robert Shahan and Chris Swoyer (1979), including a 1977 article by Quine.

Social Criticism and Philosophy of Culture

I have already mentioned the involvement of Santayana, Dewey, and others in social criticism, also a major tradition in American philosophy. Until recent decades, however, social-political philosophy was a second cousin, at best, to the mainstream interests. (See chapter 25.) Philosophy of culture has had to stay on the fringes of the family. This situation has helped to force many philosophically minded scholars interested in these subjects outside the usual haunts. The preeminent example of such a person is Lewis Mumford (1895–). Literary and social critic, aesthetician, student of cities and modern technology, and futurist, Mumford is withal a writer, one of the most consistently effective and productive in this century. Almost all his major works are still in print. Although he rarely does philosophy in the more technical sense, much of his writing rises above the ordinary canons of reflection to the philosophical. Since 1972 he has issued several large volumes of memoirs, which include material of philosophical interest. *The Transformations of Man* (1956) summarizes his evolutionary interpretation of culture.

Adams, George P., and William Pepperell Montague, eds. *Contemporary American Philosophy: Personal Statements*. 2v. New York: Macmillan, 1930. Repr.: New York: Russell & Russell, 1962.

Bertocci, Peter A., ed. *Mid-Twentieth Century American Philosophy: Personal Statements*. New York: Humanities Pr., 1974.

Black, Max, ed. *Philosophy in America*. Ithaca, N.Y.: Cornell Univ. Pr.; London: Allen & Unwin, 1965.

Blanshard, Brand, et al. *Philosophy in American Education, Its Tasks and Opportunities*. New York: Harper, 1945. (Report to American Philosophical Assn.)

Bontemps, Charles J., and S. Jack Odell, eds. *The Owl of Minerva: Philosophers on Philosophy*. New York: McGraw-Hill, 1975.

Caws, Peter, ed. *Two Centuries of Philosophy in America.* Oxford: Black-well, 1980. (Bicentennial Symposium of Philosophy, New York, 1976.)

Chisholm, Roderick M., Herbert Feigl, William E. Frankena, John Passmore, and Manley Thompson. *Philosophy.* Englewood Cliffs, N.J.: Prentice-Hall, 1974.

Cohen, Morris R. "Later Philosophy." In *Cambridge History of American Literature,* vol. 3, pp. 226–65. New York: G. P. Putnam, 1921.

Davidson, Donald, and Jaakko Hintikka, eds. *Words and Objections: Essays on the Work of W. V. Quine.* Rev. ed. Dordrecht and Boston: Reidel, 1975. (Original ed., 1969.)

Delaney, Cornelius F. *Mind and Nature: A Study of the Naturalistic Philosophies of Cohen, Woodbridge and Sellars.* Notre Dame, Ind.: Univ. of Notre Dame Pr., 1969.

————, et al. *The Synoptic Vision: Essays on the Philosophy of Wilfrid Sellars.* Notre Dame, Ind.: Univ. of Notre Dame Pr., 1977.

Donnell, Franklin H., Jr., ed. *Aspects of Contemporary American Philosophy.* Würzburg-Wien: Physica-Verlag, 1965.

Freeman, Eugene, ed. *The Abdication of Philosophy: Philosophy and the Public Good—Essays in Honor of Paul Arthur Schilpp.* La Salle, Ill.: Open Court, 1976.

Hollinger, David A. *Morris R. Cohen and the Scientific Ideal.* Cambridge, Mass.: MIT Pr., 1975.

Hook, Sidney, ed. *American Philosophers at Work: The Philosophic Scene in the United States.* New York: Criterion, 1956.

Howie, John, and Thomas O. Buford, eds. *Contemporary Studies in Philosophical Idealism.* Cape Cod, Mass.: Claude Stark, 1975.

Kallen, Horace M., and Sidney Hook, eds. *American Philosophy, Today and Tomorrow.* New York: Lee Furman, 1935.

Krikorian, Yervant H., ed. *Naturalism and the Human Spirit.* New York: Columbia Univ. Pr., 1944. Repr., 1969.

Kuklick, Bruce. *The Rise of American Philosophy.* New Haven, Conn. and London: Yale Univ. Pr., 1977.

Levi, Albert William. *Philosophy as Social Expression.* Chicago and London: Univ. of Chicago Pr., 1974.

Lewis, Clarence I. *Collected Papers.* Ed. by John D. Goheen and John L. Mothershead, Jr. Stanford, Calif.: Stanford Univ. Pr., 1970.

McDermott, John J. *The Culture of Experience: Philosophical Essays in the American Grain.* New York: New York Univ. Pr., 1976.

Morick, Harold, ed. *Challenges to Empiricism.* Belmont, Calif.: Wadsworth, 1972.

Mumford, Lewis. *The Transformations of Man.* New York: Harper & Row, 1956. Repr.: Harper Torchbook; Gloucester, Mass.: Peter Smith, 1978.

Nagel, Ernest. *Sovereign Reason and Other Studies in the Philosophy of Science.* Glencoe, Ill.: Free Pr., 1954.

Orenstein, Alex. *Willard Van Orman Quine.* Boston: Twayne, 1977.

Powell, Thomas F. *Josiah Royce.* New York: Washington Square Pr., 1967. Repr.: New York: Twayne, 1974.

Reck, Andrew J. *The New American Philosophers: An Exploration of Thought since World War II.* Baton Rouge: Louisiana State Univ. Pr., 1968.

———. *Recent American Philosophy: Studies of Ten Representative Thinkers.* New York: Random House, Pantheon, 1964.

Saydah, J. Roger. *The Ethical Theory of Clarence Irving Lewis.* Athens: Ohio Univ. Pr., 1969.

Schilpp, Paul Arthur, ed. *The Philosophy of Brand Blanshard.* 2v. La Salle, Ill.: Open Court, 1979.

———, ed. *The Philosophy of C. I. Lewis.* La Salle, Ill.: Open Court, 1968.

———, ed. *The Philosophy of George Santayana.* 2nd ed. New York: Tudor, 1951. (1st ed., 1940.)

Schneider, Herbert W. *A History of American Philosophy.* Rev. ed. New York: Columbia Univ. Pr., 1963. (1st ed., 1946.)

Sellars, Roy Wood. *Reflections on American Philosophy from Within.* Notre Dame, Ind.: Univ. of Notre Dame Pr., 1969.

Sellars, Wilfrid. *Essays in Philosophy and Its History.* Dordrecht and Boston: Reidel, 1974.

Shahan, Robert W., and Chris Swoyer, eds. *Essays on the Philosophy of W. V. Quine.* Norman: Univ. of Oklahoma Pr., 1979.

Singer, Beth J. *The Rational Society: A Critical Study of Santayana's Social Thought.* Cleveland, Ohio: Pr. of Case Western Reserve Univ., 1970.

Smith, John E. *The Spirit of American Philosophy.* Oxford and New York: Oxford Univ. Pr., 1963.

———. *Themes in American Philosophy: Purpose, Experience, and Community.* New York and London: Harper Torchbooks, 1970.

———, ed. *Contemporary American Philosophy.* 2nd series. London: Allen & Unwin, 1970.

Sprigge, Timothy L. S. *Santayana: An Examination of His Philosophy.* London and Boston: Routledge & Paul, 1974.

White, Morton G. *Science and Sentiment in America: Philosophical Thought from Jonathan Edwards to John Dewey.* Oxford and New York: Oxford Univ. Pr., 1972. (Also ed. with commentary, *Documents in the History of American Philosophy from Jonathan Edwards to John Dewey.* Oxford and New York: Oxford Univ. Pr., 1972.)

———. *Toward Reunion in Philosophy.* Cambridge, Mass.: Harvard Univ. Pr., 1956.

10

Pragmatism

In his rough sketch toward a philosophical history of pragmatism, H. S. Thayer (1968) emphasizes its efforts to integrate concerns regarding knowledge and values, meaning and action. He also aptly states that its claim to fame lies in its being a suggestive body of ideas rather than a school of thought. I would add, however, that to a fair degree this is true of all major philosophical movements. Adherents tend to agree on types of problems and methods—often not on their specific formulations—much more than they may agree on paticular doctrines. In this respect, to say "ism" is almost invariably misleading. Whether it fruitfully applies nonetheless is a matter of degree. On these criteria, for example, logical positivism has been more nearly a school of thought and existentialism less identifiable as a school than pragmatism has been. As a movement, pragmatism was attempting to clarify (usually not to simplify or reduce, in contrast to logical positivism) several types of problems, among them: (1) How are we to assure, if at all, that a notion is scientific and not merely metaphysical—that is, that it can be understood and tested operationally? (2) How are we to view religious and ethical notions in light of our more general conceptions of what is scientifically meaningful or true, or vice versa? (3) How is the meaning of a term, conception or statement to be understood in light of the fact that we go on learning from experience? (4) How are we to give warrant to assertions of truth where we feel led to assume that there is no certain base on which to judge? (5) How are we to acknowledge both the linguistic and the social determinants of meaning and truth? (6) How are our inquiries into these and other matters to be formed so as to

231

include recognition that ideas have consequences (either imaginary or real, and both either more limitedly conceptual or more directly social), and how are we to take responsibility for these consequences?

The problems have been formulated in this manner in order to highlight another feature: the recognition that doctrines and methods of inquiry are usually not, are perhaps never, isolated from each other. They interpenetrate; and it is more reasonable than not to expect them to share in patterns of social consequence. They are also formulated in an order such that they move from the primary interests of Peirce to those of James to those of Dewey and Mead. The first question is vintage Peirce, though it continues in the search for operational definitions today. The second, particularly as it relates to religion, is especially James's. Eventually Dewey was the one who drew special attention to ethics. After about 1905, moreover, Dewey became the champion of pragmatic interests, and he remained so up to World War II. In fact, his philosophy alone, among the leading pragmatists, approaches thoroughgoing pragmatism.

The third question was almost equally important to all the pragmatists, but Dewey provided its formulation and, in a sense, came to make it his life's task. The fourth is actually stated in terms that emerged as Dewey formed his later "instrumentalism" (Peirce had finally been led to distinguish his own perspective from the others' by calling it "pragmaticism"; James had finally given up trying to defend pragmatism and went on to other pursuits; this was Dewey's name for what he felt had developed). C. I. Lewis held that there is a certainty in empirical experience, in what he called "terminating judgments," and that not all ethical knowledge is empirically based. Naturalist Dewey had claimed, to the contrary, that ethics is empirically based and its method is scientific.

As to the fifth question, Peirce was more interested in linguistic determinants, as such, Dewey and Mead in wider social determinants. Peirce dwelt more with issues of meaning, Dewey with issues of truth—but in no case one to the exclusion of the other. In varying ways, all the pragmatists were concerned with question number six, but Peirce's interest was more conceptual, that of James more personal and ethical, that of Mead more sociological, that of Dewey more educational and political. It is this last drift, toward personal and social practicality, that mistakenly led to a popular identification of pragmatism with the notions that "it's meaningful if and only if it's useful," in an ordinary, down-to-earth sense, and that "it's true if it works." This view, which is indeed sometimes suggested in enthusiastic statements by James and in programmatic proposals by

Dewey, was never held by the pragmatists. In fact, they would have vehemently opposed this view, a vulgar form of pragmatism at best, in that it leaves the issue of the criteria for use and action completely undecided. This none of them wished to do.

It is in their grappling with such problems and methodological issues, then, that the ability of pragmatism to become the most influential philosophy in America during the first quarter of the twentieth century resides, together with its continuing impact upon other fields as well as within philosophy itself. Each of the major figures also developed distinctly different, full-fledged philosophies, which were not necessarily of one piece with their pragmatic ideas about meaning and truth. Thus the frequent tendency to use the term "pragmatism" to depict their philosophies as a whole is also misleading.

Among the general interpretations of pragmatism, H. S. Thayer's study (1968) is of value as a critical historical outline, and that of A. J. Ayer (1968) as a critical view from the logical positivist side (his own reading, without reference to historical context or other commentators). Israel Scheffler (1974), an analytic philosopher of education, epistemology, and science, works as a more sympathetic critic than does Ayer, sharing with the pragmatists their view that philosophy ought to use its resources to connect detail with principle, analysis with humane and practical vision. His book deals especially with theories of meaning, knowledge, and conduct in Peirce, James, Mead, and Dewey. An earlier discussion by Edward Moore (1961) on pragmatism as represented in its three New England founders—Peirce, James, and Dewey—is by one more nearly identified with their ideas. The same is true of that by Charles Morris (1970), who adds Mead. Moore sought to distill typical doctrines, Morris to display pragmatism as a cooperative movement with common themes; both recognized great differences of emphasis and solution. Recently S. Morris Eames (1977), a student of Morris and much involved with the current critical edition of Dewey's works, has attached the name "pragmatic naturalism" to the movement, again limiting treatment to the big four. His work is a very thoughtful guide to their leading ideas. David Marcell (1974) places pragmatism within the traditional American interest in "progress," interpreting it as a liberal, skeptical, scientific, activist philosophy of progress. He focuses on the thought of James, Dewey, and historian Charles Beard.

Among the later pragmatists from the 1930s on, Charles Morris especially carried forward Peirce's concern to form a comprehensive theory of signs (1971) and their relations to values (1964, both cited on p. 346), melding Mead's understanding of langugage and behavior with linguistic interests stemming from logical positivism. Abraham Kaplan has taken up these and other cues, applying them over a much broader spectrum, philosophical and cultural. Sidney Hook especially represents the social-action orientation. Of an even later generation, Richard Bernstein has written a general book on Dewey (1966), as did Hook (1939, neither cited here), and has applied Deweyan perspectives to analyses of action—personal, social, and political. All four authors are cited in other chapters—and there are many others.

Was C. I. Lewis (1883–1964) a pragmatist at all? He is sometimes listed among the major pragmatists (as by Thayer). If so, this aspect of his philosophy was restricted to his interest in conceptual analysis, more specifically to his novel thesis that the only acceptable test of the truth of a priori knowledge is a pragmatic one, a test he did not extend to empirical knowledge though he does attach it to judgments that something possesses value. But Lewis also held that philosophy is the study of the a priori, so that his analysis regarding the pragmatic test is major for him. It is also a contribution to pragmatic thought sufficiently stimulating to be noted here (Rosenthal, 1976; his major work is cited on p. 325). As is true of the other "pragmatists," his there is much more to his philosophy than a pragmatic theory of meaning or truth.

A *Monist* issue edited by John Smith (1973) gives nine "reconsiderations," mostly on special topics related to Peirce, James, or Dewey. These helpful retrospectives are yet to be accompanied by historically adequate, comprehensive appraisals. Nor do we yet have a study of related activities and influences abroad.

Ayer, Alfred J. *The Origins of Pragmatism: Studies in the Philosophy of Charles Sanders Peirce and William James.* London: Macmillan, 1968.

Eames, S. Morris. *Pragmatic Naturalism: An Introduction.* Carbondale: Univ. of Illinois Pr., 1977.

Marcell, David W. *Progress and Pragmatism: James, Dewey, Beard, and the American Idea of Progress.* Westport, Conn.: Greenwood, 1974.

Moore, Edward C. *American Pragmatism: Peirce, James, and Dewey.* New York: Columbia Univ. Pr., 1961.

Morris, Charles W. *The Pragmatic Movement in American Philosophy.* New York: Braziller, 1970.

Rosenthal, Sandra B. *The Pragmatic A Priori: A Study in the Epistemology of C. I. Lewis.* St. Louis: Green, 1976.

Scheffler, Israel. *Four Pragmatists: A Critical Introduction to Peirce, James, Mead and Dewey.* New York: Humanities Pr.; London: Routledge & Paul, 1974.

Smith, John, ed. "Pragmatism Reconsidered." *Monist* 57, no. 2:133–277 (Apr. 1973).

Thayer, Horace S. *Meaning and Action: A Critical History of Pragmatism.* Indianapolis, Ind.: Bobbs-Merrill, 1968. Repr.: Indianapolis, Ind.: Hackett, 1980 (somewhat revised).

WILLIAM JAMES (1842–1910)

Philosophy and Psychology Intertwined

Much of William James's philosophical work is not separable from his psychological studies. (In fact, his teaching both subjects started a tradition among many American colleges of having both in the same department, which lasted some three-quarters of a century.) Both make clearer than the writings of his contemporaries, Peirce and Dewey, what a threat to free intelligence the world views of absolute idealism and of other "intellectualisms," including theological ones, could seem to hold in the 1870–1914 period. James plumped for individual experience, the right to moral belief even when evidence is not settled, a testing of our ideas in scientific and practical experience, an evolutionary understanding of ideas, and what he called *A Pluralistic Universe* (1909) in the last book published during his lifetime. Although originally interested in painting (which he soon gave up, convinced he lacked ability) and biological science as careers, he was also exploring philosophical issues in the 1860s. His first appointments at Harvard were to teach anatomy and physiology in 1873 and psychology in 1875, followed by philosophy from 1879 to his resignation, at sixty-five, in 1907. James was an extremely vital, sociable man, imageful in his speech, able to gather within his circle of friends distinguished scholars of many persuasions. Intellectually, too, he was a great assembler, though not in a merely collecting-descriptive or purely phenomenological mode, in that he diligently searched for an underlying metaphysical position (a posteriori, not a priori) by which to interpret the varieties of experience.

The Principles of Psychology (1890) is usually thought to be James's greatest work. Already in this book he was emphasizing the constantly changing, though sensibly continuous, and selective, interest-bearing nature of all thought and its restriction to individual consciousness. With realist empiricists, James supposed that thought relates to reality that is independent of itself. In contrast to most empiricists, however, he allowed nothing that may appear in consciousness to be excluded in principle; evidence for well-formed understanding and belief is to be gathered by intelligent introspective means. On these bases, it was James who adopted similar themes he had heard from Peirce, Dewey and company, and in 1898 launched what he then named "pragmatism" (a term Peirce coined twenty years before) as a new movement in philosophy.

James's early essays were published as *The Will to Believe and Other Essays in Popular Philosophy* (1897). His most famous work, *The Varieties of Religious Experience: A Study in Human Nature* (1902), the 1901–2 Gifford Lectures, also represent his "early" period. The period of pragmatic controversy, which began when he was already fifty-six, includes *Pragmatism: A New Name for Some Old Ways of Thinking* (1907) with *The Meaning of Truth: A Sequel to "Pragmatism"* (1909). In the second he indicates the relation of pragmatism to radical empiricism in his philosophy. The final years, which overlap with and, in my view, do not supplant the few years in which he actually promoted pragmatism (though some have said they do) are especially represented by *Essays in Radical Empiricism* (1912). James's works are now in process of being reissued in a critical edition (1975–).

General Accounts and Collections

Overall, the literature on James is of good philosophical quality, though it is not extensive. Two biographical studies, a Pulitzer-Prize-winning philosophical survey by James's student and colleague, Ralph Barton Perry (1935), and a nonphilosophical probe into James's motivations by Gay Wilson Allen (1967), are useful complements to each other. In addition to the interpretations that cover several pragmatists, already mentioned, the following accounts of James's philosophy are of special interest. John Wild (1969) views him as a phenomenologist. Richard Stevens (1974) goes even further in analyzing compatible orientations between James and Husserl, in some detail. Patrick Dooley (1974) sees his "humanism" to be a unifying theme in his philosophy, concentrating on his early psychological works from *The Principles of Psychology* (1890) to *The Varieties of Religious Experience* (1902). That is, Dooley holds that what others have called a philosophical anthropology supplies the basis and direction for James's mature metaphysics and epistemology. Charlene Siegfried (1978) argues that James's radical empiricism, which also chiefly interested Wild and Stevens, is at the heart of his philosophy, rather than pragmatism. She includes the first full-scale analysis of his theory of relations, comparing it with the theories of Hume and Bradley. Recently Walter Corti (1976) has edited a volume of new essays on James. There is also an important volume *In Commemoration of William James* (1942) and a reference guide by Ignas Skrupskelis (1977).

Allen, Gay Wilson. *William James: A Biography.* New York: Viking, 1967.

Corti, Walter Robert, ed. *The Philosophy of William James.* New York: Adler's Foreign Books, 1977; Hamburg: Felix Meiner, 1976.

Dooley, Patrick Kiaran. *Pragmatism as Humanism: The Philosophy of William James.* Chicago: Nelson-Hall, 1974.

In Commemoration of William James, 1842–1942. New York: Columbia Univ. Pr., 1942.

James, William. *The Works of William James.* Cambridge, Mass.: Harvard Univ. Pr., 1975– . (So far, 6 volumes, 1975–79.)

Perry, Ralph Barton. *The Thought and Character of William James.* Vol. 1, *Inheritance and Vocation;* vol. 2, *Philosophy and Psychology.* Boston: Little, Brown, 1935.

Siegfried, Charlene Haddock. *Chaos and Context: A Study in William James.* Athens: Ohio Univ. Pr., 1978.

Skrupskelis, Ignas K. *William James: A Reference Guide.* Boston: G. K. Hall, 1977.

Stevens, Richard. *James and Husserl: The Foundations of Meaning.* The Hague: Nijhoff, 1974.

Wild, John D. *The Radical Empiricism of William James.* Garden City, N.Y.: Doubleday, 1969.

CHARLES SANDERS PEIRCE (1839–1914)

Status, Background, and Achievements

In principle, Charles Sanders Peirce founded pragmatism in the 1870s, though it was not launched as a movement until the late 1890s. Superbly trained in mathematics, logic, and science, already in his twenties he had become the foremost American logician. He now enjoys a reputation for originality in logic equalled only by Gottlob Frege; and some of his work, mostly unpublished, indicates that he was at the forefront of mathematical theory as well. Drawing primarily from his study of the history of logic, where he came upon Duns Scotus and the late medieval realists, he also formed an elaborate philosophical system. These occupations enabled him to write with exactness and great versatility over a broad spectrum of subjects, mostly in philosophy and science. For a number of reasons, many of these remarkable achievements have only gradually come to light, though through a number of seminal papers he has borne important influence continually since the 1860s. (See Paul Weiss's 1934 biography in Bernstein, 1965.)

Peirce was a Harvard man in an extraordinary way even for his time. The Peirces, settled in Massachusetts by 1637, had had a long, close association with the university. His father's father had been librarian there during the last five years of his life (1826–31); his father, Benjamin Peirce, Jr. (1809–80), taught mathematics and astronomy there from 1839 to his death and was the leading mathematician in America. His older brother, James Mills Peirce (1834–1906), also a mathematician, was on the faculty from 1861 to 1906, was the first dean of its graduate school (1890–95), and was dean of the faculty of arts and sciences (1895–98). Peirce himself entered Harvard early, did not adjust well, and ended in the bottom third of his class; but he picked himself up, receiving an M.A. in 1862 and an Sc.B. in chemistry summa cum laude in 1863, the first of its kind. There he also won the lifelong enthusiastic sponsorship of William James.

Peirce taught a total of only eight years, though he wanted to teach and was good at it. Had he secured an academic position, twentieth-century philosophy would no doubt have had a much greater force to contend with. There are several noticeable reasons for this serious failure. First, Peirce was a highly disciplined thinker but poorly disciplined in social respects—haughty-appearing, short-tempered, irregular in meeting his classes, prone to miss apppointments. Both qualities probably derive in large measure from his father's having rigorously supervised his education from early childhood through college. Some of what they did together was playful and creative, but the process seems to have been highly controlled withal and in later years Peirce said he wished his father had taught him more about social conduct. Furthermore, the father wanted him to be a scientist but from at least age thirteen, when he had carefully studied Richard Whately's *Elements of Logic* (1826), the son had a penchant toward logic and philosophy, which became his life's work. At the same time, he did continue in scientific work; and knowledgeable people including his father, stated that he had surpassed his father and brother in mathematics. Achievements, yes, but burdens too.

Second, Peirce divorced his wife in 1883, claiming that she had deserted him seven years earlier; although he married a lady from Nancy, France, shortly thereafter, his divorce was bound to affect his career in that climate. Third, he could not find publishers for his projects, most of which were extremely technical. Some might have been thought overly ambitious—such as in 1893 a proposed twelve volume work on philosophy and in 1902 a set of thirty-six memoirs "each complete in itself, forming a unitary system of logic in all its parts." Chances are Peirce could have pulled some of them off. He received prestigious endorsements but little further support. Fourth, much of the substantial unpublished work he did accomplish remained in unfinished form. Peirce would get them to that state and then rush into a new concentrated effort. His editors discovered mounds of such material, undated and in disarray. Hence, even now only a partly critical selection of his papers, in eight volumes (1931–35, 1958) are available. Fifth, as will be seen, although many basic themes such as his pragmatism are continual, Peirce's mind kept moving, sometimes radically changing; one idea led to another; they would not lie still.

Sixth, much of his life Peirce was poor and had to scrap to make a living. In the 1870s and 1880s he received stipends for occasional lectures and lectureships in logic and philosophy of science. From 1861 to 1891 he worked as a scientist for the U.S. Coast and Geodetic Survey, where his father was superintendent for a time (1867–74), traveling from place to place on assignment. For some years he was an assistant at the Harvard Observatory. In 1878 he published his only book, *Photometric Researches,* based on observations made there. From 1879 to 1884, when he was dismissed, he served as lecturer in logic at the newly organized Johns Hopkins University. In 1887, having obtained a small inheritance, he and his wife retired to the "wilds" of Milford, Pennsylvania, where he made some extra income writing book reviews for the *Nation,* definitions for the *Century Dictionary* (1889–91), and other short-order tasks, necessary for subsistence but distracting him from his real work. Over the last eight years of his life, William James and friends arranged a fund to keep the two alive, but by 1909 he was quite ill, and five years later he died of cancer at seventy-five.

Themes and Interpretations

Peirce's most noted essay, "How to Make Our Ideas Clear," he originally wrote in French in 1877; he translated it for publication in *Popular Science Monthly* the following year. There we find the first statement of pragmatism's key notion: "Consider what effects, which might conceivably have practical bearings, we conceive the object of our conception to have. Then, our conception of these effects is the whole of our conception of the object." Almost mathematically stated and far from vulgar pragmatism in its meaning, this statement sounds out one major continuing theme of Peirce's philosophy. In addition to the joint treatments of pragmatists already mentioned, the study by W. B. Gallie (1952) critically presents this theme in the context of his theory of knowledge and with briefer reference to his substantial contributions to metaphysics, especially cosmology. Able to use further newly edited papers (1958), Murray Murphey (1961) presents Peirce as a systematic philosopher by unveiling his underlying principles in a historical examination of his thought. During his first period (1857–65) he formed a system based on Kantian logic. In the second period (1861–70) he forged a new theory of cognition, beginning with his discovery of the irreducibility of the three syllogistic figures. A revised systematic theory of inquiry appeared in the third period (1871–84), and final revisions emerged from his discovery of quantification and set theory (1885–1914). His dream of completing a vast comprehensive system like that of Aristotle or Leibniz (synechism) never came to fruition, avers Murphey, because he was unable to use effectively his metaphysical-mathematical notion that everything is continuous.

Reflecting some of these thematic developments and changes of interest are more recent specialized studies by William Davis (1972) on his epistemology; by John Fitzgerald (1966) on developing relations of his theory of signs to his pragmatic views, a theory further examined by Douglas Greenlee (1973); by Francis Reilly (1970) on his theory of scientific method, a chronological presentation that emphasizes the systematic character of his thought; and by Joseph Esposito (1980) on his fascinating metaphysical theory of categories. A logically deeper, more analytic investigation of Peirce's philosophy of science than that of Reilly, also somewhat different in subjects covered, has recently appeared under the prolific hand of Nicholas Rescher (1978). Rescher's own trilogy (1973–77) presents a systems-theoretic methodology that answers to what he calls "pragmatic idealism." It owes much to Peirce and is an impressive latter-day example of the kind of thing Peirce was trying to do. (A later related 1979–80 trilogy by Rescher is cited on p. 426). Also helpful toward understanding the general intent and structure of Peirce's work is an examination of Peirce's reading of Duns Scotus by John Boler (1963). So far his scientific work, far more extensive than all the rest, has yet to be assessed in its relation to his philosophical thinking.

Several excellent collections mark the progress of Peirce scholarship. There are two large sets, edited first by Philip Wiener (1952) who had recently published a fine book on the role of the evolution controversy in the emergence of pragmatism (not cited here), then by

Edward Moore and Richard Robin (1964) in the same Harvard series; a handful of new general essays edited by Richard Bernstein (1965), including one by Peirce editor Paul Weiss on Peirce as a philosopher (plus his 1934 biographical summary); and a recent issue of *Monist* edited by the long-time Peirce scholar, Max Fisch (1980). A chronological edition of his *Writings,* edited by Fisch, began to appear in 1982.

Bernstein, Richard J., ed. *Perspectives on Peirce: Critical Essays on Charles Sanders Peirce.* New Haven, Conn.: Yale Univ. Pr., 1965.

Boler, John F. *Charles Peirce and Scholastic Realism: A Study of Peirce's Relation to John Duns Scotus.* Seattle: Univ. of Washington Pr., 1963.

Davis, William H. *Peirce's Epistemology.* The Hague: Nijhoff, 1972.

Esposito, Joseph L. *Evolutionary Metaphysics: The Development of Peirce's Theory of Categories.* Athens: Ohio Univ. Pr., 1980.

Fisch, Max H., et al. "The Relevance of Charles Peirce." *Monist* 63, no. 3:269–407 (July 1980).

Fitzgerald, John J. *Peirce's Theory of Signs as Foundation for Pragmatism.* The Hague: Mouton, 1966.

Gallie, W. B. *Peirce and Pragmatism.* Harmondsworth, Middlesex: Penguin, 1952. Repr.: New York: Dover, 1966.

Greenlee, Douglas. *Peirce's Concept of Sign.* The Hague: Mouton, 1973.

Moore, Edward C., and Richard S. Robin, eds. *Studies in the Philosophy of Charles Sanders Peirce.* 2nd ser. Amherst, Univ. of Massachusetts Pr., 1964.

Murphey, Murray G. *The Development of Peirce's Philosophy.* Cambridge, Mass.: Harvard Univ. Pr., 1961.

Peirce, Charles Sanders. *Collected Papers of Charles Sanders Peirce.* 8v. Vols. 1–6, ed. by Charles Hartshorne and Paul Weiss; vols. 7–8, ed. by Arthur W. Burks. Cambridge, Mass.: Harvard Univ. Pr., 1931–35, 1958.

Reilly, Francis E., S.J. *Charles Peirce's Theory of Scientific Method.* New York: Fordham Univ. Pr., 1970.

Rescher, Nicholas. *Methodological Pragmatism: A Systems-Theoretic Approach to the Theory of Knowledge.* New York: New York Univ. Pr.; Oxford: Blackwell, 1977. (Part of a trilogy with *Conceptual Idealism,* 1973, and *The Primacy of Practice,* 1973.)

———. *Peirce's Philosophy of Science: Critical Studies in His Theory of Induction and Scientific Method.* Notre Dame, Ind.: Univ. of Notre Dame Pr., 1978.

Wiener, Philip Paul, ed. *Studies in the Philosophy of Charles Sanders Peirce.* Cambridge, Mass.: Harvard Univ. Pr., 1952.

JOHN DEWEY (1859–1952)

Dewey's Development

John Dewey was a nineteenth-century philosopher through and through, who transformed his earlier views sufficiently to become

America's most reputed philosopher in the twentieth century. Had he died at age fifty-five (in 1914), rather than at ninety-two, he would have remained among the great pioneer "Golden Age" philosophers of the 1880–1918 period—with Peirce (d. 1914), James (d. 1910), Royce (d. 1916), and Santayana, who left Harvard for Rome in 1912. Instead he helped extend the Golden Age to about 1940, along with his contemporary Alfred North Whitehead (1863–1947). Whitehead was another nineteenth-century figure, at Harvard from 1924 until his death, building a new career there and presenting another, more deliberately metaphysical form of evolutionary philosophy. (It places them both to realize that Dewey was born in 1859, the year Charles Darwin's *Origin of Species* appeared. All the major pragmatists, like Whitehead, were imbued with one form of evolutionary thinking or another.) Although Dewey's method and systematic outlook were firmly established well before 1914, most of the several noted books that are still used today appeared after that time. Already in the late 1880s some basic, unchanged foundations of his later pragmatism and of his preeminent contributions to liberal sociopolitical philosophy, to progressive educational thought, and even (to his students) to liberal religion, had been laid down.

At twenty-two, Dewey had published articles in the neo-Hegelian *Journal of Speculative Philosophy,* criticizing materialism and Spinozan pantheism. As a graduate student at Johns Hopkins University, he became a devotee of the Hegelian philosophy of T. H. Green, a theistic objective idealist, through his neo-Hegelian teacher George Sylvester Morris. (He also studied with Peirce, but not out of interest, and apparently not making much use of Peirce's logic until his early forties.) Morris was also teaching part of the year at the University of Michigan, where Dewey was to join him in 1884. In the same period he studied psychology with G. Stanley Hall, who under William James had obtained Harvard's first doctorate in philosophy. Hall was later to excoriate Dewey's nonexperimental, idealist ventures in psychology. Another major influence then was a Protestant theologian, Newman Smyth, pastor of the First Congregational Church in New Haven, who had developed a "dynamic intuitionism" through the stimulus of Schleiermacher (via Ulrici and others) and of Scottish common-sense philosophers. Smyth's language and approach would dominate Dewey's writings for years to come; it was his way out of strict Hegelianism, putting him close to everyday experience and enabling him to retain his religious perspective in nontheological garb.

By 1886 Dewey was arguing in *Mind,* the leading philosophical periodical, for the position—outrageous to empiricists but not to Hegelians—that psychology and philosophy are identical in that both, as the study of self-consciousness, comprise the study of the universe in its more specific and more general aspects, respectively. Against the Hegelians, he claimed that we come to know the real world through intelligent "experience" (to become his key term), not logic. That is, scientific psychology, not logic, is the method of philosophy. Neil Coughlan (1975) rightly points out that Dewey really never dropped this systematic, prescriptive, nonempiricist, holistic outlook, though it was soon reconstructed in a more social and instrumentalist direction. Whereas James's *Principles of Psychology* (1890) was individualistic and settled upon the great variety and disjointedness of experience—as was true of urbane Cambridge compatriots such as his novelist brother Henry James and the historian Henry Adams—Dewey's *Psychology* (1887) reached for cohesion and the norm. It was on this ground that most of his teaching and writing over the next several years were to be on ethics, viewed in evolutionary perspective but against physical, materialist evolutionist positions like that of Herbert Spencer (1820–1903), and chiefly gained through a psychological analysis of behavior. This was upon his return from a short stint at the University of Minnesota to the University of Michigan, where he had already taught from 1884 to December, 1888. Now he proceeded not from the theistic, neo-Hegelian standpoint of his twenties but from a position of theological and metaphysical agnosticism.

At this distance it is perhaps difficult to realize that in Dewey's student days there were only a few American universities, and they were just beginning to create research orientations and graduate programs. This was done largely on the German model, particularly that of the University of Berlin, founded in 1810. Of the more noted nineteenth-century German philosophers, moreover, only Schopenhauer and Nietzsche were not professors. Over the six centuries before them, the only major exceptions to this rule had been Nicholas of Cusa and Leibniz. From William James on, the same was true of philosophers in America. For the most part, moreover, they have represented alternatives to theology, as became increasingly true of German philosophers after Schleiermacher, who uniquely combined both interests. By the late 1880s Dewey had completely left the evangelicalism of his Vermont youth, even his activities at the First Congregational Church in Ann Arbor. Thereafter he devoted himself to social pursuits in fulfillment of a secularized, democratic "common faith." American philosophers were to share his nontheological bent, though not completely; and they were to become social change agents only to a rather limited extent. Dewey went all out, from his University of Chicago years (1894–1904) to the long final period at Columbia University (1905–30; Emeritus, 1930–39), an intellectual pusher of liberal causes in every conceivable area (Dykhuizen, 1973). Of his greatest works, *Democracy and Education* (1916) best presents his understanding of the progressive, interactive development of education, conceived as "the continuous reconstruction of experience," and of democratic institutions. (Like many of his books, it is turgidly written yet is a clear representation of his thought.) *Experience and Nature* (1925) best presents his naturalist analysis of experience; *Logic: The Theory of Inquiry* (1939) a mature reflection upon his pragmatic method; *The Quest for Certainty* (1929), the Gifford Lectures, his pragmatic doctrine; *Reconstruction in Philosophy* (1920) his pragmatic program. *Human Nature and Conduct* (1922) best sets forth the psychological foundations of his ethics, *The Public and Its Problems* (1926) his social-political philosophy, and *Art as Experience* (1934) his aesthetics. In *Democracy and Education* Dewey defined philosophy itself as "the theory of education in its most general phases," arguing that the reconstruction of philosophy, education, and social ideals and methods must move hand in hand. This perspective goes a long way toward explaining why his chief reputation during the Columbia years was as a philosopher of education and why he remains the best-known theorist in that field.

Biographies, General Accounts, and Collections

Intellectual biographies of Dewey by George Dykhuizen (1973) and, for the pre-Chicago era, by Neil Coughlan (1975) are important for an appreciation of his role in the history of American philosophy. A substantial interpretive literature on Dewey's philosophy has never arisen, and most that does exist is of comparatively poor quality. The better overall interpretations are those in works already cited that cover several pragmatists, by Moore (1961), Thayer (1968), Morris (1970) and Scheffler (1974). William Frankena (1965, cited on p. 498) has carefully critiqued aspects of Dewey's philosophy of education from an analytic perspective. There is as yet no comprehensive critical account of the development or full scope of Dewey's philosophy.

Among the more informative collections are large ones edited by

Paul Schilpp (1939) and by Sidney Morgenbesser (1978). In between, there is a collection edited by Sidney Hook (1950), nineteen broad essays on the occasion of Dewey's ninetieth birthday, one on his educational thought, edited by Reginald Archambault (1966), and a set of new essays, mostly of a summary kind, edited by Steven Cahn (1977). From a Marxist perspective, George Novack (1975) has critiqued Dewey's pragmatism as not only a prominent manifestation of American middle class liberal thinking but, in effect, as the national philosophy of the American people. Like most Dewey studies, this one is not very tightly argued but it does show how engaging his philosophy can still be.

Probably the most significant event, philosophically speaking, is again the publication of Dewey's own writings, now being reissued in critical editions by Southern Illinois University Press (1967–). Jo Ann Boydston (1972) has edited an indispensable guide to his immense production. All of the once virtually inaccessible earlier works have come out; most of the middle and later works (1899–1953) are yet to appear. No doubt this enterprise, also gathering other tools for Dewey study, will support more accurate and useful critical analyses of his thought than have appeared so far.

Archambault, Reginald D., ed. *Dewey on Education: Appraisals.* New York: Random House, 1966.
Boydston, Jo Ann, ed. *Guide to the Works of John Dewey.* Carbondale: Southern Illinois Univ. Pr., 1972.
Cahn, Steven M., ed. *New Studies in the Philosophy of John Dewey.* Hanover, N.H.: Univ. Pr. of New England, 1977.
Coughlan, Neil. *Young John Dewey: An Essay in American Intellectual History.* Chicago and London: Univ. of Chicago Pr., 1975.
Dewey, John. *The Early Works, 1882–1898.* 5v.; *The Middle Works, 1899–1924.* 15v.; *The Later Works, 1925–1953.* ? v. Ed. by Jo Ann Boydston. Carbondale: Southern Illinois Univ. Pr., 1967– . (The first set appeared in 1967–75; vol. 1 of the second set in 1976 and vols. 10–11 in 1981; vol. 1 of the later works in 1981.)
Dykhuizen, George. *The Life and Mind of John Dewey.* Ed. by Jo Ann Boydston. Carbondale: Southern Illinois Univ. Pr., 1973.
Hook, Sidney. *John Dewey: Philosopher of Science and Freedom—A Symposium.* New York: Barnes & Noble, 1950. Repr., 1967.
Morgenbesser, Sidney, ed. *Dewey and His Critics.* New York: Journal of Philosophy, 1978.
Novak, George E. *Pragmatism versus Marxism: An Appraisal of John Dewey's Philosophy.* New York: Pathfinder, 1975.
Schilpp, Paul Arthur, ed. *The Philosophy of John Dewey.* Evanston, Ill.: Northwestern Univ. Pr., 1939.

GEORGE HERBERT MEAD (1863–1931)

George Herbert Mead was not so noticeably influential in the development of pragmatism as were the other major pragmatists, but his work on symbolism and the social self, carried forward by others at the University of Chicago, was of great importance, especially for Dewey and others who also emphasized these themes. Fresh from graduate study at Harvard and in Germany, Mead came to teach at the University of Michigan in 1891, just at the time Dewey had pumped himself up to a revolutionary mood. Dewey was enthusiastically trying to examine everything in terms of the reflex arc (which, by the time he issued his most famous essay on "The Reflex Arc in Psychology" in 1896, had become a complex interactive circuit— and, I think, a model for the complex, spiraling, antidualistic method of writing that became characteristic of Dewey); and he was conceiving action, especially social action, as the proper end of intelligent inquiry. Mead was swept up, saved, and secured by Dewey's thinking, though he went on to establish his own interpretation of the human being as social, views which during his years at the University of Chicago (1894–1931) donated essential concepts to the nascent fields of social psychology and sociology.

The current "symbolic interactionist" approach to social science (Blumer, 1969) derives chiefly from Mead, who was also influenced in his Michigan years by sociologist Charles L. Cooley. In 1894 Dewey brought Mead with him to the University of Chicago, where another previous Michigan philosopher, James Hayden Tufts (1862–1942), whom he had replaced, had preceded them. There, in the late 1890s, these men, along with psychologist James Rowland Angell, were to sponsor a new school of philosophy, which they called "pragmatism." Tufts later coauthored a textbook on *Ethics* (1908) with Dewey. David Miller (1973) has suggested both that the basis for the movement was offered in Dewey's 1896 reflex arc article and that it was especially a result of discussions with Mead, who had developed the concept of "the act," not the moment, as the unit of existence some two years before. However that may be, it is significant that all these men conversed with each other a great deal, especially Mead and Dewey.

David Miller's (1973) is a fine account of Mead's philosophy. A valuable set of new essays has been edited by Walter Corti (1973). A historical work by J. David Lewis and Richard Smith (1980) outlines the influence of pragmatism, from Peirce and James to Dewey and Mead, on Chicago sociology, especially Mead's influence. Mead did not write much. His first book, *The Philosophy of the Present* (1932), consists of unrevised lectures published posthumously. This was followed by *Mind, Self and Society* (1934), lectures on social psychology; *Movements of Thought in the Nineteenth Century* (1936); *The Philosophy of the Act* (1938); and *The Social Psychology of George Herbert Mead* (1956).

Blumer, Herbert. *Symbolic Interactionism: Perspective and Method.* Englewood Cliffs, N.J.: Prentice-Hall, 1969.

Corti, Walter Robert, ed. *The Philosophy of George Herbert Mead.* Amriswiler Bücherei, Switzerland, 1973.

Lewis, J. David, and Richard L. Smith. *American Sociology and Pragmatism: Mead, Chicago Sociology, and Symbolic Interaction.* Chicago and London: Univ. of Chicago Pr., 1980.

Mead, George Herbert. *Mind, Self and Society from the Standpoint of a Social Behaviorist.* Ed. by Charles W. Morris. Chicago: Univ. of Chicago Pr., 1934.

Miller, David L. *George Herbert Mead: Self-Language and the World.* Chicago and London: Univ. of Chicago Pr., 1973.

11

Marx and Marxism

KARL MARX (1818–1883)

Marx's Life and Thought

Though Karl Marx was baptized at age six (1824) and reared a Prussian Protestant, his family was Jewish, and Jews in Prussia lived under edicts that severely restricted their civil rights. A paternal uncle was chief rabbi of Trier, where Marx grew up, until his death in 1827; so for familial reasons alone he could not ignore what it meant to be of that oppressed class. Although he was to say some harsh things about the activities of some Jews, he also identified with and defended his people; contrary to what some critics have claimed, he was never anti-Semitic in the usual meanings of the term. From the dual heritage he came to share with his lawyer father a strong sense of calling to a life of civic responsibility, self-sacrifice, and service to humanity. By early 1837, already an unusually voracious reader, an intense, domineering arguer, and a systematizer in the German style, he had joined in his father's opposition to Hegel as well. By fall he had incensed his father (who died in May 1838 in good relations with his son) by converting to Hegel, an act he himself interpreted as a turn toward realism.

The Hegelian discipleship lasted six years, a heavily theoretical but also passionate and practical apprenticeship in social-political philosophy. In his 1841 doctoral dissertation on "The Difference between the Democritean and Epicurean Philosophy of Nature" he took over Hegel's notion that character is fate, and appears to have identified both with Epicurus's individualist devotion to self-edification and with Democritus's passion for erudition and for serious involvement with the material world. By 1846, age twenty-eight, he

248

had come to concentrate on the material side, as he would most of his life. A central thesis in Jerrold Seigel's (1978) outstanding intellectual biography, from which much of the present summary is derived, is that in adopting the Democritean emphasis Marx also took on the tension between an inner bond to philosophy and a repulsion for it that he had seen in the famous Greek thinker, who is thus a symbol of his own lifelong fate.

Already longing for social revolution, though not yet in the terms for which he is noted, Marx sought to work for change through journalism. Hence, for most of a year (1842–43) he served as a very successful editor of the liberal *Rheinische Zeitung* in Cologne, but the Prussian government closed it down. In late 1843 he moved to Paris with his new bride, Jenny, to whom he had been engaged since 1836 and who was to be a lifelong support to him and their seven children, of whom only three girls survived into adulthood. By 1844 he had given up the expectation of attaining political freedom within the conditions of the modern state and with it Hegel. Stimulated especially by the 1841–43 writings of Ludwig Feuerbach, a left-wing Hegelian, Marx began to forge a critical position of his own. Critical to a fault, in that from Marx's early years almost all his major writings began as critical denunciations of other writers. Henceforth, as the long-unpublished "Economic and Philosophic Manuscripts" of 1844 and other writings of that period show, he was to throw in his lot with the oppressed proletariat, associating Hegel with Epicurus, a philosopher idealistically removed from material reality. Following Feuerbach's lead, he "inverted" Hegel by seeking philosophical truth not in the development of ideas but in empirical knowledge, before long especially in the process of revolutionary change itself. At the same time he wrote a series of articles on Jewish rights, in which he affirmed Judaism as preeminently "the religion of practical need." (The unpublished writings of 1844–45 did not appear in German until 1931 and were not studied to any great extent until after 1945; English translations began to appear in 1959.)

Enter Frederick Engels (1820–95). The two men met in November of 1842. About a year later Engels sent Marx an essay for the *Deutsch-Französische Jahrbücher,* which he and socialist Arnold Ruge were editing. Its title: "Outlines of a Critique of Political Economy." This essay, plus one by Moses Hess "On the Essence of Money" that appeared in the yearbook in late 1843, greatly affected what Marx would write in 1844. In that year he set down a basic critique of capitalist society, an analysis of general social alienation related to the conditions of labor, and a humanistic goal of emancipation. These together set the framework, significantly revised but largely unaltered at base, for all his later efforts. Official Marxist-Leninists and Maoists, and some others, have typically held that these early liberal humanist positions are of no account and that he gave them up. There is almost always controversy over the relation between a thinker's early and later works. This has occurred over the 1844 manuscripts, which were published long after his death and thus did not figure in the initial interpretations of Marx. In my view, a careful analysis of these writings, admittedly fragmentary like almost all of his projects in the early years, cannot but yield a picture of basic continuity. Marx never gave up his early humanism. Although it was purged by fire and reforged by intense new inquiry, this is what drove his subsequent efforts to make a difference through communist theory and action. In both respect Engels was to be a fitting lifelong collaborator.

Ironically, Engels came from a wealthy business and industrial family in Calvinist-pietist Barmen; they also had large interests in Manchester, England. Engels continued to manage family-related textile firms for his livelihood until he was able to retire and live on his investments in 1869. For many years he provided the main financial support for Marx and his family.

There was room for communist interests among Barmen's burgher patricians, whose Reformed beliefs often included a strong sense of responsibility for the well-being and education of worker families and opposition to the industrial revolution. This was the environment that enabled Engels to offer a penetrating analysis of *The Condition of the Working Class in England* (1845) and to stay in business while supporting Communist revolution.

After 1844 there is little use in trying radically to separate the philosophical activities of Marx from those of Engels, who had a decisive continuing impact on his thinking. Since a considerable correspondence between them is extant and since Engels published several substantial works of his own (and dozens of newspaper articles under Marx's name), it is possible to discern some differences of methodological and doctrinal emphasis, however. From 1844 to Marx's death in 1883, for example, Engels contributed much of the dialectical structure that was central to Marx's economic analysis of social-political reality. The epoch-making pronouncements in *The German Ideology* (1846) and *The Communist Manifesto* (1848) were, in effect, only the first joint efforts of many. In the decade after

Marx's death Engels's own systematic philosophical and economic writings and his editing of Marx's unfinished manuscripts did much to establish Marxism among working-class movements. Eventually, his Hegelian emphasis after *Anti-Dühring* (1878) on dialectical materialism, with its strictly deterministic laws of history, extended even to the workings of logic and science.

Marx's own thought is quite intelligible without these narrow constraints. But this late development, which had Marx's blessing, set up a problem that has been central in Marxist thought ever since. Lenin, for example, abused it, while in the post-World War II era Western Marxists and Eastern European Marxist philosophers have recovered its more humanistic, egalitarian characteristics. The whole range of these further uses of Marx's thought, including the more closely authentic pronouncements of Engels, has been labeled "Marxism" since his death.

Until recent years, the more rigidly ideological uses of Marx's thought, especially through the medium of Engels's later writings, have generally helped keep philosophers outside Communist bloc countries from giving careful consideration to what is of philosophical interest in it. Even though Hegelian content was present throughout, and much else that is philosophical, Marx's own explicit opposition to academic philosophy after 1846 and his refusal to build a systematic philosophy of his own have also generally distracted philosophers from this task. Time and again, Marx's own obsessive search for more empirical information, which delayed and left unfinished most of his projects, seems itself to have been an escape from well-ordered philosophical inquiry. Those that have devoted themselves to digging out the philosophical undergirdings and implications of Marx's writings have usually sought to attach his thinking to another philosophical position, especially Hegelian and materialist, but also Spinozist, Kantian, positivist, Freudian, pragmatist, neo-idealist, or existentialist. Recently Carol Gould (1978) has persuasively argued that the metaphysical theory of the nature of social reality implicit in Marx's work presents to us a great, distinctly new systematic philosophy and that for the most part his concrete analyses cannot be adequately understood apart from it.

Unfortunately for Marx, until the 1880s the politics of England and central Europe were in a state of relative calm. Until the initial meeting of the First International on September 28, 1864, Marx himself was quiescent, and even then his usual role within the Communist movement was a tactical, moderating one. He felt forced to live in a situation wherein the requisites for proletarian revolution had not been met.

In the late 1850s Marx returned to philosophical inquiry, as in 1844–45 markedly Hegelian in method, language, and structure, to explain the extremely disappointing events that had occurred. After a five-year period in which he largely directed his thought to other matters, during the fall and winter of 1857–58 he worked with great intensity to set down the basic lines *(Grundrisse)* of his economic theory, this for his own clarification, not for publication. The *Grundrisse* (as it is known in translation also) is the long-missing link between the writings of 1844 and *Capital* (Vol. 1, 1867). Some 800 pages in print, it only first appeared in 1939, in the Soviet Union (a German edition), thence in Germany (1953), when it first began to get some notice, and in English translation only in 1973. This work fully displays the philosophical undergirding of his economic thought. It reexpresses the early humanism, further developing the thoroughgoing social ontology already indicated there; and it thereby sets forth the fundamentals of the economic theory which was to be more carefully elaborated, with significant changes (for example, regarding the expected falling rate of profit in capitalism) and a more pessimistic outlook, in *Capital.* The crucial, extremely innovative theory of surplus value is there. So is the key notion of alienation, directed solely and specifically to the conditions of capitalist political economy, and the related notion of individual freedom, which is seen to develop differently in different social stages and, after capitalism but still through labor activity, to bring about self-realization through self-determination and mutually supportive community.

Capital, like most of Marx's lesser projects, was never finished, though he worked on it off and on the rest of his life. After his death Engels and Karl Kautsky edited what he had prepared for the second and third volumes (with some misleading rearrangements that have only recently come to light). Driven to empirical observation, because his abstract interpretations and ideals could in his view find confirmation or refutation only in actual, changing material conditions, Marx placed his historical materialism in the forefront during those last years. But it now seems clear that historical materialism was in itself unintelligible without the revised Hegelian frame and substance of the *Grundrisse.*

General Interpretations

Among the general interpretations, the Seigel biography (1978) and the kind of analysis of Marx's social philosophy represented by

Gould (1978) are now indispensable. These effectively overthrow the exclusive stress on Marx's later economic theory long promulgated by Eastern Marxist-Leninists and in the West by French philosopher Louis Althusser (e.g., *For Marx*, 1965). To understand how the interpretive tradition has changed in the West, it is valuable to compare early studies like that of pragmatist Sidney Hook (1936) with some in the middle years like those of Jean Hyppolite (1955), who is the chief instigator of relating Hegelian to Marxian studies in France, Ernst Bloch (1950s), and Eugene Kamenka (1962), whose work on Feuerbach has already been noted. In a new preface for the 1969 edition of his book on Marx and Hegel, Hyppolite saw existentialist Marxism yielding to the new tide of structuralism à la Althusser. Within ten years this situation had greatly changed.

Sidney Hook shared a view with some European writers that pragmatism offered a corrective extension of Marxism. For about fifty years, in a series of books beginning in 1933, Hook especially represented this approach in the United States. Others not cited here who like these three viewed Marx primarily as a humanist philosopher include Erich Fromm (1961), Herbert Marcuse (1950s–1960s), Louis Dupré (1966), with the noted Marxist Yugoslavian philosopher Gajo Petrovic (1967, cited here), each from a very different standpoint. The Petrovic volume also includes some essays on general Marxist themes. Among French Marxists Roger Garaudy (cited on p. 260) especially advanced a humanist interpretation.

Theses of continuity between the early and late Marx are addressed to Marx's general social-political theory by Shlomo Avineri (1968) and to his theory of alienation by Bertell Ollman (1971). Ollman has Marx stay closer to Hegel than does Gould, who sees an Aristotelian emphasis on the independent reality of individuals who enter into social relations with each other. Similar themes are organized in a lengthy critical discussion of Marx's philosophical anthropology by Oxford social theorist John Plamenatz (1975). The latter scholars, including Gould, extend a tradition that begins most notably with Georg Lukács and is continued among later committed Marxists like Iring Fetscher (both cited on p. 260). Already in 1961 Robert Tucker had made a helpful distinction between an original Marxism, focused on self-alienated individuals, and a mature, mythic Marxism, a "scientific" socialism in which classes are placed in their stead. He saw the two commingling in writings immediately after the manuscripts of 1844, so that there is no gap between them; the first is simply the foundation of the second. The materialist conception of history, moreover, is seen to have gained its first formulation when

Marx met with Engels in Brussels in the spring of 1845. What happens, in Tucker's view, is that Marx comes to see the self-alienated individual as split (thus a "no-man") between the proletarian and the capitalist. Hence communism, for Marx, is the self regained, and self-alienation was to remain the central theme of his thought. In this respect, like many humanist interpreters of Marx, Tucker sees Marx as very modern and ahead of his time.

A brief introduction by William McBride (1977), using an intellectual history approach, typifies the discussion that has recently emerged. David McLellan (1980), who has published several books on Marx, has drawn upon some of that discussion—not quite so advanced as that in Seigel and Gould—to present sample writings by Marx with chronologically arranged biography and commentary.

Specialized Studies

Of the books already mentioned those by Seigel, Gould, Avineri, and Ollman particularly include contributions on special topics. In addition, a well-known Marx scholar John McMurtry (1978) has tried to give a precise delineation of Marx's way of explaining the human condition, sorting through the mush and muddle both of Marx's writings and of those by traditional interpreters by analyzing a few essential categories. He hopes that by such means philosophers will at last wish to accord sober attention to Marx's thought. Such attention is certainly given by Carol Gould (1978) with respect to his social interpretation of language and action, which she largely affirms. An unusually tight analytic reconstruction of his arguments about alienation, historical and philosophical materialism, morality, and dialectic by Allen Wood (1981) also presages a new stage of exact study.

Considerable agreement on Marx's theory of history was reached independently by Wood and G. A. Cohen (1978). In a solidly argued work directed against the Althusserians, Cohen defends dialectical materialism, as he believes Marx understood it, namely as the view that history is basically the growth of human productive power. Cohen uses Marx to explain, in functional terms, why economic structures enable such power to expand, and he further defends the use of functional explanations in social theory. Close in subject matter to the studies by Cohen and Wood, though different in approach, is a critical analysis of Marx's logic by the Czech Marxist Jindrich Zelený (1980). This work derives from a 1962 study in Czech on the logical structure of *Capital*, which Althusser was also proclaiming to be the essence of Marx's philosophy, or rather of his "science." However, by 1969 Althusser had given up essaying an epistemological foundation for Marxism, returning to a more open phenomenological approach. Logic, for Zelený, who relates his efforts to modern symbolic logic, is "the science of forms of thought leading to knowledge of objective truth," especially in theoretical science. He believes Marx's praxis-oriented logic enabled traditional ontology to be superseded. A huge and very different account of the discussion on Marx's conception of dialectical logic comes from Thomas Jackson (*Dialectics: The Logic of Marxism,* 1971, cited on p. 260).

Is there any tradition behind these particular ways Marx had of grounding theory in the material conditions of social-economic practice? Nicholas Lobkowicz (1967) says yes. His work starts with the Greeks and moves through Hegel to what Lobkowicz, like nearly every informed interpreter today, takes to be the crucial period for Marx, 1831–45. This theme warrants further attention, as does the closely allied theme of ethics that Kamenka, Gould, and Wood have begun to elucidate.

Was Marx a historical relativist? Tucker and Wood appear to think so; Gould does not. A closely related study by John Maguire (1978) ostensibly on Marx's theory of politics is, perhaps of necessity, rather more an account of Marx's changing reactions to political events. Still, the study is well argued and it is useful to see all these perspectives in brief compass. Other questions concerning his views of historical process are taken up by William Shaw (1978) and Melvin Rader (1979). Shaw, a student of G. A. Cohen, provides a determinist reading of Marx's views on the power of productive forces and relations of production in Marx's mature version of a historical materialist view of "the mechanics of historical evolution," elaborated after 1846. In contrast, Rader offers an organic, humanistic interpretation, referring to three models he finds in Marx's theory of history: dialectical development, a relation of base and superstructure, and organic unity. Like Cohen, Shaw tends to support a determinist, Marxian view of history (that is, a view like Marx's). Not a Marxist in any sense (that is, not following an ideological line of thought that stems from Marx), Rader does not support this theory, and he does not see it in Marx.

Althusser, Louis. *For Marx.* Tr. by Ben Brewster. New York: Pantheon, 1969. (French ed., 1965.)
Avineri, Shlomo. *The Social and Political Thought of Karl Marx.* Cambridge and New York: Cambridge Univ. Pr., 1968.

Bloch, Ernst. *On Karl Marx.* New York: Herder & Herder, 1971. (From his 3 v. work, *Das Prinzip Hoffnung.* Berlin: Aufbau-Verlag, 1953–59.)

Cohen, Gerald A. *Karl Marx's Theory of History: A Defense.* Princeton, N.J.: Princeton Univ. Pr., 1978.

Gould, Carol. *Marx's Social Ontology: Individuality and Community in Marx's Theory of Social Reality.* Cambridge, Mass.: MIT Pr., 1978.

Hook, Sidney. *From Hegel to Marx: Studies in the Intellectual Development of Karl Marx.* London: Gollancz, 1936. Repr., 1950, 1962.

Hyppolite, Jean. *Studies on Marx and Hegel.* Tr. by John O'Neill. New York: Basic Books, 1969. (French ed., 1955.)

Kamenka, Eugene. *The Ethical Foundations of Marxism.* 2nd ed. London: Routledge & Paul, 1972. (1st ed., 1962.)

Lobkowicz, Nicholas. *Theory and Practice: History of a Concept from Aristotle to Marx.* Notre Dame, Ind.: Univ. of Notre Dame Pr., 1967.

McBride, William Leon. *The Philosophy of Marx.* New York: St. Martin's Pr., 1977.

McLellan, David. *The Thought of Karl Marx: An Introduction.* 2nd ed. London: Macmillan, 1980. (1st ed., 1971.)

McMurtry, John M. *The Structure of Marx's World-View.* Princeton, N.J.: Princeton Univ. Pr., 1978.

Maguire, John M. *Marx's Theory of Politics.* Cambridge and New York: Cambridge Univ. Pr., 1978.

Ollman, Bertell. *Alienation: Marx's Conception of Man in Capitalist Society.* 2nd ed. Cambridge and New York: Cambridge Univ. Pr., 1976. (1st ed., 1971.)

Petrovic, Gajo. *Marx and the Mid-Century: A Yugoslav Philosopher Considers Karl Marx's Writings.* Garden City, N.Y.: Doubleday Anchor, 1967.

Plamenatz, John. *Karl Marx's Philosophy of Man.* Oxford: Clarendon Pr., 1975.

Rader, Melvin M. *Marx's Interpretation of History.* Oxford and New York: Oxford Univ. Pr., 1979.

Seigel, Jerrold. *Marx's Fate: The Shape of a Life.* Princeton, N.J.: Princeton Univ. Pr., 1978.

Shaw, William H. *Marx's Theory of History.* London: Hutchinson, 1978.

Tucker, Robert C. *Philosophy and Myth in Karl Marx.* 2nd ed. Cambridge and New York: Cambridge Univ. Pr., 1972. (1st ed., 1961.)

Wood, Allen W. *Karl Marx.* London and Boston: Routledge & Paul, 1981.

Zelený, Jindrich. *The Logic of Marx.* Oxford: Blackwell, 1980.

MARXISM

Varieties of Marxism

The labels "Marxist" and "Marxism" now apply to a very wide spectrum of thought, running from (1) adherence to doctrinaire positions supportive of contemporary totalitarian communism or of other versions of communism advanced by Communist parties, to (2) interpretations of Marx's own (changing) ideas, which are in important respects not assimilable to current Communist doctrine, to (3) an essentially two-class interpretation of modern historical process, in terms of a struggle between the material positions and interests of the bourgeois and of the proletariat, and (4) a broader, relativistic but still materialistic view of historical process (such as that by Georg Lukács), (5) humanist and existentialist views of history and society which draw heavily from Marx and Marxist tradition (such as those by many French intellectuals), (6) socialist thought, indebted both to Marx and Marxist thought and to other opposing or complementary sources, and (7) praxis-oriented social philosophy.

Sad to say, critics often tar numbers 5, 6, or 7 with the brush of numbers 1, 2, 3, or 4, thus showing little understanding either of the actual linkage of current with past thought or of the serious, fruitful challenges of Marx-like thinking to present-day assumptions and practices. Usually number 1-type views are so ideologically narrow and closed to critical examination as not to be philosophically respectable. This is far from the case with examples of the other types. In fact, types 3 through 7, which have normally taken deep draughts from Marx, are now a substantial presence in intelligent political theory worldwide.

Early Developments

Marxist philosophy is still heavily oriented to interpretation of Marx—understandably given his historic role in the Communist movement and given the difficulties presented in the texts. Especially among the Western Marxists and in Eastern Europe from the 1960s on, significant new developments have also been in evidence. Moreover, philosophers who have no commitment to communism in any contemporary form have also begun to take a real interest in ideas proposed by Marx and by some of the Marxists. The situation just into the 1960s is well covered by George Lichtheim's (1964) historical and critical study. No one volume as yet surveys the advances—and retreats—of the next twenty years.

The first generation of Western Marxists is most prominently represented by Georg Lukács (1885–1971), who played the leading role in introducing Marxist thought to the West, Karl Korsch (1886–1961) and Ernst Bloch (1880–1959). Among his numerous Marxist writings and cultural studies, the Hungarian Lukács's *History and Class Consciousness* (1923, tr. 1971), which takes a relativistic view, has become a classic. G. H. R. Parkinson (1977) provides a useful survey of Lukács's thought. A later German scholar much indebted to Lukács, Iring Fetscher (1967), has issued a collection of his own essays on changing conceptions of Marxism since that time. The University of Frankfurt and the New School for Social Research are among the places where Fetscher has taught. The major transmitter of a Lukács-type Marxism to France was Lucien Goldmann (1913–70), particularly through his reinterpretations of Kant (e.g., *Immanuel Kant*, 1945). Goldmann has also followed his master in doing literary studies. Recently (1978, not cited here) he has proposed a "new philosophy" woven from an encounter between that of Lukács and Heidegger.

Karl Korsch, who taught in the United States from 1936 to 1961, ended by abandoning Marxism. His 1970 book collects four essays from the 1922–30 period. Korsch was an early German Marxist theorist, much less in the Leninist organizational direction than that taken by his contemporary, the Italian Marxist Antonio Gramsci. In a 1923 book he criticized the Communist movement as a betrayal of the revolution and was condemned for this by the party. Unlike Lukács, whose ideas were similarly criticized, he did not remain a member of the movement, leaving it for good in 1928. Having fled Germany in 1933, he later taught sociology in the United States and continued to write on Marxist philosophy.

After 1933 Ernst Bloch too was attached to Marxism. Bloch waited out the war in the United States, then returned to East Germany, where he was warily accepted by the Communist regime, and in 1961 received asylum in West Germany. His early emphasis, as in his later book *A Philosophy of the Future* (1963), was on anticipatory intelligence, representing a strongly utopian, nonunilinear view of progress, a position broadly cultured and drawn only partly from a Marxian analysis of social structure. A critical account of the early period of Marxist thought, its aftermath and, in his view, eventual dissolution has come from the one-time Polish Marxist Leszek Kolakowski (1978). In a history of ideas study James Miller (1979) carries the theme of individuation and subjectivity from Marx to Jean-Paul Sartre and Maurice Merleau-Ponty, with stopovers in between.

In France since 1945

Immediately after World War II Sartre and his followers began a move toward Marxism in France, while the Marxists there began to abandon Stalinism. In a masterful study done in the history of ideas mode, Mark Poster (1975) has traced and critically analyzed the vicissitudes of these moves, seen as the dominant theme in French social thought since that time. The following summary is taken chiefly from his account. The longing for renewal after the war, he indicates, led intellectuals of most traditions to discuss Hegel's works, especially *The Phenomenology of Mind.* These were then made serious objects of study in France for the first time, through the efforts of philosophers Alexandre Kojève, a Russian emigrant, and Jean Hyppolite, who had been writing on and translating Hegel since the late 1930s. The *Phenomenology* was viewed by many French intellectuals as anticonservative, by Marxists and existentialists specifically as a way to make history intelligible.

After 1945 Marxism in France quickly came to be treated as a respectable, sophisticated philosophy. However, among committed Marxists from the mid-1930s to the mid-1950s, most notably Roger Garaudy—who by the late 1950s was initiating fruitful dialogue with other viewpoints (1970) but did not leave the party—Stalinist politics tended to hold sway even over that. Once Marx's 1844 manuscripts had been digested (they appeared in a poor French translation in 1937, in an adequate one only in 1962), Marxist humanism became the focus of debate with the existentialists. Sartre, whose radical notion of freedom became fashionable after the war and later had a great impact on the New Left, was very active in these debates, an engagement which climaxed in his 1960 *Critique of Dialectical Reason,* not itself a Marxist work though close to Marxism in his dialectical interpretation of social life. The existential phenomenologist Maurice Merleau-Ponty was much influenced by Lukács and had much to do with persuading Sartre that a concern with politics could be consistent with his other philosophical interests. Until 1955 Merleau-Ponty was close to the Communists but thereafter moved away and by 1955 was no longer involved with Marxist thought, whereas Sartre had just got going.

From early on Merleau-Ponty had firmly refused to identify with Stalinist interests. His *Adventures of the Dialectic* (1955) marks his breaking away from Marxism as well, and it includes strong criticisms of Sartre's position. After the Soviet invasion of Hungary in 1956, Sartre himself broke all association with the Communist Party, though until 1968 he put much of his energies into attempts to regenerate Marxism. During those years Marxist thought was to enter into the mainstream of French intellectual culture, along with phenomenology and structuralism. The noted Marxist Louis Althusser (1976), for example, associated himself and his dialectical materialist views with structuralism and against a phenomenological-Marxist philosophy of history. Until the late 1970s there was little interchange between the existential Marxists in France and the German critical theorists, the most notable users of Marxist philosophy in Germany since the 1960s, whose interests date from the Western Marxist activities of the Frankfurt School (1923–50). The rest of the story is nicely outlined by Mark Poster (1975) and Vincent Descombes (*Modern French Philosophy*, cited on p. 160).

Recent Developments outside France

Two 1974 volumes of collected essays by Yugoslav philosopher Mihailo Markovic show something of the growing edge in Eastern European Marxist thought, a movement far away from the official Marxism of the 1930s toward an amalgam of Marxist and other liberal, humanist thought. Markovic has been a visiting professor in the West. The essays on "humanist communism" are accompanied by a long foreword on Yugoslav philosophy by Ken Coates. The other volume shows his analytically fine-tuned attempts to form a praxis-oriented social philosophy. Marxist thought has been attractive to a number of Latin American philosophers and theologians (not translated) and to others in Third World countries. In a critical spirit some new essays by philosophers from English-speaking countries, edited by John Mepham and David-Hillel Ruben (1979), try to deepen arguments that are supportive of Marxist philosophy. Thus far, however, the notion of a distinctly Marxist philosophy has appealed only to a very small number of Anglo-American philosophers.

Althusser, Louis. *Essays in Self-Criticism.* Tr. by Grahame Lock. Atlantic Highlands, N.J.: Humanities Pr.; London: New Left Books, 1976. (Three 1973–75 essays.)

Bloch, Ernst. *A Philosophy of the Future.* Tr. by John Cumming. New York: Herder & Herder, 1970. (German ed., 1963.)

Fetscher, Iring. *Marx and Marxism.* New York: Herder & Herder, 1971. (German ed., 1967.)

Garaudy, Roger. *Marxism in the Twentieth Century.* Tr. by René Hague. London: Collins, 1969. (French ed., 1970.)

✓ Goldmann, Lucien. *Immanuel Kant.* Tr. by Robert Black. London: New Left Books, 1971. (German ed., 1945; enl. French ed., 1967.)

✓ Jackson, Thomas A. *Dialectics: The Logic of Marxism, and Its Critics—An Essay in Exploration.* New York: B. Franklin, 1971.

✓ Kolakowski, Leszek. *Main Currents of Marxism: Its Rise, Growth and Dissolution.* 3v. Tr. by P. S. Falla. Oxford: Clarendon Pr., 1978. (Polish ed., 1976–78.)

Korsch, Karl. *Marxism and Philosophy.* London: New Left Books, 1970.

Lichtheim, George. *Marxism: An Historical and Critical Study.* 2nd ed. London: Routledge & Paul, 1964. (1st ed., 1961.)

Lukács, Georg. *History and Class Consciousness: Studies in Marxist Dialectics.* Tr. by Rodney Livingstone. Cambridge, Mass.: MIT Pr., 1971. (Original German ed. 1923.)

Markovic, Mihailo. *The Contemporary Marx: Essays on Humanist Communism.* Nottingham: Spokesman Books, 1974.

———. *From Affluence to Praxis: Philosophy and Social Criticism.* Ann Arbor: Univ. of Michigan Pr., 1974.

Mepham, John, and David-Hillel Ruben, eds. *Issues in Marxist Philosophy.* 3v. Atlantic Highlands, N.J.: Humanities Pr.; Brighton: Harvester Pr., 1979.

Merleau-Ponty, Maurice. *Adventures of the Dialectic.* Tr. by Joseph Bien. Evanston, Ill.: Northwestern Univ. Pr., 1973. (French ed., 1955.)

Miller, James. *History and Human Existence: From Marx to Merleau-Ponty.* Berkeley and London: Univ. of California Pr., 1979.

Parkinson, George H. R. *Georg Lukács.* London and Boston: Routledge & Paul, 1977.

Poster, Mark. *Existential Marxism in Postwar France: From Sartre to Althusser.* Princeton, N.J.: Princeton Univ. Pr., 1975.

Sartre, Jean-Paul. *Critique of Dialectical Reason.* Vol. 1, *Theory of Practical Ensembles.* Tr. by Alan Sheridan Smith. London: New Left Books, 1976. (French ed., 1960.) (Vol. 2 not published.)

12

Existentialism

Four successive streams of thought—movements only episodically—have tumbled down to us from the early nineteenth century, each affecting somewhat the character and direction of the others as time went on: first existentialism and hermeneutics, then phenomenology, then new forms of all three, more recently an offshoot called critical theory. In various forms and combinations, all four are major options in European philosophy today.

Their provenance and formation have been chiefly European. Existentialism has important though not exclusive sources in Romantic thought and art; it comes to its first distinct expressions in Søren Kierkegaard just before mid-century, then independently and very differently in Friedrich Nietzsche about four decades later. Hermeneutics, first developed early in the century by Friedrich Schleiermacher as an entry deep into the psychological and grammatical meanings of texts, is in part a representation of Romantic interests and in part a more classically philosophical probing for linguistic detail and for dialectical form, including logical argument and architectonic structure. Both influences were dammed up for long periods—Schleiermacher's because much of his philosophy was not published until long after his death in 1834 and was not well known, Nietzsche's for a time because of false identifications of his thought with fascism, Kierkegaard's until his collected works began to appear in German after 1906 and subsequently in other languages.

Phenomenology begins in the mid-1870s with Franz Brentano's work in descriptive psychology, already discussed; but it first achieved its distinctive form in work by his student Edmund Husserl from 1900 on. Husserl (1859–1938) is an exact contemporary of John Dewey (1859–1952) and Sigmund Freud (1856–1940).

262

Critical theory is primarily associated with the work of Jürgen Habermas, the dominant German philosopher of the 1970s, whose Western social-critical Marxist orientation (which in varied forms has also attracted some prominent existentialist and phenomenological thinkers) is presented as a materialistic transformation of phenomenology; it is also both greatly indebted to the historical-interpretive, practical outlook of contemporary hermeneutical philosophy and, in the interest of "reflection," is pitted against what he takes to be its extreme context-dependency.

Several historical themes are emphasized in the major overviews of existential philosophy. First, the confluence of existential and phenomenological interests has persisted within most arms of the movement. In his introduction to the thinking of Sartre, Jaspers, Marcel, and Heidegger, James Collins (1952) appropriately included Husserl alongside Kierkegaard and Nietzsche as a major influence, especially on the existential reflections of Sartre and Heidegger. Mary Warnock (1970) later went so far—I think too far—as to claim that no one is an existential philosopher who cannot prove the parentage of Husserl's phenomenology as well as the ethical voluntarism of Kierkegaard and Nietzsche, though she admits that the two motifs clash. After those three, she has chapters only on Heidegger, Merleau-Ponty, and Sartre. As a philosophical movement, its use of concrete imagination as the way to approach the abstract has indeed been its most appealing feature, as Warnock says, but she also thinks this has brought about its eventual downfall. One cannot argue with the deliverances of concrete imagination; but without argument philosophy is not possible in the long run.

William Barrett's introduction (1958) focuses on Kierkegaard, Nietzsche, Heidegger, and Sartre in order to show the importance of existentialism as a critique of traditional forms of "rationality." Both Collins and Barrett recognize that existentialism is to be identified not as a well-defined movement but as a set of philosophical events within contemporary cultural history. Frederick Olafson (1967) depicts it as a contemporary philosophical movement that more than any other has addressed itself directly to ethical issues. He attempts to restate the existentialists' views in a manner that disengages their expression from the forbidding ontological terminology they have all employed. Olafson looks first at existentialism in its emergence and then at a selection of critical issues concerning action and values, freedom and choice, authenticity and obligation. In place of ontology Olafson interprets existential interests as expressions of a focal "conceptualizing" tendency in human life, one that is not susceptible to a reductive behavioristic analysis.

On the whole, the overviews have been interesting and suggestive but not analytically thorough or historically comprehensive. It may be that the great differences of belief and philosophical style among the major existentialists would obviate any effort to fulfill such criteria. They all share a belief in attending to the conditions of human existence first, as opposed to prior rationalist schemes, and there seems to be widespread agreement with George Schrader's view (1967) that these philosophers represent a "resurgent humanism" vis-à-vis positivist and analytic interests. Contributers to Schrader's collection of essays on each of seven thinkers—Kierkegaard, Jaspers, Heidegger, Marcel, Sartre, Albert Camus (a major French literary existentialist), and Merleau-Ponty—mirror that conception. Important features as to subject matter or method other than the humanist or existential reside in the philosophy of each major figure.

Frequently existentialism is narrowly identified with certain literary uses, especially with their focus on mere subjectivity, the irrational and the absurd. This popular misconception fits the writings of Sartre and Camus. The production of literary philosophers like Gabriel Marcel and Miguel de Unamuno (Nozick, 1971), a Spanish writer, looks very different. In part, for example, they share religious interests with Paul Tillich (1951–63) and others who have taken a more theological tack. Much twentieth-century theology has been deeply informed by existential philosophy, as has much humanistic psychology; but neither conforms to the stereotype.

Philosophers of most other persuasions have taken the search beneath the surface of behavior for the meanings of "existence" to be an idle quest, one leaving us with pronouncements too dark or indefinite to admit of refutation. At issue, however, are not the requisites of philosophy as such but very different ways of perceiving and trying to understand reality.

Barrett, William. *Irrational Man: A Study of Existential Philosophy.* Garden City, N.Y.: Doubleday, 1958.
Collins, James. *The Existentialists: A Critical Study.* Chicago: Regnery, 1952.
Nozick, Martin. *Miguel de Unamuno.* New York: Twayne 1971.
Olafson, Frederick A. *Principles and Persons: An Ethical Interpretation of Existentialism.* Baltimore, Md.: Johns Hopkins Univ. Pr., 1967.
Schrader, George Alfred, Jr., ed. *Existential Philosophers: Kierkegaard to Merleau-Ponty.* New York: McGraw-Hill, 1967.

Tillich, Paul. *Systematic Theology*. 3v. Chicago: Univ. of Chicago Pr., 1951–63.

Warnock, Mary. *Existentialism*. Oxford and New York: Oxford Univ. Pr., 1970.

SØREN KIERKEGAARD (1813–1855)

Still the best single-volume approach to the Danish philosopher, Søren Kierkegaard, also an aesthete, ethicist, social critic, and religious thinker, is Robert Bretall's (1946) well-introduced anthology. Walter Lowrie's (1962) two-volume work on his life and thought has also endured. A 3,481-page index to his collected works (McKinnon, 1970) has become an indispensable aid to research.

Kierkegaard's style is sometimes exquisitely beautiful, sometimes tortuous; routinely it penetrates to issues at the emotional depths of human experience. He attached pseudonyms to much of his "authorship," as he called it, to enable elaboration of views to which he did not necessarily subscribe and to explore them as one part of a dialectical relation, considering each to be incomplete in itself. Mark Taylor (1975) treats Kierkegaard's pseudonymous output by theme, starting with his strategy of enabling the reader's self-realization through Socratic dialogue, then following his dialectic of the stages of the existence of the self: (1) the immediate and reflective poles within the aesthetic stage, (2) the ethical stage, and (3) the religious stage, comprising Religion A and Religion B (Christianity), and ending with Taylor's own critical appraisal. John Elrod (1975) examines those same works on the thesis that, in dialectical fashion, Kierkegaard there developed an ontology, which functions as the essential unifying principle for presenting the three stages. This is done as a working out of self-structure and without any concept of Pure Being. The two George Arbaughs (1968) do something quite different, though complementary. In their guide they set forth almost all his writings (including the ethical ones) chronologically in two sets: aesthetic and Christian. This division is somewhat strained in that the explicitly Christian "edifying discourses," published in his own name, are included in the first set of nineteen, while an aesthetic mode is certainly present in many of the thirty-one Christian writings. They add a very brief account of his journals, newspaper articles, meditations, and prayers.

Among these three works, only Taylor's presents an argument specifically countering Gregor Malantschuk's noted thesis (1971 and in other works from 1953 on) that the theory of the three stages is the unifying theme of all Kierkegaard's work. In my view, Taylor is correct in seeing an extensive yet limited use of the theory, in attaching importance to Kierkegaard's own words for "stages" (not only *Stadier* but also *Spaere,* "sphere"), and in not taking the three stages as strict descriptions of developments in Kierkegaard's own life. In his excellent studies, Malantschuk had already laid out Kierkegaard's use of dialectical method in the "authorship." Although he had pointed out its pedagogical aims, a fuller treatment was to come from Ronald Manheimer (1977). In contrast to these later works, which in detail clarify Kierkegaard's performance and intent, the collection of eleven critical essays edited by Josiah Thompson (1972) offers a bewildering spectrum of interpretations, three of them by Louis Mackey (159 of the 428 pages); Mackey and Stephen Crites each add a new essay to the nine previously published.

In view of Kierkegaard's lifelong project of trying to "become" a Christian, in an effort toward self-realization, much of the literature about his thought has been set within a religious, usually Christian context. George Stack's account (1977) of his philosophical ethics lays that feature aside, as does Kierkegaard in many of his writings. Niels Thulstrup's comprehensive, chronological study (1980) of his relation to Hegel, which is crucial for his philosophy overall, has recently been translated. Displaying similarities and tensions between the two philosophies, Mark Taylor (1980) perceives both as spiritual pilgrimages toward selfhood, but with virtually opposite views of what is and is not authentic. Hegel's leads primarily to socialist emphases and Kierkegaard's leads primarily to individualist emphases among later followers.

On the whole, Kierkegaard studies have been blessed with excellent translation, notably first in German (the Jena edition, 1906 on) then in English (from the late 1930s on) and other languages.

Arbaugh, George E., and George B. Arbaugh. *Kierkegaard's Authorship: A Guide to the Writings of Kierkegaard.* London: Allen & Unwin, 1968.

Bretall, Robert. *A Kierkegaard Anthology.* Princeton, N.J.: Princeton Univ. Pr., 1946. Repr., 1973.

Elrod, John W. *Being and Existence in Kierkegaard's Pseudonymous Works.* Princeton, N.J.: Princeton Univ. Pr., 1975.

Lowrie, Walter. *Kierkegaard.* 2v. New York: Harper, 1962.

McKinnon, Alastair. *The Kierkegaard Indices to Kierkegaard's "Samlede Vaerker."* 4v. Leiden: Brill, 1970.

Malantschuk, Gregor. *Kierkegaard's Thought.* Princeton, N.J.: Princeton Univ. Pr., 1971.

Manheimer, Ronald J. *Kierkegaard as Educator*. Berkeley: Univ. of California Pr., 1977.

Stack, George J. *Kierkegaard's Existential Ethics*. University: Univ. of Alabama Pr., 1977.

Taylor, Mark C. *Journeys to Selfhood: Hegel and Kierkegaard*. Berkeley and London: Univ. of California Pr., 1980.

―――. *Kierkegaard's Pseudonymous Authorship: A Study of Time and the Self*. Princeton, N.J.: Princeton Univ. Pr., 1975.

Thompson, Josiah, ed. *Kierkegaard: A Collection of Critical Essays*. Garden City, N.Y.: Doubleday Anchor, 1972.

Thulstrup, Niels. *Kierkegaard's Relation to Hegel*. Tr. by George L. Stengren. Princeton, N.J.: Princeton Univ. Pr., 1980.

FRIEDRICH NIETZSCHE (1844–1900)

Friedrich Nietzsche is the nineteenth century's most challenging philosophical critic of Western civilization and is an abiding source for the rethinking of its aims. In the ways he pointed to individual responsibility and fought against entanglement in systems he is a founder of existential thought, though he also presents strains of positivism, as the other major existentialists do not.

No philosopher has been better served by a single interpretive volume than has Nietzsche by Walter Kaufmann's (1950, 4th ed. 1974), this despite its magisterial, sometimes vituperative dismissal of other interpreters (not unlike Nietzsche himself). Kaufmann places Nietzsche squarely within Western humanistic tradition, shows that earlier identifications of his themes of the "superman" and the "will to power" with Nazism were flagrant misreadings (initially fostered by Nietzsche's own sister), and in analytic detail displays the amazing breadth of Nietzsche's attainment as a philosopher, psychologist, and anti-Christian apologist. For the first time Kaufmann also lays out the distinct developmental lines of Nietzsche's thinking. He emphasizes that the very late notes on the will to power are indicators of an important project that can be outlined to some extent but remains unfinished; therefore they are to be used, with caution, but not as the key to Nietzsche's earlier philosophy. He holds that the climax of Nietzsche's philosophy lies in the intimate connections between his notion of the person who surpasses traditional constraints on human life and culture—the "overman" *(Übermensch)*—and his attempt to replace the modern idea of progress with the suprahistorical idea of "eternal recurrence." Unlike many other interpreters, before and after, Kaufmann views the latter concept as less an idea than a supremely joyful experience of the present moment by one whose life had been unusually marked by pain and agony.

Although Nietzsche's style is often aphoristic, his thinking is usually sustained and quite susceptible to overall interpretation. His chief aim, however, was to stimulate the reader's own critical investigation of problematic situations, frequently through shock tactics or rollicking humor. As with Kierkegaard, criticism was designed to open one to attain a moral and educational vision of one's own. Contrary to Hegel, he had no belief in the historical-dialectical truth of past systems to offer for such purposes and no picture of what they were all leading up to. At most, he was stretching toward pragmatism near the end.

It was once popular to suppose that Nietzsche's philosophy was that of a crazy man or that he grew mad in the years before his collapse in January 1889. (Thereafter his ability to think and communicate was severely restricted.) First Jaspers, who had a psychiatric background, then other scholars have thoroughly discredited these views. Nietzsche was extraordinarily productive during the 1880s and was quite lucid right up to the break, a victim probably of tertiary syphilis.

By and large, the early Nietzsche studies—through the early 1940s—are of scant value now. One marked exception is the influential summary by Karl Jaspers (1935). His major thesis, still suggestive but generally not thought to be supportable, was that Nietzsche's thought appears as a series of contradictions, both deliberate and inadvertent, contradictions that reflect ambiguities inherent in human life.

It is instructive to contrast Jaspers' book with a later influential study by Martin Heidegger (1961). Jaspers essays a synoptic view, yet one exploratory and respectful of contradiction and diversity, not regarding any one work as a magnum opus and including the posthumously published notes as important working material. In contrast, Heidegger regards the published writings as mere foreground. The account by Jaspers is an explicitly and genuinely existential interpretation; Heidegger's is neither, focusing instead on Nietzsche's role as metaphysician in enabling Being to reveal itself through the conception of an eternally recurrent will to power, thus decisively preparing the way for Heidegger's own ontology. Jaspers also discounts many of Nietzsche's principal philosophical positions except to note briefly how they relate to his own mode of existential philosophizing (out of what he calls *Existenz*), which he believes Nietzsche initiated. For Jaspers biographical, indeed interbiographical, appreciation is essential; for Heidegger it hardly figures in. Both are interesting but unfortunate reductions (Howey, 1973). Ultimately Jaspers regards Nietzsche's philosophy to be seriously deficient, because of its atheism and rejection of transcendence, and dangerous, because of its egoistic, self-destructive tendency and its supposed irrationalism. In the light of his study of both interpretations, Howey perceives an irreconcilable dualism in Nietzsche's thought between ideas oriented to cosmology and to philosophical anthropology.

Most of the important Nietzsche literature has not appeared in English. Among the representative works available, the first book by the noted Roman Catholic historian of philosophy, Frederick Copleston (1942), was on Nietzsche. Approached from a Thomistic religious standpoint, the account was also considerably influenced by Jaspers. It has value today mostly as an early exemplification of a critique frequently made. Copleston is respectful of Nietzsche's search for a higher human culture but he thinks Nietzsche's view of culture is false and pernicious. For him it is not only metaphysically nihilistic but also essentially life-negating, and it lacks any deliberate religious or social reference.

As works of scholarship Copleston's book and Arthur Danto's study (1965) are both seriously arbitrary and inaccurate. Danto's is significant for its efforts to make connections with contemporary analytic interests, which he believes Nietzsche shared to a fair extent. For him nihilism is the central concept, and his interest is largely restricted to ethical and epistemological issues.

The recent studies by Bernd Magnus (1978) and Harold Alderman (1977) are both indebted to Heidegger. Like most interpreters, however, they also find Heidegger's Nietzsche uncongenial. Magnus's work is devoted to the notion of eternal recurrence, viewed as a coherent and profound representation of the way Nietzsche's *Übermensch* would live—in a celebratory manner that transcends nihilism. Eternal recurrence is interpreted as an eternalistic countermyth to Christianized Platonism. Alderman takes *Thus Spake Zarathustra* (in four parts, 1883–92) to be the magnum opus, as is widely done. He especially points out its emphasis on the use of masks in philosophy and on the gift of speech as the means human beings have of dealing with perplexity.

Highly commendable are the somewhat more specialized works by John Wilcox (1974) on his metaethics and epistemology, by Ruediger Grimm (1977) on his mature epistemology, and by Tracy Strong (1975) on his "politics of transfiguration." Strong's percipient work is actually an overview with rare systematic reference to political ideas and implications. Previously little attention was given to this subject, since Nietzsche presents no organized text on it. Likewise, Jaspers and many others have claimed that Nietzsche had no epistemology. Both traditions were faulty in that they mistook Nietzsche's radical critique of Western philosophy and civilization as a repudiation of both metaphysics and epistemology, both morality and politics. Actually, Nietzsche called for a transformation of all these foundations of cultural thought and practice, a rebuilding on terms he himself saw only unclearly.

The collection of twenty-one essays edited by Robert Solomon (1980) is considerably diverse, dating from George Bernard Shaw's time (1896) to recent years. Six new essays cover all the major topics just mentioned.

Only recently (Mazzino Montinari and Giorgi Colli, eds., 1967–) has a critical edition of Nietzsche's writings begun to appear in German—a thirty-volume project. In English the translations by Walter Kaufmann and R. J. Hollingdale are themselves significant works of philosophical scholarship. Very few of the others are trustworthy.

Alderman, Harold. *Nietzsche's Gift.* Athens: Ohio Univ. Pr., 1977.

Copleston, Frederick C. *Friedrich Nietzsche, Philosopher of Culture.* New York: Barnes & Noble; London: Search Pr., 1975. (1st ed., 1942.) (New preface and three unpublished papers added.)

Danto, Arthur C. *Nietzsche as Philosopher.* New York: Macmillan, 1965.

Grimm, Ruediger Hermann. *Nietzsche's Theory of Knowledge.* Berlin and New York: de Gruyter, 1977.

Heidegger, Martin. *Nietzsche,* vol. 1. Tr. by David F. Krell. New York and London: Harper & Row, 1979. (Four volumes to appear, from German ed., 1961, lectures and treatises from 1936–46.)

Howey, Richard Lowell. *Heidegger and Jaspers on Nietzsche: A Critical Examination of Heidegger's and Jaspers' Interpretations of Nietzsche.* The Hague: Nijhoff, 1973.

Jaspers, Karl. *Nietzsche: An Introduction to the Understanding of His Philosophical Activity.* Tr. by Charles F. Wallraff and Frederick J. Schmitz. Tucson: Univ. of Arizona Pr., 1965. (German ed., 1935.)

Kaufmann, Walter. *Nietzsche: Philosopher, Psychologist, Antichrist.* 4th ed. Princeton, N.J.: Princeton Univ. Pr., 1974. (1st ed., 1950.)

Magnus, Bernd. *Nietzsche's Existential Imperative.* Bloomington: Indiana Univ. Pr., 1978.

Solomon, Robert C., ed. *Nietzsche: A Collection of Critical Essays.* Garden City, N.Y.: Doubleday Anchor, 1980.

Strong, Tracy B. *Friedrich Nietzsche and the Politics of Transfiguration.* Berkeley: Univ. of California Pr., 1975.

Wilcox, John T. *Truth and Value in Nietzsche: A Study of His Metaethics and Epistemology.* Ann Arbor: Univ. of Michigan Pr., 1974.

MARTIN BUBER (1878–1965)

Perhaps no Jewish religious philosopher since Maimonides has had a greater reputation outside his own religious circle than Martin Buber. This influence was chiefly due to one basic distinction, first made in his masterpiece, *I and Thou* (1922), that runs through all his thought thereafter: that between an I-Thou relation and an I-It relation. A down-to-earth, nonmystical insight, its origin was nevertheless a theological one. My relation to an "it" is to an object distant from me. That to a "thou" (or "you"—the German familiar *du*) is to one who encounters me, addresses my whole being, and in that dialogue challenges me to move toward unqualified openness and freedom, to be present in the moment of relation for its own sake, never solely because of the past. In his continual exploration of what such a relation might mean—for example, in understanding language, religious texts, life in community, socialist society, and the roles of teachers and psychotherapists—Buber ranks among the great existentialists.

The I-and-Thou project began with a theological interest, accompanied by an engagement with religious existentialism. Outlines for subsequent works never written display a predominately religious interest at that time, though often his discourse is not explicitly religious. The dialogic element came first through writings of his contemporary, Ferdinand Ebner (1882–1931), then in intimate collaboration with his close friend Franz Rosenzweig. Both of these other men had emphasized the central importance of interactive, spoken language for understanding versus the monologic thought structures of nineteenth-century German idealism and Jewish rationalism.

The introduction to Buber's thought by Malcolm Diamond (1960) is useful but very sketchy and is not philosophical. This account is corrected and greatly supplemented by the following sources. First, the large collection of thirty new essays edited by Paul Arthur Schilpp (1967) is basic for all subsequent interpretation, as are Buber's brief autobiography and his replies there. Second, Buber's own discussions with questioners takes up a quarter of *Philosophical Interrogations,* edited by Sidney and Beatrice Rome (1964) and are invaluable. Third, Grete Schaeder's large synopsis (1966) helpfully places him within the traditions of Hebrew humanism and outlines the development of his extensive work from his youth to his study with favorite university teachers, philosopher Wilhelm Dilthey and sociology founder Georg Simmel, to his dissertation on Nicholas of Cusa and Jacob Boehme, to his later studies of Hasidism, and from 1898 his distinctive role with and against Theodor Herzel in the Zionist struggle for the creation of Israel.

Buber presents a prime example of the deep involvement in religious, social, or political life by many existential philosophers. The popular reverse stereotype of self-preoccupation comes more from literature and art than from philosophy.

Buber, Martin. *I and Thou.* 2nd ed. Tr. by Ronald Gregor Smith. New York: Scribner, 1958. (1st ed., Edinburgh: T. & T. Clark, 1937; German ed., 1922.) (Another translation by Walter Kaufmann, New York: Scribner, 1970, is to be preferred in some respects.)

Diamond, Malcolm L. *Martin Buber: Jewish Existentialist.* Oxford and New York: Oxford Univ. Pr., 1960.

Rome, Sidney, and Beatrice Rome, eds. *Philosophical Interrogations of Martin Buber, John Wild, Jean Wahl, Brand Blanshard, Paul Weiss, Charles Hartshorne, Paul Tillich.* New York: Holt, Rinehart & Winston, 1964. Repr.: New York: Harper Torchbooks, 1970.

Schaeder, Grete. *The Hebrew Humanism of Martin Buber.* Tr. by Noah J. Jacobs. Detroit, Mich.: Wayne State Univ. Pr., 1973. (German ed., 1966.)

Schilpp, Paul Arthur, and Maurice Freedman, eds. *The Philosophy of Martin Buber.* La Salle, Ill.: Open Court, 1967.

KARL JASPERS (1883–1969)

For Karl Jaspers, as for Buber, interpersonal communication is an essential feature of a person's effective existence in the world. His reputation as a critic of Nazism and a philosophical prophet in post-Nazi Europe likewise marked a keen political involvement. In his sense both for the transcendent and for the severe limitations of human existence, he drew first from Kant and Nicholas of Cusa, then from Kierkegaard and Nietzsche. Dilthey also had an important effect on his way of looking at science and philosophy. Underneath is a liberalized Protestant-Augustinian faith, divested of theological doctrine and institutional ties. In 1948 he called it a "philosophical faith." In his middle years Jaspers published numerous studies of how various philosophically relevant thinkers coped with their existential predicament. Several of them—such as Lao-Tzu, Buddha, and Jesus—are not usually thought of as philosophers.

For many years, the scholarly activities of Jaspers centered in psychiatry and psychology. His "General Psychopathology" (1913) was a major work in the field; it appeared in a fourth edition after World War II. In 1921 he moved over to the philosophy department at the University of Heidelberg, where he was forced to stop teaching in 1937.He precariously waited out the war with his Jewish wife and in 1948 went to Basel, where he was professor until his death. Despite a debilitating heart condition, detected at age nineteen, Jaspers was a very productive writer. The three-volume *Philosophy* (1932, tr. 1969–71) is his chief work, articulating nearly all the basic themes he was to pursue in succeeding years. *Way to Wisdom* (1951) later sums up these themes in much briefer compass. Exploring the boundaries of reason, science, chance, suffering, death, and other conditions of human existence provides the opportunity for free decision, hence for a kind of transcendence and self-discovery. There is no final certainty, however. The philosopher's task is to learn how to live with uncertainty, how to choose freely and responsibly not having any firm and sure foundations.

Until the 1970s very little literature on Jaspers appeared in English and few of his works were translated. The best introduction to the philosophy of Jaspers available in English is by Charles Wallraff (1970). This is a brief expository work, which amply sets forth Jaspers's ideas in their own terms and in relation to what other philosophers have said, past and present. Another highly competent and sympathetic general account is given by Roman Catholic philosopher Sebastian Samay (1971). This one focuses on the interplay of metaphysical and existential issues in the functioning of philosophical reason. Oddly making no reference to either study, Leonard Ehrlich (1975) attempts an overview of his philosophy through an examination of one theme: philosophizing as a way of having faith. Ehrlich includes an examination of the notion of "ciphers" (taken by Jaspers from Pascal) as means by which transcendence ("the encompassing"), otherwise hidden and wholly other, becomes revealed in experience.

A large collection of expository and critical essays has been edited by Paul Arthur Schilpp (1957), reissued with addenda in 1981. These are accompanied by a 90-page philosophical autobiography and a 121-page reply by Jaspers.

Ehrlich, Leonard H. *Karl Jaspers: Philosophy as Faith.* Amherst: Univ. of Massachusetts Pr., 1975.

Jaspers, Karl. *Philosophy.* 3v. Tr. by E. B. Ashton. Chicago and London: Univ. of Chicago Pr., 1969–71. (German ed., 1932.)

————. *Way to Wisdom: An Introduction to Philosophy.* Tr. by Ralph Manheim. New Haven, Conn.: Yale Univ. Pr., 1954; London: Gollancz, 1951. (German ed., 1950.)

Samay, Sebastian, O.S.B. *Reason Revisited: The Philosophy of Karl Jaspers.* Notre Dame, Ind.: Univ. of Notre Dame Pr.; London: Macmillan, 1971.

Schilpp, Paul Arthur, ed. *The Philosophy of Karl Jaspers.* New York: Tudor, 1957. (48 pages added in augmented edition: Chicago: Open Court, 1981.)

Wallraff, Charles F. *Karl Jaspers: An Introduction to His Philosophy.* Princeton, N.J.: Princeton Univ. Pr., 1970.

GABRIEL MARCEL (1889–1973)

In a 1925 essay on "Existence and Objectivity" Gabriel Marcel introduced the main lines of existential thought into French philosophy. Unlike Jaspers, he had come to this point rather in reaction to idealism—especially through his engagement with F. W. J. Schelling, Josiah Royce, and F. H. Bradley—than by influence from Kierkegaard, whom he had not read, or Nietzsche. In his independently derived emphases on dialogue, communion, and cocreativity of persons he is much closer to Buber than to any other existentialist. John O'Malley (1966) has attentively explored the central place of these themes in Marcel's philosophy. Other major themes have been well captured by Kenneth Gallagher (1962), including all those featured below. No volume of critical essays on Marcel's philosophy has yet appeared in English.

Marcel's conversion to Christianity in 1929 has led some to identify him as a "Catholic" thinker. This is a misleading label, in that his thinking did not markedly change after that event. His major work, *The Mystery of Being* (1950–51), however, carries evidence evocative of Christian belief.

Because of the surpassing influence of Sartre in French existentialism, it is of interest to note the main differences in their views, seen chiefly through Marcel's eyes (1956). For Sartre, the details of experience are nauseous, their overabundance obscene; even thought is insipid. For Marcel, they bestir wonder and appreciation, though he wrenchingly acknowledges a dark side. For Sartre the necessary "freedom" of being oneself simply reveals one's life as nonbeing, a suspension from being, an absurdity. One is condemned to be free. The world is observed alone, from the terrace of a café. For Marcel, freedom is not a mere given; it is discovered and attained on the road. One's primary relation to the world is one of participation, receptivity, mutual testimony, and commitment. To grow as a person, in reflective terms, means becoming more aware of the underlying unity that ties one to other beings, one's fellow travelers. For Sartre, love is the opportunity to acquire value in the eyes of another, thus to feel that one's existence is justified; but as an ideal love is utterly unattainable. To be seen or given to by others is an intrusion and enslavement, an earthly hell. For Marcel love is essentially the positive experience of being open to each other's lives, especially of being decisively present and available *(disponible)* to each other. More, the mutually participative "we" is what constitutes human knowing and value, not the Cartesian "I" or the Sartrean exiled, alienated "I." By such means as fidelity, hope, love, and reflection, one has access to being. Therein one is not restricted to confrontation by "problems," which one can lay siege to and reduce by using established techniques; more important, one is copersonally involved in the "mystery of being," which can be known through experience and with the use of techniques but which transcends every conceivable technique.

Gallagher, Kenneth T. *The Philosophy of Gabriel Marcel.* New York: Fordham Univ. Pr., 1962. Repr., 1975.

Marcel, Gabriel. *The Mystery of Being.* 2v. Tr. by René Hague. Chicago: Regnery; London: Harvill, 1950–51. (French ed., 1951.) (Gifford Lectures, 1949–50.)

———. *The Philosophy of Existentialism.* Tr. by Manya Harari. New York: Philosophical Library, 1956. Repr.: New York: Citadel Pr., 1961. (Original ed., 1949.) (Some essays from 1933 to 1946.)

O'Malley, John B. *The Fellowship of Being: An Essay on the Concept of Person in the Philosophy of Gabriel Marcel.* The Hague: Nijhoff, 1966.

JEAN-PAUL SARTRE (1905–1980)

Jean-Paul Sartre is an eminent literary figure, whose philosophical interests permeate, sometimes overshadow, his nonphilosophical writings. His Heideggerian, Husserlian treatise, *Being and Nothingness* (1943, tr. 1956) is so far his chief claim to fame as a philosopher outside France. All the studies of his philosophy focus on that work, which refers to the themes already mentioned in contrast to Marcel's existentialism. As Joseph Catalano (1974) has emphasized in his recent brief synopsis, the book deals especially with the apparent gap between sheer contingent existence (the "for-itself") and reflective consciousness (the "in-itself"). There Sartre attempts to explain why for reflective human beings existence is prior to essence and to present the ontological grounds for authentic existence, lived in "good faith." With some adjustments, his later *Critique of Dialectical Reason* (1960, cited on p. 261) applies this position to a Marxist social philosophy. Sartre came to see his *Critique* as close to Marxism but not a Marxist work (Schilpp, 1980, p. 20), and he claims never to have thought as a Marxist. Marjorie Grene (1973) reviews both works, following the move between the two from a phenomenological dialectic of individual consciousness to a critical, experimental dialectic of society that substitutes the concept of "practical organism" for the earlier "for-itself." She does not see any marked change of position, though she detects some possible assimilations from Merleau-Ponty in a late major work on Flaubert, *Idiot of the Family* (1970–72). In the 1950s and 1960s Sartre played an important role in the formation of existential Marxism in France (Poster, 1975, cited on p. 261).

Able and typical interpretations of Sartre's ontology, within the vast but mostly undistinguished literature on the subject, are the expositions and critiques by Maurice Natanson (1951), who holds that Sartre had an inadequate phenomenological method; Wilfrid Desan (1954), who takes his existential subjectivism to be narrow and tragic; and Klaus Hartmann (1966), who finds Sartre's basic ontological views to be a positive and consistent transformation of Hegel's *Logic*. All three refer to the Husserlian and Heideggerian background and indicate ways in which he transcended it.

From within the analytic tradition, Arthur Danto (1975) admiringly abstracts five themes: absurdity, nothingness, engagement, shame, and anguish; and Phyllis Morris (1976) sympathetically discusses the notions of personal identity and responsible moral agency in his early work, relating them to recent analytic interests. The picture that emerges in both accounts is more positive than that conveyed by Marcel. In the 1960s Sartre mellowed somewhat from the stark position of his earlier years; but it has also perhaps been difficult for interpreters to believe he meant what he said in that it grates harshly against ordinary humanist sentiments.

Anthony Manser's (1966) much broader survey draws from the plays and other writings to lay out the hard core of philosophical argument that runs through them all. Mary Warnock's (1965) brief introduction is both appreciative and critical and lies close to the British analytic context. Francis Jeanson's study of Sartre (1947, tr. 1980) highlights the problem of morality and is said to be the only detailed interpretation of his work Sartre ever fully recommended. A thoroughgoing work on his ethics—a topic Sartre himself barely developed in any formal way—is yet to appear, but the examination of certain basic structures by Thomas Anderson (1979) is a good beginning.

A collection of critical essays has been edited by Mary Warnock (1971). The large Sartre volume in the Library of Living Philosophers, edited by Paul Arthur Schilpp, appeared in 1981, its twenty-eight essays themselves marking a new stage in Sartre studies. This volume lacks the usual author's autobiography and replies, because of Sartre's failing health, but includes an interview with him.

Anderson, Thomas C. *The Foundation and Structure of Sartrean Ethics.* Lawrence: Regents Pr. of Kansas, 1979.

Catalano, Joseph S. *A Commentary on Jean-Paul Sartre's "Being and Nothingness."* New York: Harper & Row, 1974.

Danto, Arthur. *Jean-Paul Sartre.* New York: Viking, 1975.

Desan, Wilfrid. *The Tragic Finale: An Essay on the Philosohy of Sartre.* Rev. ed. New York: Harper Torchbooks, 1960. (Original ed., Cambridge, Mass.: Harvard Univ. Pr., 1954.)

Grene, Marjorie. *Sartre.* New York: New Viewpoints, 1973.

Hartmann, Klaus. *Sartre's Ontology: A Study of Being and Nothingness in the Light of Hegel's Logic.* Evanston, Ill.: Northwestern Univ. Pr., 1966. (German ed., 1963.)

Jeanson, Francis. *Sartre and the Problem of Morality.* Tr. by Robert V. Stone. Bloomington: Indiana Univ. Pr., 1980. (Original French ed., 1947, with a 1965 "Postface".)

Manser, Anthony. *Sartre: A Philosophic Study.* New York: Oxford Univ. Pr.; London: Athlone Pr., 1966.

Morris, Phyllis Sutton. *Sartre's Concept of a Person: An Analytic Approach.* Amherst: Univ. of Massachusetts Pr., 1976.

Natanson, Maurice. *A Critique of Jean-Paul Sartre's Ontology.* Lincoln: Univ. of Nebraska Pr., 1951. Repr.: The Hague: Nijhoff, 1973.

Sartre, Jean-Paul. *Being and Nothingness: An Essay on Phenomenological Ontology.* Tr. by Hazel E. Barnes. New York: Philosophical Library, 1956. (French ed., 1943.)

Schilpp, Paul Arthur, ed. *The Philosophy of Jean-Paul Sartre.* La Salle, Ill.: Open Court, 1981.

Warnock, Mary. *The Philosophy of Sartre.* New York: Hillary House; London: Hutchinson, 1965.

———, ed. *Sartre: A Collection of Critical Essays.* Garden City, N.Y.: Doubleday Anchor, 1971.

MARTIN HEIDEGGER (1889–1976)

The Nouveau Ontologist

Among all the so-called existentialists, Heidegger's work is the most untypical and enigmatic. At the same time, it has attracted by far the most literature and the most devoted adherents. In fact, it is probably accurate to say—as he himself often insisted—that he is neither an existentialist nor a phenomenologist though his thought is indebted to both sources. Rather he stands peculiarly alone—a nouveau-ontologist—and is merely appropriated by advocates of both streams of thought. Generally, to philosophical readers Heidegger's writings are extraordinarily obscure and swamplike, indeed almost impenetrably so. Yet one repeatedly reads the same themes, words, and phrases, both in his work and among the diverse friendly interpretations. Something solid and significant must be going on there to have elicited such extensive interest.

Being and Time (1927, tr. 1962), his first, greatest, and most influential published treatise, employed a philosophical method he called "hermeneutic phenomenology," and the first part of this unfinished work consists of an existentialist-appearing analysis of the inauthenticity of human life in the everyday world. Heidegger characterizes this world as one into which each has been inescapably thrown, which each must make one's own, and in the particular and public dimensions of which one tends to become disastrously alienated from primal Being. What can one do in the face of such inescapable separation, loss, and finitude? In a sense, nothing. There are no clear rules. However, in some fashion the rare individual, he thinks, can overcome these obstacles, can build a destiny. How? First, by simply accepting this condition with the dread and sense of nothingness that accompanies it. Then, by searching out a future in which Being is revealed as "given" in it all, taking this anticipatory task as one's essential "concern."

Viewed in clinical perspective, Heidegger's work appears to dwell throughout especially on the universal but sometimes overwhelming depressive and paranoid features of human life. These he initially wished to deal with in a philosophically ordered way. To him, "phenomenology" then meant getting to the essence of the matter through concrete details; "hermeneutic" meant unveiling hidden meaning or truth through examination of language. In a variety of ways this interest has occupied many abstract thinkers in the twentieth century. From age seventeen it was Heidegger's overriding concern.

Heidegger's childhood and youth were steeped in Roman Catholicism. Later he gathered in Lutheran-Augustinian perspectives as well. His father was sacristan at the church in the Black Forest town of Messkirch, where he was born and died and from which area he rarely strayed during his eighty-six years. When he was seventeen a priest handed him a book by Catholic philosopher Franz Brentano, teacher of Edmund Husserl and in many respects the founder of phenomenology, on the manifold meaning of Being according to Aristotle (1862). Although he found the book hard to understand, its penetrating realism captivated him and suggested a type of vehicle that would serve his own search. This appears to have been the intellectual event that enabled him gradually to formulate his own lifetime theme over the next few years and to discover a satisfactory method for pursuing it. The theme was: What does it mean for me to exist as a human being; more specifically, what am I to do with my feelings of separation, limitation, and emptiness, and with the expectation of my own death? Still more abstractly put: "What does Being mean?" The first forms of the question, taken by themselves, might well have led to existentialism, which he only utilized in the more descriptive portions of *Being and Time,* never in any restricted fashion thereafter. The more abstract form of the question, seen as the best way to cope with the first, became his lifelong preoccupation. The method, in brief reconstruction, was: to follow whatever pathways of language and experience might lead one to primal Being, the Parmenidean One. The specific procedures took many years to work out and changed their emphasis from about 1929 on, decisively after 1934.

At the neighboring University of Freiburg Heidegger spent two years studying theology, chiefly under the influence of speculative dogmatician Carl Braig, a theological ontologist of modern idealist bent. He then moved, at age twenty-one, to the far more abstract, much less historically ensconsed resources of philosophy, though he was never to leave the religious domain entirely. In fact, the general form of his philosophy can easily be read as an abstract mirroring of the post-World War I "crisis theology," especially that of neoorthodox Karl Barth and of demythologizer Rudolf Bultmann. Against the philosophical stream since Descartes, to mine human consciousness is not the central task but rather "to listen to the voice of Being." In doing so one shakes the foundations of most previous philosophy. As his friend, Walter Biemel (1973) has written: the basic "mood" in Heidegger's thinking is that of the "time of need," finding in one's very sadness over the withdrawal of Being releasement to a new advent of Being, especially through language. This was Heidegger's way from beginning to end, and he created a great deal of idiosyncratic language in the process. In style, the textual expositions that comprise most of his lectures and writings over the years was significantly influenced by Karl Barth's epoch-making commentary on Paul's Epistle to the Romans (1918, 1921), laying out a strong line of thought against certain traditions yet fixed to the text, phrase by phrase.

The same spell that had entranced Heidegger in reading Brentano was even more pronounced in discovering Husserl's two-volume *Logical Investigations* (1900–1), which he read again and again over the next several years. His first thesis under neo-Kantian Heinrich Rickert in 1913 followed Husserl as well as Rickert and other anti-positivists of the time in opposing reduction of logic to psychological processes. His first published article (1912) had opposed the preoccupation of modern philosophy with epistemology in favor of metaphysical and historical pursuits. His 1915 thesis on Duns Scotus's views on the Being in beings and on the relation of language to Being, dedicated to Rickert, followed a period in which he was reading widely in philosophy, literature, and the sciences. Artistotle (for which he was prepared by training in the classics), the German poets Friedrich Hölderlin, Rainer Maria Rilke, and Georg Trakl, Dostoevsky's novels, Kierkegaard, Bergson, Nietzsche, and Dilthey were all major influences not only in this period but throughout. When Husserl came to Freiburg as Rickert's successor in 1916, Heidegger became his assistant. After five years in Marburg (1923–28), for him the most exciting and productive in his career, he returned to Freiburg as Husserl's successor. While in Marburg he gained a widespread reputation as an unusually provocative teacher, starting everything afresh and preparing meticulously for discussions with students through interpretation of great texts. In a reported mood of absorbed self-assurance, he basically aimed in his teaching to communicate his experience of thinking and to coax others into thinking things out for themselves. Almost all the projected seventy volumes of his works (announced on his eighty-fifth birthday in 1974), including the relatively few he actually published, come from manuscripts prepared for lectures and seminars. Normally they consisted of an examination of texts.

Just after *Being and Time* appeared in 1927, Husserl invited Heidegger to write an article with him on phenomenology for *Encyclopaedia Britannica.* Husserl's draft was published, Heidegger's not—already evidence of their considerable differences. Although Heidegger succeeded to Husserl's chair in 1928, the two never collaborated thereafter. This greatest of his works was never completed (he delivered it to his mother's deathbed—his father had died in 1924). His intention to provide a second part dealing with the question of Temporality and Being in general was not fulfilled in any of his writings. Because of this incompleteness, his beginnings have retained something of an existentialist cast to many interpreters. In the following years he nevertheless sounded less and less like either an existentialist or a phenomenologist. As it were, *Dasein* (a key term, meaning roughly being stuck in the world) took over and within it the search for *Sein* (Being). His 1929 *Kant and the Problem of Metaphysics* (tr. 1962) was in part a rejection of subjectivist approaches in philosophy, including Husserl's, and his 1929 *What Is Metaphysics?* was occupied with the problem of access to Being. Henceforth nihilism and the "darkening" of the contemporary world were viewed ontologically—even theologically, one might say, but without the doctrines or the systematics—as a falling away from Being. By publication of his next major work in 1936 on the poet Hölderlin, the shift of attention was quite apparent. Now the interest was in extracting insight into the Truth of Being from language, especially German and Greek. His own style became rather more poetical than logical. By 1964, in a lecture on "The End of Philosophy," he was summing up his interests as not in philosophy in any formal sense but in "thinking." Philosophy he then identified particularly with representational thinking and with a preoccupation with method and certainty, all of which had especially been taken over, in his view, by the scientific-technological world and the social order proper to this world.

National Socialism and After

Something else of great significance had occupied him meanwhile. In 1933–34 Heidegger experienced what can only be termed a perverse infatuation with National Socialism, believing it was Germany's only salvation. From April 1933 until his resignation from post and party in February 1934, he served as the first Nazi-supported rector of his university. During that time he was an enthusiastic advocate, though with refusals to support book burning or anti-Semitic activity. This was his last political involvement of any kind; nor did he ever publicly repudiate what either he or the Nazis had done. To many of Heidegger's interpreters the silence is deafening. Even in view of oblique comments in an interview that he permitted to be published only after his death, both his actions and his silence remain unexplained. Two features of his life would have to be included in any explanation, however. First, there is his intense regard for his native language and an allied belief in the central historic mission of German culture. He continued to use commentaries on Hölderlin for this purpose throughout the World War period. Many German intellectuals have held variants of this strong belief since the late eighteenth century, but in Heidegger it bears a virtually mystical cast, to which his fascination with what he took to be primal elements in Greek (often echoed in his idiosyncratic interpretations of German) is closely associated. Second, by 1933 the human being as an individual had drifted far away from the center of his philosophy; the individual had become ensconced in Being, along with everything else that might otherwise be understood historically. He remained in this special sense, among others, withdrawn. He did so oddly despite—or perhaps in conflictual juxtaposition with—the lyrically humanistic cast of his later writings, which sometimes contained extraordinarily penetrating and effective interpretations of texts. In that respect Heidegger presents but an extreme example of an inner inconsistency between thought and moral action that seems to have afflicted a great many humanist intellectuals of his century. Indeed, the very forcefulness of that inner conflict may explain something of the fascination he holds for other intellectuals.

Another source of attraction no doubt lies in a methodological metaphor often used by Heidegger. Thought, for him, is on the one hand like walking into a forest, where there are many interlocking paths. One must follow where they lead, and one may get lost, but one may also hope to reach a "clearing." On the other hand, thought is like such a path taken by the farmer going to his fields. Like him, one does not divagate. One goes straight to the objective. And one uses that same path to come home.

In 1944 Heidegger was removed from university teaching and put to labor on earthworks by the Nazis. After the war it was not until 1951 that the French occupation permitted him to teach again, a year before his scheduled retirement. During most of this period to his death in 1976, he was highly productive in both thinking and publication. In this fashion he attempted to make what he had announced as the "end" of philosophy, as of his life, also its culminating achievement. Thinking was to help put critical questions to treasured notions and assumptions, accompanied by art in the search for greater immediacy; and in these ways Heidegger wished to drive the participant deeper into meditation, closer to that which he presumed to be of greatest value but which may otherwise remain concealed.

Interpretations

Within the immense literature on Heidegger's thought, that in English is relatively small, but its rate of growth is still accelerating. The highly appreciative, detailed study of Jesuit William Richardson (1963) is the classic and remains basic. Two much shorter books provide excellent orientations: that by Walter Biemel (1976) and David Krell's (1977) percipient introductions to an anthology of Heidegger's basic writings. These are supplemented by an eightieth birthday Festschrift edited by John Sallis (1970); among the contributors are several substantial Heidegger interpreters. The judicious interpretation by cultural philosopher and linguist George Steiner (1979) adds a fine critical edge to their more accepting approaches. Michael Murray (1978) has gathered a broad and representative collection of essays directed to Anglo-American readers, mostly by authors who work in Anglo-American settings. These are addressed to the question "Can Heidegger be understood?"

A new translation of *Being and Time* is reported to be underway. This will no doubt stimulate further interpretive activity, as has the constant stream of translations of works by and about Heidegger in the 1970s. Joseph Fell (1979) has already nicely compared Sartre, who modeled his own philosophical masterwork after this book, and Heidegger as ontologists. In one of the best philosophical interpretations of Heidegger, Werner Marx (1960, tr. 1971) views his struggles to overcome the "substance" tradition from Aristotle to Hegel. L. M. Vail (1972) interprets and reflects upon his late ontological thinking, as in part do some European essays from a 1969 colloquium at Pennsylvania State University, edited by Joseph Kockelmans (1972).

Biemel, Walter. *Martin Heidegger: An Illustrated Study.* Tr. by J. L. Mehta. New York and London: Harcourt, Brace, 1976. (German ed., 1973.)

Fell, Joseph P. *Heidegger and Sartre: An Essay on Being and Place.* New York: Columbia Univ. Pr., 1979.

Heidegger, Martin. *Being and Time.* Tr. by John Macquarrie and Edward Robinson. New York: Harper & Row, 1962. (German ed., 1927.) (A new translation by Joan Stambaugh is in preparation. Also see Krell, below.)

Kockelmans, Joseph J., ed. *On Heidegger and Language.* Evanston, Ill.: Northwestern Univ. Pr., 1972.

Krell, David Farrell, ed. *Martin Heidegger: Basic Writings from Being and Time (1927) to the Task of Thinking (1964).* New York and London: Harper & Row, 1977.

Marx, Werner. *Heidegger and the Tradition.* Tr. by Theodore Kisiel and Murray Greene. Evanston, Ill.: Northwestern Univ. Pr., 1971. (German ed., 1960.)

Murray, Michael, ed. *Heidegger and Modern Philosophy: Critical Essays.* New Haven, Conn. and London: Yale Univ. Pr., 1978.

Richardson, William J., S.J. *Heidegger: Through Phenomenology to Thought.* The Hague: Nijhoff, 1963.

Sallis, John, ed. *Heidegger and the Path of Thinking.* Pittsburgh, Pa.: Duquesne Univ. Pr., 1970.

Steiner, George. *Martin Heidegger.* New York: Viking, 1979.

Vail, Loy M. *Heidegger and Ontological Difference.* University Park and London: Pennsylvania State Univ. Pr., 1972.

13

Phenomenology, Hermeneutics, and Critical Theory

The word "phenomenon" has had some use in philosophy and science since the late eighteenth century and was given prominence by Hegel as a virtual synonym of "appearance." Its first use in the special epistemological sense associated with phenomenology as a movement occurs in the writings of Edmund Husserl at the turn of the twentieth century, though many underlying interests were established first by Husserl's teachers Franz Brentano and Carl Strumpf. Never a unified school, each of the great variety of philosophies identified with this movement has itself undergone development. Husserl's is no exception. As the main chronicler of the movement, Herbert Spiegelberg (1960) has amply shown, during the some three decades in which Husserl interacted with adherents of the movement, his ideas markedly shifted several times and were often both among the most radical in form and the most seminal in effect. Phenomenology arose in a situation of crisis within European philosophy brought about by a rapidly maturing natural science. Would philosophy lose its status entirely, capitulate to science, or try to revise positions earlier given up? Or would it find newly defined tasks of its own? As in the various strands of analytic philosophy, the last option was the one chiefly adopted by phenomenologists. In both movements further efforts were made to provide logical and epistemological foundations for the sciences.

Before the mid-1930s phenomenology was chiefly a German affair, thereafter predominately French. Today it is a major presence in philosophy worldwide and a chief ingredient, if only through refutation, within many fields of continental European thought. In many

285

countries its impact has been evident more in nonphilosophical studies than in philosophy itself.

Participants in the movement tend to share this common aim: through description of what is attained by direct intuition to gain insight into essential structures of phenomena. In the strictest sense, gradually developed by Husserl, they not only pay special, sometimes exclusive attention to what appears subjectively in experience but apply reductive tools to ascertain how such phenomena are constituted in and by consciousness.

The most authoritative overviews of the movement are to be found in Herbert Spiegelberg's two-volume historical study (1960), now a classic, and in *Analecta Husserliana,* edited by Anna-Teresa Tymieniecka (1971–76). A synoptic study on "man's relation to reality" by Dutch phenomenologist Cornelis van Peursen (1972) appears in a long series of works in phenomenological philosophy published by Duquesne University Press. The eleven chapters include three on Husserl, one each on Augustine, Berkeley, Bergson, and Wittgenstein. An extensive listing also comes from Northwestern University Press, Indiana University Press, and Nijhoff, a great many of the books not originally in English. Van Peursen's 1972 discussion *Phenomenology and Analytic Philosophy* is supplemented by a collection of well-crafted new essays on phenomenological issues from both approaches (and others) edited by Edo Pivčević (1975).

Among the major studies in philosophical phenomenology since Husserl are that on "consciousness" by French psychiatrist Henri Ey (1968, tr. 1977) and on "the social world" by Alfred Schutz (1932, tr. 1967), the only book-length study published in his lifetime. Schutz's seminal work is extended by existential phenomenologist Maurice Natanson (1962, 1974), who treats phenomenology as "the grounding discipline" for existentialism and who also addresses related problems in the social sciences. Natanson was introduced to Husserl's thought by W. H. Werkmeister in the 1940s, an interest later intensified by contact with Schutz, then with Farber, Cairns, Gurwitsch, Spiegelberg (all mentioned below), and others. Many other American phenomenologists traveled similar routes.

Other representative studies are those by Robert Sokolowski (1978) on language and by Bernard Dauenhauer (1980) on silence. Aron Gurwitsch's (1974) essays from 1937–73 focus especially on theory of science and on related issues of the conscious "life-world"—a dual theme that permeates the phenomenological literature—as do essays in honor of Gurwitsch edited by Lester Embree (1972). Gurwitsch, who studied with Husserl, greatly influenced the spread of phenomenology in Germany, France, and the United States. Dorion Cairns was another student and friend of Husserl (from 1923 to Husserl's death in 1938); he was a long-time leading purveyor and interpreter of Husserlian phenomenology, especially at the New School in New York (1954–69). Cairns has been honored in a volume by Frederick Kersten et al. (*Phenomenology . . .*, on p. 290). Essays edited by Dale Riepe (1973) reflect themes in the materialist, naturalist phenomenology of Marvin Farber, for thirty years editor of *Philosophy and Phenomenological Research,* the chief periodical of the movement.

Dauenhauer, Bernard P. *Silence: The Phenomenon and Its Ontological Significance.* Bloomington: Indiana Univ. Pr., 1980.

Embree, Lester E., ed. *Life-World and Consciousness: Essays for Aron Gurwitsch.* Evanston, Ill.: Northwestern Univ. Pr., 1972.

Ey, Henri. *Consciousness: A Phenomenological Study of Being Conscious and Becoming Conscious.* Tr. by John H. Flodstrom. Bloomington: Indiana Univ. Pr., 1977. (From 2nd French ed., 1968; original ed., 1963.)

Gurwitsch, Aron. *Phenomenology and the Theory of Science.* Ed. by Lester Embree. Evanston, Ill.: Northwestern Univ. Pr., 1974.

Natanson, Maurice. *Literature, Philosophy and the Social Sciences: Essays in Existentialism and Phenomenology.* The Hague: Nijhoff, 1962. (1952–61 essays, supplemented by 1964–72 essays in *Phenomenology, Role and Reason: Essays on the Coherence and Deformation of Social Reality.* Springfield, Ill.: Charles C. Thomas, 1974.)

Peursen, Cornelis A. van. *Phenomenology and Analytical Philosophy.* Tr. by Rex Ambler. Pittsburgh, Pa.: Duquesne Univ. Pr., 1972.

———. *Phenomenology and Reality.* Tr. by Henry J. Koren. Pittsburgh, Pa.: Duquesne Univ. Pr., 1972.

Pivčević, Edo, ed. *Phenomenology and Philosophical Understanding.* Cambridge and New York: Cambridge Univ. Pr., 1975.

Riepe, Dale, ed. *Phenomenology and Natural Existence: Essays in Honor of Marvin Farber.* Albany: State Univ. of New York Pr., 1973.

Schutz, Alfred. *The Phenomenology of the Social World.* Tr. by George Walsh and Frederick Lehnert. Evanston, Ill.: Northwestern Univ. Pr., 1967. (From 2nd German ed., 1960; 1st ed., 1932.)

Sokolowski, Robert. *Presence and Absence: A Philosophical Investigation of Language and Being.* Bloomington: Indiana Univ. Pr., 1978.

Spiegelberg, Herbert. *The Phenomenological Movement: A Hisorical Introduction.* 2v. The Hague: Nijhoff, 1960. Repr., 1978.

Tymieniecka, Anna-Teresa, ed. *Analecta Husserliana: The Yearbook of Phenomenological Research.* Vols. 1–5 (1971–76).

EDMUND HUSSERL (1859–1938)

Edmund Husserl was forty before his philosophical thinking became strictly phenomenological, and it underwent several important changes thereafter. Only a decade later did he publish his further thinking about phenomenology as a "rigorous science." This scientific philosophy is grounded in "transcendental phenomenology," which by epistemological reduction, starting with a proposed suspension of belief and an attendant dismantling and "bracketing" of all presuppositions about reality or about the content of mental acts, gets down to "pure" rock-bottom phenomena. Herein Husserl presents a radical subjectivism, in which subjectivity is purported to be the source of all objectivities. Herein too he forms a "genetic" approach, one that is not historical in intent but examines how the constituent elements of phenomena build up from their "essences."

For a long time after his famous *Logical Investigations* (1900–1, tr. 1959–63) appeared, Husserl's further thinking was not widely known except by students and closer colleagues. This is partly because his prose is heavy, partly because translations came very slowly, partly because his student Martin Heidegger began to dominate the scene with near alternatives, and partly because there were long stretches between the initial treatise and each of his two other major works: *Ideas: General Introduction to Pure Phenomenology,* vol. 1 (1913, tr. 1931) and *Formal and Transcendental Logic* (1929, tr. 1968). Most of Husserl's work not published during his lifetime appeared in German and in French translations after 1950. They became available in English translation only from the 1960s on. Moreover, the allied theory of objects by Alexius Meinong (1853–1920), also a student of Brentano, had attracted the attention of Anglo-American philosophers over a decade before either Brentano or Husserl were known—in Britain by Bertrand Russell, G. E. Moore, C. D. Broad, and other realists, in America first by Wilbur M. Urban and other realists, much later by leading epistemologist Roderick Chisholm, who dealt extensively with the writings of both Brentano and Meinong but not of Husserl. Although Meinong did not share Husserl's interest in analysis of consciousness, both had used Brentano's work as a point of departure, moving beyond him to account for the complete range of phenomena and to form an ontological theory of objects.

Husserl was early influenced by an older student and successor of Brentano and his own teacher and colleague during the Vienna years, Carl Strumpf (1848–1936), founder of experimental phenomenology. Many psychologists of the era were also influenced by Strumpf, notably the Lewinians and Gestalt theorists. Husserl began his own distinctive search for deductive rigor and apodictic certainty through philosophy of mathematics. For a time he tried a psychological approach to overcoming defects in the foundations of mathematics, borrowing especially from the classical British empiricists and Mill. Then, partly through Gottlob Frege's example, he produced a critique of "psychologism" in favor of completely distinct logical endeavors, turning to "the things themselves" through "presuppositionless" phenomenology. This position was later supplemented by the "transcendental subjectivity" mentioned above. What seems especially to have impressed students, apart from these more formal efforts, was his insistence that each person must take radical responsibility for one's own self and one's own knowledge. In future decades this motif was to provide a strong link to existentialist interests, as did Heidegger's similar effort to break through ordinary conceptions to the very roots of experience.

An interpretation by Quentin Lauer (1958), entitled *The Triumph of Subjectivity*, was for a time the main brief introduction to Husserlian philosophy in English; it contains some inaccuracies regarding Husserl's predecessors and successors. Recently (1978) it has been issued in a second edition. Spiegelberg's much longer study (*The Phenomenological Movement*, 1960, cited on p. 287) is still the basic historical introduction. This is both a supplement to and a corrective update of Marvin Farber's classic work, which has run to three editions (1943, 1962, 1967), unchanged except for prefaces. J. N. Mohanty's (1964, 1969) short introduction to Husserl's philosophy of thinking and meaning is skillfully presented. David Carr (1974) takes the story of Husserl's philosophical development further than usual by concentrating on the more teleological, history-related thinking of his last writings (1934–37), notably his uncompleted book on *The Crisis of European Sciences* (1954, tr. by Carr in 1970). Still different general interpretations are a developmental study of Husserl's concepts of certain ("apodictic") and complete ("adequate") evidence by David Levin (1970), a study of his theory of signs by a leading Heideggerian linguist, Jacques Derrida (1967, tr. 1973), who rejects Husserl's theory of language overall, and a personal reconstruction of Husserl's thinking by Robert Sokolowski (1974) of the Catholic University of America, with special awareness of issues in political philosophy, metaphysics, and philosophy of language.

Among the numerous collections, that edited by Joseph Kockelmans (1967), Dutch emigré to the United States, has held up well; it starts with discussions on Husserl but branches out to nearer successors and to others like Sartre and Heidegger, with special reference to psychology as a paradigm "descriptive science." The collection edited by David Carr and Edward Casey (1973) gathers up important papers from the Society for Phenomenology and Existential Philosophy, with primary reference to Husserl, while that edited by Frederick Elliston and Peter McCormick (1977) includes both defenders and detractors of Husserl, including eleven new essays. The seventieth birthday Festschrift for Dorion Cairns, edited by Frederick Kersten and R. M. Zaner (1973) includes four essays by Cairns (one autobiographical) and others by major phenomenological authors. Like all the others, the *Monist* collection edited by Dagfinn Føllesdal (1975) manifests the spreading international character of studies on Husserl and the movement he started. Along with the painstaking analyses and speculative meanderings typical in this literature is often to be found that same strong sense of mission that fueled both Brentano and Husserl.

Carr, David. *Phenomenology and the Problem of History: A Study of Husserl's Transcendental Philosophy.* Evanston, Ill.: Northwestern Univ. Pr., 1974.
————, and Edward S. Casey, eds. *Explorations in Phenomenology: Papers of the Society for Phenomenology and Existential Philosophy.* The Hague: Nijhoff, 1973.
Derrida, Jacques. *Speech and Phenomena and Other Essays on Husserl's Theory of Signs.* Tr. by David B. Allison. Evanston, Ill.: Northwestern Univ. Pr., 1973. (French ed. 1967.)
Elliston, Frederick A., and Peter McCormick, eds. *Husserl: Expositions and Appraisals.* Notre Dame, Ind.: Univ. of Notre Dame Pr., 1977.
Farber, Marvin. *The Foundation of Phenomenology: Edmund Husserl and the Quest for a Rigorous Science of Philosophy.* 3rd ed. Albany: State Univ. of New York Pr., 1967. (1st ed., 1943; 2nd ed., 1962.)
Føllesdal, Dagfinn, ed. "The Philosophy of Husserl." *Monist* 59, no. 1:3–137 (Jan. 1975).
Husserl, Edmund. *The Crisis of European Sciences and Transcendental Phenomenology: An Introduction to Phenomenological Philosophy.* Tr. by David Carr. Evanston, Ill. Northwestern Univ. Pr., 1970. (German ed., 1954.)
————. *Formal and Transcendental Logic.* Tr. by Dorion Cairns. The Hague: Nijhoff, 1968. (German ed., 1929.)
————. *Ideas: General Introduction to Pure Phenomenology.* Tr. by W. R. Boyce Gibson. New York: Macmillan; London: Allen & Unwin, 1931. Repr., 1969. (This is vol. 1; the original publication of vols. 2–3 was in *Husserliana*, vols. 4–5, 1952.) (German ed., 1913.)
————. *Logical Investigations.* 2v. Tr. by J. N. Findlay. New York: Humanities Pr.; London: Routledge & Paul, 1970. (German ed., 1900–1.)
Kersten, Frederick, and Richard M. Zaner, eds. *Phenomenology: Continua-*

tion and Criticism—Essays in Memory of Dorion Cairns. The Hague: Nijhoff, 1973.

Kockelmans, Joseph J., ed. *Phenomenology: The Philosophy of Edmund Husserl and Its Interpretation.* Garden City, N.Y.: Doubleday Anchor, 1967.

Lauer, J. Quentin. *The Triumph of Subjectivity: An Introduction to Transcendental Phenomenology.* 2nd ed. New York: Fordham Univ. Pr., 1978. Repr.: *Phenomenology: Its Genesis and Prospect,* 1965. (Original ed., 1958.)

Levin, David Michael. *Reason and Evidence in Husserl's Phenomenology.* Evanston, Ill.: Northwestern Univ. Pr., 1970.

McCormick, Peter, and Frederick A. Elliston, eds., *Husserl: Shorter Works.* Notre Dame, Ind.: Univ. of Notre Dame Pr.; Brighton, Sussex: Harvester Pr., 1981.

Mohanty, Jitendranath N. *Edmund Husserl's Theory of Meaning.* 2nd ed. The Hague: Nijhoff, 1969. (1st ed., 1964.)

Sokolowski, Robert. *Husserlian Meditations: How Words Present Things.* Evanston, Ill.: Northwestern Univ. Pr., 1974.

MAURICE MERLEAU-PONTY (1908–1961)

Starting his career as a secondary school teacher (1930–35) and education school faculty member (1935–39), Maurice Merleau-Ponty joined the French army in 1939. From beginning to end existentialism and phenomenology were the two homing elements in his thought. While an infantryman and during the German occupation of France he completed his two major books in "existential phenomenology": *The Structure of Behavior* (1942, tr. 1963), mostly a critique of causal and behaviorist theories in psychology, and his masterwork *Phenomenology of Perception* (1945, tr. 1963). The second book examined what he took to be traditional prejudices regarding perception in order to foster a "return" to the things themselves, an understanding of the body as itself involving a theory of perception, and an elaboration on the theme of being-in-the-world, of knowing oneself only through relationships with the world and of the world's not being what I think but "what I live through." After teaching at the University of Lyon and the Sorbonne, in 1952 he was appointed to the prestigious chair of philosophy at the Collège de France, which he held until his death in 1961. Throughout these early works and his subsequent writings, including the very last essays posthumously collected in *Signs* (1960, tr. 1964), Husserl is his primary reference point for epistemological grounding and dialogue.

In 1945 Merleau-Ponty was a cofounder of the principal existentialist periodical *Les Temps Modernes.* He served as coeditor with his onetime fellow student and contemporary Jean-Paul Sartre for many years. He also shared with Sartre an interest in Marxism, though he did so in a very different, even crisscross fashion, abandoning Marxism and thereby breaking with Sartre over this issue, and with the periodical, in the early 1950s. His *Adventures of the Dialectic* (1955, tr. 1973, cited on p. 261—also see Mark Poster's essential 1975 study, cited there) marks the new direction in his social thought. Well to the left of Sartre during the 1940s, he was close to the Communists from 1945 to 1950 and played a crucial role in conjoining existentialist and Marxist thought during that period; but by 1955 he was no longer engaged in Marxist politics. From 1950 on, Sartre, in contrast, was moving closer to Marxism; for some years after 1955 Sartre was occupied almost exclusively with the existentialism-Marxism debate, which since 1945 had continued to be a burning issue in French intellectual and political life.

Like many philosophers in his time, Merleau-Ponty formed his views in opposition to Cartesian rationalism, dualism, and idealism. For this purpose, both Husserl's thought and Gestalt theory in psychology were indispensable aids. What emerged was something like Husserl's interest in describing structures of consciousness but without Husserl's methods of bracketing and reduction. Drawing somewhat from Husserl's latest writings, he also spoke often of a primary perceptual milieu—which Husserl called "life-world"—underlying all knowledge and science; but in opposition to Husserl he regarded this milieu or world as real in a way that transcends consciousness of it. He strove to show the interdependence of body and mind, even in perception, and thereby assigned intentional structures to body as well as to mind. In his thinking on human action—especially aesthetic, ethical, and political—he carried over these same principles, ever affirming the contingency but not the deterministic necessity either of individual choice or of political events. Marxism, he thought, was a timely device for thinking about human needs and contingencies in modern industrial society; but he eschewed its dogmatic rigidity, especially its claims to predictive power and historical mission, and the nonliberating, totalitarian features that had accrued to it.

The development of Merleau-Ponty's philosophy has been suitably outlined by John Bannan (1967) and in a collection of essays edited by Garth Gillian (1973). Samuel Mallin (1979) uses an analysis of central concepts to attempt a comprehensive treatment of his philosophy viewed as a coherent whole. Laurie Spurling (1977) explores relations in his thought between philosophy and the social sciences, including history, as expressing a dialectic between transcendental and descriptive impulses.

Bannan, John F. *The Philosophy of Merleau-Ponty*. New York: Harcourt, Brace, 1967.
Gillian, Garth, ed. *The Horizons of the Flesh: Critical Perspectives on the Thought of Merleau-Ponty*. Carbondale: Southern Illinois Univ. Pr., 1973.
Mallin, Samuel B. *Merleau-Ponty's Philosophy*. New Haven, Conn. and London: Yale Univ. Pr., 1979.
Merleau-Ponty, Maurice. *Phenomenology of Perception*. Tr. by Colin Smith. New York: Humanities Pr.; London: Routledge & Paul, 1963. (French ed., 1945.)
———. *Signs*. Tr. by Richard C. McCleary. Evanston, Ill.: Northwestern Univ. Pr., 1964. (French ed., 1960.)
Spurling, Laurie. *Phenomenology and the Social World: The Philosophy of Merleau-Ponty and Its Relation to the Social Sciences*. London and Boston: Routledge & Paul, 1977.

HERMENEUTICS AND CRITICAL THEORY

Friedrich Schleiermacher (1768–1834)

Given that we human beings are different from each other, and sometimes seem even to inhabit different worlds, how are we to convey to each other what we mean? How are we to understand what is said? In particular, how are we to grasp the meaning of each other's expressions and actions once they are recorded or to the extent that we do not have the advantage of dialogue? Supposing, further, that the items in question are ancient texts or texts from another language and culture. By what principles are we to grasp their meaning? Should religious and classical and contemporary items each be interpreted by very different principles or is there a set of general principles by which each domain is to be treated and then perhaps some additional, merely procedural canons we can use to deal with special characteristics in the diverse phenomena themselves? For example, should biblical studies have interpretive principles all their own because the scriptures are taken to be divinely inspired? Furthermore, is the task chiefly that of treating linguistic features that appear on the surface (philological ones), or is some deeper or more complex investigation called for? If so, how is this inquiry to be constituted? Such were the questions that concerned Friedrich Schleiermacher as he prepared for the first lectures on general "hermeneutics" ever given in 1805.

Schleiermacher created hermeneutics as a general historical-interpretive methodology almost single-handed. In recent decades the term hermeneutics (from a Greek verb meaning "to interpret") had been used for special methods, chiefly philological, of studying biblical, classical, and judicial texts; and it continued to be used this way long after. Since the judicial use of interpretation was quite different, he related his accounts particularly to the other two uses. By the time he first lectured on the subject in 1805 Schleiermacher had already, among other things, produced part of his classic translation of Plato into German, had joined in translating some well-known collected sermons and travel books from English, and had engaged for some ten years in exegesis of biblical texts from the Hebrew and Greek as a preacher. He had also published his famous "Romantic" works *On Religion: Addresses to Its Cultured Critics* (1799, cited on p. 482) and *Soliloquies* (1800, a partly autobiographical discourse on personal development and communication), several critical articles on literature and philosophy, and a treatise on ethics. Thereby the foundation of his perspectives on historical process—personal, institutional, and societal—had been securely laid, though he was critically to elaborate and refine them over the next thirty years. In the same period he was also setting forth his understanding of the interrelationships of disciplines within theology, which first issued in his *Brief Outline on the Study of Theology* (1811, cited on p. 7) and, as a philosopher, of their further relation to independent philosophical and historical inquiry.

Schleiermacher's earlier close relations with the Romantic circle of artists and writers occurred primarily because of an appreciation for the affective and aesthetic, this against much Enlightenment rationalism, and for the less moralistically restrained life. But his own philosophical position was on the whole distinctly different from theirs, and for at least three main reasons. First, he was struggling to form his own version of a post-Kantian critical, transcendental account of reason and ethics (with a historical and dialectical bent that was better structured and closer to social reality than that either of the other Romantics or of his later Berlin colleague Hegel tended to be). Second, he was engaged in studies and uses of language that required coming to a highly complex understanding of changing social contexts. (This brought his thinking on language very close to that of his friend Wilhelm von Humboldt, to whom linguists refer almost as a contemporary today.) Third, he worked as a professed Christian, of the Reformed branch but never subscribing to a strict dogmatic tradition, wishing to understand the place of religious experience within the whole of personal life and culture. It was out of the third interest that his hermeneutics lectures arose, at the juncture of his first appointment to a professorship, in Halle; but the methodology can only be adequately understood in relation to this overall framework.

Schleiermacher's immediate aim was to develop procedures for interpreting biblical texts that were not in principle different from those to be used in understanding any other kind of text or event. The singularity of each item was to be captured and, at the same time, its connectedness through historical or natural commonality with others within a larger context. He believed that a more or less clear core "idea" set off each process being recorded in language, and that language itself was a continually creative agent in history. The principal task of interpretation was to capture that idea and its further expression, with whatever changing nuances or additional formations could be found. From the beginning the scholar was to attend, dialectically, to the interrelation between elements internal or idiosyncratic to the item and all those factors that impinge upon it from the outside or from within the whole of which it is a part. Though less rigorously, he said, one would do the same sorts of things in attempting to gain understanding or to avoid misunderstanding in ordinary discourse.

What Schleiermacher called the "grammatical" side of hermeneutics related predominately to the external or more general features, to the social carriers of meaning; the "psychological" side (which referred to the activity of mind—mainly "conscious," or intentional—that is conveyed through human expressions and actions) related predominately to the internal features. Both early and late in his thought, the two sides were regarded as inseparably interactive. Although he emphasized the second side more than the first in his later lecture outlines, as Heinz Kimmerle pointed out in his edition (1959, tr. 1977), he did not do so in practice. In my view, the explanation resides in the fact that his hearers and colleagues had found the "psychological" aspects stranger and more difficult to grasp, as is still true of similar twentieth-century efforts, and that these aspects had given rise to greater misunderstanding. Therefore, as he routinely did in revising his published works, he concentrated on what had been misunderstood.

As yet there are some partial accounts but no systematic account of Schleiermacher's hermeneutics in English. Invaluable preparatory work has been done (and cited) by James Duke and Jack Forstman (1977) in their English edition of the hermeneutics manuscripts, most of which were not available until Kimmerle edited their German edition in 1959.

Wilhelm Dilthey (1833–1911)

Even now the tangled tales of how hermeneutics came into being are ordinarily told after the fashion of Wilhelm Dilthey, who initiated its twentieth-century phase. Raised in a Reformed parsonage and early very much taken by Schleiermacher, of whose early life he issued a now classic biography in 1870, in his twenties he gave up any specific identification as a Christian. Thereafter he displayed a pervasive interest in theoretical issues regarding history and culture and regarding relative progress in both individuals and society. Following Schleiermacher (though not often expressly so), he devoted much of his early work to establishing the independence of the cultural sciences (*Geisteswissenschaften,* today often referred to as the "human sciences") from the natural sciences. In doing this he emphasized the singular individuality and internal consciousness and coherence of cultural subjects, but not to the exclusion of the general and common; both the individual and the general were viewed as aspects of lived experience *(Erleben)* and understanding *(Verstehen)*. He never abandoned this overall view.

After about 1900 he did shift from an earlier emphasis on historical knowledge through introspection to a greater inclusion of external, public expressions. Accordingly he ceased to regard the "descriptive and analytical psychology" he had developed in the 1890s as fundamental to the cultural sciences. This is the point at which hermeneutics became especially important to him, though it had early been awakened through his study of Schleiermacher. Moreover, although Dilthey appreciated Husserl's descriptive efforts, this was done in marked divergence from phenomenology. In these respects, too, his thought is much closer to Schleiermacher's than to that of the existential phenomenologists who have since developed further versions of hermeneutical thinking.

Apparently Dilthey was closer to Schleiermacher's philosophical views than he was aware. His interpretation of Schleiermacher's hermeneutics as overly psychological, which later interpretations have routinely drawn upon, must be viewed as mistaken. In many respects, Schleiermacher's more elaborate writings and lectures in dialectic, aesthetics, and philosophy of mind, ethics and social-political philosophy, and theological method, plus his own numerous interpretive studies in theology and Greek philosophy and his commentaries on current political issues, reveal a fuller, more integrated approach to historical reality than we find in Dilthey. This difference is remarkable given the separation of over seventy years between their latest works. (To my knowledge, no one has set out to demonstrate this claim, which derives from my own knowledge of the relevant literature, but it is easily supported.) What Dilthey adds is untiring critical inquiry into nineteenth-century methodological traditions, important clarifications of issues, an articulated approach to cultural studies that emphasizes the more complex skills of understanding, a notion of biography as the basic historical science, and openness to psychoanalytically informed contributions.

Virtually all subsequent writings on hermeneutics refer in some way to Dilthey. Theodore Plantinga (1980) provides a fine overall interpretation of Dilthey's thought and its development, with special reference to the post-1900 writings.

Later Developments

Roughly in historical order, since Dilthey "hermeneutics" has come to mean at least six different things: (1) the basic theory of interpretation, especially of texts (attributed to Schleiermacher, though he did more than this); (2) a particular theory of or approach to the cultural (human) sciences (Dilthey, Emilio Betti); (3) a characteristic of philosophy that views understanding through interpretation as a basic mode of being human (Heidegger); (4) a type of existential phenomenology, that combines motifs from Dilthey, Husserl, and Heidegger and that focuses on ontological not methodological inquiry (Hans-Georg Gadamer); (5) a hermeneutic phenomenology, that uses numbers 1 through 4 as resources and that focuses on theory for interpreting cultural symbols, chiefly in texts (Paul Ricoeur); and (6) an aspect of critical theory that utilizes psychoanalytic models to detect the causes of distorted understanding and communication, purveys a somewhat Marxian analysis of material conditions, and focuses on the critique of ideology (Karl-Otto Apel and Jürgen Habermas).

Of the two main introductory accounts, Richard Palmer's (1969) concentrates on issues associated with Schleiermacher, Dilthey, Heidegger, and Gadamer, with only brief reference to Ricoeur and the considerable involvement with hermeneutical issues in contemporary theology, stimulated especially by the Heideggerian New Testament scholar Rudolf Bultmann. The latter has in itself been a great stimulus to philosophical effort. Josef Bleicher's (1980) overview more fully reflects the amazingly fertile activity of the past twenty years by including not only Heidegger, Bultmann, Gadamer, Apel, and Habermas but also the neo-Kantian phenomenologist Emilio Betti, the Marxist-materialists Hans Jörg Sandkühler and Alfred Lorenzer, and Ricoeur. All the latter philosophers have flourished in the late 1960s and 1970s. Roy Howard's (1982) introduction to a selection of current hermeneutical positions especially addresses antipositivist interests among analytic philosophers and draws above all from Ludwig Wittgenstein, Gadamer, and Habermas.

Since the 1960s hermeneutics has become a major concern in European philosophy, of a dimension and promise comparable to that of analytic philosophy in Anglo-American philosophy in the quarter century after 1945. In particular, by the late 1960s hermeneutics and the critique of ideology had become closely associated in the work of critical theorists, a combination still strongly pursued in the 1980s. Those closer to Gadamer are oriented more to ontology and existential-phenomenological analysis. Thus far only a small portion of the important books have been translated into English. Chief among them is Gadamer's principal work, *Truth and Method* (1960, tr. 1975). This treatise lays out an approach to philosophy that derives primarily from Heidegger. It takes very seriously the ways in which reality impinges upon consciousness through language and emphasizes the dialogical element in understanding. Gadamer (1900–) has sent out a continual stream of books using and talking about his method and entering into the fierce debates in print that have long characterized German philosophy. A collection of essays from 1960 to 1972 (1976) includes valuable commentary on some of these debates.

A student of Gabriel Marcel, beginning in 1935, and still closely allied to his thought, the French philosopher Paul Ricoeur (1969) turned to Husserl for greater precision. His translation of Husserl's *Ideas* in 1950 early established his reputation as a philosopher. Don Ihde's (1971) summary of his "hermeneutic phenomenology," approved by Ricoeur, indicates that by 1971 he was also engaged with French structuralism (anthropologist Claude Levi-Strauss and others) and was beginning to incorporate learnings from Anglo-American linguistics and philosophy of language. His explicit turn to hermeneutics begins with *The Symbolism of Evil* (1960, tr. 1967) and *Freud and Philosophy* (1965, tr. 1970). The focal interest from that point on has been in interpretation of symbols in texts, symbols being viewed as the place where the ambiguous, life-creating and limiting force of language is revealed most strongly and fully. His opposition to Cartesian subjectivity or self-containment has also been a distinct feature in his thinking.

Critical Theory and German Philosophy since 1945

The term "critical theory" was first associated with the efforts of a group of Western Marxist philosophers at the Institute of Social Research in Frankfurt, Germany, known as the Frankfurt School (1923–50), which operated in the United States from 1935 to 1944. It must be distinguished from interests in literary criticism, to which the word also sometimes refers. One branch of critical theory in literature, exemplified in a recent book by Michael Murray (1975), also speaks of being "the new hermeneutic" and borrows heavily from European philosophy (in his case Husserl, Heidegger, and Merleau-Ponty).

An indispensable thematic account of critical theory by David Held (1980) centers on the work of Max Horkheimer, Theodor Adorno, and Herbert Marcuse of the Frankfurt School and on their best known successor Jürgen Habermas (1929–). An intellectual history of the school by Martin Jay (1973, not cited here) is a useful accompaniment. All four theorists are characterized by their special brand of Marxism, which rejects both dialectical materialism and elements of subjectivism in Marxist humanism; their critique of both communism and capitalism; their opposition to positivism; the serious dialogue with and use of psychoanalysis (though not very clinically informed and mostly with Freud); their search through nineteenth-century German philosophy for a better undergirding of current social and aesthetic theory than is to be found in Marx; and the cooperative cross-fertilization of ideas among them and their colleagues, boosted in part by social research. In Habermas the interest in psychoanalysis seems somewhat diminished; he ranges even more widely for sources, including Anglo-American social theory; unlike his predecessors, he claims to have a solid foundational account of knowledge, language, and values; he has developed a version of hermeneutics, over which he has entered public debate with Gadamer; and he has developed a substantial method for a critique of ideology, viewed primarily as systematically distorted communication under coercive conditions.

Habermas has been a highly productive author since 1962. His style is heavily expository and polemical. The two chief works so far available to English readers are his early proposals on *Theory and Practice* (1963, tr. 1973), on the dual relationship between theory and "praxis," with special reference to Hegel and Marx, and his most influential work, *Knowledge and Human Interests* (1968, tr. 1971), where a similar reciprocity is advanced through critiques of Kant and Fichte, Hegel, Marx, the positivists Comte and Mach, Peirce, Dilthey, Nietzsche, and Freud. Closely associated with Habermas's major interests, Karl-Otto Apel (1979) has developed his own distinctive, tightly argued position, which borrows extensively from analytic logic and philosophy of language. If only for this reason, attention to his work is already being given by Anglo-American philosophers who would be put off by Habermas. So far he has not received a study of his philosophy in English.

The literature on critical theory is fast-growing. To accompany the general thematic account by Held, three works that center on Habermas are of special importance. Raymond Geuss (1981) emphasizes the critique of ideology; Russell Keat (1981) emphasizes psychoanalytic contributions to the clarification of "interest" that is basic to that critique. Thomas McCarthy (1978) notes the conjoining of hermeneutics and ideology-critique on which Habermas insists, but his more general survey features other basic themes, especially Habermas's theory of communication. All three books serve to clarify Habermas's relation to the Frankfurt School. Twelve new critical essays, including a sixty-four page reply by Habermas, have been edited by John B. Thompson and David Held (1982).

The essay by Rüdiger Bubner (*Modern German Philosophy*, 1981, cited on p. 160) on German philosophy since 1945 pays heed mainly to the development of phenomenology into hermeneutics (particularly in Heidegger and Gadamer), the amalgamation of German with foreign interests in philosophy of language (notably the hermeneutic-pragmatic communication theories of Apel and Habermas and the formal semantics of Ernst Tugendhat), contributions to philosophy of science (some of which are independent of these other trends but are in contention with them), and the nature of dialectic and its practical uses (in critical theory above all). All these movements of thought, which since 1945 have been highlighted in the fast-changing themes of hermeneutics and critical theory in middle Europe, show both vitality and increasing rigor.

Apel, Karl-Otto. *Towards a Transformation of Philosophy.* Tr. by Glyn Adey and David Frisby. London and Boston: Routledge & Paul, 1979. (Selected from a 2v. work, 1973.)
Bleicher, Josef. *Contemporary Hermeneutics: Hermeneutics as Method, Philosophy and Critique.* London and Boston: Routledge & Paul, 1980.
Gadamer, Hans-Georg. *Philosophical Hermeneutics.* Tr. and ed. by David E.

Linge. Berkeley: Univ. of California Pr., 1976. (A selection of essays from his 3v. *Kleine Schriften.*)

———. *Truth and Method.* Tr. by Garrett Barden and John Cumming. New York: Seabury Pr., 1975. (From the 2nd German ed., 1965; 1st German ed., 1960, 4th ed., 1975.) (His Plato and Hegel studies are cited in ch. 1 and ch. 6 here.)

Geuss, Raymond. *The Idea of a Critical Theory: Habermas and the Frankfurt School.* Cambridge and New York: Cambridge Univ. Pr., 1981.

Habermas, Jürgen. *Knowledge and Human Interests.* Tr. by Jeremy J. Shapiro. Boston: Beacon Pr., 1971. (German ed., 1968.)

———. *Theory and Practice.* Tr. by John Viertel. Boston: Beacon Pr., 1973. (From the 4th German ed., 1971; 1st ed., 1963.) (Abridged ed.)

Held, David. *Introduction to Critical Theory: Horkheimer to Habermas.* Berkeley and London: Univ. of California Pr., 1980.

Howard, Roy J. *Three Faces of Hermeneutics: An Introduction to Current Theories of Understanding.* Berkeley: Univ. of California Pr., 1982.

Ihde, Don. *Hermeneutic Phenomenology: The Philosophy of Paul Ricoeur.* Evanston, Ill.: Northwestern Univ. Pr., 1971.

Keat, Russell. *The Politics of Social Theory: Habermas, Freud and the Critique of Positivism.* Chicago: Univ. of Chicago Pr.; Oxford: Blackwell, 1981.

McCarthy, Thomas. *The Critical Theory of Jürgen Habermas.* Cambridge, Mass. and London: MIT Pr., 1978.

Murray, Michael E. *Modern Critical Theory: A Phenomenological Introduction.* The Hague: Nijhoff, 1975.

Palmer, Richard E. *Hermeneutics: Interpretation Theory in Schleiermacher, Dilthey, Heidegger, and Gadamer.* Evanston, Ill.: Northwestern Univ. Pr., 1969.

Plantinga, Theodore. *Historical Understanding in the Thought of Wilhelm Dilthey.* Toronto, Buffalo, and London: Univ. of Toronto Pr., 1980.

Ricoeur, Paul. *The Conflict of Interpretations: Essays in Hermeneutics.* Evanston, Ill.: Northwestern Univ. Pr., 1974. (French ed., 1969.)

Schleiermacher, Friedrich D. E. *Hermeneutics: The Handwritten Manuscripts.* Ed. by Heinz Kimmerle, tr. by James Duke and Jack Forstman. Missoula, Mont.: Scholars Pr., 1977. (German ed., 1959.)

Thompson, David B., and David Held, eds. *Habermas: Critical Debates.* Cambridge, Mass.: MIT Pr., 1982.

PART II

AREAS
OF
PHILOSOPHY

14

Contemporary
Philosophical Inquiry

Strictly speaking, the doing of philosophy, like aesthetic expression, living out a religious perspective, or making history, is not a "subject," although the study of it is. As a teacher of philosophy one would hope above all to enable students to do philosophy while studying the records of others' philosophizing. One would also hope not only to facilitate philosophy majors' knowing their subject but also to aid philosophical understanding and inquiry among those in many walks of life who are not majors or professional philosophers. In all these respects it is not so much knowing a subject as performing a range of activities that is important.

In some ways, that philosophy has become more and more of a subject in contemporary practice has gotten in the way of its being done. Yet many of the records of reflection in areas marked out by philosophy are important, sometimes indispensable means toward doing that reflection effectively now. To ignore them may lead to making serious mistakes, to being shallow-minded or losing one's way. Such is the quandary facing the contemporary reader of philosophy, who has twenty-six centuries of literature to choose from, most of it produced during the past one hundred years.

Two other difficulties must also be confronted. First, the quest for a certain base for all knowledge or for secure, normative doctrine is one that many contemporary philosophers have given up. The task now is mainly to learn how to live with uncertainty. One consequence of this change (though it also accompanies holdovers of the old quest) is the frequent concentration on analytic technique and on highly specialized problems, and such effort may require expert train-

305

ing. Second, although the noted American philosopher William James once said that the essence of philosophy is vision not technique, by 1931 his famous successor John Dewey could rightly state the following: "The chief characteristic of the present age," he said, "is its despair of any constructive philosophy—not just in its technical meaning, but in the sense of any integrated outlook and attitude." Twentieth-century philosophy has produced its share of intellectual syntheses and of the outlooks on life and tackling of life problems that often draw people to the field. The overall drift, however, has gone the other way. What the reader finds instead is very specific aids, often exquisite ones, to working out perspectives and problem-solving procedures for oneself.

THE AREAS OF PHILOSOPHY

During the first 2,200 years of its existence, very few theoretical disciplines resided outside philosophy. From the seventeenth century on there has been a gradual ingathering of distinctly philosophical issues with which members of other scholarly disciplines are not directly concerned, though many of these issues directly impinge on inquiry tasks within other disciplines and some of them in all. Since the late nineteenth century philosophy has become a profession, bearing an extremely wide band of distinctive methods and interests. (In a 1980 work, cited in chapter 1, Ben-Ami Scharfstein has given a penetrating analysis of some values and disvalues involved in philosophers' becoming professional.) Within the contemporary period, roughly 1945 to the present, it has been organized into at least sixteen major areas and numerous other subspecialties. Some of the subject matter from each area is familiar from ancient times, but each has also advanced in scope and complexity during the twentieth century, taking on new or newly formulated problems and new relationships both with other areas and with nonphilosophical disciplines. Each part of the history of philosophy has become a specialty as well. In that the leading graduate departments of philosophy have only fifteen to twenty faculty members, none is now able to cover the entire field.

In this portion of the book, sixteen areas of philosophy are arranged under two headings: the "core" areas and the "bridge" areas. Historically, those in the first set have come to serve core functions; that is, they tend to have more general reference and they are used widely in the other areas. Those in the second set more obviously relate to particular domains of experience. By using this language, however, I wish to avoid the impression that any one area is strictly foundational for others, though such a role has long been assumed for epistemology and metaphysics among most philosophers, and logic and the philosophy of language have been added to that pair by numerous philosophers in the twentieth century. The historical record yields a picture of considerable interlocking influence among the areas. This is the case especially among the core areas listed here, although for any given inquiry in one of these areas one of the bridge areas might easily provide a core function.

The order given is chiefly for ease of presentation. Theory of knowledge, logic, philosophy of language, and metaphysics are listed first because of their current prominence. Philosophy of mind and philosophy of action come next because of their close connection with the first four areas in current thinking and because looking at what is going on there gives useful perspective on values inquiry and ethics, which follow. In turn, these last two areas of the first eight suggest the greater attention to normative phenomena within all the bridge areas.

Within the second set, philosophy of science is also listed first because of its current prominence, philosophy of history next because of its equally general scope and potentially great importance within the field itself. Social-political philosophy and philosophy of law come next because of the special association with social components in decision making. Aesthetics, philosophy of religion, and philosophy of psychology and psychoanalysis follow because of their special, though far from exclusive, reference to individual life. Philosophy of education ends the list of sixteen because in it, more than any other area, lies the necessity and potential of applying all the other areas to its concerns.

RELATIONS TO OTHER DISCIPLINES

Viewed both historically and in terms of current practice, there appears to be a phase in the formation of every theoretical discipline in which it necessarily remains a part of philosophy, wherever else it may be. This was distinctly the case through the eighteenth century, since then in a much less direct and ordered way. In fact, since the late nineteenth century the initiatives for change within this relationship have normally come from the sciences; in large part, philosophy has followed their lead. A serious ill, perhaps the basic one, associated with increasing specialization is that a decreasing proportion of scientists and philosophers have much knowledge or competence in both disciplines.

Even if a given theoretical discipline has not emerged within the work of philosophers, it very soon takes on philosophical significance and depends in part on the kind of inquiry philosophers would make for its further development. Once it becomes an established discipline with technical methods and agreed results of its own it leaves philosophy, as it were, and thereafter returns only to the degree that new problems arise that are of a foundational nature or that require philosophical therapy. In this sense, philosophy as a field has continually expanded and contracted, maintaining relations to other fields in a way that is dependent on changing needs and awarenesses on both sides. In this sense, too, philosophy is both necessary and dispensable with respect to every other field of inquiry. Richard Rorty (*Philosophy and the Mirror of Nature,* 1979, cited on p. 7) aptly argues that its role is not so much that of a cultural gatekeeper, if at all, but rather more that of a wide-ranging participant in "the conversation of mankind."

Three different forms of relation to other disciplines are exemplified as follows: (1) foundational critique (Manninen and Tuomela, 1976); (2) clarifying commentary, sometimes more to bring out assumptions or to clarify concepts (Passmore, 1974), sometimes with a more prophetic edge (Barrett, 1978); and (3) application (Temkin et al., 1977). Areas of professional philosophy such as philosophy of history and philosophy of religion include all three, while some things called "philosophy of . . ." represent none of them or only one or two.

Philosophy still has its share of systematic thinkers and system builders. Such laborers, like Plato and Aristotle, suffer greater vulnerability to critique than do the journeymen essayists that populate the field today; but they too are needed to gather in what the other disciplines have to offer, to find possibly important connections that would not otherwise be imagined, to form new visions, and to prepare the way for new tasks. Rarely, as in the cases of the American Josiah Royce and the German Martin Heidegger, what is chiefly exposed by systematizers is a quite idiosyncratic consciousness; yet, as with each, this may itself be both appealing to a great many readers and stimulating of important philosophical inquiry.

In Oxford tradition the study of philosophy has been deemed central to humanistic study. The state of the field over the past half-

century has not won it such a position elsewhere. Courses in literature, art, religion, and the like have assumed surrogate roles but
ordinarily, it may be supposed, without the kinds of critical rigor or
awareness of past views that have become the charge of philosophy
as a specialty. Even at Oxford, moreover, the primary aim has been
to aid theoretical understanding, not to purvey a "philosophy of
life." This self-edifying function of philosophy remains for some,
following the Socratic injunction that the unexamined life is not
worth living. While presenting a normative position he calls "self-
actualization ethics," David Norton (1976), for example, also discusses problems of forming a philosophical foundation for patterns
of education and culture that can nurture personal development.
Richard Wasserstrom and company (1976) address several kinds of
issues relating to death. Patently, those that refer to the problem of
facing death are among the more important philosophy of life issues,
though—presumably resisted as are sex, religion, and politics—they
may not always have gotten their due. Works such as that edited by
John Cruickshank (1962) on "the novelist as philosopher" perhaps
overidentify philosophy with philosophy of life, although this study
is otherwise quite interesting.

The tangled relationships between philosophy and rhetoric since
Socrates, some of which are traced in the historical sections here,
have given rise to another set of issues concerning philosophical style
(Henze et al., 1980) and the use of rhetoric in philosophical argument (Johnstone, 1978). Chaim Perelman (1982) has abandoned the
traditional distinction between argumentative discourse in rhetoric
and in philosophy or dialectic. Insofar as problems of similar form
vex other disciplines, these too are points of intersection between
them and philosophy, which has always had to make its way between the aims of validity and persuasion.

Among the many schools of theory applied to the criticism of
literature, deconstructionism, initiated chiefly by the French literary
scholar and critic Jacques Derrida, has recently mounted a major,
extensive challenge to the claim that philosophers present or critique
"texts" in fundamentally distinctive or preferable ways. Several of
Derrida's books have been translated into English (for instance, see
citations on p. 290 and 345). A number of summary works on deconstructionist theory began to appear in the early 1980s. In a concise critical interpretation, which lays out how deconstructionist theory has evolved, Christopher Norris (1982) is especially concerned
with issues about the status of philosophical "writings."

Barrett, William. *The Illusion of Technique: A Search for Meaning in a Technological Civilization.* New York: Doubleday Anchor, 1978.

✓ Cruickshank, John, ed. *The Novelist as Philosopher: Studies in French Fiction 1935–1960.* Oxford and New York: Oxford Univ. Pr., 1962.

Henze, Donald, et al. "Philosophy as Style and Literature as Philosophy." *Monist* 63, no. 4:417–557 (Oct. 1980).

Johnstone, Henry W., Jr. *Validity and Rhetoric in Philosophical Argument: An Outlook in Transition.* University Park, Pa.: Dialogue, 1978.

Manninen, Juha, and Raimo Tuomela, eds. *Essays on Explanation and Understanding: Studies in the Foundations of Humanities and Social Sciences.* Dordrecht and Boston: Reidel, 1976.

Norris, Christopher. *Deconstruction: Theory and Practice.* New York and London: Methuen, 1982.

Norton, David L. *Personal Destinies: A Philosophy of Ethical Individualism.* Princeton, N.J.: Princeton Univ. Pr., 1976.

Passmore, John A. *Man's Responsibility for Nature: Ecological Problems and Western Traditions.* London: Duckworth, 1974.

Perelman, Chaim. *The Realm of Rhetoric.* Tr. by William Kluback. Notre Dame and London: Univ. of Notre Dame Pr., 1982. (French ed., 1977.)

Temkin, Owsei, William K. Frankena, and Sanford H. Kadish. *Respect for Life in Medicine, Philosophy and the Law.* Baltimore, Md.: Johns Hopkins Univ. Pr., 1977.

Wasserstrom, Richard, ed. "Philosophical Problems of Death." *Monist* 59, no. 2:161–283 (Apr. 1976).

RISING THEMES

Eastern/Western Philosophy

Very little comparative analysis of Eastern and Western sources has been done that is not only critical but also displays a truly knowledgeable understanding of both. A volume by Ben-Ami Scharfstein and his Israeli associates (*Philosophy East/Philosophy West,* 1978, cited on p. 158) bears these qualities. The usual effort is to interpret Eastern thought to Western readers, as in the periodicals *Philosophy East and West, Journal of Chinese Philosophy,* and *Journal of Indian Philosophy.* This is largely true of three volumes edited by Charles A. Moore (1967), fruits of the four East-West philosophers' conferences held at the University of Hawaii from 1939 to 1964. This area of inquiry is still in its infancy, held back by the relative inaccessibility of Eastern sources and by the widely held assumption that theories authentic to Eastern cultures consist primarily of mythology and of moral and religious doctrines irrelevant to modern philosophical interests.

Thus far there is little literature in English that reflects philosophical interest in Third World culture (see chapter 7).

Women

There have been very few women philosophers, though in recent decades their number has been increasing and several women have been contributing substantially to the field. This change has brought with it somewhat greater attention to issues of special concern to women, analyses of concepts related to women's existence, attributes from the experience of women, and reviews of the history of philosophy with respect to all three.

Several anthologies on women and philosophy have appeared since the special double issue of *Philosophical Forum* on this subject in 1975. This is still among the best collections and has been republished by Marx Wartofsky and Carol Gould (1976). A later work edited by Mary Vetterling-Braggin et al. (1977) is less programmatic, settling into critical investigation of several specific social issues (such as rape, androgyny, sexism and language, preferential treatment, abortion). Another book of seventeen essays edited by Vetterling-Braggin (1982), thirteen of them by women philosophers, deals with gender and sex role issues. The most extensive look into the concept of woman within the history of philosophy is gathered in Mary Brody Mahowald's 1978 work. Susan Moller Okin (*Women in Western Political Thought*, 1979, cited on p. 450) surveys the place of women in Western political traditions. A *Monist* issue edited by Mary Mothersill (1973) handles philosophical issues related to women's liberation. In one of the first sustained analyses of philosophical problems associated with feminism Carol McMillan (1982) examines tendencies to view women's biological makeup as oppressive.

Philosophy for Children

Apart from literature and history, the humanities have tended not to be well represented in elementary and secondary school curricula, either in their theory or in their design and content. This is above all true of philosophy. In the 1970s preparations have been made for a remedy of this situation among some philosophers, particularly through the leadership of Matthew Lipman. Two volumes by Lipman and associates (1978, 1980) and one by Gareth Matthews (1980) represent these new efforts.

Lipman, Matthew, and Ann Margaret Sharp, eds. *Growing Up with Philosophy*. Philadelphia, Pa.: Temple Univ. Pr., 1978.

————, Ann Margaret Sharp, and Frederick S. Oscanyan. *Philosophy in the Classroom.* 2nd ed. Philadelphia, Pa.: Temple Univ. Pr., 1980. (1st ed., n.d.)

McMillan, Carol. *Women, Reason, and Nature: Some Philosophical Problems with Feminism.* Princeton, N.J.: Princeton Univ. Pr., 1982.

Mahowald, Mary Brody. *Philosophy of Women: Classical to Current Concepts.* Indianapolis, Ind.: Hackett, 1978.

✓ Matthews, Gareth B. *Philosophy and the Young Child.* Cambridge, Mass. and London: Harvard Univ. Pr., 1980.

✓ Moore, Charles A., ed. *The Chinese Mind. The Indian Mind. The Japanese Mind.* 3v. Honolulu: East-West Center Pr., 1967.

Mothersill, Mary, ed. "Women's Liberation: Ethical, Social, and Political Issues." *Monist* 57, no. 1:1–114 (Jan. 1973).

Vetterling-Braggin, Mary, ed. *"Femininity," "Masculinity," and "Androgyny": A Modern Philosophical Discussion.* Totowa, N.J.: Littlefield, Adams, 1982.

————, Frederick A. Elliston, and Jane English, eds. *Feminism and Philosophy.* Totowa, N.J.: Littlefield, Adams, 1977.

Wartofsky, Marx, and Carol C. Gould, eds. *Women and Philosophy: Toward a Theory of Liberation.* New York: Putnam, 1976.

15

Epistemology: Theory of Knowledge

HISTORY AND CURRENT STATUS

In the broadest sense, epistemology is the philosophical interest in how and when reliable knowledge is attainable: (1) under what conditions for truth statements; (2) under what conditions for justification of knowledge claims; (3) given what assumptions as to relations between knowing subjects and known objects; and (4) given what assumptions about the social components of language and other media used to express and give meaning to beliefs. Greater sophistication on all four fronts has accrued over the some twenty-six centuries since philosophy began. During the "modern" period, since Descartes and Locke, the interests of philosophy itself have been predominately epistemological. With respect to feature number 3, a mind-body dualism, or split between the knower and the known, has generally been assumed since the seventeenth century; emphasis has been placed on investigation of what is going on in the mind, one not dependent on a very developed notion of feature number 4. Kant introduced a narrow emphasis that views epistemology as the discipline that establishes the foundations for the rest of philosophy and thereby for the sciences and the various other scholarly disciplines. In this version, there is no real separation between the concerns of science and philosophy.

What had once been the secure foundations of knowledge, wherever it occurs, for scientists like Galileo and for philosophers like Descartes and Leibniz became precisely the basic problem for Kant. After a Hegelian interlude, there was a return to this problem after the mid-nineteenth century. This occurred especially among the neo-Kantians in Germany after about 1860, in other ways among the

313

positivist followers of Auguste Comte in France and John Stuart Mill in Britain. The key questions then became: What foundations of knowledge are secure or can be made secure, if any? How and when are claims to know something warranted? A few philosophers argued that these are the basic concerns of a "scientific philosophy" and that no radical distinction between science and philosophy is to be made. Most took philosophy to be a subject in its own right. Both positions took epistemology—for some, plus metaphysics and perhaps other basic derivatives—to be the core. Thus was "philosophy" born in its usual twentieth-century mode. An increasing proportion of influential philosophers used various forms of logical and linguistic analysis for the purpose.

In twentieth-century Anglo-American philosophy subjects that since the Renaissance had been discussed under the headings of method, dialectic, rhetoric or logic, broadly conceived, have become the charge of methodology within the various scholarly disciplines, only indirectly a philosophical responsibility. For neo-Kantian Ernst Cassirer (1950) and most other philosophers until about World War II, the problem of knowledge essentially consisted of defining what scientific knowledge is and of determining how to get it. By and large, this was not true among the pragmatists, existentialists, and phenomenologists, or among the hermeneutical and critical theorists. However, in most places since the 1920s these larger goals have become the special province of philosophy of science, if that, while epistemology proper has settled upon a narrower set of problems, chiefly features number 1 and 2 or, for many recent philosophers (Roderick Chisholm perhaps chief among them), number 2 alone.

Between the two world wars, the status of "the given" was the main subject. Logical empiricist Bertrand Russell (1914) did perhaps more than any other to set up the tasks. The empirical "given"— a term first used in this sense by C. I. Lewis (1929) but accompanied by "appearances," "sense data" and other words with similar reference—was generally conceived as the certain foundation of the knowledge edifice. Most notably, John Dewey challenged that assumption throughout the period; partly for that reason, his thinking tended to be ignored by epistemologists. According to Chisholm (1964), for example, Dewey's theory of inquiry was not, strictly speaking, an epistemology at all, possessing an entirely different aim from those of seeking the secure foundations of knowledge or of ascertaining how knowledge claims are to be justified. But Chisholm himself quotes Dewey (from *Experience and Nature*) with complete favor regarding the status of "the given" as logical not primal.

In the 1950s critiques of the assumption from within analytic philosophy came especially from Max Black, Norman Malcolm (1963) and other Wittgenstein-imbued linguistic philosophers and from Wilfrid Sellars (1963). Contemporary phenomenalism, a first cousin to foundationalism (which focuses on the search for an empirical "given" as the foundation of knowledge) and not to be confused with phenomenology, was worked out in many of its details by C. I. Lewis (1946); it held that statements about physical things can be translated into statements about appearances. This alternative position was critically assessed and rejected by Chisholm (1957), W. V. O. Quine (1960) and Arthur Pap (1958) during the same period. Already in the mid-1930s Quine, himself an empiricist, had also attacked, as did Lewis later, another assumption traditionally held among empiricists: that a distinction can be upheld between the objects of analytic and synthetic judgments, or between truths of reason and truths of fact. Controversies over these assumptions have remained the major portion of the epistemological agenda since World War II.

Chisholm (1964), using the narrow definition of epistemology, has appropriately noted that in the twentieth century "most of the important contributions to the subject have been in works devoted primarily to other subjects," especially logic, philosophy of language, philosophy of science, and metaphysics. The widely used set of readings organized by Ernest Nagel and Richard Brandt (1965) derives chiefly from those "other" subjects, dealing with issues of meaning, reference, truth, universals, induction, and perception, as well as issues concerning knowledge of the external world, past events, and other minds. Accordingly, the scope of epistemology is larger for them. It consists of the systematic presentation and critique of general epistemological statements, which have the form: "The person S has greater warrant for believing h than i."

Since the early 1960s the overwhelming proportion of the epistemological literature has consisted of inquiries at or near Chisholm's conception. That emphasis alone could have led to much of the core literature in other areas of philosophy. When it has not dealt with metaepistemological issues about how to proceed in the first place, that is, how to structure effective epistemological inquiry, this further literature has related especially to skeptical arguments concerning knowledge of the external world (philosophy of science), of self-iden-

tity and other minds (philosophy of mind), of universals and necessary truths (logic and metaphysics), of values versus facts (axiology),
of the good or the right (ethics), of God (philosophy of religion) and
of the past (philosophy of history), or to skeptical arguments concerning human agency and free will (philosophy of action). Other
literature has looked especially at the social components of learning
and using reliable knowledge (notably in philosophy of language,
philosophy of education, social-political philosophy, and philosophy
of law). In several of these areas philosophers have also addressed
closely related epistemological issues about sensation and perception,
memory, anticipations of the future, inductive inference, transcendental argument, dreaming, private language and first person statements, the mind-body relation, causality, prediction, dispositions to
believe, and the ethics of belief in decision making of all kinds. In
devoting most of their books on epistemology to a number of issues
from both sets John Pollock (1974) and Garrett Vander Veer (1978)
in effect claim eminent domain for epistemology over other areas of
philosophy. This is frequently done. Almost all contemporary efforts
of an epistemological nature, moreover, have typically purported to
refute radical skepticism and have either assumed the Cartesian
search for unassailable foundations of knowledge or (among a few)
coherence as the ultimate criterion of truth. Frederick Will (1974)
has argued that the Cartesian search for justification by reference to
foundations, even in the inverse form adopted by Chisholm that
refers to self-justifying statements, ends up being an exemplification
of skepticism itself.

Imagine an increasingly complex network of issues moving out
from the core that Chisholm represents, to a large area roughly defined by Nagel and Brandt, then beyond to include central concerns
in every other area of philosophy. Add a transparent template over
this map to represent the more descriptive, ordinary-language analysis approach (for instance, J. L. Austin, 1962, and Wittgensteinian
Norman Malcolm, 1963), that attempts to show that radical skepticism refuses to acknowledge general principles underlying linguistic
mastery and communication. On this template place some lines,
partly overlapping, to indicate analytic efforts since G. E. Moore
(1903 on) to refute skepticism by reference to common sense. Finally,
place another template over it all to acknowledge the continuing
presence of skepticism itself (as in the extreme position of Peter
Unger, 1975). This network operationally designates the dominance
of epistemology in contemporary philosophy and of that portion of

modern philosophy since Descartes to which contemporary analytic philosophers have chiefly attended.

Sometimes philosophers have found themselves driven to modify their own once preferred positions because these implied skeptical conclusions. An eminent example of this powerful motive is found in C. I. Lewis's work. In his 1946 book Lewis claimed that his earlier view of knowledge in *Mind and the World Order* (1929) led to skepticism; he then formed arguments to show that there are "apprehensions of the given," what epistemologists later called beliefs that justify themselves. Within the contemporary period both are major works.

Oliver Johnson (1978) finds a marked resurgence of radical skepticism since the late 1960s, spearheaded by Arne Naess, Keith Lehrer, and Peter Unger. He devotes an entire study to this development. Is it the major task of epistemology to refute such skepticism? In searching for an alternative to the dominant foundational approach, Michael Williams (1977) thinks so, as those who accept that approach have tended to do. Arthur Danto (1968) tried to do this by showing the—to him—illusive, self-defeating error of treating semantic difficulties as if they were descriptive, empirical ones. Another tack would be simply to deny one or more premises. For example, having argued for radical skepticism in a noted 1971 article, Keith Lehrer (1974) rejects the skeptical premise that a valid claim to knowledge is a claim to certainty; he instead presents a theory of knowledge that does without certainty. A close but still more liberal account of what it takes to justify or defeat a proposition is given by Carl Ginet (1975). John Pollock (1974) associates himself with Chisholm in arguing for the position that concepts need not be analyzed only by stating their truth conditions but can best be analyzed by stating their justification conditions (see below). Accordingly, his general response to skepticism is to ask: Since we do have knowledge, what must be wrong with one or more skeptical premises that makes it possible to have the knowledge we possess, and what correct premises may be adopted in their place? Thus, the question is how, not whether, it is possible to have knowledge. This task Pollock further distinguishes from that of determining when we have knowledge, though he accepts the Gettier challenge to the effect that more than justified true belief is required for determining when.

Edmund Gettier's challenge in a now famous 1963 article has been followed by a huge literature critically reviewing the three traditional conditions stated in C. I. Lewis (1946), A. J. Ayer (1956), Chisholm

(1957) and others who have helped set the conditions for contemporary epistemological debate. In Gettier's formulation, which he rejects: "*S* knows that *P* if and only if (i) *P* is true, (ii) *S* believes that *P*, and (iii) *S* is justified in believing that *P*." George Pappas and Marshall Swain (1978) gather twenty-two key essays from that debate, five of them not published elsewhere, which they describe as depicting the main lines of study concerning the problem of knowledge over the previous decade. The excellent set of thirty new essays edited by Peter French et al. (1980) has a scope only somewhat larger. As the contents of both collections accurately indicate, the effort since about 1963 has been chiefly an American affair. A brief work by Gilbert Harman (1973) exemplifies how the post-Gettier debate could affect broader epistemological inquiry. Harman responds to radical skepticism by developing an account of knowledge that finds principles of inference to be operative from the perceptual level on up. In this fashion, he joins Wittgenstein, Quine, Wilfrid Sellars, and his nearer contemporaries Bruce Aune (1967), Keith Lehrer (1974), and William Alston (in a 1976 article and in French, 1980) in their varied critiques of foundationalism. Among the critics some (such as Michael Williams, 1977) have adopted a coherentist alternative.

OVERVIEWS AND COLLECTIONS

History

In addition to the collections just mentioned, the basic historical accounts of recent epistemology in its narrower conception have come from Roderick Chisholm (1964; in Franklin Donnell, *Aspects of Contemporary American Philosophy,* 1965, cited on p. 229; and in the second edition of his *Theory of Knowledge,* 1977). A longer and broader view is available in John Passmore's survey (*A Hundred Years of Philosophy,* 1957, cited on p. 10) of philosophy over the 100 years since Mill. Numerous other historical studies are noted in chapters 1–13. Stephen Stich's (1975) book on the classic debate over whether there are "innate ideas" includes some texts from Plato's *Meno,* Locke, Leibniz and Descartes, and nine recent essays in philosophy of language, thus marking a shift from the more metaphysical to the more linguistic side of epistemological inquiry.

Earlier twentieth-century overviews of the problems still worth consulting include the late sum-up by Bertrand Russell (1948). Another synoptic work by H. H. Price (1953) presents views close to

Russell's in many respects; but in a well-known 1932 work on perception Price had already rejected Russell's causal theory of perception (which Alvin Goldman, Marshall Swain, and others have recently tried to revive in new forms) and had sought an alternative way of understanding sense data. A modified logical positivism is offered in A. J. Ayer's overview (1956).

Recent Stages

Later stages of the debate are picked up by Arthur Danto (1968) and Chisholm (1977), who also treats the metaphysical side of some issues regarding the relation between person and object (1976). A carefully crafted Wittgensteinian approach to many of the same issues comes from Norman Malcolm (1963). In a brief, knowledgeable work, largely shriven of technicalities, Robert Ackermann (1972) nicely summarizes recent efforts. Ackermann had previously published other works in epistemology, logic, and philosophy of science.

"Cognitivism" and Metaepistemology

Oliver Johnson (1978) has applied the word "cognitivism" to the general notion that knowledge is possible. Chisholm (1966, 2nd ed. 1977) uses "critical cognitivism" for the view (as opposed to skeptics, intuitionists, and reductivists) that there are empirical truths that confer evidence, or reasonableness, upon knowledge claims, which claims are thereby "indirectly evident." Uncovering such connections, he says, is a matter of "hermeneutics," not one of simply determining what the facts are (exegesis). There is a third, metaepistemological sense of "cognitivism," however, in relation to which Chisholm is a noncognitivist versus a naturalist or nonnaturalist. That is, he rejects the assumption shared by the other two positions that epistemic principles are either true or false (excepting analytically true ones), though he agrees with the nonnaturalist position that epistemological terms cannot be defined on the basis of empirically observable qualities.

Using Gestalt psychology, Michael Polanyi (1958), a critic of foundational empiricism who emphasizes the personal accouterments of knowing and thereby the often hidden and tacit components, would be (like Chisholm) a cognitivist in the first two senses but (unlike Chisholm) probably a naturalist in the third sense. But his interest, like Dewey's, lies chiefly in practical, warrantable, and objective knowledge, not theoretical certainty, thus in the activities of getting knowledge and in the broader relations between the knower and the known. In a book of historical studies on the latter subject—stretching from Plato's *Meno* through Aristotle, Descartes, Hume, and Kant to the present—Marjorie Grene (1966) acknowledges the influence of both Polanyi and phenomenologist Maurice Merleau-Ponty. In contrast, D. M. Armstrong's work (1973) is analytical, using a naturalistic approach. He treats belief as reality-mapping and presents a modified correspondence theory of truth, such that the relation of belief-states, thoughts, or assertions to reality need not always be one-to-one.

Collections

Three general collections have already been noted: by Nagel and Brandt (1965), Pappas and Swain (1978), and French et al. (1980). In addition, a book of readings edited by Robert Swartz (1965) has been widely used and is still valuable, as is the later collection edited by Chisholm and Swartz (1973). The 1964 Oberlin Colloquium edited by Norman Care and Robert Grimm (1969) is noteworthy in that it includes several papers quite representative for that time. There Richard Popkin views epistemology since the Renaissance in terms of ever new attempts to meet the skeptical challenge (his 1979 book, *The History of Skepticism from Erasmus to Spinoza,* cited on p. 72, traces the early history); Fred Dretske anticipates his 1969 book on seeing and justification; Robert Fogelin makes a distinction between causes and reasons for doing; Chisholm points up differences between loose and popular senses of "identity" (referring to things), on the one hand, and philosophical ones (referring to persons) on the other; Jaakko Hintikka views the logic of perception as a branch of modal logic.

THEMES

Most of the issues discussed by epistemologists without leaving their own area (except in Chisholm's perspective) can be placed under three headings. Each of the general works already noted at least touches upon most of them.

Sensation and Perception

Roderick Chisholm's *Perceiving* (1957) especially marks new stages of inquiry into the epistemic roles of sensation and perception. The "history" by D. W. Hamlyn (1961) catalogs several of the main types of treatment from the Greeks up to that time, viewed in terms of current interests. Chisholm's work, like that of most in the period to follow, characteristically attempts to repair difficulties in proposals already made by making slight adjustments. J. L. Austin's *Sense and Sensibilia* (1962) is now a classic text among applications of ordinary language analysis to the task. Others took the more radical approach of simply reducing epistemic issues to issues of meaning. Among subsequent discussions in Britain, Don Locke's (1967) exercise in conceptual clarification looks at some major philosophical theories of perception and helpfully separates analysis of the question of whether we perceive external objects from that of the question of how we know that we do. He takes "sense-datum" to be a theory-neutral term. On the American side, George Pitcher (1971) offers a direct realist theory of sense perception which opposes sense-datum theory altogether. Materialist theories of mind have become popular entrées to theories of perception. D. M. Armstrong (e.g., *Belief, Truth and Knowledge,* 1973) is a well-known advocate of this approach.

Both the various recent attempts to fix up foundationalism and some proposed replacements are well represented in French et al. (1980). The recapitulation of the entire enterprise in terms of "social justification of belief" by Richard Rorty (*Philosophy and the Mirror of Nature,* 1979, cited on p. 7) is not directly represented, though some of the authors have also listened to Wilfrid Sellars's (1963) behavioristic attack on "the myth of the given" and Quine's (1960) attack on the separation of language and fact.

Some philosophers have used reflection on perception for purposes other than forming a theory of knowledge. Fred Dretske's (1969) *Seeing and Knowing,* for example, is chiefly a "descriptive" work, confined to a few specialized issues. It does not offer a theory of perception; but Dretske does draw a distinction of nonepistemic ways of seeing from primary and secondary epistemic ways, with some attention to issues regarding perceptual relativity and the functions of observation in scientific practice. In subsequent work (not cited here) Dretske has sought to apply a metaphysically materialist information and communication theory to interdisciplinary settings, distinguishing between information, viewed as raw material, and meaning, viewed as something we create. He has also explored possible relations of these interests to epistemological issues regarding sensation and perception, meaning and belief, and the status of concepts, which are quite different issues from those he is chiefly pursuing.

Meaning and Reference

Early developments in the empiricist verifiability theory of meaning, first popularized in a logical positivist form by A. J. Ayer (*Language, Truth and Logic,* 1936, cited on p. 155), are helpfully summarized by William Alston (*Philosophy of Language,* 1964, cited on p. 344). Much that is of importance in this thematic area, including discussion on issues concerning universals and necessary truth, is considered within logic, metaphysics, and philosophy of language. The problem of induction (Will, 1974) is also a major topic in logic and philosophy of science. Among the leading logical-systematic treatments of the concept of meaning as it has formed since the 1920s are those by Arthur Pap (1958), W. V. O. Quine (1960), and L. Jonathan Cohen (1962). Pap's chief aim is to clarify the distinction between necessary and contingent propositions, Quine's to destroy it. Cohen's work can be viewed in part as a linguistically sophisticated attempt to rescue it from Quine's critique, along with related distinctions between analytic and synthetic truths and what he takes to be the much more important one between what is a priori and what is not. Possible connections of such logical and semantic issues with the standard epistemological problems about justified true belief are regularly treated by Jaakko Hintikka (e.g., 1962), using what he calls "model sets."

Among the more specialized collections, "reference" is the main subject in the gathering of ten previously published papers edited by Stephen Schwartz (1977) and in the *Monist* collection edited by Dagfinn Føllesdal (1979). Here the unending controversy over the epistemic status of definite descriptions, which goes back to Gottlob Frege but was given its real start by Bertrand Russell in 1905, gets some attention. More is given to newly formulated theories about identity statements, synthetic necessary statements, and reference by some general terms that do not require the mediation of descriptions. In the Schwartz volume, use of modal, "possible worlds" semantics, which has played a prominent role in some of the newer theories, is critically examined by Alvin Plantinga.

Truth

For a great many philosophers, by far the majority in the contemporary period, "truth" has been thought of not so much as a property of something, if at all, but as a relation of correspondence between what is said or thought and facts. That is, they have held some version of a correspondence theory of truth. D. J. O'Connor (1975) examines several other recent versions, including Alfred Tarski's semantic theory, first articulated in 1931, J. L. Austin's theory, and criticisms of both by P. F. Strawson. A summary of criticisms is given by George Pitcher (1964), who features F. P. Ramsey's "redundancy" theory and then essays from or stimulated by the now famous Austin-Strawson debate of 1950 (two, by Strawson and G. J. Warnock, are new).

Austin had proposed a modified correspondence theory. Strawson took the position that "true" does not designate either a property or a relation and argued for elimination of the correspondence theory altogether. Instead, he offered a "performative" theory, according to which "true" is chiefly a performative expression (that is, an endorsement of a statement). This is meant to be a further development of Ramsey's view that to say a proposition is true is, simply and therefore redundantly, to assert the proposition itself. It is also meant to be an abandonment of the semantic theory of Rudolf Carnap, Alfred Tarski, and others, which holds that "true" is a metalinguistic property of sentences. Incidentally, it might also open the way to a tighter version of the pragmatic theory of truth, first advanced by Charles Sanders Peirce and then by John Dewey (not William James's, which they both disclaimed), but which has not received much notice in recent decades.

Are so-called truths only expressions of linguistic conventions and not strictly truths at all? Rorty and others think, with Strawson, that at any rate the correspondence theory of truth ought to be relegated to semantics. Chisholm (1964) thinks such views, including attempts to deny the distinction between analytic and synthetic truth, are examples of what Morris Cohen used to call "insurgence against reason."

The major traditional alternatives to correspondence theories have been coherence theories. Among its recent critics Michael Williams (1977) and Nicholas Rescher (1973, 1979–80), for example, have adopted coherentist positions. That of Lehrer (1974) seems to have leanings in that direction. The most noted contemporary proponent of a coherence theory of truth has been Brand Blanshard (1939), following earlier rationalists like Leibniz and Spinoza, Hegel, and various idealists. Some logical positivists, notably Otto Neurath and Carl Hempel, have adopted a coherentist position based on a mathematical model. The ultimate reference in these views resides along a scale from coherence with the system of propositions currently accepted in a given culture (the relativist extreme), to that with the system generally accepted by scientists at the time (Neurath and Hempel), to coherence with what is true of reality as a whole and therefore of its every part (Blanshard). A degrees of truth theory has been attached by most adherents in order to account for the partial, approximate state in which our actual knowledge may ordinarily be seen to exist. As with correspondence theory, attempts have been made by its more recent advocates to answer the many serious objections that have been lodged against its traditional formulations.

FUTURE PROSPECTS

Today epistemology is in a turmoil. It is easy to imagine but hard to predict what the future will bring. One could imagine, for example, that much effort will be put into trying to clear up the numerous misunderstandings and conceptual mistakes (as on meanings of "justify" and confusions between different epistemic levels) that have already been pointed out in the literature; that many epistemologists will take the turn others have already made from skepticism-oriented inquiry to philosophy of language; and that some, like Michael Dummett (1978), will use analysis of language precisely in order to put the search for foundations on a firmer footing.

As Richard Bernstein indicates in an extensive review article on Richard Rorty's 1979 book *Philosophy and the Mirror of Nature* (cited with the book on p. 7), nothing could be further than Dummett's Fregean program from Rorty's efforts to save analytic philosophy by giving up the effort to "mirror" reality and the allied search for permanent standards, criteria, and decision procedures in favor of culture-responsive practical reasoning. This critique, too, could represent or help to bring about a new turn. Or at least it might presage a return to the broader tasks of epistemology, methodology, and cultural dialogue that in recent decades have often been left to scholars outside the field of philosophy or to philosophers associated with the likes of Heidegger, Dewey, and the later Wittgenstein.

Ackermann, Robert J. *Belief and Knowledge.* Garden City, N.Y.: Doubleday Anchor, 1972.
Armstrong, David M. *Belief, Truth and Knowledge.* Cambridge and New York: Cambridge Univ. Pr., 1973.
Aune, Bruce. *Knowledge, Mind, and Nature: An Introduction to Theory of Knowledge and the Philosophy of Mind.* New York: Random House, 1967.

Austin, John L. *Sense and Sensibilia.* Reconstructed from the manuscript notes by G. J. Warnock. Oxford and New York: Oxford Univ. Pr., 1962.

Ayer, Alfred J. *The Problem of Knowledge.* New York: St. Martin's Pr.; London: Macmillan, 1956.

Blanshard, Brand. *The Nature of Thought.* 2v. New York: Macmillan; London: Allen & Unwin, 1939.

Care, Norman S., and Robert H. Grimm, eds. *Perception and Personal Identity.* Cleveland, Ohio: Pr. of Case Western Reserve Univ., 1969.

Cassirer, Ernst. *The Problem of Knowledge: Philosophy, Science and History since Hegel.* Tr. by William H. Woglom and Charles W. Hendel. New Haven, Conn. and London: Yale Univ. Pr., 1950.

Chisholm, Roderick M. *Perceiving: A Philosophical Study.* Ithaca, N.Y.: Cornell Univ. Pr., 1957.

————. *Person and Object: A Metaphysical Study.* La Salle, Ill.: Open Court; London: Allen & Unwin, 1976.

————. *Theory of Knowledge.* 2nd ed. Englewood Cliffs, N.J.: Prentice-Hall, 1977. (1st ed., 1966.)

————. "Theory of Knowledge." In *Philosophy,* pp. 233–344. Ed. by Roderick Chisholm et al. Englewood Cliffs, N.J.: Prentice-Hall, 1964.

————, and Robert J. Swartz, eds. *Empirical Knowledge: Readings from Contemporary Sources.* Englewood Cliffs, N.J.: Prentice-Hall, 1973.

Cohen, Laurence Jonathan. *The Diversity of Meaning.* 2nd ed. London: Methuen, 1966. (1st ed., 1962.)

Danto, Arthur. *Analytical Philosophy of Knowledge.* Cambridge and New York: Cambridge Univ. Pr., 1968.

Dretske, Fred I. *Seeing and Knowing.* Chicago: Univ. of Chicago Pr.; London: Routledge & Paul, 1969.

Dummett, Michael. *Truth and Other Enigmas.* Cambridge, Mass.: Harvard Univ. Pr.; London: Duckworth, 1978. (His pre-1976 essays.)

Føllesdal, Dagfinn, ed. "Truth, Meaning, and Reference." *Monist* 62, no. 2:129–258 (Apr. 1979).

French, Peter A., Theodore E. Uehling, Jr., and Howard K. Wettstein, eds. *Midwest Studies in Philosophy.* Vol. 5, *Studies in Epistemology.* Minneapolis: Univ. of Minnesota Pr., 1980.

Ginet, Carl. *Knowledge, Perception and Memory.* Dordrecht and Boston: Reidel, 1975.

Grene, Marjorie. *The Knower and the Known.* New York: Basic Books; London: Faber, 1966.

Hamlyn, D. W. *Sensation and Perception: A History of the Philosophy of Perception.* New York: Humanities Pr.; London: Routledge & Paul, 1961.

Harman, Gilbert. *Thought.* Princeton, N.J.: Princeton Univ. Pr., 1973.

Hintikka, Jaakko. *Knowledge and Belief: An Introduction to the Logic of the Two Notions.* Ithaca, N.Y.: Cornell Univ. Pr., 1962.

Johnson, Oliver A. *Skepticism and Cognitivism: A Study in the Foundations of Knowledge.* Berkeley and London: Univ. of California Pr., 1978.

Lehrer, Keith. *Knowledge.* Oxford: Clarendon Pr., 1974.

Lewis, Clarence I. *An Analysis of Knowledge and Valuation.* La Salle, Ill.: Open Court, 1946.

———. *Mind and the World Order: Outline of a Theory of Knowledge*. New York: Scribner, 1929.

Locke, Don. *Perception and Our Knowledge of the External World*. New York: Humanities Pr.; London: Allen & Unwin, 1967.

Malcolm, Norman. *Knowledge and Certainty*. Englewood Cliffs, N.J.: Prentice-Hall, 1963.

√ Nagel, Ernst, and Richard B. Brandt, eds. *Meaning and Knowledge: Systematic Readings in Epistemology*. New York: Harcourt, Brace, 1965.

O'Connor, Daniel J. *The Correspondence Theory of Truth*. London: Hutchinson, 1975; Atlantic Highlands, N.J.: Humanities Pr., 1976.

Pap, Arthur. *Semantics and Necessary Truth*. New Haven, Conn.: Yale Univ. Pr.; Oxford Univ. Pr., 1958.

√ Pappas, George S., and Marshall Swain, eds. *Essays on Knowledge and Justification*. Ithaca, N.Y.: Cornell Univ. Pr., 1978.

Pitcher, George. *A Theory of Perception*. Princeton, N.J.: Princeton Univ. Pr., 1971.

———. *Truth*. Englewood Cliffs, N.J.: Prentice-Hall, 1964.

Polanyi, Michael. *Personal Knowledge: Towards a Post-Critical Philosophy*. Chicago: Univ. of Chicago Pr.; London: Routledge & Paul, 1958.

Pollock, John L. *Knowledge and Justification*. Princeton, N.J.: Princeton Univ. Pr., 1974.

Price, Henry H. *Thinking and Experience*. Cambridge, Mass.: Harvard Univ. Pr.; London: Hutchinson, 1953.

Quine, Willard Van Orman. *Word and Object*. Cambridge, Mass.: Technology Pr. of MIT, 1960.

√ Rescher, Nicholas. *Cognitive Systematization: A Systems-Theoretic Approach to a Coherentist Theory of Knowledge*. Totowa, N.J.: Roman & Littlefield, 1979. (First of a triology with *Scepticism* and *Induction*, cited below.)

———. *The Coherence Theory of Truth*. Oxford: Clarendon Pr., 1973.

———. *Induction: An Essay on the Justification of Inductive Reasoning*. Pittsburgh, Pa.: Univ. of Pittsburgh Pr., 1980.

———. *Scepticism: A Critical Reappraisal*. Totowa, N.J.: Roman & Littlefield; Oxford: Blackwell, 1980.

Russell, Bertrand. *Human Knowledge: Its Scope and Limits*. New York: Simon & Schuster; London: Allen & Unwin, 1948.

———. *Our Knowledge of the External World as a Field for Scientific Method in Philosophy*. 2nd ed. London: Allen & Unwin, 1926. (1st ed., 1914; repr., 1956 and in other editions.)

Schwartz, Stephen P., ed. *Naming, Necessity, and Natural Kinds*. Ithaca, N.Y.: Cornell Univ. Pr., 1977.

Sellars, Wilfrid. *Science, Perception and Reality*. New York: Humanities Pr.; London: Routledge & Paul, 1963.

√ Stich, Stephen P., ed. *Innate Ideas*. Berkeley: Univ. of California Pr., 1975.

Swartz, Robert J., ed. *Perceiving, Sensing, and Knowing: A Book of Readings from Twentieth Century Sources*. Garden City, N.Y.: Doubleday Anchor, 1965.

√ Unger, Peter. *Ignorance: A Case for Scepticism*. Oxford: Clarendon Pr., 1975.

Vander Veer, Garrett L. *Philosophical Skepticism and Ordinary-Language Analysis.* Lawrence: Regents Pr. of Kansas, 1978.

Will, Frederick L. *Induction and Justification: An Investigation of Cartesian Procedure in the Philosophy of Knowledge.* Ithaca, N.Y.: Cornell Univ. Pr., 1974.

Williams, Michael. *Groundless Belief.* New Haven, Conn.: Yale Univ. Pr., 1977.

16

Logic

Overview

In the twentieth century, philosophical concerns with logic, mathematics, and language—and even in some respects with metaphysics—have become tightly intertwined. Epistemological issues are also basic to most of the literature expressly devoted to logic. This situation has come about to no small degree because of the influence of logical positivism, but numerous other changes of interest have contributed as well, as can be seen in the contrasts mentioned below.

Most of the literature cited here refers to the more strictly formal aspects of argument—that is, with such as logicians may aspire to express or represent in mathematical symbols. Thus it deals chiefly with logical composition (for example, quantification, modality, counterfactual statements, intension, and extension), inference (for example, logical truth, entailment, presuppositions, paradoxes), analyticity of statements, modes of reasoning and demonstration, and predication (for example, subjects and predicates, terms, categories, vagueness versus clarity, logical identity and necessity, properties and attributes, comparatives, and universal versus existential propositions).

Although overlaps are unavoidable and are in practice extensive, the literature cited in this section does not deal so much with the more epistemological issues of description, reference, and meaning; with the more scientific issue of causality (though there is material on probability and induction); with the more linguistic issues of tense, quotation, questioning (erotetic logic), intention, speech acts, generative semantics, language contexts, and translation; with the more

328

ethics-oriented issues of oughts and duties (deontic logic); or with the more metaphysical issues regarding time, individuals, identity, necessity, innate ideas, and ontological commitment. All these kinds of issues have nevertheless become part and parcel of specialized inquiries called logic, and most are referred to in this literature.

History

In several of the historical sections, I have already indicated some developments in the history of logic. The standard history of logic by William and Martha Kneale (1962; the latest reprint with corrections, 1978) devotes 378 of its 783 pages to the Greek beginnings, to its original, "classical" formation by Aristotle (mainly deductive, syllogistic logic), to further contributions to classical logic by the Megarians (who introduced modal concepts), Stoics (who, among other things, developed a logic of propositions), Romans (mostly as transmitters of Greek ideas) and later medieval thinkers (some more advanced than any logician before the late-nineteenth century, though still not thoroughly studied, thus cursorily treated by the Kneales), and to post-Renaissance developments through Leibniz to John Stuart Mill. The priority and influence of Gottlob Frege are especially featured in the remainder, within chapters on formal developments, philosophy of logic, philosophy of mathematics, and theory of deductive systems after Frege. Beyond this indispensable work and the more technical studies, very few English books reconstruct particular historical types or stages. Benson Mates has done this for Stoic logic (1961). Hao Wang (1974) has studied movements from mathematical thinking to philosophy. Andrezej Mostowski (1966) is among those who have briefly summarized some close relations between mathematical logic and changing foundations of mathematics over part of the twentieth century.

Typical of much writing on logic for nonspecialists, Gilbert Ryle's noted lectures (1954) on dilemmas depends very little on historical references to make the points. In contrast, James Cargile's study (1979) on paradoxes uses historical information extensively.

Introductions

Most of the numerous introductions to the philosophy of logic have emphasized symbolic logic (also called modern logic or mathematical logic) and have made considerable use of it, as in the introductions by W. V. O. Quine (1970) and Hilary Putnam (1971). Quine briefly discusses the standard topics of logical meaning and truth and considers issues about the scope of logic and the grounding of logical truth. Putnam succinctly deals with the ontological issue of whether abstract logical and mathematical entities really exist. This issue, a prolongation of the late medieval nominalist-realist debate, has attracted much attention in recent decades. Susan Haack's summary (1978), more abundant than Quine's, expertly picks its way through the thickets of nonclassical logical systems, especially modal logic (regarding what is possible versus necessary) and many-valued logic (using more than the values of true and false). This excellent book can be read without prior knowledge of the basic symbols and rules.

Fine examples of how one philosopher has put a continuing interest in the history and philosophy of logic to many philosophical uses are found in P. T. Geach's collection of some thirty-one of his previously published essays, *Logic Matters* (1972). A collection of essays edited by James Gould and Irving Copi (1978) focuses more specifically on philosophical logic itself. An early exemplary introduction to issues in symbolic logic is that by Quine (1940)—on statements, quantification, terms, extended theory of classes, relations, numbers, and syntax. A later, fuller introduction is by Alice Ambrose and Morris Lazerowitz (1962).

The great turning point toward an effort to show that mathematics itself is grounded in logic is the monumental *Principia Mathematica* (1910–13) by Alfred North Whitehead and Bertrand Russell. Russell had already published a major work on mathematical theory in 1903, independently reaching some similar conclusions but also drawing upon the seminal work of Gottlob Frege, which he had just discovered (notably his 1893 *Grundgesetze der Arithmetik,* partly translated in 1964). Recent developments in both philosophy of logic and philosophy of mathematics, with applications to philosophy, science, and computer theory, can be seen in the 1975 proceedings of the Fifth International Congress of Logic, Methodology and Philosophy, edited by Robert Butts and Jaakko Hintikka (1977). The brief introduction to philosophy of mathematics by Stephen Barker (1964) needs updating.

Some more general relations of logic to scientific thinking were highlighted in an early work by Morris R. Cohen and Ernest Nagel (1934), still worth using. Another early work, presented by John Dewey (1938) in the pragmatic vein, interprets logic as the theory of inquiry. Dewey regarded symbolic logic as at best a very small part of that theory. Dewey's basic *Essays in Experimental Logic* came out in 1903, the same year as Russell's *Principles of Mathe-matics.* The approach taken by Dewey reflects a more general use of the word "logic" to mean method or formal outline and explana-tion of procedure. His version requires an investigation of psycho-logical and social contexts in examining matters of logical meaning and truth. A third approach, by linguistic philosopher Max Black (1952), defines logic as the study of reasoning. Accordingly, his three sections are on deductive logic, on use of language and related fallacies, and on induction and scientific method. In much narrower compass, within just a portion of Black's third area, logician Arthur Burks (an editor of Peirce's works and a pioneer in computer theory) inquires into such issues as probability and induction to ex-amine the nature of scientific evidence (1977). Using patterns simi-lar to Burks's, much twentieth-century philosophy of science has been heavily logical in both interest and form, with admixtures of epistemology and metaphysics.

Three rather different accounts of logic as reasoning are by Stephen Körner (1959), John Passmore (1969), and Stephen Toulmin et al. (1979), all eminently usable. Körner emphasizes "conceptual thinking"; Passmore critically examines several modes of reasoning conspicuous in the history of philosophy; Toulmin and company study practical reasoning and argumentation in an interdisciplinary manner, with special attention to applications in law, science, the arts, management, and ethics. Within the standard tradition, Peter Geach (1980) attempts to apply formal logic to arguments in every-day language, as has much of the Anglo-American philosophical lit-erature since World War II. His topics: distribution, subjects and predicates, referring phrases, relative and indefinite pronouns, and lists.

PROBLEMS AND PROJECTS

Theoretical Approaches

Modern, mathematical logic began to develop in a systematic form with work published by Augustus De Morgan (1806–71) and George Boole (1815–64) in 1847, though, as almost always, there were predecessors. Its fuller beginning is usually attributed to Frege, from 1879 on, because of his brilliant and more comprehensive treat-ment of problems. Means for securing the independence of proposi-tional axioms to be used in mathematical logic were not found, however, until the mid-1920s. Much other basic work remained to be done, notably through stimuli from mathematicians such as Guiseppe Peano (1858–1932) and David Hilbert (1862–1943) and from philosophers such as Whitehead and Russell, Jan Łukasiewicz (1878–1956), Ludwig Wittgenstein (1889–1951), Rudolf Carnap (1891–1970), Kurt Gödel (1906–78), Alfred Tarski (1901–), Alonzo Church (1903–), and Willard Van Orman Quine (1908–). All of these thinkers contributed toward a standardization of the logical apparatus. Most held that the use of formal languages could have great philosophical significance. In an influential way Alfred Tarski (1936) attempted to make good on such optimism by constructing a correspondence theory of truth using strictly formal "metalanguage" and the related notion of a hierarchy of languages with distinct truth and falsity predicates at each level. Tarski's theory of truth has come to be very widely acepted. Ordinary language philosophers such as P. F. Strawson (1974) have expressed grave doubts about whether language can be so reduced for purposes of analysis and have therefore presented logic very differently (Strawson, 1952).

An example of an attempt to take a concept used in logic, in this case that of "existence," and to explain it in a chiefly ontological manner is given by Milton Munitz (1974). This work takes from logical theory and is meant to contribute to it but comes from a perspective radically different from any of the above, one that derives more from metaphysical and religious reflection than from modern logical tradition.

One of the earlier attempts to add one or more values to the classic true-false calculus of propositions was that of Jan Łukasiewicz in 1920. He added a neuter value. Propositions that are true or neuter were termed "possible." Nicholas Rescher (1969) has given a full-bodied historical and analytic account of these efforts, called many-valued logic. Critics have argued that proponents of these logical systems are not clear about what it means for a proposition to be truth-functional. It may be the case, as Susan Haack (1978) has argued, that, in effect, these systems simply assign standard values (truth or falsity) to nonstandard items (such as a complex sentence, part of which is true).

Modal logic is another deviation from standard (or classical) modern logic, lacking or replacing some of its vocabulary, theorems, and valid inferences. Like many-valued logic, it characteristically shares some vocabulary, theorems, and valid inferences with classical logic but also adds to that logic in these same respects. Unlike many-valued logic, it is not truth-functional. It arose especially out of the concern that the standard logical apparatus does not adequately represent various sorts of informal argument, especially those containing distinctions between "necessarily," "possibly," and "strictly implies." The relevant literature is full of tortuous discussions of epistemological issues regarding a priori versus a posteriori truths, metaphysical issues regarding necessary versus contingent truths, and more general issues regarding analytic versus synthetic truths and physical versus logical truths—plus various crossovers among those categories (such as whether there are contingent a priori truths). Treatment of these issues has played a strong role in construction of the many modal logics and in their critical assessment.

A major type of modal logic uses "possible-world semantics" in the neo-Leibnizian idiom of Saul Kripke, Jaakko Hintikka (1975), and others. This began to be developed and widely used in philosophical inquiry during the early 1960s. A notable exercise of this type is David Lewis's (1973) study of counterfactual conditional statements. As Lewis lays them out, these statements are generally of the form: "If it were the case that _____, then it would (or might) be the case that. . . ." New symbolic operators are assigned to these modes. (Other extended logics closely follow the pattern of adding operators established in modal logic. For example, epistemic logic adds symbols for "*x* knows that" and "*x* believes that"; deontic logic, for "It ought to be the case that" and "It is permitted that"; tense logic, for "now," "before time *t*," etc. A very useful dictionary of logical terms and symbols has been put together by Carol Horn Greenstein, 1978, cited in Part III on p. 509.)

Using the "possible-world semantics" approach, Raymond Bradley and Norman Swartz (1979) have recently proposed, from a resolutely ontological (realist) and antilinguistic perspective, that modal logic provides a semantic basis for much of formal logic. Their discourse is for the most part nonformal in that they wish to demonstrate its primacy for philosophical work in general. Their concern is semantic in that it investigates what it is for an argument to be valid or a proposition to be true. The predominant concern through much of the history of classical logic (including modern logic until the early 1960s) has been with discovery of formal or syntactic marks that provide assurance of the same. Work by Ruth Barcan (later Ruth Marcus, in a 1946 article on modal predicate calculus), Carnap (1947), and others in the late 1940s and 1950s prepared the way for this semantic approach, themselves drawing upon the pioneering work on modal sentence systems by C. I. Lewis (1883–1964) from 1918 on. Lewis's system S5 has become the most favored, though there are now dozens of systems.

W. V. O. Quine (e.g., *From a Logical Point of View...*, 1953) has been prominent among those who have rigorously challenged modal logic, on the grounds that it is an unnecessary extension of classical logic, that it has an excessively weak use of material implication, and that there are other philosophical difficulties, quite apart from its formal feasibility, in the interpretation of both modal sentence logic and modal predicate logic. (See Susan Haack, 1978, and Leonard Linsky, 1977, for summaries of criticisms and replies.)

Scope of Logic

Arguments on the proper scope of logic are many and varied. Quine, for example, has taken a monistic view of logic, striving for a strict, unextended formalism suitable to the requirements of physical science. In contrast, Geach (1972) takes logic to be independent of science, not continuous with it. Still others would greatly expand its scope, chiefly in ways already indicated. For example, A. N. Prior (1976) has argued that tense operators must be added and has developed an "egocentric" logic. Others would squeeze down formal logic for certain purposes—for example, by dropping distributive rules in speaking of quantum phenomena in physics. Still others (for example, Steven Toulmin, *The Philosophy of Science*, 1953, cited on p. 427) take the "instrumentalist" view that there are no correct logical systems but only internally sound ones.

A pluralist view is that there is more than one correct system of logic, either because restrictions of the standard system may be required in some contexts or in the sense that they are fully formed but competitive. Paul Feyerabend (*Against Method...*, 1975, cited on p. 424), for example, holds that a given well-formed formula may be logically true in one system and not in another because their meanings are different in the two systems. Thus the two systems are competitive; neither is necessarily incorrect. Susan Haack advocates a broad pluralist view but seems to expect more than Feyerabend that some systems cannot both be correct. She further tries to account for the revisability of logic in the sense that we can be epistemologically mistaken about what the truths of logic are. With Dewey and against Frege (and much of the tradition since Frege), she also presents some arguments for a weak, nominalist form of psychologism, one that recognizes that other mental processes and verbal behaviors are in play than those which guarantee validity of arguments. Michael Dummett (1977), having rejected both a correspondence theory of truth and the classical requirement of a two-value logic, has recently offered an intuitionist (or constructionist), anti-Platonic view, according to which logical abstractions, like mathematical ones, are mental constructions; thereby they have status only by virtue of intuitively acceptable proofs, and they may have this on their own, not as part of empirical or other nonlogical theories. Dummett's position, influenced by the later Wittgenstein, has several features in common with pragmatic approaches carved out by Peirce, Dewey, and others, that replace the term "truth" with phrases like "warranted assertibility."

Special Problems

Several perennial problem areas in the philosophy of modern logic have already been mapped out. The functioning of names and descriptive references has also comprised a major area, recently surveyed and extended by Leonard Linsky (1977). A collection of recent work on entailment has been edited by Alan Anderson et al. (1975). Another, edited by Robert Sleigh (1972), looks at the concept of necessary truth. The classic logical treatment of probability and induction by John Maynard Keynes (1921) was developed further by George von Wright (1941) and Rudolf Carnap (1950), with added studies edited by Carnap and his own editor, Richard Jeffrey (1971). Proceedings of a 1965 conference on inductive logic was edited by Imre Lakatos (1968). This has been updated in many ways by the systematic work of Arthur Burks (1977) and by that of L. Jonathan Cohen (1977), which features explication of a non-Pascalian, judicial type of probability. A brief account of statistical explanation, inference, and related problems has been put together by logician Wesley Salmon et al. (1971). A large treatise by one of the premier philosophical scholars in statistics, Henry Kyburg (1974), shows how sophisticated this area of logic has become. The same is true of a collection of essays on cellular automata edited by Arthur Burks (1970).

FUTURE PROSPECTS

In the future there are bound to be many specialists in mathematical logic, as at present. The search for reductive, symbolic means of presenting or analyzing various forms of argument is not likely to abate, though an impressive array of critiques directed at presuppositions underlying the quest has accumulated (as is noted in other

Areas of Philosophy

chapters). In particular, such logic will continue to serve computer theory and statistics. However, current trends also suggest a broadening of interest, to include what philosophers have called "method," "dialectic," "analysis of language," "practical" and "informal" reasoning, and "rhetoric" in the past. Logic as "theory of inquiry" also needs to be applied in imaginative, careful detail to the various modes of inquiry, inside and outside philosophy. For this purpose, the stimulus, except in philosophy of science, has so far come chiefly from thinkers oriented more to language, history, hermeneutics and sociocultural studies than to modern logic. All these efforts will doubtless lead as well to a more comprehensive account of logic, whatever its home base may be, and of its family network, than is now generally operative.

Ambrose, Alice, and Morris Lazerowitz. *Fundamentals of Symbolic Logic* Rev. ed. New York: Holt, Rinehart & Winston, 1962.

Anderson, Alan Ross, Nuel D. Belnap, Jr., et al. *Entailment: The Logic of Relevance and Necessity,* vol. 1. Princeton, N.Y.: Princeton Univ. Pr. 1975.

Barker, Stephen F. *Philosophy of Mathematics.* Englewood Cliffs, N.J.: Prentice-Hall, 1964.

Black, Max. *Critical Thinking: An Introduction to Logic and Scientific Thinking.* 2nd ed. Englewood Cliffs, N.J.: Prentice-Hall, 1952. (1st ed. 1946.)

Bradley, Raymond, and Norman Swartz. *Possible Worlds: An Introduction to Logic and Its Philosophy.* Indianapolis, Ind.: Hackett; Oxford: Blackwell, 1979.

Burks, Arthur W. *Chance, Cause, Reason: An Inquiry into the Nature of Scientific Evidence.* Chicago and London: Univ. of Chicago Pr., 1977.

———, ed. *Essays on Cellular Automata.* Urbana: Univ. of Illinois Pr. 1970.

Butts, Robert E., and Jaakko Hintikka, eds. *Logic, Foundations of Mathematics, and Computability Theory.* Dordrecht and Boston: Reidel, 1977 (Proceedings of the Fifth International Congress of Logic, Methodology and Philosophy of Science, 1975, Part 1. This series is an extension of *Studies in Logic and the Foundations of Mathematics,* 1964–71.)

✓ Cargile, James. *Paradoxes: A Study in Form and Predication.* Cambridge and New York: Cambridge Univ. Pr., 1979.

Carnap, Rudolf. *Logical Foundations of Probability.* Chicago: Univ. of Chicago Pr., 1950. Repr., 1962.

———. *Meaning and Necessity: A Study in Semantics and Modal Logic.* 2nd ed. Chicago: Univ. of Chicago Pr., 1956. (1st ed., 1947.)

———, and Richard C. Jeffrey, eds. *Studies in Inductive Logic and Probability,* vol. 1. Berkeley: Univ. of California Pr., 1971.

✓ Cohen, Laurence Jonathan. *The Probable and the Provable.* Oxford and New York: Oxford Univ. Pr., 1977.

Cohen, Morris R., and Ernest Nagel. *Introduction to Logic and Scientific Method.* New York: Harcourt, Brace, 1934.

Dewey, John. *Logic, the Theory of Inquiry.* New York: Holt, 1938.

Dummett, Michael A. E. *Elements of Intuitionism.* Oxford: Clarendon Pr., 1977.

Frege, Gottlob. *The Basic Laws of Arithmetic: Exposition of the System.* Tr. and ed. by Montgomery Furth. Berkeley: Univ. of California Pr., 1964. (German ed., 1893.) (Only one-fifth of the original is included.)

Geach, Peter T. *Logic Matters.* Berkeley: Univ. of California Pr.; Oxford: Blackwell, 1972.

———. *Reference and Generality: An Examination of Some Medieval and Modern Theories.* 3rd ed. Ithaca, N.Y. and London: Cornell Univ. Pr., 1980. (1st ed., 1962.)

Gould, James A., and Irving M. Copi, eds. *Contemporary Philosophical Logic.* New York: St. Martin's Pr., 1978.

Haack, Susan. *Philosophy of Logics.* Cambridge and New York: Cambridge Univ. Pr., 1978.

Hintikka, Jaakko. *The Intentions of Intentionality and Other New Models for Modalities.* Dordrecht and Boston: Reidel, 1975.

Keynes, John Maynard. *A Treatise on Probability.* London: Macmillan, 1921. Repr., 1948.

Kneale, William, and Martha Kneale. *The Development of Logic.* Oxford: Clarendon Pr., 1962. Repr. with corrections, 1978.

Körner, Stephan. *Conceptual Thinking: A Logical Inquiry.* New York: Dover, 1959.

Kyburg, Henry E., Jr. *The Logical Foundations of Statistical Inference.* Dordrecht and Boston: Reidel, 1974.

Lakatos, Imre, ed. *The Problem of Inductive Logic.* Amsterdam and New York: North Holland, 1968. (International Colloquium in the Philosophy of Science, 1965, vol. 2.)

Lewis, David K. *Counterfactuals.* Cambridge, Mass.: Harvard Univ. Pr., 1973.

Linsky, Leonard. *Names and Descriptions.* Chicago and London: Univ. of Chicago Pr., 1977.

Mates, Benson. *Stoic Logic.* Publications in Philosophy, vol. 26. Berkeley: Univ. of California Pr., 1953. Repr., 1961.

Mostowski, Andrezej. *Thirty Years of Foundational Studies: Lectures on the Development of Mathematical Logic and the Study of the Foundations of Mathematics 1930–1964.* In *Acta Philosophica Fennica,* no. 17. New York: Barnes & Noble, 1966.

Munitz, Milton K. *Existence and Logic.* New York: New York Univ. Pr., 1974.

Passmore, John A. *Philosophical Reasoning.* New York: Basic Books, 1969; London: Duckworth, 1961.

Prior, Arthur N. *The Doctrine of Propositions and Terms.* Ed. by P. T. Geach and A. J. P. Kenny. London: Duckworth, 1976.

———. *Papers in Logic and Ethics.* Ed. by P. T. Geach and A. J. P. Kenny. London: Duckworth, 1976. (Both volumes are posthumous.)

Putnam, Hilary. *Philosophy of Logic.* New York: Harper & Row, 1971.

Quine, Willard Van Orman. *From a Logical Point of View: Logico-Philosophical Essays.* 2nd ed. rev. Cambridge, Mass.: Harvard Univ. Pr., 1961. (1st ed., 1953.)

———. *Mathematical Logic.* Rev. ed. Cambridge, Mass.: Harvard Univ. Pr., 1951. (Original ed., 1940.)

———. *Philosophy of Logic.* Englewood Cliffs, N.J.: Prentice-Hall, 1970.

Rescher, Nicholas. *Many-Valued Logic.* New York: McGraw-Hill, 1969.

Russell, Bertrand. *The Principles of Mathematics.* Cambridge: Cambridge Univ. Pr., 1903.

Ryle, Gilbert. *Dilemmas.* Cambridge and New York: Cambridge Univ. Pr., 1954.

Salmon, Wesley, Richard C. Jeffrey, and James C. Greeno. *Statistical Explanation and Statistical Relevance.* Pittsburgh, Pa.: Univ. of Pittsburgh Pr., 1971.

Sleigh, Robert C., Jr., ed. *Necessary Truth.* Englewood Cliffs, N.J.: Prentice-Hall, 1972.

Strawson, P. F. *Introduction to Logical Theory.* New York: Wiley; London: Methuen, 1952.

———. *Subject and Predicate in Logic and Grammar.* New York: Barnes & Noble; London: Methuen, 1974.

Tarski, Alfred. *Logic, Semantics, Metamathematics: Papers from 1923 to 1938.* Tr. by J. H. Woodger. Oxford: Clarendon Pr., 1956. (German ed., 1936.)

Toulmin, Stephen, Richard Rieke, and Allan Janik. *An Introduction to Reasoning.* New York and London: Macmillan, 1979.

Wang, Hao. *From Mathematics to Philosophy.* London and Boston: Routledge & Paul, 1974.

Whitehead, Alfred North, and Bertrand Russell. *Principia Mathematica.* 2nd ed. 3 v. Cambridge: Cambridge Univ. Pr., 1925. (1st ed., 1910–13; repr., 1950.)

Wright, Georg Henrik von. *The Logical Problem of Induction.* 2nd rev. ed. New York: Barnes & Noble, 1957. (1st ed., his Helsinki dissertation, 1941.)

17

Philosophy of Language
and Linguistic Philosophy

Orientation

Language and logic are the philosopher's primary stock in trade. Philosophy, moreover, is a highly verbal enterprise. In a great variety of ways the functioning of language itself has been subjected to special scrutiny by philosophers in the twentieth century, starting especially with Bertrand Russell and G. E. Moore. In this pursuit many have shared Russell's hope that understanding the properties of language, perhaps first through the study and use of highly formal constructions, will aid in our understanding of the structure of the world. Others have especially shared Moore's particular hope that at least we will get some clarity about what we mean and about what can reasonably be said and what is relative nonsense.

Philosophy of language has become an area of philosophy where the examination of language is practiced, albeit a very loosely organized examination. On the other hand, philosophers have used analysis of language, often centrally and sometimes almost exclusively, to work on problems in the other areas of philosophy. This use, also quite varied as to method and intent, is frequently referred to as linguistic philosophy. Those who adopted one or more of several styles of linguistic analysis developed most prominently at Oxford from roughly 1945 to 1965 were particularly designated as "linguistic philosophers." Because these styles relied more on critical analysis of ordinary, natural language than on critical analysis of formal, artificial languages, they were also commonly called "ordinary language philosophers." Others, such as Rudolf Carnap and Bertrand Russell, continued to believe that ordinary language is too vague and

339

ambiguous, too inexplicit and too context-dependent to be adequate for philosophical purposes.

Because philosophy of language represents so much of what has occupied contemporary philosophers, hence of much treated in other chapters in this book, its actual scope and variety can only be pieced together from activities such as are noted in those other chapters. The same is true of the development of linguistic philosophy. This chapter therefore presents only a bare sketch.

In its subject matter philosophy of language is closely identified with semantics in a broad sense. Accordingly, the structure and history of this area have been presented by Donald Kalish and Norman Kretzmann (1967) under the rubric "semantics." So conceived, in a quite formal sense, philosophy of language consists principally of three parts, which move progressively from more to less abstract. These were first framed by Charles Morris in 1932 and made popular by Carnap and others. (1) Syntax deals with simple relations of linguistic signs to each other. (2) Semantics, in a narrower sense, deals with relations of those signs to other things by means of reference or structures of meaning. (3) Pragmatics examines relations of linguistic signs to what Yehoshua Bar-Hillel has called "indexical expressions," which refer to such activities as recognizing, uttering, recommending, or answering.

In a less formal sense, philosophy of language includes any critical attention to language that uses philosophical methods. Thus it may be placed—for example, as Charles Morris (1971) has done—within a broader theory of "signs" and their use. Morris called the general theory of signs "semiotics." Or the term "language" may be used to stand for nonlinguistic gestures or expressions as well, as R. G. Collingwood has done (*The Principles of Art*, 1938, cited on p. 468).

The move from syntactics to semantics among students of formal, artificial language systems is well illustrated by one of the leading figures, Rudolf Carnap (1937, 1942–43). The growing interaction with linguistics and other disciplines since the 1920s is exemplified first in a collection of new essays edited by Paul Henle (1958), then by Richard Rorty's indispensable edition, appropriately entitled *The Linguistic Turn* (1967, cited on p. 156), and more recently in a *Monist* symposium edited by Wilfrid Sellars (1976). More specific developments are noted below.

Overviews, Introductions, and Collections

When William Alston (1964) wrote his brief analytic introduction, the heyday of linguistic philosophy in the Oxfordian sense had already begun to diminish. Even that trend had many aspects; and it is fair to say that much of it has simply been absorbed into what analytic philosophers, and others, routinely do. One central and continuing aspect has been the later work of Ludwig Wittgenstein. The earliest systematic account of Wittgensteinian linguistic philosophy, still one of the best, is Friedrich Waismann's (1965), unfortunately held back for many years because of Wittgenstein's own hesitancies and therefore not so influential in itself as it deserved to be. Waismann's own independent inventiveness and concerns are conveyed in a 1968 work.

An early introduction, by N. L. Wilson (1959), views all three parts of the general framework indicated above. Recent lectures by Ian Hacking (1975) nicely show the intervening influence of linguistic philosophy, in the narrower sense, in responding to the question: "Why does language matter to philosophy?" Hacking uses several historical cases, from Thomas Hobbes to contemporaries, and in doing so indicates changing emphases in linguistic interest from that time to this. A fine introduction by Max Black (1968) draws from the American as well as the British background. Another recent work, by Jonathan Bennett (1976), uses several strands within the contemporary philosophical study of language to attempt a systematic account of communicative behavior. At a more introductory level, but also a substantial contribution in its own right, is the Wittgensteinian study by Bernard Harrison (1979).

Three large sets of readings from twentieth-century philosophers are themselves both overviews and constructive contributions to the area. That edited by Thomas Olshewsky (1969) is of the broadest scope; the one edited by Jay Rosenberg and Charles Travis (1971) sticks to key topics; that gathered by Julius Moravcsik (1974) is directed to linguists.

Successive expansions and developments in the area are particularly well tracked in seven collections, edited by Jerry Fodor and Jerrold Katz (1964), both of whom have since made further contributions; by Sidney Hook (1969); by Keith Gunderson (1975) and G. E. M. Anscombe (1975); by Samuel Guttenplan (1975), lectures dedicated to Isaiah Berlin, President of Wolfson College, Oxford, from 1966 to 1975; by Ruth Barcan Marcus (1977), a *Monist* symposium; and by Peter French et al. (1979).

THEMES AND DEVELOPMENTS

Routes Taken

Some philosophers have taken the routes mapped out by Gottlob Frege and Bertrand Russell. Bede Rundle's study of grammar (1979)

is an eminent recent example. Others have followed leads especially
from J. L. Austin (1965), Gilbert Ryle, or Ludwig Wittgenstein, illustrated in a 1963 collection edited by Charles Caton and in a 1975
collection by G. E. M. Anscombe and others. One melding of concerns in logic and language, prominent since the immediate post-
1945 period, is that of P. F. Strawson, who has followed up a collection of his papers (1971) with a treatise on "subject and predicate"
(1974) and has been particularly noted for his linguistic approaches
to logic (chapter 16) and "descriptive" metaphysics (chapter 18).
Antony Flew's (1951, 1953, 1956) editions of essays in conceptual
analysis, Oxford-style, helped build that tradition, as have Max
Black's successive collections of his own essays from 1949 to 1975.

Two major offbranches from these activities were virtually created
by Austinian John Searle (1969, 1979) and by Noam Chomsky
(1957, 1975, 1977). Searle set off a spate of interest in "speech acts,"
in the more dynamic functioning of language—as in "illocutionary"
utterances (like "aha!" or "sit!" or "I promise"), in which language
does something in itself. Searle himself developed a theory that presents the expression of symbols, words, or sentences in the performance of speech acts as the unit of linguisic communication. Thereby
he conceived theory of language as part of a theory of action (see
chapter 20). This kind of work has flourished in the 1970s. In addition to Searle's own ongoing work and a collection on pragmatics
edited by Searle and others (1980), four other works show how
rapidly and substantially this offbranch has grown: Charles Travis
(1975), Jerrold Katz (1977), David Holdcroft (1978), and Kent Bach
and Robert Harnish (1979).

Noam Chomsky has used investigations into generative, or transformational, grammar to develop explanations at a deep underlying,
"universal" level of linguistic behavior of what linguists disclose
about language descriptively. His work displays a Kantian, critical
rationalist bent. Taking his lead, Fodor, Katz, Travis, and a number
of other philosophers have made themselves experts in linguistics as
well, so that they can carry out informed interactions between the
two fields. Within Chomsky's large production, four works are singled out here. That published in 1975 is an unfinished, previously
unpublished, unrevised manuscript from nearly twenty years before.
An introduction explains the history of his thinking from his first
formal introduction to linguistics in 1947 to work by himself and
others (like Fodor and Katz, Paul Postal and Robert Lees) into the
1960s. It is the most comprehensive account Chomsky has given of

his theory of transformational grammar in the context of an overall theory of linguistics. *Syntactic Structures* (1957) is a highly influential early work. The 1973–1976 essays (1977) on his extended standard theory (EST) include suggestions in the direction of eliminating the notion of deep structures and transformational grammar. It would not be fitting to note these extremely formal investigations without noting the sense of political responsibility and interest in ideology critique for which Chomsky has also become well known. This is represented in a set of 1976 conversations with Mitsou Ronat (Chomsky, 1977) on linguistics and politics and on generative grammar. There he eschews all but a "rather abstract" connection between the two, however. Justin Leiber (1975) provides a valuable overview of Chomsky's philosophical activity.

Works presenting various admixtures of theory on meaning and semantics include Paul Ziff's early work (1960) on semantic theory, the more recently influential treatises by Katz (1972) and Fodor (1975), a critique of empirical theories by Bernard Harrison (1972), and a collection edited by Donald Davidson and Gilbert Harman (1972). Stephen Schiffer's book (1972) on "meaning," in the empiricist tradition of H. P. Grice and P. F. Strawson, overlaps more with these other works than does another analytic work by Israel Scheffler (1979), influenced also by pragmatism, on issues concerning vagueness, ambiguity, and metaphoric content in language.

European interests in language are included in chapters 11–13. A recent development in France is exemplified in Jacques Derrida's 1967 work (tr. 1976) on "grammatology." Derrida, who has sought to combine and develop features of both existential phenomenology and anthropological-psychoanalytic structuralism, has become one of the most noted European philosophers and one of the most influential figures in French intellectual life.

Special Problems

Here are some problems that have particularly interested contemporary philosophers working with language, with noteworthy examples. Language as signification and as value-transmitting (Charles Morris, 1964); as representation (Jay Rosenberg, 1974); as convention (David Lewis, 1969); as reference (Leonard Linsky, 1967; Jack Meiland 1970; David Schwartz, 1979); as presupposition (Ruth Kempson, 1975; Deirdre Wilson, 1975), though not in the general sense proposed by R. G. Collingwood; as private (O. R. Jones, 1971); as revealed in structure by artificial languages (Hilary Putnam, 1975); and as symbolism and metaphor (Philip Wheelwright, 1954, 1962; Andrew Ortony, 1979; Sheldon Sacks, 1979). The last two items are collections in a thematic area rather more richly humanistic than the others, one that has recently attracted renewed attention among philosophers. Many of these themes, but usually not this one, are also represented in collections listed earlier.

FUTURE PROSPECTS

Possibly the most reasonable thing to say about the future of linguistic philosophy and philosophy of language is that the marvelous jumble of activities is not likely to get neatly sorted out in the next several decades. Nevertheless, the several general theories that have emerged are bound to get further critical attention, to be related more closely to each other, as has begun to be done in more recent statements, and to gain enormously from new ventures in linguistics, which are already occasionally quite interactive with philsophical inquiry. Meanwhile piecemeal examination within an increasing number of thematic areas is likely to require a good deal of investment. The new interests in symbolism, metaphor, and philosophy of literature may further interact with these efforts, but the signs are still too dim to have a good hunch about this prospect.

Alston, William P. *Philosophy of Language*. Englewood Cliffs, N.J.: Prentice-Hall, 1964.
Anscombe, G. E. M., et al. *Mind and Language*. Oxford and New York: Oxford Univ. Pr., 1975.
Austin, John L. *How to Do Things with Words*. Ed. by J. O. Urmson. New York: Oxford Univ. Pr., 1965. (Original ed.: Oxford: Clarendon Pr., 1962.) (William James Lectures, Harvard University, 1955.)
Bach, Kent, and Robert M. Harnish. *Linguistic Communications and Speech Acts*. Cambridge, Mass. and London: MIT Pr., 1979.
Bennett, Jonathan. *Linguistic Behaviour*. Cambridge and New York: Cambridge Univ. Pr., 1976.
Black, Max. *Caveats and Critiques: Philosophical Essays in Language, Logic, and Art*. Ithaca, N.Y. and London: Cornell Univ. Pr., 1975.
———. *The Labyrinth of Language*. New York and London: Praeger, 1968. (Among the volumes cited here, only this one is not a collection of his essays.)
———. *Language and Philosophy: Studies in Method*. Ithaca, N.Y. and London: Cornell Univ. Pr., 1949.
———. *Margins of Precision: Essays in Logic and Language*. Ithaca, N.Y. and London: Cornell Univ. Pr., 1970.

———. *Models and Metaphors.* Ithaca, N.Y. and London: Cornell Univ. Pr.; Oxford: Oxford Univ. Pr., 1962.

———. *Problems of Analysis.* Ithaca, N.Y. and London: Cornell Univ. Pr., 1954.

Carnap, Rudolf. Studies in Semantics. Vol. 1, *Introduction to Semantics;* vol. 2, *Formalization of Logic.* Cambridge, Mass.: Harvard Univ. Pr., 1961. (Original eds., 1942–43.) (*Meaning and Necessity,* 1947, an extension of this series, moves in the direction of modal logic.)

———. *The Logical Syntax of Language.* New York: Harcourt, Brace; London: Kegan Paul, Trench, Trubner, 1937.

Caton, Charles E., ed. *Philosophy and Ordinary Language.* Urbana: Univ. of Illinois Pr., 1963.

Chomsky, Noam. *Essays on Form and Interpretation.* New York: Elsevier North-Holland, 1977.

———. *Language and Responsibility.* New York: Pantheon, 1977.

———. *The Logical Structure of Linguistic Theory.* New York: Plenum Pr., 1975.

———. *Syntactic Structures.* The Hague: Mouton, 1957.

Davidson, Donald, and Gilbert Harman, eds. *Semantics of Natural Language.* 2nd ed. Dordrecht and Boston: Reidel, 1972. (An expansion of a 1969 set of essays published in *Synthese,* vol. 21. Saul A. Kripke's essay has been reissued: *Naming and Necessity.* Rev. ed. Cambridge, Mass.: Harvard Univ. Pr., 1980.)

Derrida, Jacques. *Of Grammatology.* Tr. by Gayatri Chakravorty Spivak. Baltimore and London: Johns Hopkins Univ. Pr., 1976. (French ed., 1967.)

Flew, Antony, ed. *Essays in Conceptual Analysis.* New York: St. Martin's Pr.; London: Macmillan, 1956.

———, ed. *Logic and Language.* 1st and 2nd series. Garden City, N.Y.: Doubleday Anchor, 1965. (Original eds., Oxford: Blackwell, 1951, 1953.)

Fodor, Jerry A. *The Language of Thought.* New York: Crowell, 1975.

———, and Jerrold J. Katz, eds. *The Structure of Language.* Englewood Cliffs, N.J.: Prentice-Hall, 1964.

French, Peter A., Theodore E. Uehling, Jr., and Howard K. Wettstein, eds. *Contemporary Perspectives in the Philosophy of Language.* Minneapolis: Univ. of Minnesota Pr., 1979. (Rev. ed. of *Midwest Studies in Philosophy,* vol. 2, 1977.)

Gunderson, Keith, ed. *Language, Mind, and Knowledge.* Minnesota Studies in the Philosophy of Science, vol. 7. Minneapolis: Univ. of Minnesota Pr., 1975.

Guttenplan, Samuel, ed. *Mind and Language: Wolfson College Lectures 1974.* New York: Oxford Univ. Pr.; Oxford: Clarendon Pr., 1975.

Hacking, Ian. *Why Does Language Matter to Philosophy?* Cambridge and New York: Cambridge Univ. Pr., 1975.

Harrison, Bernard. *An Introduction to the Philosophy of Language.* New York and London: Macmillan, 1979.

———. *Meaning and Structure: An Essay in the Philosophy of Language.* New York and London: Harper & Row, 1972.

Henle, Paul, ed. *Language, Thought and Culture.* Ann Arbor: Univ. of Michigan Pr., 1958.

Holdcroft, David. *Words and Deeds: Problems in the Theory of Speech Acts.* New York: Oxford Univ. Pr.; Oxford: Clarendon Pr., 1978.

Hook, Sidney, ed. *Language and Philosophy: A Symposium.* New York: New York Univ. Pr.; London: Univ. of London Pr., 1969.

Jones, Owen R., ed. *The Private Language Argument.* New York: St. Martin's Pr.; London: Macmillan, 1971.

√ Kalish, Donald, and Norman Kretzmann. "Semantics." In *Encyclopedia of Philosophy,* vol. 7, pp. 348–406. Ed. by Paul Edwards. New York: Macmillan; London: Collier Macmillan, 1967.

Katz, Jerrold J. *Propositional Structure and Illocutionary Force: A Study of the Contribution of Sentence Meaning to Speech Acts.* Cambridge, Mass.: Harvard Univ. Pr., 1980. (Original ed., New York: Crowell, 1977.)

———. *Semantic Theory.* New York and London: Harper & Row, 1972.

Kempson, Ruth M. *Presupposition and the Delimitation of Semantics.* Cambridge and New York: Cambridge Univ. Pr., 1975.

√ Leiber, Justin. *Noam Chomsky: A Philosophic Overview.* Boston: Twayne, 1975.

Lewis, David K. *Convention: A Philosophical Study.* Cambridge, Mass.: Harvard Univ. Pr., 1969.

Linsky, Leonard. *Referring.* Atlantic Highlands, N.J.: Humanities Pr.; London: Routledge & Paul, 1967. Repr., 1980.

Marcus, Ruth Barcan, ed. "New Directions in Semantics." *Monist* 60, no. 3:303–430 (July 1977).

Meiland, Jack W. *Talking about Particulars.* London and Boston: Routledge & Paul, 1970.

Moravcsik, Julius M. E., ed. *Logic and Philosophy for Linguists: A Book of Readings.* The Hague: Mouton, 1974; Atlantic Highlands, N.J.: Humanities Pr., 1975.

Morris, Charles. *Signification and Significance: A Study of the Relations of Signs and Values.* Cambridge, Mass.: MIT Pr., 1964.

———. *Writings on the General Theory of Signs.* The Hague: Mouton, 1971.

√ Olshewsky, Thomas M., ed. *Problems in the Philosophy of Language.* New York: Holt, Rinehart & Winston, 1969.

Ortony, Andrew, ed. *Metaphor and Thought.* Cambridge and New York: Cambridge Univ. Pr., 1979.

Putnam, Hilary. *Philosophical Papers.* Vol. 1, *Mathematics, Matter and Method;* vol. 2, *Mind, Language and Reality.* Cambridge and New York: Cambridge Univ. Pr., 1975. (A 2nd ed., 1979.)

Rosenberg, Jay F. *Linguistic Representation.* Dordrecht and Boston: Reidel, 1974.

———, and Charles Travis, eds. *Readings in the Philosophy of Language.* Englewood Cliffs, N.J.: Prentice-Hall, 1971.

Rundle, Bede. *Grammar in Philosophy.* New York: Oxford Univ. Pr.; Oxford: Clarendon Pr., 1979.

Sacks, Sheldon, ed. *On Metaphor.* Chicago and London: Univ. of Chicago Pr., 1979.

Scheffler, Israel. *Beyond the Letter: A Philosophical Inquiry into Ambiguity, Vagueness and Metaphor in Language.* London and Boston: Routledge & Paul, 1979.

Schiffer, Stephen R. *Meaning.* New York: Oxford Univ. Pr.; Oxford: Clarendon Pr., 1972.

Schwarz, David S. *Naming and Referring: The Semantics and Pragmatics of Singular Terms.* New York: de Gruyter, 1979.

Searle, John R. *Expression and Meaning: Studies in the Theory of Speech Acts.* Cambridge and New York: Cambridge Univ. Pr., 1979.

———. *Speech Acts: An Essay in the Philosophy of Language.* Cambridge and New York: Cambridge Univ. Pr., 1969.

———, Ferenc Kiefer, and Manfred Bierwisch, eds. *Speech Act Theory and Pragmatics.* Dordrecht and Boston: Reidel, 1980.

Sellars, Wilfrid, ed. "Language, Thought, and the World." *Monist* 59, no. 3:306–455 (July 1976).

Strawson, P. F. *Logico-Linguistic Papers.* New York: Barnes & Noble; London: Methuen, 1971.

———. *Subject and Predicate in Logic and Grammar.* New York: Barnes & Noble; London: Methuen, 1974.

Travis, Charles. *Saying and Understanding: A Generative Theory of Illocutions.* New York: New York Univ. Pr.; Oxford: Blackwell, 1975.

Waismann, Friedrich. *How I See Philosophy.* Ed. by Rom Harré. New York: St. Martin's Pr.; London: Macmillan, 1968.

———. *The Principles of Linguistic Philosophy.* Ed. by Rom Harré. New York: St. Martin's Pr.; London: Macmillan, 1965.

Wheelwright, Philip. *The Burning Fountain: A Study in the Language of Symbolism.* Bloomington: Indiana Univ. Pr., 1954.

———. *Metaphor and Reality.* Bloomington: Indiana Univ. Pr., 1962.

Wilson, Deirdre. *Presuppositions and Non-Truth-Conditional Semantics.* New York and London: Academic Pr., 1975.

Wilson, Neil L. *The Concept of Language.* Toronto and London: Univ. of Toronto Pr., 1959.

Ziff, Paul. *Semantic Analysis.* Ithaca, N.Y.: Cornell Univ. Pr., 1960.

18

Metaphysics

The Aristotelian Program

The root meaning of the word "metaphysics" has no significance for philosophy. It was simply the title early editors of Aristotle's writings put on the material that came "after physics." But this material from Aristotle had a distinct subject matter. In appearance that subject matter remained pretty much what it had always been until the mid-twentieth century, with some expansions of interests or alternatives from age to age. Artistotle had thought of it in three ways: (1) that form of orderly thinking that is logically prior to all others (hence, "first philosophy," and at that time it might as well have been called "first science," for there was no distinction); (2) "wisdom," referring to its ultimate aim, which included really knowing and in a theoretically solid and comprehensive way; (3) "theology," referring to the knowledge of God as "pure being" (from which later tradition took the term "ontology"). Within the long history of metaphysics, some philosophers have preferred one emphasis over the other two; some have tried to combine two or three of them into a single comprehensive viewpoint.

First Philosophy

Today representatives of all eight possible combinations could probably be found, but these combinations do not include important alternatives that have developed in modern times. Thus the following distinction between seven approaches is a more useful classification. It too is one that allows for overlaps. The first three approaches are closest to Aristotle's "first philosophy" meaning. One approach is to

348

study whatever may be thought to transcend nature as it is presented by science. Examples: Plato, many classic theological metaphysicians, Immanuel Kant, but not C. I. Lewis (1929). Unfortunately, this has often been the view attributed to metaphysics by its detractors. Recently the highly reputed analytic metaphysician Anthony Quinton (1973) has aptly pointed out, to the contrary, that the ordinary procedure metaphysicians use is not pure demonstration of truths about existences that transcend all possible experience but "deductive inference from substantial premises already given and the realities whose existence he is concerned to establish are not inaccessibly beyond the world but are already within it." Second, and especially since Kant, some simply engage in a priori speculation on knowledge that cannot be established scientifically. Examples: both Kant and C. I. Lewis (the latter regarding the categories of reality, and not a set fixed once and for all). In a third view, sometimes a metaphysics consists largely or solely in a basic approach to understanding relations between appearance and reality, chaos and cosmos, the finite and the infinite, the macrocosm and the microcosm, the intelligible and the ineffable, what is and what is not and what is possible. This is not necessarily done with the aim of producing a settled, comprehensive system or of speculating beyond what science provides or what is consistent with science. Examples: naturalist George Santayana and pragmatic naturalist John Dewey (1925). Occasionally those who take such an approach hold that more than one rationally ordered view of the world is possible—for example, in Stephen Pepper's (1961) thoughts on four types of complementary "world hypotheses."

Ontology

The next two approaches are closest to Aristotle's idea of studying "being" as such. In a fourth, with the primary aims of comprehensiveness and cohesiveness, and a tendency toward speculative thought beyond scientific knowledge, the most widely practiced traditional intention has been to study the modes of being. These philosophers focus chiefly on what is presumed to "be" essence and existence, events and things (and whatever else nouns stand for, such as quantities, logical variables, fantasies, surfaces), categories, properties and relations, the ideal and the real, particulars and universals, individuals and classes, substance and attributes, change, law and cycles, continuity and identity, necessity and contingency, causation, chance and law, mind and matter, the one and the many, space and time, persons, other minds, personal identity, freedom, vital process and determinism, though not necessarily on all of these. Examples: Georg W. F. Hegel, Absolute idealist F. H. Bradley (1893), process philosopher Alfred North Whitehead, realist Paul Weiss (1958), Whiteheadian Charles Hartshorne, metaphysical mystic W. T. Stace, Schellingian-existentialist theologian Paul Tillich, neo-Thomist Jacques Maritain (1937), and existential ontologist Martin Heidegger (with the proviso that he wishes to transcend even traditional metaphysics by searching after "being beyond being").

The Standing of Traditional Metaphysics

In a fifth approach, widely used in contemporary analytic philosophy, philosophers treat the items in the fourth approach (much less often those in the first three, and even then mostly in a critical fashion) through logical-empirical analysis or through analytical description of language about them, rather than conducting a "study" of them in the context of a comprehensive system of ideas or in order to achieve such a system. A. J. Ayer and other logical positivists would accept an analytical approach to some of these items, if some meaning to them could be established through empirical verification; otherwise they are termed "nonsense."

By the 1920s the forces of positivism, empiricism, and pragmatism had a strong hold in American philosophy, mostly on a "realist" base (Fisch, 1967) and through attacks on traditional dualism (Lovejoy, 1930). The first two viewpoints, which had long been prevalent in Britain, were rapidly overtaking idealism there. All three tendencies were opposed to speculative metaphysics. When Lewis published *Mind and the World-Order* (1929, cited on p. 326) he meant his venture to be critical in the post-Kantian sense and reflective of scientific fact. For him, Whitehead's generalizing speculative approach, mostly pre-Kantian, was scarcely philosophy at all. This was representative of a widespread view of metaphysics during the 1920s through the 1940s. Brand Blanshard, who worked on his two-volume *The Nature of Thought* (1939) during the next decade, presented metaphysics as systematic but revisable. (In effect, Blanshard straddles the third and fourth approaches.) This aroused some hope that metaphysics still had something in it worth doing. In the United States by the late 1940s the revived positivist attack, led by Rudolf Carnap and other immigrants, had run out of steam, while through A. J. Ayer and others it was to continue in Britain for some time. Carnap's own move toward philosophy as semiotical analysis (concerned not with the ultimate nature of being, that is, not with metaphysics, but with the language of science and the theoretical aspects of ordinary language, combining what he called syntactic, semantic, and pragmatic analysis) presaged a general move within analytic philosophy that did not bode well for the area anywhere. On the European continent, existential, phenomenological, and Heideggerian philosophers were carrying on some of the traditional inquiries (areas one through four) but with an emphasis on experience. William Carlo (1966) represents an existential metaphysics influenced, as has almost always been the case, by phenomenology.

The Speculative, "Ism" Approach

Another, sixth approach has been current particularly since the late-eighteenth-century historians of philosophy began to classify systems of thought as "isms." Accordingly, one is asked to think of a metaphysics as an "ism" of the kind that expresses or presupposes an overarching conception of the world (a *Weltanschauung,* world-view), thus a set of basic, speculative doctrines or theories. Often the approach has been carried out in a manner that has survived from ancient times, which identifies the outlook as a "school." Examples: Aristotlianism, Thomism, Cartesianism, Hegelianism, idealism, materialism. In one distinctive version such teachings cohere with a theological position—as with Paul Tillich (cited on p. 265), whose ideas, like those of Whitehead, continue to be the subject of a great many dissertations today. In another they are an addendum, purported to be completely rational, to a presupposed theology—such as Thomism, which is still a thriving school of its own under Roman Catholic auspices. Still another version is to find reasons for what one intuitively believes on totally nontheological grounds—for example, a great deal of modern "realism," "phenomenalism," and "rationalism"—and the attempt, especially by adherents of the first two types of view, to reduce metaphysics to epistemology or linguistic analysis. Most modern thinkers who have had a philosophical interest in religion possess one of these types of metaphysics, though a great many would find the notion of subscribing to an "ism" abhorrent. They would feel this way because the very concept smacks of closed, dogmatic systems, which they wish to abjure.

For Paul Weiss (1958), founder of the highly successful *Review of Metaphysics* (1947–) and of the Metaphysical Society of America (1950), attention to speculative metaphysical issues has not only remained one of the classic occupations of philosophers but serves as a deterrent against the predations of logical positivism and its successors. He started out as a student of realist Morris R. Cohen, process philosopher Whitehead, and Thomist Étienne Gilson, and was coeditor of the works of pragmatist Charles S. Peirce. His own metaphysics is an intricate combination of several once-separate viewpoints. In a similar spirit, Andrew Reck (1972) has appropriately marked the main characteristics of "speculative philosophy" as systematic, comprehensive, explanatory, conjectural, and as metaphysical in the sense of concentrating on "ultimate" concepts of being or knowing. His own work chiefly presents representatives of realism, materialism, idealism, and process philosophy.

Further Debate

Analytic, positivist philosopher Gustav Bergmann (1954, 1960, 1964) hied to the metaphysical side, claiming for metaphysics knowledge of the world through analytical-syntactical discovery of necessary truths in an ideal language. Nevertheless the antimetaphysical (fifth) trend within analytic philosophy continued to gain ground. Contextualist Ernest Nagel (*Sovereign Reason . . . ,* 1954, cited on p. 229), for example, held that what is desirable in the place of metaphysics is context-bound inquiry, not generalizations about reality. The position of W. V. O. Quine (*From a Logical Point of View,* 1953, cited on p. 338), a logical analyst, was similar to Nagel's except that he added a structure for all cognitive discourse derived from mathematical logic. Linguistic philosopher Morris Lazerowitz (1955) claimed that metaphysical theories are mere "linguistic innovations" that fail because of an unconscious, unrealistic wish to keep the illusion of having said something profound about the world, an approach he derived from psychoanalysis. Nelson Goodman (1951, 1978) proposed linguistic analysis of what can be formulated within particular systems, not regarding any of them as metaphysically ultimate. His was a nominalist metaphysics which did not count nonindividuals among existents. In both Britain and the United States many analytic philosophers were to take the lead of Ludwig Wittgenstein, Gilbert Ryle, J. L. Austin, and others to transplant what few metaphysical issues they thought were left into syntactical analysis of language, to which semantical analysis was added.

By the 1970s everything was up for grabs again. It could reasonably be claimed that each of the antimetaphysical positions had some sort of basic presuppositions of their own that could not be analytically reduced to the foundations, usually empirical or linguistic, that they sought.

Examination of Absolute Presuppositions

A final, seventh, approach, first formally proposed by R. G. Collingwood (1940) but practiced in various ways by earlier philosophers, is the analysis of absolute presuppositions. We may ask: What notions are presupposed in the questions we ask and in the propositions we state, and how are they to be verified, if at all? We notice that some of them are simply taken for granted. How did this taking for granted come about, and in a given instance is it either justified or justifiable? For Collingwood, to analyze (disentangle and sort out) the basic, unquestioned presuppositions in our thinking is the task of metaphysics proper. Ordinarily these absolute presuppositions are not a matter of conscious choice; they tend to be unconsciously and tenaciously held; and they are difficult to give up. They are never themselves answers to questions, as Collingwood takes all propositions, either implicitly or explicitly, to be. The ultimate aim of analysis is to detect their logical efficacy in relation to the notions and propositions that presuppose them. To ask whether they are true is nonsensical, is pseudometaphysics. To ask what they are is to ask what are the occasions of their having been made or kept—that is, within what process of thought—and these are always historical questions.

Plato, Collingwood noted, used dialectic for this purpose, as have many others since. To the extent that alternative views of metaphysics assume that they are propounding what is true or are investigating whether certain propositions are true or false, they are pseudometaphysics. Various brands of positivism provide good examples, in his view, though logical positivism, in assuming that metaphysical propositions are supposed to be verified by appeal to observed facts and denying that such verification is possible, itself provides an apt refutation of pseudometaphysics.

Since the 1950s, the fifth approach has often carried elements of Collingwood's, though almost never directly referring to his proposals and not so much with its historical bent or its interest in including analysis of absolute presuppositions widely shared within a given era and of the thinking processes by which their eventual rejection, modification, or replacement occur. His later books give examples of historically oriented metaphysical analysis, especially of presuppositions about "God" and "cause" (1940), "nature" (1945), and "history" (1946, cited on p. 433).

In the eighteenth and nineteenth centuries most of what is included in epistemology today—and some aspects of logic, philosophy of science, philosophy of mind, and philosophy of action—was also a part of metaphysics. These shifts themselves suggest a rather unsteady, changing subject matter. On Collingwood's reading, nothing belongs to metaphysics except absolute presuppositions—not even relative presuppositions, which, like propositions, are answers to questions; as such, relative presuppositions can be handled within those specific areas of thought where the questions have arisen. In time, under examination some absolute presuppositions achieve relative status or become propositions, perhaps widely rejected ones, within some area of thought. This, we may suppose, is one reason why some classic subjects in metaphysics have died away or have moved to some other area of philosophy.

THEMES AND DEVELOPMENTS

Having weathered the many critical storms earlier in the century, and having changed its ways considerably under the onslaught, metaphysics underwent something of a revival in the 1970s. Consequently, the examination of metaphysical topics is very much alive in the early 1980s. Perhaps because of the continued lack of resolve in this area, there is as yet no comprehensive history of metaphysics or introduction to it. A fine brief introduction to aspects of metaphysical inquiry by W. H. Walsh (1963), written with an eye to the antimetaphysical scene in Britain, is still worth reading, as are a call to metaphysical inquiry by Dorothy Emmet (1945) and a small set of essays by British analytic philosophers edited by D. F. Pears (1957). Richard Taylor's introduction (1974) only covers topics that seem basic to him, in terms of contemporary analytic interests. Most of the topics he includes (for instance, persons and bodies, the mind as a function of the body, freedom and determinism, fate, space and time, causation, God) are often included in other areas of philosophy. Analysis of concepts is also the approach taken by Elmer Sprague (1978), who divides his brief introduction into three areas: self and person, the world, and God. A much wider array of analytic topics, more technically treated, is presented among the twenty-four new essays collected by Peter French et al. (1979).

Abraham Kaplan (*In Pursuit of Wisdom*, 1977, cited on p. 158) has helpfully distinguished between puzzles, quandaries, problems, and predicaments. Perhaps more than any other area of philosophy, over the past two or three decades metaphysical inquiry has been directed to all four. Puzzles are of our own making; the difficulties they address refer to meanings, not facts; once the meanings are cleared up, they are resolved. Among the quandaries, which do refer to facts and arise in difficult life situations, are problems, that admit of solutions but typically give rise to new problems, and predicaments, that do not allow of solutions because of the very nature of things. As to predicaments, the distinctive domain of philosophy for Kaplan, "we can only learn to live with them, cope, manage somehow." It is the latter category, I think, to which existentialist philosopher Gabriel Marcel (*The Mystery of Being*, 1950, cited on p. 275) chiefly referred when he argued that the metaphysician must deal not only, or perhaps even not so much, with problems as with mysteries. Among recent writers, Stephen Ross (1981) has picked up the theme of mystery; George Melhuish (1973) has emphasized what he takes to be "the paradoxical nature of reality." Some metaphysicians, especially since Hegel, have attempted to cope with the unruly dynamics of reality as it confronts them by forming a dialectical logic. Leslie Armour (1972) has explored this possibility. Another way of managing somehow is to form a reasoned metaphysical vision. Arthur Berndtson (1981) offers an excellent representation of this strategy, absorbing a mixture of influences in a fashion that would probably have been impossible ten or fifteen years earlier, though it is in the open-ended speculative spirit of Blanshard, Hartshorne, and Weiss. Another attempt is made, in the scientific realist vein, by J. J. C. Smart (1963), who had to move away from his earlier neo-Wittgensteinian approach to do it. More in the pragmatic-naturalist spirit of Dewey are the analytic investigations of scientific realist Wilfrid Sellars (1979), who also presents an overall vision of sorts. In a massive, systematic treatise, logician and philosopher of science Mario Bunge (1977) holds forth the conception of metaphysics as the task of staking out the main traits of the real world as it is known through science. In short, his work is a general, scientific cosmology.

Among other recognizable positions from the past, rationalism is well represented by Heilier Robinson (1975), realism by Jay Rosenberg (1980), Heideggerian phenomenology by Robert Sokolowski (1978). Materialism is given a substantial boost by Anthony Quinton (1973), examining claims about substance, essences, mental phenomena, and values; by James Cornman (1975), on the mind-body problem and perception; and by D. M. Armstrong (1978), referring to the problem of universals within scientific realism. Ever the least popular metaphysical position, materialism has gained respectability during the 1960s and 1970s. (This is not the same thing as Marxian dialectical materialism, which is mainly a historical-political thesis, but some commonality is possible between Marxist and other materialist views on relations between mind and matter.) A collection of essays on problems about universals and particulars, edited by Michael Loux (1970), displays the status of the discussion about universals among analytic philosophers by the late 1960s. One of Loux's own books (1978) presents an Aristotelian view of substances and a Platonistic view of attributes. This is an antireductionist approach, which may be contrasted with the reductionist efforts of realist Reinhardt Grossmann (1973). An analytic metaphysics that uses the concepts of essence and accident comes from Michael Slote (1975). As a result of renewed interest in modal concepts, especially among logicians, by 1979 Loux was able to edit another collection, this time on "the possible and the actual."

With respect to interests in metaphysical issues from a linguistic perspective, two approaches to problems had been set up, by Carnap and by P. F. Strawson (1959). Carnap had distinguished between existence assertions that are internal to a linguistic framework and those that are external to it and are used to propose its adoption. Anthony Quinton (1973) revises the "external" question so that it reads "how does this category work?" not "how is a proposal to adopt it to be justified?" Strawson distinguished between a descriptive metaphysics, which he believed Aristotle and Kant chiefly did and which is content to describe the actual structures of our language and thought, from a revisionary (regulative, prescriptive) metaphysics (Descartes, Leibniz, Berkeley). A number of analytic philosophers are doing metaphysics today in the descriptive style of Strawson or in the quite restricted "external" manner of Carnap or Quinton.

Among the recent treatises, several age-old problems are seen in a new light, informed by decades of analytic investigation. Exemplary works include those by Baruch Brody (1980) and Eli Hirsch (1982) on identity, by Saul Kripke (*Naming and Necessity*, 1972, cited in Davidson and Harman, p. 345) and Alvin Plantinga (1974) on necessity, by a colloquium of twelve philosophers edited by Henry Johnstone (1978) on categories, by Michael Levin (1979) on the mind-body problem, by Terence Parsons (1980) on nonexistent objects, and by David Wiggins (1980) on individuation. Most tend to look at generic issues more than to specify the features of particular genera.

Remarkable to say, all but a few of the representative authors mentioned in this chapter are cited in other chapters.

FUTURE PROSPECTS

Concluding a fine survey of major options taken from about 1930 into the 1960s, Manley Thompson (1964) noted that new possibilities from among the linguistic philosophers and contextualistic naturalists were just underway and that rising efforts among existentialists, phenomenologists, and Tillichians were likely to remain separate from those by the first two groups. With some notable exceptions (for instance, see Karl-Otto Apel, *Towards a Transformation of Philosophy*, p. 300) the separation has held. He also anticipated, however, that pre-Kantian modes of thought had about run their course, as had post-Kantian efforts to merge analytic interests with a theory about metaphysics. Neither presentiment has turned out to be correct. By 1970, in a symposium on "the future of metaphysics" edited by Robert Wood, representatives from several philosophical perspectives were indicating a rising tide of interest and showing present and possible effects on other areas of philosophy. The tide is still rising, and its effects are likely to continue their spread among the other areas.

Two other prospects were foretold by Dorothy Emmet in 1945. She wrote then: "The real problem is that our diverse worlds of thought do not make sense as a coherent unity, and probably cannot and will not do so for some time to come. For the basic suppositions underlying them are in process of a drastic reconstruction of which it is not yet possible to see the outcome." The analysis of suppositions, both in a more logical-linguistic mode and in a more Collingwoodian mode, has made significant progress since 1945, and there is much brush-clearing and replanting to be done. Emmet also pointed out that "while basic presuppositions are being overhauled, it is surely important to try to keep open lines of communication between different kinds of thinking and experience and establish some kind of modus vivendi between them." Some of this process has also occurred since 1945. It will be a major task for the next thirty-five years. Despite its obvious importance, one would be foolish to expect too much, in that this is among the touchiest, most abstract pursuits of all.

Armour, Leslie. *Logic and Reality: An Investigation into the Idea of a Dialectical System*. Assen: Van Gorcum, 1972.
Armstrong, David M. *Universals and Scientific Realism*. 2v. Cambridge and New York: Cambridge Univ. Pr., 1978.
Bergmann, Gustav. *Logic and Reality*. Madison: Univ. of Wisconsin Pr., 1964. ("Fully articulated" realism.)

————. *The Metaphysics of Logical Positivism: Papers.* 2nd ed. New York: Longmans, Green, 1967. (1st ed., 1954; repr., 1978.) (In 1954 "a reluctant phenomenalism"; in 1967, 10-page introduction added. His second essay collection, that cleared away "much of the phenomenalist debris": *Meaning and Existence.* Madison: Univ. of Wisconsin Pr., 1960.)

√ Berndtson, Arthur. *Power, Form, and Mind.* Lewisburg, Pa.: Bucknell Univ. Pr.; London and Toronto: Associated Univ. Presses, 1981.

Blanshard, Brand. *The Nature of Thought.* 2v. New York: Macmillan, 1940; London: Allen & Unwin, 1939.

Bradley, Francis H. *Appearance and Reality: A Metaphysical Essay.* 2nd ed. Oxford: Oxford Univ. Pr., 1897. (1st ed., 1893; repr.: Oxford and New York: Oxford Univ. Pr., 1969.)

Brody, Baruch A. *Identity and Essence.* Princeton, N.J.: Princeton Univ. Pr., 1980.

√ Bunge, Mario. *Treatise on Basic Philosophy.* Vols. 3–4, *Ontology.* Dordrecht and Boston: Reidel, 1977. (The other volumes in the treatise: vols. 1–2, *Semantics;* vols. 5–6, *Epistemology;* vol. 7, *Ethics.*)

Carlo, William E. *The Ultimate Reducibility of Essence to Existence in Existential Metaphysics.* The Hague: Nijhoff, 1966.

√ Collingwood, Robin G. *An Essay on Metaphysics.* Oxford: Clarendon Pr., 1940. Repr.: Chicago: Regnery-Gateway, 1971.

————. *The Idea of Nature.* Oxford: Clarendon Pr., 1945. Repr., 1960.

Cornman, James W. *Perception, Common Sense, and Science.* New Haven, Conn.: Yale Univ. Pr., 1975. (As in his examination of the mind-body problem in *Metaphysics, Reference, and Language,* Yale Univ. Pr., 1966, the problems here are presented as external to the rules of any linguistic framework and such as to "defy" any solution.)

Dewey, John. *Experience and Nature.* Chicago and London: Open Court, 1925.

Emmet, Dorothy M. *The Nature of Metaphysical Thinking.* New York: St. Martin's Pr.; London: Macmillan, 1945.

Fisch, Max, et al. "British and American Realism, 1900–1930." *Monist* 51, no. 2:159–304 (Apr. 1967). (An article by Preston Warren views the entire period; the others take special issues.)

√ French, Peter A., Theodore E. Uehling, Jr., and Howard K. Wettstein, eds. *Midwest Studies in Philosophy.* Vol. 4, *Studies in Metaphysics.* Minneapolis: Univ. of Minnesota Pr., 1979.

Goodman, Nelson. *The Structure of Appearance.* 2nd ed. Indianapolis, Ind.: Bobbs-Merrill, 1966. Repr. in a 3rd ed. in *Boston Studies in Philosophy of Science,* vol. 53. Dordrecht and Boston: Reidel, 1977. (1st ed., 1951.)

————. *Ways of Worldmaking.* Indianapolis, Ind.: Hackett, 1978.

Grossmann, Reinhardt. *Ontological Reduction.* Bloomington: Indiana Univ. Pr., 1973.

Hirsch, Eli. *The Concept of Identity.* Oxford and New York: Oxford Univ. Pr., 1982.

Johnstone, Henry W., Jr., ed. *Categories: A Symposium.* University Park: Dept. of Philosophy, Pennsylvania State Univ., 1978.

Lazerowitz, Morris. *The Structure of Metaphysics.* New York: Humanities Pr.; London: Routledge & Paul, 1955.

Levin, Michael E. *Metaphysics and the Mind-Body Problem*. New York: Oxford Univ. Pr.; Oxford: Clarendon Pr., 1979.

Loux, Michael J. *Substance and Attribute: A Study in Ontology*. Dordrecht, Boston and London: Reidel, 1978.

————, ed. *The Possible and the Actual: Readings in the Metaphysics of Modality*. Ithaca, N.Y.: Cornell Univ. Pr., 1979.

————, ed. *Universals and Particulars: Readings in Ontology*. Garden City, N.Y.: Doubleday Anchor, 1970.

Lovejoy, Arthur O. *The Revolt against Dualism: An Inquiry Concerning the Existence of Ideas*. New York: Norton, 1930.

Maritain, Jacques. *The Degrees of Knowledge*. Tr. from the 4th French ed. under supervision of Gerald B. Phelan. London: Geoffrey Bles, 1958. (1st French ed., 1932; original English ed., 1937.)

Melhuish, George. *The Paradoxical Nature of Reality*. Bristol: St. Vincent's Pr., 1973.

Parsons, Terence. *Nonexistent Objects*. New Haven, Conn. and London: Yale Univ. Pr., 1980.

Pears, David F., ed. *The Nature of Metaphysics*. New York: St. Martin's Pr.; London: Macmillan, 1957.

Pepper, Stephen C. *World Hypotheses: A Study in Evidence*. Berkeley: Univ. of California Pr.; Cambridge: Cambridge Univ. Pr., 1961.

Plantinga, Alvin. *The Nature of Necessity*. Oxford: Clarendon Pr., 1974.

Quinton, Anthony. *The Nature of Things*. London and Boston: Routledge & Paul, 1973.

Reck, Andrew J. *Speculative Philosophy: A Study of Its Nature, Types, and Uses*. Albuquerque: Univ. of New Mexico Pr., 1972.

Robinson, Heilier J. *Renascent Rationalism*. Toronto: Macmillan of Canada, 1975.

Rosenberg, Jay F. *One World and Our Knowledge of It: The Problematic of Realism in Post-Kantian Perspective*. Dordrecht, Boston and London: Reidel, 1980.

Ross, Stephen David. *Philosophical Mysteries*. Albany: State Univ. of New York Pr., 1981.

Sellars, Wilfrid. *Naturalism and Ontology*. Reseda, Calif.: Ridgeview, 1979.

Slote, Michael A. *Metaphysics and Essence*. New York: New York Univ. Pr., 1975.

Smart, James J. C. *Philosophy and Scientific Realism*. New York: Humanities Pr.; Routledge & Paul, 1963.

Sokolowski, Robert. *Presence and Absence: A Philosophical Investigation of Langue and Being*. Bloomington and London: Indiana Univ. Pr., 1978.

Sprague, Elmer. *Metaphysical Thinking*. Oxford and New York: Oxford Univ. Pr., 1978.

Strawson, P. F. *Individuals: An Essay in Descriptive Metaphysics*. Garden City, N.Y.: Doubleday Anchor, 1963; London: Methuen, 1959.

Taylor, Richard. *Metaphysics*. 2nd ed. Englewood Cliffs, N.J.: Prentice-Hall, 1974. (1st ed., 1963.)

Thompson, Manley. "Metaphysics." In *Philosophy*, pp. 125–232. Ed. by Roderick M. Chisholm et al. Englewood Cliffs, N.J.: Prentice-Hall, 1964.

Walsh, William H. *Metaphysics*. London and New York: Hutchinson, 1963.

Weiss, Paul. *Modes of Being*. Carbondale: Southern Illinois Univ. Pr., 1958. Repr., 1968.

Wiggins, David. *Sameness and Substance*. Cambridge, Mass.: Harvard Univ. Pr.; Oxford: Blackwell, 1980.

✓ Wood, Robert E., ed. *The Future of Metaphysics*. Chicago: Quadrangle, 1970.

19

Philosophy of Mind

The Scope of Inquiry

What are the meanings of our language about human mental processes? What account can be given of these processes? How is the relation of both these processes and our language about them to the physical aspects of human nature, especially the brain, to be understood? These three questions give philosophy of mind its charge today. In earlier periods, somewhat different questions were operative, and they could not be so closely related to the findings and fortunes of scientific psychology as is true in the contemporary period. Some historical studies of interest have been indicated in previous chapters; however, there is as yet no clearly delineated history of these changes. A valuable summary of six major theories of mind, mostly derived from intensive efforts since the mid-nineteenth century, was achieved by pragmatist Charles Morris (1932). It serves to remind us ✓ that the more recent options have substantial precedents; they did not spring full-grown out of nothing. Morris distinguishes mind as substance, process, relation, intentional act, substantive, and function (the last one especially from earlier pragmatists C. S. Peirce, John Dewey, and George Herbert Mead).

Through most of the twentieth century, two types of problem have taken the lion's share of attention: on relations of mind to body and on freedom versus determinism. Especially with the aid of linguistic analysis, by the late-1950s several other thematic areas had become important as well. As a result of this expansion, philosophy of mind came to be recognized as a specialized area of philosophy for the first time.

At the vanguard were three books by linguistic philosophers: Gilbert Ryle's *The Concept of Mind* (1949); Ludwig Wittgenstein's *Philosophical Investigations* (1953, cited on p. 210), translated by Gertrude E. M. Anscombe, a volume that started numerous linguistic analyses of mental acts; and Anscombe's own *Intention* (1957). John Wisdom's *Other Minds* (1952) stood out in its treatment of a major topic; so did a long 1958 essay on "The 'Mental' and the 'Physical' " by the noted American logical empiricist philosopher of science Herbert Feigl. For several decades most logical positivists, of which Feigl had been one, had tended to translate statements about mental states into statements about actual or possible behavior or about test conditions and results concerning behavior (logical behaviorism). In his lucid, tightly argued essay Feigl proposed an alternative, realist view that identifies states of direct conscious experience with configurational aspects (or types) of neuralphysiological processes—a materialist identity theory. As such, intentional acts in perception, belief, volition, and the like he regarded as matters for purely logical-semantic analysis, but they too are included in that they are describable as occurrents in direct experience. Feigl also had a great respect for psychoanalytic uncoverings of unconscious processes and so included these too, insofar as they become matters of direct experience.

Earlier historical studies, particularly on the thinking of René Descartes, John Locke, and David Hume, had helped prepare the way for these new developments, especially among linguistic philosophers, as had Wisdom's (1934) application to "problems of mind and matter" of analysis in the style of G. E. Moore. In the United States Norman Malcolm, a close associate of Wittgenstein, played a leading role in development of the area.

In *Philosophical Investigations,* Wittgenstein found a way to ask a very important question about human action. He noted that when (as we say) "I raise my arm," my arm goes up. Now: "What is left over if I subtract the fact that my arm goes up from the fact that I raise my arm?" The first book to give an extensive analysis of such problems was A. I. Melden's *Free Action* (1961, cited on p. 378). By the 1970s still another distinct area of philosophy, now called philosophy of action, had formed within the fast-developing matrix of philosophy of mind (or "philosophical psychology" as some have called it in Britain). Here I have assigned the literature on freedom to philosophy of action. (See chapter 20.)

Another clustering of literature, similarly spawned during the same period, now seems mature enough to be called a distinct area as well:

philosophy of psychology and psychoanalysis. Its basic aims are to explore issues of explanation in psychology and psychoanalysis and critically to analyze notions presupposed and concepts used in these fields. (See chapter 29.)

Is something missing? In European philosophy all three areas have typically been lumped together within the still larger category "philosophical anthropology." Within this category attempts are made to give a synoptic account of human nature. Language about the human "soul" or "spirit" (historically the first being a more Greek, the second a more Hebraic concept) is still prevalent there, whereas many empirically minded Anglo-American philosophers have been turned away from such talk by Ryle's arguments to the effect that "soul" only refers to a "ghost in the machine." In Britain and the United States, the broader perspective on human nature is carried mostly by existentialists, theologians, humanists, historians of consciousness, and theorists in psychology and psychoanalysis. Among contemporary British philosophers Antony Flew (1978) stands out as one who has traveled widely over this territory. Among American philosophers Abraham Kaplan (e.g., *In Pursuit of Wisdom*, 1977, cited on p. 158) has shown still greater breadth, though expressed more in a summary interpretive manner than in the analytic style of Flew.

Overviews, Introductions, and Collections

Some historical perspective is provided in the epoch-making books already mentioned. Additional aid comes from G. N. A. Vesey's (1965) brief survey of theories and problems. Anthony Kenny (1973) looks at views from Plato, Aristotle, Aquinas, and Descartes and appends a brief history of "intention" in ethics. Norman Malcolm (1971) refers to views of Descartes, Locke, Hume, Mill, J. J. C. Smart, Bertrand Russell, Rudolf Carnap, and others. Malcolm himself not only rejects mind-body dualism but also the identification of mind with the brain and the reduction of all psychological sentences to physical language (logical behaviorism). David Pears (1975) conjoins five essays on one's "knowing" as an agent what one is going to do with some historical essays on problems about other aspects of mind in the thinking of Hume, Russell, Wittgenstein, and moral theorist R. M. Hare. In style this volume is typical of the work of other linguistic philosophers at that time, both in its use of history chiefly to illuminate current interests and in its focus on examination of supposed cases.

In the early days, a set of 1950s essays edited by V. C. Chappell (1962) was followed by a larger collection edited by Donald Gustafson (1964). Only comparatively few non-British philosophers could yet be included in these much-used volumes. In six of ten British Academy lectures edited by P. F. Strawson (1968) leading figures in the developing area take on major themes: Ryle on thinking, A. J. Ayer on privacy, Stuart Hampshire and Strawson on freedom, Pears on predicting and deciding, and Bernard Williams on imagination and the self. A. J. Kenny (1972–73) joined a biologist, a physiologist, and a theologian in delivering Gifford Lectures on mind.

No introduction has yet offered a fully comprehensive view, a feat that would have been difficult if not impossible in this nascent period. Jerome Shaffer's brief introduction (1968), for example, is organized around the notion of "consciousness"—its nature, its subject, its relation to the body, and its role in action. This is a promising scheme, but many areas of developing inquiry are left out, as is true in the later brief treatment by Jenny Teichman (1974). Philosophers working in this area have generally preferred to work through a selection of problems in their own ways, as did Bruce Aune (1967) in his more extensive introductory work.

More advanced overviews also cover only a part of the landscape. For example, P. T. Geach (1957) examines the concept "mental acts." Kenny (1963) does a conceptual inventory of affective processes, judging, willing and other mental states, performances, and activities. Zeno Vendler (1972) develops a modified Austinian view (from J. L. Austin) about relations between speech and thought. A unifying theme in Bernard Williams's collection (1973) of his own essays, half of which are in moral theory, is that of personal identity, individuation, and continuity. All these have been major thematic areas throughout the 1960s and 1970s. Among the many philosophy of science volumes that include material on philosophy of mind, one from this period honors Feigl and features a 220-page section on several of these issues; it is edited by Paul Feyerabend and Grover Maxwell (*Mind, Matter, and Method* . . . , 1966, cited on p. 424).

By the early 1960s a widespread rejection of Cartesian mind-body dualism, in its many forms, had occurred. Such dualism had foundered, among other reasons, on the difficulty of assigning a causal relation between mind and matter if they are assumed to be two completely different kinds of entity. Accordingly, there was increased interest in either physicalism, which tended to claim that the nature of mental processes is ultimately an empirical and not a philosophical issue, and in materialistic identity theory (such as Feigl's), which regarded mental processes as physical ones at base. Physicalism is, roughly, a view that identifies mental events with physical events in the brain. In its many forms physicalism had gained a great deal of support by the early 1960s, and it tended to advocate behaviorism in psychology.

According to a recent survey of options by Jerry Fodor (1981), in which he develops aspects of his own theory, what subsequently emerged for many was a kind of nonbehaviorist, functionalist theory, one that does not envision the elimination of mentalistic concepts from the explanatory apparatus of psychological theories and thus preserves the autonomy of psychology. At the same time, it is compatible with a realist-physicalist account of mental particulars and with ascription of causal roles to those particulars in relation to stimuli, to responses, and to each other. The mind could be considered like a simple computing machine (a Turing machine). But then a host of new problems arose, so that by the late 1970s much of the activity in philosophy of mind was being devoted to these complex problems. What is needed, according to Fodor, is a theory of what it is for mental states to have propositional contents, and this need present functional theory cannot meet. Therefore he presents a "representational" theory of mind, for which he finds precedents in both Descartes and Locke, in fact in all nonbehaviorist psychologies. Mental representations, for him, are symbols that have causal roles in virtue of their formal properties. Those symbols function as objects of propositional attitude states and confer to those states their own semantic properties. Fodor does not purport, however, to have a theory of how mental representations represent.

Another recent major treatise, by Daniel Dennett (1978), also rejects both type identity theory, Turing machine functionalism, and other reductive functionalist views. He calls his view "type functionalism." One of its most interesting features is the definition of a person as a high-order intentional system—that is, one capable of reciprocal action, verbal communication, and consciousness of a special kind, which some call "self-consciousness." He further uses his concept of a person to propose a set of necessary conditions for moral personhood, conditions that can never be sufficient in that the concept is a normative ideal never reached.

Both Fodor and Dennett keep close tabs on cognitive psychology in their work. Others who have challenged the notion of a separable science of the mental include Donald Davidson (for instance, in S. C.

Brown, *Philosophy of Psychology,* 1974, cited on p. 488) and
Stephen Stich (in Andrew Woodfield, 1982). A collection of new
critical essays on functionalist theories is edited by J. I. Biro and
Robert W. Shahan (1982).

Mind-Body Problem, Materialism

The pre-Fodor/Dennett situation is captured in a symposium on the
mind-body problem edited by Chung-ying Cheng (1975), the earlier
stages in a volume of twenty-three papers on identity theory published
between 1956 and 1967, edited by C. V. Borst (1970). In addition to
the reissue of Feigl's 1958 essay with postscript (1967), other significant contributions to these issues in that period come from a collection
of new essays representing several positions edited by J. R. Smythies
(1965), from Kenneth Sayre (1976) on cybernetics, and from Stephen
Thomas (1978) on "the formal mechanics" of mind. Virtually all the
more important works are aimed either at elaborating or critically
assessing materialist theories: John O'Connor's readings (1969) on
identity theory; the *Monist* symposium by J. J. C. Smart and others
(1972); a synoptic study by James Cornman (1971); an application of
identity theory to other problems in philosophy of mind, action, ethics, law, and social-political philosophy by Edgar Wilson (1979); a
critique of physicalism by K. V. Wilkes (1978); and arguments for a
nonreductive materialism by Joseph Margolis (1978), which takes
critically into account earlier thinking by Fodor and Dennett; papers
from 1966–79 by the well-known materialist D. M. Armstrong
(1981); and a study by Mario Bunge (1980) which attempts to stay
close to psychobiological research.

Intention and Intentionality

Anscombe's 1957 essay on "intention," written in the new linguistic style, stirred up a great deal of discussion. The concept, however,
goes back to a variety of meanings developed among the phenomenologists, who continue to use the term in discussions mostly separate from those in analytic circles. John Findlay's nonanalytic exercise in Hegelian dialectic and phenomenology (1961) is aware of the
analytic discussions. It warrants comparison, if only because of the
great difference in interest and tone, with a concurrent study by
analytic philosopher Jack Meiland (1970). Two different results from
recent developments are shown in works by Judith Thomson (1977)

and Richard Aquila (1977). Some seventeen essays honoring Elizabeth Anscombe's sixtieth birthday, edited by Cora Diamond and Jenny Teichman (1979), cross several areas of philosophy—especially logic, epistemology, metaphysics, philosophy of mind, ethics, history of philosophy—as does her own work, and reflect her investigations of Wittgenstein's works, of which she has edited and translated several. Among the volume's essays are some on first person, action, and intention. Finally, Andrew Woodfield, who wrote his Oxford thesis on "teleology," has edited a volume of essays presenting a good range of current thinking on intentionality (1982).

Persons, Individuality, Identity

Several of the books already noted have included discussions on concepts of the person and related problems. An early set of essays, early as far as the contemporary discussion goes, was edited by Felix Morley (1958). A much-discussed linguistic analysis on identity of self and one's knowledge of oneself by Sidney Shoemaker (1963) followed. The development of inquiry through these and other discussions is well represented in the works by Williams (1973) and Dennett (1979) already mentioned, in companion volumes edited by John Perry (1975) and Amelie Rorty (1976), which both present new work, and in a brief study by Raziel Abelson (1977).

Other Themes

Other themes that have had importance in this fast-growing area of philosophy are represented by the following books. Mary Warnock's historical gem (1976) on imagination; Norman Malcolm's summum (1977) on memory; Malcolm's classic little book (1962) on dreaming and the collection on dreaming edited by Charles Dunlop (1977); the analysis of self-deception by Herbert Fingarette (1969), who has published widely on forensic issues, especially on the notion of responsibility; and a superb collection of very new work on emotions edited by Amelie Rorty (1980). A work rather different from any of these, though mostly analytic, comes from Leslie Armour and Edward Bartlett (1980). Stimulated throughout by R. G. Collingwood's dialectic of experience and the forms of knowledge—present as a "ghost," not by direct reference—it attempts to provide the formal, epistemological, and factual conditions for distinguishing between the inner and the outer world. The inner world has no object set at all but is made up of elements of meaning, significance, and intentionality. Aspects of Collingwood's own wide-scope philosophy of mind—he did not think much of attempts to make psychology a science beyond the level of sensations and rudimentary feelings—are summed up in his *New Leviathan* (1942, cited on p. 448). An exemplar from studies by phenomenologists is Henry Ey's *Consciousness* (1968, cited on p. 287). A respectful interpretation of six general views of mind and person is offered in a nonanalytic study by Thomist F. F. Centore (1979), who distinguishes between reductionistic and nonreductionistic materialism, psychosomaticism with and without immortality, vitalism, and reductionistic immaterialism.

Ideas about the human mind tend to have practical consequences. Three chiefly nonanalytic works provide special reminders of this: Robert Solomon's attempt (1976), in the interest of "hardheaded Romanticism," to restore emotions to the center of human life; David Norton's use (*Personal Destinies . . . ,* 1976, cited on p. 310) of reflection on mind to form an ethics of self-actualization; and Hannah Arendt's last work, *The Life of the Mind* (1978), on thinking and willing. Arendt made her reputation on *The Origins of Totaliarianism* in the immediate post-World War II period, and most of her other writings were in social-political philosophy.

FUTURE PROSPECTS

A safe prediction for this ancient yet newly constituted area of philosophy would be more of the same, and that in itself is an exciting prospect. In the 1970s there were many signs of much closer interaction with research psychology than before. Particularly because of special new interests in cognitive psychology and in the history of the emotions, I would also expect to see closer collaboration with those who do clinical and developmental studies than is yet evident.

Abelson, Raziel. *Persons: A Study in Philosophical Psychology.* New York: St. Martin's Pr.; London: Macmillan, 1977.

Anscombe, Gertrude E. M. *Intention.* 2nd ed. Ithaca, N.Y.: Cornell Univ. Pr.; Oxford: Blackwell, 1963. (1st ed., 1957).

Aquila, Richard E. *Intentionality: A Study of Mental Acts.* University Park: Pennsylvania State Univ. Pr., 1977.

Arendt, Hannah. *The Life of the Mind.* Vol. 1, *Thinking;* vol. 2, *Willing.* New York and London: Harcourt, Brace, 1978.

Armour, Leslie, and Edward T. Bartlett III. *The Conceptualization of the Inner Life.* Atlantic Highlands, N.J.: Humanities Pr., 1980.

Armstrong, David M. *The Nature of Mind and Other Essays.* Ithaca, N.Y. and London: Cornell Univ. Pr., 1981.

Aune, Bruce. *Knowledge, Mind and Nature: An Introduction to Theory of*

Knowledge and the Philosophy of Mind. New York: Random House, 1967.

Biro, John I., and Robert W. Shahan, eds. *Mind, Brain, and Function.* Norman: Univ. of Oklahoma Pr., 1982.

Borst, Clive V., ed. *The Mind-Brain Identity Theory: A Collection of Papers.* New York: St. Martin's Pr.; London: Macmillan, 1970.

Bunge, Mario. *The Mind-Body Problem: A Psychobiological Approach.* Oxford and New York: Pergamon Pr., 1980.

Centore, F. F. *Persons: A Comparative Account of the Six Possible Theories.* Westport, Conn. and London: Greenwood, 1979.

Chappell, Vere C., ed. *The Philosophy of Mind.* Englewood Cliffs, N.J.: Prentice-Hall, 1962.

Cheng, Chung-ying, ed. *Philosophical Aspects of the Mind-Body Problem.* Honolulu: Univ. of Hawaii Pr., 1975.

Cornman, James W. *Materialism and Sensations.* New Haven, Conn. and London: Yale Univ. Pr., 1971.

Dennett, Daniel C. *Brainstorms: Philosophical Essays on Mind and Psychology.* Brighton, Sussex: Harvester Pr., 1978; Montgomery, Vt.: Bradford Books, 1979.

Diamond, Cora, and Jenny Teichman, eds. *Intention and Intentionality: Essays in Honour of G. E. M. Anscombe.* Brighton, Sussex: Harvester Pr., 1979.

Dunlop, Charles E. M., ed. *Philosophical Essays on Dreaming.* Ithaca, N.Y. and London: Cornell Univ. Pr., 1977.

Feigl, Herbert, Michael Scriven, and Grover Maxwell, eds. *Concepts, Theories, and the Mind-Body Problem.* Minnesota Studies in the Philosophy of Science, vol. 2. Minneapolis: Univ. of Minnesota Pr., 1958. (Feigl's contribution was reissued, with postscript and new bibliography, as *The "Mental" and the "Physical."* Minneapolis: Univ. of Minnesota Pr., 1967.)

Findlay, John N. *Values and Intentions.* London: Allen & Unwin, 1961.

Fingarette, Herbert. *Self-Deception.* New York: Humanities Pr.; London: Routledge & Paul, 1969.

Flew, Antony. *A Rational Animal and Other Philosophical Essays.* Oxford: Clarendon Pr., 1978.

Fodor, Jerry A. *Representations: Philosophical Essays on the Foundations of Cognitive Science.* Montgomery, Vt.: Bradford Books, 1980; Cambridge, Mass.: MIT Pr., 1981.

Geach, Peter T. *Mental Acts: Their Content and Their Objects.* London: Routledge & Paul, 1957; New York: Humanities Pr., 1960.

Gustafson, Donald F., ed. *Essays in Philosophical Psychology.* Garden City, N.Y.: Doubleday Anchor, 1964.

Kenny, Anthony. *Action, Emotion and Will.* New York: Humanities Pr.; London: Routledge & Paul, 1963.

———. *The Anatomy of the Soul: Historical Essays in the Philosophy of Mind.* Oxford: Blackwell, 1973.

———, et al. *The Nature of Mind. The Development of Mind.* Edinburgh: Univ. Pr., 1972–73. (Gifford Lectures, 1971–72 and 1972–73.)

Malcolm, Norman. *Dreaming.* New York: Humanities Pr.; London: Routledge & Paul, 1962.

————. *Memory and Mind*. Ithaca, N.Y. and London: Cornell Univ. Pr., 1977.

————. *Problems of Mind: Descartes to Wittgenstein*. New York: Harper & Row; London: Allen & Unwin, 1971.

Margolis, Joseph. *Persons and Minds: The Prospects of Nonreductive Materialism*. Dordrecht and Boston: Reidel, 1978.

Meiland, Jack W. *The Nature of Intention*. New York: Barnes & Noble; London: Methuen, 1970.

Morley, Felix, ed. *Essays on Individuality*. Philadelphia: Univ. of Pennsylvania Pr., 1958.

Morris, Charles W. *Six Theories of Mind*. Chicago and London: Univ. of Chicago Pr., 1932. (6th repr., 1971.)

O'Connor, John, ed. *Modern Materialism: Readings on Mind-Body Identity*. New York: Harcourt, Brace, 1969.

Pears, David F. *Questions in the Philosophy of Mind*. New York: Barnes & Noble; London: Duckworth, 1975.

Perry, John, ed. *Personal Identity*. Berkeley and London: Univ. of California Pr., 1975.

Rorty, Amelie Oksenberg, ed. *Explaining Emotions*. Berkeley and London: Univ. of California Pr., 1980.

————, ed. *The Identities of Persons*. Berkeley and London: Univ. of California Pr., 1976.

Ryle, Gilbert. *The Concept of Mind*. New York: Barnes & Noble, 1964.

Sayre, Kenneth M. *Cybernetics and the Philosophy of Mind*. London and Boston: Routledge & Paul, 1976.

✓ Shaffer, Jerome A. *Philosophy of Mind*. Englewood Cliffs, N.J.: Prentice-Hall, 1968.

Shoemaker, Sydney. *Self-Knowledge and Self-Identity*. Ithaca, N.Y.: Cornell Univ. Pr.; Oxford: Oxford Univ. Pr., 1963.

Smart, J. J. C., et al. "Materialism Today." *Monist* 56, no. 2:149–296 (Apr. 1972).

Smythies, John R., ed. *Brain and Mind: Modern Concepts of the Nature of Mind*. New York: Humanities Pr.; London: Routledge & Paul, 1965.

Solomon, Robert C. *The Passions: The Myth and Nature of Human Emotion*. Garden City, N.Y.: Doubleday Anchor, 1976.

Strawson, P. F., ed. *Studies in the Philosophy of Thought and Action*. Oxford and New York: Oxford Univ. Pr., 1968. (Ten British Academy lectures.)

Teichman, Jenny. *The Mind and the Soul: An Introduction to the Philosophy of Mind*. New York: Humanities Pr.; London: Routledge & Paul, 1974.

Thomas, Stephen N. *The Formal Mechanics of Mind*. Ithaca, N.Y.: Cornell Univ. Pr.; Hassocks, Sussex: Harvester Pr., 1978.

Thomson, Judith Jarvis. *Acts and Other Events*. Ithaca, N.Y. and London: Cornell Univ. Pr., 1977.

Vendler, Zeno. *Res Cogitans: An Essay in Rational Psychology*. Ithaca, N.Y. and London: Cornell Univ. Pr., 1972.

Vesey, Godfrey N. A. *The Embodied Mind*. London: Allen & Unwin, 1965.

✓ Warnock, Mary. *Imagination*. Berkeley and London: Univ. of California Pr., 1976.

Wilkes, K. V. *Physicalism.* New York: Humanities Pr.; London: Routledge & Paul, 1978.

Williams, Bernard. *Problems of the Self: Philosophical Papers, 1956–1972.* Cambridge and New York: Cambridge Univ. Pr., 1973.

Wilson, Edgar. *The Mental as Physical.* London and Boston: Routledge & Paul, 1979.

Wisdom, John. *Other Minds.* 2nd ed. New York: Philosophical Library, 1966. (1st ed., Oxford: Blackwell, 1952.) (Eight papers from *Mind,* 1940–43, and later papers.)

———. *Problems of Mind and Matter.* Cambridge and New York: Cambridge Univ. Pr., 1934.

Woodfield, Andrew, ed. *Thought and Object: Essays on Intentionality.* Oxford and New York: Oxford Univ. Pr., 1982.

20

Philosophy
of Action

Questions

What is the nature of human actions? Are they free or determined? How are they significantly different from other changes in the world, if they are? Can they be explained in ways similar to those used in explaining nonhuman physical events? How are they to be told apart from each other (individuated)? In particular, what important distinctions are there, if any, between intentional movements and those that are not, particularly bodily ones? From answers to these questions, what understanding of voluntary versus involuntary and of responsible versus irresponsible actions can we gain? What accounts can be given of a person's ability and power to act (versus a mere possibility or luck)? What does one need to "have in mind" in order to act intentionally, and in what different ways can one act intentionally? What is the status of self-consciousness, emotions, wants, desires, needs, and other mental states with respect to purposive activity? What relations adhere between the causes of actions and reasons for doing them? Can reasons be causes? What constitutes rational action? How are we to know whether our beliefs about these things are accurate? Are there good reasons to suppose that human beings are or can be autonomous and responsible? In what ways might an understanding of the social characteristics of a person's mental functioning aid our getting a satisfactory answer to any of these questions, or at least our clarifying what forms the questions themselves should appropriately take?

By the 1960s enough analytic philosophers considered that it was important enough to gain ordered clarity on such issues that a whole distinct area of philosophy came into being, now called philosophy of action. Although the questions treated are interesting in themselves, the chief effects of inquiry are to link concerns in philosophy of mind with those in ethics and in all the bridge areas.

Overviews, Introductions, and Collections

Most useful for introduction to the more narrowly analytic inquiries are a chapter by Jerome Shaffer (*Philosophy of Mind*, 1968, cited on p. 370) and the brief account by Lawrence Davis (1979). Broader issues are introduced in Richard Bernstein's indispensable work, *Praxis and Action* (1971), which distinguishes concepts of action then prevalent in analytic philosophy from those set forth by Hegelians and Marxists, existentialists Søren Kierkegaard and Jean-Paul Sartre, and pragmatists C. S. Peirce and John Dewey. Bernstein's own analytically informed approach is particularly inclined toward pragmatism. A pioneering analytic inquiry by Stuart Hampshire (1960) is still an important, engaging discussion of basic issues. Hampshire's style is unusually readable while losing nothing of rigor or clarity. Another pioneering work by R. S. Peters (1958) on "motivation" is an important foundation document, though rather dated now.

The major collections, in addition to some cited in chapter 19 that include related material, are seventeen contemporary essays edited by Norman Care and Charles Landesman (1968); a systematic collection edited by Myles Brand (1970); five colloquium papers, with comments, edited by Robert Binkley et al. (1971); and proceedings from an important conference, edited by Myles Brand and Douglas Walton (1976).

Relations to moral theory are everywhere evident in the literature. A special early example is Eric D'Arcy's (1963) study of acts, circumstances, and motives with respect to moral evaluation; a recent one is Anthony Kenny's two volumes (1975, 1978) on free will and responsible action. Relations to both philosophy of mind and psychology are especially evident in books by Raimo Tuomela (1977) and Joseph Rychlak (1979). Tuomela develops a causalist, scientific realist account of action, achieved mostly through conceptual analysis. Rychlak builds on earlier "humanistic" investigations of personality theory and psychotherapy (as in his 1968 *A Philosophy of Science for Personality Theory,* cited on p. 488; also in several books since then) to consider how to think about means for attaining free, responsible action.

The Nature of Human Action

The major treatises on action from 1960 to 1980 are all chiefly explorations rather than strictly settled positions. For the most part they differ in focus, manner, and detail; and they tend to refer successively to each other within a single though diversified analytic community. From the 1960s, D. G. Brown (1968) attends especially to the point of view of the agent. Using primarily analysis of action concepts, A. R. Louch (1966) holds that the idea of a "science" of human beings or of society is untenable. He does so partly on the ground that an explanation of human action cannot be given by separating questions of fact and value. However, he uses examples from psychology and the social sciences to show that there is still plenty for them to do by way of both description and explanation. The spirit of new inquiry in this period is well captured by Richard Taylor (1966) in his emphasis on use of the concepts of "action" and "purpose," especially in the place of traditional notions of cause and effect, in trying to understand human nature. Within the same period Charles Taylor (1964) was examining some differences between an explanation of human behavior in terms of purpose or intentionality ("centralist," teleological) and a "peripheralist" (behaviorist) account, which searches for correlations. He concludes in favor of the first type, but in a way that does not preclude the possibility of more adequate theories of the second type.

By 1970 Myles Brand could appropriately announce: "We are now in the midst of an action theory revolution." Almost all the material he selects is from the 1960s. By the early 1970s, Arthur Danto (1973) had developed further and applied his earlier idea of "basic actions" (1963, in Brand 1970) on an epistemic model. Alvin Goldman (1970) had meticulously set forth a theory, first stated in his 1964 dissertation, that acts are caused by wants and beliefs. Like many others, linguistic philosopher Irving Thalberg (1972) preferred to struggle with each puzzle or enigma as it came up and not to form a cohesive theory. Although later (1977, not cited here) he did form a "component" theory of mind, he did not take a stand on several basic issues and remained skeptical about whether one could justifiably do so. Georg Henrik von Wright (1971) tried to pick his way between an intentionalist (causal) account and a teleological (means to ends) account of action, pointing out limitations in both. (When philosophers of action use "teleological" they usually refer to purposeful activity, not to functions conferred externally. There remains some issue about the ontological status of purposes, for example, as to whether some of them are "immanent" within human nature. Since the concept "purpose" is also up for analysis, "intention" often has a broader extension, so that not all human intentions are purposes.) Roy Lawrence (1972) attempted to assess some available theories by examining what experience might reveal about what motives and intentions are. Geoffrey Mortimore (1971) put together fifteen pieces on weakness of will, especially on varieties of moral weakness and of acting against one's better judgment.

By the mid-1970s Bruce Aune (1977) was in a position critically to examine several rather well-formed but tentative theories of action. He ends up arguing for a "metaphysically noncommittal" theory of agents instead, one that fastens upon intelligent action as a product of reasoning. Hence he also reviews some theories of practical reasoning, in which he finds the formal logic of practical inference no different from that of ordinary assertoric inference. Although not a few took his lead, all the other major options were alive, if not entirely well, in 1980. In that year was seen the publication of fifteen 1963–78 essays by Donald Davidson, who holds causal concepts to be essential to description and explanation of human action, and of a fresh brief analysis by Jennifer Hornsby.

Free Will and Determinism

Until the 1950s almost all philosophical writing specifically on the nature of human action was done in the service of solving the free will versus determinism issue. This is still a strong motivating force; but as many inquiries have been released from the attempt to solve this unsolvable predicament, the free will discussions have also been given new life.

Two large volumes by Mortimer Adler (1958–61) and his Institute for Philosophical Research display the ideas of freedom as a catchall perennial one, controversial since the Greeks. Adler is best known as the author of a bestseller, *How to Read a Book* (1940, not cited here), which identifies philosophical skills with those of reading books intelligently, and as a longtime advocate of placing the study of great books and their "ideas" at the core of education. In 1982 he was creating a stir in promulgating his "Paideia Proposal," which would require a standard curriculum of this kind for all children and youth, with few or no electives except at the more advanced levels.

Adler's "freedom" volumes plus three other works indicate the status and range of philosophical discussion on the topic as it entered into a more analytic phase in the 1950s. One is a proceedings volume, edited by Sidney Hook (1958), in which philosophers of several persuasions took part and which included several areas of philosophy. Challenges to traditional views of free will from "science" were much in evidence there. The second is a "preliminary inquiry" into the possibility of *Free Action* by A. I. Melden (1961), really the founding document of contemporary philosophy of action. The third is a largely Husserlian phenomenological study on voluntary action by Paul Ricoeur (1950, tr. in 1966). The first of three volumes on his philosophy of *volonté*, of which the two parts of the second, empirically oriented volume have also been translated, this one examines the essential (eidetic) structures of humans' being-in-the-world. Volume three was designed to present "poetics" as the evocation of the vision of transcendence and reconciliation. Throughout his discussions, Ricoeur assumes the Husserlian conception of intentionality as always consciousness of _____, that is, always having some object. Unlike this notion of intentionality, the one ordinarily used in analytic discourse refers to meaningful action (not necessarily voluntary, and usually but not always thought of as purposeful).

In the 1960s a great deal of effort went into new attempts to prove free will or determinism. Keith Lehrer's (1966) small collection includes good examples. The larger one edited by Bernard Berofsky (1966) is to date the most comprehensive, though the later one edited by Ted Honderlich (1973) is also of value.

In 1971 D. J. O'Connor summed up the effort by concluding that no case for either option is unassailably established. The same conclusion, I think, is to be made regarding attempts to make the two beliefs compatible. Recently John Thorp (1980), for example, has carefully examined both the compatibility option and theses that base arguments for determinism on correlations between brain events and mental events; and he has rejected them both, holding that the libertarian view is strong at its core but still faces difficulties at its periphery. It can be very worthwhile, even or especially with unsolvable problems of this kind, to clarify what can or cannot be reasonably said. This purpose is notably served in all Stuart Hampshire's writings (1959–71) on the subject and in subsequent essays by Anthony Kenny (1975–78). Kenny's 1978 book is an effective example of how such reflections might be applied to practical purposes, in this instance to criminal law. Recently Rychlak (1979) has done this for psychology and psychotherapy, and in a far-reaching set of reflections Frithjof Bergmann (1977) has done the same especially for education.

FUTURE PROSPECTS

Although much of the desired clarification that engendered the virtual creation of this area in the 1950s has been achieved, the area itself is still on the upswing. What was said about the needs and exciting prospects ahead for philosophy of mind applies here as well. Bernstein's 1971 agenda regarding inquiry into social praxis on the basis of a clarified understanding of action, and vice versa, is still timely in that the function of linking concerns in philosophy of mind with those in ethics and all the bridge areas remains constant and is as yet only minimally fulfilled.

Adler, Mortimer J. *The Idea of Freedom*. Vol. 1, *A Dialectical Examination of the Conceptions of Freedom;* vol. 2, *A Dialectical Examination of the Controversies about Freedom*. Garden City, N.Y.: Doubleday, 1958–61.

Aune, Bruce. *Reason and Action*. Dordrecht and Boston: Reidel, 1977.

Bergmann, Frithjof. *On Being Free*. Notre Dame, Ind. and London: Univ. of Notre Dame Pr., 1977.

Bernstein, Richard J. *Praxis and Action: Contemporary Philosophies of Human Activity*. Philadelphia: Univ. of Pennsylvania Pr., 1971.

Berofsky, Bernard, ed. *Free Will and Determinism*. New York: Harper & Row, 1966.

Binkley, Robert, Richard Bronaugh, and Ausonio Marras, eds. *Agent, Action, and Reason*. Toronto: Univ. of Toronto Pr.; Oxford: Blackwell, 1971.

Brand, Myles, ed. *The Nature of Human Action*. Glenview, Ill. and London: Scott, Foresman, 1970.

———, and Douglas Walton, eds. *Action Theory*. Dordrecht and Boston: Reidel, 1976. (Winnipeg Conference on Human Action, 1975.)

Brown, D. G. *Action*. Toronto and London: Univ. of Toronto Pr., 1968.

Care, Norman S., and Charles Landesman, eds. *Readings in the Theory of Action*. Bloomington and London: Indiana Univ. Pr., 1968.

Danto, Arthur C. *Analytical Philosophy of Action*. Cambridge and New York: Cambridge Univ. Pr., 1973.

D'Arcy, Eric. *Human Acts: An Essay in Their Moral Evaluation*. New York: Oxford Univ. Pr.; Oxford: Clarendon Pr., 1963.

Davidson, Donald. *Essays on Actions and Events*. New York: Oxford Univ. Pr.; Oxford: Clarendon Pr., 1980.

Davis, Lawrence H. *Theory of Action*. Englewood Cliffs, N.J.: Prentice-Hall, 1979.

Goldman, Alvin I. *A Theory of Human Action*. Englewood Cliffs, N.J.: Prentice-Hall, 1970.

Hampshire, Stuart. *Freedom of Mind and Other Essays.* Princeton, N.J.: Princeton Univ. Pr., 1971; Oxford: Clarendon Pr., 1972.

———. *Freedom of the Individual.* Expanded ed. Princeton, N.J.: Princeton Univ. Pr., 1975. (1st ed., New York: Harper & Row; London: Chatto & Windus, 1965.)

———. *Thought and Action.* New York: Viking Pr., 1960; London: Chatto & Windus, 1959.

Honderich, Ted, ed. *Essays on Freedom of Action.* London and Boston: Routledge & Paul, 1973.

Hook, Sidney, ed. *Determinism and Freedom in the Age of Modern Science.* New York: New York Univ. Pr., 1958.

Hornsby, Jennifer. *Actions.* London and Boston: Routledge & Paul, 1980.

Kenny, Anthony. *Freewill and Responsibility.* London and Boston: Routledge & Paul, 1978. (A companion volume: *Will, Freedom, and Power.* Oxford: Blackwell, 1975.)

Lawrence, Roy. *Motive and Intention: An Essay in the Appreciation of Action.* Evanston, Ill.: Northwestern Univ. Pr., 1972.

Lehrer, Keith, ed. *Freedom and Determinism.* New York: Random House, 1966.

Louch, A. R. *Explanation and Human Action.* Berkeley: Univ. of California Pr., 1966.

Melden, Abraham I. *Free Action.* New York: Humanities Pr.; London: Routledge & Paul, 1961.

Mortimore, Geoffrey, ed. *Weakness of Will.* New York: St. Martin's Pr.; London: Macmillan, 1971.

O'Connor, Daniel J. *Free Will.* Garden City, N.Y.: Doubleday Anchor, 1971.

Peters, Richard S. *The Concept of Motivation.* New York: Humanities Pr.; London: Routledge & Paul, 1958.

Ricoeur, Paul. *Freedom and Nature: The Voluntary and the Involuntary.* Tr. by Erazim V. Kohák. Evanston, Ill.: Northwestern Univ. Pr., 1966. (French ed., 1950.)

Rychlak, Joseph F. *Discovering Free Will and Personal Responsibility.* Oxford and New York: Oxford Univ. Pr., 1979.

Taylor, Charles. *The Explanation of Behavior.* New York: Humanities Pr.; London: Routledge & Paul, 1964.

Taylor, Richard. *Action and Purpose.* Englewood Cliffs, N.J.: Prentice-Hall, 1966.

Thalberg, Irving. *Enigmas of Agency: Studies in the Philosophy of Human Action.* New York: Humanities Pr.; London: Allen & Unwin, 1972.

Thorp, John. *Free Will.* London and Boston: Routledge & Paul, 1980.

Tuomela, Raimo. *Human Action and Its Explanation: A Study on the Philosophical Foundations of Psychology.* Dordrecht and Boston: Reidel, 1977.

Wright, Georg Henrik von. *Explanation and Understanding.* Ithaca, N.Y.: Cornell Univ. Pr.; London: Routledge & Paul, 1971.

21

Axiology:
Values Inquiry

The meanings of the word "value," like those of "religion," "ideology," "interest," and "feeling," have been greatly altered and extended since the eighteenth century. "Value"has the same root as the word "valor": the Latin *valere*, to be strong, to have worth. To "valorize" is to set a market price; and indeed the primary uses of "value" until the nineteenth century referred to the courage and strength of a person or to market weight or price. In the writings of Adam Smith (1723–90) and other early political economists "theory of value" referred to the second meaning, though there was an allied meaning, already articulated by Thomas Hobbes and later made prominent by Karl Marx, in which the worth or value of a man was said to reside in his labor power. In economics today "theory of value" is still directed primarily to market economics, referring to exchange values or prices, though there is also a use of "value" in welfare economics, referring to ways in which social resources are weighed and allocated.

During the late nineteenth century several distinguished German and Austrian philosophers began to use "value" to refer to a whole domain of experience over against facts. Among them, the title *Werttheorie* gradually came to be used for this kind of inquiry. In 1906 the American philosopher Wilbur M. Urban coined "axiology" as its translation. Since then "axiology" has been used, along with "value theory" and "values inquiry" and "theory of values," to refer to a distinct area of philosophy.

According to these early value theorists, values are human creations. Friedrich Nietzsche dramatically highlighted this idea in his

379

call for a "transvaluation" of all conventional cultural values. As human creations values were thought to be expressed in the effort to ascertain cognitive validity (Hermann Lotze, 1817–81) or to be contained in the activity of will and feeling (Wilhelm Windelband, 1848–1915)—both grounded in a spiritual metaphysics. Or they were held to be something like these two but logically prior to and transcendent of all being (Heinrich Rickert, 1863–1936) or to be a product of self-evidently correct judgments (Franz Brentano, 1838–1917). Or they were defined as relative and personal desires (Christian Ehrenfels, 1859–1932) or as emotive judgment with respect to actual or ideal objects (Alexius Meinong, 1853–1920). Or they were depicted as a realm of ideal, absolute essences in ranked order, borne by both persons and things but intuited and actualized by human beings (Max Scheler, 1874–1928, and Nicolai Hartmann, 1882–1950) or as a realm entailed in the crucial act of affirming that there be a world in which we participate (idealist Hugo Münsterberg, 1863–1916).

These efforts were all both energized and plagued by the desire to gain a validity and objectivity to values, believed to be a natural element of psychological experience, as solid as that attributed to facts in natural science. Consequently, they helped widen the split between fact and value, descriptive and normative discourse that became a major characteristic of twentieth-century thought (J. Prescott Johnson in Laszlo and Wilbur, 1973). One serious consequence lay in the logical positivist view that values are expressive of feeling or intention but have no meaning in themselves.

THE PERIOD 1920–1965

Since the 1920s the questions about values that have chiefly interested philosophers working in the more analytic mode have focused on the following kinds of issues: (1) whether values are natural or nonnatural properties; (2) whether they are indefinable in terms of empirical fact or whether some scientific base can be given to value attributions; (3) whether statements attributing values are analytic, synthetic, or neither; (4) whether the gap between facts and values is logically unbridgeable; (5) whether value judgments have truth value; (6) whether any value can be absolute or exists in itself or can possess a general or universal character; (7) whether values are simply emotive exclamations of commendation or approval; and (8) whether objectivity can be won for some types of value judgments by reference to ideal observers. James Olthuis (1969) has given a fine account of many of these issues in a critical study of twentieth-century moral philosophy, which has been the primary carrier of values inquiry since the 1920s.

Reputed philosophers working in the area have used "values" in several different ways: (1) what is "good" or that to which "good" is attributed (a thing or property of a thing)—as in "intrinsic versus extrinsic or instrumental values"; (2) normative beliefs or standards—as in "moral, prudential, aesthetic, and religious values," "value-system"; (3) characterizations of quality (usually comparative) versus quantitative or relatively simple descriptive or factual assertions, especially but not exclusively regarding what is in or is done by human beings—as in "valued attributes," "value-laden," and "value-free"; (4) moral goods or principles; (5) particular kinds of predisposition to act, along a scale (sometimes developmental) that reaches from simple reward-penalty responses to highly prized ends; (6) appraisals, sometimes including estimations both of worth and of what ought to be—as in the notions "value judgment" and "evaluation"—and the means, ordinarily linguistic, for making appraisals (referring to different kinds of value language: for example, "blatant," "to honor," "attractive," "authentic"); (7) depending on the theory, a synonym for desires, tastes, prizings and/or appraisings, attitudes, preferences, excellences, richness of properties, interests, feelings (for instance, of pleasure or happiness), prescriptions, gradings, or recommendations. Each of the thirteen items in number 7 has been the key term in a major philosophical definition of values, as have those in numbers 1–6.

Until recently, virtually every noted Anglo-American value theory has possessed this characteristic of a key term or concept. Apart from Bernard Bosanquet, John Laird, and J. N. Findlay, Britain has produced very few value theories; to them the Scandinavian Henrik von Wright may be added. The United States has produced a great many, through the early 1960s notably (and in rough chronological order) by Ralph Barton Perry, DeWitt H. Parker, David W. Prall, Harold Osborne, John Dewey, C. I. Lewis, Asa Hilliard, W. D. Lamont, Stephen C. Pepper, Everett W. Hall, Brand Blanshard, Charles L. Stevenson, and Paul W. Taylor. Ray Lepley (1949, 1957) edited two important symposia characteristic of that era.

Very often a philosopher writing specifically on values will hold only one of the meanings indicated above; occasionally two or more are confused with each other; at other times several kinds or levels or realms of value are discussed. So far no one theory seems adequately to encompass the entire range of phenomena, which has been fascinatingly laid out in an analysis of value language by Karl Aschenbrenner (1971). Some theories make a claim to do this, usually by attempting to reduce some or all meanings to one category. Understandably, the tendency among analytic philosophers has been to avoid use of the word value if at all possible.

FROM 1965 TO THE EARLY 1980s

By the 1960s a new turn seems to have been taken, with the following characteristics: (1) a renewed effort to form a general theory of values, still for the most part rejected in favor of specialized inquiries, particularly in ethics and aesthetics; (2) an attempt to be more inclusive both as to phenomena and as to language and concepts; and (3) greater interaction with the considerable interest in values appearing in psychology and the social sciences, an interest still increasing in the early 1980s. Not only the linguistic study by Aschenbrenner (1971) but also the unusually careful, comprehensive positions worked out by W. H. Werkmeister (1967) and Zdzistaw Najder (1975) betoken the change. In addition, Robert Hartman (1967) has proposed an unusual logical theory according to which value means fulfillment of the definition or concept of a thing. John Leslie (1979), melding ethics and metaphysics, starts from the view that the value of a thing resides in there being a reason for it to exist.

Although many philosophers have entered the discussions on behavioral science methodology, they have not tended to bring well-ordered values inquiry to it. In the behavioral sciences three conceptions of value reign, all derived more from economics than from philosophy, though some philosophers have favored them: the notions of preference, interest, and market price (for example, particularly in cost-benefit analysis). The first two come from welfare economics, which consists of an ordering of alternative allocations of social resources, usually thought of as aggregates of individual preferences, sometimes (perhaps more by noneconomists) as compositions of needs or interests. Among philosophers talking with economists, three kinds of corrective have been proposed. (1) Richard Brandt (in Sidney Hook, 1967) has pointed out a deficiency in the exclusion of moral or conventional concern for others' welfare in economic theories based on a widely used calculus of values that refers solely to what people want strictly for themselves. (2) Kurt

Baier (in Laszlo and Wilbur, 1973, and in Hook, 1967) proposes that economists use hierarchically ordered answers to various questions that concern not only preferences but also needs and interests as to "quality of life." (3) Nicholas Rescher (1969, and Laszlo and Wilbur, 1973) has argued that preferences cannot be identified with interests and that to do so is to espouse a highly questionable ideology. In his own version of an interest theory, values are always interpersonal and have reference to rational reflections upon visions of "the good life."

FUTURE PROSPECTS

In view of recent developments, I think this area of philosophy is likely to become more firmly established in future. Borrowings from other parts of philosophy can be expected to aid that process, as before. Three other kinds of contribution would also strengthen it. (1) A more detailed psychological base would help, including investigation of psychological concepts such as F. T. C. Moore's (1978) on "desire" but also learning from developmental psychology, wherein highly sophisticated views of cognitive-affective development and analyses of mental functioning are now available. (2) Allied to the first aid is the interest in hierarchical structures and levels of psychological functioning among philosophers of science (e.g., Lancelot Whyte et al., *Hierarchical Structures,* 1969). (3) Finally, some decision theorists like Isaac Levi (1980) are forming complex analyses of decision making that invite closer investigation of the roles of values and of value conflict in that domain.

Aschenbrenner, Karl. *The Concepts of Value: Foundation of Value Theory.* Dordrecht and Boston: Reidel, 1971.
Hartman, Robert S. *The Structure of Value: Foundations of Scientific Axiology.* Carbondale: Southern Illinois Univ. Pr., 1967.
Hook, Sidney, ed. *Human Values and Economic Policy.* New York: New York Univ. Pr., 1967.
Laszlo, Ervin, and James B. Wilbur, eds. *Value Theory in Philosophy and Social Science.* New York and London: Gordon and Breach Science Publishers, 1973.
Lepley, Ray, ed. *The Language of Value.* New York: Columbia Univ. Pr., 1957.
———, ed. *Value: A Cooperative Inquiry.* New York: Columbia Univ. Pr., 1949.
Leslie, John. *Value and Existence.* Totowa, N.J.: Rowman & Littlefield, 1979.

Levi, Isaac. *The Enterprise of Knowledge: An Essay on Knowledge, Credal Probability, and Chance.* Cambridge, Mass. and London: MIT Pr., 1980.

Moore, Francis C. T. *The Psychological Basis of Morality.* New York and London: Macmillan, 1978.

Najder, Zdzistaw. *Values and Evaluations.* Oxford: Clarendon Pr., 1975.

Olthuis, James H. *Facts, Values and Ethics.* 2nd ed. Assen: Van Gorcum, 1969. (1st ed., n.d.)

Rescher, Nicholas. *Introduction to Value Theory.* Englewood Cliffs, N.J.: Prentice-Hall, 1969.

Werkmeister, William H. *Man and His Values.* Lincoln: Univ. of Nebraska Pr., 1967.

Whyte, Lancelot Law, Albert B. Wilson, and Donna Wilson, eds. *Hierarchical Structures.* New York: American Elsevier, 1969. (Especially Mario Bunge, "The Metaphysics, Epistemology and Methodology of Levels," pp. 17–28.)

22

Ethics:
Moral Philosophy

The Domain of Ethics

In a general sense, ethics is ordered reflection on morality. Philosophical ethics, or moral philosophy, brings to that reflection critical analysis and constructive thinking with respect to moral language, arguments, and behavior. It comes chiefly in two parts: (1) Normative ethics attempts to construct systematic approaches to forming well-grounded substantive proposals for moral action. (2) Metaethics deals with still more formal issues. Above all, it attempts to map out the moral domain, to define the nature of morality, to analyze moral concepts, to show how moral judgments may be justified, and critically to compare various moral and ethical views.

Normative ethics is well represented within the ethical thought of individual thinkers included in chapters 2–13. Today this sort of interest is also evident among thinkers who are not professional philosophers—traditionally among religious thinkers in particular, recently among scientists. Occasionally more formal, metaethical issues are also addressed by earlier and nonanalytic philosophers, rarely by others; however, this has become the special brief of analytic philosophy in the twentieth century. Thus the more analytic work is especially featured in this chapter.

In three respects ethics may be viewed as something of a sum-up among the eight core areas. (1) Its progress in the twentieth century has relied heavily upon that in the other core areas, above all in epistemology, logic, and philosophy of language, while attention to ethical issues has also spawned much new work in other areas, especially in philosophy of mind, philosophy of action, and axiology.

385

(2) In that issues about moral conduct are important in virtually every part of human life, the scope of its possible application is very broad; therefore the potential impact on practical concerns of what is gathered into an ethical viewpoint from the other core areas is very great. (3) Ethics, like the other core areas, may have pertinence for thought in all the bridge areas; the substantive issues to which it refers have especially close ties to the content of three bridge areas: social-political philosophy, philosophy of law, and education. It is no wonder, then, that a high proportion of the investment twentieth-century philosophers have made in their field has gone into ethics. Epistemology, logic, philosophy of language, and philosophy of science are its only rivals in this regard.

Chapters 1–13 give notice of numerous works and figures in the history of ethics and of influences upon British and American ethics from continental Europe. In the twentieth century influences from current or even nineteenth-century European thinking on the analytic mainstream have not been very great. There is nothing, for example, of the enormous influence of phenomenological value theorists Franz Brentano and Max Scheler on ethical thinking in both Europe and Latin America.

Anglo-American Moral Philosophy

In America, the influence of John Dewey (1960) on ethical thinking in the first half of the twentieth century was considerable, especially (1) in his insistence on its being objectively, scientifically, and nonsupernaturally grounded and (2) in his pragmatic alternative to ethics of fixed ends. Moreover, (3) he used his reflection normatively and for moral purposes. (4) Both Dewey and R. B. Perry (e.g., 1926, not cited here) tried to form a general theory of values; Perry's was based on "interests," Dewey's focused on assessment of potential consequences. (5) Both placed great emphasis on democracy as the best means for the moral development of society. (6) Dewey went even further in exploring educational means to the fulfillment of individual and social life. (7) Finally, Dewey, who had taught psychology as early as he taught philosophy, never gave up applying psychology and what would later be called philosophy of mind and action to his understanding of moral behavior. In all these respects Dewey had great influence.

Especially on points numbered 1, 2, and 4, the next generation followed in the footsteps of both Dewey and Perry, receiving comparatively little influence from abroad. Today C. I. Lewis is perhaps the most enduringly notable among them. Recently D. W. Haslett (1974), for example, has drawn considerably upon Lewis in forming his own metaethics; and this does not seem at all strange, despite the lapse of several decades. Although Lewis held a Deweyan naturalist-empiricist theory of value, his ethical and social theory of "right" is based on a "pragmatically a priori" rational imperative "to respect the interests of others as we would call upon others to respect our own" and to do so "in every instance and for anybody" (*Our Social Inheritance,* 1957, not cited here).

These and many other moral theorists had referred their concepts of "good" basically to psychological phenomena, such as desire, interest, preference, or prizing. Were they guilty of what G. E. Moore (1903) had called "the naturalistic fallacy"? In a famous 1939 paper (in K. E. Goodpaster, 1976) William Frankena argued in the negative. To some, C. L. Stevenson (1944, 1963) added insult to Frankena's acknowledged injury by forming an emotive theory. To a great many analytic philosophers in both Britain and the United States it suggested a viable metaethical alternative to naturalism and intuitivism (to be explained below), the two most fully argued options up to that point. Many philosophers continued to believe that Moore had decisively refuted the naturalist aim of justifying moral claims on a "natural," scientific base; by the 1960s this belief had largely died out, and by that time many new and elaborate metaethical theories were available. In Stevenson's form of emotivism, itself a complex position and not readily summarized, moral statements are said to express one's approval or disapproval and one's intention to encourage that of others.

From the 1930s on, Anglo-American moral philosophy became increasingly analytic, and most attention was directed to metaethical questions. In Britain, strongly metaethical trends had already been forming in the decade before World War I, especially through the eventually towering influence of G. E. Moore. Apart from Moore's, the earlier works most cited by British moral theorists and historians date from those by C. D. Broad and W. D. Ross in 1930 (not cited here). Intuitionists (these three and many others), who believed Moore had refuted naturalism, had their heyday in the 1920s and 1930s. After the late 1930s emotivism, and later other forms of noncognitivism, supplanted intuitionism in general favor. (See the discussion of metaethics below.) By the 1970s the picture was very mixed.

Within the thirty years between 1930 and 1960, American philosophy produced little work of the analytic quality or moment of what was being published in Britain (see Frankena, 1964). In the period since the late 1950s that imbalance has been overcome.

Historical Overviews

Several brief historical overviews of moral philosophy exist in English. The classic one is by Henry Sidgwick (1838–1900): *Outlines of the History of Ethics for English Readers* (1886), updated by Alban Widgery in 1931. Although he was not intellectually a Christian, Sidgwick wrote this terse little volume primarily for ordinands of the Church of Scotland. It has set a high standard of clarity and reasoned objectivity. Along with *The Methods of Ethics* (1874, not cited here), one of the best books ever written on the subject and still in service, this brief summary has played an indispensable role in Anglo-American moral theory. An issue of *Monist* is devoted to this theme, edited by J. B. Schneewind (1974), who adds a study on Sidgwick and Victorian ethics (1977).

Among the more recent historical overviews, four must be singled out. A detailed analytical survey in *The Encyclopedia of Philosophy* (1967) is taken through the nineteenth century by Raziel Abelson and on to the early 1960s by Kai Nielsen. A more literary but analytically informed perspective comes from Alasdair MacIntyre (1966) and more of an intellectual history of still broader scope than these two from Thomist philosopher Vernon Bourke (1968), who includes Europeans and religious ethicists. A two-volume collection edited by W. D. Hudson (1974) presents monographs by British philosophers on twelve normative theories, as follows: Pamela Huby, Greek ethics; D. J. O'Connor, Aquinas and natural law; J. Kemp, ethical naturalism in Hobbes and Hume; W. D. Hudson, ethical intuitionism; H. B. Acton, Kant; W. H. Walsh, Hegelian ethics; Anthony Quinton, utilitarianism; J. N. Findlay, axiological ethics (from Franz Brentano to W. D. Ross and Nicolai Hartmann); Antony Flew, evolutionary ethics; Eugene Kamenka, Marxism; Mary Warnock, existentialism; and G. J. Warnock, contemporary moral philosophy, especially metaethics.

W. D. Hudson has contributed two valuable histories of his own, one on the modern period (1970) and one mostly on the period since Sidgwick (1980). Mary Warnock's (1960) small handbook on British ethics since 1900 is still useful. An excellent analytic "confrontation" with that tradition, especially with G. E. Moore and his influence, comes from James Olthuis (*Facts, Values and Ethics*, 1969, cited on

p. 384). Joseph Kockelmans (1972) has edited and introduced selected readings from continental European ethics, mostly since World
War II. Most of this literature is not otherwise available in English.
William Frankena (1964) covers the American scene from about
1930 to 1960.

The influence of linguistic philosophy on ethics is first betokened
by R. M. Hare's influential work *The Language of Morals* (1952).
Mary Gore Forrester (1982) offers a fine systematic account of moral
language that manifests the main developments since then. A study
by Roger Wertheimer (1972) pulls together applications to moral
language of logical interests in modality.

Introductions and Collections

R. B. Brandt's *Ethical Theory* (1959) is still the most thoroughgoing analytic introduction, though his own normative theory given
there has gone through major changes since that time and though in
metaethics the succeeding twenty years was to flourish at least as
distinctively as had the previous fifty. The main reason his book is
still useful is that the principal metaethical alternatives had been
clearly set forth by the late 1950s. It is the further debate, refinement
and, more recently, application to normative interests that make the
next period significant. A complementary introduction by John
Hospers (1961) is rich with illuminating discussion, examples and
exercises. William Frankena's (1963) slim introduction, crafted in his
usual smooth, clear style, is still widely used. A selection of his essays
on ethics has been edited by K. E. Goodpaster (1976). The various
collections of readings from that period and the next decade serve
varying, though greatly overlapping, purposes and are all gold mines.
Perhaps the most enduring is that edited by R. B. Brandt (1961). The
collection of new essays edited by Hector-Neri Casteñada and
George Nakhnikian (1963) is like a Henry Moore sculpture: solid,
reminiscent of a period, and admirable still.

Two exemplary introductions appeared near the end of the 1970s.
Though his introduction is analytic, Gilbert Harman (1977) eschews
the usual attempt to set out alternative metaethical or normative
positions in an assumedly neutral way. Instead he presents his own
account of the nature of morality, focusing on one basic problem: its
apparent immunity from observational testing. Fred Feldman's
(1978) introduction carries on the traditional effort, giving the most
persuasive, historically important arguments for and against each
theory that he can. Most of the introductory readings edited by

William Frankena and John Granrose (1974) are also organized by theories, but these are supplemented by sections on major problems and are themselves exemplifications of attempts to deal with basic problems.

Two recent collections of new essays represent the chief fruits of analytic efforts in the 1970s. A unique volume edited by Alvin Goldman and Jaegwon Kim (1979) offers sixteen essays in honor of three major figures in contemporary ethics upon their retirement, all of whom were members of the University of Michigan faculty; Richard Brandt, William Frankena, and Charles Stevenson, with bibliographies and a brief account of their careers. The set of twenty-three essays edited by Peter French et al. (1980) is also distinguished.

Theological and religious ethics have undergone marked development in the twentieth century. Only a few theologians have made full use of metaethical inquiry in philosophy, though their primary interest in normative theory and exposition has placed even these thinkers at some distance from the philosophical mainstream (e.g., see Basil Mitchell, *Morality: Religious and Secular,* 1980). James Gustafson's books, written from a Protestant Reformed (Calvinistic versus Lutheran or Anabaptist) perspective, show special acknowledgment of philosophy. Among them, a survey of contemporary theological ethics, both Roman Catholic and Protestant (1978), is especially interesting philosophically and is the best guide to that literature. Most theologians take a less optimistic view than most philosophers of human capacities to do what is right, to achieve good, or even to discern by reason what these are. This was true of Reinhold Niebuhr, with John Dewey, and possibly Bertrand Russell, publicly one of the two or three best-known ethical thinkers, philosophical or theological, in the twentieth century.

In a stunning critical study of moral theory, *After Virtue,* Alasdair MacIntyre (1981) begins with an exposé of what he takes to be the impoverishment and weakening of morality in emotivism (a popular but misleading shorthand for noncognitivism—see below). He sounds an alarm, in view of current moral disorder in the world, with a doubt that analytic philosophy can provide any convincing escape from emotivism, the debilitating effects of which are seen elsewhere in the condemnations of conventional morality by the successors of Friedrich Nietzsche and Jean-Paul Sartre. MacIntyre's work is unusual in its Collingwoodian search for the social views presupposed by each theory he rejects and for where they came from: chiefly the Enlightenment project of justifying morality and its nineteenth-century consequences in Jeremy Bentham, John Stuart Mill, Sidgwick, Moore, and pragmatism. These trends, he argues, prepared the way for the "theater of illusions" (for example, about "rights," "facts," "neutrality," "law-like generalizations," and "objectivity") that comprises much contemporary moral theory. The bulk of his book is a historical examination of views on virtue.

MacIntyre himself affirms a nonindividualistic kind of Aristotelian perspective on virtuous life and its ends. In doing so, he emphasizes selfhood, conceived as the unified narrative of a life, served by the formation of virtues as distinguished from the usual focus on single human actions; he places high value on intelligent conflict for personal and social development; against individualism, he also regards membership in local communities, wherein "goods" can be shared ("goods are not private property"), to be of the highest importance. Moral philosophy, in his view, ought to be directing its efforts on behalf of "rationality" to these realities. Although MacIntyre's arguments are familiar, on the whole, it has been a long time since a moral philosopher issued an argued challenge of these dimensions.

Metaethics and the Justification of Moral Judgments

Most of the literature so far cited concentrates on metaethics, as will be true in the rest of this chapter. The three main theoretical approaches have been: (1) naturalism, which attempts to justify moral judgments on the basis of a scientific account of human behavior; (2) nonnaturalism, or intuitionism; and (3) against these cognitivist views, noncognitivism, several versions of which center on "emotive" expression or commendation. These three alternatives exactly parallel the chief distinctions used in metaepistemology.

Intuitionism is the view that moral judgments and principles are self-justifying and self-evident, in that they are intuitively grasped. This view, most notably held by Max Scheler (1916), Sidgwick, and Moore, has had but few adherents over the past several decades. Naturalism, once prominently held by John Dewey and R. B. Perry in the United States, was the overwhelming choice of Anglo-American philosophers until the 1950s, and it has experienced a renascence of sorts, not having ever really died out, in the 1970s. In ethics "naturalism" does not have the same meaning as in other philosophical usage. A supernaturalist (for instance, a Thomist natural law theorist) can be an ethical naturalist, and a naturalist with respect to issues of metaphysics and religion can be an ethical intuitionist (for example, Moore) or an emotivist (for example, A. J. Ayer). Many now believe that Moore's once widely assumed refutation of it was not really a decisive case against ethical naturalism but rather, if at all, against the belief that moral terms can be defined in nonmoral terms. Hence what he pointed out is better referred to not as the "naturalist fallacy" but as the "definist fallacy."

Emotivism took ethics by storm over about two decades. The most influential works were by Charles Stevenson (1944), R. M. Hare (1952), and P. H. Nowell-Smith (1954), to which Henry Aiken (1962) and J. O. Urmson (1968) added later revisions. A 1911 address by Axel Hägerstrom, whose major work was translated in 1953, presaged this development; and logical positivism, especially through A. J. Ayer (*Language, Truth and Logic*, 1936, cited on p. 155), had a strong impact on its development in Anglo-American ethics. Hare (1963, 1981) developed a view beyond emotivism, usually called prescriptivism, but still noncognitive. His ongoing work provided a focus for much of the discussion over a thirty-year period.

Hare and the emotivists tend to emphasize normative neutrality in making metaethical statements and, despite some of their critics, do not adopt any form of moral nihilism as a consequence of their views. Nowell-Smith, for example, insists that public criteria are needed to decide logically proper moral claims. Jean-Paul Sartre and the existential novelist Albert Camus are highly influential examples of authors who adopted noncognitivist positions unlike those of the emotivists in these two respects.

The popular "situation ethics" (Joseph Fletcher and others) has been associated with noncognitivism in that it tends to use a loose set of rules, if that, for adjusting to different circumstances. These positions, which are in intention philosophically grounded, are also reminiscent of the views of W. D. Ross and C. D. Broad (from the 1930s, not cited here) that while the moral life is essentially lived by rules or prima facie duties (which latter ought to be kept unless other moral considerations outweigh them), there are times when we do not have a rule and simply have to adjust as best as we can. Iris Murdoch (1970) represents a later version of this view.

The easiest approach to this forest of ideas is through the introductions and readings already mentioned. One is then better able to follow discussions in the other literature cited. In addition, the following treatises are of special interest. Lawrence Becker (1973) attempts to draw up a set of procedures for the justification of moral judgments that is also meant to destroy the plausibility of moral skepticism. Earlier Abraham Edel (1963) had taken a very different but still commendable naturalist approach to forming viable methods in ethics; and in other publications (e.g., *Ethical Judgment,* 1955) he had also sought to demonstrate how science could be used as a base. These proposals retain value also for those who are not naturalists. A brand of subjectivism is exemplified in a systematic work in both metaethical and normative theory by J. L. Mackie (1977), striking the theme that morality must be "invented" and then made to function in an ordered way in changing historical circumstances. Dorothy Emmet (1979) invites the reader to consider "morality" as an "essentially contestable" concept and to regard its domain as internally complex. To view it adequately is like viewing light through a prism, which reveals many features.

Finally, two advanced works come from the hands of Alan Gewirth (1978) and Richard Brandt (1979). A *Theory of Justice* (1971, cited on p. 450) by utilitarian John Rawls should also be mentioned, since it too is a rare systematic work and has garnered considerable debate; but its chief province is social-political philosophy. Gewirth offers a "modified naturalism" that purports to justify moral principles on the ground of certain necessary and generic features of action. Not following Emmet's counsel against simplification and reduction, he nonetheless expresses a systematic impetus in organizing the whole of his massive treatment around one supreme moral principle, which is: "Act in accord with the generic rights of your recipients as well as of yourself." Brandt takes a whole fresh metaethical look at major concepts like "wanting," "good," and "rational." Then he presents substantive principles, taking the unusual step of deriving evidential support from contemporary behavioral psychology, in response to this question: "What kind of moral system for his society would it be rational for an agent to support?" In doing so, he rejects his old ideal observer theory and gives an account of "morally right," "welfare," "justice," and "equality." He rejects a simple inspection of ordinary language for these purposes, however.

In the 1960s and 1970s the general metaethical distinctions indicated above have held, but some authors cannot strictly identify their own positions as a whole with any one of them.

Normative Ethical Theories

In ethics the two main types of normative theories have been (1) deontological (literally, regarding "duties"), which emphasize rules for "right" or obligatory action, and (2) teleological, which emphasize the "good" or "humanly desirable" consequences of action.

Supernaturalist theories are also ordinarily one of the two types, though the more elaborate ethics focused on "love" are difficult to classify. Teleological theories include hedonism and egoism (Epicurus, John Locke, Thomas Hobbes, David Hume, Jeremy Bentham, John Stuart Mill, and Henry Sidgwick), self-realization theories (Friedrich Nietzsche and John Dewey, in Dewey's thought integrated with a strong social ethic), and utilitarianism (in its classic form, dating from Bentham, Mill, and Sidgwick, often called "act-utilitarianism"). Rule-utilitarianism is a combination in that it assumes there is an appropriate set of rules to guide action—for example, those an "ideal observer" would hold (Brandt, 1959); adoption of a rule is still justified with reference to desirable consequences, whereas violation of a rule cannot be. Nowell-Smith, Baier, Toulmin, Marcus G. Singer in his *Generalization in Ethics* (1961, not cited here), and possibly Mill, formed early versions of rule-utilitarianism, which is still defended and discussed, as are the other major positions. The ethics of Immanuel Kant, E. F. Carritt, W. D. Ross, H. A. Prichard, and divine command theories are deontological. To a large extent these have been replaced by rule-utilitarian theories in the contemporary period. A recent defense of hedonism comes from J. C. B. Gosling (1969) and a particularly thorough examination of utilitarianism, in its various forms the theory most held by contemporary moral theorists, by David Lyons (1965).

THEMES AND DEVELOPMENTS

Definition of Morality

Ordinarily, but not always, moral theories try to make and then assume a clear distinction between (1) convention (mores or "conventional morality," which is not strictly morality to some but includes various customs regarding acceptable behavior in a society, including matters of etiquette), (2) prudential action (which is not to be strictly identified with the exercise of "prudence," or practical wisdom, but is based on self- or group-interest), and (3) morality proper (which is a standard that one possesses by which to judge mores and which is usually taken, at the very least, to be comprised of obligations that are to apply as a matter of basic respect to all humans or sentient beings universally; sometimes other criteria are added). More often than not, it is also presupposed that an acceptable social order must itself rest on moral foundations and that on these rational persons will come to agree. The Stoics made this assumption, as have natural law theorists, whether religiously oriented or not, early modern intuitionists, and most moral philosophers since Kant. Occasionally a philosopher such as Philippa Foot (1978) will argue that favored ways of maintaining these distinctions do not uniformly hold up.

At initial appearance, some theories of value—for example, the "interest" theories of R. B. Perry (noted above) and De Witt Parker (1931, not cited here)—might suggest that prudential action would be as far as they could go; but it is still possible to hold that among various interests one may have some that are morally obligatory and must be universally applied; and prudential and moral action are not always incompatible. So one's value theory does not necessarily dictate the entirety of one's moral theory.

Is it reasonable to expect that one can form an adequate definition of morality, or designation of the moral domain, independent of a specific normative theory of moral behavior? Alan Donagan (1977) has, in effect, answered "no." He associates his fundamental moral principle—respect for every rational being, including oneself—with Hebrew-Christian tradition, though holding that it need not be religiously based. Morality is then, for him, the domain of principles and actions derived from that fundamental principle. A similar project has been undertaken by another analytic philosopher, G. J. Warnock (1971), though of broader scope and not setting down a system of primary and secondary principles as Donagan did. The general "object" of morality, for him, is to contribute to the betterment of the human predicament, namely that things are likely to go badly, by means of fostering certain rational and sympathetic dispositions, which he sketchily indicates, and deterring people from acting on others. This is but one of many attempts that have been made to aim morality essentially at goals beyond itself. In contrast, many other philosophers—for example, Peter French (1979)—try to lay out the moral domain without presenting any normative moral theory whatsoever; but French assumes that a morality is a collection of social conventions designed to guide the choices of persons. Nonetheless, much of the moral content these three accounts present as especially important is the same, at least in surface appearance.

William Frankena (1980) has probably thought about the question "What is morality?" as much as anyone. He admits that mature morality, as it is now generally conceived among moral philosophers, is a product of Judeo-Christian tradition. But his aim is to work out a rational ethics, independent of religion conceptually and in its grounding. While noting several alternative paths one could take, he defines morality in the following way: (1) It is an action-guide (which may overlap with a nonmoral one), (2) containing a value system (not necessarily overriding or ultimate and paramount), which system (3) in its essence makes judgments about how to respect humanity (as Kant said), whether in one's own person or in that of another, as an end and not just as a means (and thus is essentially social) and (4) in its enactment rests on considerations or reasons concerning the effects of actions on the lives of persons and/or sentient beings, including some animals for him, as such (including others than those immediately affected—together, what he calls "the moral point of view"). (6) Accordingly, one's moral judgments should all be as rationally defensible as possible from the moral point of view, (7) done sincerely and thereby (8) probably regarding morality as "taking precedence over all other considerations whenever it conflicts with them." Further, (9) its end includes achieving goodness or rightness (he chooses a combination of the two) in the light of principles one has adopted as a set of standards in taking the moral point of view (thus, though social, conceivably wholly at variance with the prevailing morality of one's society or social subgroup, and to some extent even desirably personal in form). In Frankena's view a morality should be used (10) both to regulate conduct and for educational purposes, and therein (11) to distinguish between what it is to be moral as opposed to immoral (but so that a person is given major credit for sincerely trying to be good or right and with room left open for ambivalence between what satisfies one's own standards versus others' standards). Only then does he lay out the general features of his own personal morality, which he takes, tentatively, to be the satisfactory one.

In each of the points in this sparse summary of Frankena's views one or more issues important in recent discussions about morality are indicated. They also touch upon all the problem areas now to be mentioned.

Is and Ought

Many of the central problems discussed in metaethics during the twentieth century have arisen from attempts to understand relations between "is-statements" and "ought-statements," between the descriptive (empirical) and the normative. Many have defined "value" in such a way—perhaps misleadingly—as to attach a fact-value distinction to the same split. D. H. Monro (1967) presents an account of typical features in the discussion over naturalist attempts to bridge the gap by reducing all ought-statements or moral judgments, except perhaps one regarding the ultimate end to be achieved (such as pleasure for hedonists), to empirical statements about means of achieving it. Monro himself argues for a subjectivist and a naturalist position. A collection of essays on "the is-ought problem" edited by W. H. Hudson (1969) includes six essays on David Hume's contention that it is logically impossible to deduce an "ought" from an "is," eleven essays on attempts either to reduce "ought" to "is" or to derive "ought" from "is," three influential essays by neonaturalists G. E. M. Anscombe and Philippa Foot, and two critiques of their arguments by D. Z. Phillips and H. O. Mounce, who argue to the contrary that there are not wants which all people have and that often wants are derived from moral beliefs, and by the noncognitive-prescriptivist R. M. Hare.

An important historical twist to the debate has come from Stuart Hampshire (1977), who contrasts two moral philosophies that chiefly diverge over their opposing view of the relation between moral theory and ordinary, established moral opinions and relates them to contemporary interests. Aristotle says the theory must be in accord with the opinions, Spinoza that moral theory requires a "moral conversion" away from ordinary opinions.

Objectivity and Subjectivity

Another set of problems has to do with what Thomas Nagel (1979) has called "the place of subjectivity in an objective world," which has been at the center of his philosophical interests. His essays are mostly, but not exclusively, on moral subjects, and he strives both to show some limits of objectivism and to make room for subjective insight and expression. The objectivist holds either that good can be predicated of some objects or activities independently of their arousing subjective states or that some things are the case whether people recognize them or not, or both. Aquinas and Kant are objectivists in both senses, as are most naturalists (quite differently in Bentham, Dewey, and idealist Brand Blanshard, 1961), some intuitionists (H. A. Prichard, W. D. Ross), and ideal observer theorists (Adam Smith; R. B. Brandt, 1959).

Another way of approaching the same issues is to parallel attempts in epistemology to answer skepticism, only this time with respect to moral knowledge. This is nicely represented in a sustained argument by Renford Bambrough (1979), which focuses on relations between emotion and understanding. He attempts to offer "a direct proof" of the objectivity of morals and with it a refutation of subjectivism.

An allied defense of reason is given by Stanley Rosen (1969) over against the nihilistic—"everything is permitted" (Friedrich Nietzsche)—consequences of various detachments of "reasonable" from the moral "good." In Rosen's view this split and the nihilism that flows from it were defined by Nietzsche, elaborated by Martin Heidegger, expressed by Ludwig Wittgenstein, ordinary language philosophy and emotivism but prepared for even earlier by modern rationalism and historicism. Rosen writes in the spirit of vigilance against nihilism as a perennial danger.

One way an emotivist can consistently retain an element of objectivity is to refer it to the requirements of a moral community, even of an imagined and ideal one, but without reducing the importance of personal moral autonomy. This is what Henry David Aiken (1962) has done. Others have retained order, if not strict objectivity, (1) by insisting on criteria of reasonableness or of good moral thinking, or by moving away from the usual emotivist base altogether either (2) to affirm that ought-statements are imperatives or (3) to make fulfillment of criteria like prescriptivity and universalizability essential to morality, each of these moves made while maintaining a noncognitivist perspective. Hare has done all three.

Relativism

Is morality culturally relative? Since E. A. Westermarck's 1932 extended defense of relativism, not cited here, there have been only occasional efforts to look at this problem with some care. John Dewey's naturalist approach (1960) assumed relativism but also stood for developing agreement, ultimately through democratic and allied educational procedures. A study by Benjamin Llamzon (1978) helpfully contrasts Dewey's relativism with ethical absolutism as represented by Kant. Only two major attempts have been made by philosophers to study morality anthropologically: R. B. Brandt's 1954 study of the Hopi Indians and John Ladd's 1957 study of the Navahos, neither cited here. Ladd's study led him to adopt an emotivist position. May and Abraham Edel have also used cultural anthropology prominently, among other scientific bases used in support of a naturalist position. A small collection of essays on ethical relativism by philosophers and anthropologists, edited by John Ladd (1973), left a need for more detailed analysis only recently fulfilled in a collection of eleven essays from the 1970s on both moral and cognitive relativism, edited by Michael Krausz and Jack Meiland (1982). Also important are articles by Gilbert Harman in Goldman (1978) and in French (1980) and by Frankena and David Cooper in French (1980).

Both relativism and subjectivism are critically examined by Roger Trigg (1973), who emphasizes the rationality of commitment.

Egoism and Altruism

Does the moral point of view exclude egoism? That is, is it essentially altruistic? If the latter, how are moral obligations to oneself to be included, if at all, or are self-regarding actions to be thought of as solely or chiefly prudential? In philosophical ethics these questions did not become a serious area of debate until the seventeenth century, with Thomas Hobbes. Altruistic virtues did not occur among those held high by Plato and Aristotle. In medieval views no distinction was made between what I would owe to myself and to others, since all good was generally held to be formed by divine love and directed by divine command.

Is altruism merely a disguise for self-seeking (Hobbes), at base identical with it (Earl of Shaftesbury), compatible with it (Bishop Joseph Butler), or to our long-term self-interest (William Paley), or independent though necessary and coexistent (David Hume)? These positions are all held today, but the strict altruistic position rejects each one. For example, Kurt Baier (1958) views moralities as means of social control and as special forms of practical reasoning directed to that end. He holds that even the enlightened egoist, who observes social rules unless he or she has good evidence to suppose that personal benefit will outweigh doing so, does not hold the moral point of view. Arguments against volitional skepticism by Thomas Nagel (1970) lead him to accept altruism as a basic condition of practical reasoning. That is, altruism does not depend on taste, sentiment, or arbitrary choice but on our reasons for action being subject to "the formal condition of objectivity, which depends in turn on our ability to view ourselves from both the personal and impersonal standpoints, and to engage in reasoning to practical conclusions from both of those standpoints." Nicholas Rescher (1975), likewise, acknowledges a prominent but not predominant or decisive role of "vicarious affects" as motivators in actual practice but accords them a key role in the measure of moral and social theories. His own theory counters a view widely held among utilitarians and other theorists, in that he regards altruism as essential to morality and not ultimately reducible to self-interest. David Lyons's critical examination (1965) of utilitarianism is also important in this regard. A core element in altruism as it is viewed by most philosophers is that of respect for persons. This notion is reviewed both analytically and to some extent historically by R. S. Downie and Elizabeth Telfer (1970), who argue that it permits a naturalistic or nonnaturalistic but not a prescriptivist metaethics.

These four works pretty well cover the range of recent treatments of the egoism-altruism issues among those who do not already assume egoism. Some would take a mediate but still nonegoistic position of the following kind: that obligations to oneself may be moral ones insofar as one treats oneself equally as a member of the moral community (however that may be defined) and does not accord oneself privilege in that respect.

The Recipients of Moral Action

To whom, or what, should moral obligation extend? Stephen Clark (1977) critically examines arguments on attribution of moral status to animals. He builds an Aristotelian-Christian oriented case for gardening and guarding the natural world and thereby according some animals some rights but denying them others that humans would have. A normative work by Peter Singer (1979), which issues from a utilitarian perspective but makes room for other views, places taking the life of animals in the midst of issues about abortion, euthanasia, and aid to the poor. A collection edited by R. I. Sikora and Brian Barry (1978) considers what intrinsic value should be placed, if any, on the preservation of humankind and our obligations to future generations. As presented, these are relatively new features in discussions of the scope of morality. The three books well represent the turn to a more ecological and ecumenical framework that a few moral philosophers were taking from the late 1960s on. (By "ecumenical" I mean a concern for the whole inhabited world, from the Greek *oikumene,* and a concern to achieve rational agreement on policy from many points of view, derivative from the contemporary ecumenical movement among Christian churches. It is not a term of trade in ethics; but some now bear the concern it connotes and I recommend it.)

Human Rights

Ronald Dworkin (*Taking Rights Seriously,* 1977, cited on p. 448) has tentatively suggested a classification of political theories into goal-based (teleological), rule-based (deontological and, I suppose, including rule-utilitarianism), and right-based theories. Picking up that suggestion, J. L. Mackie (in French et al., 1980) has recently proposed that a moral theory could be right-based, so that the fundamental right, from which other rights, goals, or duties are logically derived, would be "the right of persons progressively to choose how they shall live." (By "progressively" he means not once-for-all or conclusively but in successive and changing choices.) More: he proposes that "there cannot be an acceptable moral theory that is not right-based." A. I. Melden (1978) seems to be making a similar proposal. He speaks of a basic, inalienable right of persons "to pursue their interests." He regards this one basic right and other derivative but absolute human rights to be matters of "moral dignity," such that persons are able to demand, and all others are obligated to give them, treatment as equal members of the community of human beings. These proposals both differ from some other moral theories in that (1) they assign absolute, not prima facie, status to the basic and derived human rights, (2) they conceive of these rights as basic, not as derivative from goals or duties, and (3) they make according these rights essential to the moral point of view, to such an extent that all other rights, goals, rules, or duties would seem to have only a derived and subsidiary status. Without using the notion of rights, Frankena and others appear to have an understanding of what is basic in the moral point of view that assumes a similar principle. So far a right-based theory has not been fully worked out, however, though earlier works like that of A. J. M. Milne on *Freedom and Rights* (1968) display an inclination toward the task. Alan Gewirth's (1978) recent theory, noted in an earlier section, largely centers in a conception of rights; and some (such as Alan Donagan, 1977) have argued that John Rawls's moral theory is at base a theory of human rights.

Moral Psychology

Sidgwick once wrote: "All important ethical notions are also psychological, except perhaps the fundamental antitheses of 'good' and 'bad,' 'right' and 'wrong,' with which psychology, as it treats of what is and not of what ought to be, is not directly concerned." This statement helped set a widely accepted tradition that gives scientific psychology and philosophy of mind entrée into a considerable range of ethical inquiries. Psychology, which like ethics deals with human beings individually, along with politics (and jurisprudence), which do not, and theology, which relies on revelation, he termed "cognate subjects." In ethical analysis a great deal of piecemeal work of a psychological nature has been done over the past century. Each of the metaethical approaches has a somewhat different interest in these materials. For example, there are writings on (1) pleasure and pains, desiring, wanting, intending; (2) moral agency, motivation, interest, deciding, choosing, free will, freedom and compulsion, ability to act, and exercise of that ability; (3) other-regarding feelings like sympathy and concern; (4) self-knowledge, self-deceit, and self-control; (5) conscience, sense of duty or suitability, and guilt. Rarely, however, has moral psychology been performed or applied in a systematic fashion. Maurice Mandelbaum's *The Phenomenology of Moral Experience* (1955), which purports to present a nonnormative, structural account, is still the most comprehensive effort. Mandelbaum is a phenomenologist, influenced by Scheler and by intuitionist Dietrich von Hildebrand. Lawrence Blum's study (1980) of "altruistic emotions" such as sympathy, compassion, and human concern is also unusual, as are sections of Richard Brandt's 1979 work in which he ransacks "empirical" (mostly behaviorist) psychology to search for what a "rational" person might want, take pleasure in, and choose to do. For the most part, psychoanalytic theory and developmental psychology have been ignored in ethics; analytic philosophers who have done a fair amount of moral psychology, especially since Wittgenstein, generally do not evidence a close reading of psychology in any of its forms.

Among Sidgwick's three cognate subjects, there has been somewhat more interaction with politics and jurisprudence, very little either way with theology.

Virtues, Vices, and Moral Character

Normative inquiry among Greek and Roman moral theorists dealt heavily with moral character, particularly with the fostering of certain moral excellences or virtues. This strong interest continued into modern times. It has been a weak interest in contemporary analytic philosophy, as in the writings of Hume, Kant, Mill, Moore, Ross, and Prichard before them, and not a very strong one among other nontheological moral theorists. Between World War II and recent years two notable exceptions have been Frankena's writings in philosophy of education and some chapters in Henrik von Wright's *The Varieties of Goodness* (1963, not cited here). Peter Geach's recent account (1977) of the four classic "cardinal" virtues (wisdom or prudence, justice, temperance, and courage) and of the three classic "theological" virtues (faith, hope, and love or charity) combines a knowledge both of that long tradition and of contemporary interests in moral philosophy. A set of ten *Monist* essays by Frankena and others (1970) well represents contemporary interests in the subject, including H. A. Prichard's question, in a famous 1912 article, about whether a duty is not simply something to be followed and his view that any attempt to provide further justification rests on the "mistake" of thinking this is needed. More specific interests in moral development and moral education, stirred up especially by the work of cognitive developmental psychologist Lawrence Kohlberg during the 1970s, have not yet taken monograph form.

Recently two naturalistic accounts of virtues and vices have been set forth. James Wallace (1978) has sought to provide a naturalistic basis for the value placed on certain character traits within human communities that enable them to function well. He singles out conscientiousness, benevolence, courage, and restraint (the latter two especially represent the individual's abilities to mold feelings and desires into plans that do not produce undue discord within the community or among themselves and to carry them out). Philippa Foot's attempts to renew naturalism, which a great many moral philosophers had thought was defunct, and to form alternatives to contemporary efforts to derive morality from reason, have attracted much controversy since the late 1950s. A collection of her essays (1978) is headed by a new one on "Virtues and Vices." In my view, this topic area is not likely to regain its once-honored spot in moral philosophy until there is greater interest in what psychological studies might reveal about the development of moral capacities generally. This interest is displayed somewhat in Alasdair MacIntyre's *After Virtue* (1981), most of which is an examination of classic theories of virtue and their practical consequences.

Practical Reasoning and Responsibility

Because of the primary interest in justification of moral judgments in contemporary analytic ethics, two aspects of the moral process itself have received increasing attention: the nature of practical reasoning and related issues regarding moral responsibility. As an approach to normative philosophy, David A. J. Richards (1971), for example, has presented a systematic account and theory of the concept "reasons for action," one close to the work of John Rawls, his teacher. The account includes principles used in making rational, moral choices, whether for action or for advising and the like, and examines the case of rationality and that of morality in parallel fashion. Joel Feinberg (1970) represents a growing interaction among philosophy of mind, philosophy of law, and ethics with respect to the concept "responsibility." The theory of responsibility, as he develops it, attempts to distinguish three types of action that may be seen from a moral point of view—those that are obligatory, permissible, and wrong—and to give an account of cases wherein an agent may or may not be held responsible for his or her action or be deserving of others' action. The issue of free will versus determinism is a separate one, which he has not taken up; I have assigned it here to philosophy of action.

Earlier authors not cited here, such as Stephen Toulmin (1950), Geoffrey Russell Grice (1967) and linguistic philosopher David P. Gauthier (1963) had examined especially the place of reasoning in moral discourse (sometimes versus prudential discourse): particularly its use in establishing grounds of rights, obligations, and judgments as to what is good or better and its use in coming to decisions. In trying to stay close to common sense usage, Toulmin had provided a critique of objectivist, subjectivist, and imperativist approaches to ethics and a rough alternative that retains features emphasized in each. Toulmin has continued this interest in a work on logic (*An Introduction to Reasoning*, 1979, cited on p. 338). Baier (1958) and Aiken (1962), cited above, took up similar tasks, in the effort to show how practical reasoning is used to justify moral judgments on a cognitive, not only on an emotive, basis. Drawing in part from Michael Polanyi, J. M. Brennan (1977) presents a cognitivist approach (but rejecting basic aspects of both naturalism and nonnaturalism as well as noncognitivism), which takes moral concepts to be "open-textured"; morally neutral facts, he contends, do not enter into moral discourse. These are all typical efforts.

By the mid-1970s practical reasoning was established as a major subject, mainly referred to morality. A logical, epistemological, and metaphysical account of practical thinking in general is given, for example, by Stephen Körner (1976, following one on "conceptual thinking" in 1959, cited on p. 337), a "primarily phenomenological" (versus metaphysical) investigation by another analytic philosopher, Hector-Neri Casteñada (1974). Both refer especially to morality. Out of a background that conjoins law and morals, Joseph Raz has done particularly detailed inquiry into the nature and functions of practical reasoning. Through him and a few others, this has become a key element in philosophy of law over the past two decades. Raz (1978) has edited a collection of essays on the subject, wherein the reference of "practical" covers a wider spectrum, not so exclusively focused on morality.

Practical Uses: Normative Ethics

The preoccupation with metaethics in twentieth-century moral theory has been roundly criticized from several quarters, but without a very impressive effort to remedy the situation. Normative writings that have not taken benefit from metaethics often seem unclear, ill-ordered, and poorly argued. Exceptions are available in several recent collections of essays on personal and social issues, not cited here, such as those edited by Richard T. De George (1966), Harry K. Girvetz (1974), Tom L. Beauchamp (1974), James Rachels (1975), and by Thomas A. Mappes and Jane S. Zembaty (1977). The best, most comprehensive of the lot, edited by John Arthur (1981), is cited here, as are Jonathan Glover's systematic account (1977) of death-related issues and L. W. Sumner's on abortion (1981). Environmental issues are treated in a collection of original essays edited by K. E. Goodpaster and K. M. Sayre (1979) and in John Passmore's book on ecologically sensitive responsibility (*Man's Responsibility for Nature*, 1974, cited on p. 310). Other issues about treatment of persons, animals, and future generations have been discussed in works cited in an earlier section of this chapter.

FUTURE PROSPECTS

Ethics has been a steadily developing, broadening area over the past one hundred years and will no doubt continue to be so in virtually every part and in its interactions with other areas of philosophy. In addition to those interactions, the greatest changes over the next twenty years will come through greater attention to normative social issues and to developmental psychology.

Abelson, Raziel, and Kai Nielsen. "History of Ethics." In *Encyclopedia of Philosophy*, vol. 3, pp. 87–113. Ed. by Paul Edwards. New York: Macmillan; London: Collier Macmillan, 1967.

Aiken, Henry David. *Reason and Conduct: New Bearings in Moral Philosophy*. New York: Knopf, 1962.

Arthur, John, ed. *Morality and Moral Controversies*. Englewood Cliffs, N.J.: Prentice-Hall, 1981.

Baier, Kurt. *The Moral Point of View: A Rational Basis of Ethics*. Ithaca, N.Y.: Cornell Univ. Pr., 1958. Repr., abridged ed., 1965.

Bambrough, Renford. *Moral Skepticism and Moral Knowledge*. Atlantic Highlands, N.J.: Humanities Pr., 1979.

Becker, Lawrence C. *On Justifying Moral Judgements*. New York: Humanities Pr.; London: Routledge & Paul, 1973.

Blanshard, Brand. *Reason and Goodness*. New York: Macmillan; London: Allen & Unwin, 1961.

Blum, Lawrence A. *Friendship, Altruism, and Morality*. London and Boston: Routledge & Paul, 1980.

Bourke, Vernon J. *History of Ethics*. Garden City, N.Y.: Doubleday, 1968.

Brandt, Richard B. *Ethical Theory: The Problems of Normative and Critical Ethics*. Englewood Cliffs, N.J.: Prentice-Hall, 1959.

———. *A Theory of the Good and the Right*. Oxford and New York: Oxford Univ. Pr., 1979.

———. *Value and Obligation: Systematic Readings in Ethics*. New York: Harcourt, Brace, 1961.

Brennan, John M. *The Open-Texture of Moral Concepts*. New York: Barnes & Noble; London: Macmillan, 1977.

Casteñada, Hector-Neri. *The Structure of Morality*. Springfield, Ill.: C. C. Thomas, 1974.

———, and George Nakhnikian, eds. *Morality and the Language of Conduct*. Detroit, Mich.: Wayne State Univ. Pr., 1963.

Clark, Stephen R. L. *The Moral Status of Animals*. Oxford: Clarendon Pr., 1977.

Dewey, John. *Theory of the Moral Life*. Ed. by Arnold Isenberg. New York: Holt, Rinehart & Winston, 1960.

Donagan, Alan. *The Theory of Morality*. Chicago: Univ. of Chicago Pr., 1977.

Downie, Robert S., and Elizabeth Telfer. *Respect for Persons*. New York: Schocken, 1970.

Edel, Abraham. *Ethical Judgment: The Use of Science in Ethics*. Glencoe, Ill.: Free Pr., 1955.

———. *Method in Ethical Theory*. Indianapolis, Ind.: Bobbs-Merrill; London: Routledge & Paul, 1963.

Emmet, Dorothy. *The Moral Prism*. New York: St. Martin's Pr., 1979; London: Macmillan, 1978.

Feinberg, Joel. *Doing and Deserving: Essays in the Theory of Responsibility*. Princeton, N.J.: Princeton Univ. Pr., 1970.

Feldman, Fred. *Introductory Ethics*. Englewood Cliffs, N.J.: Prentice-Hall, 1978.

Foot, Philippa. *Virtues and Vices and Other Essays in Moral Philosophy*. Berkeley: Univ. of California Pr.; Oxford: Blackwell, 1978.

Forrester, Mary Gore. *Moral Language*. Madison and London: Univ. of Wisconsin Pr., 1982.

Frankena, William K. "Ethical Theory." In *Philosophy*, pp. 345–464. Ed. by Roderick M. Chisholm et al. Englewood Cliffs, N.J.: Prentice-Hall, 1964.

———. *Ethics*. 2nd ed. Englewood Cliffs, N.J.: Prentice-Hall, 1972. (1st ed., 1963.)

———. *Thinking about Morality*. Ann Arbor: Univ. of Michigan Pr., 1980. (Originally in *Monist* 63, no. 1:1–68 (Jan. 1980), followed by commentaries by Alan Gewirth, G. J. Warnock, and Harald Ofstad, and by a reply by Frankena, 69–128. See Goodpaster for his collected essays.)

———, et al. "Virtue and Moral Goodness." *Monist* 54, no. 1:1–153 (Jan. 1970).

———, and John T. Granrose, eds. *Introductory Readings in Ethics.* Englewood Cliffs, N.J.: Prentice-Hall, 1974.

French, Peter A. *The Scope of Morality.* Minneapolis: Univ. of Minnesota Pr., 1979.

———, Theodore E. Uehling, Jr., and Howard K. Wettstein, eds. *Midwest Studies in Philosophy.* Vol. 3, *Studies in Ethical Theory.* Minneapolis: Univ. of Minnesota Pr., 1980.

Geach, Peter T. *The Virtues.* Cambridge and New York: Cambridge Univ. Pr., 1977.

Gewirth, Alan. *Reason and Morality.* Chicago and London: Univ. of Chicago Pr., 1978.

Glover, Jonathan. *Causing Death and Saving Lives.* New York and Harmondsworth, Middlesex: Penguin, 1977.

Goldman, Alvin I., and Jaegwon Kim, eds. *Values and Morals: Essays in Honor of William Frankena, Charles Stevenson, and Richard Brandt.* Dordrecht and Boston: Reidel, 1978.

Goodpaster, K. E., ed. *Perspectives on Morality: Essays by William K. Frankena.* Notre Dame, Ind. and London: Univ. of Notre Dame Pr., 1976.

———, and K. M. Sayre, eds. *Ethics and the Problems of the 21st Century.* Notre Dame, Ind. and London: Univ. of Notre Dame Pr., 1979.

Gosling, Justin C. B. *Pleasure and Desire: The Case for Hedonism Reviewed.* Oxford: Clarendon Pr., 1969.

Gustafson, James M. *Protestant and Roman Catholic Ethics: Prospects for Rapprochement.* Chicago and London: Univ. of Chicago Pr., 1978.

Hampshire, Stuart. *Two Theories of Morality.* Oxford and New York: Oxford Univ. Pr., 1977.

Hare, R. M. *Freedom and Reason.* Oxford and New York: Oxford Univ. Pr., 1963.

———. *The Language of Morals.* Oxford and New York: Oxford Univ. Pr., 1952.

———. *Moral Thinking: Its Levels, Method and Point.* New York: Oxford Univ. Pr.; Oxford: Clarendon Pr., 1981.

Harman, Gilbert. *The Nature of Morality: An Introduction to Ethics.* Oxford and New York: Oxford Univ. Pr., 1977.

Haslett, D. W. *Moral Rightness.* The Hague: Nijhoff, 1974.

Hospers, John. *Human Conduct: An Introduction to the Problems of Ethics.* New York: Harcourt, Brace, 1961.

Hudson, William D. *A Century of Moral Philosophy.* New York: St. Martin's Pr.; London: Macmillan, 1980.

———. *Modern Moral Philosophy.* London: Macmillan, 1970.

———, ed. *The Is-Ought Question: A Collection of Papers on the Central Problem in Moral Philosophy.* London: Macmillan, 1969.

———, ed. *New Studies in Ethics.* 2v. New York and London: Macmillan, 1974. (Twelve studies on classical and modern theories, originally published as paperbacks, 1967–73.)

Kockelmans, Joseph J., ed. *Contemporary European Ethics: Selected Readings.* Garden City, N.Y.: Doubleday Anchor, 1972.

Körner, Stephan. *Experience and Conduct: A Philosophical Inquiry into Practical Thinking.* Cambridge and New York: Cambridge Univ. Pr., 1976.

Krausz, Michael, and Jack W. Meiland, eds. *Relativism: Cognitive and Moral.* Notre Dame, Ind. and London: Univ. of Notre Dame Pr., 1982.

Ladd, John, ed. *Ethical Relativism.* Belmont, Calif.: Wadsworth, 1973.

Llamzon, Benjamin S. *Reason, Experience and the Moral Life: Ethical Absolutism and Relativism in Kant and Dewey.* Washington, D.C.: Univ. Pr. of America, 1978.

Lyons, David. *Forms and Limits of Utilitarianism.* New York: Oxford Univ. Pr.; Oxford: Clarendon Pr., 1965.

MacIntyre, Alasdair. *After Virtue: A Study in Moral Theory.* Notre Dame, Ind.: Univ. of Notre Dame Pr.; London: Duckworth, 1981.

———. *A Short History of Ethics.* New York and London: Macmillan, 1966.

Mackie, John L. *Ethics: Inventing Right and Wrong.* New York and Harmondsworth, Middlesex: Penguin, 1977.

Mandelbaum, Maurice. *The Phenomenology of Moral Experience.* Glencoe, Ill.: Free Pr., 1955.

Melden, A. I. *Rights and Persons.* Berkeley: Univ. of California. Pr., 1978.

Milne, Alan J. M. *Freedom and Rights.* New York: Humanities Pr.; London: Allen & Unwin, 1968.

Mitchell, Basil. *Morality: Religious and Secular: The Dilemma of the Traditional Conscience.* New York: Oxford Univ. Pr.; Oxford: Clarendon Pr., 1980.

Monro, David H. *Empiricism and Ethics.* Cambridge and New York: Cambridge Univ. Pr., 1967.

Moore, George E. *Ethics.* New York: Holt; London: Oxford Univ. Pr., 1912.

———. *Principia Ethica.* Cambridge: Cambridge Univ. Pr., 1903.

Murdoch, Iris. *The Sovereignty of Good.* New York: Schocken, 1971; London: Routledge & Paul, 1970.

Nagel, Thomas. *Mortal Questions.* Cambridge and New York: Cambridge Univ. Pr., 1979.

———. *The Possibility of Altruism.* Oxford: Clarendon Pr., 1970. Repr.: Princeton, N.J.: Princeton Univ. Pr., 1978.

Nowell-Smith, Patrick H. *Ethics.* New York and Harmondsworth, Middlesex: Penguin, 1954.

Raz, Joseph, ed. *Practical Reasoning.* Oxford and New York: Oxford Univ. Pr., 1978.

Rescher, Nicholas. *Unselfishness: The Role of the Vicarious Affects in Moral Philosophy and Social Theory.* Pittsburgh, Pa.: Univ. of Pittsburgh Pr., 1975.

Richards, David A. J. *A Theory of Reasons for Action.* Oxford: Clarendon Pr., 1971.

Rosen, Stanley. *Nihilism: A Philosophical Essay.* New Haven, Conn. and London: Yale Univ. Pr., 1969.

Scheler, Max. *Formalism in Ethics and Non-Formal Ethics of Values: A

New Attempt toward the Foundation of an Ethical Personalism. 5th rev. ed. Tr. by Manfred S. Frings and Roger L. Funk. Evanston, Ill.: Northwestern Univ. Pr., 1973. (1st German ed., 1916.)

Schneewind, Jerome B. *Sidgwick's Ethics and Victorian Moral Philosophy.* Oxford: Clarendon Pr., 1977.

——, ed. "Sidgwick and Moral Philosophy." *Monist* 58, no. 3:349–517 (July 1974).

Sidgwick, Henry. *Outlines of the History of Ethics for English Readers.* 6th ed. enl. New York: St. Martin's Pr.; London: Macmillan, 1967. (6th ed., 1931; 1st ed., 1886.) (Ch. 5 by Alban G. Widgery.)

Sikoria, R. I., and Brian Barry, eds. *Obligations to Future Generations.* Philadelphia, Pa.: Temple Univ. Pr., 1978.

Singer, Peter. *Practical Ethics.* Cambridge and New York: Cambridge Univ. Pr., 1979.

Stevenson, Charles L. *Ethics and Language.* New Haven, Conn.: Yale Univ. Pr., 1944. (Reprinted in numerous editions.)

——. *Facts and Values: Studies in Ethical Analysis.* New Haven, Conn. and London: Yale Univ. Pr., 1963.

Sumner, L. W. *Abortion and Moral Theory.* Princeton, N.J.: Princeton Univ. Pr., 1981.

Trigg, Roger. *Reason and Commitment.* Cambridge and New York: Cambridge Univ. Pr., 1973.

Urmson, James O. *The Emotive Theory of Ethics.* Oxford and New York: Oxford Univ. Pr., 1968.

Wallace, James D. *Virtues and Vices.* Ithaca, N.Y. and London: Cornell Univ. Pr., 1978.

Warnock, Geoffrey J. *The Object of Morality.* London: Methuen, 1971.

Warnock, Mary. *Ethics since 1900.* 3rd ed. Oxford and New York: Oxford Univ. Pr., 1978. (1st ed., 1960.)

Wertheimer, Roger. *The Significance of Sense: Meaning, Modality, and Morality.* Ithaca, N.Y. and London: Cornell Univ. Pr., 1972.

23

Philosophy
of Science

Introduction: Scientific Change and Revolution

Since the late nineteenth century, the preponderance of investment in philosophy of science has gone to several standard problems. Many of them are apparently intractable, at least given the basic epistemological, logical, and metaphysical assumptions usually held. Over the past twenty years the glamour stocks have been a rather different set of issues, concerning scientific change and revolution. Debate over these issues has gradually changed the conditions of thought to such a degree that nearly all other issues in this area of philosophy may, perhaps must, now be considered in their light.

Twenty years ago, Herbert Feigl (1964) could plausibly make the claim that although individual approaches and procedures differ greatly "there is perhaps a larger measure of agreement in this field than in any other area of philosophy." This is no longer the case, if it ever was. With the exception of G. E. Moore, all the more notable British philosophers of the early twentieth century—Russell, Whitehead, Collingwood, Popper, and Wittgenstein (in two phases)—contributed eminently to philosophy of science. Among them only Russell, Popper, and the early Wittgenstein comport with Feigl's chiefly logical-empirical type of consensus. Nor in many respects do the great American pragmatists fit it, or the neo-Kantian idealist Ernst Cassirer, the phenomenologists, the hermeneutical thinkers, or their nearer successors also active in philosophy of science. Two qualifications to this general distinction should be made: (1) the Americans and Europeans just mentioned (except Cassirer) were chiefly interested in psychology or the social sciences, whereas most others in the

410

area dealt largely with the natural sciences; (2) Feigl and a few others would have included some interests they would call "pragmatic." Feigl's own focus on issues of reliability and intersubjective testability of knowledge (public, beyond the individual), and his formalist manner of addressing these issues, have also come under much critical scrutiny since 1964.

The shift in emphasis, portrayed in some detail by Harold Brown (1977), has come about especially through historical study and analysis of actual scientific practice—spurred by early efforts like Michael Polanyi's *Personal Knowledge* (1958, cited on p. 326), Norwood Hanson's *Patterns of Discovery* (1958), Stephen Toulmin's *Foresight and Understanding* (1961, not cited here), Thomas Kuhn's *The Structure of Scientific Revolutions* (1962), and essays by Paul Feyerabend from that same period.

As it turns out, not deliberately at first, these historically minded philosophers carried into their investigations assumptions of a hermeneutical sort; and many of these assumptions as applied to philosophy of science were presaged by R. G. Collingwood. The strict distinction between contexts of discovery and contexts of justification or validation made by Hans Reichenbach (1951) and generally presupposed by logical-empirical thinkers was now broken down; thereby contributions to philosophical inquiry about science from history, psychology, and the social sciences became not only desirable but necessary in the view of many philosophers. Philosophical analysis itself was not to be restricted either to the context of justification or to supposedly given structures of science but was to center on its changing, sometimes revolutionary process.

Since *The Structure of Scientific Revolutions* (1962) appeared, Thomas Kuhn has been in the eye of the storm. In retrospect, this position may be seen to derive as much from his mediate posture with respect to alternatives as much as from his bold proposals. A spectrum of key figures representing the drift away from logical positivism in philosophy of science to an emphasis on the shaping forces of historical context would move from Carnap and Hempel, to Popper and Lakatos, to Kuhn, to Collingwood and Toulmin, to Feyerabend, who contends that scientific behavior is in a sense "anarchical." Kuhn has used historical case studies to indicate that scientific knowledge is intrinsically a group product and to register a distinction between the relatively fixed and serene structures or "paradigms" in "normal" science and the unpredictable, unruly habits of science in its "revolutionary" mode, wherein rival theories have "in-

commensurable" characteristics and communication among participants is at best partial. In more recent years he has been led, chiefly
by Quine's arguments, to examine the different languages that proponents of different theories speak, "languages expressing different
cognitive commitments, suitable for different worlds."

Because he referred to long periods of normality, Kuhn has been
frequently misunderstood to have been referring only to episodes on
the grand scale. Actually, the more interesting part of his account is
its claim that little revolutions are going on all the time, as a regular
feature of science. This is what requires a conceptual change in the
performance of both history and philosophy of science. We do not
need to wait for the Newtons and Einsteins to see revolution going
on. In a collection of his essays (1977) Kuhn acknowledges that he
used "pardigm" unclearly and in several ways in his now classic
book. He distinguishes two senses that he wishes to employ. First,
"paradigm" designates all the shared commitments of a scientific
community (its "disciplinary matrix"), especially including formal,
symbolic generalizations, models, and certain concrete problem solutions regarded as exemplary (or paradigmatic). These are highly interactive and complex. The last item provides the second meaning of
"paradigm," to which he has drawn special attention.

Critics of both Kuhn and Feyerabend have often misunderstood
them in one particularly striking way, contending that for them
choices between rival theories or paradigms must be irrational. Not
at all. But both have tried to show that the functioning of rationality
in science is always limited and that choices may well significantly
include nonrational factors (this does not make them necessarily
counter-rational or merely a matter of feeling). In keeping with time-
honored skeptical tradition, Feyerabend has been particularly effective in raising doubts about the presumed eternity or efficacy of
prevailing conceptions of rationality and in opposing them from a
different value standpoint from what prevails now. His startling
book *Against Method* (1975) was written in this spirit. His *Science in
a Free Society* (1978) in effect reviews much of the debate over the
new philosophy of science, already joined in the first book, and
advances it further. This time, the overriding aim is to argue for the
position that the adherents of rationality, as one kind of social tradition among many, should have no more status in affecting public
policy than those of other traditions. He has claimed from the beginning that in some periods rationalism in some form may be good
medicine; in this period, this age of "professionalized incompetence,"

such "anarchy," he believes, is the medicine we need. Thus, in quite radical but reasoned fashion, Feyerabend conjoins history and philosophy, science and politics.

Among the interpretations of this paradigm shift in philosophy of science, that of Harold Brown (1979) stops short of Feyerabend on the continuum mentioned just above. Among the opposing alternatives, that of Larry Laudan (1977) is notable for its ordered commitment to the kind of rationality Feyerabend opposes. A volume edited by Imre Lakatos and Alan Musgrave (1970) consists of an essay by Kuhn originally prepared for the Schilpp volume on Popper (cited on p. 203), discussions of it by Popper, Lakatos, Kuhn, Toulmin, Feyerabend, J. W. N. Watkins, L. Pearce Williams, and Margaret Masterman, and replies by Kuhn. Gary Gutting (1980) has edited a fine collection of fourteen previously published essays (1967–79) on Kuhn's philosophy, with special emphasis on applications in the social sciences and in history of science. A collection of new essays edited by Karin Knorr et al. (1975) looks at broader issues of scientific development "after the Kuhnian revolution," with special reference to determinants and controls of social science development.

Collections

For two decades three series of collections have dominated the field: *Boston Studies in the Philosophy of Science* (1963–), in sixty-six volumes by 1981; *Minnesota Studies in the Philosophy of Science* (1956–), in nine volumes by 1978; and the *University of Pittsburgh Series in the Philosophy of Science* (1962–), edited by Robert Colodny, in five volumes by 1972. For general purposes, and to trace discussion on major issues over the past twenty years, the following volumes are especially notable among them: Herbert Feigl and Grover Maxwell, eds. (*Minnesota Studies*, vol. 3, 1962); Michael Radner and Stephen Winokur, eds. (*Minnesota Studies*, vol. 4, 1970); Roger Buck and Robert Cohen, eds. (*Boston Studies*, vol. 8, 1971, honoring Rudolf Carnap); and R. S. Cohen et al. (*Boston Studies*, vol. 39, 1976, honoring Imre Lakatos). The University of Western Ontario also has its own series (to at least vol. 14, 1978). The Philosophy of Science Association published its own biennial proceedings in 1976 (Suppe and Asquith, 1976–77), earlier ones in *Boston Studies*. Prominent among the other collections is a 1959 proceedings from a section of the American Association for the Advancement of Science (Feigl and Maxwell, 1961); a volume honoring Herbert Feigl (Feyerabend and Maxwell, 1966); and one on natural science problems edited by Dudley Shapere (1965). Proceedings of an important 1960 international congress were edited by three early leaders in this area: Ernest Nagel, Patrick Suppes, and Alfred Tarski (1962). These follow upon other valuable collections in the 1950s and early 1960s edited by Bernard Baumrin, by Arthur Danto and Sidney Morgenbesser, by Philipp Frank, by Henry E. Kyburg, Jr., and Ernest Nagel, by Edward H. Madden, and by Philip P. Wiener (not cited here). In no other area of philosophy are collections of current work so numerous or so prominent.

Historical Developments

Since conceptions of the philosophy of science have been changing, the story of its own developments can also be expected to change. Using the older assumptions, Gerd Buchdahl's account (1969) of the origins from Descartes to Kant is a significant work. The thirteen historical studies on fifteenth- to nineteenth-century theories of scientific method by Ralph Blake et al. (1960) are also useful. Dudley Shapere's study (1974) on Galileo and I. Bernard Cohen's on Newton (1980) enter somewhat into the newer discussions about what goes on in scientific revolutions. One of the early philosophical histories in the new style, by Norwood Hanson (1958), examined the role of such notions as "observation," "facts," and "causality" in the discovery of theories in microphysics. A collection of essays from the 1960s by intellectual historian Gerald Holton (1973) is particularly noteworthy for his attention to the use of "thematic imagination" in scientific theory construction. A *Minnesota Studies* volume edited by Roger Stuewer (1970) is an apt sign of the changing times. It includes among its thirteen items an indication from Feigl of how he thinks historians and logicians could work together, an indication by Mary Hesse of some difficulties in trying to separate "internal" from "external" influences on science, a distinction by Gerd Buchdahl between "conceptual," "constitutive," and "architectonic" components in choosing hypotheses, with reference to Newton, and a scathing brief critique of contemporary philosophy of science—"a subject with a great past"—by Paul Feyerabend.

Early twentieth-century developments are particularly well represented by P. W. Bridgman (1927), the father of "operational" thinking, on the logic of modern physics; by Hans Reichenbach (1951) on the rise of "scientific philosophy"; and by Morris Cohen (1931), who more than anyone fostered the development of this field in American philosophy during the 1920s and 1930s, on the understanding of scientific method at that time. The ideas conveyed in these works have probably influenced American education more than any since. From the 1930s on, German and Vienna Circle immigrants to the United States principally modeled their formalist, axiomatic approaches to philosophy of science after mathematics. Their influence was far less pronounced in Britain, where only a minority joined R. B. Braithwaite in pursuit of similar formal interests. In the United States Otto Neurath is especially to be mentioned for his dream (from the 1920s to his death in 1954) of a multivolume encyclopedia, visual thesaurus, and other means of aiding unification of the sciences on a logical-empirical basis. Monographs prepared for the *International Encyclopedia of Unified Science* edited by Neurath, Rudolf Carnap, and Charles Morris include important works by philosophers as diverse in both method and viewpoint as John Dewey, Carl Hempel, Abraham Edel, and Thomas Kuhn. Although he never came close to getting his dream, the entrepreneurship of Neurath, along with Feigl and other European emigrés who shared his passionate advocacy of scientific philosophy, did much to advance the field.

Sharp turns away from the received view that dominated the period from the 1920s to the 1950s are chronicled by Stephen Toulmin (1977) and Frederick Suppe (1977). Suppe's massive volume includes his own 350 pages analyzing aspects of the change and essays by David Bohm, I. Bernard Cohen, Hempel, Kuhn, Hilary Putnam, Shapere, and Suppes—all leaders in the 1970s debates.

For a long time, the book of readings edited by Feigl and May Brodbeck (1953) was a major resource; it is still valuable. Carl Hempel's clear analyses of scientific methods and concepts were also highly influential (as in his 1952 monograph and in other essays collected in 1965; see Nicholas Rescher, 1969). Both are steeped in the logical-empirical tradition. In his radical critique of that tradition, Richard Rorty (e.g., *Philosophy and the Mirror of Nature*, 1979, cited on p. 7) has especially singled out Wilfrid Sellars (1968 and earlier writings)—and from a different standpoint W. V. O. Quine, also a "holist"—as one who saw justification of belief as a matter of conversation, of social practice, not of a special relation between words and objects, not as reductive or atomistic, and not as built upon anything certain. Sellars, a psychological nominalist, has based scientific rationality not on its having a firm, unchanging logical or empirical foundation but on its being a self-corrective enterprise. In a different way, the same basic point has been argued by Karl Popper.

Popper's *Logic of Scientific Discovery* (1934, tr. 1959) had an enormous influence in the 1960s and 1970s, as has his follow-up book (1963) and major debates in which he subsequently played a critical and provocative role. The most noted among his numerous, often seriously misunderstood contributions is his critique of the logical positivists' demarcation of science from metaphysics in terms of a principle of verifiability, which to them made metaphysics nonsense. Himself a professed realist, Popper considered metaphysics essential to all knowledge and science. He distinguished it from science in that science must always carry not verifiability but falsifiability within it as the primary criterion of scientific rigor and growth. (The Vienna-born Popper was never a logical positivist, and he has not thought of formal elements or of an empirical base in ways the logical empiricists have tended to do. In recent years he has nonetheless fought hard against what he took to be tendencies toward subjectivism and irrationalism in Polanyi, Kuhn, and others.) Both criteria have been deemed inadequate by critics. Among them is Hungarian-born Imre Lakatos (d. 1974), for many years a colleague of Popper at the London School of Economics. A careful critic of positivism who has nonetheless kept his roots in positivist-formalist soil, Lakatos was interested primarily in the logic of mathematical discovery (1976) and in a mathematical orientation to inquiry about science (1978, vol. 2). His most noted thesis in philosophy of science (1978, vol. 1) is that because there are so many factors in scientific change, some of them quite idiosyncratic and uncontrollable, and because single episodes or experiments are rarely decisive in themselves, the basic criterion is the formation and success of long-term "research programs." In that Lakatos has devoted much attention to the question of how these programs function and Popper to the progress of science through theoretical conjecture and refutation, both their philosophies move decisively in the direction of the new philosophy of science, though both have lodged important criticisms against it.

Numerous philosophically minded scientists have also contributed to this area over the years, Alfred Einstein (Schilpp, 1949) chief among them. Gerard Radnitzky's survey (1968) of contemporary schools of metascience devotes one volume to those in English-speaking areas; in the other he draws on hermeneutic, dialectic, psychoanalytic, critical, and other approaches to form his own philosophical anthropology as a groundplan for the study of scientific enterprises. Paul Feyerabend's *Against Method* (1975)—written in part to "tease" his friend Lakatos about nonrationalist implications in his otherwise eminently formalist writings—and his follow-up book (1978), discussed above, are strongly affirmative of science but sharply critical of "rationality" held by the generation of philosophers born before 1920. The unusually trenchant rhetorical features of his style should not blind the reader to his well-reasoned, timely arguments, which also serve as an informed commentary on the history of the field since about 1950. The collection edited by Peter Asquith and Henry Kyburg (1979) surveys some recent developments and literature in twenty-eight topical areas; it includes a 111-item dissertation bibliography (1961–77) and a list of forty-two proceedings and colloquia.

Introduction and Overviews

Hints of the newer perspectives are already present in Stephen Toulmin's 1953 introduction, though he did not begin his decade-long occupation with historical studies until 1954. Toulmin applied a Wittgensteinian analysis of "language games" to a functional taxonomy of explanatory procedures in varying types of scientific inquiry. The larger, quite clearly written, posthumous introduction of 1962 by Arthur Pap (1921–59) is still well within the logical-empirical tradition, as are the popular introduction by Morris Cohen's noted successor, Ernest Nagel (1961) and the highly reputed introduction to philosophy of natural science by Carl Hempel (1966). Nagel and Pap catch up much that was prominently summarized in the 1950s by Gustav Bergmann, Philipp Frank, John Kemeny, and Henryk Mehlberg (not cited here). David Hull (1974) deals with biological science. Comparison of Hull's treatment with one even fifteen years earlier (such as that by Morton Beckner, 1959, not cited here) indicates some development, as does comparison with an early work on physics (such as that by Milic Capek, 1961, not cited here). Another brief starter book, by Karel Lambert and Gordon Brittan (1970), presents a summary of the "classical" position (for example, that held by Carnap, Feigl, Hempel, Nagel, and Reichenbach), then some objections to it, in four topic areas, all formalist in content: mathematics, explanation, confirmation and acceptability, and the limits of science. A larger, popular synthesis by Marx Wartofsky (1968) covers a much wider area, adding chapters on the genesis of science and on the biological and human sciences to the usual discussions of methods and concepts. A more up-to-date introduction is needed.

Seven quite diverse nonintroductory overviews display many of the developing issues. Israel Scheffler (1963) uses empiricist-linguistic analytic tools to study three problem areas—explanation, significance, confirmation—basic to a theory of scientific structure. In an unusual synoptic work David Hawkins (1964) treats of numerous familiar topics in philosophy of science and in doing so attempts to build conceptual bridges between various aspects of experience inside and outside both mathematics and science to several other philosophical concerns, especially in philosophy of mind, axiology, ethics, and social philosophy. Carl Hempel (1965) combines revisions of eleven previously published technical essays (1942–64) in four orthodox formalist areas—confirmation, induction and rational belief, cognitive significance, structure and function of scientific concepts and theories, and explanation—and adds a 165-page monograph on explanation. In Britain Mary Hesse and Rom Harré have offered strong opposition to the positivist, deductivist elements in the thinking of Hempel, Carnap, and others. A systematic work by Harré (1970) systematically argues for an alternative brand of realism. A major opus by Mary Hesse (1980) registers critical variations on the theme of scientific change and much else. A collection of papers (1951–69) by Patrick Suppes, in contrast, stays with the more conventional approach and is filled with mathematical and logical analyses. *The Legacy of Logical Positivism,* edited by Peter Achinstein and Stephen Barker (1969), joins support by Feigl and Hempel to critiques by Hesse, Hanson, Hilary Putnam, Michael Scriven, Dudley Shapere, Toulmin, and the editors. Shapere's important "Notes toward a Post-Positivist Interpretation of Science" in that collection is foreshadowed in a 1965 book on philosophy of natural science that he edited. There he introduces a set of eight previously published essays that present "logical" approaches (Carnap, Pap, Hempel, and Richard Rudner) and "historical" ones (Pierre Duhem, Toulmin, Hesse, and Kuhn).

Is scientific advance registered by increasing probability (Carnap), by discrete verifications (the logical positivists) or falsifications (Popper), by revolutions (Kuhn), by growing consensus (Polanyi), by progressive versus degenerating research programs, conducted over long periods (Lakatos), or what? The debate goes on.

THEMATIC AREAS

Typically, the themes discussed in conferences and symposia in the field are numerous, interlocking, and complex. The same is true of individual contributions. Therefore it is more meaningful to speak of thematic areas, realizing that the central concern by which each is designated gathers to it many other concerns. Here I distinguish six thematic areas.

1. *Causality.* Four decades ago, R. G. Collingwood (*An Essay on Metaphysics,* 1940, cited on p. 358) distinguished three main senses of the word "cause" as they have developed for historical, practical, and theoretical purposes, respectively, and indicated confusions between them often made in scientific contexts. The formal aspects of his analysis have been quite typical within treatments of causality since then; the historical aspects have been much less marked. Mario Bunge's (1959) study represents what debates over the next two decades came to, as does a more conventional study by Victor Lenzen (1959, not cited here). An excellent volume of fourteen readings, mostly from the 1960s and 1970s, and masterfully introduced by Ernest Sosa (1975) lays out a restricted set of theoretic problems that reside in current conceptions of causality, including three early papers: a now classic 1926 paper by C. J. Ducasse on observability of causal relations and papers by Roderick Chisholm (1955) and Wilfrid Sellars (1958) on "counterfactuals." Such writers often take Hume's extreme skepticism on the knowability of causation to be the one most notable historic position to beat, for to accept his view may imply that science is irrational. Among the more systematic accounts are a critique of the Humean theory and its close successors, the regularity theories, by Rom Harré and E. H. Madden (1975). J. L. Mackie's exposition of a regularity theory (1974) begins with an analysis of Hume's arguments. Some links with the issue of determinism are examined by another prominent theorist, Henrick von Wright (1974), whose view is more divergent from Hume's. Von Wright holds that whether determinism is universal is an open question but that in any case free human agency is compatible with determinism. Much of the discussion has derived from an effort to ascertain what sort of lawlike connections must be assumed if particular facts are to be explained scientifically. A probabalistic approach to this problem is outlined by Brian Skyrms (1980).

2. *Law and Explanation.* What relations hold between functional laws, prediction, and explanation in science? How are we to determine where any one of these is theoretically not possible to achieve? Is teleological (functional) explanation justifiable, particularly with respect to self-regulating systems? Such questions have evoked much debate among philosophers of science. Early stages of the debate have been recapitulated by R. B. Braithwaite (1953). Whereas some philosophers have greatly restricted the areas within which explana-

tion is thought to be supportable, a synoptic approach by Ernest Nagel (1961), directed to a wider audience, assumes extensive and diverse modes of scientific explanation. A later collection of essays (1935–77) by Nagel (1979) includes defenses of his views as an "unreconstructed empirical rationalist" over against the new critics. Carl Hempel (1965) has analyzed the purported logical structures of three basic types: the deductive-nomological, the inductive-statistical, and the deductive-statistical, each of which involves reference to what he calls "covering laws." Two studies, by Jaakko Hintikka and Unto Remes (1974) on analytic method and its origin in geometry and by Peter Bieri et al. (1979) on the use of transcendental arguments in the conceptual framework of science versus alternative positions, represent the continuing development of formalist analysis.

All these writings are by positivists (though not logical positivists in the strict sense), as is that of von Wright (1971), who offers some brief historical perspective in presenting his analysis of recent efforts to consider what is implied in taking a causal-determinist versus an intentional (teleological or quasi-teleological) approach to scientific explanation and scientific laws. Another analytic account, which keeps positivist views critically in sight throughout, is that of Peter Achinstein (1971). He attempts to steer a course between positivist and historicist approaches. Blending historical and philosophical investigation, Willard Humphreys (1968) examines alternative theories of physical science on the view that each is organized around ways to identify, clarify, and explain anomalies. A symposium of four papers with comments and replies, edited by Stephan Körner (1975), briefly displays what the discussion on explanation has come to. A linguistic analysis by Achinstein is followed by accounts of teleological, theoretical, and ideological explanation by Peter Geach, Wesley Salmon, and J. L. Mackie, respectively.

3. *Probability and Induction.* A treatise on probability and induction by logician William Kneale (1949) succinctly lays out the main issues that have been repeatedly worked over during the past thirty years. Recent thinking is represented in one of the *Minnesota Studies* volumes (Maxwell and Anderson, 1975), with emphasis on the status of so-called inductive inferences and on confirmation of hypotheses and theories (see Feigl and Maxwell, 1961, pp. 265–86). The allied ideal of objectivity is examined and supported by Israel Scheffler (1967), in response to somewhat misperceived attacks by people like Polanyi and Kuhn. Various meanings of simplicity as a formal condition are sorted out by Elliott Sober (1975), whose own detailed

analytic theory is based on the notion of the kinds and amounts of information a hypothesis can supply in answer to certain kinds of questions.

4. *Information and Inference.* How are inferences to be formed, on what basis, and with reference to what kinds of information? Wesley Salmon (1967) has briefly but systematically investigated this topic area, Mary Hesse (1974) more extensively and diverging more from conventional approaches. In this "logic of science" Hesse proffers a middle way between more formalist and more historical-relativist positions, borrowing heavily from the interpretation of science enunciated by Pierre Duhem seventy-five years ago and adopted by Quine as a network of concepts related by law, one in which only pragmatic, relative distinctions are made between the "observable" and the "theoretical." Unlike some, she has not given up correspondence rules to do this. A collection of essays edited by Hintikka and Suppes (1970) presents equally careful analyses.

5. *Concept Formation and Change.* A now classic monograph by Hempel (1952) on fundamentals of concept formation is a necessary reference point for all subsequent studies. Divergent approaches have been taken by Achinstein (1968) and, with special reference to collectivities, as in the intellectual disciplines, by Toulmin (1972). Identifying his position as "critical scientific realism" and working very much in the mathematical-semantic style of Hintikka, Raimo Tuomela (1973) uses model theory, a development of mathematical logic, to analyze the nature, elimination, and use of theoretical concepts. His examples are taken chiefly from the social sciences. Until the 1970s the most sophisticated analyses of concept formation and change in science tended to emphasize the similarities between natural and social science, as with Tuomela. The scope of the thirteen colloquium essays on conceptual change edited by Glenn Pearce and Patrick Maynard (1973) go even beyond science; some take notice of recent antipositivist critiques, but there is little explicit reference to possible differences in various modes of science. One of the most dramatic changes in physics, that from earlier conceptions of space and time to the idea of "space-time" are examined by Lawrence Sklar (1974) and in a collection of new essays edited by John Earman et al. (1977). This subject had been significantly treated by Adolf Grünbaum (1963, not cited here).

6. *Unity of Science.* What has happened to Neurath's dream of a unified science? Certainly it remains a purportedly high value among scientists, yet one readily and consistently given up. The hope some

philosophers have kept for a "science of science" is so strong as to be a modern version of "faith seeking understanding" (Augustine, Anselm). With critical reservations, Robert Causey (1977) keeps Neurath's dream alive, as does Mario Bunge (1973) in the limited sense of methodological unity, but as a very remote ideal. Causey accepts a particular type of reductionist program, as has generally been the case in discussions since Neurath and before, only now with a much greater accumulation of tools and examples to work with. As Robert McRae (1961) indicates, this theoretical aspiration was already a philosophical "problem" in the centuries from Bacon to Kant. Lindley Darden and Nancy Maull (1974) have set apart the phenomenon of interfield theories for study. The need for such theories and their development have been mainsprings of advance in this century. That interdisciplinary approaches to inquiry on scientific and other problems are still very difficult to organize, despite the well-established fruits that have come of them, is perhaps testimony enough to collective and nonrational elements in science.

FUTURE PROSPECTS

The current revolution in philosophy of science, at least as significant as the logical empiricist one in the 1920s and 1930s, is barely underway. So far, its greatest effects on scientific practice and on the public use of science are in the social sciences (treated separately here). This is to be expected for two reasons. First, aspects of the natural science models on which much social science has been constructed are now seen to be inaccurate, inadequate, or confused. Therefore other models are being strenuously sought—and this activity will surely increase. Second, several of the disciplines that are being used to form a more adequate description of actual practice in the natural sciences are among the social sciences. Whether this is a sixty-year swing of the cultural pendulum, as Toulmin (1977) surmises, is an interesting question. Certainly these shifts of emphasis from formal to functional, and the like, have been seen before in art, science, and philosophy.

My own opinion is that the systems complexity of social life and of its interface with science will demand a greater systems awareness from philosophers of science. If this occurs, the vast pendulum swings seen in the past will be replaced by more intricate movements. A necessary component of this change will be a far greater attention to the operation of values in both science and philosophy of science and to interactions between the conduct and uses of each. Apart from the considerable literature on physics and science-related mathematics, debates more directly related to values issues and issues of application have so far centered largely on isolated areas such as biological explanation, sociobiology, philosophy of medicine, technology, decision theory in social science, and statistical mechanics.

Achinstein, Peter. *Concepts of Science: A Philosophical Analysis.* Baltimore, Md.: Johns Hopkins Univ. Pr., 1968.
———. *Law and Explanation.* Oxford and New York: Oxford Univ. Pr., 1971.
Achinstein, Peter, and Stephen F. Barker, eds. *The Legacy of Logical Positivism: Studies in the Philosophy of Science.* Baltimore, Md.: Johns Hopkins Univ. Pr., 1969.
Asquith, Peter D., and Henry E. Kyburg, Jr., eds. *Current Research in Philosophy of Science.* East Lansing, Mich.: Philosophy of Science Assn., 1979.
Bieri, Peter, Rolf P. Horstmann, and Lorenz Krüger, eds. *Transcendental Arguments and Science: Essays in Epistemology.* Dordrecht and Boston: Reidel, 1979.
Blake, Ralph M., Curt J. Ducasse, and Edward H. Madden. *Theories of Scientific Method: The Renaissance through the Nineteenth Century.* Seattle and London: Univ. of Washington Pr., 1960.
Braithwaite, Richard B. *Scientific Explanation: A Study of the Function of Theory, Probability and Law in Science.* Cambridge and New York: Cambridge Univ. Pr., 1953.
Bridgman, Percy W. *The Logic of Modern Physics.* New York: Macmillan, 1938. (Original ed., 1927.)
Brown, Harold I. *Perception, Theory and Commitment: The New Philosophy of Science.* Chicago: Precedent Publishing, 1977; Chicago: Univ. of Chicago Pr., 1979.
Buchdahl, Gerd. *Metaphysics and the Philosophy of Science: The Classical Origins. Descartes to Kant.* Oxford: Blackwell, 1969.
Buck, Roger C., and Robert S. Cohen, eds. *PSA 1970: In Memory of Rudolf Carnap.* Boston Studies in the Philosophy of Science, vol. 8. Dordrecht and Boston: Reidel, 1971.
Bunge, Mario. *Causality: The Place of the Causal Principle in Modern Science.* Cambridge, Mass.: Harvard Univ. Pr., 1959.
———. *The Methodological Unity of Science.* Dordrecht and Boston: Reidel, 1973.
Causey, Robert L. *The Unity of Science.* Dordrecht and Boston: Reidel, 1977.
Cohen, I. Bernard. *The Newtonian Revolution: With Illustrations of the Transformation of Scientific Ideas.* Cambridge and New York: Cambridge Univ. Pr., 1980.
Cohen, Morris R. *Reason and Nature.* 2nd rev. ed. Glencoe, Ill.: Free Pr., 1953. (1st ed., 1931.)

Cohen, Robert S., P. K. Feyerabend, and M. W. Wartofsky, eds. *Essays in Memory of Imre Lakatos. Boston Studies in the Philosophy of Science,* vol. 39. Dordrecht and Boston: Reidel, 1976.

Colodny, Robert G., ed. University of Pittsburgh Series in the Philosophy of Science. Vol. 1, *Frontiers of Science and Philosophy.* Pittsburgh, Pa.: Univ. of Pittsburgh Pr., 1962; London: Allen & Unwin, 1964. Vol. 2, *Beyond the Edge of Certainty: Essays in Contemporary Science and Philosophy.* Englewood Cliffs, N.J.: Prentice-Hall, 1965. Vol. 3, *Mind and Cosmos: Explorations in the Philosophy of Science.* Pittsburgh, Pa.: Univ. of Pittsburgh Pr., 1966. Vol. 4, *The Nature and Function of Scientific Theories: Essays in Contemporary Science and Philosophy.* Pittsburgh, Pa.: Univ. of Pittsburgh Pr., 1970. Vol. 5, *Paradigms and Paradoxes: The Philosophical Challenges of the Quantum Domain.* Pittsburgh, Pa.: Univ. of Pittsburgh Pr., 1972.

Darden, Lindley, and Nancy Maull. "The Unity of Science: Interfield Theories." In *Contributed Papers: Fifth International Congress of Logic, Methodology, and Philosophy of Science,* pp. v–108. London and Ontario: International Union of History and Philosophy of Science, 1974.

Earman, John, Clark Glymour, and John Stachel, eds. *Foundations of Space-Time Theories.* Minnesota Studies in the Philosophy of Science, vol. 8. Minneapolis: Univ. of Minnesota Pr., 1977.

Feigl, Herbert. "Philosophy of Science." In *Philosophy,* pp. 465–540. Ed. by Roderick M. Chisholm et al. Englewood Cliffs, N.J.: Prentice-Hall, 1964.

———, and May Brodbeck, eds. *Readings in the Philosophy of Science.* New York: Appleton-Century-Crofts, 1953.

———, and Grover Maxwell, eds. *Current Issues in the Philosophy of Science.* New York: Holt, Rinehart & Winston, 1961. (American Assn. for the Advancement of Science, 1959.)

———, and ———, eds. *Scientific Explanation, Space, and Time.* Minnesota Studies in the Philosophy of Science, vol. 3. Minneapolis: Univ. of Minnesota Pr., 1962.

Feyerabend, Paul K. *Against Method: Outline of an Anarchistic Theory of Knowledge.* New York: Schocken; London: Verso, 1978. (Original ed., 1975.) (A portion was first published in *Minnesota Studies in the Philosophy of Science,* vol. 4, 1970.)

———. *Science in a Free Society.* London: NOB, 1978.

———, and Grover Maxwell, eds. *Mind, Matter, and Method: Essays in Philosophy and Science in Honour of Herbert Feigl.* Minneapolis: Univ. of Minnesota Pr.; Oxford: Oxford Univ. Pr., 1966.

Gutting, Gary, ed. *Paradigms and Revolutions: Applications and Appraisals of Thomas Kuhn's Philosophy of Science.* Notre Dame, Ind.: Univ. of Notre Dame Pr., 1980.

Hanson, Norwood R. *Patterns of Discovery.* Cambridge and New York: Cambridge Univ. Pr., 1958.

Harré, Rom. *The Principles of Scientific Thinking.* Chicago: Univ. of Chicago Pr., 1970.

———, and E. H. Madden. *Causal Powers: A Theory of Natural Necessity.* Totowa, N.J.: Roman & Littlefield, 1975.

Hawkins, David. *The Language of Nature: An Essay in the Philosophy of*

Science. San Francisco and London: Freeman, 1964. (Rev. ed. forthcoming.)

Hempel, Carl G. *Aspects of Scientific Explanation and Other Essays in the Philosophy of Science.* New York: Free Pr., 1965.

————. *Fundamentals of Concept Formation in Empirical Science. International Encyclopedia of Unified Science,* vol. 2, no. 7. Chicago: Univ. of Chicago Pr., 1952.

————. *Philosophy of Natural Science.* Englewood Cliffs, N.J.: Prentice-Hall, 1966.

Hesse, Mary. *Revolutions and Reconstruction in the Philosophy of Science.* Bloomington and London: Indiana Univ. Pr., 1980.

————. *The Structure of Scientific Inference.* Berkeley: Univ. of California Pr., 1974.

Hintikka, Jaakko, and Patrick Suppes, ed. *Information and Inference.* Dordrecht and Boston: Reidel, 1970.

————, and Unto Remes. *The Method of Analysis: Its Geometrical Origin and Its General Significance.* Dordrecht and Boston: Reidel, 1974.

Holton, Gerald. *Thematic Origins of Scientific Thought: Kepler to Einstein.* Cambridge, Mass.: Harvard Univ. Pr., 1973.

Hull, David L. *Philosophy of Biological Science.* Englewood Cliffs, N.J.: Prentice-Hall, 1974.

Humphreys, Willard C. *Anomalies and Scientific Theories.* San Francisco: Freeman, 1968.

Kneale, William. *Probability and Induction.* Oxford: Clarendon Pr., 1949.

Knorr, Karin D., Herman Strasser, and Hans G. Zilian, eds. *Determinants and Controls of Scientific Development.* Dordrecht and Boston: Reidel, 1975.

Körner, Stephan, ed. *Explanation: Papers and Discussions.* New Haven, Conn.: Yale Univ. Pr., 1975.

Kuhn, Thomas S. *The Essential Tension: Selected Studies in Scientific Tradition and Change.* Chicago: Univ. of Chicago Pr., 1977.

————. *The Structure of Scientific Revolutions.* 2nd ed. *International Encyclopedia of Unified Science,* vol. 2, no. 2. Chicago: Univ. of Chicago Pr., 1970. (1st ed., 1962.)

Lakatos, Imre. *Philosophical Papers.* Vol. 1, *The Methodology of Scientific Research Programmes;* vol. 2, *Mathematics, Science and Epistemology.* Cambridge and New York: Cambridge Univ. Pr., 1978.

————. *Proofs and Refutations: The Logic of Mathematical Discovery.* Ed. by John Worrall and Elie Faber. Cambridge and New York: Cambridge Univ. Pr., 1976.

————, and A. E. Musgrave, eds. *Criticism and the Growth of Knowledge.* Cambridge and New York: Cambridge Univ. Pr., 1970.

Lambert, Karel, and Gordon G. Brittan, Jr. *An Introduction to the Philosophy of Science.* Englewood Cliffs, N.J.: Prentice-Hall, 1970.

Laudan, Larry. *Progress and Its Problems: Towards a Theory of Scientific Growth.* Berkeley and London: Univ. of California Pr., 1977.

Mackie, John L. *The Cement of the Universe: A Study of Causation.* Oxford: Clarendon Pr., 1974.

McRae, Robert. *The Problem of the Unity of the Sciences: Bacon to Kant.* Toronto: Univ. of Toronto Pr.; Oxford: Oxford Univ. Pr., 1961.

Maxwell, Grover, and Robert M. Anderson, Jr., eds. *Induction, Probability and Confirmation.* Minnesota Studies in the Philosophy of Science, vol. 6. Minneapolis: Univ. of Minnesota Pr., 1975.

Nagel, Ernest. *The Structure of Science: Problems in the Logic of Scientific Explanation.* New York: Harcourt, Brace, 1961. Repr.: Indianapolis, Ind.: Hackett, 1979.

———. *Teleology Revisited and Other Essays in the Philosophy and History of Science.* New York: Columbia Univ. Pr., 1979.

———, Patrick C. Suppes, and Alfred Tarski, eds. *Logic, Methodology, and Philosophy of Science: Proceedings of the 1960 International Congress.* Stanford, Calif.: Stanford Univ. Pr., 1962.

Neurath, Otto, Rudolf Carnap, and Charles Morris, eds. *International Encyclopedia of Unified Science.* 2v. Chicago: Univ. of Chicago Pr., 1938–69. (Issued in 10 parts each vol.)

Pap, Arthur. *Introduction to the Philosophy of Science.* New York: Free Pr. of Glencoe; London: Eyre & Spottiswood, 1962.

Pearce, Glen, and Patrick Maynard, eds. *Conceptual Change.* Dordrecht and Boston: Reidel, 1973.

Popper, Karl. *Conjectures and Refutations: The Growth of Scientific Knowledge.* London: Routledge & Paul, 1963.

———. *The Logic of Scientific Discovery.* New York: Basic Books; London: Hutchinson, 1959. (German ed., 1934.)

Radner, Michael, and Stephan Winokur, eds. *Analyses of Theories and Methods of Physics and Psychology.* Minnesota Studies in the Philosophy of Science, vol. 4. Minneapolis: Univ. of Minnesota Pr., 1970.

Radnitzky, Gerald. *Contemporary Schools of Metascience.* Chicago: Regnery, 1973; Göteberg, 1968.

Reichenbach, Hans. *The Rise of Scientific Philosophy.* Berkeley: Univ. of California Pr., 1951.

Rescher, Nicholas, ed. *Essays in Honor of Carl G. Hempel.* Dordrecht and Boston: Reidel, 1969.

Salmon, Wesley C. *The Foundations of Scientific Inference.* Pittsburgh, Pa.: Univ. of Pittsburgh Pr., 1967.

Scheffler, Israel. *The Anatomy of Inquiry: Philosophical Studies in the Theory of Science.* New York: Knopf, 1963.

———. *Science and Subjectivity.* Indianapolis, Ind.: Bobbs-Merrill, 1967.

Schilpp, Paul Arthur, ed. *Albert Einstein: Philosopher-Scientist.* 3rd ed. La Salle, Ill.: Open Court, 1970. (1st ed., 1949.)

Sellars, Wilfrid. *Science and Metaphysics: Variations on Kantian Themes.* New York: Humanities Pr.; London: Routledge & Paul, 1968.

Shapere, Dudley. *Galileo: A Philosophical Study.* Chicago: Univ. of Chicago Pr., 1974.

———, ed. *Philosophical Problems of Natural Science.* New York: Macmillan, 1965.

Sklar, Lawrence. *Space, Time, and Spacetime.* Berkeley: Univ. of California Pr., 1974.

Skyrms, Brian. *Causal Necessity: A Pragmatic Investigation of the Necessity of Laws.* New Haven, Conn. and London: Yale Univ. Pr., 1980.

Sober, Elliott. *Simplicity.* Oxford: Clarendon Pr., 1975.

Sosa, Ernest, ed. *Causation and Conditionals.* Oxford and New York: Oxford Univ. Pr., 1975.

Stuewer, Roger H., ed. *Historical and Philosophical Perspectives of Science.* Minnesota Studies in the Philosophy of Science, vol. 5. Minneapolis: Univ. of Minnesota Pr., 1970.

Suppe, Frederick, ed. *The Structure of Scientific Theories.* 2nd ed. Urbana: Univ. of Illinois Pr., 1977. (1st ed., 1974.)

———, and Peter D. Asquith, eds. *PSA 1976.* 2v. East Lansing, Mich.: Philosophy of Science Assn., 1976–77.

Suppes, Patrick C. *Studies in the Methodology and Foundations of Science.* Dordrecht and Boston: Reidel, 1969. (Selected papers from 1951–69.)

Toulmin, Stephen. "From Form to Function: Philosophy and History of Science in the 1950s and Now." *Daedalus* 106, no. 3:143–62 (Summer 1977).

———. *Human Understanding.* Vol. 1. Princeton, N.J.: Princeton Univ. Pr.; Oxford: Clarendon Pr., 1972. (Two volumes were to follow.)

———. *The Philosophy of Science: An Introduction.* London: Hutchinson, 1953.

Tuomela, Raimo. *Theoretical Concepts.* New York: Springer, 1973.

Wartofsky, Marx W. *Conceptual Foundations of Scientific Thought: An Introduction to the Philosophy of Science.* New York: Macmillan, 1968.

Wright, George Henrik von. *Causality and Determinism.* New York: Columbia Univ. Pr., 1974.

———. *Explanation and Understanding.* London: Routledge & Paul, 1971.

24

Philosophy
of History

The Tasks of Historical Inquiry

Contemporary philosophy of history is chiefly an analytical and critical pursuit, not a speculative one, for foxes not hedgehogs. In a distinguished essay on Leo Tolstoy, Isaiah Berlin (1953) referred to the purveyors of more speculative interpretations as hedgehogs in that, as the Greek poet Archilochus said: "The fox knows many things, but the hedgehog knows one big thing." Although Tolstoy was by nature a fox, says Berlin, in his great historical novel *War and Peace* (1863–73) he viewed history as following inexorable cosmic law. Among philosophers foxes are content to look at the smaller pieces and not to seek an overall vision.

Until the eighteenth century the more speculative philosophical interpretations of the meaning of human history stemmed very largely from religious sources. Among these, East or West, Judeo-Christian sources have been distinctive in that they contain a strongly teleological element, which places moral as well as salvific purpose at the core of historical process. Augustine's conception of a confrontation between the divine and human orders in his *City of God* (413–27) dominated Western conceptions until the nineteenth century. Although to twentieth-century scholars Giambattista Vico is the great eighteenth-century pioneer in the transition to more modern views of historical patterns, both speculative and critical, his thinking bore little influence in his own time.

Late eighteenth-century efforts to carve out an "enlightened" conception of universal historical development by Johann Gottfried Herder and Immanuel Kant spearheaded the more comprehensive

428

synoptic attempts of Georg W. F. Hegel, then of Auguste Comte, Herbert Spencer, and Karl Marx in the nineteenth century. In the twentieth century nonphilosophers Oswald Spengler and Arnold Toynbee have been the most noted. They have been joined especially by numerous theological interpreters, who have also dealt with historical origins and culminations or "end times" (eschatology) as philosophers have not tended to do.

Most contemporary philosophers of history would agree with the more speculative interpreters that human nature is historical, and so they spend time looking critically at the subject and procedures of historical inquiry: at historical knowledge, historical narrative and interpretation, and historical theory and its underlying presuppositions. Mostly conceptual analysis is used to examine the nature, intelligibility, and justifiability of proposals in each of these categories. "History" itself comes out not as a given but as an essentially contested concept. They would tend not to agree with the "old" interpreters that human history overall is developmental, not at least according to any readily ascertainable patterns or not as something for philosophers to concern themselves about (see Raymond Polin in Yirmiahu Yovel, 1978).

Historicism

Among several eminent German philosophers and historians in the nineteenth century a tendency emerged (1) to view human events especially in their singularity, (2) to try to understand the diverse relationships of these events to general but changing patterns or to evolutionary trends, but in a dynamic and concrete manner, (3) to examine all human products in this historical fashion, and (4) to affirm for such inquiry—sometimes for the social sciences generally, on this basis—a scientific status distinctly different from that of the natural sciences. Proponents experienced these tasks as a decisive turning point in the consciousness of self and world. Even their most noted critics, who from the 1920s on have dubbed several quite divergent descriptions of historical theory "historicism" (see Pietro Rossi in Leonard Krieger, 1975), have tended to agree with this judgment. Many of these critics followed Ernst Troeltsch (1922, not cited here), otherwise congenial to historicism, in a concern that many such theories could end in individualism, relativism, or skepticism with regard to "meanings" in history. An early work in contemporary Anglo-American critical philosophy of history by Maurice Mandelbaum (1938), for example, focuses on the issues of relativism and skepticism, though it was not his intention to offer a critique of "historicism" as such. Karl Popper's famous 1944–45 critique is considerably off the mark, and his definition brought further confusion into an already cloudy area of scholarship; but he too worked on important issues regarding theories of historical evolution that would not likely have arisen without the "historicists" (John Passmore in Krieger, 1975).

In fact there is no such overall thing as "historicism," but rather a diverse set of interests, problems, and solutions, almost all of which share the four general characteristics I have indicated above. From the early 1800s, Friedrich Schleiermacher is the original proponent of a more hermeneutical approach to historical reality, one which fulfills those characteristics. Wilhelm Dilthey followed. Different proposals claiming an empirical "scientific" status for history by the great critical historians Barthold Georg Niebuhr, Leopold von Ranke, and their successors (see Krieger, 19975) intervened, as did the dynamic, politically infused vision of historical development by Georg W. F. Hegel, which is still a leading factor in German historiography. Dilthey was the most prominent "historicist" of his century, Benedetto Croce (1966), who among other things emphasized history as an expression of current interests, of the early twentieth century.

Contemporary critical philosophy of history stands on the shoulders of historicism, broadly defined. An outstanding account of the nineteenth-century background, which itself advances the discussion considerably, comes from Hayden White (1973). A *Monist* symposium on epistemological issues related to historicism, edited by Richard Rorty (1977), displays the richness of current discussion. That the "old" speculative trend is still lively is betokened in a study by Michael Murray (1970), which dates the "modern" era in philosophy of history from Joachim of Flora (1145–1202), finds its culmination in Hegel, and perceives new openings in Heidegger. Haskell Fain (1970) argues for a rapprochement between critical and speculative approaches and for greater historical attentiveness in philosophical inquiry overall.

Overviews, Introductions, and Collections

A substantial collection of readings edited by Patrick Gardiner (1959) runs interpretations of historical process from Vico to R. G. Collingwood, who made it his career to reflect on the nature of historical investigation and its importance in philosophical inquiry.

Gardiner then reprints eighteen critical essays on classical theories, on explanation and laws, and on history and the social sciences. In effect, this volume sums up the markedly new stage of discussion signaled by Mandelbaum (1938), solidified in Collingwood's still only partly digested new ventures from the 1930s (1946), brought into analytic discourse by Carl Hempel's famous 1942 article, "The Function of General Laws in History" (in Gardiner, 1959; also see restatements of his "covering law" theory in Sidney Hook, 1963, and William Dray, 1966), by W. H. Walsh (1951), and by William Dray (1957), the latter especially in his critique of Hempel.

The division of idealist versus positivist views advanced by W. H. Walsh in his pioneering 1951 introduction is no longer serviceable, though it is true that the idealists tended to refuse assimilation of history to a natural science paradigm; but the work itself is still useful. The brief general introduction by William Dray (1964) is also standard. That by Arthur Danto (1965) centers on issues regarding historical narrative and explanation. That by Ronald Atkinson (1978) accepts the distinction between analytic and "substantive" approaches (in most respects similar to that between critical and speculative) and, like him, leans to the analytic side. His introduction is topical: knowledge of the past, objectivity, explanation, causation, and values. The succession of introductions nicely shows the developing discussion, mostly among analytic philosophers.

Indicative in like manner are the collections edited by Sidney Hook (1963) and William Dray (1966), the *Monist* symposium by John Smith et al. (1969) and that edited by Richard Rorty (1977), and the proceedings edited by Yirmiahu Yovel (1978).

THEMES AND DEVELOPMENTS

The major thematic areas in contemporary philosophy of history have already been pointed out. On that of historical knowledge and understanding, Morton White (1965) represents the effort to assimilate historical inquiry to a natural science paradigm. Alternatives have been outlined in chapter 23; some further literature related to the social sciences is noted in chapter 25. A naturalist approach of a more Aristotelian variety is offered by John Herman Randall (1958). Jack Meiland (1965) presents a "constructionist," skeptical position. Against historical realists, Leon Goldstein (1976) later takes a somewhat similar position, that the past is "constituted" by historical research. That is the only "objectivity" we are going to get, in his view. Another well-argued work by Murray Murphey (1973) also emphasizes the necessary use of theoretical constructs for "knowing" the past; he holds that those theories are postulated to explain not only past objects and events but also the consequences of statements about them, including present consequences. In certain respects, this concern comes close to what Collingwood claimed in affirming that historical inquiry is essentially the "reenactment" of past thinking, encapsulated in the present, and that by its very nature history must therefore be continually revised. In the lingo of subsequent philosophy of action, Collingwood's view was that history deals primarily with intentional and other kinds of action (not exclusively, because there are other kinds of data used as framework and evidence). Based on the more advanced discussions on "action," Rex Martin (1977) took up the Collingwoodian theme anew.

In current discussions the understanding of "action" is a major topic, as are questions about action "events," for example: how nearly individual are they, and do they exist in any of the ways things do? Further, is rational historical knowledge possible? Long ago, Søren Kierkegaard, founder of existentialism, said "no." Have we learned anything since that would strengthen a "yes"? Especially, do we have sufficient clarity about explanation and the possible operation of laws to serve this purpose? What scope of description is appropriate for explaining a historical action or set of actions? What is the appropriate relation between our descriptions of the results of such events (conceived as occurrences of action) and their consequences for further human action? And how are we to account for actions that are not consciously intended or not thought out or understood by the agent (psychohistory)? Some of these issues are tackled by Frederick Olafson (1979) in an attempt to join phenomenologist and analytic approaches to explanation of human action. He regards the subject matter of all historical accounts to be human actions, the structure of which is dictated by methods of interpretation. Mandelbaum (1977) presents arguments against this position and against another currently popular line, which is that history is fictional narrative. One way of characterizing current theories of history in general would be to indicate to what degree and in what ways the "fictive" element is included.

Another focal interest in recent decades is a reflection of the free will/determinism debate. Since Jean-Jacques Rousseau the assertion of free will and specifically of the capacity of individuals to achieve their own personal development has been a major feature or presupposition in liberal theories of history. Taking that line, Isaiah Berlin (1955) has argued against the doctrine of historical inevitability, which has led to further considerations about whether historical process is nonetheless irreversible.

On explanation, Patrick Gardiner (1952) early took a direction less extreme than that of Morton White (1965)—one closer to Popper than to Hempel—regarding historical inquiry as somewhat different yet basically subject to the requirements of science. W. B. Gallie (1964), with William Dray (1957), rejects that direction, while moving still further away than Dray in emphasizing the narrative character of historical discourse; Arthur Danto (1965) tries an intermediate position.

FUTURE PROSPECTS

Labeling, misconstrual, and talking past each other occurs in every area of philosophy, as elsewhere. Perhaps these practices have had a more deterring effect on the growth of this area than is true of most. In any case, some signs of more accurate responsiveness have appeared and may be expected to become a trend.

Other directions for the future are suggested by these renewed interests: (1) in interpretive, reenactive procedures, (2) in understanding how consequences of past actions right up to the present, and even in a pragmatic anticipatory sense into the future, may or must be related to such procedures, and (3) in very tentative forays into the once-rejected domain of speculative or substantive philosophy of history.

Atkinson, Ronald F. *Knowledge and Explanation in History: An Introduction to the Philosophy of History.* Ithaca, N.Y. and London: Cornell Univ. Pr., 1978.

Berlin, Isaiah. *The Hedgehog and the Fox: An Essay on Tolstoy's View of History.* New York: Simon & Schuster; London: Weidenfeld & Nicolson, 1953.

———. *Historical Inevitability.* Oxford and New York: Oxford Univ. Pr., 1955.

Collingwood, Robin G. *The Idea of History.* New York: Oxford Univ. Pr.; Oxford: Clarendon Pr., 1946.

Croce, Benedetto. *Philosophy, Poetry, History: An Anthology of Essays.* Tr. and intro. by Cecil Sprigge. Oxford and New York: Oxford Univ. Pr., 1966.

Danto, Arthur C. *Analytical Philosophy of History.* Cambridge and New York: Cambridge Univ. Pr., 1965.

Dray, William H. *Law and Explanation in History.* New York: Oxford Univ. Pr.; Oxford: Clarendon Pr., 1957.

———. *Philosophy of History.* Englewood Cliffs, N.J.: Prentice-Hall, 1964.

———, ed. *Philosophical Analysis and History.* New York and London: Harper & Row, 1966.

Fain, Haskell. *Between Philosophy and History: The Resurrection of Speculative Philosophy of History within the Analytic Tradition.* Princeton, N.J.: Princeton Univ. Pr., 1970.

Gallie, W. B. *Philosophy and the Historical Understanding.* 2nd ed. New York: Schocken Books, 1968. (1st ed., London: Chatto & Windus, 1964.)

Gardiner, Patrick. *The Nature of Historical Explanation.* Oxford and New York: Oxford Univ. Pr., 1952.

———, ed. *Theories of History: Readings from Classical and Contemporary Sources.* Glencoe, Ill.: Free Pr., 1959.

Goldstein, Leon J. *Historical Knowing.* Austin and London: Univ. of Texas Pr., 1976.

Hook, Sidney, ed. *Philosophy and History: A Symposium.* New York: New York Univ. Pr., 1963.

Krieger, Leonard, Pietro Rossi, John Passmore, and Hayden V. White. *Essays on Historicism.* Beiheft 14 of History and Theory: Studies in the Philosophy of History. Middletown, Conn.: Wesleyan Univ. Pr., 1975.

Mandelbaum, Maurice. *The Anatomy of Historical Knowledge.* Baltimore, Md.: Johns Hopkins Univ. Pr., 1977.

———. *The Problem of Historical Knowledge: An Answer to Relativism.* New York: Liveright, 1938.

Martin, Rex. *Historical Explanation: Re-enactment and Practical Inference.* Ithaca, N.Y. and London: Cornell Univ. Pr., 1977.

Meiland, Jack W. *Skepticism and Historical Knowledge.* New York: Random House, 1965.

Murphey, Murray G. *Our Knowledge of the Historical Past.* Indianapolis, Ind.: Bobbs-Merrill, 1973.

Murray, Michael E. *Modern Philosophy of History: Its Origin and Destination.* The Hague: Nijhoff, 1970.

Olafson, Frederick A. *The Dialectic of Action: A Philosophical Interpretation of History and the Humanities.* Chicago and London: Univ. of Chicago Pr., 1979.

Popper, Karl R. *The Poverty of Historicism.* 2nd ed. Boston: Basic Books; London: Routledge & Paul, 1960. (Original ed., 1944–45.)

Randall, John Herman, Jr. *Nature and Historical Experience: Essays in Naturalism and in the Theory of History.* New York: Columbia Univ. Pr., 1958.

Rorty, Richard, ed. "Historicism and Epistemology." *Monist* 53, no. 1:445–582 (Oct. 1977).

Smith, John E., et al. "Philosophy of History." *Monist* 53, no. 1:1–133 (Jan. 1969).

Walsh, William H. *Philosophy of History: An Introduction.* 2nd ed. New York: Harper Torchbooks, 1960; London: Hutchinson, 1958. (1st ed., 1951.)

White, Hayden. *Metahistory: The Historical Imagination in Nineteenth-Century Europe.* Baltimore, Md.: Johns Hopkins Univ. Pr., 1973.

White, Morton. *Foundations of Historical Knowledge.* New York and London: Harper & Row, 1965.

Yovel, Yirmiahu, ed. *Philosophy of History and Action: Papers Presented at the First Jerusalem Philosophical Encounter, December 1974.* Dordrecht and Boston: Reidel; Jerusalem: Magnes Pr., 1978.

25

Social-Political
Philosophy

The Social-Political Domain

Suppose you were to accept some such characterization of morality as that of William Frankena, summarized in chapter 22. Add to that a placing of the locales of moral activity at four interlocking levels: (1) the personal, such that you could have self-regarding obligations, directed to yourself as equal to all other members of the human race, possessed of human dignity, and worthy of respect; (2) the interpersonal, mostly one-on-one; (3) the group, comprised of family relations and group participation in the great variety of areas in which we have social relations and form our social identities; and (4) the political, which refers to ways in which the life of all is arranged and goods are distributed within a society and internationally. This is a scheme I would use. Accordingly, the first two levels are those ordinarily treated in moral philosophy, though some philosophers are more attuned than others to interactions among all four levels. The last two levels are the usual domain of social-political philosophy. Moreover, just as some philosophers working on the first two levels may take special heed to conventional or prudential matters, the choice partly depending on their initial point of view about morality, so do those working primarily on the second two levels. The activities to which this larger range of choices at the second two levels is directed makes up the general subject matter of social-political philosophy.

Today probably most of the topics of social-political philosophy—often called "political philosophy" for short—are more familiar, even to the relatively untutored, than are those of any other area of

436

philosophy. Readily they weave into the fabric of our common life. Social and political theory is discussed not only by philosophers but also by social scientists, historians, media commentators, politicians, and social activists, not infrequently with depth and finesse. Nevertheless the philosophers, who alone are featured here, have their own distinctive methods and concerns to bring to the scholarly and public conversation.

(As a supplement to the historical surveys given below, see the index under "Social-political philosophy" and under their own names for the several references to individual thinkers. Recent theory by nonphilosophers is especially important in this area and comprises a large literature; such coverage is beyond the scope of this study, however, so must be sought elsewhere.)

The Tradition—Sustained, Broken, and Revived

The great moments in the past came with Plato and Aristotle, the Romans and Augustine, the medieval to Renaissance views of natural law and of the state, responses to Machiavelli on the art of politics, then the first systematic modern statement by Thomas Hobbes, followed by John Locke, Jean-Jacques Rousseau, Georg W. F. Hegel, John Stuart Mill, Karl Marx, T. H. Green, and the British idealists. Developments of thought among these and other political theorists have been chronicled in George Sabine's (1937) outstanding intellectual history. From Hobbe's *Leviathan* (1651) through the nineteenth century, political theory was a steady and prominent part of Anglo-American philosophical tradition. It generally had an important role to play in continental European philosophy as well.

In numerous writings John Dewey (e.g., *The Public and Its Problems,* 1927) applied the grand tradition to the special problems of a growing democratic society and to a critique of schemes alternative to democracy, efforts in which he was especially succeeded by Sidney Hook (e.g., *Philosophy and Public Policy,* 1980) throughout another long career. From the 1920s to the 1960s the paucity of effort among British philosophers, dominated by analytic interests, was simply highlighted by the many popular writings of Bertrand Russell, since he too held firmly to the fact/value, analytic/normative split generally presupposed and regarded such work as of relatively minor philosophical importance. Until the 1970s the only twentieth-century work in political philosophy that might deserve to be measured "great" by past standards was *The New Leviathan* by R. G. Collingwood (1942), written by a man recovering from stroke and in great haste but responsive to the rising crisis of civilization he had been among the few to perceive in the 1930s. And this work was largely ignored at the time. Since Augustine most of the other notable theoretical statements had also been made in response to widespread public crisis.

In 1956, a quite knowledgeable philosopher, Peter Laslett, pronounced this area of philosophy "dead." He attributed its death chiefly to logical positivism and its analytic successors. It is true that until the 1960s only a few philosophers, most notably T. D. Weldon, were applying analytic methods to social-political problems. Nor was it thriving outside analytic circles, with notable exceptions like "natural rights" theorist Leo Strauss (1953). Only with the public crises from the mid-1960s onward did a new era of reflection open up at last, by the early 1980s one unprecedented in quality and in scope.

HISTORY AND CURRENT STATUS

The Long View

A history of political theory from the perspective of more recent knowledge and conceptualization has yet to be written. Until then, George Sabine's classic history (1937) may be accompanied by works such as the following. First there is C. B. Macpherson's fresh analysis (1973) of doctrines and presuppositions centering on "possessive individualism" among the seventeenth-eighteenth century founders of modern liberal thought. As L. T. Hobhouse's classic summary (1911) of liberalism best shows, the term "liberal" here refers to a tradition opposed to monarchy, state absolutism, and the like, not to the contemporary liberal/conservative distinction. One of the most illuminating analyses of the latter distinction has come from Ronald Dworkin (in Stuart Hampshire, 1978). Renaissance and Reformation thought has been outlined at length by Quentin Skinner (1978). A work of major importance by J. G. A. Pocock (1975) traces focal issues from Machiavelli and early sixteenth-century Florentine political thought to Anglo-American thought in the seventeenth to nineteenth centuries. He conceives these issues to be necessary ingredients in present-day views of historical and political processes and of alienation from those processes. In a study on the treatment of women in Western political philosophy, especially in Plato, Aristotle, Rousseau, and Mill, Susan Moller Okin (1979) finds that the only place within that tradition where women are included on the same terms as men is within the guardian class in Plato's *Republic*.

Twentieth-Century Thought

Since John Stuart Mill, most elements of political theory favored by British philosophers have been utilitarian, and the issues have generally been engaged on the soil of moral theory. Attempts to improve on these elements remained the focus of attention in the 1970s. This emphasis has been so strong that Melvin Richter (*The Politics of Conscience,* 1964, cited on p. 149) has had to insert the reminder that the British idealists had a great impact on British political thought and reform in the late nineteenth and early twentieth centuries. The same was true of related educational practice, as Peter Gordon and John White (*Philosophers as Educational Reformers,* 1979, cited on p. 148) have shown. Until recently continental Europe chiefly brought the actual occasions and prophetic assessments of Western crisis (Oswald Spengler, Edmund Husserl, Martin Heidegger, Karl Jaspers, Jose Ortega y Gasset, Nicolai Berdyaev, and others) that would lead to new thought. It did not contribute so much to philosophical substance. An early exception is to be found in the seminal work of Max Scheler (1924) on issues that arise within the search for an effective sociology of knowledge.

Particularly through the continual waves of liberal-progressive thought, reform, and historical inquiry—which have been well studied outside philosophy—American political theory has been in flux throughout the century. All these movements have tended to be suspicious of excessive formalism and to enter into the flow of vital social reality. Yet in 1949 Morton White, surveying the half-century before the wrenching depression of the 1930s, rued the virtual demise of this way of thinking in American social thought. In a noted review of this same era in educational thought and practice, taken into the mid-1950s, Lawrence Cremin (not cited here) came to the same conclusion. John Dewey was the only professional philosopher among the main purveyors of this progressive tradition, most of whom had died by the early 1930s.

In the period just after World War II, political philosophy tended to concentrate on a comparative assessment of communism, fascism, and democracy; and this trend continued for some years. Karl Popper's semihistorical treatise on *The Open Society and Its Enemies* (1945) set the stage in Britain. Both that work and Michael Oakeshott's conservative-rationalist essays (1962) represent the predominantly formalist tradition there. In either Britain, Europe, or America it was unusual to find careful analyses as are performed in the essays on justice and political argument by Chaim Perelman (1963), professor of logic and ethics at the University of Brussels.

Exemplary, influential works from the period between roughly 1945 and 1965 are those on liberty by F. A. Hayek (1960) and Isaiah Berlin (1969, picking up a theme he first articulated in his famous inaugural lecture of 1958). For the first time in a systematic way, Stanley Benn and R. S. Peters (1959) applied the newer analytic techniques to democratic political theory. In presenting "a cautious Utilitarianism which takes full account of the principle of impartiality," they presage much of the succeeding discussion, especially in Britain. Four collections represent the new trends in America: a Nomos volume on justice edited by Carl Friedrich and John Chapman (1963), two mostly analytic works on justice edited by Frederick Olafson (1961) and Richard Brandt (1962)—actually, also including treatments of freedom and equality, the other two principles usually discussed and compared—and the opening of Peter Laslett's social-political philosophy series in 1956 (in five volumes through 1979, which move from predominately nonanalytic to mainly analytic approaches, as did the area overall). Recent works by Hanna Fenichel Pitkin (1972) and John Danford (1978) show that the thought of Ludwig Wittgenstein has relevance for social-political inquiry. So far the chief influence seems to have occurred indirectly, at first most noticeably in philosophy of law, from about 1960 on, then in other areas as well.

A medley of theoretical approaches starts off the new era in a collection edited by Richard De George (1966). In his book on "radical liberalism" Arnold Kaufmann (1968), an analytic philosopher who was a founder of the "teach-in" movement in 1965, more immediately met the challenges to conventional thinking from the civil rights movement and the New Left, in both of which he was an active but critical participant. The renewed interest in "human rights" is indicated in a *Monist* collection edited by Herbert Morris (1968). A book by Terrence Tice (1976) presents moral, political, and legal issues caught up in concerns about "student rights," which date especially from the 1965–75 period.

"Civil disobedience" likewise became an important theme. Carl Cohen (1971), who had edited a 1970 *Monist* symposium on it (not cited here), gave it systematic treatment. Hugo Bedau (1969), who has also written extensively on political and criminal justice issues, edited a book of essays on it. More recently Ted Honderich (1976) has discussed the broader theme of "political violence."

Several varieties of politically oriented theologies gained a large following from the 1960s on, though some had been essentially formed a decade or more earlier. Among the many figures, the Protestants included Paul Lehmann, Jürgen Moltmann, Dorothee Soelle, James Cone, Richard Shaull, José Míguez Bonino, and Frederick Herzog; the Roman Catholics included J. B. Metz, Gustavo Gutierrez, Rosemary Ruether, and J. L. Segundo. "Liberation theology" was a catchword for some of these interests, "black theology" and "feminist theology" for a few. Although the writings of such theologians were not intended to purvey philosophical content, as such, some of them were philosophically informed; occasionally the influence flowed in the other direction.

Finally, the Nomos series, dating from 1958, includes a multidisciplinary volume on "equality" edited by J. Roland Pennock and John Chapman (1967). This principle, unlike those of freedom and justice, has rarely been put forth as the basic political principle; but it has risen in importance since the 1960s. So have the themes of social, political, and (or versus) legal obligation, featured in a 1970 Nomos volume edited by these two men and in a systematic work, both historically grounded and responsive to debates of the 1970s, by A. John Simmons (1979).

Connections with Ethical and Legal Theory

Still another Nomos volume edited by Pennock and Chapman (1979) indicates one among many thematic areas of common interest among the domains explored by moral, political, and legal theory. In this instance the theme is "compromise." Machiavelli has especially bequeathed the following question to political philosophy: To what extent should the restraints that may apply to private morality also be placed upon political action and public policy? A fine little volume by Stuart Hampshire (1978) with Bernard Williams, Thomas Nagel, T. M. Scanlon, and Ronald Dworkin tackles issues central to this problem. Literature on practical reasoning and on practical uses of moral theory has been noted in chapter 22; related materials follow in chapter 26. Perelman's (1963) volume includes some fresh thinking on political argument, to which Brian Barry (1965) devoted an entire treatise. The pertinent rules of argument have since become a major concern in all three domains. Another connecting tissue is the concept of "rights." In chapter 22 some works are noted that take a "rights" approach to basic moral theory, not relegating it to the social-political and legal domains alone.

Overviews, Introductions, and Collections

Melvin Richter (1980) has edited an excellent overview of major tasks in the current practice of political philosophy—the study of texts, the recognition of political philosophers as historical actors, analytic work, coming to an understanding with Marxism, interacting with the social sciences, entering into political decision making, and legal and political education—something of an agenda for the 1980s and beyond. Richter's own fifty-four-page introduction places these items in historical perspective. A much-used brief introduction by Joel Feinberg (1973) deals mainly with freedom and coercion, legal and human rights, and social justice. A collection of his essays (1980) expands on these same themes. An example of a more European approach comes from hermeneutical phenomenologist Paul Ricoeur (1974), whose writing is also close to concerns debated among the European churches. Other examples of both European and Anglo-American thought are cited in chapters 7 and 11–13, while Anglo-American thought is further represented in chapters 8–10.

The two main treatises of the 1970s, much-debated and on a par with the greater works of past centuries, were John Rawls's *A Theory of Justice* (1971), which presents a considerably modified utilitarianism, and Robert Nozick's *Anarchy, State and Utopia* (1974), which argues for the libertarian position that only a "minimal state, limited to the narrow functions of protection against force, theft, fraud, enforcement of contracts, and so on," is justified with respect to the more fundamental rights of individuals. (More about these below.) A third volume, by Ronald Dworkin (1977), which carefully defends a liberal theory of law based on an underlying moral conception of individual rights, also warrants the ascription of greatness.

A few collections sum up the growing variety of interests in the area. Those by Laslett and others culminate in a 1979 volume of thirteen essays; while contributors to earlier volumes were mostly British, these are mostly American and two are from Australia. This is reflective of a growing predominance of Americans working in the area. Of chiefly British provenance is a collection edited by Ted Honderich (1976); of chiefly American provenance is possibly the largest collection of original essays in social-political philosophy ever made, edited by Peter French et al. (1982). Both are analytic in approach. Collections on specific subjects will be mentioned below.

Basic Principles

Most of the works already indicated deal with basic principles and the corresponding rights in some fashion, for these are the main substance of any well-formed political philosophy. Historically speaking, the list of "human rights" that are frequently mentioned has grown within the modern age. They are usually thought of as universally binding moral ideals or rights and are ordinarily subsumed under the principles of freedom, justice, or equality. Two recent collections of essays capture what the discussion on human rights has come to. All contributors to Alan Rosenbaum's (1980) sizable volume of international perspectives on the foundations, meanings, and applications of human rights are philosophers. Rosenbaum's own forty-two-page essay includes a historical survey and an account of recent views. In the smaller collection edited by Australians Eugene Kamenka and Alice Ehr-Soon Tay (1978), four philosophers join five others (from jurisprudence, sociology, and political science) in presenting basic analyses of the concept.

In addition to the Benn and Peters (1959) volume, several have been devoted to the general theory of democracy, and it would be the ultimate aim of most Anglo-American political philosophers to contribute to such a theory. Particularly representative of these efforts are a 1971 *Monist* symposium by Carl Cohen and others, essays by C. B. Macpherson (1973), and a large systematic work by J. Roland Pennock (1979). As Macpherson (1962) has indicated especially well, the notion of "property rights" has been of major importance in the history of liberal-democratic theory. In a clear, parsimonious manner, Lawrence Becker (1977) presents general and coordinated arguments for justification of private property based on concepts of labor, utility (including economic considerations), and political liberty; and he either rejects or considers the possible merits of other considerations. In these respects, contemporary philosophers would generally regard this as a model work. Viewed from Marxist and socialist perspectives its content leaves much to be desired. These viewpoints, however, do not yet play much of a role in mainline Anglo-American social-political philosophy. Although Dewey's views can be construed as offering a mediating position, outside education circles they have not been much discussed in recent decades.

Is there one basic political principle that should order social life in general and in relation to which other principles are derivative or subsidiary? Both justice and freedom have been so conceived. A tendency to emphasize freedom, or liberty, shows up in the writings of Berlin, Hayek, and Kaufman, already cited. In a collection edited by Robert Cunningham (1979), philosophers Joseph Raz, Ronald Dworkin, Tibor Machan, Rolf Sartorius, and Cunningham join scholars from other fields in appraising Hayek's position. A volume edited by Alan Ryan (1979) offers essays on freedom in honor of Berlin.

Works on justice by Perelman, Olafson, and Brandt have already been noted. This principle has always been particularly attractive to ethical deontologists and rule-utilitarians, though not exclusively. John Rawls's modified utilitarian view (1971) of justice was the chief reference for much of the discussion on justice and other related issues during the 1970s. Within the huge literature specifically focused on Rawls's arguments, the following are especially notable: critical examinations by Brian Barry (1973) and Robert Paul Wolff (1977), a collection gathering the first wave of response edited by Norman Daniels (1975), and an extensive treatment on egalitarian liberalism especially developed in opposition to Rawls by Vinit Haksar (1979). Haksar rejects Rawls's view that judgments of intrinsic value regarding human beings, even some human beings and some forms or ways of human life (perfectionism) should be bypassed in a theory of justice.

Two comprehensive discussions of justice, by David Miller (1976) and J. R. Lucas (1980), are also reflective of the Rawls debate but chiefly go their own ways. Both are historically oriented and use conceptual analysis. Miller includes a critique of theories by David Hume, Herbert Spencer, and Peter Kropotkin (each representing a type of theory) and concludes with an "interpretive sociology." This final social application attempts to show how an emphasis on one of the three distinct, conflicting elements of the idea "social justice"— protection of rights, according of deserts, and distribution by need—leads to a different form of society: hierarchical, market, and egalitarian, respectively (the third in theory only, so far). Primitive societies, he holds, do not possess an idea of social justice but organize around a notion of the common good.

Robert Nozick's book (1974) defending a libertarian position, like

Rawls's book, engendered much controversy. Jeffrey Paul (1981) has collected twenty critical essays on his views, including six on his entitlement (versus distributive) theory of social justice.

Philosophy of Social Science

The issues typically considered in philosophy of psychology and psychoanalysis (chapter 29) somewhat overlap with those treated in philosophy of social science; and some philosophers would derive them both completely from a general philosophy of science (chapter 23), following a natural science paradigm. In any case, the complex set of social factors that must be considered in any thorough scrutiny of the social sciences would seem to require special treatment. Such treatment, moreover, should be performed in close association with, if not dependence on, social-political theory and practice. Therefore, for the present at least, a comfortable niche can be found for it within social-political philosophy.

Each type of position surveyed in chapters 10–13 has wrought its own distinct approaches to philosophy of social science—pragmatist, Marxist, existentialist, phenomenological, hermeneutical approaches, and the hybrid critical theory approach. These as well as the analytic discussions have been directed primarily to five thematic areas: (1) the explanation and prediction of social behavior, (2) the relation of values to theory formation and selection, (3) the place of normative practical thinking in social discourse, (4) the comparative status of individual action and social process (the "holist" position is defined by its not reducing the basis for understanding social processes to individual action), and (5) specific methods of inquiry and interpretation. Theoretical frameworks used in general critiques of ideologies and social-political theories also draw from these thematic areas.

All five areas are represented in some fashion in positivist May Brodbeck's large collection (1968) of readings, though such a collection would have to be very differently organized by the early 1980s. Only numbers 1 and 2 are included among the eight new studies recently edited by Christopher Hookway and Philip Pettit (1978). Peter Winch's partly Wittgensteinian essay, *The Idea of a Social Science and Its Relation to Philosophy* (1963), much referred to, deals mostly with number 1. He closely associates his constructive views with R. G. Collingwood's historical-contextual way of distinguishing social science tasks from those of the natural sciences. Among the Europeans, Karl-Otto Apel (1967) especially uses linguistic analysis to consider such issues (number 1). Max Scheler (1924) and his followers tend to start by assigning a significant role to values (number 2) then move to other issues. Abraham Edel's essays (1979), accrued over four decades, also center on the attempt to break down the fact-value split, still assumed in most other philosophy of social science.

Area number 3 is featured in Hector-Neri Castañeda's work (1975), which is based on a comprehensive theory of action. Castañeda attempts to bypass the theory of values by presenting them as simply representations of facts about wants, intentions, and the like. Although every theorist has to take some position on the individual action versus holistic understanding of social process, no single philosophical work represents this interest (number 4). Abraham Kaplan's *The Conduct of Inquiry* (1964) offers a more pragmatic account of all five areas, as had Dewey's work overall; it does not bypass theory of values and deals much more with specific kinds of method (number 5) than usual. The collection edited by Werner Leinfellner and Eckehart Köhler deals largely with number 5, as does the integrated effort of Rom Harré and P. F. Secord (1972).

Few introductions to philosophy of social science are yet available. Among the books just listed, those by Winch, Brodbeck, Kaplan, and Hookway and Pettit serve diverse introductory purposes. The brief analytic introduction by Richard Rudner (1966) treats mostly thematic areas numbers 1 and 2, and it places special emphasis on teleological and functional systems. Alan Ryan (1970) offers an introduction of slightly broader scope. So far no single work grasps the entire range of debate over their foundations, functions, and methods that has flourished among the social sciences themselves since the mid-1960s.

Practical Applications

All the works reported in this chapter bear possible implications for actual social or scientific practice. Some writings, however, are directed to specific types of practical application. This has been a distinctive mark of the writings of John Dewey and Sidney Hook. Some additional works that stem more directly from moral than from social-political theory have already been cited in chapter 22. Here, as there, almost all the important ones have appeared since the late 1960s, but with a comparative time-lag of several years on the whole. Representative of the growing scope of involvement by philosophers in matters of public policy are the 1972 *Monist* collection by Richard Wasserstrom and others; his own recent volume (1980); the collections on ethical issues in government, edited by Norman Bowie (1981); and on foreign policy issues, edited by Henry Shue

(1980). The collection on parenting issues, edited by Onora O'Neill and William Ruddick (1979), is reflective of recent interests in children's rights. That on issues of social-economic growth and planning, edited by Joseph Grunfeld (1979), is a particularly surprising latecomer given the widespread knowledge of national and global crises related to these issues since the late 1960s.

FUTURE PROSPECTS

Precisely these practical themes are likely to elicit far more extensive effort among social-political philosophers over the next twenty years than has been exercised over the past several decades. There will no doubt also be proportionately greater attention to political education issues, already highlighted in the 1980 Richter volume.

Increased investment is also to be expected not only in philosophy of social science but also in its interactions with ideology (taken as the larger concept) and with social-political theory. As in the rest of ethics, broadly conceived, the best work will tend to be that which is well grounded in historical, presuppositional, and conceptual analysis and which is thoroughly argued. Two additional criteria, that have not often been placed on such work, are those of contextual awareness, timeliness, and pertinence to long-term concerns about humane survival. To be "practical" in anything more than an ad hoc or prudential sense, these philosophical efforts will have to adopt an empirically informed, long-term, future-responsive view; and to do this they will have to rely on interdisciplinary cooperation.

Economics is so far heavily neglected among the social sciences that have received specific critical treatment. Perhaps economics is more appropriately referred to not as a separate "field," despite the current fashion, but as a set of factors operative in any general social-political ideology or theory. In any case, particular conceptions of economic factors are presupposed and dominant in virtually every social system today, and these conceptions require philosophical examination.

Apel, Karl-Otto. *Analytic Philosophy of Language and the Geisteswissenschaften.* Dordrecht and Boston: Reidel, 1967.
Barry, Brian. *The Liberal Theory of Justice: A Critical Examination of the Principal Doctrines in "A Theory of Justice" by John Rawls.* New York: Oxford Univ. Pr.; Oxford: Clarendon Pr., 1973.
———. *Political Argument.* New York: Humanities Pr.; London: Routledge & Paul, 1965.

Becker, Lawrence C. *Property Rights: Philosophic Foundations.* London and Boston: Routledge & Paul, 1977.

Bedau, Hugo, ed. *Civil Disobedience: Theory and Practice.* New York: Pegasus, 1969.

Benn, Stanley I., and R. S. Peters. *Social Principles and the Democratic State.* London: Allen & Unwin, 1959. Repr. as *The Principles of Political Thought.* New York: Free Pr., 1964.

Berlin, Isaiah. *Four Essays on Liberty.* Oxford and New York: Oxford Univ. Pr., 1969.

Bowie, Norman E., ed. *Ethical Issues in Government.* Philadelpia, Pa.: Temple Univ. Pr., 1981.

Brandt, Richard B., ed. *Social Justice.* Englewood Cliffs, N.J.: Prentice-Hall Spectrum Book, 1962.

Brodbeck, May, ed. *Readings in the Philosophy of the Social Sciences.* New York: Macmillan; London: Collier Macmillan, 1968.

Castañeda, Hector-Neri. *Thinking and Doing: The Philosophical Foundations of Institutions.* Dordrecht and Boston: Reidel, 1975.

Cohen, Carl. *Civil Disobedience: Conscience, Tactics, and the Law.* New York and London: Columbia Univ. Pr., 1971.

――――, et al. "Foundations of Democracy." *Monist* 55, no. 1:1–159 (Jan. 1971).

Collingwood, Robin G. *The New Leviathan.* Oxford: Clarendon Pr., 1942.

Cunningham, Robert L., ed. *Liberty and the Rule of Law.* College Station: Texas A & M Univ. Pr., 1979.

Danford, John W. *Wittgenstein and Political Philosophy: A Reexamination of the Foundations of Social Science.* Chicago and London: Univ. of Chicago Pr., 1978.

Daniels, Norman, ed. *Reading Rawls: Critical Studies on Rawls' A Theory of Justice.* New York: Basic Books; Oxford: Blackwell, 1975.

De George, Richard T., ed. *Ethics and Society: Original Essays on Contemporary Moral Problems.* Garden City, N.Y.: Doubleday Anchor, 1966.

Dewey, John. *The Public and Its Problems.* New York: Henry Holt, 1927. Repr.: Denver: Alan Swallow, n.d.

✓ Dworkin, Ronald. *Taking Rights Seriously.* Cambridge, Mass.: Harvard Univ. Pr., 1977.

Edel, Abraham. *Science, Ideology and Value.* Vol. 1, *Analyzing Concepts in Social Science;* vol. 2, *Exploring Fact and Value.* New Brunswick, N.J.: Transaction Books, 1979–80.

Feinberg, Joel. *Rights, Justice, and the Bounds of Liberty: Essays in Social Philosophy.* Princeton, N.J. and Guildford, Surrey: Princeton Univ. Pr., 1980. (Previously published essays, 1964–78.)

――――. *Social Philosophy.* Englewood Cliffs, N.J.: Prentice-Hall, 1973.

✓ French, Peter A., Theodore E. Uehling, Jr., and Howard K. Wettstein, eds. *Midwest Studies in Philosophy.* Vol. 7, *Social and Political Philosophy.* Minneapolis: Univ. of Minnesota Pr., 1982.

Friedrich, Carl J., and John W. Chapman, eds. *Justice. Nomos* 6. New York: Atherton Pr., 1963.

Grunfeld, Joseph, ed. *Growth in a Finite World.* Philadelphia, Pa.: Franklin Institute Pr., 1979.

Haksar, Vinit. *Equality, Liberty and Perfectionism.* Oxford and New York: Oxford Univ. Pr., 1979.

Hampshire, Stuart, et al. *Public and Private Morality.* Cambridge and New York: Cambridge Univ. Pr., 1978.

Harré, Rom, and P. F. Secord. *The Explanation of Social Behavior.* Totowa, N.J.: Littlefield, Adams, 1973; Oxford: Blackwell, 1972.

Hayek, Friedrich A. *The Constitution of Liberty.* Chicago: Univ. of Chicago Pr.; London: Routledge & Paul, 1960.

Hobhouse, L. T. *Liberalism.* Oxford: Oxford Univ. Pr., 1911. Repr., with Introduction by Alan P. Grimes, New York: Oxford Univ. Pr., 1964.

Honderich, Ted. *Political Violence.* Ithaca, N.Y.: Cornell Univ. Pr.; Oxford: Blackwell, 1976.

————, ed. *Social Ends and Political Means.* London and Boston: Routledge & Paul, 1976.

Hook, Sidney. *Philosophy and Public Policy.* Carbondale: Southern Illinois Univ. Pr.; London: Feffer & Simons, 1980. (Previously published essays, 1945–78.)

Hookway, Christopher, and Philip Pettit, eds. *Action and Interpretation: Studies in the Philosophy of the Social Sciences.* Cambridge and New York: Cambridge Univ. Pr., 1978.

Kamenka, Eugene, and Alice Ehr-Soon Tay, eds. *Human Rights.* New York: St. Martin's Pr., 1978.

Kaplan, Abraham. *The Conduct of Inquiry.* San Francisco: Chandler, 1964.

Kaufman, Arnold S. *The Radical Liberal: New Man in American Politics.* New York: Atherton Pr., 1968.

Laslett, Peter, ed. *Philosophy, Politics, and Society: A Collection.* New York: Macmillan; Oxford: Blackwell, 1956. The 2nd–5th series were also edited by Laslett and others, with the title *Philosophy, Politics, and Society,* each time published by Blackwell: 2nd–3rd ser., with W. G. Runciman (New York: Barnes & Noble, 1962, 1967); 4th ser., with W. G. Runciman and Quentin Skinner (New York: Barnes & Noble, 1972); 5th ser., with James Fishkin (New Haven, Conn.: Yale Univ. Pr., 1979).

Leinfellner, Werner, and Eckehart Köhler, eds. *Developments in the Methodology of Social Science.* Dordrecht and Boston: Reidel, 1974.

Lucas, J. R. *On Justice.* New York: Oxford Univ. Pr.; Oxford: Clarendon Pr., 1980.

Macpherson, Crawford B. *Democratic Theory: Essays in Retrieval.* New York: Oxford Univ. Pr.; Oxford: Clarendon Pr., 1973.

————. *The Political Theory of Possessive Individualism: Hobbes to Locke.* New York: Oxford Univ. Pr.; Oxford: Clarendon Pr., 1962.

Miller, David. *Social Justice.* New York: Oxford Univ. Pr.; Oxford: Clarendon Pr., 1976.

Morris, Herbert, et al. "Human Rights." *Monist* 52, no. 4:475–639 (Oct. 1968).

Nozick, Robert. *Anarchy, State and Utopia.* New York: Basic Books; Oxford: Blackwell, 1974.

Oakeshott, Michael. *Rationalism in Politics and Other Essays.* London: Methuen, 1962.

Okin, Susan Moller. *Women in Western Political Thought*. Princeton, N.J. and Guildford, Surrey: Princeton Univ. Pr., 1979.

Olafson, Frederick A., ed. *Justice and Social Policy*. Englewood Cliffs, N.J.: Prentice-Hall, 1961.

O'Neill, Onora, and William Ruddick, eds. *Having Children: Philosophical and Legal Reflections on Parenting*. Oxford and New York: Oxford Univ. Pr., 1979.

Paul, Jeffrey, ed. *Reading Nozick: Essays on Anarchy, State and Utopia*. Totowa, N.J.: Rowman & Littlefield, 1981.

Pennock, James Roland. *Democratic Political Theory*. Princeton, N.J. and Guildford, Surrey: Princeton Univ. Pr., 1979.

———, and John W. Chapman, eds. *Compromise in Ethics, Law, and Politics*. Nomos 21. New York: New York Univ. Pr., 1979.

———, eds. *Equality*. Nomos 9. New York: Atherton Pr., 1967.

———, eds. *Political and Legal Obligation*. Nomos 12. New York: Atherton Pr., 1970.

Perelman, Chaim. *The Idea of Justice and the Problem of Argument*. Tr. by John Petrie. New York: Humanities Pr.; London: Routledge & Paul, 1963. (A collection of his essays.)

Pitkin, Hanna Fenichel. *Wittgenstein and Justice: On the Significance of Ludwig Wittgenstein for Social and Political Thought*. Berkeley and London: Univ. of California Pr, 1972.

Pocock, J. G. A. *The Machiavellian Moment: Florentine Political Thought and the Atlantic Republican Tradition*. Princeton, N.J. and London: Princeton Univ. Pr., 1975.

Popper, Karl. *The Open Society and Its Enemies*. Rev. ed. Princeton, N.J.: Princeton Univ. Pr., 1950. (Original ed., London: Routledge & Paul, 1945; 4th rev. ed., 1961.) (Original vol. 1, *The Spell of Plato;* vol. 2, *The High Tide of Prophecy;* especially Aristotle, Hegel, and Marx.)

Rawls, John. *A Theory of Justice*. Cambridge, Mass.: Belknap Pr. of Harvard Univ. Pr., 1971; Oxford: Oxford Univ. Pr., 1972.

Richter, Melvin, ed. *Political Theory and Political Education*. Princeton, N.J. and Guildford, Surrey: Princeton Univ. Pr., 1980.

Ricouer, Paul. *Political and Social Essays*. Ed. by David Stewart and Joseph Bien. Athens: Ohio Univ. Pr., 1974.

Rosenbaum, Alan S., ed. *The Philosophy of Human Rights: International Perspectives*. Westport, Conn.: Greenwood, 1980.

Rudner, Richard S. *Philosophy of Social Science*. Englewood Cliffs, N.J.: Prentice-Hall, 1966.

Ryan, Alan. *The Philosophy of the Social Sciences*. New York: Pantheon, 1970.

———, ed. *The Idea of Freedom: Essays in Honour of Isaiah Berlin*. Oxford and New York: Oxford Univ. Pr., 1979.

Sabine, George H. *A History of Political Theory*. Rev. ed. New York: Holt, 1950. (Original ed., 1937.)

Scheler, Max. *Problems of a Sociology of Knowledge*. Ed. by Kenneth W. Stikkers, tr. by Manfred S. Frings. London and Boston: Routledge and Paul, 1980. (Original German ed., 1924.)

Shue, Henry. *Basic Rights: Subsistence, Affluence, and U.S. Foreign Policy*.

Princeton, N.J. and Guildford, Surrey: Princeton Univ. Pr., 1980. (From Center for Philosophy and Public Policy.)

Simmons, A. John. *Moral Principles and Political Obligations.* Princeton, N.J. and Guildford, Surrey: Princeton Univ. Pr., 1979.

Skinner, Quentin. *The Foundations of Modern Political Thought.* Vol. 1, *The Renaissance;* vol. 2, *The Age of Reformation.* Cambridge and New York: Cambridge Univ. Pr., 1978.

Strauss, Leo. *Natural Right and History.* Chicago: Univ. of Chicago Pr., 1953.

Tice, Terrence N. *Student Rights, Decisionmaking, and the Law.* ERIC/ Higher Education Research Report No. 10. Washington, D.C.: American Assn. for Higher Education, 1976.

Wasserstrom, Richard A. *Philosophy and Social Issues: Five Studies.* Notre Dame, Ind. and London: Univ. of Notre Dame Pr., 1980.

————, et al. "Philosophy and Public Policy." *Monist* 56, no. 1:1–139 (Jan. 1972).

White, Morton. *Social Thought in America: The Revolt against Formalism.* New York: Viking Pr., 1949.

Winch, Peter. *The Idea of a Social Science and Its Relation to Philosophy.* New York: Humanities Pr.; London: Routledge & Paul, 1963.

Wolff, Robert Paul. *Understanding Rawls: A Reconstruction and Critique of A Theory of Justice.* Princeton, N.J. and Guildford, Surrey: Princeton Univ. Pr., 1977.

26

Philosophy
of Law

What are the relative functions of law and authority in achieving public order, how are they grounded, and why should one obey them? In what does a just order consist, and how is justice to be upheld and fostered? Philosophy of law begins with serious reflection on these questions among the Sophists in the late fifth century B.C., with their conflicts with Socrates, and with the systematic efforts of Plato and Aristotle. Apart from special references to laws, however, it was indistinguishable as a subject from morals and politics. The Sophists tended to regard law as convention and to regard obedience only as a matter of promoting one's self-interest, except those (like Callicles in Plato's *Gorgias*) who believed that rule of the strongest is a law of nature. Socrates, Plato, and Aristotle rejected all three views. For them, law is rooted in human nature, in a reasoned understanding of moral virtue, and in the harmonizing requirements of justice; it seeks the common good.

Scarcely any major area of concern to legal philosophers today was not treated by these men, although what was specifically meant by such questions as they raised and by the concepts they used to respond has been largely replaced by other meanings and formulations over the centuries. Most notably, a strong and varied natural law tradition emerged out of these early efforts. This occurred first through the effect of Stoic thought on Roman law, where a distinction was made between laws that apply to all nature, to all societies, or to a particular society (civil law). As legal theory came to be integrated with theology, all these other forms of law tended to be contrasted with and held under the ultimate authority of divine law.

452

Building on systematization of the Church's canon law in the previous century, in the thirteenth century Thomas Aquinas placed all law within a hierarchical divine order and under specific standards of right reason. In his view, all human laws are subject to the natural law, which God has ordained. From the sixteenth through the nineteenth centuries issues of legislative, executive, and judicial power with respect to law, of international law, of equality and freedom under or as (sovereign) expressions of the law, and of challenge to natural law traditions formed as societies and social visions changed.

Jeremy Bentham (1748–1832) and his early followers revolutionized jurisprudence (the theory of legal practices) and led the way to important legal reforms in England. Their thinking moved swiftly in the direction of the utilitarian and positivist views that have had increasing acceptance in Anglo-American legal theory since the mid-nineteenth century. Utilitarian views distinctively require criteria for maximizing good within a society or overall, without reference to a fixed nonsocietal standard. Legal positivist views hold that the laws of a society are conventions and do not necessarily cohere with the precepts of an ideal morality or with religious doctrine.

A century later analytic philosopher Herbert Hart drew from the seminal thinking of John Austin (1790–1859) in both respects. In his bringing knowledge of contemporary logic, philosophy of language, philosophy of action, ethics, and social-political philosophy to bear on issues of legal theory Hart is generally deemed to have provided a service to Anglo-American philosophy of law as great as Bentham's to jurisprudence. He has even made it more difficult to separate the concerns of jurisprudence from those of philosophy directed to legal issues. In both Britain and America the field had lain virtually dormant since the 1930s. Both lawyer and philosopher, Hart took interest in the combination, quickened by close association with Oxford philosophers Gilbert Ryle and Stuart Hampshire as they did military intelligence work together during World War II. He joined them at Oxford after the war, then gained the Chair of Jurisprudence there in 1952. This he resigned in 1968 to devote more time to a coeditorship of Bentham's writings and membership on the Monopolies Commission of the United Kingdom. His first book, *Causation in the Law* (1959), jointly authored with another Oxford jurist A. M. Honoré, masterfully demonstrated the rootage of legal concepts in ordinary discourse. Since publication of Hart's most famous book *The Concept of Law* (1961), much of the awakening in legal philosophy has related closely to his ongoing work. Neil MacCormick's first volume

(1981) in a projected series on legal theorists not only critically reviews Hart's work in its interaction with that of predecessors and contemporaries but also displays something of that influence. A volume of sixteen substantial essays honoring Hart on his seventieth birthday, edited by P. M. S. Hacker and Joseph Raz (1977), shows that the influence was still waxing then.

Because of the great renascence of legal philosophy since about 1960, the very terms by which an adequate history of previous efforts could be written have altered. No historical survey as yet reflects this change. Nevertheless, that by Huntington Cairns (1949) is still serviceable, as is that of political theorist Carl Friedrich (1963).

In the United States legal theory took on a varied realist, sociological, sometimes pragmatic cast, most notably through the long career of Roscoe Pound (1870–1964), whose *Jurisprudence* (1950) is a monument to these early efforts. Until recent decades, very few American philosophers wrote in this area. The outstanding exception was Morris R. Cohen (1880–1947), who was a collaborator of Pound. His activities and essays (1933) had a great deal to do with keeping the area alive. The classic volume of readings prepared by him and his son Felix Cohen (1951, not cited here) is still of historical value. For practical purposes it has been superseded by the collection edited by Joel Feinberg and Hyman Gross (1980).

Two excellent overviews of the main issues, both brief but full, come from Martin Golding (1975) and Thomas Morawetz (1980). Each uses both analysis of concepts and discussion of normative issues. Although each reveals his own views, this aim is emphasized more by Golding, while Morawetz's method serves especially to bring the reader into the discussion and to survey a variety of arguments that have been or could be used. Three sets of essays, edited by Robert Summers (1968, 1971) and A. W. B. Simpson (1973), together with the Hacker and Raz volume (1977), well represent the status of inquiries on basic themes within the 1960 to 1977 period.

THEMES

The philosophy of law has become an intricate web of issues. In the following section I sort out some of these, not so much to reveal what is specifically at issue as to indicate the types of interlocking concerns that have become characteristic.

1. First then: What is the nature of the law itself? What does it mean to speak of a legal system? On what assumptions about its

proper functions in society is it to be studied, and with what methods? Where, for example, is normative versus descriptive discourse appropriate, and how is that matter to be decided? In all these respects the debate along the spectrum between traditional natural law theories and strictly positivist theories has been of crucial significance. Toward the latter extreme, the neo-Kantian Hans Kelsen (e.g., 1967), perhaps continental Europe's greatest twentieth-century jurist, presents a "pure theory" of law, one purportedly divorced from historical, sociological, moral, or ideological elements. The task of philosophy of law, for him, is to provide the conceptual basis for law conceived strictly as a descriptive science. The legal system is, pure and simple, a hierarchical system of imposed norms and sanctions. The ground of validity for these norms lies in an originating, nonpositive presupposition he calls a "basic norm." Kelsen retired from the University of California at Berkeley in 1952, after having taught in the United States since 1940. He had already labored in this vineyard over thirty years before 1940. A collection of his essays (1957) includes more applied uses of his theory.

Hart's analytic jurisprudence owes a great deal to Kelsen's analysis of norms, as does Joseph Raz's much-noted book *The Concept of a Legal System* (1970). But against both, Hart takes the more Humean position that the obligatoriness of norms is founded in attitudes; consistent with this position, he also holds that while legal activity essentially refers to rules, legal discretion relies on nonlegal factors as well and that the law cannot be a closed normative system. On the other hand, Ronald Dworkin (*Taking Rights Seriously,* 1977, cited on p. 448), Hart's successor in the Oxford chair and the most prominent critic of Hart's positivism, argues for a nonpositivist view that grounds the law and legal decision making in particular moral rights and principles.

A good deal of the philosophical discussion about theory of law centers on the nature and functioning of norms, no matter what the assumptions of participants may be; and the approach is often made through a more general account of practical action and practical reason. In an important work Joseph Raz (1975), for example, has explored the general theory of norms with special application to law, using an analysis of legal discourse largely derived from Kelsen and directed to a refutation of natural law theory. Raz especially contributes to a theory of norms by using relations of these kinds of rules to reasons for action. He distinguishes between rules (categorical and permissive) that are reasons for action of a special type and rules (power-conferring) that he takes to be logically related to such reasons. After giving a general account of the operating of normative systems he considers the unique functioning of norms in legal systems, which to him include the mark of comprehensiveness and the claim to be supreme. Similarly the Scandinavian Alf Ross (1968) performed an analysis of directive speech and the concept of a norm, followed by an account of deontic ("duty"-oriented) logic as applied especially, but not solely, to legal settings. Ross studies laws chiefly in their role as directives to courts.

At the natural law end of the spectrum, though from a non-Thomistic standpoint, Lon Fuller (e.g., 1964) argues that the normative force of law is sustainable only on extralegal grounds, which he believes have a universal character. Iredell Jenkins (1980) attempts a systematic theory of positive law but as a type of natural law investigation. That is, with Fuller he views law within the context of the human enterprise as a whole and as a development within larger evolutionary and historical processes. Theodore Benditt (1978) combines a critique of American legal realism (Pound, Cohen, and others) with a critique of Dworkin in defense of what he calls a functional natural law position.

2. What is the status of judicial decisions, and how are they to be made? Every theorist also addresses this question. Having adopted a Hartian positivist position, Neil MacCormick (1978), for example, analyzes the use of arguments in judicial decision making and discusses the relation of these phenomena to legal theory. He agrees with Dworkin that arguments from principles are used and that the law is not value-free. He also argues, however, that many rules, as well as principles, identify rights; but he sees principles as relatively general norms that serve to rationalize rules or sets of rules, and he holds, with Hart, that rules are themselves recognized through what he calls institutive rules. So the framework is still positivist.

Increasingly, discussion of this kind draws from work in ethics. Thomas Perry (1976) presents a notable example. Perry especially uses dialogue with R. M. Hare's much-noted prescriptivism in ethics to develop a new approach to the question: Can moral judgments or statements be justified by rational argument, and if so, how? He attempts, particularly against naturalist descriptivist positions, an account which assumes that there are no self-evident moral standards yet which finds validation of good moral reasoning in nonmoral terms. He includes examination of analogues in judicial reasoning and displays what he takes to be a moral component in the duty judges have to use various criteria to validate legal rules. Neither, he thinks, is done in such a way as to claim, unlike political philosopher John Rawls and others, that morally reasonable people can always be expected to agree.

3. What, then, are the possible relations of morality to law, which are justified, and how is this to be done? A debate between Lon Fuller and Herbert Hart in the *Harvard Law Review* of 1957–58 set up the contemporary form of this discussion. Each has subsequently developed his position further: Fuller especially in his book *The Morality of Law* (1964), Hart in his major work *The Concept of Law* (1961) and elsewhere, notably in two brief volumes (not cited here) on *Law, Liberty and Morality* (1963) and *The Morality of the Criminal Law* (1965). Dworkin's already classic analysis in *Taking Rights Seriously* (1977), mentioned above, is the third main referent in current discussion. Several closely related questions are also frequently addressed, recently in a systematic way by Joseph Raz (1979), namely: What authority should we acknowledge as due to the law? More particularly, wherein lies its moral authority, and what conditions must it satisfy to be deserving of moral respect? What meaning can be given to the notions of a right to dissent or to practice civil disobedience?

In what he called works on "critical morality" as applied to law, in distinction from analytical jurisprudence, Hart, like most other legal philosophers, has written mainly about criminal law. Hart's approach to practical issues emphasizes the functioning of both substantive and procedural rules in law as a particular kind of social rule (that is, "positive" in this special sense), not necessarily linked to morality. He also stresses the openendedness of the positive law, the status of which is continually subject to judicial discretion. As a liberal, critical moralist he also maintains a commitment to the sovereignty of individual conscience and to the freedom and responsibility of individuals. In this respect he joins Dworkin and other critics of positivism in their opposition to any ideology, whether conservative or so-called liberal or socialist, that does not uphold that commitment. Hart has been misunderstood as though he did not accept the dependence of legal authority on extralegal moral considerations. He does. But whereas coercion makes for compliance according to John Austin and the natural bond of lived relationships between people for Iredell Jenkins, it is the validity of the law itself that achieves this purpose for Hart. Has he begged the question? The debate continues.

4. There are further questions of a more practical nature, not all of

them directly concerned with morality. For example, as Jenkins (1980) applies his theory of law to practical problems he especially asks: What are the conditions of legal effectiveness? When is the legal apparatus overloaded and abused? What are its proper limits? He takes positive law to be not so much the direction of the sovereign (as John Austin thought), as instead an agent of social forces and a reflection of an actual social order, whose task it is to discover the direction those forces seek, to criticize and correct them, and to implement their realization. He vigorously opposes the use of law proposed by Pound and others for "social engineering" or social planning and reform. Hart and Dworkin, among others, strongly disagree.

5. Within the criminal law, in particular, what are the grounds of responsibility before the law and of innocence or punishment under the law? The usual types of approach already mentioned are well represented in a 1968 work by Hart. Among the more recent systematic works on the theory of criminal law is one by Hyman Gross (1979). Herbert Morris's (1979) philosophical approach to issues of legal punishment and responsibility is based on investigations in moral psychology on phenomena such as guilt, shame, and suffering. Further studies can be expected, based in part on material available from philosophy of mind.

FUTURE PROSPECTS

Because this area of philosophy is growing at a rapid pace, and on the basis of developments so far, one would also expect to see the following features ahead: (1) Further clarifying analysis of concepts, arguments, positions, and practices, using new tools from other parts of philosophy; (2) on the basis of these efforts, a greater share in revision of the more specific theories used or espoused in law; (3) more prominence given to the theme of judicial hermeneutics, or theory of interpretation; (4) new philosophical ventures in the understanding of social decision making and conflict utilization and of the relations of legal institutions to others in these respects; and (5) further examination of the notion of human rights and its implications for international law.

Benditt, Theodore M. *Law as Rule and Principle: Problems of Legal Philosophy.* Stanford: Calif.: Stanford Univ. Pr., 1978.
Cairns, Huntington. *Legal Philosophy from Plato to Hegel.* Baltimore, Md.: Johns Hopkins Univ. Pr., 1949.

Cohen, Morris. *Law and the Social Order: Essays in Legal Philosophy.* Hamden, Conn.: Archon Books, 1967. (Original ed., 1933.)

Feinberg, Joel, and Hyman Gross, eds. *Philosophy of Law.* 2nd ed. Belmont, Calif.: Wadsworth, 1980. (1st ed., 1975.)

Friedrich, Carl J. *The Philosophy of Law in Historical Perspective.* 2nd ed. Chicago: Univ. of Chicago Pr., 1963. (German ed., 1955.)

Fuller, Lon. *The Morality of Law.* 2nd ed. New Haven, Conn.: Yale Univ. Pr., 1969. (1st ed., 1964.)

Golding, Martin P. *Philosophy of Law.* Englewood Cliffs, N.J.: Prentice-Hall, 1975.

Gross, Hyman. *A Theory of Criminal Law.* Oxford and New York: Oxford Univ. Pr., 1979.

Hacker, P. M. S., and Joseph Raz, eds. *Law, Morality, and Society: Essays in Honour of H. L. A. Hart.* Oxford: Clarendon Pr., 1977.

Hart, Herbert L. A. *The Concept of Law.* Oxford: Clarendon Pr., 1961.

———. *Punishment and Responsibility.* Oxford and New York: Oxford Univ. Pr., 1968.

———, and A. M. Honoré. *Causation in the Law.* Oxford: Clarendon Pr., 1959.

Jenkins, Iredell. *Social Order and the Limits of Law: A Theoretical Essay.* Princeton, N.J.: Princeton Univ. Pr., 1980.

Kelsen, Hans. *Pure Theory of Law.* Berkeley: Univ. of California Pr., 1967. (Repr., 1978; from German ed., 1960; 1st German ed., 1934.)

———. *What Is Justice? Justice, Law, and Politics in the Mirror of Science.* Berkeley: Univ. of California Pr., 1957.

MacCormick, Neil. *H. L. A. Hart.* Stanford, Calif.: Stanford Univ. Pr., 1981.

———. *Legal Reasoning and Legal Theory.* Oxford and New York: Oxford Univ. Pr., 1978.

Morawetz, Thomas. *The Philosophy of Law: An Introduction.* New York and London: Macmillan, 1980.

Morris, Herbert. *On Guilt and Innocence: Essays in Legal Philosophy and Moral Psychology.* Berkeley: Univ. of California Pr., 1979.

Perry, Thomas D. *Moral Reasoning and Truth: An Essay in Philosophy and Jurisprudence.* Oxford: Clarendon Pr., 1976.

Pound, Roscoe. *Jurisprudence.* 5v. St. Paul, Minn.: West, 1950.

Raz, Joseph. *The Authority of Law: Essays on Law and Morality.* Oxford: Clarendon Pr., 1979.

———. *The Concept of a Legal System: An Introduction to the Theory of Legal System.* Oxford: Clarendon Pr., 1970.

———. *Practical Reason and Norms.* London: Hutchinson, 1975.

Ross, Alf. *Directives and Norms.* New York: Humanities Pr.; London: Routledge & Paul, 1968.

Simpson, A. W. B., ed. *Oxford Essays in Jurisprudence.* 2nd series. Oxford: Clarendon Pr., 1973.

Summers, Robert S., ed. *Essays in Legal Philosophy.* Berkeley: Univ. of California Pr., 1968.

———, ed. *More Essays in Legal Philosophy: General Assessments of Legal Philosophies.* Berkeley: Univ. of California Pr., 1971.

27

Aesthetics:
Philosophy of Art

HISTORY AND PRESENT STATUS

Early History

Until modern times, aesthetics chiefly purveyed objectivist theories of beauty, occasionally descending from the sublime to the radiance of homely pleasures. Such theories were ordinarily accompanied by a conception of art as craft, viewing art works as artifacts made for some preconceived purpose (see R. G. Collingwood's critique, 1938). Fascination with the concept of beauty has not disappeared; witness the Thomist works by Jacques Maritain (1953) and Francis Kovach (1974), Robert O'Connell's study of Augustine (1978), the new analytic account by Guy Sircello (1975), and the earlier analytic treatment of some basic problems by Harold Osborne (1953). All five works retain a concept of beauty, the first three much more accepting of traditional views, the last two much more critical. Studies on "why Plato banished the artists" from his envisioned republic by Iris Murdoch (1977) and on the ancient "prelude" to aesthetics by Eva Schaper (1968) remind us that theoretical attention to beauty was itself a mixed blessing even among the Greeks.

By the eighteenth century, philosophical interest had begun to expand from accounts of beauty as an objective property of things to inquiry about the nature of art, taste, and aesthetic experience, which itself may be taken to go beyond the bounds of art. Monroe Beardsley (1966) has depicted many of these changes in an analytic mode that sharply contrasts with the classic idealist history by Bernard Bosanquet (1892) but not so greatly with the comprehensive three-volume history of aesthetics through the seventeenth century by Wladyslaw Tatarkiewicz (1970; also his 1980 work on modern

460

themes) or the briefer history by Harold Osborne (1968), both of whom are philosophers using a history of ideas approach.

Kant

Kant's thinking is especially important within this modern shift because it raises crucial issues about the foundations of judgment and points toward later efforts to build a comprehensive aesthetic theory. According to Kant, judgments of taste, in contrast to moral and scientific judgments, are based on feeling and claim universal validity only subjectively, through the free play of imagination and understanding. Although Kant's own writings on aesthetics have been among the classic texts, until very recently they have not been subjected to the same analytic scrutiny accorded his other works. Eva Schaper (1979) has begun to make up for this lack, as has Donald Crawford (1974), both using the rest of his critical philosophy to shed light on his theory of aesthetic judgment and (between them) on his views of aesthetic beauty, perception, fiction, and form. Paul Guyer (1979) has given a complementary account of Kant's developing ideas on taste from the 1760s to the *Critique of Judgment* (1790) and subsequent ethical work. What these authors have achieved is yet to be supplemented by studies on the cultural and biographical occasions underlying Kant's aesthetic thought and on the specific changes his questions have undergone since the late eighteenth century.

Form versus Expression

Many of the changes are reflected in inquiries about the functions of form versus expression in art. For example, Clive Bell's *Art* (1914), a small but long-influential work, was produced under the sway of G. E. Moore, whose view was that "good" cannot be defined but is a quality applied to some actions or states of affairs that cannot be broken down into parts. (The only things good in themselves are states of mind.) Moore argued that when one tries to define good in terms of other qualities it always remains an "open question" as to whether the quality consistently applies. Bell took "significant form" to be the same sort of quality, the only one essential to all objects that provoke an assumedly isolable type of emotion, called aesthetic. Works of art he defined as objects possessing that form, according to subjective, individual taste.

Despite Bell's belief that people who are of "robust intellect" and "for whom art is a constant source of passionate emotion" would see the truth of his theory, critics so possessed have not complied. Bell did not reason out his position thoroughly. Had he done so, he might have seen it to be open to the kinds of objections Moore's intuitionist view of "good" attracted. Nevertheless, as an opening gambit Bell's theory proved useful, especially on two accounts. First, Bell's approach suggested a way to think about how to expel from the domain of art certain objects that are felt to be beautiful but are intuited not to belong on that ground alone, and to exclude certain experiences, even appreciative ones, that come from qualities in works of art but do not come across as art (Bell thought all representation was of this sort). That is, in such a fashion one might be able to assign a special character to certain artifacts that enables critical judgment about them as art. Second, by attending to significant form as the essential evocative quality in art one is incited to analyze out those formal aspects of artifacts in detail. D. W. Prall (1936), for example, later applied a quite similar position to the analysis of art, this time adding the feature of immediate, exclusive attention to "aesthetic surface"—a notion borrowed from John Dewey (1934)—such that the aesthetic is vaguely taken to be "the top" of all experience whatsoever.

In articulating factual bases for an alternative, expressive theory in his 690-page masterwork (1940), Theodore M. Greene affirmed the element of intrinsic satisfaction inherent in these more formalist theories but went beyond this to emphasize the expressive and communicative aspects of the work of art—taking it, moreover, not only in its formal parts but as a whole. In doing so, Greene also proposed a theory of artistic truth as propositional. This subsidiary position has a certain initial plausibility, given his belief that the complex, diverse nature of reality is such that it can be genuinely grasped through a rational understanding of available data, but it has not stood up under scrutiny from John Hospers (1946) and others. The crux of Hospers' critique was that we must be able to identify conventional rules by which to know what assertions would refer to in nonverbal media like color or sound, but this we cannot do. However, the task of determining in what ways expression and communication might help to define art or to play a role in some art remains prominent to this day.

In this period, others had also made a special effort to identify formal criteria of aesthetic quality, notably DeWitt Parker, John Dewey, and Stephen Pepper; none of these philosophers, however, was a formalist.

Recent Approaches

Other nonformalists such as Arnold Isenberg (1973) continued to pursue aspects of the more traditional game, while Monroe Beardsley (1958), and many analytic philosophers to follow, restricted their attention to questions about the meaning and truth of critical statements, leaving aside so-called psychological questions about the causes and effects of works of art. Joseph Margolis (1965) took a similar tack. Both, like Virgil Aldrich (1963), have nevertheless maintained an interest in distinguishing aesthetic perception from other kinds. Another analytic philosopher, Jerome Stolnitz (1960), on the other hand, has retained interest in a broader range of aesthetic experience as part of a metacritical theory. Both approaches have survived in current thought (H. Gene Blocker, 1979; Dickie and Sclafani, 1977; Margolis, 1981).

Although Joseph Margolis's first edition of the anthology *Philosophy Looks at the Arts* (1962) already showed the rapidly growing sophistication of analytic thinking on aesthetics, the markedly new edition of 1978 (which retains only five 1962 items and adds nineteen) evidences considerable further progress. Among collections, the turn to a new language-sensitive, analytic aesthetics was first displayed in that edited by William Elton (1954), thence notably by those edited by Morris Weitz (1959; 2nd ed., 1970); Beardsley and Schneller (1967, from the *Journal of Aesthetics and Art Criticism*); Harold Osborne (1968, from the *British Journal of Aesthetics*); and Benjamin Tilghman (1973), the last showing especially the influence of Wittgenstein. (Osborne was editor of the British journal from its founding in 1960 to his retirement in 1977.)

A wider spectrum of approaches is included in the collection edited by Howard Kiefer and Milton Munitz (1970), not so distant as are the others from the conventional hodgepodge in Melvin Rader's much-used collections (1935; 3rd ed., 1960). The more broadly humanistic discussion of the relation of aesthetic value in art to other domains by Rader and Jessup (1976) is also unusual in that it purports to offer a general theory of value. In contrast, Morris Weitz never uses "value" as a term in his *Opening Mind: A Philosophical Study of Humanistic Concepts* (1977) and reiterates his argument from a noted 1956 article that, strictly speaking, even a theory of art is not possible. In its use the concept of art is open, he had argued. But a theory of art either presupposes or entails the claim that it is closed—that is, governed by necessary and sufficient criteria that correspond to the definitive properties of art; and this claim is false. Weitz's position has been assailed but not destroyed, in my view; and it retains high merit, coming as it does from the skeptical side of inquiry. Most contemporary aesthetics, from whatever quarter, have presupposed that the search for definitive conditions, properties, or criteria is appropriate and a theory of art possible.

FURTHER THEMES AND DEVELOPMENTS

Aesthetic Attitude

One way to conduct the search for well-formed theory has been to focus on the possibility of a general aesthetic attitude in experience, an attitude somehow heightened in art. For example, in an influential 1913 article Edward Bulloch (in Rader) asked whether "psychical distance" is necessary in the experience of art. The question is still being debated. More specifically, it might be framed as follows: Must one be able to step away from any interests or affections external to the encounter itself? Or: Might it be the proper aesthetic attitude not strictly to maintain distance but, say, to cultivate "disinterested and sympathetic attention to and contemplation of any object of awareness whatever, for its own sake alone" (Stolnitz, 1960)? In any case, is the aesthetic object that we appreciate and to which we apply criticism to be defined simply as the object obtained by the aesthetic attitude? Joseph Margolis (1965) and George Dickie (1974) have offered telling arguments against taking the affirmative position, indeed against assigning any meaningful role to a so-called aesthetic attitude at all. Further empirical studies will be needed to help settle the matter, though none can be expected to decide the conceptual issues involved. In an allied effort, Karl Aschenbrenner (1974) has performed a meticulously ordered empirical examination of concepts used in aesthetic criticism, relying on quotations to illumine issues of usage. One interesting finding is that critics tend to use the same appraisive concepts in looking at all the various areas of art and whether they refer to the artist or to the work of art.

Three Current Tasks

Consideration of these questions also remains open to influence from at least three other directions. (1) Further attempts to see how or whether a distinctly aesthetic domain must be fitted into an overall view of human nature and development (for example, through such a program as R. G. Colingwood began in *Speculum Mentis*,

1924); (2) further exploration over the full range of affective, attitudinal, interest-bearing, principled phenomena and over other features of discrimination that are seen to accompany, or somewhat inform, or perhaps essentially determine certain kinds of perceptual experience that may justifiably be called aesthetic, though possibly on other grounds (for instance, through investigations of the sort the great French phenomenologist aesthetician, Mikel Dufrenne, set in motion, 1973); and (3) further understanding of the social meanings of art.

The third task has been undertaken in part by the Polish Marxist, Stanislaw Ossowski (1978). One of the most highly developed systematic theories so far achieved, by the Czech thinker Jan Mukařovský (1978), began with a structuralist position, which he had come to in the 1930s, countering any attention to subject-object interaction that ignores either its determination by social norms or its semiotic functions. In the 1940s, under the influence of phenomenology, he attempted to account more specifically for those universal features of individuals that enable us to be creative participants in the aesthetic process and thereby to realize ourselves vis-à-vis the external world. From an analytic standpoint, George Dickie (1974) offers an "institutional" theory of art, which focuses on "the nonexhibited characteristics that works of art have in virtue of being embedded in an institutional matrix," which he called "the artworld," and takes these characteristics to be essential and defining. His definition of aesthetic object is similarly formed; it emphasizes conventions used to present certain features of works of art, which conventions locate the aesthetic object contained in works of art.

Style

Of late, issues regarding style have had a history like that of aesthetic attitude. In the Berel Lang symposium (1979), for example, some of the authors (especially Svetlana Alpers) question whether the very notion of style is warranted. For the most part, however, contributors accept its importance and proceed to examine verbal, visual, and musical representations of style, though none emerges with a general theory.

Intentionality, Expression, and Communication

The classic works presenting an expression theory of art, first by the Italian idealist Benedetto Croce (1902) and in some respects more thoroughly by R. G. Collingwood (1924, 1938) have attracted much criticism. Croce's theory, however, has been chiefly known only through his early work. His *Poetry and Literature* (1936, tr. 1981), at least his third try at a systematic aesthetics, indicates efforts that deserve greater notice. If the artist's intentionality through the exercise of expressive or other communicative functions is to be included within a comprehensive theory of art, as many still believe it must, their arguments and proposals will continue to warrant close attention. Guy Sircello (1972) has put together numerous critical counters that would have to be dealt with if tighter modified versions of their expression theories are to be formed. Alan Tormey (1971) has set forth arguments supporting a theory limited to expressive properties, properties defined as denoting intentional states of persons but wholly contained within the constituent parts of art works themselves. Allied issues, that were focal in Collingwood's theory and are now widely discussed, have to do with the nature of art works as objects (especially Richard Wollheim, 1980), with the nature of imagination and aesthetic consciousness (Mary Warnock, 1976; Roger Scrutton, 1974; and the phenomenologists), with art as language, particularly as symbolic or metaphorical, and with the variety of relations between the artist and the audience that may be conveyed through works of art.

Since Bertrand Russell's early epistemological essays (e.g., "Mysticism and Logic," 1914), the predominant tendency among analytic philosophers has been to lump all or most nonpropositional language into one category called "emotive." In my view, Ernst Cassirer's *Philosophy of Symbolic Forms* (1923–31) sets up a potentially richer analysis of how different symbolic forms and their emotive components determine different modes of thought. Suzanne Langer's *Philosophy in a New Key* (1942) gave expression to this alternative approach, which she further developed in her later works, focusing especially on the high symbolic functions of art. As clearly as I can make out, in her more fully developed view works of art are to be taken in their entirety, not broken down into isolated elements. As such, they are seen to be revelatory. That is, the whole work is an "expressive form," used by projection abstractly and imaginatively to present a semblance of what human feeling (sensation or emotion, perhaps not necessarily both) apprehends (namely, the artist's "ideas") in actual life. In art actual life often means extraordinary life, what one might never experience were it not for the work of art itself. Attending closely to the language of artists and related metaphorical discourse, she has eventually (1953, and in later works) formed a systematic philosophy of mind to account for such phenomena.

Grand Theory versus Analytic Investigation

Here a distinction is in order between grand theory and analytic investigation. What grand theory offers by way of vision, scope, and suggestiveness it tends to lack in rigor and clarity, the cardinal virtues of more analytic approaches. The analytically minded ordinarily turn away from the grander schemes of Croce, Collingwood, Dewey, Greene, Langer, Mukařovský, and company to deal with finer-tuned problems and puzzles. This alternative approach is displayed, for example, in the excellent recent set of articles on symbols, representations, and other language-like features of art in *Monist* (Beardsley, 1974) and in Nelson Goodman's stimulating work on "symbolic systems" (1968), to which all these authors refer.

FUTURE PROSPECTS

Within philosophy, the most promising aesthetic inquiries at present seem to be coming from close contact with specific aesthetic activity combined with recent analytic work in epistemology, philosophy of language, and philosophy of mind. Other areas that may deserve equal consideration have been indicated. Through such efforts the grand theories just mentioned may well gain force, with modification, rather than simply drop by the wayside because of the greater current interest in analytic detail.

Aldrich, Virgil. *Philosophy of Art.* Englewood Cliffs, N.J.: Prentice-Hall, 1963.

Aschenbrenner, Karl. *The Concepts of Criticism.* Dordrecht and Boston: Reidel, 1974.

Beardsley, Monroe C. *Aesthetics from Ancient Greece to the Present: A Short History.* New York: Macmillan, 1966.

———. *Aesthetics: Problems in the Philosophy of Criticism.* 2nd ed. Indianapolis, Ind. and Cambridge: Hackett, 1981. (1st ed., 1958.) (Added: a 47-page "Afterword—1980." His papers have been collected in the book *The Aesthetic Point of View,* ed. by Donald Callen and Michael Wreen. Ithaca, N.Y. and London: Cornell Univ. Pr., 1981.)

———, ed. "Languages of Art." *Monist* 58, no. 2:175–348 (Apr. 1974).

———, and Herbert M. Schneller, eds. *Aesthetic Inquiry: Essays on Art Criticism and the Philosophy of Art.* Belmont, Calif.: Dickenson, 1967.

Bell, Clive. *Art.* New York: Stokes; London: Chatto & Windus, 1914.

Blocker, H. Gene. *Philosophy of Art.* New York: Scribner, 1979.

Bosanquet, Bernard. *A History of Aesthetic.* New York: Macmillan, 1892. Repr., 1934.

Cassirer, Ernst. *Philosophy of Symbolic Forms.* 3v. Tr. by Ralph Manheim. New Haven, Conn.: Yale Univ. Pr., 1953–57. (German ed., 1923–31.) (His brief *Essay on Man,* Yale Univ. Pr., 1944, is a synopsis of this work.)

Collingwood, Robin G. *The Principles of Art.* Oxford: Clarendon Pr., 1938.

———. *Speculum Mentis.* Oxford: Clarendon Pr., 1924.

Crawford, Donald W. *Kant's Aesthetic Theory.* Madison: Univ. of Wisconsin Pr., 1974.

Croce, Benedetto. *Aesthetic.* Rev. ed. Tr. by Douglas Ainslie. New York: Noonday Pr., 1953. (Italian ed., 1902.) (Actually translated by R. G. Collingwood.)

———. *Poetry and Literature: An Introduction to Its Criticism and History.* Tr. with introduction and notes by Giovanni Gullace. Carbondale: Southern Illinois Univ. Pr., 1981. (1st Italian ed., 1936; 6th ed., 1963.)

Dewey, John. *Art as Experience.* New York: Minton, Balch, 1934.

Dickie, George. *Art and the Aesthetic: An Institutional Analysis.* Ithaca, N.Y.: Cornell Univ. Pr., 1974.

———, and R. J. Sclafani, eds. *Aesthetics: A Critical Anthology.* New York: St. Martin's Pr., 1977.

Dufrenne, Mikel. *The Phenomenology of Aesthetic Experience.* Tr. by Edward S. Casey et al. Evanston, Ill.: Northwestern Univ. Pr., 1973. (French ed., 1953.)

Elton, William, ed. *Aesthetics and Language.* New York: Philosophical Library, 1954.

Goodman, Nelson. *Languages of Art: An Approach to a Theory of Symbols.* 2nd ed. Indianapolis, Ind.: Hackett, 1976. (1st ed., Indianapolis, Ind.: Bobbs-Merrill, 1968; Oxford Univ. Pr., 1969.)

Greene, Theodore Meyer. *The Arts and the Art of Criticism.* Princeton, N.J.: Princeton Univ. Pr., 1940.

Guyer, Paul. *Kant and the Claims of Taste.* Cambridge, Mass.: Harvard Univ. Pr., 1979.

Hospers, John. *Meaning and Truth in the Arts.* Chapel Hill: Univ. of North Carolina Pr., 1946. Repr., 1964.

Isenberg, Arnold. *Aesthetics and the Theory of Criticism: Selected Essays.* Ed. by William Callaghan et al. Chicago: Univ. of Chicago Pr., 1973.

Kiefer, Howard E., and Milton K. Munitz, eds. *Perspectives in Education, Religion, and the Arts.* Albany: State Univ. of New York Pr., 1970.

Kovach, Francis J. *Philosophy of Beauty.* Norman: Univ. of Oklahoma Pr., 1974.

Lang, Berel, ed. *The Concept of Style.* Philadelphia: Univ. of Pennsylvania Pr., 1979.

Langer, Suzanne K. *Feeling and Form: A Theory of Art.* New York: Scribner's, 1953.

———. *Philosophy in a New Key.* Cambridge, Mass.: Harvard Univ. Pr., 1942.

Margolis, Joseph Z. *Art and Philosophy.* Atlantic Highlands, N.J.: Humanities Pr., 1981.

———. *The Language of Art and Art Criticism: Analytic Questions in Aesthetics.* Detroit, Mich.: Wayne State Univ. Pr., 1965.

————. *Philosophy Looks at the Arts: Contemporary Readings in Aesthetics*. Rev. ed. Philadelphia, Pa.: Temple Univ. Pr., 1978. (1st ed., New York: Scribner's, 1962.)

Maritain, Jacques. *Creative Intuition in Art and Poetry*. New York: Pantheon, 1953.

Mukařovský, Jan. *Structure, Sign and Function*. Tr. and ed. by John Burbank and Peter Steiner. New Haven, Conn. and London: Yale Univ. Pr., 1978.

Murdoch, Iris. *The Fire and the Sun: Why Plato Banished the Artists*. Oxford: Clarendon Pr., 1977.

O'Connell, Robert J., S.J. *Art and the Christian Intelligence in St. Augustine*. Cambridge, Mass.: Harvard Univ. Pr., 1978.

Osborne, Harold. *Aesthetics and Art Theory: An Historical Introduction*. London: Longmans, Green, 1968.

————. *Theory of Beauty*. New York: Philosophical Library, 1953; London: Routledge & Paul, 1952.

————, ed. *Aesthetics in the Modern World*. London: Thames & Hudson, 1968.

Ossowski, Stanislaw. *The Foundations of Aesthetics*. Tr. by Janina and Witold Rodzinski. Dordrecht and Boston: Reidel, 1978.

Prall, David W. *Aesthetic Analysis*. New York: Crowell, 1936.

Rader, Melvin, ed. *A Modern Book of Esthetics: An Anthology*. 3rd ed. New York: Holt, Rinehart & Winston, 1960. (1st ed., 1935; 2nd ed., 1953.)

————, and Bertram Jessup. *Art and Human Values*. Englewood Cliffs, N.J.: Prentice-Hall, 1976.

Russell, Bertrand. *Mysticism and Logic and Other Essays*. London: Longmans, Green, 1918. Repr.: New York: Norton, 1929.

Schaper, Eva. *Prelude to Aesthetics*. London: Allen & Unwin, 1968.

————. *Studies in Kant's Aesthetics*. Edinburgh: Edinburgh Univ. Pr., 1979.

Scrutton, Roger. *Art and Imagination: A Study in the Philosophy of Mind*. New York: Barnes & Noble, 1974.

Sircello, Guy. *Mind and Art: An Essay on the Varieties of Expression*. Princeton, N.J.: Princeton Univ. Pr., 1972.

————. *A New Theory of Beauty*. Princeton, N.J.: Princeton Univ. Pr., 1975.

Stolnitz, Jerome. *Aesthetics and Philosophy of Art Criticism: A Critical Introduction*. Boston: Houghton Mifflin, 1960.

Tatarkiewicz, Wladyslaw. *History of Aesthetics*. 2v. Ed. by C. Barrett. New York: Humanities Pr.; The Hague: Mouton, 1970–74. (Polish ed., 1960.)

————. *A History of Six Ideas: An Essay in Aesthetics*. Tr. by Christopher Kasparek. The Hague: Nijhoff, 1980. (Modern themes.)

Tilghman, Benjamin R., ed. *Language and Aesthetics: Contributions to the Philosophy of Art*. Lawrence: Univ. Pr. of Kansas, 1973.

Tormey, Alan. *The Concept of Expression: A Study in Philosophical Psychology and Aesthetics*. Princeton, N.J.: Princeton Univ. Pr., 1971.

Warnock, Mary. *Imagination*. Berkeley: Univ. of California Pr., 1976.

Weitz, Morris. *The Opening Mind: A Philosophical Study of Humanistic Concepts*. Chicago: Univ. of Chicago Pr., 1977.

————. *Problems in Aesthetics: An Introductory Book of Readings.* 2nd ed. New York: Macmillan, 1970. (1st ed., 1959.)

Wollheim, Richard *Art and Its Objects.* 2nd ed. Cambridge and New York: Cambridge Univ. Pr., 1980. (1st ed., 1968.) (The 2nd ed. adds six essays.)

28

Philosophy of
Religion

THE RELIGIOUS DOMAIN

Somewhat metaphorically, religion may be characterized as centering in one's feeling at home in the universe and in the way one deals with the feeling of not being at home. So conceived, it is pervasive; it is also fundamentally a matter of development and of degree, not a one-time or a final achievement. In its expression, moreover, it can be as confused, as isolated, or as integrated in relation to other aspects of human life as anything else. Because we are social beings, an individual usually carries religion—or reactions against particular "religious" points of view—with some historical orientation and group reference in mind. To this extent, mores and doctrines are necessary components. However, this is also why religion sometimes gets mistakenly reduced to mere morality or "religious" doctrine.

The first attempts to define religion in a systematic way occurred in the eighteenth century, largely as part of the Enlightenment project of carving up domains of experience so that each could find its distinct place within an encyclopedic outline. Consequently, there are, of course, many other definitions or characterizations than the one I have just sketched. This one is very close to that offered by the Berlin philosopher and theologian, Friedrich Schleiermacher (1768–1834), generally acknowledged to have been at once founder of the modern study of religion and father of modern theology, in his famous treatise *On Religion: Addresses in Response to Its Cultured Critics* (1799, tr. 1969).

Schleiermacher's emphasis, however, was on "the feeling of absolute dependence." By this he did not mean to exclude one's feeling or being personally free and independent. Rather, he wished to point to

471

the experience of human events—indeed, of all other events—as being both immediately and ultimately bound by the rest of the world and in particular by God. In ontological perspective, events are inescapably related to, even participative of, the *Universum*. In historical perspective, human events possess social context and refer to some representation or awareness of the ultimate (God). One's own feelings and awarenesses or perspectives were at the core, moreover, because Schleiermacher thought of religion as, at least potentially, the most exquisitely personal experience in life.

Among those after Schleiermacher who came to think of religion in psychological terms, Sigmund Freud a century later took it to be primarily a form of regression to a primal state (such as an "oceanic feeling" of the sort mystics report). Today a psychoanalytic interpretation might well view it primarily in relation to the lifelong development of separation-individuation. The first phases of this process culminate in the young child's capacity to negotiate a social world beyond the dyadic relationship with which each of us begins. For a time there is much magic and fantasy in these efforts, many of which still center in the home, whatever its form. The next phases culminate in adolescence and young adulthood, in those social settings where these exist to some degree in more than a physical sense. Here one, in effect, leaves one's home. Even if one never leaves physically, there is now the possibility of making one's own way, of not being bound to home as one was in the earlier years. One becomes "one's own person" and now, in a much broader fashion that may include a philosophical or theological understanding of one's place in the entire social and physical universe, creates one's own home. Moving toward debility and death is the final great stage of separation-individuation. (See Tice, "A Psychoanalytic Perspective," 1980, cited on p. 500.)

Except in relatively unintegrated or superficial ways, philosophy of religion is so dependent on the development of human consciousness itself—in all its personal, social, and intellectual dimensions—that it could not have formed very substantially until modern times. In a study of Hume, Kant, and Hegel, James Collins (1967) has placed the crucial period of emergence at about 1730 to 1830. On the other hand, because in the West philosophy itself was for most of its history largely dominated by Judeo-Christian theology and in the East by other specific religious traditions, even today the subjects and terms of debate heavily reflect highpoints in the premodern literature. Authors such as Plato and Aristotle, Augustine, Anselm, and Aquinas still provide many of the great texts used for analysis.

Currently organization of the area is determined by two sets of problems. The first set has to do with the nature and existence of God and sometimes with other theological issues. The second set is directed to whatever is regarded to be religious experience: religious language, religious belief and understanding (versus skepticism), and the relation of religion to other domains of experience. Along a spectrum in between are ways of looking at peculiarly religious problems—notably, immortality, freedom, the existence of evil, prayer, mysticism, religious ethics, and the possibility of divine revelation as a distinct source of knowledge in comparison with reason and experience.

APPROACHES

It is easier to negotiate the relevant literature if some distinctions between different kinds of philosophically minded thinkers interested in religion are kept in mind. For some of these, "religion" essentially means "religious thought." For most, it is a phenomenon of much broader scope, but they tend to concentrate on ideas rather than experiences. Nine categories may be distinguished, each well represented not only in the past but also in twentieth-century thought: (1) primarily philosophers of religion—David Hume, Immanuel Kant, William Alston, James Collins, Antony Flew, John Hick, George Mavrodes, Alvin Plantinga, Ian Ramsey, and most others cited here (typically, all but a couple of these profess a religious faith, and all but Collins are Protestants in background); (2) primarily philosophically minded religious thinkers—Christian existentialist Søren Kierkegaard, Jewish existentialists Martin Buber and Franz Rosenzweig, and liberal Henry Nelson Wieman; (3) primarily philosophically minded students of religious experience—Rudolf Otto, William James, William Ernest Hocking, W. T. Stace, and Ninian Smart; (4) primarily philosophical humanists and humanistic critics of religion—Georg W. F. Hegel, neo-Hegelian Ludwig Feuerbach, positivist Auguste Comte, pragmatist John Dewey, and empiricists Bertrand Russell and Paul Edwards; (5) primarily nonhumanist advocates of a metaphysical-religious outlook—Baruch Spinoza, Gottfried Wilhelm Leibniz, Arthur Schopenhauer, Henri Bergson, Charles Sanders Peirce, Josiah Royce, Samuel Alexander, Alfred North Whitehead, Charles Hartshorne, Peter Bertocci, and Brand Blanshard.

In addition, there are four mainly theological categories, first those who are: (6) primarily philosophical advocates of or apologists for a particular (type of) religion—Anselm, John Oman, William Temple, John Baillie, F. R. Tennant, and E. L. Mascall (all these men are Christians and are from Britain, where this approach has long been a strong tradition); (7) primarily theologians but philosophically astute—Christians Augustine, Karl Barth, and Emil Brunner, and Jewish theologian Abraham Heschel. (8) In a few cases the thinker is substantially both a philosopher and a theologian—preeminently Thomas Aquinas, Friedrich Schleiermacher, and Paul Tillich.

(9) There is also a special sense of "philosophical theology," inaugurated by Schleiermacher (*Brief Outline on the Study of Theology*, 1811, cited on p. 7), the chief purpose of which is not to defend the faith to outsiders or even to support religious belief for insiders (number 6) but to offer historical-critical clarification of concepts used in a given church community, in comparison with those used elsewhere, and to provide critique of "diseased deviations" in either doctrine or polity within it. The importance of this activity is underscored by Schleiermacher's proposition that "everyone's philosophical theology essentially includes within it the principles of his whole theological way of thinking."

Besides the apologists (number 6), some of the philosophers mentioned above also do more than a little theological work—most notably, Kierkegaard, Wieman, Mascall, and Hick; and some who are primarily philosophers of religion (number 1) also do apologetic work (number 6).

Although any one thinker may ply several of these trades, nearly all tend to stick to one of them. In that each group has much that is of immediate value for the other groups, they nevertheless constitute a single philosophical community.

Once the choice of approach is made, inquiry still tends to be significantly colored by religious or theological orientation. Steven Katz (1975) shows this for Jewish philosophers. Islamic philosophers have rarely figured in modern discussions, but Sayyed Hossein Nasr's Gifford Lectures (1981) well represent that general orientation. Roman Catholic thought helps form the language and interests of Anthony Kenny (1979), Peter Geach (1977), and James Collins (1967). None of these three much-published authors quite represents the traditional interests purveyed among Roman Catholic theologians, however. Although much of the modern discussion in philosophy of religion has been shaped by skeptical challenges, as in epistemology, skepticism itself is a distinctive approach in Antony Flew's (1966) and Kai Nielsen's writing (1973). Antiskepticism reaches high intensity in R. S. Heimbeck's logical-critical study (1969) of "metatheological skepticism." A nonsupernaturalist, Wittgensteinian "fideist" position in the middle-ground, such as that of Dewi Phillips (1976, and in his noted 1966 book *The Concept of Prayer,* not cited here), is committed neither to skepticism nor to theism, against which most skeptical arguments are directed.

"Natural theology" is a tradition of Christian thought since the scholastics, which reached movement strength in the seventeenth and eighteenth centuries. Its primary assumption is that there are religiously significant propositions about God, nature, and faith that are grounded not on revelation but on unaided reason. This tradition dominated philosophical thinking about religion almost unchallenged (except in certain theological quarters) from the late eighteenth century until the 1950s, when other options began to get clearer focus and wider use. Among twentieth-century theologians, Karl Barth especially represents opposition to natural theology; Emil Brunner supports it. Among the philosophers George Thomas (1970) presents a good latter-day example of the older style of natural theology, conceived as a part of philosophy, not theology per se.

Especially in the United States, one option to natural theology derives especially from pragmatist William James's *Varieties of Religious Experience* (1902, not cited here) and other of his writings and from idealist William Ernest Hocking (1912). In 1981 two full-scale studies of James's philosophy of religion appeared, by Henry Levinson and Robert Vanden Burgt, the first since Julius Seelye Bixler's in 1926. Levinson's has a more scholarly, Vanden Burgt's a more apologetic aim. More recently, Ninian Smart (e.g., 1973) has produced numerous studies on religious phenomena, East and West, viewed through philosophical spectacles. A second, closely related set of options is that of practical, religious mysticism (Quakers Rufus Jones and Douglas Steere) and metaphysical mysticism (W. T. Stace). Idealists like Josiah Royce and W. M. Urban have remained closer to natural theology, as have empiricists like D. C. Mackintosh, Henry Nelson Wieman, H. D. Lewis (1959) and John Smith (1968), rationalists like Brand Blanshard (1974), and the metaphysical personalist school of Borden Parker Bowne, E. S. Brightman, and Peter Bertocci (1979).

Pragmatism yielded a third major option to natural theology, that of substituting a natural and changing social faith (that later commentators have called a social ideology or a civic religion) for a supernatural one bound to some religious institution. John Dewey's *A Common Faith* (1934, not cited here) especially marks this approach. The metaphysical reflections of Alfred North Whitehead have given rise to a fourth major option, that of process theology. From the philosophy side this movement has been engendered especially by Charles Hartshorne (e.g., 1948) throughout his long career. A Hartshorne Festschrift edited by William Reese and Eugene Freeman (1964) emphasizes metaphysical, logical, and epistemological issues.

CONTEMPORARY THEMES AND DEVELOPMENTS

The 1950s

Until the 1950s all but a small portion of the philosophy literature on religion related chiefly to philosophical theism. That is, the main alternatives argued over were those of believers, agnostics, atheists, deists, pantheists, or panpsychists with respect to a theistic concept of God. This concept was thought of either in a more metaphysical or in a more anthropomorphic sense. Particularly after A. J. Ayer's *Language, Truth and Logic* (1936), logical positivists and their logical empiricist successors began to refer to religious belief itself as "nonsense" on the ground that what religious language claims to represent cannot be empirically verified. A volume of essays edited by Antony Flew and Alasdaire MacIntyre (1955) well represents the stir that had been aroused by the 1950s. In a much-noted 1955 lecture, empiricist R. B. Braithwaite argued that this situation only points to the fact that religious assertions, like moral ones, have a very different function from those that are empirically verifiable, namely to express one's intention to follow a specified policy of behavior. In *Faith and Knowledge* (1957, not cited here), on the other hand, John Hick attempted to base a theistic position on an empirical-verificationist foundation.

Ordinary language philosophers entered into the fray with efforts to clarify the meaning (or nonsense) of religious language over an increasingly wider field. Ian Ramsey's (1957) work particularly betokens this approach, as does a set of Oxford essays edited by Basil Mitchell (1957) and in the United States Frederick Ferré's *Language, Logic and God* (1961). Writings by D. Z. Phillips and Ninian Smart, already mentioned, also used ordinary language analysis for their purposes.

The 1960s to the Early 1970s

The chief efforts of the 1960s were also addressed to issues newly raised by the verification controversy and by attempts to apply methods of logical and linguistic analysis to the age-old problems. The early 1960s essays of William Alston nicely exemplify these continuing interests, as do his (uncollected) essays twenty years later. John Hick has modified his position somewhat, but his numerous subsequent publications have used an empiricist approach to both philosophical and theological problems. A 1964 volume he edited while teaching philosophy at Princeton Theological Seminary puts the continuing debate in bold relief, including contributions from Alston, MacIntyre, H. H. Price, and other notables, as does his own volume (1963). Antony Flew (1966) attempts to develop and examine a case for Christian theism (God and immortality) against what he and many others at that time took to be the "irrationalist" position of Karl Barth. His collected essays published a decade later (not cited here) evidence a general consistency of view over the following period.

In the early 1970s two collections intended as textbooks indicated how far the new analytic ventures had gone. That edited by Baruch Brody (1974) combined classical texts to which these philosophers had often referred with examples of recent analytic discussions on the nature and existence of God, God talk, God's relation to the world, the relation of human beings to God, immortality, and resurrection. The collected edited by Malcolm Diamond and Thomas Litzenburg (1973) traced verificationism and ended with essays by Alvin Plantinga arguing that it is insupportable, and by Wesley Salmon and Michael Tooley arguing that modifications give it staying power. At that time Basil Mitchell (1973), twenty years earlier a member of the Wittgensteinian group called "the Metaphysicals," argued for the view that religious faith is justified in its character as an unconditional existential choice. He also attempted to show the similarities and differences of the kind of choice in comparison with many other kinds people reasonably make.

What had been accomplished? Certainly the terms of discourse had been clarified as never before. As supplements, even alternatives, to ordinary language analyses, two rigorously logical-analytical works on justification of belief in God show this advance particularly well, by Alvin Plantinga (1967) and George Mavrodes (1970).

The classical arguments for the existence of God had also been thoroughly reviewed and new, tighter versions had been proposed. In addition to the two textbooks already mentioned, John Hick (1964) edited a useful volume of classic texts on the major arguments with some recent essays, Alvin Plantinga (1965) a similar one on the ontological argument, and Donald Burrill (1967) on the cosmological argument. All three were analytic, as is Richard Swinburne's recent synopsis (1979). A potpourri of approaches was gathered in a *Monist* symposium by Charles Hartshorne (1970) and others. Later Richard Campbell (1976) concocted a fresh study of Anselm's *Proslogion* of 1078, wherein the ontological argument was given its first substantial form. Campbell not only opposed Barth's dismissal of the Cartesian-Kantian tradition in analyzing Anselm's argument, which he presents in symbolic logic and accepts as valid. He also took an approach alternative to that tradition. It is questionable whether Campbell's analysis obviates Barth's main point, which is based on the fact that Anselm's work is presented as a prayer and thereby as an exercise in faith seeking understanding, not as an exercise in natural theology as this is conceived by modern philosophers. Similar issues as to their intention and use adhere to analyses of the other classic arguments.

Other yields had come in discussions of the problem that evil exists in the face of a supposedly omnipotent, good, and loving God. The most thoroughgoing, engaging historical treatment came from John Hick (1966), who adopted a Schleiermacherian position. Edward Madden and Peter Hare (1968) referred to further contemporary arguments, including a number by nonanalytic writers. Some tightly argued 1971–72 lectures on the subject by Thomist analytic philosopher Peter Geach (1977) expanded to other subjects such as animal pain, original sin, freedom, hope, hell, and divine providence.

From the skeptical-critical side came an unusual set of finely crafted, provocative articles by Paul Edwards (1967) on atheism, life, asking the "why" questions, common consent arguments for the existence of God, and panpsychism.

Since the Mid-1970s

The Geach lectures presage a significant change of scope and direction that appeared in books by the late 1970s, the first major shift in two decades. Between them, and with much overlap of subject matter, if not content, five collections display the extraordinarily fulsome harvest: those edited by Stuart Brown (1977), Linwood Urban and Douglas Walton (1978), C. F. Delaney (1978), Frederick Crosson (1981)—all on aspects of religious belief—and above all that edited by Steven Cahn and David Shatz on *Contemporary Philosophy of*

Religion (1982). Further work was being done on arguments for the existence of God (such as Anthony Kenny's 1979 book on philosophers' views of divine omniscience, foreknowledge, and omnipotence, and William Rowe's historically based 1975 study on the cosmological argument); on religious language (such as Patrick Sherry's 1977 Wittgensteinian exploration of what the nature of religious "language-games" and "forms of life" would be, if there are any); and the problem of evil (as in Alvin Plantinga, 1975, with an essay on the cosmological, teleological, and ontological arguments). But the five collections mentioned show that the limelight had moved to the kind of investigations that used to be in the charge of systematic theologians. I believe that Schleiermacher's injunction about the task of philosophical theology, quoted earlier, was being rediscovered in this period and that the eventual effects on theological work itself should be profound. Already these collections contained important thinking about the divine attributes (especially divine omnipotence vis-à-vis human freedom), the intelligibility of the universe, divine action in time and the issue of God's timelessness and omnipresence, miracles, religious feelings, worship and ritual, the rationality of religious belief, religion as an autonomous form of life, mysticism, life after death, and relations between world religions.

Recent books by individuals have also begun to manifest these changes. A critical examination of the notion that God is "timeless" by Nelson Pike (1970) and reflections on psychic research by H. H. Price (1972), for example, were both written in a somewhat earlier methodological frame but are indicative, respectively, of the return to specific theological problems and the broadening scope of inquiry that was to come. (Empiricist Price had given the 1960 Gifford Lectures on *Belief,* not cited here, and Pike had been an earlier contributor to the analytic debates on God and evil.) These changes are exemplified particularly well in a Kantian affirmation of "religious reason" by Ronald Green (1978), a monograph by Ben-Ami Scharfstein (1973), and two collections on "mysticism" edited by William Earle in *Monist* (1976) and by Steven Katz (1978), an attempt to base religious epistemology on hope rather than belief by James Muyskens (1979), a systematic treatise on death, eternal life, and eschatology (last things) by John Hick (1976), a work on "the coherence of theism" by Richard Swinburne (1977), and a study of "paradox and identity" in theology by R. T. Herbert (1979). Renewed interest in theological ethics is also manifest.

FUTURE PROSPECTS

Future prospects for this now burgeoning area of philosophy seem to be well indicated in the recent works just noted. The broadening of the scope of interest will no doubt continue, as will the careful, analytic attention to matters that used to be handled mostly by systematic theologians. Perhaps secular critique of the sort Paul Edwards did in 1967 will be renewed—probably closer to his analytic, reflective approach than to the sometimes frenetic "God is dead" dialectic that was fashionable in the late 1960s. Perhaps positive, naturalist efforts of the kind John Dewey once made will be added to it. In any case, one of the most exciting, productive periods in the history of this area was definitely going on in the late 1970s and early 1980s, and no evidence of its stopping is apparent.

Alston, William P. "Philosophy of Religion: Problems of," "Religion: Naturalistic Reconstructions of, Psychological Explanations of," "Religious Language," "Teleological Argument for the Existence of God." *Encyclopedia of Philosophy,* vols. 6–7. Ed. by Paul Edwards. New York: Macmillan; London: Collier Macmillan, 1967.
———, ed. *Religious Belief and Philosophical Reflection.* New York: Harcourt, Brace, 1963.
Bertocci, Peter A. *The Person God Is.* New York: Humanities Pr.; London: Allen & Unwin, 1970.
Blanshard, Brand. *Reason and Belief.* London: Allen & Unwin, 1974; New Haven, Conn.: Yale Univ. Pr., 1975. (Based on Gifford Lectures and Noble Lectures at Harvard.)
Brody, Baruch A., ed. *Readings in the Philosophy of Religion: An Analytic Approach.* Englewood Cliffs, N.J.: Prentice-Hall, 1974.
Brown, Stuart C., ed. *Reason and Religion.* Ithaca, N.Y.: Cornell Univ. Pr., 1977.
Burrill, Donald, ed. *The Cosmological Argument.* New York: Doubleday, 1967.
Cahn, Steven M., and David Shatz, eds. *Contemporary Philosophy of Religion.* Oxford and New York: Oxford Univ. Pr., 1982.
Campbell, Richard. *From Belief to Understanding.* Canberra: Australian National Univ. Pr., 1976.
Collins, James. *The Emergence of Philosophy of Religion.* New Haven, Conn. and London: Yale Univ. Pr., 1967.
Crosson, Frederick, ed. *The Autonomy of Religious Belief: A Critical Inquiry.* Notre Dame, Ind. and London: Univ. of Notre Dame Pr., 1981.
Delaney, C. F., ed. *Rationality and Religious Belief.* Notre Dame, Ind. and London: Univ. of Notre Dame Pr., 1979.
Diamond, Malcolm L., and Thomas V. Litzenburg, Jr., eds. *The Logic of God: Theology and Verification.* Indianapolis, Ind.: Bobbs-Merrill, 1973.

Earle, William, ed. "The Philosophy of Mysticism." *Monist* 59, no. 4:463–586 (Oct. 1976).

Edwards, Paul. "Atheism," "Common Consent Arguments for the Existence of God," "Life, Meaning and Value of," "Panpsychism," "Why." *Encyclopedia of Philosophy.* Ed. by Paul Edwards. New York: Macmillan; London: Collier Macmillan, 1967.

Ferré, Frederick. *Language, Logic and God.* New York: Harper & Row; London: Eyre & Spottiswoode, 1961.

Flew, Antony. *God and Philosophy.* New York: Harcourt, Brace; London: Hutchinson, 1966.

———, and Alasdaire MacIntyre, eds. *New Essays in Philosophical Theology.* London: SCM Pr., 1955.

Geach, Peter T. *Providence and Evil: The Stanton Lectures, 1971–1972.* New York and Cambridge : Cambridge Univ. Pr., 1977.

Green, Ronald M. *Religious Reason: The Rational and Moral Basis of Religious Belief.* Oxford and New York: Oxford Univ. Pr., 1978.

Hartshorne, Charles. *The Divine Relativity: A Social Conception of God.* New Haven, Conn.: Yale Univ. Pr., 1948.

———, et al. "The Philosophic Proofs of God's Existence." *Monist* 54, nos. 2–3:159–459 (April, July 1970).

Heimbeck, Raeburne S. *Theology and Meaning: A Critique of Metatheological Scepticism.* Stanford, Calif.: Stanford Univ. Pr.; London: Allen & Unwin, 1969.

Herbert, Robert T. *Paradox and Identity in Theology.* Ithaca, N.Y. and London: Cornell Univ. Pr., 1979.

Hick, John. *Death and Eternal Life.* New York and London: Harper & Row, 1976.

———. *Evil and the God of Love.* Rev. ed. New York and London: Harper & Row, 1978. (Brief chapter added updating original 1966 ed.)

———. *Philosophy of Religion,* 2nd ed. Englewood Cliffs, N.J.: Prentice-Hall, 1973. (1st ed., 1963.)

———, ed. *The Existence of God.* New York and London: Collier Macmillan, 1964.

———, ed. *Faith and the Philosophers.* New York: St. Martin's; London: Macmillan, 1964.

Hocking, William Ernest. *The Meaning of God in Human Experience: A Philosophic Study of Religion.* New Haven, Conn.: Yale Univ. Pr., 1912. Repr., 1963.

Katz, Steven T., ed. *Jewish Philosophers.* Jerusalem: Keter, 1975.

———, ed. *Mysticism and Philosophical Analysis.* Oxford and New York: Oxford Univ. Pr., 1978.

Kenny, Anthony. *The God of the Philosophers.* New York: Oxford Univ. Pr.; Oxford: Clarendon Pr., 1979.

Levinson, Henry S. *The Religious Investigations of William James.* Chapel Hill: Univ. of North Carolina Pr., 1981.

Lewis, Hywel D. *Our Experience of God.* London: Allen & Unwin, 1959; New York: Macmillan, 1960.

Madden, Edward H., and Peter H. Hare. *Evil and the Concept of God.* Springfield, Ill.: Thomas, 1968.

482 Areas of Philosophy

Mavrodes, George I. *Belief in God.* New York: Random House, 1970.

Mitchell, Basil. *The Justification of Religious Belief.* New York and London: Macmillan, 1973. Repr.: Oxford and New York: Oxford Univ. Pr., 1981.

———, ed. *Faith and Logic: Oxford Essays in Philosophical Theology.* London: Allen & Unwin, 1957.

Muyskens, James L. *The Sufficiency of Hope: The Conceptual Foundations of Religion.* Philadelphia, Pa.: Temple Univ. Pr., 1979.

Nasr, Seyyed Hossein. *Knowledge and the Sacred.* New York: Crossroad, 1981. (Gifford Lectures, 1981.)

Nielsen, Kai. *Scepticism.* New York: St. Martin's; London: Macmillan, 1973.

Phillips, Dewi Z. *Religion without Explanation.* Oxford: Blackwell, 1976.

Pike, Nelson. *God and Timelessness.* London: Routledge & Paul, 1970.

Plantinga, Alvin. *God and Other Minds: A Study of the Rational Justification of Belief in God.* Ithaca, N.Y.: Cornell Univ. Pr., 1967.

———. *God, Freedom, and Evil.* New York: Harper & Row, 1974; London: Allen & Unwin, 1975.

———, ed. *The Ontological Argument.* New York: Macmillan, 1965.

Price, Henry H. *Essays in the Philosophy of Religion.* Oxford: Clarendon Pr., 1972. (Sarum Lectures, Oxford, 1971.)

Ramsey, Ian T. *Religious Language: An Empirical Placing of Theological Language.* London: SCM Pr., 1957.

Reese, William L., and Eugene Freeman, eds. *Process and Divinity: The Hartshorne Festschrift, Philosophical Essays.* La Salle, Ill.: Open Court, 1964.

Rowe, William L. *The Cosmological Argument.* Princeton, N.J.: Princeton Univ. Pr., 1975.

Scharfstein, Ben-Ami. *Mystical Experience.* Oxford: Blackwell, 1973.

Schleiermacher, Friedrich. *On Religion: Addresses in Response to Its Cultured Critics.* Tr. with introduction and notes by Terrence N. Tice. Richmond, Va.: John Knox Pr., 1969.

Sherry, Patrick. *Religion, Truth and Language-Games.* New York: Barnes & Noble; London: Macmillan, 1977.

Smart, Ninian. *The Phenomenon of Religion.* New York and London: Macmillan, 1973.

Smith, John E. *Experience and God.* Oxford and New York: Oxford Univ. Pr., 1968.

Swinburne, Richard G. *The Coherence of Theism.* New York: Oxford Univ. Pr.; Oxford: Clarendon Pr., 1977.

———. *The Existence of God.* New York: Oxford Univ. Pr.; Oxford: Clarendon Pr., 1979. (A sequel, making a trilogy with these two, is to follow, entitled *Faith and Reason.*)

Thomas, George F. *Philosophy and Religious Belief.* New York: Scribner, 1970.

Urban, Linwood, and Douglas N. Walton, eds. *The Power of God: Readings on Omnipotence and Evil.* Oxford and New York: Oxford Univ. Pr., 1978.

Vanden Burgt, Robert J. *The Religious Philosophy of William James.* Chicago: Nelson-Hall, 1981.

29

Philosophy of Psychology and Psychoanalysis

The chief aims of the philosophy of psychology and psychoanalysis are critically to analyze presuppositions, theories, methods, and concepts in these fields, to contribute to developing theory and modes of explanation, and to facilitate interaction between them and other areas of philosophy—at present, especially philosophy of mind and philosophy of action.

Beginning in the late nineteenth century, when psychology was emerging as a distinct science, psychology was taught in the philosophy department in many colleges and universities in the United States or in conjoint departments. William James and John Dewey were well known for their teaching and publications in both fields. In some places this pattern continued into the 1950s. As the two fields have developed and separated, each has presented new problems and possibilities to the other; but not infrequently these have not been received. Psychoanalysis, which effectively began with publication of Sigmund Freud's *Interpretation of Dreams* in 1900 (enlarged and revised five times through 1919; first translated in 1913), developed slowly in medical schools and separate institutes. It did not really come into its own in Britain and America until after World War II. Its work in developmental psychology, and especially on expressions of unconscious mental functioning, has received comparatively little notice among philosophers or experimental psychologists. Particularly in recent decades, there has been a significant flow the other way, however. In short, the untapped potentials for interactions among these three fields are very great.

This area of philosophy, therefore, is quite young. The systematic

483

effort of Charles Wallraff (1961) to think out relations between empirical studies and philosophical theory has as yet no successor. A valuable collection of twelve essays on explanation, mostly by philosophers, was edited by Robert Borger and Frank Cioffi (1970) and includes substantial critiques by philosophers, psychologists, and sociologists with author replies. This publication was unusual, however, even in 1970. A brief introduction by the linguistic philosopher Jerry Fodor (1968) on explanation by direct reference to psychological states has fared better, in that in the 1970s he and other philosophers developed considerable interest in cognitive psychology (see chapter 19). The interest was so intensive, in fact, that apart from idiom and modes of argument it is sometimes difficult in these writings to know where one field ends and the other begins. Jerome Neu's treatise (1977) stands almost alone in attempting to apply historic philosophical positions to the practice of therapy. No doubt Ludwig Wittgenstein's recently published (1980) *Remarks on the Philosophy of Psychology* will stir up further investigations, especially among linguistic philosophers.

Closely related works on mind, action, and moral psychology have already been mentioned in chapters 19, 20, and 22, and Karl Aschenbrenner's study of value concepts in chapter 21. Some include essays explicitly on philosophy of psychology. Apart from these, seven recent works betoken the major emergent themes in philosophy of psychology: anthologies of contributions by both philosophers and psychologists edited by S. C. Brown (1974) and Neil Bolton (1979); Ned Block's readings (1980–81); Wade Savage's edition of essays (1978) from a 1975 conference on cognitive psychology, which emphasized computational and information-processing models of cognitive processes; a set of *Monist* essays on cognition edited by William Alston (1978); a gathering of philosophical and psychological reflections on "the self," edited by Theodore Mischel (1977); and Jeff Coulter's combination of linguistic philosophy and ethnomethodology (1979) to understand "the social construction of mind." These writings from the 1970s tend to follow current trends in philosophy of mind and action. Consequently they are familiar in both content and method to anyone who reads in those areas and thus little additional comment on them is necessary at this point. Unfortunately, the same is not generally true of philosophical writings on psychoanalysis.

Often philosophers and psychologists joined in these ventures, occasionally both in the same person. The concept of "action" is also brought to the fore in many of the more recent writings. That is, psychology is conceived primarily as a scientific investigation of human actions.

Not many earlier volumes are noteworthy. The first volume in the Minnesota Studies in the Philosophy of Science, edited by Herbert Feigl and Michael Scriven (1956), included essays on both psychology and psychoanalysis. Half of Edward Madden's little book (1962) is on philosophical problems in psychoanalysis; the rest relates mostly to Gestalt psychology, learning theory, and *verstehende* psychology (Wilhelm Dilthey and others). Joseph Rychlak (1968), who writes for the most part from within psychology, provides some philosophical investigation of personality theory. Theodore Mischel (1969), one of the rare breed who ranges comfortably on either side, joined philosophers A. I. Melden, R. S. Peters, and Stephen Toulmin with four psychologists to consider conceptual frameworks for psychological studies.

PSYCHOANALYSIS

A 1946 essay by analytic philosopher John Wisdom, "Philosophy and Psycho-Analysis," headlines a 1953 collection of his essays, mostly on other subjects, and is mainly a general approach to understanding "philosophical conflicts." Another philosopher named J. O. Wisdom (cited on p. 107 and in Charles Hanly, 1970) is one of the very few who have closely associated themselves with psychoanalysis; his views are allied with the ideas of Melanie Klein, a nonmainstream analyst whose school has had a wide following in Britain and Latin America. An unparalleled effort to bring a psychoanalytic orientation to bear on understanding the lives and choices of philosophers, by Ben-Ami Scharfstein (*The Philosophers*, 1980, cited on p. 7), has already been mentioned; for the most part, he does this in a manner which, I think rightly, guards against wild interpretation.

It is not possible to do creditable analysis of a person or of a piece of writing without having strong evidence of thoughts and fantasies that reveal patterns of action and of inner conflict, usually hidden. The possibility of psychobiography, psychoanalytic literary criticism, and allied efforts lies in the clinical experience that even though it ordinarily takes years of intensive analysis to reveal, work through, and gain insight into one's basic intrapsychic conflicts and patterns, the analyst can usually detect particular trends among them in the initial interviews. The questions of confirmation and disconfirmation, of explanation, and of application remain for the analyst, who must constantly be ready for new information and surprises and must not be overly influenced by earlier impressions. Nevertheless, we all do develop patterns of character and complex predispositions to act and choose which our ordinary words, expressions, and actions reveal, sometimes with startling clarity. Philosophers are no exception; nor are the works of philosophers. In a very broad way Morris Lazerowitz (1977; and 1955, cited on p. 358) has used this insight to expose what he takes to be illusive innovations in philosophical language and theory.

The primary interests in philosophy of psychoanalysis, however, are directed to psychoanalysis itself, particularly to issues about the scientific status and effects of its concepts, methods, presuppositions, and theories. An early collection of twenty-eight essays edited by Sidney Hook (1959) dealt almost entirely with such issues; a few were by psychoanalysts and psychologists, the remainder by philosophers. This was succeeded by a symposium of twelve essays edited by Charles Hanly and Morris Lazerowitz (1970), three by analysts, one by the noted psychoanalytic ethnologist George Devereux, one by sociologist Lewis Feuer, and the rest by philosophers; a *Monist* symposium of seven philosophers edited by William Alston (1972); and a Richard Wollheim edition (1974) of critical essays, some of them new, by twenty-two philosophers. Wollheim also wrote one of the several recent biographies of Freud.

Individual works of similar importance have come from Alasdair MacIntyre (1958) on the concept "unconscious motivation"; Herbert Fingarette (1963; also 1969, cited on p. 369), presenting several conceptual analyses and applications of psychoanalysis, viewed as "a responsible tool of inquiry," to an understanding of his own life and to the issue of "self-transformation"; Michael Sherwood (1969) on explanation; and studies by hermeneutical phenomenologist Paul Ricoeur (1970; see chapter 13) on the nature and tasks of interpretation. Sherwood's study is a critical analysis of some claims in psychoanalytic theory, but it could be applied to other theories as well. Ricoeur's is more a personal reading and reinterpretation of Freud than a critical scrutiny of psychoanalytic theory.

Serious limitations in almost all these writings include (1) an undue concentration on a few notions in Freud and the earlier literature of psychoanalysis, the mainstream of which has developed considerably as a clinically and observationally based science since the 1920s; (2) a lack of indepth experience either with psychoanalytic process or with critical thought about that process among contemporary analysts; and (3) a habit, borne chiefly of logical empiricism, of focusing on epistemological issues concerning justification of belief. Nevertheless some valuable, informed analysis and critique appear within these writings, reflective especially of a growing sophistication in philosophy of mind, and thereby give a promising foretaste of things to come. None of the great twentieth-century philosophers appears to have had more than a brush with psychoanalysis. Although Freud himself was an empiricist, a naturalist, a materialist, and a positivist of sorts, psychoanalytic thinking ran counter to the prevailing emphases on finding simple, reductive surface-empirical models of experience, on securing a single type of foundation and methodology for the sciences, and on elaborating a kind of "rationality" that is almost bound to regard much of the unconscious material Freud unearthed as disturbingly vague, mythical or irrational, and therefore unamenable to rational ordering.

FUTURE PROSPECTS

For some years to come, the fortunes of this area are likely to follow those of the parent areas rather closely. Divergences from this pattern will occur as more philosophers become intimately knowledgeable in academic psychology, clinical psychology, developmental psychology, and psychoanalysis and as more practitioners of those disciplines gain greater facility in philosophy. Otherwise, a pattern very familiar from the past history of philosophy is likely to prevail: that of repeating the same unclarified puzzles, inadequately informed definition and treatment of problems, limiting distinctions and partial theories over and over again. As in the past, much philosophical investment—some of it fruitful—will go into worrying over details. It will take some new and inescapable information sufficiently to dislodge philosophers from these efforts to enable them to begin to raise new questions and to grasp a larger, more integrated picture. This process is perhaps especially significant in philosophy of psychology since within the twentieth century psychology has taken upon itself an increasingly broad scope of investigations into human nature and human action. In this respect, psychoanalysis is not far behind.

Alston, William P., ed. "Philosophy and Psychoanalysis." *Monist* 56, no. 3:313–464 (July 1972).
———, ed. "The Philosophy and Psychology of Cognition." *Monist* 61, no. 4:501–637 (Oct. 1978).

Block, Ned, ed. *Readings in Philosophy of Psychology.* 2v. Cambridge, Mass.: Harvard Univ. Pr., 1980–81.

Bolton, Neil, ed. *Philosophical Problems in Psychology.* New York and London: Methuen, 1979.

✓ Borger, Robert, and Frank Cioffi, eds. *Explanation in the Behavioral Sciences.* Cambridge and New York: Cambridge Univ. Pr., 1970.

Brown, Stuart C., ed. *Philosophy of Psychology.* New York: Barnes & Noble; London: Macmillan, 1974. (Royal Institute of Philosophy Conference, University of Kent, 1971.)

✓ Coulter, Jeff. *The Social Construction of Mind: Studies in Ethnomethodology and Linguistic Philosophy.* New York and London: Macmillan, 1979.

Feigl, Herbert, and Michael Scriven, eds. *The Foundations of Science and the Concepts of Psychology and Psychoanalysis.* Minnesota Studies in the Philosophy of Science, vol. 1. Minneapolis: Univ. of Minnesota Pr., 1956.

Fingarette, Herbert. *The Self in Transformation: Psychoanalysis, Philosophy, and the Life of the Spirit.* New York and London: Basic Books, 1963.

✓ Fodor, Jerry A. *Psychological Explanation: An Introduction to the Philosophy of Psychology.* New York: Random House, 1968.

Hanly, Charles, and Morris Lazerowitz, eds. *Psychoanalysis and Philosophy.* New York: International Universities Pr., 1970.

Hook, Sidney, ed. *Psychoanalysis, Scientific Method, and Philosophy: A Symposium.* New York: Grove Pr., 1959.

Lazerowitz, Morris. *The Language of Philosophy: Freud and Wittgenstein.* Boston Studies in the Philosophy of Science, vol. 55. Dordrecht and Boston: Reidel, 1977.

✓ MacIntyre, Alasdair C. *The Unconscious: A Conceptual Analysis.* New York: Humanities Pr.; London: Routledge & Paul, 1958.

Madden, Edward H. *Philosophical Problems of Psychology.* New York: Odyssey Pr., 1962.

Mischel, Theodore, ed. *Human Action: Conceptual and Empirical Issues.* New York: Academic Pr., 1969.

———, ed. *The Self: Psychological and Philosophical Issues.* Totowa, N.J.: Rowman & Littlefield; Oxford: Blackwell, 1977.

✓ Neu, Jerome. *Emotion, Thought and Therapy: A Study of Hume and Spinoza and the Relationship of Philosophical Theories of the Emotions to Psychological Theories of Therapy.* New York: Humanities Pr.; London: Routledge & Paul, 1977.

Ricoeur, Paul. *Freud and Philosophy: An Essay on Interpretation.* Tr. by Denis Savage. New Haven, Conn.: Yale Univ. Pr., 1970. (Terry Lectures at Yale University, 1961, and 1962 lectures at the University of Louvain.)

✓ Rychlak, Joseph F. *A Philosophy of Science for Personality Theory.* Boston: Houghton Mifflin, 1968.

Savage C. Wade, ed. *Perception and Cognition: Issues in the Foundations of Psychology.* Minnesota Studies in the Philosophy of Science, vol. 9. Minneapolis: Univ. of Minnesota Pr., 1978.

✓ Sherwood, Michael. *The Logic of Explanation in Psychoanalysis.* New York: Academic Pr., 1969.

✓ Wallraff, Charles F. *Philosophical Theory and Psychological Fact: An Attempt at Synthesis.* Tucson: Univ. of Arizona Pr., 1961.

Wisdom, John. *Philosophy and Psycho-analysis.* Oxford: Blackwell, 1953.
Wittgenstein, Ludwig. *Remarks on the Philosophy of Psychology.* 2v. Ed. by G. E. M. Anscombe and G. H. von Wright; tr. by G. E. M. Anscombe. Oxford and New York: Oxford Univ. Pr., 1980.
Wollheim, Richard, ed. *Freud: A Collection of Critical Essays.* Garden City, N.Y.: Doubleday Anchor, 1974.

30

Philosophy
of Education

Among all the areas of philosophy, philosophy of education is pecu-
liar in its modern identification with a set of professional activities.
Moreover, those activities contain or imply the broadest possible
scope of public concerns.

Philosophy of art, religion, science, and history (to mention only
the most obvious examples) may also include professional interests.
These philosophical endeavors, however, have not become a regular
part of initiation or advanced study in the fields mentioned. Or they
are so only in very limited ways. For example, philosophical concerns
are included in discussions of the theory of art criticism among academic students of art, in the curricula of theological seminaries and
departments of religion, and in still more restricted ways in discussions of scientific theory among scientists and of historiography
among historians.

As to public concerns, the field has not produced specialists in the
philosophy of social work, public health, or medicine. The closest
neighbor would be found within the tradition of jurisprudence in
law, where a few philosophers of law have attached themselves. But
every school of education provides instruction in philosophy of education. There at least a smattering of it is often a requirement, or it is
presented as an option alongside sociology and history of education
and as a subject for advanced study. In the United States this is often
done in departments of social foundations of education or, very recently, of educational policy, planning, and administration, as well as
in many philosophy departments. In the numerous branches of the
education profession, which now extends into every profession and

490

into every area of public life, elements of philosophical interest are sustained within its endless concerns about professional conduct and about educational theory, policy making, evaluation, and planning.

John Dewey, widely reputed to be the most eminent modern philosopher of education, once made a case for regarding philosophy itself as "the theory of education in its most general phases." This proposal rested on a conception of education as "the process of forming fundamental dispositions, intellectual and emotional, toward nature and fellow men" (and women), the process, moreover, that enables the continuous, critical intelligent "reconstruction of experience." Whether one accepts this metaview of philosophy or not, there can be no doubt that education, seen from either a more descriptive or a more comprehensive and normative point of view, is potentially an important ingredient in every area of human experience. (This would be true, for example, if one defined education, as I do, as any process of learning conducive to human growth in which the learner is an active participant. The need to clarify what such terms could mean drives one from a descriptive to a normative task.) At the present stage in the evolution of consciousness and culture, therefore, a thoroughly systematic philosophical outlook would include education not only in its overarching or linking functions but also distinctively in every part, with somewhat different questions and concerns in each one.

THEMES AND DEVELOPMENTS

No comprehensive history of the philosophy of education yet exists, though there are a number of intellectual histories of educational ideas. Perhaps none was really possible before, if now, for lack of adequate conceptualization. In any case, the body of detailed, sustained historical-critical studies necessary to undergird such a task is itself small. Most of the books in this field are introductory texts, and most of the rest are anthologies of topical essays.

In the broadest sense, the classical texts would be drawn from those that interpret the development of human intelligence and culture. In a narrower sense, the texts would deal especially with pedagogy and with the functioning and place of formal educational institutions in society. Early on the second list would be Plato's *Republic* (see Werner Jaeger's *Paideia*, 1939, cited on p. 17 and Robin Barrow's *Plato, Utilitarianism and Education*, 1975, cited on p. 32). Among the great philosophers the list would also include

Aristotle, Kant, and Dewey (all three studied from an analytic viewpoint by William Frankena, 1965); Augustine and Aquinas; Locke and Rousseau (1979); Bertrand Russell (1932; see Park, 1963); Jacques Maritain (1943); and Alfred North Whitehead (1929); though after the medieval period numerous lesser-known writers are also of importance.

Joseph Chambliss (1968) has studied the nineteenth-century origins of philosophy of education as a discipline in the United States. He claims it was not really established as a "distinct" field until about 1913. Twentieth-century developments in America can be traced, in part, through three yearbooks of the National Society for the Study of Education, two edited by Nelson Henry (1942, 1955), one by analytic philosopher Jonas Soltis (1981), who had issued his own introduction (1968), and a companion volume taken from *Teachers College Record* (1979), also edited by Soltis. An only somewhat historical introduction to mid-twentieth-century philosophy of education in Great Britain comes from two leaders among the predominately analytic school there, Paul Hirst and R. S. Peters (1970). This may be supplemented by a collection of essays in conceptual analysis edited by Glenn Langford and D. J. O'Connor (1973).

In large part, the field has grown toward maturity only with revival of the Philosophy of Education Society (in the United States) and the Philosophy of Education Society of Great Britain after World War II. Its primary form has been the "schools of philosophy" or "ism" approach, which is still pervasive among introductory texts but has increasingly been challenged by analytic and problem-oriented approaches in recent years. Within the leadership of the field the "ism" approach diminished slowly during the late 1950s and 1960s and was overtaken by analytic approaches, chiefly addressed to concepts, in the 1970s.

In Britain this change was first prominently evidenced in D. J. O'Connor's introduction (1957), which opposed systematic efforts in favor of "occasional and fragmentary glimpses of enlightenment." On the American scene, books by Israel Scheffler (the first in 1960) and a collection edited by B. Othanel Smith and Robert Ennis (1961) heralded the would-be takeover by analytic philosophers. The 1968 *Monist* volume by the noted moral philosopher William Frankena et al. has contributions from several approaches, none of them strictly identified with an "ism," including an appeal from Brand Blanshard, a leading spirit in American philosophy, for a merging of analytic and speculative sensibilities. Among the recent introductions James

McClellan's (1976) is representative of the type of conceptual analysis that has ruled that approach for nearly three decades. The introduction by William Frankena (1965) is strictly analytic but has more than the usual interest in systematic definition and breadth of reference; it includes brief readings from Dewey, Maritain, and Peters. That by Clive Beck (1974) bears strong analytic qualities but is more traditional. Sidney Hook's (1963) broad-sweeping liberal-social emphasis is especially reminiscent of John Dewey and does not partake of the new analytic trend. Reginald Archambault, like many others during the 1950s and 1960s, traveled to England for study; he brought back a volume of new essays by British philosophers (1965). James Doyle (1973), in return, later published a volume in England mostly written by Americans, both signs of the growing intercontinental (regrettably, not yet international) character of the field. Almost all these efforts have tended toward narrowly defined, piecemeal investigations, using various forms of linguistic (not exclusively ordinary language) analysis.

R. S. Peters has been the leading light in Britain during most of the 1950–80 period. In 1967 Peters edited a significant collection of eleven new essays (and one old one) on the concept of education, nearly all by English philosophers. A large volume edited by two other leaders, R. F. Dearden and P. H. Hirst with Peters (1972), inaugurated the International Library of the Philosophy of Education established under his general editorship. Hirst and Peters (1970) had already offered an introduction to philosophy of education in Great Britain in the Students Library of Education.

The "ism" approach has itself taken several forms. Among the more notable examples, Theodore Brameld's (1955) continues to have influence, particularly in applying "isms" to educational problems viewed in sociocultural context. He distinguished between progressivism (as cultural transition), essentialism (as cultural conservatism), and perennialism (as cultural regression). Among many others, G. Max Wingo (1965) took up the same themes, arguing that in practice American educational thought is essentialist and conservative, then noting liberal protests (progressivism and pragmatism) and protests from perennialism, Marxism, and existentialism. It has also long been popular for philosophers of education to set forth their own ideas as representative of idealism, classical realism, perennialism (chiefly neo-Thomist), or pragmatism. To these have been added existentialism (especially from the early 1950s to the mid-1960s—e.g., George Kneller, *Existentialism and Education*, 1958), phenomenological existentialism (from the mid-1960s on—e.g., Donald Vandenberg, *Being and Education,* 1971, and the David Denton collection, 1974), to which interests from hermeneutics (e.g., Maxine Greene, *Landscapes of Learning,* 1978) and even critical theory have been attached in the last few years. Nowadays it is fashionable to add still more isms such as logical empiricism, analytic philosophy, Marxism, and various new brands of social reconstructionism or experimentalism.

TOPICS

Historically, issues regarding aims, curriculum, and administration have dominated the field. Issues of aims are implicit if not always explicit in almost all discussions, though R. S. Peters (e.g., in Frankena, *Philosophy of Education,* 1965) has argued that concrete reference to rules and procedures is more fruitful, because less vague, than references to aims. However, sophisticated philosophical examination of the details of administrative theory is nascent at best. The quite new emphasis on the closely related area of policy studies is perhaps best exemplified by rigorous work from Thomas Green and company (1980) and to a small degree within philosophical critiques of educational research (as in complementary volumes edited by Lawrence Thomas, 1972, and by Harry Broudy et al., 1972) through the interest in obtaining usable knowledge. The emphasis in the research critiques, however, has so far been on scrutiny of the long-dominant behaviorist patterns and on awareness of the need to investigate newer paradigms of research á la Thomas Kuhn, Imre Lakatos, Paul Feyerabend, and others (see chapter 23). It has long been an assumption in educational circles that the "results of science" can be readily applied to educational purposes, an assumption that has contributed to mistaken expectations from and overblown claims by "experts." Some of the leading educational theorists and philosophers are beginning to register doubts about this widespread belief.

The philosophical investigation of contemporary curriculum theory is also still far from well developed in its details. The principal philosophical views, moreover, have focused largely, sometimes exclusively, on "forms of knowledge" understood as separate classes of true propositions. The most influential of these theories among philosophers in recent years is that of Paul Hirst (1974, and in Archambault, 1965). He originally distinguished seven basic forms—mathematics, physical sciences, religion, literature and the fine arts, philosophy, history, and the human sciences—but later replaced the last two with moral judgment and the understanding of our own and others' minds. This theory has only just begun to get substantial criticism from other analytic philosophers—for example, by Jane Martin (in Soltis, 1981), who deems it "narrow and intolerant." Her own collection of readings on curriculum (1970) already displayed greater diversity. In his understanding of the complexity of curricular processes and issues, as in other areas, John Dewey would seem still to be far ahead of the field. An example of a leading philosophical contributor to curriculum theory who was greatly influenced by Dewey but emphasized bodies of knowledge in a manner not very different from Hirst and most others is Joseph Schwab (1978), especially in science education. The "forms of knowledge" positions tended to hold that not only K–12 education but also "liberal education" at the postsecondary level should be built upon a few basic disciplines, thus conceived.

Unlike Dewey's these theories have also tended to be rather removed from the practices of teaching and schooling. The same is true of the main theories of teaching—as Donna Kerr has pointed out (in Soltis, 1981). Although Dewey has been as famous among educators for his emphasis on reflective thinking and problem solving (e.g., *How We Think*, 1933), this limited conception cannot be squared even with his earlier thought (1916), on which during the three decades after 1916 he built further noncognitive, aesthetic, organizational, and sociocultural elements (see Joe Burnett in Soltis, 1979). The volumes of Dewey appraisals edited by Reginald Archambault (1966) and R. S. Peters (1977) are of interest but must be supplemented by more rigorous, systematic, and historically adept efforts. As it seems to me, dealing with Dewey's challenges still belongs near the top of the agenda. One still timely challenge, for example, is presented in his 1938 book, a critique of both progressive and conventional schools. Progressive schooling is an extremely diverse tradition, well established long before Dewey began writing about it. Although Dewey strongly supported the liberal tendencies it represented—as he would support the "alternatives" movement today—it is a mistake to attribute its philosophy to him. Often the progressive outlook was more attuned to Romanticism, Rousseau, and unreflective reaction to restrictions in conventional schooling than to Dewey. The critical editing of Dewey's works by Southern Illinois University's Center for Dewey Studies (1960–) is providing much that is needed for a better informed appraisal and use of his work.

How can people learn so as to develop moral and intellectual virtue and so as to find their appropriate places in society? What forms of teaching are most fitting for such purposes, what organizational structures, and how administered? Is indoctrination, for example, an acceptable procedure? Are the requirements of educative process different for various cultural groups or at the several stages of life? How are purportedly educational processes to be studied and evaluated, and with what potential effects on educational decision making, policy making, and planning? Moreover, how are such issues to be understood, ordered, and thought about? Will the very answer to this last question be different depending on one's values or on one's metaphysical orientation, and if so what account is to be given of this? These are the kinds of questions to which detailed attention is being given in contemporary philosophy of education.

In recent decades the primary emphasis has been on epistemological aspects of these questions, increasingly with reference to psychological theories and studies on cognitive development. Most contributors to a volume on this subject edited by Theodore Mischel (1971), for example, are philosophers; a few psychologists are joined there by Lawrence Kohlberg, whose Kantian use of Jean Piaget's theories for inquiry into moral education has reopened this topic and helped place it in bold relief for some twenty years. The collection on "educational judgments" edited by James Doyle (1973), mostly by leading American analytic philosophers, represents the analytic trend. So far the main work on moral development and moral education has been done by psychologists. An interdisciplinary work on the subject edited by Clive Beck et al. (1971) presaged a continuing buildup of effort into the early 1980s and presumably beyond. A synoptic treatise by R. S. Peters (1966) and similar ventures by John Wilson and others in Britain have tended to deal less specifically with developmental issues than those in the United States. On both sides of the Atlantic almost all this literature, however, presupposes at most a three-stage development from premoral or primitive moral functioning to customary morality to mature morality, sticking rather close to Piaget or to behaviorist social learning theory. This was still true of the *Monist* symposium (1974) by William Frankena et al. More recently there are some slight signs of greater attention to the enormous complexities and nuances of development as these are made manifest in psychoanalytic investigations (e.g., Tice, "A Psychoanalytic Perspective," 1980).

Questions about the nature and appropriateness of indoctrination (e.g., Snook, *Indoctrination and Education,* 1972) have been a major interest for many years, combining concerns about teaching and learning. As is true of many questions in this field, there seems to be no end in sight, though in this case inquiry has definitely yielded valuable clarification. That is, one who has benefited from the literature should be able to know exactly what one is talking about on this issue and to take a well-grounded position. In a noted 1970 study (the original, 1961 version was an analytic philosophy of history dissertation), Jane Roland Martin examines several things it can mean to explain something to someone and for the person to understand this. The approach is typical among the better conceptual analyses on these topics. A collection of his own essays on "reason and teaching" by one of her teachers, Israel Scheffler (1973), also exemplifies this approach.

Philosophical reflection addressed to specific life stages is rare. The usual assumption is that the overall task of education is to get the individual up to "adult" functioning, but that too is not defined developmentally. Some thoughts about higher education were gathered at the end of a long and notable career as a philosopher of education by John Brubacher (1977). William Frankena (1980) has edited a set of new essays on graduate education by philosophers. A fine example of how philosophical thought can be directed to issues of professional education is that on political education edited by Melvin Richter (*Political Theory and Political Education,* 1980, cited on p. 450).

In essential ways the subject matter of philosophy of education interacts with every other area of philosophy. Recognition especially of the interplay with aesthetics, epistemology, ethics, logic, metaphysics, social philosophy, and philosophy of science is given in the 1981 yearbook edited by Jonas Soltis.

FUTURE PROSPECTS

In future, philosophy of education can be expected to take greater advantage of its built-in scope. In doing this, philosophers will need to develop a historical-analytic critique of language and assumptions found in educational theory over the entire range of current concerns, inside and outside of the school. It would be appropriate to use such a critique, plus the considerable gains already made through conceptual analysis, for more systematic, integrative purposes, as John Dewey did several generations ago. It is more likely, however, that philosophers will develop even more specific contributions to a critical understanding not only of curriculum and teaching, their major interests in the past, but also of organizational life, policy options, evaluative process, and planning. Given the fast-growing knowledge about personal development both in childhood and through all later stages in the life cycle, they can also be expected to relate their thinking about educational views and processes more closely to that knowledge. Finally, educational philosophers can also be expected to be more involved in cross currents of educational thinking around the globe, including efforts within the developing countries to form ideas and policies more pertinent to their own situations than those earlier borrowed from the West.

Archambault, Reginald D., ed. *Dewey on Education: Appraisals*. New York: Random House, 1966.

————, ed. *Philosophical Analysis and Education*. New York: Humanities Pr.; London: Routledge & Paul, 1965.

Beck, Clive. *Educational Philosophy and Theory: An Introduction*. Boston: Little, Brown, 1974.

————, B. S. Crittenden, and E. V. Sullivan, eds. *Moral Education: Interdisciplinary Approaches*. Toronto: Univ. of Toronto Pr., 1971.

Brameld, Theodore. *Philosophies of Education in Cultural Perspective*. New York: Dryden, 1955.

Broudy, Harry S., Robert Ennis, and Leonard I. Krimmerman, eds. *Philosophy of Educational Research*. New York: Wiley, 1972. (An American Educational Research Assn. volume.)

Brubacher, John S. *On the Philosophy of Higher Education*. San Francisco: Jossey-Bass, 1977.

Chambliss, Joseph J. *The Origins of American Philosophy of Education: Its Development as a Distinct Discipline, 1808–1913*. The Hague, Nijhoff, 1968.

Dearden, R. F., P. H. Hirst, and R. S. Peters, eds. *Education and the Development of Reason*. London and Boston: Routledge & Paul, 1972.

Denton, David E., ed. *Existentialism and Phenomenology in Education: Collected Essays*. New York and London: Teachers College Pr., 1974.

Dewey, John. *Democracy and Education: Introduction to the Philosophy of Education*. New York: Macmillan, 1916. Repr., 1966.

————. *Experience and Education*. New York: Macmillan, 1938.

————. *How We Think: A Restatement of the Relation of Reflective Thinking to the Educative Process*. Boston: Heath, 1933.

Doyle, James F., ed. *Educational Judgments: Papers in the Philosophy of Education*. London and Boston: Routledge & Paul, 1973.

Frankena, William K. *Philosophy of Education*. New York: Macmillan, 1965.

————. *Three Historical Philosophies of Education*. Chicago: Scott, Foresman, 1965. (Aristotle, Kant, and Dewey.)

————, ed. *The Philosophy and Future of Graduate Education*. Ann Arbor: Univ. of Michigan Pr., 1980.

————, ed. "The Philosophy of Moral Education." *Monist* 58, no. 4:541–693 (Oct. 1974).

————, et al. "Philosophy of Education." *Monist* 52, no. 1:1–132 (Jan. 1968).

Green, Thomas F., David P. Ericson, and Robert M. Seidman. *Predicting the Behavior of the Educational System*. Syracuse, N.Y.: Syracuse Univ. Pr., 1980.

Greene, Maxine. *Landscapes of Learning*. New York: Teachers College Pr., 1978.

Henry, Nelson B., ed. *Modern Philosophies and Education: The Fifty-fourth Yearbook of the National Society for the Study of Education*. Chicago: Univ. of Chicago Pr., 1955.

————, ed. *Philosophies of Education: The Forty-first Yearbook of the National Society for the Study of Education*. Part I. Bloomington, Ill.: Public School Pub. Co., 1942.

Hirst, Paul H. *Knowledge and the Curriculum: A Collection of Philosophical Papers*. London and Boston: Routledge & Paul, 1974.

————, and R. S. Peters. *The Logic of Education*. New York: Humanities Pr., 1971; London: Routledge & Paul, 1970.

Hook, Sidney. *Education for Modern Man*. New York: Knopf, 1963.

Kneller, George F. *Existentialism and Education*. New York: Philosophical Library, 1958.

Langford, Glenn, and D. J. O'Connor, eds. *New Essays in the Philosophy of Education*. London and Boston: Routledge & Paul, 1973.

McClellan, James E. *Philosophy of Education*. Englewood Cliffs, N.J.: Prentice-Hall, 1976.

Maritain, Jacques. *Education at the Crossroads*. New Haven, Conn.: Yale Univ. Pr., 1943.

Martin, Jane R. *Explaining, Understanding, and Teaching*. New York: McGraw-Hill, 1970.

————, ed. *Readings in the Philosophy of Education: A Study of Curriculum*. Boston: Allyn & Bacon, 1970.

Mischel, Theodore, ed. *Cognitive Development and Epistemology*. New York: Academic Pr., 1971.

O'Connor, Daniel J. *An Introduction to the Philosophy of Education*. London: Routledge & Paul, 1957.

Park, Joe. *Bertrand Russell on Education*. Columbus: Ohio State Univ. Pr., 1963.

Peters, Richard S. *Ethics and Education*. New York: Scott, Foresman, 1967; London: Allen & Unwin, 1966.

————, ed. *The Concept of Education*. New York: Humanities Pr.; London: Routledge & Paul, 1967.

————, ed. *John Dewey Reconsidered*. London and Boston: Routledge & Paul, 1977.

Rousseau, Jean-Jacques. *Emile, or On Education*. Tr. by Allan Bloom. New York: Basic Books, 1979. (With Introduction, pp. 3–59 and Notes, pp. 481–95.)

Russell, Bertrand. *Education and the Modern World.* New York: Norton; London: Allen & Unwin, 1932. (Published in London under the title *Education and the Social Order.*)

Scheffler, Israel. *The Language of Education.* Springfield, Ill.: Thomas, 1960.

———. *Reason and Teaching.* Indianapolis, Ind.: Bobbs-Merrill; London: Routledge & Paul, 1973.

Schwab, Joseph J. *Science, Curriculum and Liberal Education: Selected Essays.* Ed. by Ian Westbury and Niel J. Wilkof. Chicago: Univ. of Chicago Pr., 1978.

Smith, B. Othanel, and Robert H. Ennis, eds. *Language and Concepts in Education.* Chicago: Rand McNally, 1961.

Snook, I. A. *Indoctrination and Education.* London and Boston: Routledge & Paul, 1972.

———, ed. *Concepts of Indoctrination: Philosophical Essays.* London: Routledge & Paul, 1972.

Soltis, Jonas F. *An Introduction to the Analysis of Educational Concepts.* Reading, Mass.: Addison-Wesley, 1968.

———, ed. *Philosophy and Education: Eightieth Yearbook of the National Society for the Study of Education.* Part I. Chicago: Univ. of Chicago Pr., 1981.

———, ed. "Philosophy of Education since Mid-Century." *Teachers College Record* 81, no. 2:127–247 (Winter 1979). (This issue, plus Winter 1981 issues of *Harvard Educational Review* and *Educational Theory,* are devoted to critique of the Yearbook.)

Thomas, Lawrence G., ed. *Philosophical Redirection of Educational Research, Seventy-first Yearbook of the National Society for the Study of Education.* Part I. Chicago: Univ. of Chicago Pr., 1972.

Tice, Terrence N. "A Psychoanalytic Perspective." In *Moral Development and Socialization,* pp. 161–200. Ed. by Myra Windmiller, Nadine Lambert, and Elliot Turiel. Boston and London: Allyn & Bacon, 1980.

Vandenberg, Donald. *Being and Education: An Essay in Existential Phenomenology.* Englewood Cliffs, N.J.: Prentice-Hall, 1971.

Whitehead, Alfred North. *The Aims of Education.* New York: Macmillan, 1929.

Wingo, G. Max. *Philosophies of Education: An Introduction.* 2nd ed. Lexington, Mass. and London: D. C. Heath, 1974. (1st ed., 1965.)

PART III

REFERENCE WORKS

Bibliography

Baatz, Charles A. *The Philosophy of Education: A Guide to Information Sources.* Detroit, Mich.: Gale, 1980. 344p.
A topically arranged annotated bibliography for both scholar and non-scholar. The first chapter serves as an introduction to the volume. The following chapters contain brief introductions followed by bibliographies on topics such as philosophers, ideals, curricula, causality, instruments, and philosophies of education. Author, title, and subject indexes.

Bibliographie de la Philosophie. Bulletin Trimestriel. (Bibliography of Philosophy. A Quarterly Bulletin.) Paris: Librairie Philosophique, J. Vrin, 1937– . v.1– .
This bibliography is published under the sponsorship of several international organizations and encompasses books published throughout the world on philosophy and related subjects. Substantial abstracts are provided for works published for the first time. Citations only are provided for reprints, translations, new editions, and paperbacks. The abstracts are initialed, and a key to such appears at the beginning of each quarterly issue. The dimensions, pagination, and price are also noted. The abstracts appear in the language of the original publication if it was written in English, French, German, Italian, or Spanish. Otherwise, the abstracts are written in English or French. No evaluations of the works are provided. Each issue is divided into subject areas, such as philosophical psychology, aesthetics, culture and education, and reference books and miscellany. The final issue of the year provides indexes of books, of names, including both citers and citees, and of publishers. This last index is organized geographically.

Bibliographies of Famous Philosopers Series. Ed. by Richard H. Linebeck. Bowling Green, Ohio: Philosophy Documentation Center, Bowling Green State Univ., 1974– .
For the most part, these volumes provide listings alphabetically under headings referring to aspects of the philosopher's thought and are not indexed or chronologically arranged. They provide listings of each philosopher's writings and of works about the philosopher. Volumes have been issued on Bergson, Heidegger, Husserl, Marcel, Merleau-Ponty, Santayana, Sartre, Whitehead, and Wittgenstein. Others are forthcoming.

Borchardt, Dietrich Hans. *How to Find Out in Philosophy and Psychology.* Oxford: Pergamon Pr., 1968. 97p.
Aimed at the layperson and the undergraduate student, this book provides an introduction to general works on philosophy and psychology. Biblio-

503

graphical essays treat types of materials, such as encyclopedias, dictionaries, bibliographies, and reviewing journals, as well as societies and associations. This work deals with materials in most Western languages but concentrates on English-language sources. Two indexes, one to the works cited in the text and the other to subjects, conclude this volume.

Bowman, Mary Ann. *Western Mysticism: A Guide to the Basic Works.* Chicago: American Library Assn., 1978. 113p.

This selective guide to works about non-Oriental mysticism includes both the Eastern Orthodox and Jewish traditions. The titles are classified into four chapters covering the philosophical, historical, practical, and experiential aspects of mysticism. Three additional chapters survey "Oriental Mysticism in Western Contexts," "Mystical and Contemplative Writings," and "Mystical Expression in Literature." Materials covering the occult are excluded. An author, title, and subject index provides further access. An appendix suggests first purchase choices for libraries.

DeBrie, G. A. *Bibliographica Philosophica 1934–1945.* Vol. 1, *Bibliographia Historiae Philosophiae;* vol. 2, *Bibliographia Philosophiae.* Bruxellis: Editiones Spectrum, 1950, 1954. 664, 798p.

Ready English access.

DeGeorge, R. T. *A Guide to Philosophical Bibliography and Research.* New York: Appleton-Century-Crofts, 1971. 141p.

This is an annotated bibliography for the field of philosophy. It includes dictionaries, encyclopedias, histories of philosophy, philosophical classics, bibliographical tools and specialized bibliographies, library and trade catalogs, philosophical journals, guides to writing and publishing, and biographical sources. It closes with information and works concerning philosophical professional life.

Guerry, Herbert. *A Bibliography of Philosophical Bibliographies.* Westport, Conn.: Greenwood, 1977. 332p.

This volume lists over 2,300 philosophical bibliographies published either as monographs, as parts of books, or in periodicals. Works in many languages are included. Some items are annotated, most often to indicate the number of items contained in the bibliography. The first part of the work lists bibliographies of individual philosophers. In the second part are subject bibliographies. An index of compilers completes the work.

Harvard University Library. *Widener Library Shelflist.* Vol. 42–43, *Philosophy and Psychology.* Cambridge, Mass.: Harvard Univ. Pr., 1973.

This includes a list of 59,000 books, periodicals, and pamphlets. The work is divided into four parts: (1) the classification schedule, (2) the entries in shelflist order, (3) the same items in chronological order by date of publication, and (4) authors and titles.

Jasenas, Michael. *A History of the Bibliography of Philosophy.* New York: Olms, 1973. 188p.

Jasenas' work consists of bibliographic essays discussing bibliographies of philosophy published in Western languages between 1592 and 1960. The major chapter headings are for Renaissance bibliographies of philosophy, bibliographies and the rise of modern philosophy, bibliographies of the German Aufklärung, post-Kantian bibliographies, variety in the twentieth century, and tradition and progress. The essays deal with influences upon the bibliographers as well as with the contents of the bibliographies. Appended are a bibliography of works used in the investigation, a bibliography of bibliographies discussed, and a list of other bibliographies of philosophy, 1615–1960. Also appended is a short title list of major philosophical works discussed in standard histories of philosophy. An index of names concludes the volume.

Koren, Henry J. *Research in Philosophy: A Bibliographical Introduction to Philosophy and a Few Suggestions for Dissertations.* Pittsburgh: Duquesne Univ. Pr., 1966. 203p.
Six chapters comprise this guide to philosophical literature. The first chapter discusses books, including proper ways of handling them. Chapters two through five list, respectively, monographs, periodicals, reference books, and bibliographic tools useful in philosophical research. Annotations accompany some of these items, and a narrative passage introduces each section. The last chapter of this book gives guidelines for writing theses.

Lindley, R. C., and J. M. Shorter. *The Philosophy of Mind: A Bibliography.* Part 1, *The Self.* Oxford: Sub-Faculty of Philosophy, 1977. 76p.
The listings are largely of twentieth-century works, especially recent ones, both books and articles. These are topically ordered. Part 2 of this volume was to be on Philosophy of Action.

McLean, George F. *An Annotated Bibliography of Philosophy in Catholic Thought, 1900–1964.* Philosophy in the 20th Century: Catholic and Christian, v.1. New York: Ungar, 1967. 371p.
This annotated bibliography lists works written between 1900 and 1964 dealing with the writings or influence of Scholastics such as St. Augustine, St. Thomas Aquinas, and other influential churchmen, together with more recent works on personalist, existential, or phenomenological philosophy. In general, works on the history of philosophy are not included. The first part of the book is divided into thirteen chapters covering such topics as research instruments, logic, epistemology, psychology, metaphysics, theodicy, ethics, and aesthetics. The second part of the book lists works dealing with schools of Christian philosophy. The entries, arranged alphabetically, give basic bibliographic information, brief annotations, a note indicating the suggested level of readership, and citations to major reviews of the work. An author index is appended.

———, ed. *A Bibliography of Christian Philosophy and Contemporary Issues.* Philosophy in the 20th Century: Catholic and Christian, v. 2. New York: Ungar, 1967. 312p.
This is a select, unannotated bibliography of books and articles written

between 1934 and 1964 on themes such as man, love, freedom, culture, language, and God. The book is divided into eight chapters dealing with Christian philosophy, contemporary philosophy, philosophy and technology, philosophy of man and God, the problem of God in a secular culture, religious knowledge and language, moral philosophy, and teaching philosophy. Each chapter is subdivided by topic, with entries listed alphabetically by author. An appendix of doctoral dissertations in philosophy in the Catholic universities of the United States and Canada and an author index complete the work.

Matczak, Sebastian A. *Philosophy: Its Nature, Methods and Basic Sources.* New York: Learned Publications, 1975. 280p.

Matczak's work is primarily bibliographical and gives emphasis to works written in or translated into English, since the volume is addressed primarily to English-speaking students. The book is divided into five major parts with numerous subdivisions by form, country, and subject. The first part contains short essays, each appended by a bibliography, on the nature of philosophy. The second part lists general and specific bibliographies, and the third cites descriptive sources, such as biographies and encyclopedias. The fourth section contains lists of periodicals and guides to them. The final part lists and provides some information on institutions, such as societies, academies, associations, and libraries. An index of names and a select bibliography are appended.

————. *Philosophy: A Select, Classified Bibliography of Ethics, Economics, Law, Politics, Sociology.* Louvain: Nauwelaerts, 1970. 308p.

Addressed primarily to English-speaking students, Matczak's bibliography cites books and articles on ethics per se and on the related fields mentioned in the title insofar as they deal with philosophical questions. Each major area is finely subdivided chronologically, geographically, and/or by subject. Within subdivisions, the arrangement is alphabetical by author. An index of authors is appended.

Neu, Jerome, and Richard Rorty. "A Bibliography of Writings in English on Linguistic Method in Philosophy and Related Issues 1930–1965." In *The Linguistic Turn: Recent Essays in Philosophical Method,* pp. 361–93. Ed. by Richard Rorty. Chicago: Univ. of Chicago Pr., 1967.

This is a select bibliography, alphabetically arranged and including mainly works in analytic philosophy. It is the fullest available on the 1930–65 period.

Peacocke, C. A. B., and Dana Scott. *A Selective Bibliography of Philosophical Logic.* Study Aids, vol. 1, 3rd ed. Rev. by Martin Davies and Graeme Forbes. Oxford: Sub-Faculty of Philosophy, Sept. 1978. 125p. (Also by Davies and Forbes: *Supplement.* Oct. 1980. 23p.)

This is not a systematic list, but it contains up-to-date references to both books and articles, chiefly British. The entries are arranged by topics.

The Philosopher's Index. Bowling Green, Ohio: Bowling Green State Univ., 1967– .
This quarterly publication is an international index with abstracts to philosophical periodicals, including interdisciplinary journals that publish articles relating to philosophy. Each issue has a subject index and an author index with full bibliographic data, as well as a separate book review index indicating the sources of the reviews. In addition, this work has a three-volume, retrospective index that lists works published in the United States between 1940 and 1967.

Philosopher's Index: A Retrospective Index to U.S. Publications from 1940. Bowling Green, Ohio: Philosophy Documentation Center, 1978. 3v.
This retrospective guide to the *Philosophers Index* covers books published from 1940 to 1976 and journal articles from 1940 to 1966. The citations found within this index are for scholarly works published in the United States on philosophical issues. Two of the three volumes comprise a subject index to citations; the third volume is arranged by authors and includes citations and abstracts.

Philosophical Books; A Quarterly Review. Leicester: Leicester Univ. Pr. 1960– . v.1– .
Each issue of this journal, now published three times a year, contains approximately twenty signed, critical reviews of selected, recently published books on philosophical topics.

Rand, Benjamin, comp. *Bibliography of Philosophy, Psychology, and Cognate Subjects.* New York: Macmillan, 1905, 1933. Repr.: New York: Peter Smith, 1949. 2v.
This work forms the third volume of James Baldwin's *Dictionary of Philosophy and Psychology.* Approximately 60,000 unannotated citations to books and articles are included. The first volume covers bibliography and the history of philosophy, including works both by and about 600 philosophers. The second volume covers the topics of systematic philosophy, logic, aesthetics, philosophy of religion, ethics, and psychology. Each of these has form divisions, such as dictionaries, periodicals, and bibliographies as well as subject divisions, such as insanity and idiocy, casuistry, evolution, and syllogisms. With each subdivision, the entries are arranged alphabetically by the author.

Shield, Allan. *A Bibliography of Bibliographies in Aesthetics.* San Diego, Calif.: San Diego State Univ. Pr., 1975. 79p.
A selected bibliography of works in the English language published between 1900 and 1972 containing bibliographies or bibliographical articles on aesthetics. Full citations to journals and books are arranged by topic. Contains an author-title index.

Tobey, Jeremy L. *The History of Ideas: A Bibliographical Introduction.* Vol. 1, *Classical Antiquity* (1975); vol. 2, *Medieval and Early Modern Europe* (1977). Santa Barbara, Calif.: Clio.

Tobey has written a series of integrated, connected bibliographic essays on works dealing with philosophy, science, aesthetics, and religion. Each of these sections is divided by several form and subject headings. An introduction explores works on the history of ideas and general bibliographic sources. The guide is selective rather than comprehensive and somewhat stresses works in English. An index of periodicals and an author-title index are included.

Wainwright, William J. *Philosophy of Religion: An Annotated Bibliography of Twentieth-Century Writings in English.* New York and London: Garland, 1978. 776p.
This selected listing of articles and books is arranged in the following divisions: divine attributes, arguments for existence of God, problem of evil, mysticism and religious experience, miracles, faith and revelation, religious language, justification of religious belief.

Dictionaries and Encyclopedias

Angeles, Peter Adam. *Dictionary of Philosophy.* New York: Harper & Row, 1981. 326p.
A dictionary of important terms and concepts for the beginning philosophy student. This alphabetically arranged volume contains many cross-references and gives some etymologies. An index of philosophers appears at the end, giving birth and death dates and listing the pages on which their concepts appear.

Edwards, Paul, ed. *The Encyclopedia of Philosophy.* New York: Macmillan and Free Pr., 1969. 8v.
This work was sponsored by the Association for Philosophical Research, and the directors of this group are chosen from leading universities. The editorial board includes eighty-one philosophers from eleven nations. The contributors include mathematicians, physicists, biologists, psychologists, and sociologists. The contributors came from twenty-four nations and many schools of philosophy. The bulk of the articles are by scholars from the United States and Great Britain. The editor is against authoritarianism, but has allowed many points of view in this work, although the analytical, empirical, and linguistic schools predominate.
The work deals with major philosophical problems and philosophers with signed articles and annotated bibliographies with many topics. The level of difficulty is indicated in the bibliographies. Volume six includes analytical annotations of reference works under the topic headings, "philosophical dictionaries and encyclopedias" and "philosophical journals."

Great Treasury of Western Thought. Mortimer J. Adler and Charles Van Doren, eds. New York: R. R. Bowker, 1977. 1771p.
Most of the entries in this work are long, averaging over 100 words. The quotations are taken primarily from the works of the outstanding philoso-

phers, dramatists, scientists, novelists, and poets of all time, including people such as St. Thomas Aquinas, Homer, Tolstoy, Aristotle, Darwin, and Shakespeare. In addition to having a reference use, the work can be used to gain an introduction to what such major thinkers have said of topics central to human experiences. The *Treasury* consists of twenty chapters on broad subjects such as "language," "emotion," "history," and "religion." Each chapter is further divided into smaller topics, and within these the quotations are arranged chronologically. Access to the volume is provided by author and subject-proper name indexes.

Greenstein, Carol Horn. *Dictionary of Logical Terms and Symbols.* New York: Van Nostrand Reinhold, 1978. 188p.

This resource presents alternative notational systems in logic, item by item, including notations for tense logic, epistemic logic, doxastic logic, and deontic logic as well. Among the additional material is that on logical gate notation, program flowchart symbols, diagrams, truth tables in both truth functional and binary form, abbreviations, a glossary of logical terms, and a bibliography.

The Harper Dictionary of Modern Thought. Alan Bullock and Oliver Stallybrass, eds. New York: Harper & Row, 1977. 684p.

Concepts in current use in a wide range of fields in the sciences, social sciences, and humanities are discussed in this work. Art, philosophy, information science, recent history, physics, economics, literature, biology, and political science are some of the areas covered. The dictionary attempts to place each term in the context of modern thought as a whole; thus, numerous cross-references are provided. Suggested books for further reading are listed at the end of some of the articles. The volume has no biographical entries. Important modern thinkers are listed, however, with reference to articles in which their ideas are discussed.

Lacey, A. R. *A Dictionary of Philosophy.* London: Routledge & Paul, 1976. 239p.

Lacey's work is addressed to the layperson and the beginning student and stresses definitions and discussions of the problems and questions involved in logical and epistemological terms and concepts. Also included are some eighty brief biographical sketches and entries from the fields of ethics and aesthetics. Within all these areas, the emphasis is on English-speaking philosophy. Bibliographies are appended to many of the entries, and cross-references are noted as necessary. Examples of entries include John Duns Scotus, substance, denial of antecedent, essence, imperative, and truth table.

Nauman, St. Elmo, Jr. *Dictionary of American Philosophy.* New York: Philosophical Library, 1973. 273p.

Nauman has compiled sketches on almost 150 American philosophers, both living and dead. Included are those persons who have influenced American thought as well as professional philosophers who have developed analytical constructs and/or speculative systems. The sketches deal with both the lives and thoughts of such persons as John Dewey, Mortimer Adler, Albert

Einstein, Thomas Paine, Eric Hoffer, and Paul Tillich. The biographies are preceded by a survey of American philosophy and by a chronology of philosophers. A few photographs are included.

————. *The New Dictionary of Existentialism*. New York: Philosophical Library, 1971. 166p.

Nauman has sought to provide a guide to the technical terminology contained in the writings of the major philosophical and psychological existentialists. The literary existentialists are generally accorded secondary importance, with Sartre constituting an exception because of his dual role. The entries frequently note word derivations and provide a general explanation of the term as well as extracts from writings of existentialists illustrating their particular conceptions and orientations. One finds, for example, discussions of such terms as death, bad faith, individual, good, and subjectivity. Biographical sketches, focusing on ideas propounded, are also included for such existentialists as Heidegger, Jaspers, and Kierkegaard. A bibliography is appended.

Peters, Francis E. *Greek Philosophical Terms. A Historical Lexicon*. New York: New York Univ. Pr., 1967. 234p.

This dictionary is addressed to persons with an intermediate level of knowledge of Greek philosophy. Several definitions may be provided for a given term, and textual references to Greek philosophers appear throughout the definitions. Cross-references assist the reader in gaining a fuller understanding of concepts. The body of the work is introduced by an essay on language and philosophy; and the volume terminates with an annotated English-Greek index.

Reese, W. L. *Dictionary of Philosophy and Religion: Eastern and Western Thought*. Atlantic Highlands, N.J.: Humanities Pr., 1980. 644p.

Also encyclopedic in function, not only a dictionary, this work includes brief definitions and historical references for terms, both analytical and historical accounts of a wide range of topics, individuals, and movements, and sketches of several areas of philosophy. Select bibliographies are attached to many of the entries and considerable cross-referencing.

Rosenthal, M., and P. Yudin, eds. *A Dictionary of Philosophy*. Moscow: Progress, 1967. 494p.

This dictionary contains entries for both persons and terms, such as Fichte, Lomonosov, Plotinus, paradoxes, inference, and deism. Many of the discussions employ Marxian terminology; and several of the entries deal with the interface between philosophy and society or social issues. Word derivations are sometimes noted, and cross-references are plentiful. A glossary of foreign words and phrases current in philosophical literature is appended.

Urmson, James O., ed. *The Concise Encyclopedia of Western Philosophy and Philosophers*. 2nd ed. New York: Hawthorn Books, 1975. 319p.

This work, addressed to the nonspecialist reader, contains four principal categories of entries in one alphabetical order. The contributors have provided articles on technical terms, on positions or schools formed in response to philosophical questions, on individual philosophers, and on currents of philosophical study. Thus, one finds articles on such topics as atomism, Plotinus, Skeptics, materialism, logical positivists, and aesthetics. Terms mentioned in an article that are more fully explored in another article are printed in boldface type. The length of the articles ranges from a paragraph on deontology to several pages on Immanuel Kant. No attempt has been made to provide "answers" to those long-standing philosophical questions on which philosophers have disputed through the ages. Black and white photographs are generously provided, and the book contains a few color plates. At the end are some notes on the contributors and a bibliography that covers periods, individuals, and fields of study.

Wiener, Philip P., ed. *Dictionary of the History of Ideas. Studies of Selected Pivotal Ideas.* New York: Scribner, 1973–74. 4v.
This work was written by scholars from many countries, especially by those with an interdisciplinary approach. It is a study of pivotal topics in intellectual history and methods of writing about such topics and includes an index volume. There are studies of three sorts: cross-cultural studies limited to a given period, studies that trace an idea from antiquity to later periods, and studies that explain the meaning of an idea and its development in the minds of its leading proponents.
The work has the following framework:

1. The history of ideas about the external order of nature studied by the physical and biological sciences, ideas also present in common usage, imaginative literature, myths about nature, metaphysical speculation.
2. The history of ideas about human nature in anthropology, psychology, religion, and philosophy as well as in literature and common sense.
3. The history of ideas in literature and the arts in aesthetic theory and literary criticism.
4. The history of ideas about or attitudes to history, historiography, and historical criticism.
5. The historical development of economic, legal, and political ideas and institutions, ideologies and movements.
6. The history of religious and philosophical ideas.
7. The history of formal, mathematical, logical, linguistic, and methodological ideas. (Pref., p. viii)
   The purpose of these studies of the historical interrelationships of ideas is to help establish some sense of the unity of human thought and its cultural manifestations in a world of ever-increasing specialization and alienation. (Ibid.)

Digests and Handbooks

Burr, John R. *Handbook of World Philosophy: Contemporary Developments since 1945.* Westport, Conn.: Greenwood, 1980. 641p.
An international work containing descriptive essays about philosophic thought, trends, activities, and philosophers throughout various regions and countries since 1945. The essays are arranged by region and then by country

and are followed by notes and selected bibliographies. The appendixes include a directory of philosophical organizations and a list of meetings. There are subject and philosopher indexes.

Klibansky, Raymond, ed. *Philosophy in the Mid-Century.* 4v. Florence: La Nuova Italia Editrice, 1958–59.

————, ed. *Contemporary Philosophy: A Survey.* 4v. Florence: Italia Editrice, 1968–71.

The first set surveys the period 1948–55. The second surveys 1956–67 and is organized as follows. Vol. 1: logic and foundations of mathematics (August 1968); vol. 2: philosophy of science (August 1968); vol. 3: metaphysics, phenomenology, language and structure (1969); vol. 4: ethics, aesthetics, law, religion, politics, historical and dialectical materialism, and sections on philosophy in Eastern Europe, Asia, and Latin America (1971). About half of the chapters are in English, half in French, and a few in German.

Magill, Frank N., ed. *Masterpieces of World Philosophy in Summary Form.* New York: Harper & Row, 1961. 1166p.

This volume contains summaries of 200 works of philosophy. While European and American writings occupy most of the volume, the works of a few Oriental philosophers, such as Tseng Tzu, Chuang Chou, S'ankara, Confucius, and Sarvepalli Radhakrishnan also receive essay reviews. The arrangement is chronological from Anaximander and Heraclitus to Paul Tillich and Ludwig Wittgenstein. For each entry, the philosopher's dates, the type of work, the date of publication, and the principal ideas advanced are noted in addition to the provisions of the essay summary. A glossary of some 250 common philosophical terms is an added feature. An alphabetical list of titles and an author index are also included.

Directories

Bahm, Archie, et al., eds. *Directory of American Philosophers.* Bowling Green, Ohio: Philosophy Documentation Center, 1962/63– .

This is a biennial publication that provides information on activities in the United States and Canada. Parts I and II are a directory of colleges and universities. For each institution in the United States data are provided on accreditation, type of control, type of student body, type of academic calendar, its level and kinds of offerings, enrollments, highest level of instruction in philosophy, the college division under which philosophy is taught, and the telephone number of that division.

Following the information on each university or college is a list of the faculty members who teach philosophy. For each, the highest degree earned, rank, and area of specialty is given. Information on assistantships and fellowships is also provided.

Data on societies, journals, and publishers are also given in Parts I and II. Part III is made of "late reports." Part IV provides statistics on sizes of philosophy departments, highest level of specialization in philosophy, and the number of philosophers in each state or province. Part V is made up of indexes.

Cormier, Ramona, et al. *International Directory of Philosophy and Philosophers 1980–81.* 10th ed. Bowling Green, Ohio: Philosophy Documentation Center, 1980.

This work does not contain information on activities in the United States and Canada. The data were gathered by questionnaires and, with the exception of the material on international organizations, are arranged by country. Under each country data are given on universities and colleges, institutes and research centers, associations and societies, journals and publishers.

Information provided on universities includes name, date of founding, source of financial support, name and address of the department of philosophy, names of the faculty members, their rank and field of specialty, enrollment, enrollment in philosophy courses, types of degrees offered, and number of advanced degrees awarded in philosophy during the past five years.

Information on research centers includes date of founding, address, purpose, activities, addresses of officers, membership data and publications.

Information provided for associations and societies is similar. Data on journals include date of founding, number and address of editors, purpose, sponsor, frequency, circulation, number of philosophical articles per year, book review section, publishers' name and address, and subscription price.

Information on publishers includes date of founding, address, journals published, and series published.

Whitbeck, Caroline, ed. *A Directory of Women in Philosophy.* Bowling Green, Ohio: Philosophy Documentation Center, 1978. 80p.

An alphabetical listing of women in philosophy, giving their fields of specialization, up to six of their publications, plus address, phone number, degrees, and position held. Indexed by both state and fields of specialization.

Dissertation Index

Bechtle, Thomas C., and Mary F. Riley. *Dissertations in Philosophy Accepted at American Universities, 1861–1975.* New York: Garland, 1978. 537p.

This work lists 7,503 theses in philosophy which have been accepted at 115 universities. The volume is well indexed.

Series

Arguments of the Philosophers. London and Boston: Routledge & Paul, 1973– .

This series specializes in analyses of major arguments put forth by leading philosophers. It includes volumes on Berkeley, Descartes, Hume, Kant, Meinong, Plato, Russell, Santayana, Schopenhauer, Socrates, and Wittgenstein. The material is at an advanced level but is clearly presented.

Boston Studies in the Philosophy of Science. Dordrecht and Boston: Reidel, 1963– .
The first volume of Boston Studies in the Philosophy of Science, edited by Marx W. Wartofsky, appeared as Proceedings of the 1961–62 Boston Colloquium for the Philosophy of Science. Robert S. Cohen joined Wartofsky in editing the extended series, which now includes more than sixty volumes published. The series has included many special volumes as well as proceedings, some of them translations of European philosophers, collected essays, and Festschriften.

Foundations of Philosophy. Englewood Cliffs, N.J.: Prentice-Hall, 1963– .
Most of the major areas of philosophy have been introduced by analytic philosophers in these slim volumes. They are intended for introductory use.

Library of Living Philosophers. Ed. by Paul Arthur Schilpp. Chicago: Open Court, 1939– .
By 1982 extensive volumes on each of sixteen philosophers had appeared. Each contains critical essays on the thought of a given philosopher, a comprehensive bibliography, and an autobiography and reply to the critics by the individual philosopher. Those treated include: Blanshard, Broad, Buber, Carnap, Cassirer, Dewey, Einstein, Jaspers, Lewis, Moore, Popper, Radhakrishnan, Russell, Santayana, Sartre, and Whitehead. Forthcoming: volumes on Marcel, Quine, and von Wright.

Midwest Studies in Philosophy. Ed. by Peter A. French, Theodore E. Uehling, Jr., and Howard K. Wettstein. Minneapolis: Univ. of Minnesota Pr., 1976– .
Seven large volumes of analytic studies had appeared by 1982, each comprised of new essays within an area of philosophy. As of May 1982 there were volumes on: history of philosophy, philosophy of language, ethical theory, metaphysics, epistemology, the foundations of analytic philosophy, and social and political philosophy, all edited by the same authors. The volume on analytic philosophy is cited in chapter 7, the others in Part II.

Modern Studies in Philosophy. New York: Doubleday Anchor, 1966– .
Each volume includes a set of critical essays on the work of a particular philosopher, some of them previously published, and an introduction. The over two dozen volumes cover most historical periods, from the Presocratics to twentieth-century philosophers Ludwig Wittgenstein and Noam Chomsky. These volumes are meant to accompany study of the original texts. They partly serve as an introduction to the subject; however, many of the essays are of a technical nature.

Oxford Readings in Philosophy. Ed. by G. J. Warnock. Oxford and New York: Oxford Univ. Pr., 1967– .
Each volume offers a short selection of previously published articles, usu-

ally within an entire area of philosophy. Volumes like those on perception and theory of meaning are exceptions.

Synthese Library. Dordrecht: Reidel, 1959– .

A distinguished source since 1959; by 1979 in its 136th volume. The series includes the Boston Studies in Philosophy of Science and other monographs on logic, philosophy of mathematics, epistemology, methodology, sociology and knowledge and philosophy of science, and mathematical methods used in the social and behavioral sciences.

AUTHOR-TITLE INDEX

Aaron, R. I. *John Locke,* 95
The Abdication of Philosophy (Schilpp),
 E. Freeman, ed., 223, 229
Abelard. *Sic et Non,* 63
Abelson, R. *Persons,* 367, 368
———, and K. Kielsen. "History of Eth-
 ics," 388, 405
Abortion and Moral Theory, L. W.
 Sumner, 405, 409
The Achilles of Rationalist Arguments, B.
 L. Mijuskovic, 97, 102
Achinstein, P. *Concepts of Science,* 421,
 423; *Law and Explanation,* 420, 423
———, and S. F. Barker, eds. *The Leg-
 acy of Logical Positivism,* 154, 418,
 423
Ackermann, R. J. *Belief and Knowledge,*
 319, 324; *The Philosophy of Karl Pop-
 per,* 202, 203
Action, D. G. Brown, 374, 377
Action and Intrpretation, C. Hookway
 and P. Pettit, eds., 445, 449
Action and Purpose, R. Taylor, 374, 378
Action, Emotion and Will, A. Kenny,
 364, 369
Action Theory, M. Brand and D. Walton,
 eds., 373, 377
Actions, J. Hornsby, 375, 378
Acts and Other Events, J. J. Thomson,
 366, 370
Adams, G. P. and W. P. Montague, eds.
 Contemporary American Philosophy,
 222, 228
Adey, G., tr. *See* Apel, K.-O, *Towards.*
Adkins, A. W. H. *From the Many to the
 One,* 30, 31; *Merit and Responsibility,*
 30, 31

Adler, M. J. *How to Read a Book,* 375;
 The Idea of Freedom, 375, 377
———, and C. Van Doren, eds. *Great
 Treasury of Western Thought,* 508
Advancement of Learning, F. Bacon, 77,
 143
Adventures of Ideas, A. N. Whitehead,
 212, 215
Adventures of the Dialetic (Marxism),
 M. Merleau-Ponty, 259, 261, 292
Aesthetic, B. Croce, 465, 468
Aesthetic Analysis, D. W. Prall, 462, 469
Aesthetic Inquiry, M. C. Beardsley and
 H. M. Schneller, eds., 463, 467
The Aesthetic Point of View, M. C.
 Beardsley, 463, 467
Aesthetics, M. C. Beardsley, 463, 467
Aesthetics, G. Dickie and R. J. Sclafani,
 eds., 463, 468
Aesthetics and Art Theory, H. Osborne,
 461, 469
Aesthetics and Language, W. Elton, ed.,
 463, 468
*Aesthetics and Philosophy of Art Criti-
 cism,* J. Stolnitz, 463, 464, 469
Aesthetics and the Theory of Criticism,
 A. Isenberg, 463, 468
*Aesthetics from Ancient Greece to the
 Present,* M. C. Beardsley, 460, 467
Aesthetics in the Modern World, H. Os-
 borne, ed., 463, 469
After Virtue, A. MacIntyre, 390, 403, 408
Against Method, P. K. Feyerabend, 334,
 412, 416, 424
An Age of Crisis (18th c.), L. G. Crocker,
 98, 102
Agent, Action, and Reason, R. Binkley,

517

R. Bronaugh and A. Marras, eds., 373, 377
Aiken, H. D. *Reason and Conduct,* 391, 398, 404, 405
The Aims of Education, A. N. Whitehead, 492, 500
Albert Einstein, P. A. Schilpp, ed., 416, 426
Albert the Great, F. J. Kovach and R. W. Shahan, eds., 64, 68
Alderman, H. *Nietzsche's Gift,* 269, 270
Aldrich, V. *Philosophy of Art,* 463, 467
Alexander, S. *Space, Time and Deity,* 166
Alexander, W. H. *Johann Georg Hamann,* 100, 101
Alexius Meinong on Objects of Higher Order and Husserl's Phenomenology, M. L. Schubert Kalsi, 132, 135
Algozin, K. W., ed. *See* O'Malley, J. J.
Alienation (Marx), B. Ollman, 253, 254, 256
The Alienation of Reason (Positivism), L. Kolakowski, 128–30, 135
Allan, D. J. *The Philosophy of Aristotle,* 37, 45
Allen, G. W. *William James: A Biography,* 236, 237
Allen, R. E. *Plato's 'Euthyphro' and Earlier Theory of Forms,* 30; *Socrates and Legal Obligation,* 31; *see also* Furley, D. J., *Studies,* and Heller, A.
———, ed. *Studies in Plato's Metaphysics,* 30, 31
———, and D. J. Furley, eds. *Studies in Presocratic Philosophy* (v. 2), 13, 14, 16
Allison, D. B., tr. *See* Derrida, J., *Speech.*
Allison, H. E. *The Kant-Eberhard Controversy,* 116, 121
Alston, W. P. *Philosophy of Language,* 322, 340, 344; "Philosophy of Religion," etc., 473, 477, 480
———, ed. "Philosophy and Psychoanalysis," 486, 487; "The Philosophy and Psychology of Cognition," 484, 487; *Religious Belief,* 476, 480
Althusser, L. *Essays in Self-Criticism,* 259, 260; *For Marx,* 253, 255
Ambler, R., tr. *See* Peursen, C. A., *Phenomenology and Analytical Philosophy.*
Ambrose, A. and M. Lazerowitz. *Fundamentals of Symbolic Logic,* 330, 336

———, ———, eds. *G. E. Moore,* 187, 188; *Ludwig Wittgenstein,* 209
American Philosophers at Work, S. Hook, ed., 222, 229
American Philosophy, Today and Tomorrow, H. M. Kallen and S. Hook, eds., 222, 229
American Pragmatism, E. C. Moore, 234, 244
American Sociology and Pragmatism, J. D. Lewis and R. L. Smith, 246, 247
Analecta Husserliana, A.-T. Tymieniecka, ed., 286, 287
Analyses of Theories and Methods of Physics and Psychology, M. Radner and S. Winokur, eds., 413, 426
An Analysis of Knowledge and Valuation, C. I. Lewis, 315, 317, 325
Analysis of Sensations, E. Mach, 131
Analytic Philosophy of Language and the Geisteswissenschaften, K.-O. Apel, 445, 447
The Analytic Tradition in Philosophy, M. Corrado, 154, 155
Analytical Philosophy, R. J. Butler, ed., 169, 171
Analytical Philosophy of Action, A. C. Danto, 374, 377
Analytical Philosophy of History, A. C. Danto, 431, 433
Analytical Philosophy of Knowledge, A. C. Danto, 317, 319, 325
Anarchy, State and Utopia, R. Nozick, 442, 444, 449
The Anatomy of Historical Knowledge, M. Mandelbaum, 432, 434
The Anatomy of Inquiry, I. Scheffler, 417, 426
The Anatomy of the Soul, A. Kenny, 363, 369
Anaximander and the Origins of Greek Cosmology, C. H. Kahn, 14, 17
Ancilla to the Pre-Socratic Philosophers (tr. Diels fragments), K. Freeman, 12, 17
Anderson, A. R., N. D. Belnap, et al. *Entailment,* 335, 336
Anderson, M. L., tr. *See* Maritain, J., *Bergsonian Philosophy.*
Anderson, R. M., ed. *See* Maxwell, G.
Anderson, T. C. *The Foundation and Structure of Sartrean Ethics,* 277
Andersson, T. J. *Polis and Psyche* (Plato), 31, 32

Angeles, P. A. *Dictionary of Philosophy*, 508

An Annotated Bibliography of Philosophy in Catholic Thought, 1900–1964, G. F. McLean, 505

Anomalies and Scientific Theories, W. C. Humphreys, 420, 425

Anscombe, G. E. M. *Intention*, 362, 366, 368; *An Introduction to Wittgenstein's Tractatus*, 207, 209; *see also* Wittgenstein, L., *Philosophical Investigations* and *Remarks*

———, et al. *Mind and Language*, 341, 342, 344

Anselm. *Proslogion*, 478

Apel, K.-O. *Analytic Philosophy of Language and the Geisteswissenschaften*, 445, 447; *Towards a Transformation of Philosophy*, 300, 357

Appearance and Reality, F. H. Bradley, 148, 350, 358

Aquila, R. E. *Intentionality*, 367, 368

Aquinas (St. Thomas). *Summa Contra Gentiles*, 53, 64; *Summa Theologiae*, 64

Aquinas, F. C. Copleston, 65, 67

Aquinas, A. Kenny, ed., 65, 68

Aquinas and Natural Law, D. J. O'Connor, 65, 68

Arbaugh, G. E. and G. B. *Kierkegaard's Authorship*, 265, 266

Archaic Logic, R. A. Prier, 16, 18

Archambault, R. D., ed. *Dewey on Education*, 245, 494, 495, 498; *Philosophical Analysis and Education*, 492, 494, 498

The Architecture of the Intelligible Universe in the Philosophy of Plotinus, A. H. Armstrong, 48, 49

Árdal, P. S. *Passion and Value in Hume's Treatise*, 108, 109

Ardley, G. *Berkeley's Renovation of Philosophy*, 104, 106

Arendt, H. *The Life of the Mind*, 368; *The Origins of Totalitarianism*, 368

The Argument and the Action of Plato's Laws, L. Strauss, 31, 33

Arguments of the Philosophers, 513

The Aristotelian Ethics, A. Kenny, 43, 46

Aristotle. *De Motu Animalium*, 43, 46

Aristotle, W. Jaeger, 24, 25, 35, 36, 45

Aristotle, G. E. R. Lloyd, 37, 46

Aristotle, J. M. E. Moravcsik, ed., 36, 37, 41, 44, 46

Aristotle, J. H. Randall, 37, 46

Aristotle, W. D. Ross, 25, 36, 46

Aristotle and His School, F. Grayeff, 35, 45

Aristotle and Plato in the Mid-Fourth Century, I. Düring and G. E. L. Owen, eds., 37, 45

Aristotle and the Arabs, F. E. Peters, 57, 68

Aristotle and the Problem of Value, W. J. Oates, 44, 46

Aristotle on Emotion, W. W. Fortenbaugh, 43, 45

Aristotle on Memory, R. Sorabji, 43, 46

Aristotle's Concept of Dialectic, J. D. G. Evans, 38, 39, 45

Aristotle's Conception of Ontology, W. Leszl, 41, 46

Aristotle's Criticism of Plato and the Academy, H. Cherniss, 13, 36, 45

Aristotle's Criticism of Presocratic Philosophy, H. Cherniss, 24, 36, 45

Aristotle's De Motu Animalium, M. C. Nussbaum, 43, 46

Aristotle's Man, R. L. Clark, 42, 45

Aristotle's School, J. P. Lynch, 34, 36, 46

Aristotle's System of the Physical World, F. Solmsen, 41, 46

Aristotle's Theory of the Will, A. Kenny, 44, 45

Armour, L. *Logic and Reality*, 355, 357

———, and E. T. Bartlett. *The Conceptualization of the Inner Life*, 367, 368

Armstrong, A. H. *The Architecture of the Intelligible Universe in the Philosophy of Plotinus*, 48, 49; *Plotinian and Christian Studies*, 48, 49

———, ed. *The Cambridge History of Later Greek and Early Medieval Philosophy*, 48, 49, 51, 56

Armstrong, D. M. *Belief, Truth and Knowledge*, 320, 321, 324; *The Nature of Mind and Other Essays*, 366, 368; *Universals and Scientific Realism*, 355, 357; *see also* Martin, C. B.

Art, C. Bell, 461–62, 467

Art and Human Values, M. Rader and B. Jessop, 463, 469

Art and Imagination, R. Srutton, 466, 469

Art and Its Objects, R. Wollheim, 466, 470

Art and Philosophy, J. Margolis, 463, 468

Art and the Aesthetic, G. Dickie, 464, 465, 468
Art and the Christian Intelligence in St. Augustine, R. J. O'Connell, 56, 460, 469
Art as Experience, J. Dewey, 244, 462, 468
The Art of Memory, F. A. Yates, 43, 46
Arthur, J., ed. *Morality and Moral Controversies,* 405
Articles on Aristotle, J. Barnes, M. Schofield and R. Sorabji, eds., 37, 44, 45
The Arts and the Art of Criticism, T. M. Greene, 462, 468
Aschenbrenner, K. *The Concepts of Criticism,* 464, 467; *The Concepts of Value,* 382, 383, 484; *see also* Bochenski, I. M.
Ashton, E. B., tr. *See* Jaspers, K., *Philosophy.*
Aspects of Aristotle's Logic, R. Bosley, 39, 45
Aspects of Contemporary American Philosophy, F. H. Donnell, ed., 222, 229
Aspects of Scientific Explanation, C. G. Hempel, 415, 418, 420, 425
Asquith, P. D. and H. E. Kyburg, Jr., eds. *Current Research in Philosophy of Science,* 417, 423; *see also* Suppe, F., *PSA 1976*
"Atheism," etc., P. Edwards, 473, 478, 480, 481
Atkinson, R. F. *Knowledge and Explanation in History,* 431, 433
Auguste Comte and Positivism, J. S. Mill, 127, 135
Augustine. *City of God,* 428; *Confessions,* 55; *De Doctrina Christiana,* 60
Augustine, R. A. Markus, ed., 56, 68
Aune, B. *Kant's Theory of Morals,* 116, 121; *Knowledge, Mind and Nature,* 318, 324, 364, 368; *Reason and Action,* 375, 377
Austin, J. L. *How to Do Things with Words,* 168, 342, 344; *Philosophical Papers,* 168, 171; *Sense and Sensibilia,* 168, 316, 321, 325; *see also* Fann, K. T.
The Authority of Law, J. Raz, 457, 459
Autobiography, R. G. Collingwood, 5, 6, 186–87, 196
Autobiography, G. Vico, 99
The Autobiography of Bertrand Russell, B. Russell, 179, 181

The Autonomy of Religious Belief, F. Crosson, ed., 478, 480
Avineri, S. *The Social and Political Thought of Karl Marx,* 253–55
Ayer, A. J. *Language, Truth and Logic,* 153, 155, 188, 322, 392, 476; *The Origins of Pragmatism,* 233, 234; *Part of My Life,* 165–66, 171; *The Problem of Knowledge,* 317, 319, 325; *Russell and Moore,* 163, 171; *see also* Macdonald, G. F. (1979 Festschrift)
———, ed. *Logical Positivism,* 154, 155
———, et al. *The Revolution in Philosophy,* 169, 171
Ayers, M. *See* Ree, J., *Philosophy.*
Ayers, R. H. *Language, Logic, and Reason in the Church Fathers,* 58, 67
al-Azm, S. J. *The Origins of Kant's Arguments in the Antinomies,* 116, 121

Baatz, C. A. *The Philosophy of Education: A Guide to Information Sources,* 503
Bach, K. and R. M. Harnish. *Linguistic Communications and Speech Acts,* 342, 344
Back to Kant, T. E. Willey, 133, 135
Bacon, F. *Advancement of Learning,* 77, 143
Bahm, A., et al., eds. *Directory of American Philosophers,* 512
Baier, K. *The Moral Point of View,* 399, 404, 405
Baird, A. W. S. *Studies in Pascal's Ethics,* 84, 85
Baker, G. P. and P. M. S. Hacker. *Wittgenstein—Understanding and Meaning,* 208, 209
Baldwin, J. *See* Rand, B.
Bambrough, R. *Moral Scepticism and Moral Knowledge,* 397, 406
———, ed. *New Essays on Plato and Aristotle,* 30, 32; *Plato, Popper and Politics,* 202, 203
Bannan, J. F. *The Philosophy of Merleau-Ponty,* 292, 293
Barcan, R. *See* Marcus, R. B.
Barden, G., tr. *See* Gadamer, H.-G., *Truth.*
Barker, E. *Greek Political Theory,* 30, 32
Barker, J. *Strange Contrarieties* (Pascal), 84, 85
Barker, S. F. *Philosophy of Mathematics,* 330, 336

Barnes, H. E., tr. *See* Sartre, J.-P., *Being.*

Barnes, J. *The Presocratic Philosophers,* 14, 17; *see also* Schofield, M.

———, M. Schofield and R. Sorabji, eds. *Articles on Aristotle,* 37, 44, 45

Barrett, C., ed. *See* Tatarkiewicz, W.

Barrett, W. *The Illusion of Technique,* 308, 310; *Irrational Man* (Existentialism), 263, 264

Barrow, R. *Plato, Utilitarianism and Education,* 31, 32, 491

Barry, B. *The Liberal Theory of Justice* (Rawls), 444, 447; *Political Argument,* 441, 447; *see also* Sikoria, R. I.

Barth, K. *Protestant Theology in the Nineteenth Century,* 124, 134

Bartlett, E. T. *See* Armour, L.

The Basic Laws of Arithmetic, G. Frege, 330, 337

Basic Rights, H. Shue, 446, 450

Bayle, P. *Dictionnaire historique et critique,* 85, 104

Beard, R. W., ed. *See* Copi, I. M.

Beardsley, M. C. *The Aesthetic Point of View,* 463, 467; *Aesthetics,* 463, 467; *Aesthetics from Ancient Greece to the Present,* 460, 467

———, ed. "Languages of Art," 467

———, and H. M. Schneller, eds. *Aesthetic Inquiry,* 463, 467

Bechtle, T. C. and M. F. Riley. *Dissertations in Philosophy Accepted at American Universities, 1861–1975,* 513

Beck, C. *Educational Philosophy and Theory,* 493, 498

Beck, C. B., B. S. Crittenden and E. V. Sullivan, eds. *Moral Education,* 496, 498

Beck, L. J. *The Metaphysics of Descartes,* 81, 82

Beck, L. W. *A Commentary on Kant's Critique of Practical Reason,* 114, 121, 220; *Early German Philosophy,* 98–99, 101; *Studies in the Philosophy of Kant,* 120, 121

———, ed. *Kant Studies Today,* 120, 121; "Thomas Aquinas 1274–1974," 65, 67

———, et al. "Philosophy of the History of Philosophy," 6

Becker, L. C. *On Justifying Moral Judgements,* 392, 406; *Property Rights,* 443, 448

Bedau, H., ed. *Civil Disobedience,* 440, 448

Being and Education, D. Vandenberg, 494, 500

Being and Existence in Kierkegaard's Pseudonymous Works, J. W. Elrod, 265, 266

Being and Nothingness, J.-P. Sartre, 275, 277

Being and Time, M. Heidegger, 278, 281, 283

Belaief, G. *Spinoza's Philosophy of Law,* 87

Belief, H. H. Price, 479

Belief and Knowledge, R. J. Ackermann, 319, 324

Belief in God, G. I. Mavrodes, 473, 477, 482

Belief, Truth and Knowledge, D. M. Armstrong, 320, 321, 324

Bell, C. *Art,* 461–62, 467

Bell, D. *Frege's Theory of Judgement,* 133, 134

Belnap, N. D. *See* Anderson, A. R.

Benditt, T. M. *Law as Rule and Principle,* 456, 458

Benn, S. I. and R. S. Peters. *Social Principles and the Democratic State,* 440, 443, 448

Bennett, J. *Kant's Analytic,* 115, 121; *Kant's Dialectic,* 115, 121; *Linguistic Behaviour,* 341, 344; *Locke, Berkeley, Hume,* 95

Bergmann, F. *On Being Free,* 377

Bergmann, G. *Logic and Reality,* 154, 352, 357; *Meaning and Existence,* 352, 358; *The Metaphysics of Logical Positivism,* 352, 358; *Realism* (Brentano and Meinong), 132, 134

Bergson, H. *Creative Evolution,* 127; *The Two Sources of Morality and Religion,* 127

Bergson and Modern Physics, M. Čapek, 127, 134

Bergsonian Philosophy and Thomism, J. Maritain, 127, 135

Berkeley, G. *An Essay Towards a New Theory of Vision,* 103; *Philosophical Commentaries,* 104; *A Treatise Concerning the Principles of Human Knowledge,* 103, 106

Berkeley, H. M. Bracken, 106

Berkeley, G. Pitcher, 106, 107

Berkeley, I. C. Tipton, 106, 107

Berkeley, G. J. Warnock, 106, 107
Berkeley and Malebranche, A. A. Luce, 104, 106
Berkeley's Analysis of Perception, J. Stack, 105, 107
Berkeley's Renovation of Philosophy, G. Ardley, 104, 106
Berkovits, E. *Major Themes in Modern Philosophies of Judaism*, 157, 158
Berlin, I. *Four Essays on Liberty*, 440, 444, 448; *The Hedgehog and the Fox*, 428, 433; *Historical Inevitability*, 433; *Vico and Herder*, 99, 101; *see also* Ryan, A., *The Idea of Freedom* (1979 Festschrift)
Berndtson, A. *Power, Form, and Mind*, 355, 358
Bernstein, R. J. *Praxis and Action*, 157, 373, 377; *see also* Rorty R., *Philosophy*
————, ed. *Perspectives on Peirce*, 237, 241
Berofsky, B., ed. *Free Will and Determinism*, 376, 377
Bertocci, P. A. *The Person God Is*, 473, 475, 480
————, ed. *Mid-Twentieth Century American Philosophy*, 222, 228
Bertrand Russell, D. Pears, ed., 180, 181
Bertrand Russell and the British Tradition in Philosophy, D. Pears, 177, 180, 181
Bertrand Russell Memorial Volume, G. W. Roberts, ed., 180, 181
Bertrand Russell on Education, J. Park, 492, 499
Bertrand Russell's Philosophy, G. Nakhnikian, ed., 180, 181
Bertrand Russell's Theory of Knowledge, E. Eames, 180, 181
Between Philosophy and History, H. Fain, 430, 434
Beyond Epistemology (Hegel), F. G. Weiss, ed., 141, 142
Beyond the Letter, I. Scheffler, 343, 347
Bibliographica Philosophica, 1934–1945, G. A. De Brie, 504
Bibliographie de la Philosophie, 503
Bibliographies of Famous Philosophers Series, R. H. Linebeck, ed., 503
A Bibliography of Bibliographies in Aesthetics, A. Shield, 507
A Bibliography of Christian Philosophy and Contemporary Issues, G. F. McLean, ed., 505

A Bibliography of Philosophical Bibliographies, H. Guerry, 504
Bibliography of Philosophy, Psychology, and Cognate Subjects, B. Rand, comp., 507
"A Bibliography of Writings in English on Linguistic Method in Philosophy and Related Issues 1930–1965," J. Neu and R. Rorty, 506
Biemel, W. *Martin Heidegger*, 280, 283
Bien, J., ed. *See* Merleau-Ponty, M., *Adventures*; Ricoeur, P., *Political*.
Bieri, P., R. P. Horstmann and L. Krüger, eds. *Transcendental Arguments and Science*, 420, 423
Bierwisch, M., ed. *See* Searle, J. R., *Speech Act Theory*.
Bigger, C. P. *Participation*, 25, 32
Binkley, R., R. Bronaugh and A. Marras, eds. *Agent, Action, and Reason*, 373, 377
Binkley, T. *Wittgenstein's Language*, 206, 208, 209
Biro, J. I. and R. W. Shahan, eds. *Mind, Brain, and Function*, 366, 369; *see also* Shahan, R. W., *Spinoza*
The Birth of Tragedy, F. Nietzsche, 19, 21
Black, M. *Caveats and Critiques*, 342, 344; *A Companion to Wittgenstein's Tractatus*, 207, 209; *Critical Thinking*, 331, 336; *The Labyrinth of Language*, 341, 344; *Language and Philosophy*, 342, 344; *Margins of Precision*, 342, 344; *Models and Metaphors*, 342, 345; *Problems of Analysis*, 342, 345
————, ed. *Philosophy in America*, 222, 228
Black, R., tr. *See* Goldmann, L., *Immanuel Kant*.
Blackwell, K., ed. *See* Thomas, J. E.
Blake, R. M., C. J. Ducasse and E. H. Madden. *Scientific Method*, 414, 423
Blanshard, B. *The Nature of Thought*, 323, 325, 350, 358; *Reason and Belief*, 473, 475, 480; *Reason and Goodness*, 397, 406; *see also* Rome, S.
————, et al. *Philosophy in American Education*, 222, 228
Bleicher, J. *Contemporary Hermeneutics*, 297, 300
Bloch, E. *On Karl Marx*, 253, 256; *A Philosophy of the Future*, 257, 258, 260

Block, N., ed. *Readings in Philosophy of Psychology*, 484, 487

Blocker, H. G. *Philosophy of Art*, 463, 467

Bloom, A., tr. *See* Rousseau, J.-J., *Emile.*

Blum, A. F. *Theorizing*, 39, 45

Blum, L. A. *Friendship, Altruism, and Morality*, 402, 406

Blumer, H. *Symbolic Interactionism*, 246, 247

Boas, G. *Dominant Themes of Modern Philosophy*, 74, 79; *Rationalism in Greek Philosophy*, 49

———, H. Cherniss, et al. *Studies in Intellectual History*, 5, 6

Bochenski, I. M. *Contemporary European Philosophy*, 157–58, 159

Boehner, P. *Medieval Logic*, 58, 67

Boethius. *Consolation of Philosophy*, 55

Bogen, J. *Wittgenstein's Philosophy of Language*, 208, 209

Boler, J. F. *Charles Peirce and Scholastic Realism* (Duns Scotus), 65, 240, 241

Bolotin, D. *Plato's Dialogue on Friendship* ("Lysis"), 31, 32

Bolton, N., ed. *Philosophical Problems in Psychology*, 484, 488

Bonansea, B. M., ed. *See* Ryan, J. K. *Bonaventure and Aquinas*, R. W. Shahan, ed., 64, 69

Bonner, S. F. *Education in Ancient Rome*, 60, 67

Bontemps, C. J. and C. J. Odell, eds. *The Owl of Minerva* (American philosophy), 223, 228

Borchardt, D. H. *How to Find Out in Philosophy and Psychology*, 503

Borger, R. and F. Cioffi, eds. *Explanation in the Behavioral Sciences*, 484, 488

Borst, C. V., ed. *The Mind-Brain Identity Theory*, 366, 369

Bosanquet, B. *A History of Aesthetic*, 460, 467

Boscherini, E. G. *Lexicon Spinozanum*, 87

Bosley, R. *Aspects of Aristotle's Logic*, 39, 45

Boston Studies in the Philosophy of Science, 514

The Bounds of Sense (Kant), P. F. Strawson, 115, 121

Bourke, V. J. *History of Ethics*, 388, 406

Bowden, J., tr. *See* Barth, K.

Bowie, N. E., ed. *Ethical Issues in Government*, 446, 448

Bowman, M. A. *Western Mysticism: A Guide to the Basic Works*, 504

Boyd, W. *The Educational Theory of Jean Jacques Rousseau*, 111, 113

Boydston, J. A. *Guide to the Works of John Dewey*, 245; *see also* Dykhuizen, G.; Dewey, J., *Works*

Bracken, H. M. *Berkeley*, 106

Bradley, F. H. *Appearance and Reality*, 148, 350, 358

Bradley, R. and N. Swartz. *Possible Worlds*, 333, 336

Bradley's Metaphysics and the Self, G. L. Vander Veer, 148, 149

Brain and Mind, J. R. Smythies, ed., 366, 370

Brainstorms, D. C. Dennett, 365, 367, 369

Braithwaite, R. B. *Scientific Explanation*, 419, 423

Brameld, T. *Philosophies of Education in Cultural Perspective*, 493, 498

Brand, M., ed. *The Nature of Human Action*, 373, 374, 377

———, and D. Walton, eds. *Action Theory*, 373, 377

Brandt, R. B. *Ethical Theory*, 389, 394, 397, 406; *The Philosophy of Schleiermacher*, 125, 134; *A Theory of the Good and the Right*, 393, 402, 406; *Value and Obligation*, 389, 406; *see also* Goldman, A. and J. Kim (1978 Festschrift); Nagel, E., *Meaning and Knowledge*

———, ed. *Social Justice*, 440, 444, 448

Brazill, W. J. *The Young Hegelians*, 126, 134

Brendel, O. J. *Symbolism of the Sphere*, 11, 17

Brennan, J. M. *The Open-Texture of Moral Concepts*, 404, 406

Bretall, R. *A Kierkegaard Anthology*, 265, 266

Brewster, B., tr. *See* Althusser, L., *For Marx.*

Bricke, J. *Hume's Philosophy of Mind*, 108, 109

Bridgman, P. W. *The Logic of Modern Physics*, 414, 423

Brief Outline on the Study of Theology, F. Schleiermacher, 5, 7, 294, 474

Brinton, C. *Ideas and Men*, 9, 10

British Analytic Philosophy, B. A. O. Williams and A. Montefiore, eds., 169, 172
"British and American Realism," M. Fisch et al., 350, 358
British Philosophy in Mid-Century, C. A. Mace, ed., 163, 169, 171
Brittan, G. G. *See* Lambert, K.
Broad, C. D. *Leibniz,* 90
Brodbeck, M., ed. *Readings in the Philosophy of the Social Sciences,* 445, 448; *see also* Feigl, H., *Readings*
Brody, B. A. *Identity and Essence,* 356, 358
———, ed. *Readings in the Philosophy of Religion,* 477, 480
Bronaugh, R., ed. *See* Binkley, R.
Broudy, H. S., R. Ennis and L. I. Krimmerman, eds. *Philosophy of Educational Research,* 494, 498
Brown, D. G. *Action,* 374, 377
Brown, H. I. *Perception, Theory and Commitment,* 411, 413, 423
Brown, K. C., ed. *Hobbes Studies,* 92, 93
Brown, S. C., ed. *Philosophy of Psychology,* 366, 484, 488; *Reason and Religion,* 478, 480; *see also* Mays, W.
Brown, T. K., tr. *See* Nelson, L.
Brown, V., ed. *See* Stern, S. M.
Brubacher, J. S. *On the Philosophy of Higher Education,* 497, 498
Brumbaugh, R. S. *Plato for the Modern Age,* 30, 32
Buber, M. *I and Thou,* 271, 272
Bubner, R. *Modern German Philosophy,* 159, 160, 300
Buchdahl, G. *Metaphysics and the Philosophy of Science,* 414, 423
Buck, R. C. and R. S. Cohen, eds., *PSA 1970,* 413, 423
Buford, T. O., ed. *See* Howie, J.
Bullock, A. and O. Stallybrass, eds. *The Harper Dictionary of Modern Thought,* 509
Bunge, M. *Causality,* 418, 423; *The Methodological Unity of Science,* 422, 423; *The Mind-Body Problem,* 366, 369; *Treatise on Basic Philosophy,* 355, 358
Burbank, J., tr. and ed. *See* Mukařovský, J.
Burkert, W. *Lore and Science in Ancient Pythagoreanism,* 14, 17
Burks, A. W. *Chance, Cause, Reason,* 331, 335, 336

———, ed. *Essays on Cellular Automata,* 335, 336; *see also* Peirce, C. S., *Collected Papers*
Burnet, J. *Early Greek Philosophy,* 12, 17
The Burning Fountain (Symbolism), P. Wheelwright, 344, 347
Burnyeat, M., ed. *See* Honderich, T.; Schofield, M.
Burr, J. R. *Handbook of World Philosophy,* 158, 511
Burrill, D., ed. *The Cosmological Argument,* 477, 480
Burtt, E. A. *The Metaphysical Foundations of Modern Science,* 74, 79
Butler, R. J., ed. *Analytical Philosophy,* 169, 171; *Cartesian Studies,* 82
Butts, R. E. and J. Hintikka, eds. *Logic, Foundations of Mathematics, and Computability Theory,* 330, 336

Cahn, S. M., ed. *New Studies in the Philosophy of John Dewey,* 245
———, and D. Shatz, eds. *Contemporary Philosophy of Religion,* 478, 480
Cailliet, E. *Pascal,* 84, 85
Cairns, D. *See* Husserl, E., *Formal;* Kersten, F. (1973 Festschrift).
Cairns, H. *Legal Philosophy from Plato to Hegel,* 454, 458
Callaghan, W., et al., eds. *See* Isenberg, A.
Callen, D., ed. *See* Beardsley, M. C., *Aesthetic Point of View.*
The Cambridge History of Later Greek and Early Medieval Philosophy, A. H. Armstrong, ed., 48, 49, 51, 56
The Cambridge History of Later Medieval Philosophy, N. Kretzmann, ed., 52, 68
Cameron, D. *The Social Thought of Rousseau and Burke,* 112, 113
Campbell, R. *From Belief to Understanding,* 478, 480
Capaldi, N. *David Hume,* 108, 109
Čapek, M. *Bergson and Modern Physics,* 127, 134
Capital, K. Marx, 252
Care, N. S. and R. H. Grimm, eds. *Perception and Personal Identity,* 320, 325
———, and C. Landesmann, eds. *Readings in the Theory of Action,* 373, 377

The Career of Philosophy, J. H. Randall, 9, 10

Cargile, J. *Paradoxes*, 329, 336

Carlo, W. E. *The Ultimate Reducibility of Essence to Existence in Existential Metaphysics*, 351, 358

Carnap, R. *Formalization of Logic*, 340, 345; *Introduction to Semantics*, 340, 345; *Logical Foundations of Probability*, 335, 336; *The Logical Structure of the World and Pseudoproblems in Philosophy*, 153, 155; *Meaning and Necessity*, 333, 336, 340, 345; *Philosophy and Logical Syntax*, 153, 155; *see also* Buck, R. C. (1971 Festschrift); Neurath, O.

———, and R. C. Jeffrey, eds. *Studies in Inductive Logic and Probability*, 335, 336

Carr, D. *Phenomenology and the Problem of History* (Husserl), 289, 290; *see also* Husserl, E., *Crisis*

———, and E. S. Casey, eds. *Explorations in Phenomenology*, 290

Carr, H. W. *Leibniz*, 90

Carré, M. H. *Phases of Thought in England*, 143, 148

Cartesian Essays, B. Magnus and J. B. Wilbur, eds., 82, 83

Cartesian Studies, R. J. Butler, ed., 82

The Case of Wagner, F. Nietzsche, 19, 21

Casey, E. S., ed. *See* Carr, D.

———, et al., tr. *See* Dufrenne, M.

Cassirer, E. *Essay on Man*, 466, 468; *The Individual and the Cosmos in Renaissance Philosophy*, 71, 72; *The Philosophy of the Enlightenment*, 97, 102; *Philosophy of Symbolic Forms*, 466, 468; *The Problem of Knowledge*, 314, 325; *Rousseau, Kant, Goethe*, 110, 113; *Symbol, Myth and Culture*, 152, 155

Casteñada, H.-N. *The Structure of Morality*, 404, 406; *Thinking and Doing*, 446, 448

———, and G. Nakhnikian, eds. *Morality and the Language of Conduct*, 389, 406

Catalano, J. S. *A Commentary on Jean-Paul Sartre's "Being and Nothingness,"* 275, 277

Categories, H. W. Johnstone, ed., 356, 358

Caton, C. E., ed. *Philosophy and Ordinary Language*, 342, 345

Caton, H. *The Origin of Subjectivity* (Descartes), 81, 82

Causal Necessity, B. Skyrms, 419, 426

Causal Powers, R. Harré and E. H. Madden, 419, 424

Causality, M. Bunge, 418, 423

Causality and Determinism, G. H. von Wright, 419, 427

Causation and Conditionals, E. Sosa, ed., 419, 427

Causation in the Law, H. L. A. Hart and A. M. Honoré, 453, 459

Causey, R. L. *The Unity of Science*, 422, 423

Causing Death and Saving Lives, J. Glover, 405, 407

Caveats and Critiques, M. Black, 342, 344

Cavell, S. *The Claims of Reason* (Wittgenstein), 209

Caws, P., ed. *Two Centuries of Philosophy in America*, 216, 219, 221, 227, 229

The Cement of the Universe, J. L. Mackie, 419, 425

Centore, F. F. *Persons*, 368, 369

A Century of Moral Philosophy, W. D. Hudson, 388, 407

Challenges to Empiricism, H. Morick, ed., 223, 229

Chambliss, J. J. *The Origins of American Philosophy of Education*, 492, 498

Chance, Cause, Reason, A. W. Burks, 331, 335, 336

Chaos and Context (James), C. H. Siegfried, 236, 237

Chapman, J. W., ed. *See* Friedrich, C. J.; Pennock, J. R.

Chappell, V. C., ed. *Hume*, 109; *The Philosophy of Mind*, 364, 369

Charles Peirce and Scholastic Realism (Duns Scotus), J. F. Boler, 65, 240, 241

Charles Peirce's Theory of Scientific Method, F. E. Reilly, 240, 241

Charlesworth, M. J. *Philosophy and Linguistic Analysis*, 170, 171

Charvet, J. *The Social Problem in the Philosophy of Rousseau*, 112, 113

Cheng, C., ed. *Philosophical Aspects of the Mind-Body Problem*, 366, 369

Cherniak, S., tr. *See* Hyppolite, J., *Genesis*.

Cherniss, H. *Aristotle's Criticism of Plato and the Academy,* 13, 36, 45; *Aristotle's Criticism of Presocratic Philosophy,* 24, 36, 45; *The Riddle of the Early Academy,* 24, 32; lecture in Allen, R. E., *Studies,* 13; *see also* Boas, G., *Studies*
The Chinese Mind, C. A. Moore, ed., 310, 312
Chisholm, R. M. *Perceiving,* 315, 317–18, 320, 325; *Person and Object,* 319, 325; *Theory of Knowledge,* 318, 319, 325; "Theory of Knowledge," 314, 315, 318, 323, 325
———, ed. *Realism and the Background of Phenomenology,* 131, 134
———, H. Feigl, W. E. Frankena, J. Passmore and M. Thompson. *Philosophy* (American), 220, 229
———, and R. J. Swartz, eds. *Empirical Knowledge,* 320, 325
Chomsky, N. *Essays on Form and Interpretation,* 342, 343, 345; *Language and Responsibility,* 342, 343, 345; *The Logical Structure of Linguistic Theory,* 342, 345; *Syntactic Structures,* 342, 343, 345
Christian, W. A. *An Interpretation of Whitehead's Metaphysics,* 214
The Christian Philosophy of Saint Augustine, E. Gilson, 56, 67
The Christian Philosophy of Saint Thomas Aquinas, E. Gilson, 65, 67
The Christian Scholar in the Age of the Reformation, E. H. Harbison, 70, 72
The Christian Tradition, J. Pelikan, 52, 53, 68
Cioffi, F., ed. *See* Borger, R.
City of God, Augustine, 428
Civil Disobedience, H. Bedau, ed., 440, 448
Civil Disobedience, C. Cohen, 440, 448
The Claim of Reason (Wittgenstein), S. Cavell, 209
Clarity Is Not Enough (Linguistic Philosophy), H. D. Lewis, ed., 170, 171
Clark, H. R. *Philosophy and Its History,* 6
Clark, M. *Logic and System* (Hegel), 140, 141
Clark, R. W. *The Life of Bertrand Russell,* 180, 181
Clark, S. R. L. *Aristotle's Man,* 42, 45; *The Moral Status of Animals,* 400, 406

Clarke, F. P. *See* Ross, J. F. (1971 Festschrift).
Classical Rhetoric and Its Christian and Secular Tradition from Ancient to Modern Times, G. A. Kennedy, 59, 68
Clegg, J. S. *The Structure of Plato's Philosophy,* 30, 32
Cognitive Development and Epistemology, T. Mischel, ed., 496, 499
Cognitive Systematization, N. Rescher, 323, 326
Cohen, C. *Civil Disobedience,* 440, 448
———, et al. "Foundations of Democracy," 443, 448
Cohen, G. A. *Karl Marx's Theory of History,* 254–56
Cohen, I. B. *The Newtonian Revolution,* 414, 423
Cohen, L. J. *The Diversity of Meaning,* 322, 325; *The Probable and the Provable,* 335, 336
Cohen, M. R. "Later Philosophy" (American), 216–18, 229; *Law and the Social Order,* 454, 456, 459; *Reason and Nature,* 217, 414, 423
———, and E. Nagel. *Introduction to Logic and Scientific Method,* 330, 337
Cohen, R. S., ed. *See* Boston Studies; Buck, R. C.
———, P. K. Feyerabend and M. W. Wartofsky, eds. *Essays in Memory of Imre Lakatos,* 413, 424
The Coherence of Theism, R. G. Swinburne, 479, 482
The Coherence Theory of Truth, N. Rescher, 323, 326
Colish, M. L. *The Mirror of Language,* 59, 67
Collected Papers, C. I. Lewis, 226, 229
Collected Papers, C. S. Peirce, 239, 241
Collected Papers, G. Ryle, 165, 172
Collected Works, J. S. Mill, 145, 149
Collingwood, R. G. *Autobiography,* 5, 6, 186–87, 196; *An Essay on Metaphysics,* 353–54, 358, 419; *Essay on Philosophical Method,* 22, 32, 188, 196, 197; *Essays in the Philosophy of Art,* 196, 197; *Essays in the Philosophy of History,* 196, 197; *Faith and Reason,* 196, 197; *The Idea of History,* 353, 431, 433; *The Idea of Nature,* 28, 32, 189, 353, 358; *The New Leviathan,* 91, 188, 196, 197, 368, 437, 448; *The*

Principles of Art, 188, 340, 460, 465–66, 468; *Speculum Mentis,* 166, 188, 192, 193, 464, 465, 468; other works, 188, 193, 195
——, tr. *See* Croce, B., *Aesthetic* and *Philosophy of . . . Vico;* Ruggiero, G.
——, and R. P. Wright. *The Roman Inscriptions of Britain,* 195, 197
Collingwood and the Reform of Metaphysics, L. Rubinoff, 196, 198
Collins, J. *The Emergence of Philosophy of Religion,* 472–74, 480; *The Existentialists,* 263, 264; *Interpreting Modern Philosophy,* 5, 6, 101
Colodny, R. G., ed. *University of Pittsburgh Series in the Philosophy of Science,* vols. 1–5, 413, 424
A Commentary on Jean-Paul Sartre's "Being and Nothingness," J. S. Catalano, 275, 277
A Commentary on Kant's Critique of Practical Reason, L. W. Beck, 114, 121, 220
A Commentary to Kant's Critique of Pure Reason, N. K. Smith, 114, 121
A Common Faith, J. Dewey, 475
The Common Place Books, 1919–1953, G. E. Moore, 187
A Companion to Wittgenstein's Philosophical Investigations, G. Hallett, 208, 209
A Companion to Wittgenstein's Tractatus, M. Black, 207, 209
Compromise in Ethics, Law, and Politics, J. R. Pennock and J. W. Chapman, eds., 441, 450
Comte, A. *Cour de philosophie positive,* 128
The Concept of a Legal System, J. Raz, 455, 459
The Concept of Education, R. S. Peters, ed., 493, 499
The Concept of Expression, A. Tormey, 466, 469
The Concept of Identity, E. Hirsch, 356, 358
The Concept of Language, N. L. Wilson, 341, 347
The Concept of Law, H. L. A. Hart, 453, 457, 459
The Concept of Matter, E. McMullin, 41, 46
The Concept of Mind, G. Ryle, 167, 362, 370

The Concept of Motivation, R. S. Peters, 373, 378
The Concept of Prayer, D. Z. Phillips, 475
The Concept of Style, B. Lang, ed., 465, 468
The Concepts of Criticism, K. Aschenbrenner, 464, 467
Concepts of Indoctrination, I. A. Snook, ed., 497, 500
Concepts of Science, P. Achinstein, 421, 423
The Concepts of Value, K. Aschenbrenner, 382, 383, 484
Concepts, Theories, and the Mind-Body Problem, H. Feigl, M. Scriven and G. Maxwell, eds., 362, 366, 369
Conceptual Change, G. Pearce and P. Maynard, eds., 421, 426
Conceptual Foundations of Scientific Thought, M. W. Wartofsky, 417, 427
Conceptual Thinking, S. Körner, 331, 337
The Conceptualization of the Inner Life, L. Armour, 367, 368
The Concise Encyclopedia of Western Philosophy and Philosophers, J. O. Urmson, ed., 510
The Condition of the Working Class in England, F. Engels, 250
The Conduct of Inquiry, A. Kaplan, 446, 449
Confessions, Augustine, 55
Confessions, J.-J. Rousseau, 111
The Conflict of Interpretations, P. Ricoeur, 298, 301
Conjectures and Refutations, K. Popper, 416, 426
Consciousness, H. Ey, 286, 287, 368
Consequences of Pragmatism, R. Rorty, 115, 156, 415
Considerations on Representative Government, J. S. Mill, 145
Consolation of Philosophy, Boethius, 55
The Constitution of Liberty, F. A. Hayek, 440, 444, 449
Contemporary American Philosophy, G. P. Adams and W. P. Montague, eds., 222, 228
Contemporary American Philosophy, J. E. Smith, ed., 222, 230
Contemporary Aspects of Philosophy, G. Ryle, ed., 170, 172
Contemporary British Philosophy, H. D. Lewis, ed., 157, 168, 171

Contemporary British Philosophy, J. H. Muirhead, ed., 162, 172

Contemporary European Ethics, J. J. Kockelmans, ed., 389, 408

Contemporary European Philosophy, I. M. Bochenski, 157–58, 159

Contemporary French Philosophy, C. Smith, 159, 160

Contemporary Hermeneutics, J. Bleicher, 297, 300

The Contemporary Marx, M. Markovic, 260, 261

Contemporary Perspectives in the Philosophy of Language, P. A. French, T. E. Uehling and H. K. Wettstein, eds., 341, 345

Contemporary Philosophical Logic, J. A. Gould and I. M. Copi, eds., 330, 337

Contemporary Philosophy, F. C. Copleston, 158

Contemporary Philosophy, R. Klibansky, ed., 159, 512

Contemporary Philosophy of Religion, S. M. Cahn and D. Shatz, eds., 478, 480

Contemporary Schools of Metascience, G. Radnitzsky, 416, 426

Contemporary Studies in Philosophical Idealism, J. Howie and T. O. Buford, eds., 225, 229

Convention, D. K. Lewis, 343, 346

Cooper, J. M. *Reason and Human Good in Aristotle,* 44, 45

Copi, I. M., ed. See Gould, J. A.

———, and R. W. Beard, eds. *Essays on Wittgenstein's Tractatus,* 207, 209

Copleston, F. C. *Aquinas,* 65, 67; *Contemporary Philosophy,* 158; *Friedrich Nietzsche,* 269, 270; *A History of Philosophy,* 8, 10

Cormier, R., et al. *International Directory of Philosophy and Philosophers,* 513

Cornford, F. M. *From Religion to Philosophy,* 11, 17; *Plato and Parmenides,* 14, 17; *Plato's Cosmology,* 13, 17; *Principium Sapientiae,* 12, 17

———, ed. and tr. *The Republic of Plato,* 31, 32

Cornforth, M. C. *Marxism and the Linguistic Philosophy,* 170, 171; *The Open Philosophy and the Open Society* (Popper), 202, 203

Cornman, J. W. *Materialism and Sensa-*

tions, 366, 369; *Metaphysics, Reference, and Language,* 355, 358; *Perception, Common Sense, and Science,* 355, 358

Corpus Aristotelicum, 35, 56

Corrado, M. *The Analytic Tradition in Philosophy,* 154, 155

The Correspondence Theory of Truth, D. J. O'Connor, 323, 326

Corti, W. R., ed. *The Philosophy of George Herbert Mead,* 246, 247; *The Philosophy of William James,* 236, 237

The Cosmological Argument, D. Burrill, ed., 477, 480

The Cosmological Argument, W. L. Rowe, 479, 482

Coughlan, N. *Young John Dewey,* 243–45

Coulter, J. *The Social Construction of Mind,* 484, 488

Coulter, J. A. *The Literary Microcosm* (Neoplatonists), 48, 49

Counterfactuals, D. K. Lewis, 333, 337

Cour de philosophie positive, A. Comte, 128

Cozens, B., tr. See Barth, K.

Cranston, M. and R. S. Peters, eds. *Hobbes and Rousseau,* 93, 113

Crawford, D. W. *Kant's Aesthetic Theory,* 461, 468

Creative Evolution, H. Bergson, 127

Creative Intuition in Art and Poetry, J. Maritain, 460, 469

The Crisis of European Sciences and Transcendental Phenomenology, E. Husserl, 289, 290

Crites, S. *In the Twilight of Christendom* (Hegel and Kierkegaard), 138, 141

Critical Essays on the Philosophy of R. G. Collingwood, M. Krausz, ed., 190, 197, 198

A Critical Exposition of the Philosophy of Leibniz, B. Russell, 90, 91

A Critical History of Western Philosophy, D. J. O'Connor, 9, 10

The Critical Theory of Jürgen Habermas, T. McCarthy, 300, 301

Critical Thinking, M. Black, 331, 336

Criticism and the Growth of Knowledge, I. Lakatos and A. E. Musgrave, eds., 413, 425

Critique of Dialectical Reason, J.-P. Sartre, 259, 261, 276

A Critique of Jean-Paul Sartre's Ontology, M. Natanson, 276, 277
Critique of Judgment, I. Kant, 114
A Critique of Karl Popper's Methodology, I. Johansson, 202, 203
A Critique of Linguistic Philosophy, C. W. K. Mundle, 170, 172
Critique of Practical Reason, I. Kant, 113–15, 117, 119
Critique of Pure Reason, I. Kant, 113, 116
Crittenden, B. S., ed. *See* Beck, C. B.
Croce, B. *Aesthetic*, 193, 465, 468; *The Philosophy of Giambattista Vico*, 100, 102; *Philosophy, Poetry, History*, 430, 433; *Poetry and Literature*, 466, 468
Crocker, L. G. *An Age of Crisis* (18th c.), 98, 102; *Nature and Culture* (18th c.), 98, 102
Crombie, I. M. *An Examination of Plato's Doctrines*, 30, 32
Crosson, F., ed. *The Autonomy of Religious Belief*, 478, 480
Cruickshank, J., ed. *The Novelist as Philosopher*, 309, 310
The Culture of Experience, J. J. McDermott, 217, 229
Cumming, J., tr. *See* Bloch, E., *A Philosophy;* Gadamer, H.-G., *Truth.*
Cunningham, G. W. *The Idealistic Argument in Recent British and American Philosophy*, 220
Cunningham, R. L., ed. *Liberty and the Rule of Law*, 444, 448
Curley, E. M. *Descartes Against the Skeptics*, 81, 83; *Spinoza's Metaphysics*, 86, 88
Current Issues in the Philosophy of Science, H. Feigl and G. Maxwell, eds., 413, 424
Current Research in Philosophy of Science, P. D. Asquith and H. E. Kyburg, Jr., eds., 417, 423
Cybernetics and the Philosophy of Mind, K. M. Sayre, 366, 370

Danford, J. W. *Wittgenstein and Political Philosophy*, 440, 448
Daniels, N., ed. *Reading Rawls*, 444, 448
Danto, A. C. *Analytical Philosophy of Action*, 374, 377; *Analytical Philosophy of History*, 431, 433; *Analytical Philosophy of Knowledge*, 317, 319,

325; *Jean-Paul Sartre*, 276, 277; *Nietzsche as Philosopher*, 269, 270
D'Arcy, E. *Human Acts*, 373, 377
Darden, L. and N. Maull. "The Unity of Science: Interfield Theories," 422, 424
Darwin, C. *Origin of Species*, 218, 242
Dauenhauer, B. P. *Silence*, 286, 287
David Hume, N. Capaldi, 108, 109
David Hume, D. G. C. McNabb, 108, 109
David Hume, K. R. Merrill and R. W. Shahan, eds., 108, 109
David Hume, G. P. Morice, ed., 109
David Hume, D. F. Morton, 107, 109
David Hume, D. F. Norton and R. H. Popkin, eds., 108, 110
Davidson, D. *Essays on Actions and Events*, 375, 377
———, and G. Harman, eds. *Semantics of Natural Language*, 343, 345
———, and J. Hintikka, eds. *Words and Objections* (Quine), 228, 229
Davidson, H. M. *The Origin of Certainty* (Pascal), 84, 85
Davies, M. *See* Peacocke, C. A. B.
Davis, L. H. *Theory of Action*, 373, 377
Davis, W. H. *Peirce's Epistemology*, 240, 241
De Brie, G. A. *Bibliographica Philosophica 1934–1945*, 504
De Doctrina Christiana, Augustine, 60
De George, R. T. *A Guide to Philosophical Bibliography and Research*, 504
———, ed. *Ethics and Society*, 440, 448
De la recherche de la vérité, N. Malebranche, 104
De Motu Animalium, Aristotle, 43, 46
Dearden, R. F., P. H. Hirst and R. S. Peters, eds. *Education and the Development of Reason*, 493, 498
Death and Eternal Life, J. Hick, 479, 481
Debbins, W., ed. *See* Collingwood, R. G., *Essays in the Philosophy of History.*
Deconstruction, C. Norris, 310
The Degrees of Knowledge, J. Maritain, 350, 359
Delaney, C. F. *Mind and Nature* (Cohen, Woodbridge, R. W. Sellars), 226, 229
———, et al. *The Synoptic Vision* (W. Sellars), 228, 229
———, ed. *Rationality and Religious Belief*, 478, 480
Democracy and Education, J. Dewey, 244, 495, 498

Author-Title Index

Democratic Political Theory, J. Pennock, 443, 450

Democratic Theory, C. B. Macpherson, 443, 449

Dennett, D. C. *Brainstorms,* 365, 367, 369

Denton, D. E., ed. *Existentialism and Phenomenology in Education,* 494, 498

Derrida, J. *Of Grammatology,* 343, 345; *Speech and Phenomena and Other Essays on Husserl's Theory of Signs,* 289, 290

Desan, W. *The Tragic Finale* (Sartre), 276, 277

Descartes, R. *Discours de la méthode,* 80; *Meditationes,* 80–81; *Principia Philosophiae,* 80

Descartes, W. Doney, ed., 81–83

Descartes, M. Hooker, ed., 81–83

Descartes, S. V. Keeling, 81, 83

Descartes, A. Kenny, 81, 83

Descartes, J. Ree, 81, 83

Descartes, B. Williams, 81, 83

Descartes, M. D. Wilson, 81, 83

Descartes Against the Skeptics, E. M. Curley, 81, 83

Descombes, V. *Modern French Philosophy,* 159, 160, 260

Despland, M. *Kant on History and Religion,* 118, 121

Determinants and Controls of Scientific Development, K. D. Knorr, H. Strasser and H. G. Zilian, eds., 413, 425

Determinism and Freedom in the Age of Modern Science, S. Hook, ed., 376, 378

The Development of Arabic Logic, N. Rescher, 57, 69

The Development of Bertrand Russell's Philosophy, R. Jager, 174, 180, 181

The Development of Kant's Ethics, K. Ward, 116, 122

The Development of Logic, W. Kneale and M. Kneale, 329, 337

The Development of Logical Empiricism, J. Joergensen, 154, 155

The Development of Mind, A. Kenny et al., 364, 369

The Development of Peirce's Philosophy, M. G. Murphey, 240, 241

The Development of Plato's Ethics, J. Gould, 31, 32

Developments in the Methodology of So-cial Science, W. Leinfellner and E. Köhler, eds., 446, 449

Dewey, J. *Art as Experience,* 244, 462, 468; *A Common Faith,* 475; *Democracy and Education,* 244, 495, 498; *Essays in Experimental Logic,* 330; *Experience and Education,* 244, 495, 498; *Experience and Nature,* 244, 314, 349, 358; *How We Think,* 495, 498; *Logic, the Theory of Inquiry,* 244, 330, 337; *Psychology,* 243; *The Public and Its Problems,* 244, 437, 448; *Reconstruction in Philosophy,* 5, 6, 9, 222; *Theory of the Moral Life,* 386, 396, 406; *Works,* 245; other works, 242, 244

Dewey and His Critics, S. Morgenbesser, ed., 245

Dewey on Education, R. D. Archambault, ed., 245, 494, 495, 498

The Dialectic of Action, F. A. Olafson, 432, 434

Dialectics (Marxism), T. A. Jackson, 255, 260

Dialogue and Dialectic (Plato), H.-G. Gadamer, 31, 32

Dialogues Concerning Natural Religion, D. Hume, 107–8

Dialogues of Alfred North Whitehead, A. N. Whitehead, 212, 214, 215

Diamond, C. and J. Teichman, eds. *Intention and Intentionality,* 367, 369

Diamond, M. L. *Martin Buber,* 271, 272

———, and T. V. Litzenburg, Jr., eds. *The Logic of God,* 477, 480

Dickie, G. *Art and the Aesthetic,* 464, 465, 468

———, and R. J. Sclafani, eds. *Aesthetics,* 463, 468

Dictionary of American Philosophy, S. E. Nauman, Jr., 509

Dictionary of Logical Terms and Symbols, C. H. Greenstein, 333, 509

Dictionary of Philosophy, P. A. Angeles, 508

A Dictionary of Philosophy, A. R. Lacey, 509

A Dictionary of Philosophy, M. Rosenthal and P. Yudin, eds., 510

Dictionary of Philosophy and Religion: Eastern and Western Thought, W. L. Reese, 159, 510

Dictionary of the History of Ideas, P. P. Wiener, ed., 511

Dictionnaire historique et critique, P. Bayle, 85, 104

Diels, H. and W. Kraus, eds. *Die Fragmente der Vorsokratiker,* 12, 17; *see also* Freeman, K.

Dienstag, J. I., ed. *Studies in Maimonides and St. Thomas Aquinas,* 57, 67

Dilemmas, G. Ryle, 329, 338

Dillon, J. *The Middle Platonists,* 48, 49

Dilman, I. *Induction and Deduction* (Wittgenstein), 209; *Morality and the Inner Life* (Plato's "Gorgias"), 31, 32

Directives and Norms, A. Ross, 456, 459

Directory of American Philosophers, A. Bahm et al., eds., 512

A Directory of Women in Philosophy, C. Whitbeck, ed., 513

Discours de la méthode, R. Descartes, 80

Discourse on the Origins of Inequality, J.-J. Rousseau, 112

Discourse on the Sciences and the Arts, J.-J. Rousseau, 112

Discovering Free Will and Personal Responsibility, J. F. Rychlak, 373, 378

Discovering the Mind, W. Kaufmann, 5, 6

Dissertations in Philosophy Accepted at American Universities, 1861–1975, T. C. Bechtle and M. F. Riley, 513

The Dissolution of the Medieval Outlook, G. Leff, 67, 68

The Diversity of Meaning, L. J. Cohen, 322, 325

The Divine Relativity, C. Hartshorne, 473, 475, 481

Divine Substance, G. Stead, 42, 46

The Doctrine of Being in the Aristotelian Metaphysics, J. Owens, 41–42, 46

The Doctrine of Propositions and Terms, A. N. Prior, 334, 337

Documents in the History of American Philosophy, M. G. White, ed., 221, 230

Dodds, E. R. *The Greeks and the Irrational,* 12, 17

Doing and Deserving, J. Feinberg, 404, 406

Domandi, Mario, tr. *See* Cassirer, E., *Individual.*

Dominant Themes of Modern Philosophy, G. Boas, 74, 79

Donagan, A. *The Later Philosophy of R. G. Collingwood,* 197; *The Theory of Morality,* 395, 406; *see also* Collingwood, R. G., *Essays in the Philosophy of Art*

Doney, W., ed. *Descartes,* 81–83

Donnell, F. H., Jr., ed. *Aspects of Contemporary American Philosophy,* 222, 229

Dooley, P. K. *Pragmatism as Humanism* (James), 236, 237

Doubt and Dogmatism (Hellenistic), M. Schofield, M. Burnyeat and J. Barnes, eds., 47, 50

Dover, K. J. *Greek Popular Morality in the Time of Plato and Aristotle,* 30, 32

The Downfall of Cartesianism, 1673–1712, R. A. Watson, 82, 83

Downie, R. S. and E. Telfer. *Respect for Persons,* 400, 406

Doyle, J. F., ed. *Educational Judgments,* 493, 496, 498

Dray, W. H. *Law and Explanation in History,* 430, 433, 434; *Philosophy of History,* 431, 434

———, ed. *Philosophical Analysis and History,* 430, 431, 434

Dreaming, N. Malcolm, 367, 369

Dretske, F. I. *Seeing and Knowing,* 321, 325

Ducasse, C. J. *See* Blake, R. M.

Dufrenne, M. *The Phenomenology of Aesthetic Experience,* 465, 468

Duke, J., tr. *See* Schleiermacher, F., *Hermeneutics.*

Dummett, M. A. E. *Elements of Intuitionism,* 335, 337; *Frege,* 132, 134; *Truth and Other Enigmas,* 167, 169, 324, 325

Dunlop, C. E. M., ed. *Philosophical Essays on Dreaming,* 367, 369

Dunn, J. *The Political Thought of John Locke,* 95

Düring, I. and G. E. L. Owen, eds. *Aristotle and Plato in the Mid-Fourth Century,* 37, 45

Dworkin, R. *Taking Rights Seriously,* 400, 422, 448, 455, 457

Dykhuizen, G. *The Life and Mind of John Dewey,* 244, 245

Eames, E. R. *Bertrand Russell's Theory of Knowledge,* 180, 181

Eames, S. M. *Pragmatic Naturalism,* 233, 234

Earle, W., ed. "The Philosophy of Mysticism," 479, 481

Early German Philosophy, L. W. Beck, 98–99, 101

Early Greek Philosophy, J. Burnet, 12, 17

Earman, J., C. Glynmour and J. Stachel, eds. *Foundations of Space-Time Theories*, 421, 424

Edel, A. *Ethical Judgment*, 393, 406; *Method in Ethical Theory*, 392, 406; *Science, Ideology and Value*, 446, 448

Edmund Husserl's Theory of Meaning, J. N. Mohanty, 289, 291

Education and the Development of Reason, R. F. Dearden, P. H. Hirst and R. S. Peters, eds., 493, 498

Education and the Modern World, B. Russell, 178, 492, 500

Education at the Crossroads, J. Maritain, 492, 499

Education for Modern Man, S. Hook, 493, 499

Education in Ancient Rome, S. F. Bonner, 60, 67

Educational Judgments, J. F. Doyle, ed., 493, 496, 498

Educational Philosophy and Theory, C. Beck, 493, 498

The Educational Theory of Jean-Jacques Rousseau, W. Boyd, 111, 113

Edwards, P. "Atheism," etc., 473, 478, 480, 481

——, ed. *The Encyclopedia of Philosophy*, 158, 508

Ehrlich, L. H. *Karl Jaspers*, 273

Eight Philosophers of the Italian Renaissance, P. O. Kristeller, 70, 72

Eighteenth-Century British Logic and Rhetoric, W. S. Howell, 98, 102

Einstein, A. *See* Schilpp. P. A.

Elements of Intuitionism, M. E. Dummett, 335, 337

Elements of Logic, R. Whately, 238

Ellenburg, S. *Rousseau's Political Philosophy*, 112, 113

Elliston, F. A., ed. *See* Vetterling-Braggin, M.

——, and P. McCormick, eds. *Husserl: Expositions and Appraisals*, 290; *see also* McCormick, P.

Elrod, J. W. *Being and Existence in Kierkegaard's Pseudonymous Works*, 265, 266

Elton, W., ed. *Aesthetics and Language*, 463, 468

The Embodied Mind, G. N. A. Vesey, 363, 370

Embree, L. E., ed. *Life-World and Consciousness*, 286, 287; tr., *see* Gurwitsch, A., *Phenomenology*

The Emergence of Philosophy of Religion, J. Collins, 472–74, 480

The Emergence of Probability, I. Hacking, 76, 79

Emile, or On Education, J.-J. Rousseau, 111–12, 492, 499

Emmet, D. M. *The Moral Prism*, 393, 406; *The Nature of Metaphysical Thinking*, 354, 357, 358

Emotion, Thought and Therapy, J. Neu, 484, 488

The Emotive Theory of Ethics, J. O. Urmson, 392, 409

Empedocles' Cosmic Cycle, D. O'Brien, 14, 18

Empirical Knowledge, R. M. Chisholm and R. J. Swartz, eds., 320, 325

The Encyclopedia of Philosophy, P. Edwards, ed., 508

Engel, S. M. *Wittgenstein's Doctrine of the Tyranny of Language*, 207, 209

Engels, F. *The Condition of the Working Class in England*, 250; other works, 250–52

English, J., ed. *See* Vetterling-Braggin, M.

English Philosophy Since 1900, G. J. Warnock, 162, 163, 172

The English Utilitarians, L. Stephen, 145, 149

Enigmas of Agency, I. Thalberg, 374, 378

The Enlightenment, P. Gay, 97, 102

Ennis, R. H., ed. *See* Broudy, H. S.; Smith, B. O.

Enquiries, D. Hume, 107

Entailment, A. R. Anderson, N. D. Belnap, et al., 335, 336

The Enterprise of Knowledge, I. Levi, 383, 384

Epicurus, J. M. Rist, 48, 50

The Epistemology of G. E. Moore, E. D. Klemke, 187, 188

Equality, J. R. Pennock and J. W. Chapman, eds., 441, 450

Equality, Liberty and Perfectionism, V. Haksar, 444, 449

Erdmann, J. E. *History of Philosophy*, 8, 10

Ernst Cassirer, S. Itzkoff, 152, 155

Ericson, D. P. *See* Green, T. F.

Ermarth, M. *Wilhelm Dilthey*, 125, 134
Esposito, J. L. *Evolutionary Metaphysics* (Peirce), 240, 241; *Schelling's Idealism and Philosophy of Nature*, 123, 134
An Essay on Human Understanding, J. Locke, 75, 85, 94–95
Essay on Man, E. Cassirer, 466, 468
An Essay on Metaphysics, R. G. Collingwood, 353–54, 358, 419
Essay on Philosophical Method, R. G. Collingwood, 22, 32, 188, 196, 197
An Essay Towards a New Theory of Vision, G. Berkeley, 103
Essays in Analysis, B. Russell, 180, 181
Essays in Conceptual Analysis, A. Flew, ed., 169, 342, 345
Essays in Experimental Logic, J. Dewey, 330
Essays in Hegelian Dialectic, Q. Lauer, 140, 142
Essays in Honor of Carl G. Hempel, N. Rescher, ed., 415, 426
Essays in Honour of Jaakko Hintikka, E. Saarinen, et al., eds., 154, 156
Essays in Legal Philosophy, R. S. Summers, ed., 454, 459
Essays in Memory of Imre Lakatos, R. S. Cohen, P. K. Feyerabend and M. W. Wartofsky, eds., 413, 424
Essays in Philosophical Psychology, D. F. Gustafson, ed., 364, 369
Essays in Philosophy and Its History, W. Sellars, 227, 230
Essays in Self-Criticism, L. Althusser, 259, 260
Essays in the Philosophy of Art, R. G. Collingwood, 196, 197
Essays in the Philosophy of History, R. G. Collingwood, 196, 197
Essays in the Philosophy of Religion, H. H. Price, 479, 482
Essays on Actions and Events, D. Davidson, 375, 377
Essays on Aristotle's Ethics, A. O. Rorty, ed., 37, 44, 46
Essays on Bertrand Russell, E. D. Klemke, ed., 180, 181
Essays on Cellular Automata, A. W. Burks, ed., 335, 336
Essays on Explanation and Understanding, J. Manninen and R. Ruomela, 308, 310
Essays on Form and Interpretation, N. Chomsky, 342, 343, 345
Essays on Freedom of Action, T. Honderich, ed., 376, 378
Essays on Frege, E. D. Klemke, ed., 132, 135
Essays on Historicism, L. Krieger, P. Rossi, J. Passmore and H. V. White, 429, 430, 434
Essays on Individuality, F. Morley, ed., 367, 370
Essays on Islamic Philosophy and Science, G. F. Hourani, ed., 57, 68
Essays on Knowledge and Justification, G. S. Pappas and M. Swain, eds., 318, 320, 326
Essays on the Philosophy of Leibniz, M. Kulstad, ed., 90, 91
Essays on the Philosophy of W. V. Quine, R. Shahan and C. Swoyer, eds., 228, 230
Essays on Wittgenstein, I. M. Copi and R. W. Beard, eds., 207, 209
Essays on Wittgenstein, E. D. Klemke, ed., 209, 210
Essays on Wittgenstein in Honour of G. H. von Wright, J. Hintikka, ed., 209
Essential Articles for the Study of Francis Bacon, B. Vickers, 77, 79
The Essential Tension, T. S. Kuhn, 412, 425
Ethica, B. Spinoza, 86
The Ethical Foundations of Marxism, E. Kamenka, 253, 255, 256
Ethical Issues in Goverment, N. E. Bowie, ed., 446, 448
Ethical Judgment, A. Edel, 393, 406
Ethical Relativism, J. Ladd, ed., 398, 408
Ethical Theory, R. B. Brandt, 389, 394, 397, 406
"Ethical Theory," W. K. Frankena, 388, 389, 406
The Ethical Theory of Clarence Irving Lewis, J. R. Saydah, 226, 230
Ethics, W. K. Frankena, 389, 406
Ethics, J. L. Mackie, 393, 408
Ethics, G. E. Moore, 186–87, 408
Ethics, P. H. Nowell-Smith, 392, 408
Ethics and Education, R. S. Peters, 496, 499
Ethics and Language, C. L. Stevenson, 389, 392, 409
Ethics and Society, R. T. De George, ed., 440, 448
Ethics and the Problems of the 21st Cen-

tury, K. E. Goodpaster and K. M. Sayre, eds., 405, 407

Ethics Since 1900, M. Warnock, 388, 409

The European Mind, 1680–1715, P. Hazard, 74, 79

European Positivism in the Nineteenth Century, W. M. Simon, 128, 135

Evans, J. D. G. *Aristotle's Concept of Dialectic*, 38, 39, 45

Evil and the Concept of God, E. H. Madden and P. H. Hare, 478, 481

Evil and the God of Love, J. Hick, 478, 481

Evolution and the Founders of Pragmatism, P. P. Wiener, 220

Evolutionary Metaphysics (Peirce), J. L. Esposito, 240, 241

Ewing, A. C. *Idealism*, 146, 148

———, ed. *The Idealist Tradition from Berkeley to Blanshard*, 146, 148

An Examination of Logical Positivism, J. R. Weinberg, 220

An Examination of Plato's Doctrine, I. M. Crombie, 30, 32

Exegesis and Argument (Vlastos Festschrift), E. Lee, A. P. D. Mourelatos and R. Rorty, eds., 14, 18

Existence and Logic, M. K. Munitz, 332, 337

The Existence of God, J. Hick, ed., 477, 481

The Existence of God, R. G. Swinburne, 478, 482

Existential Marxism in Postwar France, M. Poster, 258, 260, 261, 276, 292

Existential Philosophers, G. A. Schrader, ed., 264

Existentialism, M. Warnock, 263, 265

Existentialism and Education, G. F. Kneller, 493, 499

Existentialism and Phenomenology in Education, D. E. Denton, ed., 494, 498

The Existentialists, J. Collins, 263, 264

Experience and Conduct, S. Körner, 404, 408

Experience and Education, J. Dewey, 244, 495, 498

Experience and Ethics, D. H. Monro, 396, 408

Experience and God, J. E. Smith, 475, 482

Experience and Nature, J. Dewey, 244, 314, 349, 358

Explaining Emotions, A. O. Rorty, ed., 367, 370

Explaining, Understanding, and Teaching, J. R. Martin, 497, 499

Explanation, S. Körner, ed., 420, 425

Explanation and Human Action, A. R. Louch, 374, 378

Explanation and Understanding, G. H. von Wright, 374, 378, 420, 427

Explanation in the Behavioral Sciences, R. Borger and F. Cioffi, eds., 484, 488

The Explanation of Behavior, C. Taylor, 374, 378

The Explanation of Social Behavior, R. Harré and P. F. Secord, 446, 449

Explorations in Phenomenology, D. Carr and E. S. Casey, eds., 290

Expression and Meaning, J. R. Searle, 342, 347

Ey, H. *Consciousness*, 286, 287, 368

F. H. Bradley, R. Wollheim, 148, 149

Faber, E., ed. *See* Lakatos, I., *Proofs.*

Facets of Plato's Philosophy, W. H. Werkmeister, ed., 29, 30, 33

Fackenheim, E. L. *The Religious Dimension in Hegel's Thought*, 138, 141

Facts and Values, C. L. Stevenson, 387, 409

Facts, Values and Ethics, J. H. Olthuis, 381, 384, 388

Fain, H. *Between Philosophy and History*, 430, 434

Faith and Knowledge, J. Hick, 476

Faith and Logic, B. Mitchell, ed., 476, 482

Faith and Reason, R. G. Collingwood, 196, 197

Faith and Reason, R. G. Swinburne, 482

Faith and the Philosophers, J. Hick, ed., 477, 481

The Faith of Reason (18th c.), C. Frankel, 98, 102

Falla, P. S., tr. *See* Kolakowski, L., *Main Currents.*

Fann, K. T., ed. *Symposium on J. L. Austin*, 169, 171

Farber, M. *The Foundation of Phenomenology* (Husserl), 289, 390; *see also* Riepe, D. (1973 Festschrift)

Feeling and Form, S. K. Langer, 466, 468

Feigl, H. "Philosophy of Science," 410, 424; *see also* Feyerabend, P. K. and G. Maxwell (1966 Festschrift)

———, and M. Brodbeck, eds. *Readings in the Philosophy of Science,* 415, 424

———, and G. Maxwell, eds. *Current Issues in the Philosophy of Science,* 413, 424; *Scientific Explanation, Space, and Time,* 413, 424

———, and M. Scriven, eds. *The Foundations of Science and the Concepts of Psychology and Psychoanalysis,* 485, 488

———, ———, and G. Maxwell, eds. *Concepts, Theories, and the Mind-Body Problem,* 362, 366, 369

Feinberg, J. *Doing and Deserving,* 404, 406; *Rights, Justice, and the Bounds of Liberty,* 442, 448; *Social Philosophy,* 442, 448

———, and H. Gross, eds. *Philosophy of Law,* 454, 459

Feldman, F. *Introductory Ethics,* 389, 406

Fell, J. P. *Heidegger and Sartre,* 283

The Fellowship of Being (Marcel), J. B. O'Malley, 274, 275

"Femininity," "Masculinity," and "Androgyny," M. Vetterling-Braggin, ed., 311, 312

Feminism and Philosophy, M. Vetterling-Braggin, F. A. Elliston and J. English, eds., 311, 312

Ferrater Mora, J. *Philosophy Today,* 158

Ferré, F. *Language, Logic and God,* 476, 481

Fetscher, I. *Marx and Marxism,* 253, 258, 260

Feuerbach, M. W. Wartofsky, 126, 135

Feyerabend, P. K. *Against Method,* 334, 412, 416, 424; *Science in a Free Society,* 412, 417, 424; *see also* Cohen, R. S.

———, and G. Maxwell, eds. *Mind, Matter and Method,* 364, 413, 424

Fichte, Marx and the German Philosophical Tradition, T. Rockmore, 123, 135

Fifty Years of Hume Scholarship, R. Hall, 108, 109

Fin-de-Siècle Vienna, C. E. Schorske, 204, 210

Finch, H. L. *Wittgenstein: The Early Philosophy,* 207, 209; *Wittgenstein: The Later Philosophy,* 208, 209

Findlay, J. N. *Hegel: A Re-examination,* 140, 141; *Meinong's Theory of Objects and Value,* 132, 134; *Plato,* 25, 28, 32; *Values and Intentions,* 366, 369

———, tr., *see* Husserl, E., *Logical Investigations*

Fingarette, H. *Self-Deception,* 367, 369, 486; *The Self in Transformation,* 486, 488

The Fire and the Sun (Plato), I. Murdoch, 31, 33, 460, 469

Fisch, M., et al. "British and American Realism, 1900–1930," 350, 358; "The Relevance of Charles Peirce," 241

Fishkin, J. *See* Laslett, P.

Fitzgerald, J. J. *Peirce's Theory of Signs,* 240, 241

Flew, A. *God and Philosophy,* 473, 474, 477, 481; *Hume's Philosophy of Belief,* 108, 109; *An Introduction to Western Philosophy,* 9, 10; *A Rational Animal and Other Philosophical Essays,* 363, 369

———, ed. *Essays in Conceptual Analysis,* 169, 342, 345; *Logic and Language,* 169, 342, 345

———, and A. MacIntyre, eds. *New Essays in Philosophical Psychology,* 476, 481

Flodstrom, J. H., tr. *See* Ey, H.

Fodor, J. A. *The Language of Thought,* 343, 345; *Psychological Explanation,* 484, 488; *Representations,* 365, 369

———, and J. J. Katz, eds. *The Structure of Language,* 341, 345

Fogelin, R. J. *Wittgenstein,* 208, 209

Føllesdal, D., ed. "The Philosophy of Husserl," 290; "Truth, Meaning, and Reference," 322, 325

Foot, P. *Virtues and Vices and Other Essays in Moral Philosophy,* 395, 403, 406

For Marx, L. Althusser, 253, 255

Forbes, G. *See* Peacocke, C. A. B.

Foresight and Understanding, S. Toulmin, 411

Formal and Transcendental Logic, E. Husserl, 288, 290

The Formal Mechanisms of Mind, S. N. Thomas, 366, 370

Formalism in Ethics and Non-Formal Ethics of Values, M. Scheler, 133, 391, 408

Formalization of Logic, R. Carnap, 340, 345

The Formative Years of R. G. Colling-wood, W. M. Johnston, 190, 198
Forms and Limits of Utilitarianism, D. Lyons, 394, 400, 408
Forrester, M. G. *Moral Language,* 389, 406
Forstman, J., tr. *See* Schleiermacher, F., *Hermeneutics.*
Fortenbaugh, W. W. *Aristotle on Emotion,* 43, 45
The Foundation and Structure of Sartrean Ethics, T. C. Anderson, 277
The Foundation of Phenomenology (Husserl), M. Faber, 289, 290
The Foundations of Aesthetics, S. Ossowski, 465, 469
The Foundations of Analytic Philosophy, P. A. French, T. E. Uehling, and H. K. Wettstein, eds., 154, 155
"Foundations of Democracy," C. Cohen, et al., 443, 448
Foundations of Historical Knowledge, M. White, 431, 435
The Foundations of Modern Political Thought, Q. Skinner, 438, 451
Foundations of Philosophy (series), 514
The Foundations of Science and the Concepts of Psychology and Psychoanalysis, H. Feigl and M. Scriven, eds., 485, 488
The Foundations of Scientific Inference, W. C. Salmon, 421, 426
Foundations of Space-Time Theories, J. Earman, C. Glynmour, and J. Stachel, eds., 421, 424
Foundations of the Metaphysics of Morals, I. Kant, 114
The Foundations of Wittgenstein's Late Philosophy, E. K. Specht, 208, 210
Four Essays on Liberty, I. Berlin, 440, 444, 448
Four Pragmatists, I. Scheffler, 233, 234, 244
Fourfold Root of the Principle of Sufficient Reason, A. Schopenhauer, 127
Die Fragmente der Vorsokratiker, H. Diels and W. Krans, eds., 12, 17
Fralin, R. *Rousseau and Representation,* 112, 113
Francis Bacon: Discovery and the Art of Discourse, L. Jardine, 78, 79
Franciscan Philosophy at Oxford in the Thirteenth Century, D. E. Sharp, 63, 69

Frankel, C. *The Faith of Reason* (18th c.), 98, 102
Frankena, W. K. "Ethical Theory," 388, 389, 406; *Ethics,* 389, 406; *Philosophy of Education,* 493, 494, 498; *Thinking About Morality,* 395–96, 406; *Three Historical Philosophies of Education,* 244, 492, 498; *see also* Goldman, A. and J. Kim (1978 Festschrift); Goodpaster, K., *Perspectives;* Temkin, O.
———, et al. "Philosophy of Education," 492, 499; "Virtue and Moral Goodness," 403, 407
———, ed. *The Philosophy and Future of Graduate Education,* 497, 499; "The Philosophy of Moral Education," 496, 499
———, and J. T. Granrose, eds. *Introductory Readings in Ethics,* 390, 407
Frankfurt, H. G., ed. *Leibniz,* 89, 90
Fraser, R. *The Language of Adam,* 78, 79, 111
Free Action, A. I. Melden, 362, 376, 378
Free Will, D. J. O'Connor, 376, 378
Free Will, J. Thorp, 376, 378
Free Will and Determinism, B. Berofsky, ed., 376, 377
Freedman, M., ed. *See* Schilpp, P. A., *Philosophy of Martin Buber.*
Freedom and Determinism, K. Lehrer, ed., 376, 378
Freedom and History, H. D. Lewis, 168, 171
Freedom and Independence, J. N. Shklar, 139, 142
Freedom and Nature, P. Ricoeur, 376, 378
Freedom and Reason, R. M. Hare, 392, 407
Freedom and Resentment and Other Essays, P. F. Strawson, 154, 156
Freedom and Rights, A. J. M. Milne, 401, 408
Freedom of Mind and Other Essays, S. Hampshire, 376, 378
Freedom of the Individual, S. Hampshire, 376, 378
Freeman, E., ed. *The Abdication of Philosophy* (Schilpp), 223, 229; *see also* Reese, W. L., *Process*
———, and M. Mandelbaum, eds. *Spinoza,* 87, 88
Freeman, K. *Ancilla to the Pre-Socratic*

Philosophers (tr. Diels fragments), 12, 17; *The Pre-Socratic Philosophers: A Companion to Diels*, 12, 17

Freewill and Responsibility, A. Kenny, 373, 376, 378

Frege, G. *The Basic Laws of Arithmetic*, 330, 337

Frege, M. A. E. Dummett, 132, 134

Frege's Theory of Judgement, D. Bell, 133, 134

French, P. A. *The Scope of Morality*, 395, 407

————, T. E. Uehling and H. K. Wettstein, eds. *Contemporary Perspectives in the Philosophy of Language*, 341, 345; *The Foundations of Analytic Philosophy*, 154, 155; *Midwest Studies in Philosophy* (series), 514; *Social and Political Philosophy*, 443, 448; *Studies in Epistemology*, 318, 320, 321, 325; *Studies in Ethical Theory*, 390, 399, 401, 407; *Studies in Metaphysics*, 354, 358

Freud, S. *Interpretation of Dreams*, 483

Freud, R. Wollheim, ed., 486, 489

Freud and Philosophy, P. Ricoeur, 398, 486, 488

Friedrich, C. J. *The Philosophy of Law in Historical Perspective*, 454, 459

————, and J. W. Chapman, eds. *Justice*, 440, 448

Friedrich Nietzsche, F. C. Copleston, 269, 270

Friedrich Nietzsche and the Politics of Transfiguration, T. B. Strong, 269, 270

Friendship, Altruism, and Morality, L. A. Blum, 402, 406

Frings, M. S. *Max Scheler*, 134

————, ed., *Max Scheler (1874–1928)*, 134

————, tr., *see* Scheler, M.

Frisby, D., tr. *See* Apel, K.-O., *Towards*.

From a Logical Point of View, W. V. O. Quine, 334, 338, 352

From Affluence to Praxis, M. Markovic, 260, 261

From Belief to Understanding, R. Campbell, 478, 480

From Descartes to Hume, L. E. Loeb, 101, 102

"From Form to Function: Philosophy and History of Science in the 1950s and Now," S. Toulmin, 415, 422, 427

From Hegel to Marx, S. Hook, 252, 256

From Hegel to Nietzsche, K. Löwith, 124, 135

From Mathematics to Philosophy, H. Wang, 329, 338

From Platonism to Neoplatonism, P. Merlan, 48, 49

From Religion to Philosophy, F. M. Cornford, 11, 17

From the Many to the One, A. W. H. Adkins, 30, 31

Fuller, L. *The Morality of Law*, 456, 457, 459

Fundamentals of Concept Formation in Empirical Science, C. G. Hempel, 415, 421, 425

Fundamentals of Symbolic Logic, A. Ambrose and M. Lazerowitz, 330, 336

Funk, R. L., tr. *See* Scheler, M., *Formalism.*

Furley, D. J. *Two Studies in the Greek Atomists*, 14, 17

————, and R. E. Allen, eds. *Studies in Presocratic Philosophy* (v. 1), 12, 14, 17; *see also* Allen, R. E., *Studies* (v. 2).

Furth, M., tr. and ed. *See* Frege G.

The Future of Metaphysics, R. E. Wood, ed., 357, 360

G. E. Moore, A. Ambrose and M. Lazerowitz, eds., 187, 188

G. W. F. Hegel, S. Rosen, 141, 142

Gadamer, H.-G. *Dialogue and Dialectic* (Plato), 31, 32; *Hegel's Dialectic*, 140, 141; *Philosophical Hermeneutics*, 298, 300; *Truth and Method*, 298, 301

Galileo, D. Shapere, 414, 426

Gallagher, K. T. *The Philosophy of Gabriel Marcel*, 274, 275

Gallie, W. B. *Peirce and Pragmatism*, 240, 241; *Philosophy and the Historical Understanding*, 433, 434

Galston, W. A. *Kant and the Problem of History*, 118, 121

Garaudy, R. *Marxism in the Twentieth Century*, 253, 259, 260

Gardiner, P. *The Nature of Historical Explanation*, 433, 434; *Schopenhauer*, 126–27, 134

————, ed. *Theories of History*, 430–31, 434

Garforth, F. W. *John Stuart Mill's Theory of Education*, 145, 148

Gaskin, J. C. A. *Hume's Philosophy of Religion*, 108, 109

Gay, P. *The Enlightenment,* 97, 102

Geach, P. T. *Logic Matters,* 330, 334, 337; *Mental Acts,* 364, 369; *Providence and Evil,* 474, 481; *Reference and Generality,* 331, 337; *Truth, Love, and Immortality* (McTaggart), 148; *The Virtues,* 402, 407; *see also* Prior, A. N.

Gellner, E. *Words and Things* (Linguistic Philosophy), 170, 171

Generalization in Ethics, M. G. Singer, 394

Genesis and Structure of Hegel's Phenomenology of Spirit, J. Hyppolite, 138, 141

Georg Lukács, G. H. R. Parkinson, 257, 261

George Herbert Mead, D. L. Miller, 246, 247

Geuss, R. *The Idea of a Critical Theory,* 300, 301

Gewirth, A. *Reason and Morality,* 393, 401, 407; *see also* Frankena, W. K., *Thinking*

Giambattista Vico, G. Tagliacozzo and H. V. White, eds., 100, 102

Gibson, W. R. B., tr. *See* Husserl, E., *Ideas.*

Gilbert, N. W. *Renaissance Concepts of Method,* 71, 72

Gillian G., ed. *The Horizons of the Flesh* (Merleau-Ponty), 292, 293

Gilson, E. *The Christian Philosophy of Saint Augustine,* 56, 67; *The Christian Philosophy of Saint Thomas Aquinas,* 65, 67; *History of Philosophy in the Middle Ages,* 51, 67; *see also* Maurer, A. A.

Ginet, C. *Knowledge, Perception and Memory,* 317, 325

Glover, J. *Causing Death and Saving Lives,* 405, 407

Glymour, C., ed. *See* Earman, J.

God and Other Minds, A. Plantinga, 477, 482

God and Philosophy, A. Flew, 473, 474, 477, 481

God and Timelessness, N. Pike, 479, 482

God, Freedom, and Evil, A. Plantinga, 473, 479, 482

The God of the Philosophers, A. Kenny, 474, 479, 481

Goheen, J. D., ed. *See* Lewis, C. I., *Collected Papers.*

Golding, M. P. *Philosophy of Law,* 454, 459

Goldman, A. I. *A Theory of Human Action,* 374, 377

———, and J. Kim, eds. *Values and Morals,* 390, 399, 407

Goldmann, L. *Immanuel Kant,* 120, 258, 260

Goldstein, L. J. *Historical Knowing,* 431, 434

Goodman, N. *Languages of Art,* 467, 468; *The Structure of Appearance,* 352, 358; *Ways of Worldmaking,* 352, 358

Goodpaster, K. E., ed. *Perspectives on Morality* (Frankena essays), 387, 389, 407

———, and K. M. Sayre, eds. *Ethics and the Problems of the 21st Century,* 405, 407

Gordon, P. and J. White. *Philosophers as Educational Reformers* (British Idealism), 147, 148, 439

Gosling, J. C. B. *Plato,* 30, 32; *Pleasure and Desire,* 394, 407

———, ed. *Plato's Philebus,* 30, 32

Gould, C. *Marx's Social Ontology,* 251, 253–56; *see also* Wartofsky, M.

Gould, J. *The Development of Plato's Ethics,* 31, 32

Gould, J. A. and I. M. Copi, eds. *Contemporary Philosophical Logic,* 330, 337

Graham, K. *J. L. Austin,* 170, 171

Grammar in Philosophy, B. Rundle, 341, 346

The Grammar of Justification (Wittgenstein), J. T. E. Richardson, 207, 210

Granrose, J. T., ed. *See* Frankena, W. K., *Introductory Readings.*

Grayeff, F. *Aristotle and His School,* 35, 45

The Great Chain of Being, A. O. Lovejoy, 5, 7

Great Treasury of Western Thought, M. Adler and C. Van Doren, eds., 508

Greek into Arabic, R. Walzer, 57, 69

Greek Philosophical Terms, F. E. Peters, 510

Greek Political Theory, E. Barker, 30, 32

Greek Popular Morality in the Time of Plato and Aristotle, K. T. Dover, 30, 32

Greek Skepticism, C. L. Stough, 48, 50

The Greeks and the Irrational, E. R. Dodds, 12, 17

Green, R. M. *Religious Reason,* 479, 481

Green, T. F., D. P. Ericson and R. M. Seidman. *Predicting the Behavior of the Educational System,* 494, 499

Greene, Maxine. *Landscapes of Learning,* 494, 499

Greene, Murray. *Hegel on the Soul,* 140, 141

———, tr., *see* Marx, W.

Greene, T. M. *The Arts and the Art of Criticism,* 462, 468

Greene, W. C. *Moira,* 12, 17

Greenlee, D. *Peirce's Concept of Sign,* 240, 241

Greeno, J. G. *See* Salmon, W.

Greenstein, C. H. *Dictionary of Logical Terms and Symbols,* 333, 509

Grene, M. *The Knower and the Known,* 320, 325; *Philosophy In and Out of Europe,* 158; *Sartre,* 276, 277

———, ed. *Spinoza,* 87, 88

Grimm, Robert H., ed. *See* Care, N. S.

Grimm, Ruediger H. *Nietzsche's Theory of Knowledge,* 269, 270

Grimsley, R. *The Philosophy of Rousseau,* 111, 113

Gross, H. *A Theory of Criminal Law,* 458, 459; *see also* Feinberg, J., *Philosophy of Law*

Grossmann, R. *Meinong,* 132, 134; *Ontological Reduction,* 356, 358; *Reflections on Frege's Philosophy,* 132, 134

Groundless Belief, M. Williams, 317, 318, 323, 327

Growing Up With Philosophy, M. Lipman and A. M. Sharp, eds., 311

Growth in a Finite World, J. Grunfeld, ed., 447, 448

Grundrisse, K. Marx, 252

Grunfeld, J., ed. *Growth in a Finite World,* 447, 448

Guerry, H. *A Bibliography of Philosophical Bibliographies,* 504

A Guide to Philosophical Bibliography and Research, R. T. De George, 504

Guide to the Works of John Dewey, J. A. Boydston, 245

Gullace, G., tr. and ed. *See* Croce, B., *Poetry.*

Gulley, N. *Plato's Theory of Knowledge,* 31, 32

Gunderson, K., ed. *Language, Mind, and Knowledge,* 341, 345

Gurwitsch, A. *Phenomenology and the Theory of Science,* 286, 287; *see also* Embree, L. E. (1972 Festschrift)

Gustafson, D. F., ed. *Essays in Philosophical Psychology,* 364, 369

Gustafson, J. M. *Protestant and Roman Catholic Ethics,* 390, 407

Guthrie, W. K. C. *A History of Greek Philosophy,* 14, 17; *see also* Cornford, F. M., *Principium.*

Gutmann, J., tr. *See* Cassirer, E., *Rousseau.*

Guttenplan, S., ed. *Mind and Language,* 341, 345

Gutting, G., ed. *Paradigms and Revolutions,* 413, 424

Guttmann, J. *Philosophies of Judaism,* 57, 67

Guyer, P. *Kant and the Claims of Taste,* 461, 468

H. L. A. Hart, N. MacCormick, 453, 459

Haack, S. *Philosophy of Logics,* 330, 332, 334, 337

Habermas, J. *Knowledge and Human Interests,* 300, 301; *Theory and Practice,* 299, 301

Habermas: Critical Debates, J. B. Thompson and D. Held, eds., 300, 301

Hacker, P. M. S. *Insight and Illusion* (Wittgenstein), 207, 209; *see also* Baker, G. P.

———, and J. Raz, eds. *Law, Morality, and Society,* 454, 459

Hacking, I. *The Emergence of Probability,* 76, 79; *Why Does Language Matter to Philosophy?* 341, 345

Hague, R., tr. *See* Garaudy, R.; Marcel, G., *Mystery.*

Hahm, D. E. *The Origins of Stoic Cosmology,* 48, 49

Haksar, V. *Equality, Liberty and Perfectionism,* 444, 449

Hall, J. C. *Rousseau,* 112, 113

Hall, R. *Fifty Years of Hume Scholarship,* 108, 109

Hallett, G. *A Companion to Wittgenstein's Philosophical Investigations,* 208, 209

Halliday, R. J. *John Stuart Mill,* 145, 148

Hamann, J. G. *Socratic Memorabilia,* 100

Hamlyn, D. W. *Schopenhauer,* 126–27, 135; *Sensation and Perception,* 320, 325

Hampshire, S. *Freedom of the Individual,* 376, 378; *Freedom of Mind and Other Essays,* 376, 378; *Spinoza,* 87, 88; *Thought and Action,* 373, 378; *Two Theories of Morality,* 397, 407

———, et al. *Public and Private Morality,* 438, 441, 449

Handbook of World Philosophy, J. R. Burr, 158, 511

Hanly, C. and M. Lazerowitz, eds. *Psychoanalysis and Philosophy,* 485, 486, 488

Hanson, N. R. *Patterns of Discovery,* 411, 414, 424

Harari, M., tr. *See* Marcel, G., *Philosophy.*

Harbison, E. H. *The Christian Scholar in the Age of the Reformation,* 70, 72

Hare, P. H. *See* Madden, E. H., *Evil.*

Hare, R. M. *Freedom and Reason,* 392, 407; *The Language of Morals,* 389, 392, 407; *Moral Thinking,* 392, 407

Harman, G. *The Nature of Morality,* 389, 407; *Thought,* 318, 325; *see also* Davidson, D., *Semantics*

Harnish, R. *See* Bach, K.

The Harper Dictionary of Modern Thought, A. Bullock and O. Stallybrass, eds., 509

Harré, R. *The Principles of Scientific Thinking,* 418, 424; *see also* Waismann, F., *How I See Philosophy* and *Principles*

———, and E. H. Madden, *Causal Powers,* 419, 424

———, and P. E. Secord. *The Explanation of Social Behavior,* 446, 449

Harris, H. S. *Hegel's Development Toward the Sunlight (1770–1801),* 138, 141

Harris, R. B., ed. *The Significance of Neoplatonism,* 48, 49

Harrison, B. *An Introduction to the Philosophy of Language,* 341, 345; *Meaning and Structure,* 343, 345

Harrison, J. *Hume's Moral Epistemology,* 108, 109

Hart, H. L. A. *The Concept of Law,* 453, 457, 459; *Law, Liberty and Morality,* 457; *The Morality of the Criminal Law,* 457; *Punishment and Responsibility,* 458, 459; *see also* Hacker, P. M. S. (1977 Festschrift)

———, and A. M. Honoré. *Causation in the Law,* 453, 459

Hartman, D. *Maimonides,* 58, 68

Hartman, E. *Substance, Body and Soul* (Aristotle), 42, 45

Hartman, R. S. *The Structure of Value,* 382, 383

Hartmann, K. *Sartre's Ontology,* 276, 277

Hartshorne, C. *The Divine Relativity,* 473, 475, 481; *Whitehead's Philosophy,* 214; *see also* Peirce, C. S.; Reese, W. L. and E. Freeman (1964 Festschrift); Rome, S.

———, et al. "The Philosophic Proofs for God's Existence," 478, 481

Harvard Univ. Library. *Widener Library Shelflist,* v. 42–43: *Philosophy and Psychology,* 504

Has History Any Meaning? (Popper), B. T. Wilkins, 202, 203

Haslett, D. W. *Moral Rightness,* 387, 407

Having Children, O. O'Neill and W. Ruddick, eds., 447, 450

Hawkins, D. *The Language of Nature,* 418, 424

Hayek, F. A. *The Constitution of Liberty,* 440, 444, 449

Hazard, P. *The European Mind, 1680–1715,* 74, 79

The Hebrew Humanism of Martin Buber, G. Schaeder, 271, 272

Heckman, J., tr. *See* Hyppolite, J., *Genesis.*

The Hedgehog and the Fox, I. Berlin, 428, 433

Hegel, G. W. F. *The Phenomenology of Mind,* 136–39, 259

Hegel, W. A. Kaufmann, 138, 139, 141, 142

Hegel, A. MacIntyre, ed., 141, 142

Hegel, C. Taylor, 141, 142

Hegel: A Re-examination, J. N. Findlay, 140, 141

Hegel and After, R. Schacht, 125, 135

Hegel and the History of Philosophy, J. J. O'Malley, K. W. Algozin and F. G. Weiss, eds., 141, 142

Hegel Bibliography, K. Steinhauer, ed., 141, 142

Hegel on the Soul, M. Greene, 140, 141

Hegelian Ethics, W. H. Walsh, 140, 142

Hegelianism, J. E. Toews, 126, 135
Hegel's Development Toward the Sunlight (1770–1801), H. S. Harris, 138, 141
Hegel's Dialectic, H.-G. Gadamer, 140, 141
Hegel's Philosophy of History, B. T. Wilkins, 140, 142
Hegel's Political Philosophy, Z. A. Pelczynski, ed., 139, 142
Hegel's Retreat from Eleusis, G. A. Kelly, 139, 142
Hegel's Social and Political Thought, D. P. Verene, ed., 139, 142
Heidegger, M. *Being and Time,* 278, 281, 283; *Nietzsche,* 268, 270; other works, 281
Heidegger, W. J. Richardson, 283, 284
Heidegger and Jaspers on Nietzsche, R. L. Howey, 269, 270
Heidegger and Modern Philosophy, M. Murray, ed., 283, 284
Heidegger and Ontological Difference, L. M. Vail, 283, 284
Heidegger and Sartre, J. P. Fell, 283
Heidegger and the Path of Thinking, J. Sallis, ed., 283, 284
Heidegger and the Tradition, W. Marx, 283, 284
Heimbeck, R. S. *Theology and Meaning,* 475, 481
Held, D. *Introduction to Critical Theory,* 299, 301; *see also* Thompson, J. B.
Hellenistic Philosophy, A. A. Long, 48, 49
Heller, A. *Renaissance Man,* 71, 72
Helton, T., ed. *See* Kristeller, P. O., *Renaissance Thought and Its Sources.*
Hempel, C. G. *Aspects of Scientific Explanation,* 415, 418, 420, 425; *Fundamentals of Concept Formation in Empirical Science,* 415, 421, 425; *Philosophy of Natural Science,* 417, 425; *see also* Rescher, N., ed. (1969 Festschrift)
Hendel, C. W. *Studies in the Philosophy of David Hume,* 107, 109
———, tr., *see* Cassirer, E., *Problem*
Henle, P., ed. *Language, Thought and Culture,* 340, 346
Henry, D. P. *Medieval Logic and Metaphysics,* 51, 68
Henry, N. B., ed. *Modern Philosophies and Education,* 492, 499; *Philosophies of Education,* 492, 499

Henze, D., et al. "Philosophy as Style and Literature as Philosophy," 309, 310
Heraclitus, G. S. Kirk, 14, 18
Herbert, R. T. *Paradox and Identity in Theology,* 479, 481
Hermeneutic Phenomenology (Ricoeur), D. Ihde, 298, 301
Hermeneutics, R. E. Palmer, 5, 297, 301
Hermeneutics, F. D. E. Schleiermacher, 295, 301
Hesse, M. *Revolutions and Reconstruction in the Philosophy of Science,* 418, 425; *The Structure of Scientific Inference,* 421, 425
Hessing, S., ed. *Speculum Spinozanum, 1677–1977,* 87, 88
Hick, J. *Death and Eternal Life,* 479, 481; *Evil and the God of Love,* 478, 481; *Faith and Knowledge,* 476; *Philosophy of Religion,* 473, 474, 477, 481
———, ed. *The Existence of God,* 477, 481; *Faith and the Philosophers,* 477, 481
Hierarchical Structures, L. L. Whyte, A. B. Wilson and D. Wilson, eds., 383, 384
Highet, G., tr. *See* Jaeger, W., *Paideia.*
Himmelfarb, G. *On Liberty and Liberalism* (Mill), 145, 148
Hinnant, C. H. *Thomas Hobbes,* 93; *Thomas Hobbes: A Reference Guide,* 93
Hintikka, J. *The Intentions of Intentionality and Other New Models for Modalities,* 333, 337; *Knowledge and Belief,* 322, 325; *Time and Necessity* (Aristotle), 41, 44, 45
———, ed. *Essays on Wittgenstein in Honour of G. H. von Wright,* 209; *see also* Butts, R. E.; Davidson, D., *Words;* Saarinen, E. (1979 Festschrift)
———, and U. Remes. *The Method of Analysis,* 420, 425
———, and P. Suppes, eds. *Information and Inference,* 421, 425
Hirsch, E. *The Concept of Identity,* 356, 358
Hirst, P. H. *Knowledge and the Curriculum,* 494, 499; *see also* Dearden, R. F.
———, and R. S. Peters. *The Logic of Education,* 492, 493, 499
Historical and Philosophical Perspectives of Science, R. H. Stuewer, ed., 414, 427

The Historical Constitution of St. Bona-venture's Philosophy, J. F. Quinn, 65, 69

Historical Explanation, R. Martin, 432, 434

Historical Inevitability, I. Berlin, 433

Historical Knowing, L. J. Goldstein, 431, 434

Historical Understanding in the Thought of Wilhelm Dilthey, T. Plantinga, 297, 301

"Historicism and Epistemology," R. Rorty, ed., 430, 431, 434

The Historiography of the History of Philosophy, J. A. Passmore, ed., 4, 6, 7

History and Class Consciousness (Marxism), G. Lukács, 253, 257–58, 261

History and Human Existence (Marxism), J. Miller, 258, 261

History and Truth in Hegel's Phenomenology, M. Westphal, 139, 142

History as a Science (Collingwood), W. J. Van Der Dussen, 197, 198

History, Man, and Reason (19th c.), M. Mandelbaum, 125, 135

A History of Aesthetic, B. Bosanquet, 460, 467

History of Aesthetics, W. Tatarkiewicz, 460, 469

A History of American Philosophy, H. W. Schneider, 217, 218, 230

History of Christian Philosophy in the Middle Ages, E. Gilson, 51, 67

A History of English Philosophy to 1900, W. R. Sorley, 143, 149

History of English Thought in the Eighteenth Century, L. Stephen, 98, 102

"History of Ethics," R. Abelson and K. Nielsen, 388, 405

History of Ethics, V. J. Bourke, 388, 406

A History of European Liberalism, G. Ruggiero, 193

A History of Greek Philosophy, W. K. C. Guthrie, 14, 17

The History of Ideas: A Bibliographical Introduction, J. L. Tobey, 507

History of Modern Philosophy, H. Høffding, 160

A History of Philosophy, F. C. Copleston, 8, 10

History of Philosophy, J. E. Erdmann, 8, 10

A History of Philosophy, F. Thilly, 8, 10

A History of Philosophy, W. Windelband, 8, 10

A History of Political Theory, G. H. Sabine, 437, 438, 450

The History of Scepticism from Erasmus to Spinoza, R. H. Popkin, 72, 76, 220, 320

A History of Six Ideas (Aesthetics), W. Tatarkiewicz, 460, 469

A History of the Bibliography of Philosophy, M. Jasenas, 504

A History of Western Philosophy, W. T. Jones, 9, 10

A History of Western Philosophy, B. Russell, 8, 10, 178

Hobbes, T. *Leviathan,* 91, 437

Hobbes, R. S. Peters, 93

Hobbes and Rousseau, M. Cranston and R. S. Peters, eds., 93, 113

Hobbes on Civil Association, M. Oakeshott, 91–93

Hobbes Studies, K. C. Brown, ed., 92, 93

Hobbes's System of Ideas, J. W. N. Watkins, 92, 93

Hobhouse, L. T. *Liberalism,* 438, 449

Hochberg, H. I. *Thought, Fact, and Reference* (Logical Atomism), 154, 155

Hocking, W. E. *The Meaning of God in Human Experience,* 473, 475, 481

Høffding, H. *History of Modern Philosophy,* 160

Holdcroft, D. *Words and Deeds,* 342, 346

Hollinger, D. A. *Morris R. Cohen and the Scientific Ideal,* 226, 229

Holton, G. *Thematic Origins of Scientific Thought,* 414, 425

Honderich, T. *Political Violence,* 441, 449

———, ed. *Essays on Freedom of Action,* 376, 378; *Social Ends and Political Means,* 442, 449

———, and M. Burnyeat, eds. *Philosophy as It Is,* 156, 158

Honoré, A. M. *See* Hart, H. L. A., *Causation.*

Hook, S. *Education for Modern Man,* 493, 499; *From Hegel to Marx,* 252, 256; *John Dewey,* 245; *Philosophy and Public Policy,* 437, 449

———, ed. *American Philosophers at Work,* 222, 229; *Determinism and Freedom in the Age of Modern Science,* 376, 378; *Human Values and Economic Policy,* 382–83; *Language and*

Philosophy, 341, 346; *Philosophy and History,* 431, 434; *Psychoanalysis, Scientific Method, and Philosophy,* 486, 488; *see also* Kallen, H. M.

Hooker, M., ed. *Descartes,* 81–83; *Leibniz,* 90

Hookway, C. and P. Pettit, eds. *Action and Interpretation,* 445, 449

The Horizons of the Flesh (Merleau-Ponty), G. Gilliam, ed., 292, 293

Hornsby, J. *Actions,* 375, 378

Horstmann, R. P., ed. See Bieri, P.

Hospers, J. *Human Conduct,* 389, 407; *Meaning and Truth in the Arts,* 462, 468

Hostler, J. *Leibniz's Moral Philosophy,* 90

Hourani, A., ed. See Stern, S. M.

Hourani, G. F., ed. *Essays on Islamic Philosophy and Science,* 57, 68

How I See Philosophy, F. Waismann, 341, 347

How Philosophy Uses Its Past, J. H. Randall, 5, 7

How to Do Things with Words, J. L. Austin, 168, 342, 344

How to Find Out in Philosophy and Psychology, D. H. Borchardt, 503

How to Read a Book, M. J. Adler, 375

How We Think, J. Dewey, 495, 498

Howard, R. J. *Three Faces of Hermeneutics,* 298, 301

Howell, W. S. *Eighteenth-Century British Logic and Rhetoric,* 98, 102; *Logic and Rhetoric in England, 1500–1700,* 77–79, 98

Howey, R. L. *Heidegger and Jaspers on Nietzsche,* 269, 270

Howie, J. and T. O. Buford, eds. *Contemporary Studies in Philosophical Idealism,* 225, 229

Hudson, W. D. *A Century of Moral Philosophy,* 388, 407; *Modern Moral Philosophy,* 388, 407

———, ed. *The Is-Ought Question,* 397, 407; *New Studies in Ethics,* 388, 407

Hull, D. L. *Philosophy of Biological Science,* 417, 425

Human Action, T. Mischel, ed., 484, 488

Human Action and Its Explanation, R. Tuomela, 373, 378

Human Acts, E. D'Arcy, 373, 377

Human Conduct, J. Hospers, 389, 407

Human Knowledge, B. Russell, 318, 326

Human Rights, E. Kamenka and E.-S. Tay, eds., 443, 449

"Human Rights," H. Morris, et al., 440, 449

Human Understanding, S. Toulmin, 421, 427

Human Values and Economic Policy, S. Hook, ed., 382–83

Hume, D. *Dialogues Concerning Natural Religion,* 107–8; *Enquiries,* 107; *A Treatise of Human Nature,* 107–8

Hume, V. C. Chappell, ed., 109

Hume, D. W. Livingston and J. T. King, eds., 109

Hume, T. Penelhum, 109, 110

Hume, B. Stroud, 108, 110

Hume and the Enlightenment, B. Todd, ed., 108, 110

Hume, Newton, and the Design Argument, R. H. Hurlbutt, 108, 109

Hume Studies, A. Meinong, 132

Hume's Intentions, J. A. Passmore, 108, 110

Hume's Moral Epistemology, J. Harrison, 108, 109

Hume's Philosophical Development, J. H. Noxon, 109, 110

Hume's Philosophy of Belief, A. Flew, 108, 109

Hume's Philosophy of Mind, J. Bricke, 108, 109

Hume's Philosophy of Religion, J. C. A. Gaskin, 108, 109

Humphreys, W. C. *Anomalies and Scientific Theories,* 420, 425

A Hundred Years of Philosophy, J. A. Passmore, 9, 10, 318

Hurlbutt, R. H. *Hume, Newton, and the Design Argument,* 108, 109

Husserl, E. *The Crisis of European Sciences and Transcendental Phenomenology,* 289, 290; *Formal and Transcendental Logic,* 288, 290; *Ideas,* 288, 290, 298; *Logical Investigations,* 280, 288, 290

Husserl and Frege, J. N. Mohanty, 133, 135

Husserl: Expositions and Appraisals, F. A. Elliston and P. McCormick, eds., 290

Husserl: Shorter Works, P. McCormick and F. A. Elliston, eds., 291

Husserlian Meditations, R. Sokolowski, 289, 291

Hyppolite, J. *Genesis and Structure of Hegel's Phenomenology of Spirit*, 138, 141; *Studies on Marx and Hegel*, 253, 256

I and Thou, M. Buber, 271, 272
The Idea of a Critical Theory, R. Geuss, 300, 301
The Idea of a Social Science and its Relation to Philosophy, P. Winch, 445, 451
The Idea of Freedom, M. J. Adler, 375, 377
The Idea of Freedom, A. Ryan, ed., 444, 450
The Idea of History, R. G. Collingwood, 353, 431, 433
The Idea of Justice and the Problem of Argument, Ch. Perelman, 440, 441, 444, 450
The Idea of Nature, R. G. Collingwood, 28, 32, 189, 353, 358
Idealism, A. C. Ewing, 146, 148
Idealist Epilogue, G. R. G. Mure, 146, 149
The Idealist Tradition from Berkeley to Blanshard, A. C. Ewing, ed., 146, 148
The Idealistic Argument in Recent British and American Philosophy, G. W. Cunningham, 220
Ideas, E. Husserl, 288, 290, 298
Ideas and Men, C. Brinton, 9, 10
The Identities of Persons, A. O. Rorty, ed., 367, 370
Identity and Essence, B. Brody, 356, 358
Idiot of the Family, J.-P. Sartre, 276
Ignorance: A Case for Scepticism, P. Unger, 316–17, 326
Ihde, D. *Hermeneutic Phenomenology* (Ricoeur), 298, 301
The Illusion of Technique, W. Barrett, 308, 310
Imagination, M. Warnock, 367, 370, 466, 469
Immanuel Kant, L. Goldmann, 120, 258, 260
The Imposition of Method (Descartes, Locke), P. A. Schouls, 75, 79, 82, 94
In Commemoration of William James, 1842–1942, 237
In Our Image and Likeness (Italian humanism), C. Trinkaus, 71, 73
In Pursuit of Truth (Popper Festschrift), P. Levinson, ed., 198, 203

In Pursuit of Wisdom, A. Kaplan, 156, 158, 354, 363
In the Interest of the Governed (Bentham), D. Lyons, 145, 149
In the Twilight of Christendom (Hegel, Kierkegaard), S. Crites, 138, 141
The Indian Mind, C. A. Moore, ed., 310, 312
The Individual and Society in the Middle Ages, W. Ullmann, 63, 65, 69
The Individual and the Cosmos in Renaissance Philosophy, E. Cassirer, 71, 72
Individuals, P. F. Strawson, 169, 356, 359
Indoctrination and Education, I. A. Snook, 497, 500
Induction, N. Rescher, 323, 326
Induction and Deduction (Wittgenstein), I. Dilman, 209
Induction and Justification, F. L. Will, 316, 322, 327
Induction, Probability and Confirmation, G. Maxwell and R. M. Anderson, eds., 420, 426
Infinity in the Presocratics, L. Sweeney, 13, 18
Information and Inference, J. Hintikka and P. Suppes, eds., 421, 425
Innate Ideas, S. P. Stich, ed., 318, 326
Inquiries into Medieval Philosophy, J. F. Ross, ed., 62, 69
Insight and Illusion (Wittgenstein), P. M. S. Hacker, 207, 209
Intellectual Experiments of the Greek Enlightenment, F. Solmsen, 13, 18
Intention, G. E. M. Anscombe, 362, 366, 368
Intention and Intentionality, C. Diamond and J. Teichman, eds., 367, 369
Intentionality, R. E. Aquila, 367, 368
The Intentions of Intentionality and Other New Models for Modalities, J. Hintikka, 333, 337
International Directory of Philosophy and Philosophers, R. Cormier, et al., 513
International Encyclopedia of Unified Science, O. Neurath, R. Carnap and C. Morris, eds., 415, 426
Interpretation of Dreams, S. Freud, 483
An Interpretation of Whitehead's Metaphysics, W. A. Christian, 214
Interpreting Modern Philosophy, J. Collins, 5, 6, 101

An Introduction to Augustine, R. E. Meagher, 56, 68

Introduction to Critical Theory, D. Held, 299, 301

Introduction to Logic and Scientific Method, M. R. Cohen and E. Nagel, 330, 337

Introduction to Logical Theory, P. F. Strawson, 332, 338

An Introduction to Reasoning, S. Toulmin, R. Rieke and Allan Janik, 331, 338, 404

Introduction to Semantics, R. Carnap, 340, 345

An Introduction to the Analysis of Educational Concepts, J. F. Soltis, 492, 500

An Introduction to the Philosophy of Education, D. J. O'Connor, 492, 499

An Introduction to the Philosophy of Language, B. Harrison, 341, 345

An Introduction to the Philosophy of Science, K. Lambert and G. G. Brittan, 417, 425

Introduction to the Philosophy of Science, A. Pap, 417, 426

Introduction to Value Theory, N. Rescher, 383, 384

An Introduction to Western Philosophy, A. Flew, 9, 10

An Introduction to Wittgenstein, G. E. M. Anscombe, 207, 209

Introductory Ethics, F. Feldman, 389, 406

Introductory Readings in Ethics, W. K. Frankena and J. T. Granrose, eds., 390, 407

Irrationalism (Existentialism), W. Barrett, 263, 264

Irwin, T. *Plato's Moral Theory*, 31, 32

The Is-Ought Question, W. D. Hudson, ed., 397, 407

Isenberg, A. *Aesthetics and the Theory of Criticism*, 463, 468; *see also* Dewey, J., *Theory of the Moral Life*

Ishiguro, H. *Leibniz's Philosophy of Logic and Language*, 90, 91

Islamic Philosophy and the Classical Tradition, S. M. Stern, A. Hourani and V. Brown, eds., 57, 69

Issues in Marxist Philosophy, J. Mepham and D.-H. Ruben, eds., 260, 261

Itzkoff, S. *Ernst Cassirer*, 152, 155

J. L. Austin, K. Graham, 170, 171

Jackson, T. A. *Dialectics* (Marxism), 255, 260

Jacobs, N. J., tr. *See* Schaeder, G.

Jaeger, W. *Aristotle*, 24, 25, 35, 36, 45; *Paideia*, 12, 13, 17, 491; *The Theology of the Early Greek Philosophers*, 12, 17

Jager, R. *The Development of Bertrand Russell's Philosophy*, 174, 180, 181

James, W. *Pragmatism*, 236; *The Principles of Psychology*, 235; *The Varieties of Religious Experience*, 236, 475; *The Works of William James*, 236, 237; other works, 236

James and Husserl, R. Stevens, 236, 237

James and John Stuart Mill, B. Mazlich, 145, 149

James and John Stuart Mill, J. M. Robson and M. Laine, eds., 145, 149

Janik, A. and S. Toulmin. *Wittgenstein's Vienna*, 131, 204, 207, 210; *see also* Toulmin, S., *An Introduction*

The Japanese Mind, C. A. Moore, ed., 310, 312

Jardine, L. *Francis Bacon: Discovery and the Art of Discourse*, 78, 79

Jasenas, M. *A History of the Bibliography of Philosophy*, 504

Jaspers, K. *Nietzsche*, 268, 270; *Philosophy*, 273; *Way to Wisdom*, 273, 274

Jaynes, J. *The Origin of Consciousness*, 11, 17

Jean-Paul Sartre, A. Danto, 276, 277

Jeanson, F. *Sartre and the Problem of Morality*, 277

Jeffrey, R. C. *See* Carnap, R., *Studies*; Salmon, W.

Jenkins, I. *Social Order and the Limits of Law*, 456–58, 459

Jeremy Bentham, B. Parekh, ed., 145, 149

Jessup, B. *See* Rader, M., *Art*.

Jewish Philosophers, S. T. Katz, ed., 474, 481

Jewish Philosophy in Modern Times, N. Rotenstreich, ed., 124, 135

Joachim, H. H. *Spinoza's Tractatus De Intellectus Emmendatione*, 86, 88; *A Study of the Ethics of Spinoza*, 86, 88

Joergensen, J. *The Development of Logical Empiricism*, 154, 155

Johann Georg Hamann, W. H. Alexander, 100, 101

Johann Georg Hamann, J. C. O'Flaherty, 100, 102

Johansson, I. *A Critique of Karl Popper's Methodology*, 202, 203

John Dewey, S. Hook, 245

John Dewey Reconsidered, R. S. Peters, ed., 495, 499

John Duns Scotus, 1265–1965, J. K. Ryan and B. M. Bonansea, eds., 66, 69

John Locke, R. I. Aaron, 95

John Locke, J. D. Mabbott, 95

John Locke, D. J. O'Connor, 94, 96

John Locke, J. W. Yolton, ed., 95, 96

John Stuart Mill, R. J. Halliday, 145, 148

John Stuart Mill, A. Ryan, 145, 149

John Stuart Mill and Representative Government, D. F. Thompson, 145, 149

John Stuart Mill's Theory of Education, F. W. Garforth, 145, 148

Johnson, O. A. *Skepticism and Cognitivism*, 317, 319, 325

Johnston, W. M. *The Formative Years of R. G. Collingwood*, 190, 198

Johnstone, H. W. *Validity and Rhetoric in Philosophical Argument*, 310

———, ed. *Categories*, 356, 358

Jones, H. and J. H. Muirhead. *The Life and Philosophy of Edward Caird*, 147, 149

Jones, O. R., ed. *The Private Language Argument*, 343, 346

Jones, W. T. *A History of Western Philosophy*, 9, 10

Josiah Royce, T. F. Powell, 224, 229

Journeys to Selfhood: Hegel and Kierkegaard, M. C. Taylor, 266, 267

Jurisprudence, R. Pound, 454, 456, 459

Justice, C. J. Friedrich and J. W. Chapman, eds., 440, 448

Justice and Social Policy, F. A. Olafson, ed., 440, 444, 450

The Justification of Religious Belief, B. Mitchell, 477, 482

Kadish, S. H. *See* Temkin, O.

Kahn, C. H. *Anaximander and the Origins of Greek Cosmology*, 14, 17

Kalish, D. and N. Kretzmann. "Semantics," 340, 346

Kallen, H. M. and S. Hook, eds. *American Philosophy, Today and Tomorrow*, 222, 229

Kamenka, E. *The Ethical Foundations of Marxism*, 253, 255, 256; *The Philosophy of Ludwig Feuerbach*, 126, 135; *see also* Passmore, J., *Historiography*

———, and Tay, E.-S., eds. *Human Rights*, 443, 449

Kant, I. *Critique of Judgment*, 114; *Critique of Practical Reason*, 113–14, 116; *Critique of Pure Reason*, 113, 115, 117, 119; *Foundations of the Metaphysics of Morals*, 114; *Prolegomena to Any Future Metaphysics*, 114; *Religion within the Limits of Reason Alone*, 114; other works, 117–18

Kant, R. C. S. Walker, 115, 122

Kant, W. H. Werkmeister, 120, 122

Kant, R. P. Wolff, ed., 121, 122

Kant and the Claims of Taste, P. Guyer, 461, 468

Kant and the Philosophy of History, Y. Yovel, 120, 122

Kant and the Problem of History, W. A. Galston, 118, 121

Kant as Philosophical Anthropologist, P. van de Pitte, 117, 121

The Kant-Eberhard Controversy, H. E. Allison, 116, 121

Kant on History and Religion, M. Despland, 118, 121

Kant Studies Today, L. W. Beck, ed., 120, 121

Kant's Aesthetic Theory, D. W. Crawford, 461, 468

Kant's Analytic, J. Bennett, 115, 121

Kant's Concept of Teleology, J. D. McFarland, 118, 121

Kant's Criticism of Metaphysics, W. H. Walsh, 115, 122

Kant's Critique of Pure Reason, T. E. Wilkerson, 115, 122

Kant's Dialectic, J. Bennett, 115, 121

Kant's Rational Theology, A. W. Wood, 118, 122

Kant's Theory of Morals, B. Aune, 116, 121

Kant's Transcendental Logic, T. K. Swing, 116, 121

Kaplan, A. *The Conduct of Inquiry*, 446, 449; *In Pursuit of Wisdom*, 156, 158, 354, 363; *The New World of Philosophy*, 156, 158

Karl Jaspers, L. H. Ehrlich, 273

Karl Jaspers, C. F. Wallraff, 273, 274

Karl Marx, A. W. Wood, 254–56

Karl Marx's Philosophy of Man, J. Plamenatz, 253, 256

Karl Marx's Theory of History, G. A.
Cohen, 254–56
Karl Popper, A. O'Hear, 202, 203
Kasparek, C., tr. *See* Tatarkiewicz, W., *A
History of Six Ideas.*
Katz, J. J. *Propositional Structure and Il-
locutionary Force,* 342, 346; *Semantic
Theory,* 343, 346; *see also* Fodor,
J. A., *Structure*
Katz, S. T., ed. *Jewish Philosophers,* 474,
481; *Mysticism and Philosophical
Analysis,* 479, 481
Kaufman, A. S. *The Radical Liberal,* 440,
444, 449
Kaufmann, W. A. *Discovering the Mind,*
5, 6; *Hegel,* 138, 139, 141, 142;
Nietzsche, 267, 270
———, tr., *see* Buber, M.; Nietzsche, F.,
Birth
Keat, R. *The Politics of Social Theory*
(Habermas), 300, 301
Keeling, S. V. *Descartes,* 81, 83
Kelly, E. *Max Scheler,* 134, 135
Kelly, G. A. *Hegel's Retreat from Eleusis,*
139, 142
Kelsen, H. *Pure Theory of Law,* 455,
459; *What Is Justice?* 455, 459
Kempson, R. M. *Presupposition and the
Delimitation of Semantics,* 343, 346
Kennedy, G. A. *Classical Rhetoric and Its
Christian and Secular Tradition from
Ancient to Modern Times,* 59, 68
Kenny, A. *Action, Emotion and Will,*
364, 369; *The Anatomy of the Soul,*
363, 369; *The Aristotelian Ethics,* 44,
45; *Aristotle's Theory of the Will,* 43,
46; *Descartes,* 81, 83; *Freewill and Responsibility,* 373, 376, 378; *The God
of the Philosophers,* 474, 479, 481;
Will, Freedom, and Power, 373, 376,
378; *Wittgenstein,* 208, 210
———, ed. *Aquinas,* 65, 68
———, et al. *The Nature of Mind,* 364,
369; *The Development of Mind,* 364,
369
Kenny, A. J. P., ed. *See* Prior, A. N.
Kersten, F. and R. M. Zaner, eds. *Phenomenology,* 287, 290
Keynes, J. M. *A Treatise on Probability,*
335, 337
Kiefer, F., ed. *See* Searle, J. R., *Speech
Act Theory.*
Kiefer, H. E., ed. *Perspectives in Education, Religion, and the Arts,* 463, 468

Kierkegaard, W. Lowrie, 265, 266
Kierkegaard, J. Thompson, ed., 266, 267
A Kierkegaard Anthology, R. Bretall,
265, 266
Kierkegaard as Educator, R. J. Man-
heimer, 266, 267
*The Kierkegaard Indices to Kierkegaard's
Samlede Vaerker,* A. McKinnon, 265,
266
Kierkegaard's Authorship, G. E. and
G. B. Arbaugh, 265, 266
Kierkegaard's Existential Ethics, G. J.
Stack, 266, 267
*Kierkegaard's Pseudonymous Author-
ship,* M. C. Taylor, 265, 267
Kierkegaard's Relation to Hegel, N.
Thulstrup, 266, 267
Kierkegaard's Thought, G. Malantschuk,
265, 266
Kim, J., ed. *See* Goldman, A., *Values.*
Kimmerle, H., ed. *See* Schleiermacher, F.,
Hermeneutics.
King, J. T., ed. *See* Livingston, D. W.
King-Farlow, J., ed. *See* Shiner, R. A.
Kirk, G. S. *Heraclitus,* 14, 18
———, and J. E. Raven. *The Presocratic
Philosophers,* 12, 17
Kisiel, T., tr. *See* Marx, W.
Klein, J. *Plato's Trilogy,* 31, 32
Klein, K. H. *Positivism and Christianity,*
154, 156
Klemke, E. D. *The Epistemology of G. E.
Moore,* 187, 188
———, ed. *Essays on Bertrand Russell,*
180, 181; *Essays on Frege,* 132, 135;
Essays on Wittgenstein, 209, 210;
*Studies in the Philosophy of G. E.
Moore,* 187, 188
Klibansky, R., ed. *Contemporary Phi-
losophy,* 159, 512; *Philosophy in the
Mid-Century,* 159, 512
———, and H. J. Paton, eds. *Philosophy
and History,* 4, 5, 7
Klubertanz, G. P. *St. Thomas on Anal-
ogy,* 65, 68
Kneale, W. *Probability and Induction,*
413, 420, 425
———, and M. Kneale. *The Development of Logic,* 329, 337
Kneller, G. F. *Existentialism and Education,* 493, 499
Knorr, K. D., H. Strasser and H. G. Zilian, eds. *Determinants and Controls of
Scientific Development,* 413, 425

The Knower and the Known, M. Grene, 320, 325
Knowledge, K. Lehrer, 317, 318, 323, 325
Knowledge and Belief, J. Hintikka, 322, 325
Knowledge and Certainty, N. Malcolm, 314, 316, 319, 326
Knowledge and Explanation in History, R. F. Atkinson, 431, 433
Knowledge and Human Interests, J. Habermas, 300, 301
Knowledge and Justification, J. Pollock, 316, 317, 326
Knowledge and Reality in Plato's Philebus, R. A. Shiner, 30, 33
Knowledge and the Curriculum, P. H. Hirst, 494, 499
Knowledge and the Sacred, S. H. Nasr, 474, 482
Knowledge, Mind and Nature, B. Aune, 318, 324, 364, 368
Knowledge, Perception and Memory, C. Ginet, 317, 325
Kockelmans, J. J., ed. *Contemporary European Ethics,* 389, 408; *On Heidegger and Language,* 283; *Phenomenology* (Husserl), 289, 291
Koelln, F. C. A., tr. *See* Cassirer, E., *Philosophy of the Enlightenment.*
Kohák, E. V., tr. *See* Ricoeur, P., *Freedom.*
Köhler, E., ed. *See* Leinfellner, W.
Kolakowski, L. *The Alienation of Reason* (Positivism), 128–30, 135; *Main Currents of Marxism,* 258, 260
Kolenda, K., ed. *Studies in Philosophy,* 169, 171; *see also* Ryle, G., *On Thinking*
Koren, H. J. *Research in Philosophy,* 505; *see also* Peursen, C. A. van, *Phenomenology and Reality.*
Körner, S. *Conceptual Thinking,* 331, 337; *Experience and Conduct,* 404, 408
———, ed. *Explanation,* 420, 425
Korsch, K. *Marxism and Philosophy,* 257–58, 260
Kovach, F. J. *Philosophy of Beauty,* 460, 468
———, and R. W. Shahan, eds. *Albert the Great,* 64, 68; *see also* Shahan, R. W.
Krans, W., ed. *See* Diels, H.

Kraus, E. M. *The Metaphysics of Experience* (Whitehead), 214
Krausz, M., ed. *Critical Essays on the Philosophy of R. G. Collingwood,* 190, 197, 198
———, and J. M. Meiland, eds. *Relativism,* 399, 408
Krell, D. F., ed. *Martin Heidegger,* 283, 284
———, tr., *see* Heidegger, M., *Nietzsche*
Kretzmann, N., ed. *The Cambridge History of Later Medieval Philosophy,* 52, 68; *see also* Kalish, D.
Krieger, L., P. Rossi, J. Passmore and H. V. White. *Essays on Historicism,* 429, 430, 434
Krikorian, Y. H., ed. *Naturalism and the Human Spirit,* 226, 229
Krimmerman, L. I., ed. *See* Broudy, H. S.
Kripke, S. A. *Naming and Necessity,* 345 (Davidson)
Kristeller, P. O. *Eight Philosophers of the Italian Renaissance,* 70, 72; *Medieval Aspects of Renaissance Learning,* 70, 72; *Renaissance Thought and Its Sources* (includes *Renaissance Concepts of Man* and *Renaissance Thought*), 70, 72; *Renaissance Thought and the Arts,* 70, 72; *Studies in Renaissance Thought and Letters,* 70, 72
Krüger, L., ed. *See* Bieri, P.
Kuhn, T. S. *The Essential Tension,* 412, 425; *The Structure of Scientific Revolutions,* 411–12, 425
Kuklich, B. *The Rise of American Philosophy,* 218, 229
Kulstad, M., ed. *Essays on the Philosophy of Leibniz,* 90, 91
Kyburg, H. E. *The Logical Foundations of Statistical Inference,* 335, 337; *see also* Asquith, P. D.

The Labyrinth of Language, M. Black, 341, 344
Lacey, A. R. *A Dictionary of Philosophy,* 509
Lackey, D., ed. *See* Russell, B., *Essays.*
Ladd, J., ed. *Ethical Relativism,* 398, 408
Laine, M., ed. *See* Robson, J. M.
Lakatos, I. *Philosophical Papers,* 416, 425; *Proofs and Refutations,* 416, 425; *see also* Cohen, R. S. et al. (1976 Festschrift)

———, ed. *The Problem of Inductive Logic,* 335, 337

———, and A. E. Musgrave, eds. *Criticism and the Growth of Knowledge,* 413, 425

Lambert, K. and G. G. Brittan. *An Introduction to the Philosophy of Science,* 417, 425

Landesman, C., ed. *See* Care, N. S.

Landscapes of Learning, M. Greene, 494, 499

Lang, B., ed. *The Concept of Style,* 465, 468

Langer, S. K. *Feeling and Form,* 466, 468; *Philosophy in a New Key,* 466, 468

Langford, G. and D. J. O'Connor, eds. *New Essays in the Philosophy of Education,* 492, 499

Language and Aesthetics, B. R. Tilghman, ed., 463, 469

Language and Concepts in Education, B. O. Smith and R. H. Ennnis, eds., 492, 500

Language and Philosophy, M. Black, 342, 344

Language and Philosophy, S. Hook, ed., 341, 346

Language and Responsibility, N. Chomsky, 342, 343, 345

Language, Logic and God, F. Ferré, 476, 481

Language, Logic and Reason in the Church Fathers, R. H. Ayers, 58, 67

Language, Mind, and Knowledge, K. Gunderson, ed., 341, 345

The Language of Adam, R. Fraser, 78, 79, 111

The Language of Art and Art Criticism, J. Margolis, 463, 468

The Language of Education, I. Scheffler, 492, 500

The Language of Morals, R. M. Hare, 389, 392, 407

The Language of Nature, D. Hawkins, 418, 424

The Language of Philosophy: Freud and Wittgenstein, M. Lazerowitz, 5, 7, 486, 488

The Language of Thought, J. A. Fodor, 343, 345

The Language of Value, R. Lepley, ed., 381, 383

Language, Thought and Culture, P. Henle, ed., 340, 346

"Language, Thought and the World," W. Sellars, ed., 340, 347

Language, Truth and Logic, A. J. Ayer, 153, 155, 188, 322, 392, 476

"Languages of Art," M. C. Beardsley, ed., 467

Languages of Art, N. Goodman, 467, 468

Laslett, P., ed. *Philosophy, Politics, and Society,* 438, 440, 442, 449; *see also* Locke, J., *Two Treatises*

Laszlo, E. and J. B. Wilbur, eds. *Value Theory in Philosophy and Social Science,* 380, 383

"Later Philosophy" (American), M. R. Cohen, 216–18, 229

The Later Philosophy of R. G. Collingwood, A. Donagan, 197

Laudan, L. *Progress and Its Problems,* 413, 425

Lauer, J. Q. *Essays in Hegelian Dialectic,* 140, 142; *Phenomenology,* 289, 291; *A Reading of Hegel's Phenomenology of Spirit,* 139, 142; *The Triumph of Subjectivity* (Husserl), 289, 291

Law and Explanation, P. Achinstein, 420, 423

Law and Explanation in History, W. H. Dray, 430, 433, 434

Law and the Social Order, M. R. Cohen, 454, 456, 459

Law as Rule and Principle, T. M. Benditt, 456, 458

Law, Liberty and Morality, H. L. A. Hart, 457

Law, Morality, and Society, P. M. S. Hacker and J. Raz, eds., 454, 459

Lawrence, N. M. *Whitehead's Philosophical Development,* 214

Lawrence, R. *Motive and Intention,* 375, 378

Lazerowitz, M. *The Language of Philosophy: Freud and Wittgenstein,* 5, 7, 486, 488; *The Structure of Metaphysics,* 352, 358, 486; *see also* Ambrose, A.; Hanly, C.

Leclerc, I. *Whitehead's Metaphysics,* 214
———, ed. *The Relevance of Whitehead,* 214, 215

Lee, E. N., A. P. D. Mourelatos and R. Rorty, eds. *Exegesis and Argument* (Vlastos Festschrift), 14, 18

Leff, G. *The Dissolution of the Medieval Outlook,* 67, 68; *Medieval Thought,*

51, 52, 68; *William of Ockham*, 66, 68
The Legacy of Logical Positivism, P. Achinstein and S. F. Barker, eds., 154, 418, 423
Legal Philosophy from Plato to Hegel, H. Cairns, 454, 458
Legal Reasoning and Legal Theory, N. MacCormick, 456, 459
Lehnert, F., tr. *See* Schutz, A.
Lehrer, K. *Knowledge*, 317, 318, 323, 325
————, ed. *Freedom and Determinism*, 376, 378
Leiber, J. *Noam Chomsky*, 343, 346
Leibniz, G. W. *Theodicée*, 88
Leibniz, D. C. Broad, 90
Leibniz, H. W. Carr, 90
Leibniz, H. G. Frankfurt, ed., 89, 90
Leibniz, M. Hooker, ed., 90
Leibniz, N. Rescher, 90, 91
Leibniz and Philosophical Analysis, R. M. Yost, 90, 91
Leibniz's Moral Philosophy, J. Hostler, 90
Leibniz's Philosophy of Logic and Language, H. Ishiguro, 90, 91
Leinfellner, E., et al., eds. *Wittgenstein and His Impact on Contemporary Thought*, 209, 210
Leinfellner, W. and E. Köhler, eds. *Developments in the Methodology of Social Science*, 446, 449
Lemos, R. M. *Rousseau's Political Philosophy*, 112, 113
Lepley, R., ed. *The Language of Value*, 381, 383; *Value*, 381, 383
Leslie, J. *Value and Existence*, 382, 383
Leszl, W. *Aristotle's Conception of Ontology*, 41, 46; *Logic and Metaphysics in Aristotle*, 38, 46
Levi, A. W. *Philosophy as Social Expression*, 5, 7, 223, 229
Levi, I. *The Enterprise of Knowlwedge*, 383, 384
Leviathan, T. Hobbes, 91, 437
Levin, D. M. *Reason and Evidence in Husserl's Phenomenology*, 289, 291
Levin, M. E. *Metaphysics and the Mind-Body Problem*, 356, 359
Levinson, H. S. *The Religious Investigations of William James*, 475, 481
Levinson, P., ed. *In Pursuit of Truth* (Popper Festschrift), 198, 203

Levy, P. *Moore*, 161, 163, 184, 188
Lewis, C. I. *An Analysis of Knowledge and Valuation*, 315, 317, 325; *Collected Papers*, 226, 229; *Mind and the World Order*, 218, 314, 317, 326, 350; *Our Social Inheritance*, 387
Lewis, D. K. *Convention*, 343, 346; *Counterfactuals*, 333, 337
Lewis, H. D. *Freedom and History*, 168, 171; *Our Experience of God*, 475, 481
————, ed. *Clarity Is Not Enough* (Linguistic Philosophy), 170, 171; *Contemporary British Philosophy*, 157, 168, 171
Lewis, J. D. and R. L. Smith. *American Sociology and Pragmatism*, 246, 247
Lewy, C., ed. *See* Broad, C. D.
Lexicon Spinozanum, E. Boscherini, 87
The Liberal Theory of Justice (Rawls), B. Barry, 444, 447
Liberalism, L. T. Hobhouse, 438, 449
Liberty and the Rule of Law, R. L. Cunningham, ed., 444, 448
Library of Living Philosophers (series), P. A. Schilpp, ed., 514
Lichtheim, G. *Marxism*, 257, 261
The Life and Mind of John Dewey, G. Dykhuizen, 244, 245
The Life and Philosophy of Edward Caird, H. Jones and J. H. Muirhead, 147, 149
The Life of Bertrand Russell, R. W. Clark, 180, 181
The Life of David Hume, E. C. Mossner, 108, 110
The Life of Reason, G. Santayana, 226
The Life of the Mind, H. Arendt, 368
Life-World and Consciousness, L. E. Embree, ed., 286, 287
The Limits of Analysis, S. Rosen, 152, 156
Lindley, R. C. and J. M. Shorter. *The Philosophy of Mind: A Bibliography*, 505
Linebeck, R. H., ed. *Bibliographies of Famous Philosophers Series*, 503
Linge, D. E., tr. and ed. *See* Gadamer, H.-G., *Philosophical Hermeneutics*.
Linguistic Analysis and Phenomenology, W. Mays and S. C. Brown, eds., 170, 172
Linguistic Behavior, J. Bennett, 341, 344
Linguistic Communication and Speech

Acts, K. Bach and R. M. Harnish, 342, 344

Linguistic Representation, J. F. Rosenberg, 343, 346

The Linguistic Turn, R. Rorty, ed., 154, 156, 340

Linsky, L. *Names and Descriptions,* 334, 335, 337; *Referring,* 343, 346

Lipman, M. and A. M. Sharp, eds. *Growing Up with Philosophy,* 311

————, ————, and F. S. Oscanyan. *Philosophy in the Classroom,* 311, 312

The Literary Microcosm (Neoplatonists), J. A. Coulter, 48, 49

Literature, Philosophy and the Social Sciences, M. Natanson, 286, 287

Litzenburg, T. V., ed. *See* Diamond, M. L.

Livingston, D. W. and J. T. King, eds. *Hume,* 109

Livingstone, R., tr. *See* Lukacs, G.

Llamson, B. S. *Reason, Experience and the Moral Life* (Kant and Dewey), 398, 408

Lloyd, G. E. R. *Aristotle,* 37, 46; *Magic, Reason, and Experience,* 12, 18; *Polarity and Analogy,* 14–15, 18

Lobkowicz, N. *Theory and Practice* (Marx), 254, 256

Lock, G., tr. *See* Althusser, L., *Essays.*

Locke, D. *Perception and Our Knowledge of the External World,* 321, 326

Locke, J. *An Essay on Human Understanding,* 75, 85, 94–95; *Two Treatises of Government,* 94, 95

Locke and Berkeley, C. B. Martin and D. M. Armstrong, eds., 95, 106

Locke, Berkeley, Hume, J. Bennett, 95

Loeb, L. E. *From Descartes to Hume,* 101, 102

Loemker, L. E. *Struggle for Synthesis* (17th c.), 76, 79, 90

Logic and Knowledge: Essays 1901–1950, B. Russell, 180, 181

Logic and Language, A. Flew, ed., 169, 342, 345

Logic and Metaphysics in Aristotle, W. Leszl, 38, 46

Logic and Philosophy for Linguists, J. M. E. Moravcsik, ed., 341, 346

Logic and Reality, L. Armour, 355, 357

Logic and Reality, G. Bergmann, 154, 352, 357

Logic and Reality in Leibniz's Metaphysics, G. H. R. Parkinson, 90, 91

Logic and Rhetoric in England, 1500–1700, W. S. Howell, 77–79, 98

Logic and System, M. Clark, 140, 141

Logic, Foundations of Mathematics, and Computability Theory, R. E. Butts and J. Hintikka, eds., 330, 336

Logic Matters, P. T. Geach, 330, 334, 337

Logic, Methodology, and Philosophy of Science, E. Nagel, P. C. Suppes and A. Tarski, eds., 414, 426

The Logic of Analogy (Aquinas), R. M. McInerny, 65, 68

The Logic of Education, P. H. Hirst and R. S. Peters, 492, 493, 499

The Logic of Explanation in Psychoanalysis, M. Sherwood, 486, 488

The Logic of God, M. C. Diamond and T. V. Litzenburg, eds., 477, 480

The Logic of Marx, J. Zelený, 254, 256

The Logic of Modern Physics, P. W. Bridgman, 414, 423

The Logic of Scientific Discovery, K. Popper, 154, 198–99, 202, 416, 426

The Logic of William of Ockham, E. A. Moody, 220

Logic, Semantics, Metamathematics, A. Tarski, 332, 338

Logic, the Theory of Inquiry, J. Dewey, 244, 330, 337

Logical Foundations of Probability, R. Carnap, 335, 336

The Logical Foundations of Statistical Inference, H. E. Kyburg, 335, 337

Logical Investigations, E. Husserl, 280, 288, 290

Logical Positivism, A. J. Ayer, ed., 154, 155

The Logical Problem of Induction, G. H. von Wright, 335, 338

The Logical Structure of Linguistic Theory, N. Chomsky, 342, 345

The Logical Structure of the World and Pseudoproblems in Philosophy, R. Carnap, 153, 155

Logico-Linguistic Papers, P. F. Strawson, 342, 347

Lombard, P. *Sentences,* 54, 66

Long, A. A. *Hellenistic Philosophy,* 48, 49

————, ed. *Problems in Stoicism,* 48, 49

Lore and Science in Ancient Pythagoreanism, W. Burkert, 14, 17

Louch, A. R. *Explanation and Human Action*, 374, 378
Loux, M. J. *Substance and Attribute*, 356, 359
———, ed. *The Possible and the Actual*, 356, 359; *Universals and Particulars*, 356, 359
Lovejoy, A. O. *The Great Chain of Being*, 5, 7; *The Revolt Against Dualism*, 350, 359
Lowe, V. *Understanding Whitehead*, 214, 215
Löwith, K. *From Hegel to Nietzsche*, 124, 135
Lowrie, W. *Kierkegaard*, 265, 266
Lucas, J. R. *On Justice*, 444, 449
Luce, A. A. *Berkeley and Malebranche*, 104, 106
Ludwig Wittgenstein, A. Ambrose and M. Lazerowitz, eds., 209
Ludwig Wittgenstein, D. Pears, 208, 210
Lukács, G. *History and Class Consciousness* (Marxism), 253, 257–58, 261; *The Young Hegel*, 138, 142
Luckhardt, C. G., ed. *Wittgenstein*, 204, 207, 208, 210
Lynch, J. P. *Aristotle's School*, 34, 36, 46
Lynch, L. E. M., tr. *See* Gilson, E., *Christian Philosophy of Saint Augustine*.
Lyons, D. *Forms and Limits of Utilitarianism*, 394, 400, 408; *In the Interest of the Governed* (Bentham), 145, 149

Mabbott, J. D. *John Locke*, 95
McBride, W. L. *The Philosophy of Marx*, 254, 256
McCarthy, T. *The Critical Theory of Jürgen Habermas*, 300, 301
McCleary, R. C., tr. *See* Merleau-Ponty, M., *Signs*.
McClellan, J. E. *Philosophy of Education*, 493, 499
MacCormick, N. *H. L. A. Hart*, 453, 459; *Legal Reasoning and Legal Theory*, 456, 459
McCormick, P. and F. A. Elliston, *Husserl: Shorter Works*, 291; *see also* Elliston, F. A.
McCosh, J. *Scottish Philosophy*, 143, 149
McDermott, J. J. *The Culture of Experience*, 217, 229
MacDonald, G. F., ed. *Perception and Identity*, 169, 171

Mace, C. A., ed. *British Philosophy in Mid-Century*, 163, 169, 171
McFarland, J. D. *Kant's Concept of Teleology*, 118, 121
McGuiness, B., ed. *See* Waismann, F., *Philosophical Papers*.
Mach, E. *Analysis of Sensations*, 131
The Machiavellian Moment, J. G. A. Pocock, 438, 450
McInerny, R. M. *The Logic of Analogy* (Aquinas), 65, 68; *St. Thomas Aquinas*, 65, 68
MacIntyre, A. *After Virtue*, 390, 403, 408; *A Short History of Ethics*, 388, 408; *The Unconscious*, 486, 488
———, ed. *Hegel*, 141, 142; *see also* Flew, A., *New Essays*
McKeon, R., et al. "Philosophy of Duns Scotus," 66, 68
Mackie, J. L. *The Cement of the Universe*, 419, 425; *Ethics*, 393, 408
McKinnon, A. *The Kierkegaard Indices to Kierkegaard's Samlede Vaerker*, 265, 266
McLean, G. F. *An Annotated Bibliography of Philosophy in Catholic Thought, 1900–1964*, 505
———, ed. *A Bibliography of Christian Philosophy and Contemporary Issues*, 505
McLellan, D. *The Thought of Karl Marx*, 254, 256
McMillan, C. *Women, Reason, and Nature*, 311, 312
McMullin, E. *The Concept of Matter*, 41, 46
McMurtry, J. M. *The Structure of Marx's World-View*, 254, 256
McNabb, D. G. C. *David Hume*, 108, 109
Macpherson, C. B. *Democratic Theory*, 443, 449; *The Political Theory of Possessive Individualism*, 438, 443, 449
Macquarrie, J., tr. *See* Heidegger, M., *Being*.
McRae, R. *The Problem of the Unity of the Sciences*, 422, 425
McTaggart, J. M. E. *The Nature of Existence*, 166; *Studies in the Hegelian Dialectic*, 140, 142
Madden, E. H. *Philosophical Problems of Psychology*, 485, 488; *see also* Blake, R. M.

————, and P. H. Hare. *Evil and the Concept of God,* 478, 481

Magee, B., ed. *Modern British Philosophy,* 170, 172

————, et al. *Men of Ideas,* 170, 172

Magic, Reason, and Experience, G. E. R. Lloyd, 12, 18

Magill, F. N., ed. *Masterpieces of World Philosophy in Summary Form,* 512

Magnus, B. *Nietzsche's Existential Imperative,* 269, 270

————, and J. B. Wilbur, eds. *Cartesian Essays,* 82, 83

Maguire, J. M. *Marx's Theory of Politics,* 255, 256

Mahoney, E. P., ed. *See* Kristeller, P. O., *Medieval Aspects.*

Mahowald, M. B. *Philosophy of Women,* 311, 312

Maimonides, D. Hartman, 58, 68

Main Currents of Marxism, L. Kolakowski, 258, 260

Major Themes in Modern Philosophies of Judaism, E. Berkovits, 157, 158

Malantschuk, G. *Kierkegaard's Thought,* 265, 266

Malcolm, N. *Dreaming,* 367, 369; *Knowledge and Certainty,* 314, 316, 319, 326; *Memory and Mind,* 367, 370; *Problems of Mind,* 363, 370

Malebranche, N. *De la recherche de la vérité,* 104

Mallin, S. B. *Merleau-Ponty's Philosophy,* 292, 293

Man and His Values, W. H. Werkmeister, 382, 384

Mandelbaum, M. *The Anatomy of Historical Knowledge,* 432, 434; *History, Man, and Reason* (19th c.), 125, 135; "On the Historiography of Philosophy," 6, 7, 120; *The Phenomenology of Moral Experience,* 402, 408; *The Problem of Historical Knowledge,* 429, 431, 434; *see also* Freeman, E.; Passmore, J. A., *Historiography*

Manheim, R., tr. *See* Cassirer, E., *Philosophy of Symbolic Forms;* Jaspers, K., *Way to Wisdom*

Manheimer, R. J. *Kierkegaard as Educator,* 266, 267

Manninen, J. and R. Tuomela. *Essays on Explanation and Understanding,* 308, 310

Man's Responsibility for Nature, J. A. Passmore, 308, 310, 405

Manser, A. *Sartre,* 276, 277

Manuel, F. E. *A Portrait of Isaac Newton,* 79

Many-Valued Logic, N. Rescher, 332, 338

Marcel, G. *The Mystery of Being,* 274, 275, 355; *The Philosophy of Existentialism,* 274, 275

Marcell, D. W. *Progress and Pragmatism,* 233, 234

Marcus, R. B., ed. "New Directions in Semantics," 341, 346

Marcuse, H. *Reason and Revolution,* 139, 142

Margins of Precision, M. Black, 342, 344

Margolis, J. *Art and Philosophy,* 463, 468; *The Language of Art and Art Criticism,* 463, 468; *Persons and Minds,* 366, 370; *Philosophy Looks at the Arts,* 463, 469

Maritain, J. *Bergsonian Philosophy and Thomism,* 127, 135; *Creative Intuition in Art and Poetry,* 460, 469; *The Degrees of Knowledge,* 350, 359; *Education at the Crossroads,* 492, 499

Markovic, M. *The Contemporary Marx,* 260, 261; *From Affluence to Praxis,* 260, 261

Markus, R. A., ed. *Augustine,* 56, 68

Marras, A., ed. *See* Binkley, R.

Marsh, R. C., ed. *See* Russell, B., *Logic and Knowledge.*

Martin, C. B. and D. M. Armstrong, eds. *Locke and Berkeley,* 95, 106

Martin, J. R. *Explaining, Understanding, and Teaching,* 497, 499

————, ed. *Readings in the Philosophy of Education,* 495, 499

Martin, R. *Historical Explanation,* 432, 434

Martin, R. M., ed. "Nominalism: Past and Present," 66, 68

Martin Buber, M. L. Diamond, 271, 272

Martin Heidegger, W. Biemel, 280, 283

Martin Heidegger, D. F. Krell, ed., 283, 284

Martin Heidegger, G. Steiner, 283, 284

Marx, K. *Capital,* 252, 254; *Grundrisse,* 252; other works, 249–51

Marx, W. *Heidegger and the Tradition,* 283, 284

Marx and Marxism, I. Fetscher, 253, 258, 260

Marx and the Mid-Century, G. Petrovic, 253, 256
Marxism, G. Lichtheim, 257, 261
Marxism and Philosophy, K. Korsch, 257–58, 260
Marxism and the Linguistic Philosophy, M. C. Cornforth, 170, 171
Marxism in the Twentieth Century, R. Garaudy, 253, 259, 260
Marx's Fate, J. Seigel, 249, 252, 254, 256
Marx's Interpretation of History, M. M. Rader, 255, 256
Marx's Social Ontology, C. Gould, 251, 253–56
Marx's Theory of History, W. H. Shaw, 255, 256
Marx's Theory of Politics, J. M. Maguire, 255, 256
Masterpieces of World Philosophy in Summary Form, F. N. Magill, ed., 512
Masters, R. D. *The Political Philosophy of Rousseau,* 112, 113
Matczak, S. A. *Philosophy: A Select, Classified Bibliography of Ethics, Economics, Law, Politics, Sociology,* 506; *Philosophy: Its Nature, Methods and Basic Sources,* 506
Materialism and Sensations, J. W. Cornman, 366, 369
"Materialism Today," J. J. C. Smart et al., 366, 370
Mates, B. *Stoic Logic,* 220, 329, 337
Mathematical Logic, W. V. O. Quine, 330, 338
Matson, W., et al. *See* Saw, R. L.
Matthews, E., tr. *See* Bubner, R.
Matthews, G. B. *Philosophy and the Young Child,* 311, 312
Maull, N. *See* Darden, L.
Maurer, A. A. *Medieval Philosophy,* 51, 68
Mavrodes, G. I. *Belief in God,* 473, 477, 482
Max Scheler, M. S. Frings, 134
Max Scheler, E. Kelly, 134, 135
Max Scheler (1874–1928), M. S. Frings, 134
Maxwell, G., ed. *See* Feigl, H.; Feyerabend, P. K.
———, and R. M. Anderson, eds. *Induction, Probability and Confirmation,* 420, 426
Maynard, P., ed. *See* Pearce, G.
Mays, W. and S. C. Brown, eds. *Linguistic Analysis and Phenomenology,* 170, 172
Mazlich, B. *James and John Stuart Mill,* 145, 149
Mead, G. H. *Mind, Self and Society,* 247; other works, 247
Meagher, R. E. *An Introduction to Augustine,* 56, 68
Meaning, S. R. Schiffer, 343, 347
Meaning and Action: A Critical History of Pragmatism, H. S. Thayer, 231–33, 235, 244
Meaning and Existence, G. Bergmann, 352, 358
Meaning and Knowledge, E. Nagel and R. Brandt, eds., 315, 320, 326
Meaning and Necessity, R. Carnap, 333, 336, 340, 345
Meaning and Structure, B. Harrison, 343, 345
Meaning and Truth in the Arts, J. Hospers, 462, 468
The Meaning of God in Human Experience, W. E. Hocking, 473, 475, 481
Medieval Aspects of Renaissance Learning, P. O. Kristeller, 70, 72
Medieval Logic, P. Boehner, 58, 67
Medieval Logic and Metaphysics, D. P. Henry, 51, 68
Medieval Philosophy, A. A. Maurer, 51, 68
Medieval Thought, G. Leff, 51, 52, 68
Meditationes, R. Descartes, 80–81
Mehta, J. L., tr. *See* Biemel, W.
Meiland, J. W. *The Nature of Intention,* 366, 370; *Scepticism and Historical Knowledge,* 431, 434; *Talking about Particulars,* 343, 346; *see also* Krausz, M.
Meinong, A. *Hume Studies,* 132
Meinong, R. Grossmann, 132, 134
Meinong's Theory of Objects and Value, J. N. Findlay, 132, 134
Melden, A. I. *Free Action,* 362, 376, 378; *Rights and Persons,* 401, 408
Melhuish, G. *The Paradoxical Nature of Reality,* 355, 359
Memory and Mind, N. Malcolm, 367, 370
Men and Citizens (Rousseau), J. N. Shklar, 112, 113
Men of Ideas, B. Magee, et al., 170, 172
Mental Acts, P. T. Geach, 364, 369

The Mental as Physical, E. Wilson, 366, 371

Mepham, J. and D.-H. Ruben, eds. *Issues in Marxist Philosophy*, 260, 261

Merit and Responsibility, A. W. H. Adkins, 30, 31

Merlan, P. *From Platonism to Neoplatonism*, 48, 49; *Monopsychism, Mysticism, Metaconsciousness* (Neoaristotelians, Neoplatonists), 48, 49

Merleau-Ponty, M. *Adventures of the Dialectic* (Marxism), 259, 261, 292; *Phenomenology of Perception*, 291, 293; *Signs*, 291, 293; *The Structure of Behavior*, 291

Merleau-Ponty's Philosophy, B. Mallin, 292, 293

Merrill, K. R. and R. W. Shahan, eds. *David Hume*, 108, 109

Metahistory (19th c.), H. White, 430, 435

Metaphor and Reality, P. Wheelwright, 344, 347

Metaphor and Thought, A. Ortony, ed., 344, 346

The Metaphysical Foundations of Modern Science, E. A. Burtt, 74, 79

Metaphysical Thinking, E. Sprague, 354, 359

Metaphysics, R. Taylor, 354, 359

"Metaphysics," M. Thompson, 357, 359

Metaphysics, W. H. Walsh, 354, 359

Metaphysics and Essence, M. A. Slote, 356, 359

Metaphysics and the Mind-Body Problem, M. E. Levin, 356, 359

Metaphysics and the Philosophy of Science, G. Buchdahl, 414, 423

The Metaphysics of Descartes, L. J. Beck, 81, 82

The Metaphysics of Experience (Whitehead), E. M.Krans, 214

The Metaphysics of Logical Positivism, G. Bergmann, 352, 358

Metaphysics, Reference, and Language, J. W. Cornman, 355, 358

Method in Ethical Theory, A. Edel, 392, 406

The Method of Analysis, J. Hintikka and U. Remes, 420, 425

Methodological Pragmatism, N. Rescher, 240, 241

The Methodological Unity of Science, M. Bunge, 422, 423

The Methods of Ethics, H. Sidgwick, 146, 388

Michalos, A. C. *The Popper-Carnap Controversy*, 202, 203

Mid-Twentieth Century American Philosophy, P. A. Bertocci, ed., 222, 228

The Middle Ages and Philosophy, A. C. Pegis, 60, 68

The Middle Platonists, J. Dillon, 48, 49

Midwest Studies in Philosophy (series), P. A. French, T. E. Uehling and H. K. Wettstein, eds., 514

Miguel de Unamuno, M. Nozick, 264

Mijuskovic, B. L. *The Achilles of Rationalist Arguments*, 97, 102

Mill, J. S. *Auguste Comte and Positivism*, 127, 135; *Collected Works*, 145, 149; *Considerations on Representative Government*, 145; *On Liberty*, 145; *System of Logic*, 77, 128, 143

Mill, J. B. Schneewind, ed., 146, 149

Miller, D. *Social Justice*, 444, 449

Miller, D. L. *George Herbert Mead*, 246, 247

Miller, J. *History and Human Existence* (Marxism), 258, 261

Milne, A. J. M. *Freedom and Rights*, 401, 408; *The Social Philosophy of English Idealism*, 147, 149

Minar, E. L., tr. *See* Burkert, W.

Mind and Art, G. Sircello, 466, 469

Mind and Language, G. E. M. Anscombe, et al., 341, 342, 344

Mind and Language, S. Guttenplan, ed., 341, 345

Mind and Nature (Cohen, Woodbridge, R. W. Sellars), C. F. Delaney, 226, 229

The Mind and the Soul, J. Teichman, 364, 370

Mind and the World Order, C. I. Lewis, 218, 314, 317, 326, 350

The Mind-Body Problem, M. Bunge, 366, 369

The Mind-Brain Identity Theory, C. V. Borst, ed., 366, 369

Mind, Brain, and Function, J. I. Biro and R. W. Shahan, eds., 366, 369

Mind, History, and Dialectic (Collingwood), L. O. Mink, 196, 198

Mind, Matter and Method, P. K. Feyerabend and G. Maxwell, eds., 364, 413, 424

Mind, Self and Society, G. H. Mead, 247

Mink, L. O. *Mind, History, and Dialectic* (Collingwood), 196, 198
The Mirror of Language, M. L. Colish, 59, 67
Mischel, T., ed. *Cognitive Development and Epistemology*, 496, 499; *Human Action*, 484, 488; *The Self*, 485, 488
Mitchell, B. *The Justification of Religious Belief*, 477, 482; *Morality*, 390, 408
———, ed. *Faith and Logic*, 476, 482
Models and Metaphors, M. Black, 342, 345
A Modern Book of Esthetics, M. Rader, ed., 463, 464, 469
Modern British Philosophy, B. Magee, ed., 170, 172
Modern Critical Theory, M. E. Murray, 299, 301
Modern French Philosophy, V. Descombes, 159, 160, 260
Modern German Philosophy, R. Bubner, 159, 160, 300
Modern Materialism, J. O'Connor, ed., 366, 370
Modern Moral Philosophy, W. D. Hudson, 388, 407
Modern Philosophies and Education, N. B. Henry, ed., 492, 499
Modern Philosophy, G. Ruggiero, 193
Modern Philosophy of History, M. E. Murray, 430, 434
Modern Studies in Philosophy, 514
Modes of Being, P. Weiss, 350, 351, 360
Modes of Thought, A. N. Whitehead, 212–15
Mohanty, J. N. *Edmund Husserl's Theory of Meaning*, 289, 291; *Husserl and Frege*, 133, 135
Moira, W. C. Greene, 12, 17
Monopsychism, Mysticism, Metaconsciousness (Neoaristotelians, Neoplatonists), P. Merlan, 48, 49
Monro, D. H. *Empiricism and Ethics*, 396, 404
Montague, W. P., ed. *See* Adams, G. P.
Montefiore, A., ed. *See* Williams, B. A. O.
Moody, E. A. *The Logic of William of Ockham*, 220; *Studies in Medieval Philosophy, Science, and Logic*, 58, 68
Mooney, M., ed. *See* Kristeller, P. O., *Renaissance Thought and Its Sources*.
Moore, C. A., ed. *The Chinese Mind*, 310, 312; *The Indian Mind*, 310, 312; *The Japanese Mind*, 310, 312

Moore, E. C. *American Pragmatism*, 234, 244
———, and R. S. Robin, eds. *Studies in the Philosophy of Charles Sanders Peirce*, 241
Moore, F. C. T. *The Psychological Basis of Morality*, 383, 384
Moore, G. E. *The Common Place Books, 1919–1953*, 187; *Ethics*, 186–87, 408; *Philosophical Papers*, 187, 188; *Philosophical Studies*, 187, 188; *Principia Ethica*, 161, 185, 387, 408; *Some Main Problems of Philosophy*, 186, 187, 188
Moore, P. Levy, 161, 163, 184, 188
The Moral and Political Philosophy of David Hume, J. B. Stewart, 108, 110
Moral Education, C. B. Beck, B. S. Crittenden and E. V. Sullivan, eds., 496, 498
Moral Language, M. G. Forrester, 389, 406
The Moral Philosophy of George Berkeley, P. J. Olscamp, 105, 107
The Moral Point of View, K. Baier, 399, 404, 405
Moral Principles and Political Obligations, A. J. Simmons, 441, 451
The Moral Prism, D. Emmet, 393, 406
Moral Reasoning and Truth, T. D. Perry, 456, 459
Moral Rightness, D. W. Haslett, 387, 407
Moral Scepticism and Moral Knowledge, R. Bambrough, 397, 406
The Moral Status of Animals, S. R. L. Clark, 400, 406
Moral Thinking, R. M. Hare, 392, 407
Morality, B. Mitchell, 390, 408
Morality and Moral Consciousness, J. Arthur, ed., 405
Morality and the Inner Life (Plato's "Gorgias"), I. Dilman, 31, 32
Morality and the Language of Conduct, H.-N. Casteñada and G. Nakhnikian, eds., 389, 406
The Morality of Law, L. Fuller, 456, 457, 459
The Morality of the Criminal Law, H. L. A. Hart, 611
Moravcsik, J. M. E., ed. *Aristotle*, 36, 37, 41, 44, 46; *Logic and Philosophy for Linguists*, 341, 346; *Patterns in Plato's Thought*, 30, 32

Morawetz, T. *Wittgenstein and Knowledge,* 209, 210; *The Philosophy of Law,* 454, 459

More Essays in Legal Philosophy, R. S. Summers, ed., 454, 459

Morgenbesser, S., ed. *Dewey and His Critics,* 245

Morice, G. P., ed. *David Hume,* 109

Morick, H., ed. *Challenges to Empiricism,* 223, 229

Morley, F., ed. *Essays on Individuality,* 367, 370

Morris, C. W. *The Pragmatic Movement in American Philosophy,* 233, 234, 244; *Signification and Significance,* 343, 346; *Six Theories of Mind,* 361, 370; *Writings on the General Theory of Signs,* 340, 346; *see also* Mead, G. H., *Mind;* Neurath, O.

Morris, H. *On Guilt and Innocence,* 458, 459

———, et al. "Human Rights," 440, 449

Morris, P. S. *Sartre's Concept of a Person,* 276, 277

Morris R. Cohen and the Scientific Ideal, D. A. Hollinger, 226, 229

Mortal Questions, T. Nagel, 397, 408

Mortimore, G. W., ed. *Weakness of Will,* 375, 378

Morton, D. F. *David Hume,* 107, 109

Mossner, E. C. *The Life of David Hume,* 108, 110; *see also* Todd, W. B. (1974 Festschrift)

Mostowski, A. *Thirty Years of Foundational Studies* (Mathematics, Logic), 329, 337

Mothershead, J. L., ed. *See* Lewis, C. I., *Collected Papers.*

Mothersill, M., ed. "Women's Liberation," 311, 312

Motive and Intention, R. Lawrence, 375, 378

Mourelatos, A. P. D. *The Route of Parmenides,* 14, 18

———, ed. *The Pre-Socratics,* 13, 18; *see also* Lee, E. N.

Muirhead, J. H. *The Platonic Tradition in Anglo-Saxon Philosophy* (Idealism), 146, 149; *see also* Jones, H.

———, ed. *Contemporary British Philosophy,* 162, 172

Mukařovský, J. *Structure, Sign and Function,* 465, 469

Mumford, L. *The Transformations of Man,* 228, 229

Mundle, C. W. K. *A Critique of Linguistic Philosophy,* 170, 172

Munitz, M. K. *Existence and Logic,* 332, 337; *see also* Kiefer, H. E.

Murdoch, I. *The Fire and the Sun* (Plato), 31, 33, 460, 469; *The Sovereignty of Good,* 392, 408

Mure, G. R. G. *Idealist Epilogue,* 146, 149; *A Study of Hegel's Logic,* 140, 142

Murphey, M. G. *The Development of Peirce's Philosophy,* 240, 241; *Our Knowledge of the Historical Past,* 432, 434

Murray, M. E. *Modern Critical Theory,* 299, 301; *Modern Philosophy of History,* 430, 434

———, ed. *Heidegger and Modern Philosophy,* 283, 284

Musgrave, A. E., ed. *See* Lakatos, I., *Criticism.*

Muyskens, J. L. *The Sufficiency of Hope,* 479, 482

My Philosophical Development, B. Russell, 179, 181

The Mystery of Being, G. Marcel, 274, 275, 355

Mystical Experience, B.-A. Scharfstein, 479, 482

Mysticism and Logic and Other Essays, B. Russell, 174, 177, 466, 469

Mysticism and Philosophical Analysis, S. T. Katz, ed., 479, 481

Nagel, E. *Sovereign Reason,* 225, 229, 352; *The Structure of Science,* 417, 420, 426; *Teleology Revisited,* 420, 426; *see also* Cohen, M. R., *Introduction*

———, and R. Brandt, eds. *Meaning and Knowledge,* 315, 320, 326

———, P. C. Suppes and A. Tarski, eds. *Logic, Methodology, and Philosophy of Science,* 414, 426

Nagel, T. *Mortal Questions,* 397, 408; *The Possibility of Altruism,* 399, 408

Najder, Z. *Values and Evaluations,* 382, 384

Nakhnikian, G., ed. *Bertrand Russell's Philosophy,* 180, 181; *see also* Casteñada, H.-N., *Morality*

Names and Descriptions, L. Linsky, 334, 335, 337
Naming and Necessity, S. A. Kripke, 345 (Davidson)
Naming and Referring, D. S. Schwarz, 343, 347
Naming, Necessity, and Natural Kinds, S. P. Schwartz, ed., 322, 326
Nasr, S. H. *Knowledge and the Sacred,* 474, 482
Natanson, M. *A Critique of Jean-Paul Sartre's Ontology,* 276, 277; *Literature, Philosophy and the Social Sciences,* 286, 287; *Phenomenology, Role and Reason,* 286, 287
Natural Right and History, L. Strauss, 438, 451
Naturalism and Ontology, W. Sellars, 355, 359
Naturalism and the Human Spirit, Y. H. Krikorian, ed., 226, 229
Nature and Culture (18th c.), L. G. Crocker, 98, 102
Nature and Historical Experience, J. H. Randall, 431, 434
The Nature of Existence, J. M. E. McTaggart, 166
The Nature of Historical Explanation, P. Gardiner, 433, 434
The Nature of Human Action, M. Brand, ed., 373, 374, 377
The Nature of Intention, J. W. Meiland, 366, 370
The Nature of Metaphysical Thinking, D. M. Emmet, 354, 357, 358
The Nature of Metaphysics, D. F. Pears, ed., 354, 359
The Nature of Mind, A. Kenny et al., 364, 369
The Nature of Mind and Other Essays, D. M. Armstrong, 366, 368
The Nature of Morality, G. Harman, 389, 407
The Nature of Necessity, A. Plantinga, 356, 359
The Nature of Things, A. Quinton, 349, 355, 356, 359
The Nature of Thought, B. Blanshard, 323, 325, 350, 358
Nauman, St. E. *Dictionary of American Philosophy,* 509; *The New Dictionary of Existentialism,* 510
Necessary Truth, R. C. Sleigh, 335, 338

Necessity, Cause and Blame (Aristotle), R. Sorabji, 44, 46
Nelson, L. *Socratic Method and Critical Philosophy,* 152, 156
Neu, J. *Emotion, Thought and Therapy,* 484, 488
——, and R. Rorty. "A Bibliography of Writings in English on Linguistic Method in Philosophy and Related Issues 1930–1965," 506
Neurath, O., R. Carnap and C. Morris, eds. *International Encyclopedia of Unified Science,* 415, 426
The New American Philosophers (since 1945), A. J. Reck, 221, 229
The New Dictionary of Existentialism, St. E. Nauman, 510
"New Directions in Semantics," R. B. Marcus, ed., 341, 346
New Essays in Philosophical Theology, A. Flew and A. MacIntyre, eds., 476, 481
New Essays in the Philosophy of Education, G. Langford and D. J. O'Connor, eds., 492, 499
New Essays on Plato and Aristotle, R. Bambrough, ed., 30, 32
New Essays on Plato and the Pre-Socratics, R. A. Shiner and J. King-Farlow, eds., 13, 18
The New Leviathan, R. G. Collingwood, 91, 188, 196, 197, 368, 437, 448
New Studies in Berkeley's Philosophy, W. E. Steinkraus, ed., 106, 107
New Studies in Ethics, W. D. Hudson, ed., 388, 407
New Studies in Hegel's Philosophy, W. E. Steinkraus, ed., 141, 142
New Studies in the Philosophy of Descartes, N. K. Smith, 80, 83
New Studies in the Philosophy of John Dewey, S. M. Cahn, ed., 245
A New Theory of Beauty, G. Sircello, 460, 469
A New World of Philosophy, A. Kaplan, 156, 158
The Newtonian Revolution, I. B. Cohen, 414, 423
Nicholl, D., tr. *See* Bochenski, I. M.
Nielsen, K. *Skepticism,* 474, 482; *see also* Abelson, R.
Nietzsche, F. *The Birth of Tragedy,* 19, 21; *The Case of Wagner,* 19, 21; *Thus Spake Zarathustra,* 269

Nietzsche, M. Heidegger, 268, 270

Nietzsche, K. Jaspers, 268, 270

Nietzsche, W. Kaufmann, 267, 270

Nietzsche, R. C. Solomon, ed., 270

Nietzsche as Philosopher, A. C. Danto, 269, 270

Nietzsche's Existential Imperative, B. Magnus, 269, 270

Nietzsche's Gift, H. Alderman, 269, 270

Nietzsche's Theory of Knowledge, R. H. Grimm, 269, 270

Nihilism, S. Rosen, 398, 408

Noam Chomsky, J. Leiber, 343, 346

"Nominalism: Past and Present," R. M. Martin, ed., 66, 68

Nonexistent Objects, T. Parsons, 356, 359

Norris, C. *Deconstruction*, 310

Norton, D. F. and R. H. Popkin, eds. *David Hume*, 108, 110

Norton, D. L. *Personal Destinies*, 309, 310, 368

Novak, G. E. *Pragmatism versus Marxism*, 245

The Novelist as Philosopher, J. Cruick-shank, ed., 309, 310

Nowell-Smith, P. H., *Ethics*, 392, 408

Noxon, J. H. *Hume's Philosophical Development*, 109, 110

Nozick, M. *Miguel de Unamuno*, 264

Nozick, R. *Anarchy, State and Utopia*, 442, 444, 449; *Philosophical Explanations*, 157, 158

Nussbaum, M. C. *Aristotle's De Motu Animalium*, 43, 46

Oakeshott, M. *Hobbes on Civil Association*, 91–93; *Rationalism in Politics and Other Essays*, 439, 449

Oates, W. J. *Aristotle and the Problem of Value*, 44, 46

The Object of Morality, G. J. Warnock, 395, 409

Objective Knowledge, K. Popper, 198, 203

Obligations to Future Generations, R. I. Sikoria and B. Barry, eds., 400, 409

O'Brien, D. *Empedocles' Cosmic Cycle*, 14, 18

The Occult Philosophy in the Elizabe-than Age, F. A. Yates, 71, 73

O'Connell, R. J. *Art and the Christian Intelligence in St. Augustine*, 56, 460, 469

O'Connor, D. J. *Aquinas and Natural Law*, 65, 68; *The Correspondence Theory of Truth*, 323, 326; *Free Will*, 376, 378; *An Introduction to the Philosophy of Education*, 492, 499; *John Locke*, 94, 96

———, ed. *A Critical History of Western Philosophy*, 9, 10; *see also* Langford, G.

O'Connor, J., ed. *Modern Materialism*, 366, 370

Odell, S. J., ed. *See* Bontemps, C. J.

Of Grammatology, J. Derrida, 343, 345

O'Flaherty, J. C. *Johann Georg Hamann*, 100, 102

Ofstad, H. *See* Frankena, W. K., *Thinking*.

O'Hear, A. *Karl Popper*, 202, 203

Okin, S. M. *Women in Western Political Thought*, 438, 450

Olafson, F. A. *The Dialectic of Action*, 432, 434; *Principles and Persons* (Existentialism), 263, 264

———, ed. *Justice and Social Policy*, 440, 444, 450

Ollman, B. *Alienation* (Marx), 253, 254, 256

Olscamp, P. J. *The Moral Philosophy of George Berkeley*, 105, 107

Olshewsky, T. M., ed. *Problems in the Philosophy of Language*, 341, 346

Olson, R. *Scottish Philosophy and British Physics, 1750–1880*, 144, 149

Olthuis, J. H. *Facts, Values and Ethics*, 381, 384, 388

O'Malley, J. B. *The Fellowship of Being* (Marcel), 274, 275

O'Malley, J. J., K. W. Algozin and F. G. Weiss, eds. *Hegel and the History of Philosophy*, 141, 142

On Being Free, F. Bergmann, 377

On Guilt and Innocence, H. Morris, 458, 459

On Heidegger and Language, J. J. Kockelmans, ed., 283

On Justice, J. R. Lucas, 444, 449

On Justifying Moral Judgments, L. A. Becker, 392, 406

On Karl Marx, E. Bloch, 253, 256

On Liberty, J. S. Mill, 145

On Liberty and Liberalism (Mill), G. Himmelfarb, 145, 148

On Metaphor, S. Sacks, ed., 344, 346

On Religion, F. Schleiermacher, 294, 471, 482

"On the Historiography of Philosophy," M. Mandelbaum, 6, 7, 120

On the Philosophy of Higher Education, J. S. Brubacher, 497, 498

On Thinking, G. Ryle, 165, 172

One and Many in Presocratic Philosophy, M. C. Stokes, 13, 18

One World and Our Knowledge of It, J. F. Rosenberg, 355, 359

O'Neill, J., tr. *See* Hyppolite, J., *Studies.*

O'Neill, O. and W. Ruddick, eds. *Having Children,* 447, 450

Ong, W. J. *Ramus, Method, and the Decay of Dialogue,* 72

The Ontological Argument, A. Plantinga, ed., 477, 482

Ontological Reduction, R. Grossmann, 356, 358

Ontological Relativity and Other Essays, W. V. O. Quine, 154, 156

The Open Philosophy and the Open Society (Popper), M. C. Cornforth, 202, 203

The Open Society and its Enemies, K. Popper, 198, 202, 439, 450

The Open-Texture of Moral Concepts, J. M. Brennen, 404, 406

The Opening Mind, M. Weitz, 463, 469

Orenstein, A. *Willard Van Orman Quine,* 228, 229

The Origin of Consciousness, J. Jaynes, 11, 17

Origin of Species, C. Darwin, 218, 242

The Origin of Subjectivity (Descartes), H. Caton, 81, 82

The Origins of American Philosophy of Education, J. J. Chambliss, 492, 498

The Origins of Certainty (Pascal), H. M. Davidson, 84, 85

The Origins of Kant's Arguments in the Antinomies, S. J. al-Azm, 116, 121

The Origins of Pragmatism, A. J. Ayer, 233, 234

The Origins of Stoic Cosmology, D. E. Hahm, 48, 49

The Origins of Totalitarianism, H. Arendt, 368

Ortony, A., ed. *Metaphor and Thought,* 344, 346

Osborne, H. *Aesthetics and Art Theory,* 461, 469; *Theory of Beauty,* 460, 469
———, ed. *Aesthetics in the Modern World,* 463, 469

Oscanyan, F. S. *See* Lipman, M.

Ossowski, S. *The Foundations of Aesthetics,* 465, 469

Other Minds, J. Wisdom, 362, 371

Our Experience of God, H. D. Lewis, 475, 481

Our Knowledge of the External World, B. Russell, 163, 176, 314, 326

Our Knowledge of the Historical Past, M. G. Murphey, 432, 434

Our Social Inheritance, C. I. Lewis, 387

Outlines of the History of Ethics, H. Sidgwick, 146, 388, 409

Owen, G. E. L., ed. *See* Düring, I.

Owens, J. *The Doctrine of Being in the Aristotelian Metaphysics,* 41–42, 46
———, ed. "Parmenides Studies Today," 14, 18

The Owl of Minerva (American Philosophy), C. J. Bontemps and S. J. Odell, eds., 223, 228

Oxford Essays in Jurisprudence, A. W. B. Simpson, ed., 454, 459

Oxford Readings in Philosophy (series), G. J. Warnock, ed., 514

PSA 1970, R. C. Buck and R. S. Cohen, eds., 413, 423

PSA 1976, F. Suppe and P. D. Asquith, eds., 413, 427

Paideia, W. Jaeger, 12, 13, 17, 491

Palmer, R. E. *Hermeneutics,* 5, 297, 301

Pap, A. *Introduction to the Philosophy of Science,* 417, 426; *Semantics and Necessary Truth,* 315, 322, 326

Papers in Logic and Ethics, A. N. Prior, 334, 337

Pappas, G. S. and M. Swain, eds. *Essays on Knowledge and Justification,* 318, 320, 326

Paradigms and Revolutions, G. Gutting, ed., 413, 424

Paradox and Identity in Theology, R. T. Herbert, 479, 481

Paradoxes, J. Cargile, 329, 336

The Paradoxical Nature of Reality, G. Melhuish, 355, 359

Parekh, B., ed. *Jeremy Bentham,* 145, 149

Park, J. *Bertrand Russell on Education,* 492, 499

Parkinson, G. H. R. *Georg Lukács,* 257, 261; *Logic and Reality in Leibniz's Metaphysics,* 90, 91

"Parmenides Studies Today," J. Owens, ed., 14, 18

Parsons, T. *Nonexistent Objects,* 356, 359

Part of My Life, A. J. Ayer, 165–66, 171

Participation, C. P. Bigger, 25, 32

Pascal, G. *Pensées,* 84–85; *Provincial Letters,* 84

Pascal, E. Cailliet, 84, 85

Passion and Value in Hume's Treatise, P. S. Árdal, 108, 109

The Passions, R. C. Solomon, 368, 370

Passmore, J. A. *Hume's Intentions,* 108, 110; *A Hundred Years of Philosophy,* 9, 10, 318; *Man's Responsibility for Nature,* 308, 310, 405; *Philosophical Reasoning,* 331, 337; "Philosophical Scholarship in the United States, 1930–1960," 6–8, 143; *see also* Krieger, L.

———, ed. *The Historiography of the History of Philosophy,* 4, 6, 7

Paton, H. J. *See* Klibansky, R.

Patterns in Plato's Thought, J. Moravcsik, ed., 30, 32

Patterns of Discovery, N. R. Hanson, 411, 414, 424

Paul, J., ed. *Reading Nozick,* 445, 450

Peacocke, C. A. B. and D. Scott, rev. by M. Davies and G. Forbes. *A Selective Bibliography of Philosophical Logic,* 506

Pearce, G. and P. Maynard, eds. *Conceptual Change,* 421, 426

Pears, D. *Bertrand Russell and the British Tradition in Philosophy,* 177, 180, 181; *Ludwig Wittgenstein,* 208, 210; *Questions in the Philosophy of Mind,* 363, 370

———, ed. *Bertrand Russell,* 180, 181

Pears, D. F., ed. *The Nature of Metaphysics,* 354, 359

Pegis, A. C. *The Middle Ages and Philosophy,* 60, 68

Peirce, C. S. *Collected Papers,* 239, 241

Peirce and Pragmatism, W. B. Gallie, 240, 241

Peirce's Concept of Sign, D. Greenlee, 240, 241

Peirce's Epistemology, W. H. Davis, 240, 241

Peirce's Philosophy of Science, N. Rescher, 240, 241

Peirce's Theory of Signs, J. J. Fitzgerald, 240, 241

Pelczynski, Z. A., ed. *Hegel's Political Philosophy,* 139, 142

Pelikan, J. *The Christian Tradition,* 52, 53, 68

Penelhum, T. *Hume,* 109, 110

Pennock, J. R. *Democratic Political Theory,* 443, 450

———, and J. W. Chapman, eds. *Compromise in Ethics, Law, and Politics,* 441, 450; *Equality,* 441, 450; *Political and Legal Obligation,* 441, 450

Pensées, B. Pascal, 84–85

Pepper, S. C. *World Hypotheses,* 349, 359

Perceiving, R. M. Chisholm, 315, 317–18, 320, 325

Perceiving, Sensing, and Knowing, R. J. Swartz, ed., 320, 326

Perception and Cognition, C. W. Savage, ed., 484, 488

Perception and Identity, G. F. Macdonald, ed., 169, 171

Perception and Our Knowledge of the External World, D. Locke, 321, 326

Perception and Personal Identity, N. Care and R. H. Grimm, eds., 320, 325

Perception, Common Sense, and Science, J. W. Cornman, 355, 358

Perception, Theory and Commitment, H. I. Brown, 411, 413, 423

Perelman, Ch. *The Idea of Justice and the Problem of Argument,* 440, 441, 444, 450; *The Realm of Rhetoric,* 310

Perry, J., ed. *Personal Identity,* 367, 370

Perry, R. B. *The Thought and Character of William James,* 220, 236, 237

Perry, T. D. *Moral Reasoning and Truth,* 456, 459

Person and Object, R. M. Chisholm, 319, 325

The Person God Is, P. A. Bertocci, 473, 475, 480

Personal Destinies, D. L. Norton, 309, 310, 368

Personal Identity, J. Perry, ed., 367, 370

Personal Knowledge, M. Polanyi, 319, 326, 411

Persons, R. Abelson, 367, 368

Persons, F. F. Centore, 368, 369

Persons and Minds, J. Margolis, 366, 370

Perspectives in Education, Religion, and the Arts, H. E. Kiefer, ed., 463, 468

Perspectives on Morality (Frankena essays), K. E. Goodpaster, ed., 387, 389, 407

Perspectives on Peirce, R. J. Bernstein, ed., 237, 241

Peters, F. E. Aristotle and the Arabs, 57, 68; Greek Philosophical Terms, 510

Peters, R. S. The Concept of Motivation, 373, 378; Ethics and Education, 496, 499; Hobbes, 93; see also Benn, S. I.; Cranston, M.; Dearden, R. F.; Hirst, P. H.

———, ed. The Concept of Education, 493, 499; John Dewey Reconsidered, 495, 499

Petrie, J., tr. See Perelman, Ch.

Petrovic, G. Marx and the Mid-Century, 253, 256

Pettegrove, J. P., tr. See Cassirer, E., Philosophy of the Enlightenment.

Pettit, P., ed. See Hookway, C.

Peursen, C. A. van. Phenomenology and Analytical Philosophy, 286, 287; Phenomenology and Reality, 286, 287

Phases of Thought in England, M. H. Carré, 143, 148

Phelan, G. B., tr. See Maritain, J., Degrees.

The Phenomenological Movement, H. Spiegelberg, 220, 285–87, 289

Phenomenology, F. Kersten and R. M. Zaner, eds., 287, 290

Phenomenology (Husserl), J. J. Kockelmans, eds., 289, 291

Phenomenology, J. Q. Lauer, 289, 291

Phenomenology and Analytical Philosophy, 286, 287

Phenomenology and Natural Existence, D. Riepe, ed., 287

Phenomenology and Philosophical Understanding, E. Pivcevic, ed., 286, 287

Phenomenology and Reality, C. A. van Peursen, 286, 287

Phenomenology and the Problem of History (Husserl), D. Carr, 289, 290

Phenomenology and the Social World (Merleau-Ponty), L. Spurling, 292, 293

Phenomenology and the Theory of Science, A. Gurwitsch, 286, 287

The Phenomenology of Aesthetic Experience, M. Dufrenne, 465, 468

The Phenomenology of Mind, G. W. F. Hegel, 136–39, 259

The Phenomenology of Moral Experience, M. Mandelbaum, 402, 408

Phenomenology of Perception, M. Merleau-Ponty, 291, 293

The Phenomenology of the Social World, A. Schutz, 286, 287

Phenomenology, Role and Reason, M. Natanson, 286, 287

The Phenomenon of Religion, N. Smart, 473, 475, 476, 482

Phillips, D. L. Wittgenstein and Scientific Knowledge, 209, 210

Phillips, D. Z. The Concept of Prayer, 475; Religion Without Explanation, 474, 476, 482

The Philosophers, B.-A. Scharfstein, 5, 7, 174, 306, 485

Philosophers as Educational Reformers, P. Gordon and J. White, 147, 148, 439

The Philosopher's Index, 507

Philosopher's Index: A Retrospective Index to U.S. Publications from 1940, 507

"The Philosophic Proofs for God's Existence," C. Hartshorne et al., 478, 481

Philosophical Analysis, J. O. Urmson, 163, 172

Philosophical Analysis and Education, R. D. Archambault, ed., 492, 494, 498

Philosophical Analysis and History, W. H. Dray, ed., 430, 431, 434

Philosophical Aspects of the Mind-Body Problem, C. Cheng, ed., 366, 369

Philosophical Books, 507

Philosophical Commentaries, G. Berkeley, 104

"Philosophical Disagreement," N. Rescher, 22, 33

Philosophical Essays on Dreaming, C. E. M. Dunlop, ed., 367, 369

Philosophical Explanations, R. Nozick, 157, 158

Philosophical Hermeneutics, H.-G. Gadamer, 298, 300

Philosophical Interrogations, S. and B. Rome, eds., 271, 272

Philosophical Investigations, L. Wittgenstein, 205–8, 210, 362

Philosophical Mysteries, S. D. Ross, 355, 359

Philosophical Papers, J. L. Austin, 168, 171

Philosophical Papers, I. Lakatos, 416, 425

Philosophical Papers, G. E. Moore, 187, 188

Philosophical Papers, H. Putnam, 343, 346

Philosophical Papers, F. Waismann, 151, 156

Philosophical Problems in Psychology, N. Bolton, ed., 484, 488

"Philosophical Problems of Death," R. Wasserstrom, ed., 309, 310

Philosophical Problems of Natural Science, D. Shapere, ed., 414, 426

Philosophical Problems of Psychology, E. H. Madden, 485, 488

Philosophical Reasoning, J. A. Passmore, 331, 337

Philosophical Redirection of Educational Research, L. Thomas, 494, 500

"Philosophical Scholarship in the United States, 1930–1960," J. A. Passmore, 6–8, 143

Philosophical Skepticism and Ordinary-Language Analysis, G. L. Vander Veer, 316, 327

Philosophical Studies, G. E. Moore, 187, 188

Philosophical Theory and Psychological Fact, C. F. Wallraff, 484, 488

Philosophies of Education, N. B. Henry, ed., 492, 499

Philosophies of Education, G. M. Wingo, 493, 500

Philosophies of Education in Cultural Perspective, T. Brameld, 493, 498

Philosophies of Judaism, J. Guttmann, 57, 67

Philosophy, R. Chisholm, H. Feigl, W. E. Frankena, J. Passmore and M. Thompson, 220, 229

Philosophy, K. Jaspers, 273

Philosophy: A Select, Classified Bibliography of Ethics, Economics, Law, Politics, Sociology, S. A. Matczak, 506

Philosophy and an African Culture, K. Wiredu, 159, 160

Philosophy and Education, J. F. Soltis, ed., 492, 495, 497, 500

The Philosophy and Future of Graduate Education, W. K. Frankena, ed., 497, 499

Philosophy and History, S. Hook, ed., 431, 434

Philosophy and History, R. Klibansky and H. J. Paton, eds., 4, 5, 7

Philosophy and Its History, H. R. Clark, 6

Philosophy and Its Past, J. Ree, M. Ayers and A. Westoby, 7

Philosophy and Linguistic Analysis, M. J. Charlesworth, 170, 171

Philosophy and Logical Syntax, R. Carnap, 153, 155

Philosophy and Myth in Karl Marx, R. C. Tucker, 253, 255, 256

Philosophy and Ordinary Language, C. E. Caton, ed., 342, 345

"Philosophy and Psychoanalysis," W. A. Alston, ed., 486, 487

Philosophy and Psychoanalysis, J. Wisdom, 485, 489

"The Philosophy and Psychology of Cognition," W. A. Alston, ed., 484, 487

Philosophy and Public Policy, S. Hook, 437, 449

"Philosophy and Public Policy," R. A. Wasserstrom et al., 446, 451

Philosophy and Religious Belief, G. F. Thomas, 475, 482

Philosophy and Scientific Realism, J. J. C. Smart, 355, 359

Philosophy and Social Issues, R. A. Wasserstrom, 446, 451

Philosophy and the Historical Understanding, W. B. Gallie, 433, 434

Philosophy and the Mirror of Nature, R. Rorty, 4, 7, 155, 223, 308, 321, 324, 415

Philosophy and the Young Child, G. B. Matthews, 311, 312

Philosophy as It Is, T. Honderich and M. Burnyeat, eds., 156, 158

Philosophy as Social Expression, A. W. Levi, 5, 7, 223, 229

"Philosophy as Style and Literature as Philosophy," D. Henze et al., 309, 310

Philosophy East/Philosophy West, B.-A. Scharfstein, ed., 157, 158, 310

Philosophy in a New Key, S. K. Langer, 466, 468

Philosophy in America, M. Black, ed., 222, 228

Philosophy in American Education, B. Blanshard et al., 222, 228

Philosophy In and Out of Europe, M. Grene, 158

Philosophy in the Classroom, M. Lipman, A. M. Sharp and F. S. Oscanyan, 311, 312

Philosophy in the Mid-Century, R. Klibansky, ed., 159, 512

Philosophy: Its Nature, Methods and Basic Source, S. A. Matczak, 506

Philosophy Looks at the Arts, J. Margolis, 463, 469

The Philosophy of Alfred North Whitehead, P. A. Schilpp ed., 211, 214, 215

The Philosophy of Aristotle, D. J. Allan, 37, 45

Philosophy of Art, V. Aldrich, 463, 467

Philosophy of Art, H. S. Blocker, 463, 467

Philosophy of Beauty, F. J. Kovach, 460, 468

The Philosophy of Bertrand Russell, P. A. Schilpp, ed., 178, 180, 181

Philosophy of Biological Science, D. L. Hull, 417, 425

The Philosophy of Brand Blanshard, P. A. Schilpp, ed., 224, 230

The Philosophy of C. D. Broad, P. A. Schilpp, ed., 163, 172

The Philosophy of C. I. Lewis, P. A. Schilpp, ed., 226, 230

The Philosophy of David Hume, N. K. Smith, 108, 110

"Philosophy of Duns Scotus," R. McKeon et al., 66, 68

Philosophy of Education, W. K. Frankena, 493, 494, 498

"Philosophy of Education," W. K. Frankena et al., 492, 499

Philosophy of Education, J. E. McClellan, 493, 499

The Philosophy of Education: A Guide to Information Sources, C. A. Baatz, 503

"Philosophy of Education Since Mid-Century," J. F. Soltis, ed., 492, 495, 500

Philosophy of Educational Research, H. S. Broudy, R. Ennis and L. I. Krimmerman, eds., 494, 498

The Philosophy of Ernst Cassirer, P. A. Schilpp, ed., 152, 156

The Philosophy of Existentialism, G. Marcel, 274, 275

The Philosophy of G. E. Moore, P. A. Schilpp, ed., 183, 187, 188

The Philosophy of Gabriel Marcel, K. T. Gallagher, 274, 275

The Philosophy of George Herbert Mead, W. R. Corti, ed., 246, 247

The Philosophy of George Santayana, P. A. Schilpp, ed., 227, 230

The Philosophy of Giambattista Vico, B. Croce, 100, 102

The Philosophy of Hegel, W. T. Stace, 140, 142

Philosophy of History, W. H. Dray, 431, 434

"Philosophy of History," J. E. Smith et al., 431, 434

Philosophy of History, W. H. Walsh, 431, 434

Philosophy of History and Action, Y. Yovel, ed., 429, 431, 435

The Philosophy of Human Rights, A. S. Rosenbaum, ed., 443, 450

"The Philosophy of Husserl," D. Føllesdal, ed., 290

Philosophy of Jean-Paul Sartre, P. A. Schilpp, 276–77

The Philosophy of John Dewey, P. A. Schilpp, ed., 245

The Philosophy of Karl Jaspers, P. A. Schilpp, ed., 273, 274

The Philosophy of Karl Popper, R. J. Ackermann, 202, 203

Philosophy of Language, W. P. Alston, 322, 340, 344

Philosophy of Law, J. Feinberg and H. Gross, eds., 454, 459

Philosophy of Law, M. P. Golding, 454, 459

The Philosophy of Law, T. Morawetz, 454, 459

The Philosophy of Law in Historical Perspective, C. J. Friedrich, 454, 459

Philosophy of Logic, H. Putnam, 329, 337

Philosophy of Logic, W. V. O. Quine, 329, 338

Philosophy of Logics, S. Haack, 330, 332, 334, 337

The Philosophy of Ludwig Feuerbach, E. Kamenka, 126, 135

The Philosophy of Martin Buber, P. A. Schilpp and M. Freedman, eds., 271, 272

The Philosophy of Marx, W. L. McBride, 254, 256

Philosophy of Mathematics, S. F. Barker, 330, 336

The Philosophy of Merleau-Ponty, J. F. Bannan, 292, 293

The Philosophy of Mind, V. C. Chappell, ed., 364, 369

Philosophy of Mind, J. A. Shaffer, 364, 370, 373
The Philosophy of Mind: A Bibliography, R. C. Lindley and J. M. Shorter, 505
"The Philosophy of Moral Education," W. K. Frankena, ed., 496, 499
"The Philosophy of Mysticism," W. Earle, ed., 479, 481
Philosophy of Natural Science, C. G. Hempel, 417, 425
Philosophy of Psychology, S. C. Brown, ed., 366, 484, 488
"Philosophy of Religion," etc., W. P. Alston, 473, 477, 480
Philosophy of Religion, J. Hick, 473, 474, 477, 481
Philosophy of Religion: An Annotated Bibliography, W. J. Wainwright, 508
The Philosophy of Rousseau, R. Grimsley, 111, 113
The Philosophy of Rudolf Carnap, P. A. Schilpp, ed., 154, 156
The Philosophy of Sartre, M. Warnock, 276, 277
The Philosophy of Sarvepalli Radhakrishnan, P. A. Schilpp, ed., 157, 158
The Philosophy of Schleiermacher, R. B. Brandt, 125, 134
"Philosophy of Science," H. Feigl, 410, 424
The Philosophy of Science, S. Toulmin, 334, 417, 427
A Philosophy of Science for Personality Theory, J. F. Rychlak, 373, 485, 488
Philosophy of Social Science, R. S. Rudner, 446, 450
The Philosophy of Socrates, G. Vlastos, ed., 19, 21
The Philosophy of Spinoza, H. A. Wolfson, 86, 88, 220
Philosophy of Symbolic Forms, E. Cassirer, 466, 468
The Philosophy of the Enlightenment, E. Cassirer, 97, 102
A Philosophy of the Future, E. Bloch, 257, 258, 260
"Philosophy of the History of Philosophy," L. W. Beck et al., 6
The Philosophy of the Kalam, H. A. Wolfson, 56, 69
The Philosophy of the Social Sciences, A. Ryan, 446, 450
The Philosophy of William James, W. R. Corti, ed., 236, 237

Philosophy of Women, M. B. Mahowald, 311, 312
Philosophy, Poetry, History, B. Croce, 430, 433
Philosophy, Politics, and Society, P. Laslett, ed., 438, 440, 442, 449
Philosophy Today, J. Ferrater Mora, 158
Physicalism, K. V. Wilkes, 366, 371
Pike, N. *God and Timelessness,* 479, 482
Pitcher, G. *Berkeley,* 106, 107; *A Theory of Perception,* 321, 326; *Truth,* 323, 326
———, ed. *Wittgenstein, the Philosophical Investigations,* 208, 210; *see also* Wood, O. P.
Pitkin, H. F. *Wittgenstein and Justice,* 440, 450
Pitte, F. P. van de. *Kant as Philosophical Anthropologist,* 117, 121
Pivčević, E., ed. *Phenomenology and Philosophical Understanding,* 286, 287
Plamenatz, J. *Karl Marx's Philosophy of Man,* 253, 256
Plamondon, A. L. *Whitehead's Organic Philosophy of Science,* 214, 215
Plantinga, A. *God and Other Minds,* 477, 482; *God, Freedom, and Evil,* 473, 479, 482; *The Nature of Necessity,* 356, 359
———, ed. *The Ontological Argument,* 477, 482
Plantinga, T. *Historical Understanding in the Thought of Wilhelm Dilthey,* 297, 301
Plato. *Lysis, see* Bolotin, D.; *Philebus, see* Gosling, J. C. B.; *The Republic, see* Cornford, F. M.
Plato, J. N. Findlay, 25, 28, 32
Plato, J. C. B. Gosling, 30, 32
Plato, G. Vlastos, ed., 24, 30, 33
Plato and Parmenides, F. M. Cornford, 14, 17
Plato for the Modern Age, R. S. Brumbaugh, 30, 32
Plato on Knowledge and Reality, N. P. White, 30, 33
Plato, Popper and Politics, R. Bambrough, ed., 202, 203
Plato, Utilitarianism and Education, R. Barrow, 31, 32, 491
Platonic Studies, G. Vlastos, 15, 18, 28, 29
The Platonic Tradition in Anglo-Saxon

Philosophy (Idealism), J. H. Muirhead, 146, 149

Plato's Analytic Method, M. Sayre, 30, 33

Plato's Cosmology, F. M. Cornford, 13, 17

Plato's Dialogue on Friendship ("Lysis"), D. Bolotin, 31, 32

Plato's Earlier Dialectic, R. Robinson, 19, 21, 27, 30

Plato's 'Euthyphro' and Earlier Theory of Forms, R. E. Allen, 30

Plato's Later Epistemology, W. G. Runciman, 31, 33

Plato's Moral Theory, T. Irwin, 31, 32

Plato's Philebus, J. C. B. Gosling, ed., 30, 32

Plato's Progress, G. Ryle, 25–28, 33

Plato's Theory of Ideas, W. D. Ross, 23, 24, 33

Plato's Theory of Knowledge, N. Gulley, 31, 32

Plato's Trilogy, J. Klein, 31, 32

Plato's Universe, G. Vlastos, 13, 18

Plattner, M. F. *Rousseau's State of Nature,* 111, 113

Pleasure and Desire, J. C. B. Gosling, 394, 407

Plotinian and Christian Studies, A. H. Armstrong, 48, 49

Plotinus, J. M. Rist, 48, 50

Pocock, J. G. A. *The Machiavellilan Moment,* 438, 450

Poetry and Literature, B. Croce, 466, 468

Polanyi, M. *Personal Knowledge,* 319, 326, 411

Polarity and Analogy, G. E. R. Lloyd, 14–15, 18

Polis and Psyche (Plato), T. J. Andersson, 31, 32

Polish Analytical Philosophy, H. Skolimowski, 159, 160

Political and Legal Obligation, J. R. Pennock and J. W. Chapman, eds., 441, 450

Political and Social Essays, P. Ricoeur, 442, 450

Political Argument, B. Barry, 441, 447

The Political Philosophy of Hobbes, L. Strauss, 92, 93

The Political Philosophy of Hobbes, H. Warrender, 92–93

The Political Philosophy of Rousseau, R. D. Masters, 112, 113

Political Theory and Political Education, M. Richter, ed., 442, 447, 450, 497

The Political Theory of Possessive Individualism, C. B. Macpherson, 438, 443, 449

The Political Thought of John Locke, J. Dunn, 95

Political Violence, T. Honderich, 441, 449

The Politics of Conscience (T. H. Green, Idealism), M. Richter, 147, 149, 439

The Politics of Motion (Hobbes), T. A. Spragens, 93

The Politics of Social Theory (Habermas), R. Keat, 300, 301

Pollock, J. *Knowledge and Justification,* 316, 317, 326

Pompa, L. *Vico,* 99, 102

Popkin, R. H. *The History of Scepticism from Erasmus to Spinoza,* 72, 76, 220, 320; *see also* Norton, D. F.

Popper, K. *Conjectures and Refutations,* 416, 426; *The Logic of Scientific Discovery,* 154, 198–99, 202, 416, 426; *Objective Knowledge,* 198, 203; *The Open Society and Its Enemies,* 198, 202, 439, 450; *The Poverty of Historicism,* 198, 202, 430, 434; other works, 198; *see also* Levinson, P. (1982 Festschrift)

The Popper-Carnap Controversy, A. C. Michalos, 202, 203

Port-Royal Logic, 77, 84

A Portrait of Isaac Newton, F. E. Manuel, 79

Positivism and Christianity, K. H. Klein, 154, 156

The Possibility of Altruism, T. Nagel, 399, 408

The Possible and the Actual, M. J. Loux, ed., 356, 359

Possible Worlds, R. Bradley and N. Swartz, 333, 336

Poster, M. *Existential Marxism in Postwar France,* 258, 260, 261, 276, 292

Pound, R. *Jurisprudence,* 454, 456, 459

The Poverty of Historicism, K. R. Popper, 198, 202, 430, 434

Powell, T. F. *Josiah Royce,* 224, 229

Power, Form, and Mind, A. Berndtson, 355, 358

The Power of God, L. Urban and D. N. Walton, eds., 478, 482

Practical Ethics, P. Singer, 400, 409

Practical Reason and Norms, J. Raz, 455, 459
Practical Reasoning, J. Raz, ed., 405, 408
The Pragmatic A Priori (C. I. Lewis), S. B. Rosenthal, 234
The Pragmatic Movement in American Philosophy, C. W. Morris, 233, 234, 244
Pragmatic Naturalism, S. M. Eames, 233, 234
Pragmatism, W. James, 236
Pragmatism as Humanism (James), P. K. Dooley, 236, 237
"Pragmatism Reconsidered," J. Smith, ed., 235
Pragmatism versus Marxism, G. E. Novak, 245
Prall, D. W. *Aesthetic Analysis*, 462, 469
Praxis and Action, R. J. Bernstein, 157, 373, 377
Predicting the Behavior of the Educational System, T. F. Green, D. P. Ericson and R. M. Seidman, 494, 499
Prelude to Aesthetics, E. Schaper, 460, 469
Presence and Absence, R. Sokolowski, 286, 287, 355, 359
The Presocratic Philosophers, J. Barnes, 14, 17
The Pre-Socratic Philosophers, G. S. Kirk and J. E. Raven, 12, 17
The Pre-Socratic Philosophers: A Companion to Diels, K. Freeman, 12, 17
The Pre-Socratics, A. P. D. Mourelatos, ed., 13, 18
Presupposition and the Delimitation of Semantics, R. M. Kempson, 343, 346
Presuppositions and Non-Truth-Conditional Semantics, D. Wilson, 343, 347
Preus, A. *Science and Philosophy in Aristotle's Biological Works*, 41, 46
Price, H. H. *Relief*, 479; *Essays in the Philosophy of Religion*, 479, 482; *Thinking and Experience*, 318–19, 326
Price, L., ed. *See* Whitehead, A. N., *Dialogues.*
Prier, R. A. *Archaic Logic*, 16, 18
Priestley, E. F. L., ed. *See* Mill, J. S., *Collected Works.*
Principia Ethica, G. E. Moore, 161, 185, 387, 408
Principia Mathematica, A. N. Whitehead and B. Russell, 153, 175, 178, 206, 211–12, 330, 338

Principia Philosophiae, R. Descartes, 80
Principium Sapientiae, F. M. Cornford, 12, 17
Principles and Persons (Existentialism), F. A. Olafson, 263, 264
The Principles of Art, R. G. Collingwood, 188, 340, 460, 465–66, 468
The Principles of Linguistic Philosophy, F. Waismann, 341, 347
The Principles of Mathematics, B. Russell, 162, 175, 176, 184, 204, 330–31, 338
The Principles of Psychology, W. James, 235
The Principles of Scientific Thinking, R. Harré, 418, 424
Prior, A. N. *The Doctrine of Propositions and Terms*, 334, 337; *Papers in Logic and Ethics*, 334, 337
The Private Language Argument, O. R. Jones, ed., 343, 346
Probability and Hume's Inductive Scepticism, D. C. Stove, 109, 110
Probability and Induction, W. Kneale, 413, 420, 425
The Probable and the Provable, L. J. Cohen, 335, 336
The Problem of Historical Knowledge, M. Mandelbaum, 429, 431, 434
The Problem of Inductive Logic, I. Lakatos, ed, 335, 337
The Problem of Knowledge, A. J. Ayer, 317, 319, 325
The Problem of Knowledge, E. Cassirer, 314, 325
The Problem of the Unity of the Sciences, R. McRae, 422, 425
Problems in Aesthetics, M. Weitz, 463, 470
Problems in Stoicism, A. A. Long, ed., 48, 49
Problems in the Philosophy of Language, T. M. Olshewsky, ed., 341, 346
Problems of a Sociology of Knowledge, M. Scheler, 439, 445, 450
Problems of Analysis, M. Black, 342, 345
Problems of Mind, N. Malcolm, 363, 370
Problems of Mind and Matter, J. Wisdom, 362, 371
Problems of the Self, B. Williams, 364, 367, 371
Process and Divinity (Hartshorne), W. L. Reese and E. Freeman, eds., 476, 482

Process and Reality, A. N. Whitehead, 166, 212–15
Progress and Its Problems, L. Lauden, 413, 425
Progress and Pragmatism, D. W. Marcell, 233, 234
Prolegomena to Any Future Metaphysics, I. Kant, 114
Proofs and Refutations, I. Lakatos, 416, 425
Property Rights, L. C. Becker, 443, 448
Propositional Structure and Illocutionary Force, J. J. Katz, 342, 346
Proslogion, Anselm, 478
Protestant and Roman Catholic Ethics, J. M. Gustafson, 390, 407
Protestant Theology in the Nineteenth Century, K. Barth, 124, 134
Providence and Evil, P. T. Geach, 474, 481
Provincial Letters, B. Pascal, 84
Psychoanalysis and Philosophy, C. Hanly and M. Lazerowitz, eds., 485, 486, 488
Psychoanalysis, Scientific Method, and Philosophy, S. Hook, ed., 486, 488
"A Psychoanalytic Perspective" (Moral Development), T. Tice, 472, 496, 500
The Psychological Basis of Morality, F. C. T. Moore, 383, 384
Psychological Explanation, J. Fodor, 484, 488
Psychology, J. Dewey, 243
The Public and Its Problems, J. Dewey, 244, 437, 448
Public and Private Morality, S. Hampshire et al., 438, 441, 449
Punishment and Responsibility, H. L. A. Hart, 458, 459
Pure Theory of Law, H. Kelsen, 455, 459
Putnam, H. *Philosophical Papers*, 343, 346; *Philosophy of Logic*, 329, 337

Questions in the Philosophy of Mind, D. Pears, 363, 370
Quine, W. V. O. *From a Logical Point of View*, 334, 338, 352; *Mathematical Logic*, 330, 338; *Ontological Relativity and Other Essays*, 154, 156; *Philosophy of Logic*, 329, 338; *A System of Logistic*, 228; *Word and Object*, 315, 321, 322, 326
Quinn, J. F. *The Historical Constitution of St. Bonaventure's Philosophy*, 65, 69
Quinton, A. *The Nature of Things*, 349, 355, 356, 359

Rader, M. M. *Marx's Interpretation of History*, 255, 256
———, ed. *A Modern Book of Esthetics*, 463, 464, 469
———, and B. Jessup. *Art and Human Values*, 463, 469
The Radical Empiricism of William James, J. D. Wild, 236, 237
The Radical Liberal, A. S. Kaufman, 440, 444, 449
Radner, M. and S. Winokur, eds. *Analyses of Theories and Methods of Physics and Psychology*, 413, 426
Radnitzky, G. *Contemporary Schools of Metascience*, 416, 426
Ramsey, I. T. *Religious Language*, 473, 476, 482
Ramus, Method, and the Decay of Dialogue, W. J. Ong, 72
Rand, B., comp. *Bibliography of Philosophy, Psychology, and Cognate Subjects*, 507
Randall, J. H. *Aristotle*, 37, 46; *The Career of Philosophy*, 9, 10; *How Philosophy Uses Its Past*, 5, 7; *Nature and Historical Experience*, 431, 434
A Rational Animal and Other Philosophical Essays, A. Flew, 363, 369
The Rational Society (Santayana), B. Singer, 227, 230
Rational Theology and Christian Philosophy in England in the Seventeenth Century, J. Tulloch, 76, 79
Rationalism in Greek Philosophy, G. Boas, 49
Rationalism in Politics and Other Essays, M. Oakeshott, 439, 449
Rationality and Religious Belief, C. F. Delaney, ed., 478, 480
Raven, J. E. *See* Kirk, G. S.
Rawls, J. *A Theory of Justice*, 393, 442, 444, 450
Raz, J. *The Authority of Law*, 457, 459; *The Concept of a Legal System*, 455, 459; *Practical Reason and Norms*, 455, 459
———, ed. *Practical Reasoning*, 405, 408; *see also* Hacker, P. M. S.

Reading Nozick, J. Paul, ed., 445, 450

A Reading of Hegel's Phenomenology of Spirit, Q. Lauer, 139, 142

Reading Rawls, N. Daniels, ed., 444, 448

Readings in Philosophy of Psychology, N. Block, ed., 484, 487

Readings in the Philosophy of Education, J. R. Martin, ed., 495, 499

Readings in the Philosophy of Language, J. F. Rosenberg and C. Travis, eds., 341, 346

Readings in the Philosophy of Religion, B. Brody, ed., 477, 480

Readings in the Philosophy of Science, H. Feigl and M. Brodbeck, eds., 415, 424

Readings in the Philosophy of the Social Sciences, M. Brodbeck, ed., 445, 448

Readings in the Theory of Action, N. S. Care and C. Landesmann, eds., 373, 377

Realism (Brentano and Meinong), G. Bergmann, 132, 134

Realism and the Background of Phenomenology, R. M. Chisholm, ed., 131, 134

The Realm of Rhetoric, Ch. Perelman, 310

Realms of Being, G. Santayana, 226

Reason and Action, B. Aune, 375, 377

Reason and Belief, B. Blanshard, 473, 475, 480

Reason and Commitment, R. Trigg, 399, 409

Reason and Conduct, H. D. Aiken, 391, 398, 404, 405

Reason and Conduct in Hume and His Predecessors, S. Tweyman, 108, 110

Reason and Evidence in Husserl's Phenomenology, D. M. Levin, 289, 291

Reason and Goodness, B. Blanshard, 397, 406

Reason and Human Good in Aristotle, J. M. Cooper, 44, 45

Reason and Morality, A. Gewirth, 393, 401, 407

Reason and Nature, M. R. Cohen, 217, 414, 423

Reason and Religion, S. C. Brown, ed., 478, 480

Reason and Revolution, H. Marcuse, 139, 142

Reason and Teaching, I. Scheffler, 497, 500

Reason, Experience and the Moral Life

(Kant and Dewey), B. S. Llamson, 398, 408

Reason Revisited (Jaspers), S. Samay, 273, 274

Recent American Philosophy, A. J. Reck, 221, 230

Reck, A. J. *The New American Philosophers* (since 1945), 221, 229; *Recent American Philosophy,* 221, 230; *Speculative Philosophy,* 352, 359

Reconstruction in Philosophy, J. Dewey, 5, 6, 9, 222

Ree, J. *Descartes,* 81, 83

———, M. Ayers and A. Westoby. *Philosophy and Its Past,* 7

Reese, W. L. *Dictionary of Philosophy and Religion: Eastern and Western Thought,* 159, 510

———, and E. Freeman, eds. *Process and Divinity* (Hartshorne), 476, 482

Reference and Generality, P. T. Geach, 331, 337

Referring, L. Linsky, 343, 346

Reflections on American Philosophy from Within, R. W. Sellars, 224, 230

Reflections on Frege's Philosophy, R. Grossmann, 132, 134

Reflections on Kant's Philosophy, W. H. Werkmeister, ed., 115, 121, 122

Reichenbach, H. *The Rise of Scientific Philosophy,* 154, 411, 414, 426

Reilly, F. E. *Charles Peirce's Theory of Scientific Method,* 240, 241

Relativism, M. Krausz and J. M. Meiland, eds., 399, 408

"The Relevance of Charles Peirce," M. H. Fisch et al., 241

The Relevance of Whitehead, I. Leclerc, ed., 214, 215

Religion, Truth and Language-Games, P. Sherry, 479, 482

Religion Within the Limits of Reason Alone, I. Kant, 114

Religion Without Explanation, D. Z. Phillips, 474, 475, 482

Religious Belief, W. P. Alston, ed., 476, 480

The Religious Dimension in Hegel's Thought, E. L. Fackenheim, 138, 141

The Religious Investigations of William James, H. S. Levinson, 475, 481

Religious Language, I. T. Ramsey, 473, 476, 482

The Religious Philosophy of William James, R. J. Vanden Burgt, 475, 482
Religious Reason, R. M. Green, 479, 481
Remarks on the Philosophy of Psychology, L. Wittgenstein, 484, 489
Remes, U., ed. *See* Hintikka, J., *Method*.
Renaissance Concepts of Man, P. O. Kristeller, 72
Renaissance Concepts of Method, N. W. Gilbert, 71, 72
Renaissance Man, A. Heller, 71, 72
Renaissance Thought and Its Sources, P. O. Kristeller, 70, 72
Renaissance Thought and the Arts, P. O. Kristeller, 70, 72
Renascent Rationalism, H. J. Robinson, 355, 359
Repercussions of the Kalam in Jewish Philosophy, H. A. Wolfson, 57, 69
Representations, J. A. Fodor, 365, 369
The Republic of Plato, F. M. Cornford, ed., 31, 32
Res Cogitans, Z. Vendler, 364, 370
Rescher, N. *Cognitive Systematization*, 323, 326; *The Coherence Theory of Truth*, 323, 326; *The Development of Arabic Logic*, 57, 69; *Induction*, 323, 326; *Introduction to Value Theory*, 383, 384; *Leibniz*, 90, 91; *Many-Valued Logic*, 332, 338; *Methodological Pragmatism*, 240, 241; *Peirce's Philosophy of Science*, 240, 241; "Philosophical Disagreement," 22, 33; *Scepticism*, 323, 326; *Studies in Arabic Philosophy*, 57, 69; *Unselfishness*, 399, 408
———, ed. *Essays in Honor of Carl G. Hempel*, 415, 426
Research in Philosophy, H. J. Koren, 505
Respect for Life in Medicine, Philosophy and the Law, O. Temkin, W. K. Frankena and S. H. Kadish, 308, 310
Respect for Persons, R. S. Downie and E. Telfer, 400, 406
The Revolt Against Dualism, A. O. Lovejoy, 350, 359
The Revolution in Philosophy, A. J. Ayer et al., eds., 169, 171
Revolutions and Reconstruction in the Philosophy of Science, M. Hesse, 418, 425
Rhetoric and Philosophy in Renaissance Humanism, J. Seigel, 71, 72

Richards, D. A. J. *A Theory of Reasons for Action*, 403, 408
Richardson, J. T. E. *The Grammar of Justification* (Wittgenstein), 207, 210
Richardson, W. J. *Heidegger*, 283, 284
Richter, M. *The Politics of Conscience* (T. H. Green, Idealism), 147, 149, 439
———, ed. *Political Theory and Political Education*, 442, 447, 450, 497
Ricoeur, P. *The Conflict of Interpretations*, 298, 301; *Freedom and Nature*, 376, 378; *Freud and Philosophy*, 298, 486, 488; *Political and Social Essays*, 442, 450; *The Symbolism of Evil*, 410
The Riddle of the Early Academy, H. Cherniss, 24, 32
Rieke, R. *See* Toulmin, S., *An Introduction*.
Riepe, D., ed. *Phenomenology and Natural Existence*, 287
Rights and Persons, A. I. Melden, 401, 408
Rights, Justice, and the Bounds of Liberty, J. Feinberg, 442, 448
The Rights of Reason (Kant), S. M. Shell, 118, 121
Riley, M. F. *See* Bechtle, M. F.
The Rise of American Philosophy, B. Kuklick, 218, 229
The Rise of Scientific Philosophy, H. Reichenbach, 154, 411, 414, 426
Rist, J. M. *Epicurus*, 48, 50; *Plotinus*, 48, 50; *Stoic Philosophy*, 48, 50
———, ed. *The Stoics*, 48, 50
Roberts, G. W., ed. *Bertrand Russell Memorial Volume*, 180, 181
Robin, R. S., ed. *See* Moore, E. C., *Studies*.
Robinson, E., tr. *See* Heidegger, M., *Being*.
Robinson, H. J. *Renascent Rationalism*, 355, 359
Robinson, R. *Plato's Earlier Dialectic*, 19, 21, 27, 30
———, tr., *see* Jaeger, W., *Aristotle*
Robson, J. M. and M. Laine, eds. *James and John Stuart Mill*, 145, 149
Rockmore, T. *Fichte, Marx and the German Philosophical Tradition*, 123, 135
Rodzinski, J. and W., tr. *See* Ossowski, S.
The Roman Inscriptions of Britain, R. G. Collingwood and R. P. Wright, 195, 197

Rome, S. and B., eds. *Philosophical Interrogations*, 271, 272

Rorty, A. O., ed. *Essays on Aristotle's Ethics*, 37, 44, 46; *Explaining Emotions*, 367, 370; *The Identities of Persons*, 367, 370

Rorty, R. *Consequences of Pragmatism*, 155, 156, 415; *Philosophy and the Mirror of Nature*, 5, 7, 155, 223, 308, 321, 324, 415; *see also* Lee, E. N.; Neu, J., "A Bibliography"

———, ed. "Historicism and Epistemology," 430, 431, 434; *The Linguistic Turn*, 154–56, 340

Rosen, S. *G. W. F. Hegel*, 141, 142; *The Limits of Analysis*, 152, 156; *Nihilism*, 398, 408

Rosenbaum, A. S., ed. *The Philosophy of Human Rights*, 443, 450

Rosenberg, J. F. *Linguistic Representation*, 343, 346; *One World and Our Knowledge of It*, 335, 359

———, and C. Travis, eds. *Readings in the Philosophy of Language*, 341, 346

Rosenthal, M. and P. Yudin, eds. *A Dictionary of Philosophy*, 510

Rosenthal, S. B. *The Pragmatic A Priori* (C. I. Lewis), 234

Ross, A. *Directives and Norms*, 456, 459

Ross, J. F., ed. *Inquiries into Medieval Philosophy*, 62, 69

Ross, S. D. *Philosophical Mysteries*, 355, 359

Ross, W. D. *Aristotle*, 25, 36, 46; *Plato's Theory of Ideas*, 23, 24, 33

Rossi, P. *See* Krieger, L.

Rotenstreich, N., ed. *Jewish Philosophy in Modern Times*, 124, 135

Rousseau, J.-J. *Confessions*, 111; *Discourse on the Origins of Inequality*, 112; *Discourse on the Sciences and the Arts*, 112; *Emile, or On Education*, 111–12, 492, 499; *The Social Contract*, 111–12

Rousseau, J. C. Hall, 112, 113

Rousseau and Representation, R. Fralin, 112, 113

Rousseau, Kant, Goethe, E. Cassirer, 110, 113

Rousseau's Political Philosophy, S. Ellensburg, 112, 113

Rousseau's Political Philosophy, R. M. Lemos, 112, 113

Rousseau's State of Nature, M. F. Plattner, 111, 113

The Route of Parmenides, A. P. D. Mourelatos, 14, 18

Rowe, W. L. *The Cosmological Argument*, 479, 482

Royal Institute of Philosophy. *Understanding Wittgenstein*, 209, 210

Ruben, D.-H., ed. *See* Mepham, J.

Rubinoff, L. *Collingwood and the Reform of Metaphysics*, 196, 198; *see also* Collingwood, R. G., *Faith and Reason*

Ruddick, W., ed. *See* O'Neill, O.

Rudner, R. S. *Philosophy of Social Science*, 446, 450

Ruggiero, G. *A History of European Liberalism*, 193; *Modern Philosophy*, 193

Runciman, W. G. *Plato's Later Epistemology*, 31, 33; *see also* Laslett, P.

Rundle, B. *Grammar in Philosophy*, 341, 346

Russell, B. *The Autobiography of Bertrand Russell*, 179, 181; *A Critical Exposition of the Philosophy of Leibniz*, 89–91; *Education and the Modern World*, 178, 492, 500; *Essays in Analysis*, 180, 181; *A History of Western Philosophy*, 8, 10, 178; *Human Knowledge*, 318, 326; *Logic and Knowledge: Essays, 1901–1950*, 180, 181; *My Philosophical Development*, 179, 181; *Mysticism and Logic and Other Essays*, 174, 177, 466, 469; *Our Knowledge of the External World*, 163, 176, 314, 326; *The Principles of Mathematics*, 162, 175, 176, 184, 204, 330–31, 338; *see also* Whitehead, A. N., *Principia Mathematica*; other works, 176–79

Russell, R. M. Sainsbury, 180, 181

Russell and Moore, A. J. Ayer, 163, 171

Russell in Review, J. E. Thomas and K. Blackwell, eds., 180, 181

Ryan, A. *John Stuart Mill*, 145, 149; *The Philosophy of the Social Sciences*, 446, 450

———, ed. *The Idea of Freedom*, 444, 450

Ryan, J. K. and B. M. Bonansea, eds. *John Duns Scotus, 1265–1965*, 66, 69

Rychlak, J. F. *Discovering Free Will and Personal Responsibility*, 373, 378; *A Philosophy of Science for Personality Theory*, 373, 485, 488

Ryle, G. *Collected Papers*, 165, 172; *The Concept of Mind*, 167, 362, 370; *Dilemmas*, 329, 338; *On Thinking*, 165, 172; *Plato's Progress*, 25–28, 33; "Taking Sides in Philosophy," 22, 33; *see also* Kolenda, K.
———, ed. *Contemporary Aspects of Philosophy*, 170, 172
Ryle, O. P. Wood and G. Pitcher, eds., 169, 172

Saarinen, E., et al., eds. *Essays in Honour of Jaakko Hintikka*, 154, 156
Sabine, G. H. *A History of Political Theory*, 437, 438, 450
Sacks, S., ed. *On Metaphor*, 344, 346
Sainsbury, R. M. *Russell*, 180, 181
St. Thomas Aquinas, R. M. McInerny, 65, 68
St. Thomas Aquinas, 1274–1974, 65, 69
St. Thomas on Analogy, G. P. Klubertanz, 65, 68
Sallis, J., ed. *Heidegger and the Path of Thinking*, 283, 284
Salmon, W. C. *The Foundations of Scientific Inference*, 421, 426
———, ed. *Zeno's Paradoxes*, 14, 18
———, R. C. Jeffrey and J. G. Greeno. *Statistical Explanation and Statistical Relevance*, 335, 338
Samay, S. *Reason Revisited* (Jaspers), 273, 274
Sameness and Substance, D. Wiggins, 356, 360
Sandbach, F. H. *The Stoics*, 48, 50
Santas, G. X. *Socrates*, 19–21
Santayana, G. *The Life of Reason*, 226; *Realms of Being*, 226; *Scepticism and Animal Faith*, 226
Santayana, T. L. S. Sprigge, 227, 230
Sartre, J.-P. *Being and Nothingness*, 275, 277; *Critique of Dialectical Reason*, 259, 261, 276; *Idiot of the Family*, 276
Sartre, M. Grene, 276, 277
Sartre, A. Manser, 276, 277
Sartre, M. Warnock, ed., 277
Sartre and the Problem of Morality, F. Jeanson, 277
Sartre's Concept of a Person, P. S. Morris, 276, 277
Sartre's Ontology, K. Hartmann, 276, 277

Savage, C. W., ed. *Perception and Cognition*, 484, 488
Savage, D., tr. *See* Ricoeur, P., *Freud*.
Saw, R. L., et al. "Spinoza," 87, 88
Saydah, J. R. *The Ethical Theory of Clarence Irving Lewis*, 226, 230
Saying and Understanding, C. Travis, 342, 347
Sayre, K. M. *Cybernetics and the Philosophy of Mind*, 366, 370; *Plato's Analytic Method*, 30, 33; *see also* Goodpaster, K. E., *Ethics*.
Scepticism, N. Rescher, 323, 326
Scepticism and Animal Faith, G. Santayana, 226
Scepticism and Historical Knowledge, J. W. Meiland, 431, 434
Schacht, R. *Hegel and After*, 125, 135
Schaeder, G. *The Hebrew Humanism of Martin Buber*, 271, 272
Schaper, Eva. *Prelude to Aesthetics*, 460, 469; *Studies in Kant's Aesthetics*, 461, 469
Scharfstein, B.-A. *Mystical Experience*, 479, 482; *The Philosophers*, 5, 7, 174, 306, 485
———, ed. *Philosophy East/Philosophy West*, 157, 158, 310
Scheffler, I. *The Anatomy of Inquiry*, 417, 426; *Beyond the Letter*, 343, 347; *Four Pragmatists*, 233, 234, 244; *The Language of Education*, 492, 500; *Reason and Teaching*, 497, 500; *Science and Subjectivity*, 420, 426
Scheler, M. *Formalism in Ethics and Non-Formal Ethics of Values*, 133, 391, 408; *Problems of a Sociology of Knowledge*, 439, 445, 450
Schelling's Idealism and Philosophy of Nature, J. L. Esposito, 123, 134
Schiffer, S. R. *Meaning*, 343, 347
Schilpp, P. A., ed. *Albert Einstein*, 416, 426; *Library of Living Philosophers* (series), 514; *The Philosophy of Alfred North Whitehead*, 211, 214, 215; *The Philosophy of Bertrand Russell*, 178, 180, 181; *The Philosophy of Brand Blanshard*, 224, 230; *The Philosophy of C. D. Broad*, 163, 172; *The Philosophy of C. I. Lewis*, 226, 230; *The Philosophy of Ernst Cassirer*, 152, 156; *The Philosophy of G. E. Moore*, 183, 187, 188; *The Philosophy of George Santayana*, 227, 230; *The Philosophy*

of *Jean-Paul Sartre*, 276–77; *The Philosophy of John Dewey*, 245; *The Philosophy of Karl Jaspers*, 273, 274; *The Philosophy of Karl Popper*, 202, 203; *The Philosophy of Rudolf Carnap*, 154, 156; *The Philosophy of Sarvepalli Radhadrishnan*, 157, 158; *see also* Freeman, E. (1976 Festschrift)
———, and M. Freedman, eds. *The Philosophy of Martin Buber*, 271, 272
Schleiermacher, F. *Brief Outline on the Study of Theology*, 5, 7, 294, 474; *Hermeneutics*, 295, 301; *On Religion*, 294, 471, 482; *Soliloquies*, 294
Schleiermacher Bibliography, T. N. Tice, 125, 135
Schmitz, F. J., tr. *See* Jaspers, K., *Nietzsche*.
Schneewind, J. B. *Sidgwick's Ethics and Victorian Moral Philosophy*, 146, 149, 388, 409
———, ed. *Mill*, 146, 149; "Sidgwick and Moral Philosophy," 146, 149, 388, 409
Schneider, H. W. *A History of American Philosophy*, 217, 218, 230
Schneller, H. M., ed. *See* Beardsley, M. C., *Aesthetic Inquiry*.
Schofield, M., ed. *See* Barnes, J.
———, M. Burnyeat and J. Barnes, eds. *Doubt and Dogmatism* (Hellenistic), 47, 50
Schopenhauer, A. *Fourfold Root of the Principle of Sufficient Reason*, 127; *The World as Will and Idea*, 127
Schopenhauer, P. Gardiner, 126–27, 134
Schopenhauer, D. W. Hamlyn, 126–27, 135
Schorske, C. E. *Fin-de-Siècle Vienna*, 204, 210
Schouls, P. A. *The Imposition of Method* (Descartes, Locke), 75, 79, 82, 94
Schrader, G. A., ed. *Existential Philosophers*, 264
Schubert Kalsi, M.-L. *Alexius Meinong on Objects of Higher Order and Husserl's Phenomenology*, 132, 135
Schutz, A. *The Phenomenology of the Social World*, 286, 287
Schwab, J. J. *Science, Curriculum and Liberal Education*, 495, 500
Schwartz, S. P., ed. *Naming, Necessity, and Natural Kinds*, 322, 326

Schwarz, D. W. *Naming and Referring*, 343, 347
Science and Metaphysics, W. Sellars, 416, 426
Science and Philosophy in Aristotle's Biological Works, A. Preus, 41, 46
Science and Sentiment in America, M. G. White, 221, 227, 230
Science and Subjectivity, I. Scheffler, 420, 426
Science and the Modern World, A. N. Whitehead, 212–15
Science, Curriculum and Liberal Education, J. J. Schwab, 495, 500
Science, Ideology and Value, A. Edel, 446, 448
Science in a Free Society, P. K. Feyerabend, 412, 417, 424
Science, Perception and Reality, W. Sellars, 315, 321, 326
Scientific Explanation, R. B. Braithwaite, 419, 423
Scientific Explanation, Space, and Time, H. Feigl and G. Maxwell, eds., 413, 424
Scienza Nuova, G. Vico, 99
Sclafani, R. J., ed. *See* Dickie, G., *Aesthetics*.
The Scope of Morality, P. A. French, 395, 407
Scott, D. *See* Peacocke, C. A. B.
Scottish Philosophy, J. McCosh, 143, 149
Scottish Philosophy and British Physics, 1750–1880, R. Olson, 144, 149
Scriven, M., ed. *See* Feigl, H., *Concepts and Foundations*.
Scrutton, R. *Art and Imagination*, 466, 469
Searle, J. R. *Expression and Meaning*, 342, 347; *Speech Acts*, 342, 347
———, F. Kiefer and M. Bierwisch, eds. *Speech Act Theory and Pragmatics*, 342, 347
Seeing and Knowing, F. I. Dretske, 321, 325
Seidman, R. M. *See* Green, T. F.
Seigel, J. *Marx's Fate*, 249, 252, 254, 256; *Rhetoric and Philosophy in Renaissance Humanism*, 71, 72
A Selective Bibliography of Philosophical Logic, C. A. B. Peacocke and D. Scott, rev. by M. Davies and G. Forbes, 506
The Self, T. Mischel, ed., 485, 488

Self-Deception, H. Fingarette, 367, 369, 486

The Self in Transformation, H. Fingarette, 486, 488

Self-Knowledge and Self-Identity, S. Shoemaker, 367, 370

Sellars, R. W. *Reflections on American Philosophy from Within,* 224, 230

Sellars, W. *Essays in Philosophy and Its History,* 227, 230; *Naturalism and Ontology,* 355, 359; *Science and Metaphysics,* 415, 426; *Science, Perception and Reality,* 315, 321, 326

————, ed. "Language, Thought and the World," 340, 347

Semantic Analysis, P. Ziff, 343, 347

Semantic Theory, J. J. Katz, 343, 346

"Semantics," D. Kalish and N. Kretzmann, 340, 346

Semantics and Necessary Truth, A. Pap, 315, 322, 326

Semantics of Natural Language, D. Davidson and G. Harman, eds., 343, 345

Sensation and Perception, D. W. Hamlyn, 320, 325

Sense and Sensibilia, J. L. Austin, 168, 316, 321, 325

Sentences, P. Lombard, 54, 66

The Seventeenth Century Background, B. Willey, 74, 79

Shaffer, J. A. *Philosophy of Mind,* 364, 370, 373

Shahan, R. W. and F. J. Kovach, eds., *Bonaventure and Aquinas,* 64, 69; *see also* Kovach, F. J.; Merrill, K. R.

————, and J. I. Biro, eds. *Spinoza,* 87, 88

————, and C. Swoyer, eds. *Essays on the Philosophy of W. V. Quine,* 228, 230

Shapere, D. *Galileo,* 414, 426

————, ed. *Philosophical Problems of Natural Science,* 414, 426

Shapiro, J. J., tr. *See* Habermas, J., *Knowledge.*

Sharp, A. M. *See* Lipman, M.

Sharp, D. E. *Franciscan Philosophy at Oxford in the Thirteenth Century,* 63, 69

Shatz, D., ed. *See* Cahn, S. M.

Shaw, W. H. *Marx's Theory of History,* 255, 256

Shell, S. M. *The Rights of Reason* (Kant), 118, 121

Sherry, P. *Religion, Truth and Language-Games,* 479, 482

Sherwood, M. *The Logic of Explanation in Psychoanalysis,* 486, 488

Shield, A. *A Bibliography of Bibliographies in Aesthetics,* 507

Shiner, R. A. *Knowledge and Reality in Plato's Philebus,* 30, 33

————, and J. King-Farlow, eds. *New Essays on Plato and the Pre-Socratics,* 13, 18

Shklar, J. N. *Freedom and Independence,* 139, 142; *Men and Citizens* (Rousseau), 112, 113

Shoemaker, S. *Self-Knowledge and Self-Identity,* 367, 370

Shook, L. K., tr. *See* Gilson, E., *Christian Philosophy of Saint Thomas Aquinas.*

A Short History of Ethics, A. MacIntyre, 388, 408

A Short History of Medieval Philosophy, J. R. Weinberg, 51, 69

Shorter, J. M. *See* Lindley, R. C.

Shue, H. *Basic Rights,* 446, 450

Sic et Non, Abelard, 63

Sidgwick, H. *The Methods of Ethics,* 146, 388; *Outlines of the History of Ethics,* 146, 388, 409

"Sidgwick and Moral Philosophy," J. B. Schneewind, ed., 146, 149, 388, 409

Sidgwick's Ethics and Victorian Moral Philosophy, J. B. Schneewind, 146, 149, 388, 409

Siegfried, C. H. *Chaos and Context* (James), 236, 237

The Significance of Neoplatonism, R. B. Harris, ed., 48, 49

The Significance of Sense, R. Wertheimer, 389, 409

Signification and Significance, C. Morris, 343, 346

Signs, M. Merleau-Ponty, 291, 293

Sikoria, R. I. and B. Barry, eds. *Obligations to Future Generations,* 400, 409

Silence, B. P. Dauenhauer, 286, 287

Silverman, D. W., tr. *See* Guttmann, J.

Simmons, A. J. *Moral Principles and Political Obligations,* 441, 451

Simon, W. M. *European Positivism in the Nineteenth Century,* 128, 135

Simplicity, E. Sober, 420, 426

Simpson, A. W. B., ed. *Oxford Essays in Jurisprudence,* 454, 459

Sinclair, E. M., tr. *See* Strauss, L., *Political Philosophy.*

Singer, B. *The Rational Society* (Santayana), 227, 230

Singer, M. G. *Generalization in Ethics,* 394

Singer, P. *Practical Ethics,* 400, 409

Sircello, G. *Mind and Art,* 466, 469; *A New Theory of Beauty,* 460, 469

Six Theories of Mind, C. W. Morris, 361, 370

Skepticism, K. Nielsen, 474, 482

Skepticism and Cognitivism, O. A. Johnson, 317, 319, 325

Skinner, Q. *The Foundations of Modern Political Thought,* 438, 451; *see also* Laslett, P.

Sklar, L. *Space, Time, and Spacetime,* 421, 426

Skolimowski, H. *Polish Analytical Philosophy,* 159, 160

Skrupskelis, I. K. *William James: A Reference Guide,* 237

Skyrms, B. *Causal Necessity,* 419, 426

Sleigh, R. C., ed. *Necessary Truth,* 335, 338

Slote, M. A. *Metaphysics and Essence,* 356, 359

Smart, J. J. C. *Philosophy and Scientific Realism,* 355, 359

———, et al. "Materialism Today," 366, 370

Smart, N. *The Phenomenon of Religion,* 473, 475, 476, 482

Smith, A. S., tr. *See* Sartre, J.-P., *Critique.*

Smith, B. O. and R. H. Ennis, eds. *Language and Concepts in Education,* 492, 500

Smith, C. *Contemporary French Philosophy,* 159, 160

———, tr., *see* Merleau-Ponty, M., *Phenomenology.*

Smith, J. E. *Experience and God,* 475, 482; *The Spirit of American Philosophy,* 227, 230; *Themes in American Philosophy,* 222, 230

———, ed. *Contemporary American Philosophy,* 222, 230; "Pragmatism Reconsidered," 235

———, et al. "Philosophy of History," 431, 434

Smith, N. K. *A Commentary to Kant's 'Critique of Pure Reason,'* 114, 121; *New Studies in the Philosophy of Descartes,* 80, 83; *The Philosophy of David Hume,* 108, 110; *Studies in the Cartesian Philosophy,* 80, 83

Smith, P. C., tr. *See* Gadamer, H.-G., *Dialogue* and Hegel's *Dialectic.*

Smith, R. G., tr. *See* Buber, M.

Smith, R. L. *See* Lewis, J. D.

Smythies, J. R., ed. *Brain and Mind,* 366, 370

Snook, I. A. *Indoctrination and Education,* 497, 500

———, ed. *Concepts of Indoctrination,* 497, 500

Sober, E. *Simplicity,* 420, 426

Social and Political Philosophy, P. A. French, T. E. Uehling and H. K. Wettstein, eds., 443, 448

The Social and Political Thought of Karl Marx, S. Avineri, 253–55

The Social Construction of Mind, J. Coulter, 484, 488

The Social Contract, J.-J. Rousseau, 111–12

Social Ends and Political Means, T. Honderich, ed., 442, 449

Social Justice, R. B. Brandt, ed., 440, 444, 448

Social Justice, D. Miller, 444, 449

Social Order and the Limits of Law, I. Jenkins, 456–58, 459

Social Philosophy, J. Feinberg, 442, 448

The Social Philosophy of English Idealism, A. J. M. Milne, 147, 149

Social Principles and the Democratic State, S. I. Benn and R. S. Peters, 440, 443, 448

The Social Problem in the Philosophy of Rousseau, J. Charvet, 112, 113

Social Thought in America, M. White, 439, 451

The Social Thought of Rousseau and Burke, D. Cameron, 112, 113

Socrates, G. X. Santas, 19–21

Socrates, A. E. Taylor, 19, 21

Socratic and Legal Obligation, R. E. Allen, 31

Socratic Memorabilia, J. G. Hamann, 100

Socratic Method and Critical Philosophy, L. Nelson, 152, 156

Sokolowski, R. *Husserlian Meditations,* 289, 291; *Presence and Absence,* 286, 287, 355, 359

Soliloquies, F. Schleiermacher, 294

Solmsen, F. *Aristotle's System of the Physical World*, 41, 46; *Intellectual Experiments of the Greek Enlightenment*, 13, 18

Solomon, R. C. *The Passions*, 368, 370
——, ed. *Nietzsche*, 270

Soltis, J. F. *An Introduction to the Analysis of Educational Concepts*, 492, 500
——, ed. *Philosophy and Education*, 492, 495, 497, 500; "Philosophy of Education Since Mid-Century," 492, 495, 500

Some Main Problems of Philosophy, G. E. Moore, 186, 187, 188

Sorabji, R. *Aristotle on Memory*, 43, 46; *Necessity, Cause and Blame* (Aristotle), 44, 46; *see also* Barnes, J.

Sorley, W. R. *A History of English Philosophy to 1900*, 143, 149

Sosa, E., ed. *Causation and Conditionals*, 419, 427

Sovereign Reason, E. Nagel, 225, 229, 352

The Sovereignty of Good, I. Murdoch, 392, 408

Space, Time and Deity, S. Alexander, 166

Space, Time, and Spacetime, L. Sklar, 421, 426

Specht, E. K. *The Foundations of Wittgenstein's Late Philosophy*, 208, 210

Speculative Philosophy, A. J. Reck, 352, 359

Speculum Mentis, R. G. Collingwood, 166, 188, 192, 193, 464, 465, 468

Speculum Spinozanum, 1677–1977, S. Hessing, ed., 87, 88

Speech Act Theory and Pragmatics, J. R. Searle, F. Kiefer and M. Bierwisch, eds., 342, 347

Speech Acts, 342, 347

Speech and Phenomena and Other Essays on Husserl's Theory of Signs, J. Derrida, 289, 290

Spiegelberg, H. *The Phenomenological Movement*, 220, 285–87, 289

Spinoza, B. *Ethica*, 86; *Tractatus de Intellectus Emendatione*, 86; *Tractatus Theologico-politicus*, 86

Spinoza, E. Freeman and M. Mandelbaum, eds., 87, 88

Spinoza, M. Grene, ed., 87, 88

Spinoza, S. Hampshire, 87, 88

"Spinoza," R. L. Saw et al., 87, 88

Spinoza, R. Shahan and J. I. Biro, eds., 87, 88

Spinoza's Critique of Religion, L. Strauss, 87, 88

Spinoza's Metaphysics, E. M. Curley, 86, 88

Spinoza's Philosophy of Man, J. Wetlesen, ed., 87, 88

Spinoza's Philosophy of the Law, G. Belaief, 87

Spinoza's Tractatus De Intellectus Emendatione, H. H. Joachim, 86, 88

The Spirit of American Philosophy, J. E. Smith, 227, 230

Spivak, G. C., tr. *See* Derrida, J., *Of Grammatology*.

Spragens, T. A. *The Politics of Motion* (Hobbes), 93

Sprague, E. *Metaphysical Thinking*, 354, 359

Sprigge, C., tr. *See* Croce, B., *Philosophy*.

Sprigge, T. L. S. *Santayana*, 227, 230

Spurling, L. *Phenomenology and the Social World* (Merleau-Ponty), 292, 293

Stace, W. T. *The Philosophy of Hegel*, 140, 142

Stachel, J., ed. *See* Earman, J.

Stack, G. J. *Berkeley's Analysis of Perception*, 105, 107; *Kierkegaard's Existential Ethics*, 266, 267

Stallybrass, O., ed. *See* Bullock, A.

Stambaugh, J., tr. *See* Heidegger, M., *Being and Time*.

Statistical Explanation and Statistical Relevance, W. Salmon, R. C. Jeffrey and J. G. Greeno, 335, 338

Stead, G. C. *Divine Substance*, 42, 46

Steiner, G. *Martin Heidegger*, 283, 284

Steiner, P., tr. and ed. *See* Mukařovský, J.

Steinhauer, K., ed. *Hegel Bibliography*, 141, 142

Steinkraus, W. E., ed. *New Studies in Berkeley's Philosophy*, 106, 107; *New Studies in Hegel's Philosophy*, 141, 142

Stengren, G. L., tr. *See* Thulstrup, N.

Stenius, E. *Wittgenstein's Tractatus*, 207, 210

Stephen, L. *The English Utilitarians*, 145, 149; *History of English Thought in the Eighteenth Century*, 98, 102

Stern, S. M., A. Hourani and V. Brown, eds. *Islamic Philosophy and the Classical Tradition*, 57, 69

Stevens, R. *James and Husserl*, 236, 237

Stevenson, C. L. *Ethics and Language,* 387, 392, 409; *Facts and Values,* 387, 409; *see also* Goldman, A. and J. Kim (1978 Festschrift)
Stewart, D., ed. *See* Ricoeur, P., *Political.*
Stewart, J. B. *The Moral and Political Philosophy of David Hume,* 108, 110
Stich, S. P., ed. *Innate Ideas,* 318, 326
Stoic Logic, B. Mates, 220, 329, 337
Stoic Philosophy, J. M. Rist, 48, 50
The Stoics, J. M. Rist, ed., 48, 50
The Stoics, F. H. Sandbach, 48, 50
Stokes, M. C. *One and Many in Presocratic Philosophy,* 13, 18
Stolnitz, J. *Aesthetics and Philosophy of Art Criticism,* 463, 464, 469
Stone, R. V., tr. *See* Jeanson, F.
Stough, C. L. *Greek Skepticism,* 48, 50
Stove, D. C. *Probability and Hume's Inductive Scepticism,* 108, 110
Strange Contrarieties (Pascal), J. Barker, 84, 85
Strasser, H., ed. *See* Knorr, K. D.
Strauss, L. *The Argument and the Action of Plato's Laws,* 31, 33; *Natural Right and History,* 438, 451; *The Political Philosophy of Hobbes,* 92, 93; *Spinoza's Critique of Religion,* 87, 88
Strawson, P. F. *The Bounds of Sense* (Kant), 115, 121; *Freedom and Resentment and Other Essays,* 154, 156; *Individuals,* 169, 356, 359; *Introduction to Logical Theory,* 332, 338; *Logico-Linguistic Papers,* 342, 347; *Subject and Predicate in Logic and Grammar,* 332, 338, 342, 347
———, ed. *Studies in the Philosophy of Thought and Action,* 169, 172, 364, 370
Strong, T. B. *Friedrich Nietzsche and the Politics of Transfiguration,* 269, 270
Stroud, B. *Hume,* 109, 110
The Structure of Appearance, N. Goodman, 352, 358
The Structure of Behavior, M. Merleau-Ponty, 291
The Structure of Language, J. A. Fodor and J. J. Katz, eds., 341, 345
The Structure of Marx's World-View, J. M. McMurtry, 254, 256
The Structure of Metaphysics, M. Lazerowitz, 352, 358, 486
The Structure of Morality, H. N. Casteñada, 404, 406

The Structure of Plato's Philosophy, J. S. Clegg, 30, 32
The Structure of Science, E. Nagel, 417, 420, 426
The Structure of Scientific Inference, M. Hesse, 421, 425
The Structure of Scientific Revolutions, T. S. Kuhn, 411–12, 425
The Structure of Scientific Theories, F. Suppe, ed., 415, 427
The Structure of Value, R. S. Hartman, 382, 383
Structure, Sign and Function, J. Mukařovský, 465, 469
Struggle for Synthesis (17th c.), L. E. Loemker, 76, 79, 90
Student Rights, Decisionmaking and the Law, T. Tice, 440, 451
Studies in Arabic Philosophy, N. Rescher, 57, 69
Studies in Epistemology, P. A. French, T. E. Uehling and H. K. Wettstein, eds., 318, 320, 321, 325
Studies in Ethical Theory, P. A. French, T. E. Uehling and H. K. Wettstein, eds., 390, 399, 401, 407
Studies in Inductive Logic and Probability, R. Carnap and R. C. Jeffrey, eds., 335, 336
Studies in Intellectual History, G. Boas, H. Cherniss et al., 5, 6
Studies in Kant's Aesthetics, E. Schaper, 461, 469
Studies in Maimonides and St. Thomas Aquinas, J. I. Dienstag, ed., 57, 67
Studies in Medieval Philosophy, Science, and Logic, E. A. Moody, 58, 68
Studies in Metaphysics, P. A. French, T. E. Uehling and H. K. Wettstein, eds., 354, 358
Studies in Pascal's Ethics, A. W. S. Baird, 84, 85
Studies in Philosophy, K. Kolenda, ed., 169, 171
Studies in Plato's Metaphysics, R. E. Allen, ed., 30, 31
Studies in Presocratic Philosophy, R. E. Allen and D. J. Furley, eds., 13, 16
Studies in Presocratic Philosophy, D. J. Furley and R. E. Allen, eds., 12, 14, 17
Studies in Renaissance Thought and Letters, P. O. Kristeller, 70, 72
Studies in the Cartesian Philosophy, N. K. Smith, 80, 83

Studies in the Hegelian Dialectic, J. M. E. McTaggart, 140, 142
Studies in the Methodology and Foundations of Science, P. C. Suppes, 418, 427
Studies in the Philosophy of Charles Sanders Peirce, E. C. Moore and R. S. Robin, eds., 241
Studies in the Philosophy of Charles Sanders Peirce, P. P. Wiener, ed., 240, 241
Studies in the Philosophy of David Hume, C. W. Hendel, 107, 109
Studies in the Philosophy of G. E. Moore, E. D. Klemke, ed., 187, 188
Studies in the Philosophy of Kant, L. W. Beck, 120, 121
Studies in the Philosophy of Thought and Action, P. F. Strawson, ed., 169, 172, 364, 370
Studies in the Philosophy of Wittgenstein, P. Winch, ed., 209, 210
Studies on Marx and Hegel, J. Hyppolite, 253, 256
A *Study of Hegel's Logic,* G. R. G. Mure, 140, 142
A *Study of the Ethics of Spinoza,* H. H. Joachim, 86, 88
Stuewer, R. H., ed. *Historical and Philosophical Perspectives of Science,* 414, 427
Subject and Predicate in Logic and Grammar, P. F. Strawson, 332, 338, 342, 347
Substance and Attribute, M. J. Loux, 356, 359
Substance, Body and Soul (Aristotle), E. Hartman, 42, 45
The Sufficiency of Hope, J. L. Muyskens, 479, 482
Sullivan, E. V., ed. *See* Beck, C. B.
Summa Contra Gentiles, Aquinas, 53, 64
Summa Theologiae, Aquinas, 64
Summers, R. S., ed. *Essays in Legal Philosophy,* 454, 459; *More Essays in Legal Philosophy,* 454, 459
Sumner, L. W. *Abortion and Moral Theory,* 405, 409
Suppe, F., ed. *The Structure of Scientific Theories,* 415, 427
———, and P. D. Asquith, eds. *PSA 1976,* 413, 427
Suppes, P. C. *Studies in the Methodology and Foundations of Science,* 418, 427;

see also Hintikka, J., *Information;* Nagel, E., *Logic*
Swain, M., ed. *See* Pappas, G. S.
Swartz, N. *See* Bradley, R.
Swartz, R. J., ed. *Perceiving, Sensing, and Knowing,* 320, 326; *see also* Chisholm, R. M., *Empirical Knowledge*
Sweeney, L. *Infinity in the Presocratics,* 13, 18
Swinburne, R. G. *The Coherence of Theism,* 479, 482; *The Existence of God,* 478, 482; *Faith and Reason,* 482
Swing, T. K. *Kant's Transcendental Logic,* 116, 121
Swoyer, C., ed. *See* Shahan, R. W., *Essays.*
Symbol, Myth and Culture, E. Cassirer, 152, 155
Symbolic Interactionism, H. Blumer, 246, 247
The Symbolism of Evil, P. Ricoeur, 298
Symbolism of the Sphere, O. J. Brendel, 11, 17
Symposium on J. L. Austin, K. T. Fann, ed., 169, 171
The Synoptic Vision (W. Sellars), C. F. Delaney et al., 228, 229
Syntactic Structures, N. Chomsky, 342, 343, 345
Synthese Library, 515
System of Logic, J. S. Mill, 77, 128, 143
A *System of Logistic,* W. V. O. Quine, 228
Systematic Theology, P. Tillich, 264, 265

Tagliacozzo, G. and H. V. White, eds. *Giambattista Vico,* 100, 102
Taking Rights Seriously, R. Dworkin, 400, 442, 448, 455, 457
"Taking Sides in Philosophy," G. Ryle, 22, 33
Talking about Particulars, J. W. Meiland, 343, 346
Tarski, A. *Logic, Semantics, Metamathematics,* 332, 338; *see also* Nagel, E., *Logic*
Tatarkiewicz, W. *History of Aesthetics,* 460, 469; *A History of Six Ideas* (Aesthetics), 460, 469
Tay, A. E.-S., ed. *See* Kamenka, E., *Human Rights.*
Taylor, A. E. *Socrates,* 19, 21
Taylor, C. *The Explanation of Behavior,* 374, 378; *Hegel,* 141, 142

Taylor, M. C. *Journeys to Selfhood: Hegel and Kierkegaard*, 266, 267; *Kierkegaard's Pseudonymous Authorship*, 265, 267

Taylor, R. *Action and Purpose*, 374, 378; *Metaphysics*, 354, 359

Teichman, J. *The Mind and the Soul*, 364, 370; *see also* Diamond, C.

Teleology Revisited, E. Nagel, 420, 426

Telfer, E. *See* Downie, R. S.

Temkin, O., W. K. Frankena and S. H. Kadish. *Respect for Life in Medicine, Philosophy and the Law*, 308, 310

Thalberg, I. *Enigmas of Agency*, 374, 378

Thayer, H. S. *Meaning and Action: A Critical History of Pragmatism*, 231–33, 235, 244

Thematic Origins of Scientific Thought, G. Holton, 414, 425

Themes in American Philosophy, J. E. Smith, 222, 230

Theodicée, G. W. Leibniz, 88

Theology and Meaning, R. S. Heimbeck, 475, 481

The Theology of the Early Greek Philosophers, W. Jaeger, 12, 17

Theoretical Concepts, R. Tuomela, 421, 427

Theories of History, P. Gardiner, ed., 430–31, 434

Theories of Scientific Method, R. M. Blake, C. J. Ducasse and E. H. Madden, 414, 423

Theorizing, A. F. Blum, 39, 45

Theory and Practice, J. Habermas, 299, 301

Theory and Practice (Marx), N. Lobkowicz, 254, 256

Theory of Action, L. H. Davis, 373, 377

Theory of Beauty, H. Osborne, 460, 469

A Theory of Criminal Law, H. Gross, 458, 459

A Theory of Human Action, A. E. Goldman, 374, 377

A Theory of Justice, J. Rawls, 393, 442, 444, 450

Theory of Knowledge, R. M. Chisholm, 318, 319, 325

"Theory of Knowledge," R. M. Chisholm, 314, 315, 318, 323, 325

The Theory of Morality, A. Donagan, 395, 406

A Theory of Perception, G. Pitcher, 321, 326

A Theory of Reasons for Action, D. A. J. Richards, 403, 408

A Theory of the Good and the Right, R. B. Brandt, 393, 402, 406

Theory of the Moral Life, J. Dewey, 386, 396, 406

Thilly, F. *A History of Philosophy*, 8, 10

Thinking About Morality, W. K. Frankena, 395–96, 406

Thinking and Doing, H.-N. Casteñada, 446, 448

Thinking and Experience, H. H. Price, 318–19, 326

Thirty Years of Foundational Studies (Mathematical Logic), A. Mostowski, 329, 337

Thomas, G. F. *Philosophy and Religious Belief*, 475, 482

Thomas, J. E. and K. Blackwell, eds. *Russell in Review*, 180, 181

Thomas, L. *Philosophical Redirection of Educational Research*, 494, 500

Thomas, S. N. *The Formal Mechanics of Mind*, 366, 370

"Thomas Aquinas 1274–1974," L. W. Beck, ed., 65, 67

Thomas Hobbes, C. H. Hinnant, 93

Thomas Hobbes: A Reference Guide, C. H. Hinnant, 93

Thompson, D. F. *John Stuart Mill and Representative Government*, 145, 149

Thompson, J., ed. *Kierkegaard*, 266, 267

Thompson, J. B. and D. Held, eds. *Habermas: Critical Debates*, 300, 301

Thompson, M. "Metaphysics," 357, 359

Thomson, J. J. *Acts and Other Events*, 366, 370

Thorp, J. *Free Will*, 376, 378

Thought, G. Harman, 318, 325

Thought and Action, S. Hampshire, 373, 378

Thought and Object, A. Woodfield, ed., 366, 367, 371

The Thought and Character of William James, R. B. Perry, 220, 236, 237

Thought, Fact, and Reference (Logical Atomism), H. I. Hochberg, 154, 155

The Thought of Karl Marx, D. McLellan, 254, 256

Three Historical Philosophies of Education, W. K. Frankena, 244, 492, 498

Three Faces of Hermeneutics, R. J. Howard, 298, 301

Thulstrup, N. *Kierkegaard's Relation to Hegel*, 266, 267

Thus Spake Zarathustra, F. Nietzsche, 269

Tice, T. N. "A Psychoanalytic Perspective" (Moral Development), 472, 496, 500; *Schleiermacher Bibliography*, 125, 135; *Student Rights, Decision-making, and the Law*, 440, 451

———, tr., *see* Schleiermacher, F., *Brief Outline* and *On Religion*

Tilghman, B. R., ed. *Language and Aesthetics*, 463, 469

Tillich, P. *Systematic Theology*, 264, 265; *see also* Rome, S.

Time and Necessity (Aristotle), J. Hintikka, 41, 44, 45

Tipton, I. C. *Berkeley*, 106, 107

Tobey, J. L. *The History of Ideas: A Bibliographical Introduction*, 507

Todd, W. B., ed. *Hume and the Enlightenment*, 108, 110

Toews, J. E. *Hegelianism*, 126, 135

Tolstoy, L. *War and Peace*, 428

Tormey, A. *The Concept of Expression*, 466, 469

Toulmin, S. *Foresight and Understanding*, 411; "From Form to Function: Philosophy and History of Science in the 1950s and Now," 415, 422, 427; *Human Understanding*, 421, 427; *The Philosophy of Science*, 334, 417, 427; *see also* Janik, A.

———, R. Rieke and A. Janik. *An Introduction to Reasoning*, 331, 338, 404

Toward a Reunion in Philosophy, M. G. White, 223, 230

Towards a Transformation of Philosophy, K.-O. Apel, 300, 357

Tractatus de Intellectus Emendatione, B. Spinoza, 86

Tractatus Logico-Philosophicus, L. Wittgenstein, 166, 177, 204–8, 210

Tractatus Theologico-politicus, B. Spinoza, 86

The Tragic Finale (Sartre), W. Desan, 276, 277

Transcendental Arguments and Science, P. Bieri, R. P. Horstmann and L. Krüger, eds., 420, 423

Transcendentals and Their Function in the Metaphysics of Duns Scotus, A. Wolter, 66, 69, 220

The Transformations of Man, L. Mumford, 228, 229

Travis, C. *Saying and Understanding*, 342, 347

A Treatise Concerning the Principles of Human Knowledge, G. Berkeley, 103, 106

A Treatise of Human Nature, D. Hume, 107–8

Treatise on Basic Philosophy, M. Bunge, 355, 358

A Treatise on Probability, J. M. Keynes, 335, 337

Trigg, R. *Reason and Commitment*, 399, 409

Trinkaus, C. *In Our Image and Likeness* (Italian Humanism), 71, 73

The Triumph of Subjectivity (Husserl), J. Q. Lauer, 289, 291

Truth, G. Pitcher, 323, 326

Truth and Method, H.-G. Gadamer, 298, 301

Truth and Other Enigmas, M. Dummett, 167, 169, 324, 325

Truth and Value in Nietzsche, J. T. Wilcox, 269, 271

Truth, Love and Immortality (McTaggart), P. T. Geach, 148

"Truth, Meaning, and Reference," D. Føllesdal, ed., 322, 325

Tucker, R. C. *Philosophy and Myth in Karl Marx*, 253, 255, 256

Tufts, J. H., tr. *See* Windelband, W.

Tulloch, J. *Rational Theology and Christian Philosophy in England in the Seventeenth Century*, 76, 79

Tuomela, R. *Human Action and Its Explanation*, 373, 378; *Theoretical Concepts*, 421, 427

Turbayne, C. M., ed. *See* Berkeley, G., *A Treatise*.

Tweyman, S. *Reason and Conduct in Hume and His Predecessors*, 108, 110

Two Centuries of Philosophy in America, P. Caws, ed., 216, 219, 221, 227, 229

The Two Sources of Morality and Religion, H. Bergson, 127

Two Studies in the Greek Atomists, D. J. Furley, 14, 17

Two Theories of Morality, S. Hampshire, 397, 407

Two Treatises of Government, J. Locke, 94, 95

Tymieniecka, A.-T., ed. *Analecta Husserliana,* 286, 287

Uehling, T. E., ed. *See* French, P. A.
Ullmann, W. *The Individual and Society in the Middle Ages,* 63, 65, 69
The Ultimate Reducibility of Essence to Existence in Existential Metaphysics, W. E. Carlo, 351, 358
The Unconscious, A. C. MacIntyre, 486, 488
The Unconscious Sources of Berkeley's Philosophy, J. O. Wisdom, 103–4, 107, 485
Understanding Rawls, R. P. Wolff, 444, 451
Understanding Whitehead, V. Lowe, 214, 215
Understanding Wittgenstein, Royal Institute of Philosophy, 209, 210
Unger, P. *Ignorance: A Case for Scepticism,* 316–17, 326
The Unity of Science, R. L. Causey, 422, 423
"The Unity of Science: Interfield Theories," L. Darden and N. Maull, 422, 424
Universals and Particulars, M. J. Loux, ed., 356, 359
Universals and Scientific Realism, D. M. Armstrong, 355, 357
University of Pittsburgh Series in the Philosophy of Science, vols. 1–5, R. G. Colodny, ed., 413, 424
Unselfishness, N. Rescher, 399, 408
Urban, L. and D. N. Walton, eds. *The Power of God,* 478, 482
Urmson, J. O. *The Emotive Theory of Ethics,* 392, 409; *Philosophical Analysis,* 163, 172
———, ed. *The Concise Encyclopedia of Western Philosophy and Philosophers,* 510; *see also* Austin, J. L., *How to Do Things wtih Words* and *Philosophical Papers*

Vail, L. M. *Heidegger and Ontological Difference,* 283, 284
Validity and Rhetoric in Philosophical Argument, H. W. Johnstone, 310
Value, R. Lepley, ed., 381, 383
Value and Existence, J. Leslie, 382, 383
Value and Obligation, R. B. Brandt, 389, 406

The Value of the Individual, K. J. Weintraub, 111, 113
Value Theory in Philosophy and Social Science, E. Laszlo and J. B. Wilbur, eds., 380, 383
Values and Evaluations, Z. Najder, 382, 384
Values and Intentions, J. N. Findlay, 366, 369
Values and Morals, A. I. Goldman and J. Kim, eds., 390, 399, 407
Vandenberg, D. *Being and Education,* 494, 500
Vanden Burgt, R. J. *The Religious Philosophy of William James,* 475, 482
Van Der Dussen, W. J. *History as a Science* (Collingwood), 197, 198
Vander Veer, G. L. *Bradley's Metaphysics and the Self,* 148, 149; *Philosophical Skepticism and Ordinary-Language Analysis,* 316, 327
Van Doren, C., ed. *See* Adler, M., *Great Treasury.*
The Varieties of Goodness, G. H. von Wright, 402
The Varieties of Religious Experience, W. James, 236, 475
Vendler, Z. *Res Cogitans,* 364, 370
Verene, D. P. *Vico's Science of Imagination,* 100, 102
———, ed. *Hegel's Social and Political Thought,* 139, 142; *see also* Cassirer, E., *Symbol*
Vesey, G. N. A. *The Embodied Mind,* 363, 370
Vetterling-Braggin, M., ed. *"Femininity," "Masculinity," and "Androgyny,"* 311, 312
———, F. A. Elliston and J. English, eds. *Feminism and Philosophy,* 311, 312
Vickers, B., ed. *Essential Articles for the Study of Francis Bacon,* 77, 79
Vico, G. *Autobiography,* 99; *Scienza Nuova,* 99
Vico, L. Pompa, 99, 102
Vico and Herder, I. Berlin, 99, 101
Vico's Science of Imagination, D. Verene, 100, 102
Viertel, J., tr. *See* Habermas, J., *Theory.*
"Virtue and Moral Goodness," W. K. Frankena et al., 403, 407
The Virtues, P. T. Geach, 402, 407
Virtues and Vices, J. D. Wallace, 403, 409

Virtues and Vices and Other Essays in Moral Philosophy, P. Foot, 395, 403, 406

Vlastos, G. *Platonic Studies,* 15, 18, 28, 29; *Plato's Universe,* 13, 18; articles in Allen, R. E., *Studies,* 13; review of Cornford in Furley, D., *Studies,* 12; *see also* Lee, E. N. (1973 Festschrift)
———, ed. *The Philosophy of Socrates,* 19, 21; *Plato,* 24, 30, 33

Wahl, J. *See* Rome, S.
Wainwright, W. J. *Philosophy of Religion: An Annotated Bibliography,* 508
Waismann, F. *How I See Philosophy,* 341, 347; *Philosophical Papers,* 151, 156; *The Principles of Linguistic Philosophy,* 341, 347
Walford, D. E., tr. *See* Specht, E. K.
Walker, R. C. S. *Kant,* 115, 122
Wallace, J. D. *Virtues and Vices,* 403, 409
Wallraff, C. F. *Karl Jaspers,* 273, 274; *Philosophical Theory and Psychological Fact,* 484, 488
———, tr., *see* Jaspers, K., *Nietzsche*
Walsh, G., tr. *See* Schutz, A.
Walsh, W. H. *Hegelian Ethics,* 140, 142; *Kant's Criticism of Metaphysics,* 115, 122; *Metaphysics,* 354, 359; *Philosophy of History,* 431, 434; *see also* Passmore, J., ed., *Historiography*
Walton, D., ed. *See* Brand, M., *Action Theory.*
Walton, D. N. *See* Urban, L.
Walzer, R. *Greek into Arabic,* 57, 69; *see also* Stern, S. M. (1972 Festschrift)
Wang, H. *From Mathematics to Philosophy,* 329, 338
War and Peace, L. Tolstoy, 428
Ward, K. *The Development of Kant's Ethics,* 116, 122
Warnock, G. J. *Berkeley,* 106, 107; *English Philosophy Since 1900,* 162, 163, 172; *The Object of Morality,* 395, 409
———, ed. *Oxford Readings in Philosophy* (series), 514; *see also* Austin, J. L., *Philosophical Papers* and *Sense and Sensibilia;* Frankena, W. K., *Thinking*
Warnock, M. *Ethics Since 1900,* 388, 409; *Existentialism,* 263, 265; *Imagination,* 367, 370, 466, 469; *The Philosophy of Sartre,* 276, 277
———, ed. *Sartre,* 277

Warren, P. *See* Fisch, M.
Warrender, H. *The Political Philosophy of Hobbes,* 92–93
Wartofsky, M. W. *Conceptual Foundations of Scientific Thought,* 417, 427; *Feuerbach,* 126, 135; *see also* Boston Studies; Cohen, R. S.
———, and C. C. Gould, eds. *Women and Philosophy,* 311, 312
Wasserstrom, R. A. *Philosophy and Social Issues,* 446, 451
———, et al. "Philosophy and Public Policy," 446, 451
———, ed. "Philosophical Problems of Death," 309, 310
Watkins, J. W. N. *Hobbes's System of Ideas,* 92, 93
Watson, R. A. *The Downfall of Cartesianism, 1673–1712,* 82, 83
Way to Wisdom, K. Jaspers, 273, 274
Ways of Worldmaking, N. Goodman, 352, 358
Weakness of Will, G. W. Mortimore, ed., 375, 378
Weinberg, J. R. *An Examination of Logical Positivism,* 220; *A Short History of Medieval Philosophy,* 51, 69
Weintraub, K. J. *The Value of the Individual,* 111, 113
Weiss, F. G., ed. *Beyond Epistemology* (Hegel), 141, 142; *see also* O'Malley, J. J.
Weiss, P. *Modes of Being,* 350, 351, 360; *see also* Peirce, C. S.; Rome, S.
Weitz, M. *The Opening Mind,* 463, 469; *Problems in Aesthetics,* 463, 470
Werkmeister, W. H. *Kant,* 120, 122; *Man and His Values,* 382, 384
———, ed. *Facets of Plato's Philosophy,* 29, 30, 33; *Reflections on Kant's Philosophy,* 115, 121, 122
Wertheimer, R. *The Significance of Sense,* 389, 409
Westbury, I., ed. *See* Schwab, J. J.
Western Mysticism: A Guide to the Basic Works, M. A. Bowman, 504
Westoby, A. *See* Ree, J., *Philosophy.*
Westphal, M. *History and Truth in Hegel's Phenomenology,* 139, 142
Wetlesen, J., ed. *Spinoza's Philosophy of Man,* 87, 88
Wettstein, H. K., ed. *See* French, P. A.
What Is Justice? H. Kelsen, 455, 459
Whately, R. *Elements of Logic,* 238

Wheelwright, P. *The Burning Fountain* (Symbolism), 344, 347; *Metaphor and Reality*, 344, 347

Whitbeck, C., ed. *A Directory of Women in Philosophy*, 513

White, H. V. *Metahistory* (19th c.), 430, 435; *see also* Krieger, L.; Tagliacozzo, G.

White, J. *See* Gordon, P.

White, M. G. *Foundations of Historical Knowledge*, 431, 435; *Science and Sentiment in America*, 221, 227, 230; *Social Thought in America*, 439, 451; *Toward Reunion in Philosophy*, 223, 230

———, ed. *Documents in the History of American Philosophy*, 221, 230

White, N. P. *Plato on Knowledge and Reality*, 30, 33

Whitehead, A. N. *Adventures of Ideas*, 212, 215; *The Aims of Education*, 492, 500; *Dialogues of Alfred North Whitehead*, 212, 214, 215; *Modes of Thought*, 212–15; *Process and Reality*, 166, 212–15; *Science and the Modern World*, 212–15; other works, 210, 212

———, and B. Russell. *Principia Mathematica*, 153, 175, 178, 206, 211–12, 330, 338

Whitehead's Metaphysics, I. Leclerc, 214

Whitehead's Organic Philosophy of Science, A. L. Plamondon, 214, 215

Whitehead's Philosophical Development, N. M. Lawrence, 214

Whitehead's Philosophy, C. Hartshorne, 214

Why Does Language Matter to Philosophy? I. Hacking, 341, 345

Whyte, L. L., A. B. Wilson and D. Wilson, eds. *Hierarchical Structures*, 383, 384

Widener Library Shelflist, v. 42–43: *Philosophy and Psychology*, Harvard Univ. Library, 504

Widgery, A. G. *See* Sidgwick, H., *Outlines.*

Wiener, P. P. *Evolution and the Founders of Pragmatism*, 220

———, ed. *Dictionary of the History of Ideas*, 511; *Studies in the Philosophy of Charles Sanders Peirce*, 240, 241

Wiggins, D. *Sameness and Substance*, 356, 360

Wilbur, J. B., ed. *See* Laszlo, E.; Magnus, B.

Wilcox, J. T. *Truth and Value in Nietzsche*, 269, 271

Wild, J. D. *The Radical Empiricism of William James*, 236, 237; *see also* Rome, S.

Wilhelm Dilthey, M. Ermarth, 125, 134

Wilkerson, T. E. *Kant's Critique of Pure Reason*, 115, 122

Wilkes, K. V. *Physicalism*, 366, 371

Wilkins, B. T. *Has History Any Meaning?* (Popper), 202, 203; *Hegel's Philosophy of History*, 140, 142

Wilkof, N. J., ed. *See* Schwab, J. J.

Will, F. L. *Induction and Justification*, 316, 322, 327

Will, Freedom, and Power, A. Kenny, 373, 376, 378

Willard Van Orman Quine, A. Orenstein, 228, 229

Willey, B. *The Seventeenth Century Background*, 74, 79

Willey, T. E. *Back to Kant*, 133, 135

William James: A Biography, G. W. Allen, 236, 237

William James: A Reference Guide, I. K. Skrupskelis, 237

William of Ockham, G. Leff, 66, 68

Williams, B. *Descartes*, 81, 83; *Problems of the Self*, 364, 367, 371

Williams, B. A. O. and A. Montefiore, eds. *British Analytic Philosophy*, 169, 172

Williams, M. *Groundless Belief*, 317, 318, 323, 327

Wilson, A. B., ed. *See* Whyte, L. L.

Wilson, Deirdre. *Presuppositions and Non-Truth-Conditional Semantics*, 343, 347

Wilson, Donna, ed. *See* Whyte, L. L.

Wilson, E. *The Mental as Physical*, 366, 371

Wilson, M. D. *Descartes*, 81, 83

Wilson, N. L. *The Concept of Language*, 341, 347

Winch, P. *The Idea of a Social Science and Its Relation to Philosophy*, 445, 451

———, ed. *Studies in the Philosophy of Wittgenstein*, 209, 210

Windelband, W. *A History of Philosophy*, 8, 10

Windmiller, M., N. Lambert and E. Turiel, eds. *Moral Development and Socialization. See* Tice, T. N., "A Psychoanalytic Perspective."
Wingo, G. M. *Philosophies of Education,*
493, 500
Winokur, S., ed. *See* Radner, M.
Wiredu, K. *Philosophy and an African
Culture,* 159, 160
Wisdom, J. *Other Minds,* 362, 371; *Philosophy and Psycho-analysis,* 485,
489; *Problems of Mind and Matter,*
362, 371
Wisdom, J. O. *The Unconscious Sources
of Berkeley's Philosophy,* 103–4, 107,
485
Wittgenstein, L. *Philosophical Investigations,* 205–8, 210, 362; *Remarks on
the Philosophy of Psychology,* 484,
489; *Tractatus Logico-Philosophicus,*
166, 177, 204–8, 210; other works,
205–6
Wittgenstein, R. J. Fogelin, 208, 209
Wittgenstein, A. Kenny, 208, 210
Wittgenstein, C. G. Luckhardt, ed., 204,
207, 208, 210
*Wittgenstein and His Impact on Contem-
porary Thought,* E. Leinfellner et al.,
eds., 209, 210
Wittgenstein and Justice, H. F. Pitkin,
440, 450
Wittgenstein and Knowledge, T. Mora-
wetz, 209, 210
Wittgenstein and Political Argument,
J. W. Danford, 440, 448
Wittgenstein and Scientific Knowledge,
D. L. Phillips, 209, 210
*Wittgenstein on the Foundations of
Mathematics,* C. Wright, 209, 210
Wittgenstein: The Early Philosophy,
H. L. Finch, 207, 209
Wittgenstein: The Later Philosophy,
H. L. Finch, 208, 209
*Wittgenstein, the Philosophical Investiga-
tions,* G. Pitcher, ed., 208, 210
*Wittgenstein—Understanding and Mean-
ing,* G. P. Baker and P. M. S. Hacker,
208, 209
*Wittgenstein's Doctrine of the Tyranny
of Language,* S. M. Engel, 207, 209
Wittgenstein's Language, T. Binkley,
206, 208, 209
Wittgenstein's Philosophy of Language,
J. Bogen, 208, 209

Wittgenstein's Tractatus, E. Stenius, 207,
210
Wittgenstein's Vienna, A. Janik and S.
Toulmin,131, 204, 207, 210
Woglom, W. H., tr. *See* Cassirer, E.,
Problem.
Wolff, R. P. *Understanding Rawls,* 444,
451
———, ed. *Kant,* 121, 122
Wolfson, H. A. *The Philosophy of Spi-
noza,* 86, 88, 220; *The Philosophy of
the Kalam,* 56, 69; *Repercussions of
the Kalam in Jewish Philosophy,* 57,
69
Wollheim, R. *Art and Its Objects,* 446,
470; *F. H. Bradley,* 148, 149
———, ed. *Freud,* 486, 489
Wolter, A. *Transcendentals and Their
Function in the Metaphysics of Duns
Scotus,* 66, 69, 220
Women and Philosophy, M. Wartofsky
and C. C. Gould, eds., 311, 312
Women in Western Political Thought,
S. M. Okin, 438, 450
Women, Reason, and Nature, C. McMil-
lan, 311, 312
"Women's Liberation," M. Mothersill,
ed., 311, 312
Wood, A. W. *Kant's Rational Theology,*
118, 122; *Karl Marx,* 254–56
Wood, L. *See* Thilly, F.
Wood, O. P. and G. Pitcher, eds. *Ryle,*
169, 172
Wood, R. E., ed. *The Future of Meta-
physics,* 357, 360
Woodfield, A., ed. *Thought and Object,*
366, 367, 371
Woodger, J. H., tr. *See* Tarski, A.
Word and Object, W. V. O. Quine, 315,
321, 322, 326
Words and Deeds, D. Holdcroft, 342,
346
Words and Objectives (Quine), D. Da-
vidson and J. Hintikka, eds., 228, 229
Words and Things (Linguistic Philoso-
phy), E. Gellner, 170, 171
Works, J. Dewey, 245
The Works of William James, W. James,
236, 237
The World as Will and Idea, A. Schopen-
hauer, 127
World Hypotheses, S. C. Pepper, 349,
359
Worrall, J., ed. *See* Lakatos, I., *Proofs.*

Wreen, M., ed. *See* Beardsley, M. C., *Aesthetic Point of View.*

Wright, C. *Wittgenstein on the Foundations of Mathematics,* 209, 210

Wright, G. H. von. *Causality and Determinism,* 419, 427; *Explanation and Understanding,* 374, 378, 420, 427; *The Logical Problem of Induction,* 335, 338; *The Varieties of Goodness,* 402; *see also* Hintikka, J., ed. (1976 Festschrift); Wittgenstein, L., *Remarks*

Wright, R. P. *See* Collingwood, R. G., *Roman Inscriptions.*

Writings on the General Theory of Signs, C. W. Morris, 340, 346

Yates, F. A. *The Art of Memory,* 43, 46; *The Occult Philosophy in the Elizabethan Age,* 71, 73

Yolton, J. W., ed. *John Locke,* 95, 96

Yost, R. M. *Leibniz and Philosophical Analysis,* 90, 91

The Young Hegel, G. Lukacs, 138, 142

The Young Hegelians, W. J. Brazill, 126, 134

Young John Dewey, N. Coughlan, 243–45

Yovel, Y. *Kant and the Philosophy of History,* 120, 122

———, ed. *Philosophy of History and Action,* 429, 431, 435

Yudin, P., ed. *See* Rosenthal, M.

Zaner, R. M., ed. *See* Kersten, F.

Zelený, J. *The Logic of Marx,* 254, 256

Zeno's Paradoxes, W. C. Salmon, ed., 14, 18

Ziff, P. *Semantic Analysis,* 343, 347

Zilian, H. G., ed. *See* Knorr, K. D.

SUBJECT INDEX

Names in parentheses refer to authors.

Abelard, 52, 61–63, 111
Academy, *see* Plato
Action, philosophy of, 157, 190, 263, 272, 316, 354, 362, 367, 372–78, 432, 446, 483, 484; "act," "action," 43, 87, 157, 246, 364, 374–75, 432; bibliography, 377 (Binkley), 505; culpability, responsibility, 44, 48, *see also* Ethics; free will and determinism, 375–77, *see also* Freedom; linguistic analysis, 362. *See also* Intentionality; Mind, philosophy of; Teleological concepts; Will.
Action, H. B., 388
Adler, Felix, 6 (Kaufmann)
Adorno, Theodor, 299
Aesthetics, 97, 114, 115, 117, 121, 134, 146, 188–90, 226, 265, 294, 296, 331, 376, 460–70, 497; aesthetic attitude, 464; beauty, 28, 460; bibliography, 507; form vs. expression, 461–62, 465–66; social meanings of art, 465; style, 465. *See also* Arts; Literature; Metaphor; Symbols.
African philosophy, 159
Agricola, Rudolph, 78
Albert the Great, 64
Alexander, Samuel, 131, 166, 473
Alexander of Macedon, 33
Alienation, 137, 252–54, 275, 278, 438
Alpers, Svetlana, 465
Alston, William, 318, 344, 477, 480, 484, 487
Althusser, Louis, 253–55, 259, 260
Ambrose, 54
American Philosophical Association, 222
American philosophy, 6, 166, 168, 213, 216–47, 286, 288, 350–51, 363, 381,

442, 492; 18th c., 98, 124; Golden Age, 217, 219, 242
Analogy, *see* Method, philosophical
Analytic and synthetic, 75, 315, 322, 323, 328, 380; Kant (vs. predecessors), 115, 120
Analytic philosophy, 124, 150–56, 158, 219, 222, 227, 298, 300, 315, 317, 341, 350, 352, 372, 380, 385, 438, 492; as deteriorated Hegelianism, 152; British, 161–72; methods, 163–65, 168; relations to phenomenology, 286; varieties of, 164–65
Anaximander, 14
Andronicus of Rhodes, 35
Angell, James Rowland, 246
Annas, Julia, 37
Anscombe, G. E. M., 43, 209, 344, 362, 367, 368, 397
Anselm, 52, 58–62, 143, 422, 472, 474, 478
Anthropology, 398
Anthropology, philosophical, 140, 236, 269, 363, 416; 18th c., 98, 117–18; basis for political thought, 91, 253; human malleability, 125; man a "thinking reed," 84; man in image and likeness of God, 71; Renaissance man, 71
Antiochus of Ascalon, 48
Apel, Karl-Otto, 297, 298, 300, 357, 445, 447
Apollonian vs. Dionysian, 19
Apostles (club), 161, 163, 182, 184–85
Aquinas, 25, 52–53, 58–59, 64–66, 223; analogy, use of, 65; Aristotle, study of, 64; "chief scholastic," 61; education, 492; ethics, 397; law, 453;

588 Subject Index

logic and semiotics, 59; Maimonides and, 57; mind, 363; natural order, law, 63, 388; religion, 472, 474; synthesis of scholastic learning, 64. *See also* Thomism.

Arcesilaus (Skeptic), 47
Arguments, *see* Method, philosophical
Aristotle, 30, 33–46, 49, 58, 167, 253, 256 (Lobkowicz), 320; actuality and potentiality, 37, 42; aesthetics, 38, 39, 42, 43; analytics (logic), 28, 36, 38; anthropology, 38, 42, 44; Arabic studies and translations, 36, 42, 56–57; Brentano on, 279; *Categories*, 36–38, 62; character, development of, 44; cosmology, 15–16; *De Memoria et Reminiscentia*, 43; *De Motu Animalium*, 43; definition, 38; demonstration, 39; development of his thought, 37; dialectic, 28, 37–39, *see also Topics* (below); dualism, 25, 41; economics, 44; education, 492; emotion and cognition, 42; empirical tasks, 39–40; ethics, 37, 39, 42–44; eudaimonia, 44; *Eudemian Ethics*, 24, 36, 43, 44; final causes, 37, 42; form and matter, 37; Heidegger and, 280; history, 44; introduction to the West, 64; law, 44, 452; logic, 14–16, 21, 28, 37, 38; Lyceum, 33; *Magna Moralia*, 36, 43–44; Maimonides, use by, 57; mathematics, 40; matter, materialist, 41, 42; metaphysics, 37–38, 279, 348–50, 356; *Metaphysics*, 35, 36, 41–42; methodology, 37, 39; mind, 363; necessity, 44; *Nichomachean Ethics*, 36, 43–44, 391, 397, 399; on Socrates, 20; ontology, 39, 348; organon, 36, 38; Peripatetics, 34–36; Plato and, 22–28; poetics, 36, 43; politics, 36, 38, 43–44, 56, 437; practical reason, 43; Presocratics and, 24; *Protrepticus*, 24, 36; psychology, 38, 42; rhetoric, 27, 36, 43, 60; scholastics on, 36, 42, 61, 64, 65; sciences, 36, 37, 39, 40–41; Spinoza and, 86; substance (vs. genera and species), 41, 42, 355, 356; teleology, 41; theology, 41, 42; *Topics*, 28, 36, 38–40; transmission of writings, 34–35; "unity" of, 36; values, 44; will, 43; women, 438; works, authentic, 36, 38
Arts, 47, 70, 127; literature, letters, 70; music, 59; poetry, 43, 70, 79 (Willey); rejection of, 119; *see also* Aesthetics

Artz, Frederick B., 51
Astronomy, 13, 47, 59
Athens: Academy, *see* Plato; Hellenistic, 47; Lyceum, *see* Aristotle; Neoplatonic school, 36; succeeded by Constantinople, 55
Atomism, 89, 174, 415; analytic, 151, 163–64; Democritean, 13, 14; Russellian, 163, 174, 175, 184, 192
Augustine, 4, 25, 52–56, 58, 111, 143, 286, 422; aesthetics, 46, 460; autobiography, biography, 55, 111; *City of God*, 54, 428, 437; dialectic, 60; education, 492; *Enchiridion*, 54; Franciscans and, 64–66; Heidegger and, 279; humanistic, the, 63; influence in 17th c., 76, 84; Jaspers and, 272; language, philosophy of, 58–59; logic, 59; Neoplatonic vs. Pauline elements, 53, 56; religion, 472, 474; rhetoric, 59–60; universals, 62; Wittgenstein and, 208
Austin, J. L., 37, 104, 165, 167–70, 316, 323, 352, 364
Austin, John, 91, 453, 457, 458
Autobiography: 6, 188, 196 (Collingwood); 55 (Augustine); 79 (Vico); 111 (Rousseau); 170 (British); 179 (Russell); 187 (Moore); 202 (Popper); 222 (American); 224 (R. W. Sellars); 290 (Cairns); 294 (Schleiermacher); 514 (Library of Living Philosophers). *See also* Biography.
Avenarius, Richard, 129
Averroes, 57
Avicenna, 57, 66
Axiology, value theory, 132–34, 221, 316, 379–84, 386–88, 395, 396, 463, *see also* Value
Ayer, A. J., 153–55, 164–67, 169–71, 187, 207, 234, 317, 319, 350, 364, 392, 476

BBC (British Broadcasting Corp.), 170, 179
Bacon, Francis, 77–78, 143
Bacon, Roger, 64, 129
Baier, Kurt, 383, 399, 404, 405
Baillie, John, 473
Bar-Hillel, Yehoshua, 340
Barth, Karl, 58, 124, 134, 279–80, 474, 475, 477, 478
Bauer, Bruno, 136
Baumrin, Bernard, 414
Beard, Charles A., 233

Subject Index

Beauchamp, Tom L., 405
Beck, Lewis White, 6, 67, 101, 115, 121
Beckner, Morton, 417
Being, 38, 39, 41, 58, 275, 278, 349; and value, 45; chain of, 7 (Lovejoy); philosophy of, 157; see also Metaphysics: ontology
Bentham, Jeremy, 128, 143–44, 391, 394, 397, 453
Berdyaev, Nicolai, 439
Bergmann, Gustav, 130, 132, 134, 153–55, 352, 357–58, 417
Bergson, Henri, 123, 127, 129, 130, 157, 280, 286, 473; bibliography, 503
Berkeley, George, 95, 98, 101, 102–7, 121, 129, 137, 146, 286, 356, 513
Berlin, Isaiah, 99, 100, 167, 341, 423, 428, 433, 440, 444
Berlin, University of, 99, 126, 136, 243
Bernard, Claude, 129
Bertocci, Peter A., 222, 225, 475; bibliography, 229 (Howie)
Betti, Emilio, 297, 298
Bibliographies, 503–8, see also under specific items
Biography, 4, 119–20, 268, 297, 306; 55 (Augustine); 79 (Newton); 84 (Pascal); 103 (Berkeley); 108 (Hume); 111 (Rousseau); 125 (Schleiermacher); 138 (Hegel); 143 (the Scots); 145 (the Mills); 147 (Caird); 180 (Russell); 184 (Moore); 236 (James); 237 (Peirce); 244 (Dewey); 252, 254 (Marx); 265 (Kierkegaard); 267 (Nietzsche); 271–72 (Buber); 283 (Heidegger); see also Autobiography
Biology, 127, 417, see also Evolutionary views
Bixler, Julius Seelye, 475
Black, Max, 207, 222, 315, 331, 341, 342
Blanshard, Brand, 146, 219, 221, 222, 224–25, 272 (Rome); 323–24, 350, 355, 381, 397, 473, 475, 514; bibliography, 514
Bloch, Ernst, 253, 257, 258
Bloom, Allan, 111
Bloomsbury Group, 163, 185
Blumberg, A. E., 153
Boehme, Jacob, 272
Boethius, 55, 62, 63
Bohm, David, 415
Boltzmann, Ludwig, 131
Bonaventure, 52, 61, 64–65

Boodin, John Elof, 221
Boole, George, 331
Bosanquet, Bernard, 147–48, 162, 381
Boström, Christopher Jacob, 159
Bourgeois thought, 124, 126
Bowne, Bordon Parker, 225, 475
Bracken, Harry M., 106
Bradley, F. H., 147–48, 162, 185, 236, 274, 350
Braig, Carl, 279
Braithwaite, R. B., 163, 415, 419, 476
Brandt, Richard B., 125, 382, 389, 390, 393, 394, 397, 398, 402, 440
Bréhier, Emile, 62, 82
Brentano, Franz, 123, 131–32, 262, 279, 285, 288, 290, 380, 386, 388
Brightman, Edgard Sheffield, 221, 475
British Academy, 169, 186, 195, 364
British philosophy, 124, 143–49, 159, 161–215, 288, 350, 363, 381, 437, 493; English Renaissance, 143; founding of modern, 82, 94, 101; history of, 9, 98, 143. See also Analytic philosophy; Cambridge; Oxford.
Broad, C. D., 81, 90, 132, 148, 163, 184, 208, 288, 387, 392, 514; bibliography, 514
Brouwer, L. E. J., 205, 207
Brunner, Emil, 474, 475
Bruno, Giordano, 70, 71
Buber, Martin, 6 (Kaufmann), 157, 271–72, 274, 473, 514; bibliography, 272 (Schaeder), 514
Buchdahl, Gerd, 414
Buchler, Justus, 221
Buddha, 272
Bühler, Karl, 199
Bulloch, Edward, 464
Bultmann, Rudolf, 279, 297
Burckhardt, Jacob, 72 (Kristeller)
Burke, Edmund, 112
Burnett, Joe, 495
Burnyeat, M. F., 37, 156
Butler, Joseph, 399

Caird, Edward, 147
Cairns, Dorion, 287, 290
Calvin, John, 54, 70
Cambridge, University of, 147, 148, 153, 161–63, 165, 174, 179, 182–86, 203–5, 210, 212
Cambridge Platonists, 76, 98
Camus, Albert, 264, 392
Cantor, Georg, 175

Capek, Milic, 417
Carlyle, Thomas, 147
Carnap, Rudolf, 152, 153, 155, 168, 202, 413, 415, 514; analysis of artificial languages, 165, 339–40; bibliography, 514; biography, 152–53, 514; inductive logic and probability, 335; language, philosophy of, 340, 350; logical postivism, 153, 350; mathematical logic, 332; metaphysics, 356; mind, 363; science, 201, 411, 417, 418; semantics and modal logic, 323, 333, 335, 340; syntactics, 153, 340
Carritt, E. F., 394
Cartesians, 83 (Watson), see also Descartes
Cassirer, Ernst, 4, 7 (Klibansky), 71, 97, 110, 152, 314, 410, 466, 514; bibliography, 514
Cause, causation, causality, 46 (Sorabji), 48, 57, 95, 101, 105, 353, 354, 374–75, 414, 419, 431, 453
Certainty, uncertainty, 28, 81, 83, 85 (Davidson), 151, 175, 201, 202, 206, 211, 231, 232, 244, 273, 281, 288, 289, 305, 314, 316–17, 319
Chadwick, Henry, 56
Charvet, John, 112, 113
Chisholm, Roderick, 131, 132, 220, 288, 314–23, 419
Chomsky, Noam, 342–43
Christ, 53, 54, 56; see also Jesus; Theology
Christendom, 55, 138
Christian philosophy, 53–56, 274, 474–75; bibliography, 505–6. See also Medieval philosophy; Religion, philosophy of.
Christianity, 265, 267, 294; East and West, 54. See also Christ; Jesus; Religion; Theology.
Church, Alonzo, 332
Cicero, 60, 77
Clarke, Samuel, 116
Clement of Alexandria, 25
Coates, Ken, 260
Cohen, Felix, 454
Cohen, Hermann, 157
Cohen, I. Bernard, 414, 415, 423
Cohen, Morris R., 216–18, 226, 229 (Delaney, Hollinger), 323, 330, 352, 414, 417, 454, 456
Coleridge, Samuel Taylor, 147
Colet, John, 70

Collingwood, R. G., 188–98; aesthetics, 188–90, 460, 464–66; bibliography, 198 (Rubinoff); biography, 5, 162, 165, 166, 188–96, 203; causality, 419; forms of experience, 166, 189, 192, 367; history, philosophy of, 189, 193, 196–97, 432, 445; history and philosophy, 189, 193–97, 430–31; language, 340; political critique, 188, 194–96, 437; presuppositions (metaphysics), 190, 196, 343, 353–54, 357, 390; question-and-answer method, 5, 193, 196; religion, 188–90, 196; Roman Britain studies, 194–95; Ruskin and, 190–93; science, 410–11; translations, 100, 193
Common sense: Hume's ethics, 107; in metaphysics, 103, 105; in 19th c. philosophy, 144, 218, 242; Moore, 164, 181–82, 316
Comte, Auguste, 127–29, 300, 314, 429, 473
Consciousness, 267, 279, 286, 288, 292, 295, 298, 313, 364, 365, 376; birth of, 11, 16; Cartesian "subjectivity," 81, 275; development of, 138, 472, 491; dialectic of, 126, 136; eternal, 147; species-consciousness, 126; "world"-construction by, 130, 286; see also Unconscious
Cone, James, 441
Constantinople, University of, 55
Continental European philosophy, 101, 157, 159, 170–71, 285, 298, 351, 386, 439
Cooley, Charles L., 246
Cooper, David, 399
Cosmology, early, 11–14, 15. See also Astronomy; Metaphysics; Physics; Science.
Couturat, Louis, 89, 90
Cremin, Lawrence, 439
Crites, Stephen, 138, 141, 266
Critical theory, 223, 262, 297, 299–300, 314, 494
Croce, Benedetto, 100, 193–94, 430, 465–66
Cudworth, Ralph, 76
Culture, philosophy of, 228, 269–70, 296–97, 310, 324, 380, 464, 491
Curley, E. M., 81, 86, 87, 89, 90

Danto, Arthur, 82, 269, 276, 317, 319, 374, 414, 431

Darwin, Charles, 129, 242, *see also* Evolutionary views
Daub, Karl, 136
d'Autrecourt, Nicholas, 129
Davidson, Donald, 43, 228, 343, 365, 375
De George, Richard T., 405, 440
De Morgan, Augustus, 331
De Wulf, Maurice, 61
Death, 279, 309, 405, 472, *see also* Immortality
Deconstructionism, 223, 309
Dedekind, Julius Wilhelm Richard, 175
Definitions, *see* Method, philosophical
Deism, 85, 98, 102, 105
Democritus, 13, 14 (Atomists), 248–49
Derrida, Jacques, 289, 309, 343
Descartes, René (and Cartesian views), 80–83, 223, 313, 320, 362, 414, 513; bibliography, 83 (Doney); biography, 80, 85; certain foundations, search for, 81, 316; a founder of "modern" philosophy, 75, 78, 82, 101, 313; innate ideas, 318; mind-body dualism, 81–82, 292, 363–65; positivism, 129; rationalist metaphysics, 80–82, 94, 101, 292, 356; skeptical method, 77, 81; subjectivity, idealism, 116, 275, 279, 292, 313, *see also* Cartesians
Determinism, *see* Freedom
Dewey, John, 5, 179, 233, 234 (Marcell, Moore, Scheffler), 241–45, 246, 314, 349, 415, 462, 495, 514; action, 157, 373; aesthetics, 462; bibliography, 245 (Boydston), 514; biography, 217, 218, 221, 241–44, 262, 390, 514; certainty, against the quest for, 244, 314, 319; constructive philosophy, metaphysics, 306, 349; democratic social thought, 243–45, 437–39, 443–44, 446; education, 244, 245, 444, 491–93, 495, 497; ethics, 386, 390, 391, 394, 397, 398; James and, 235–36; logic, theory of inquiry, 244, 330, 446; mind, 361; naturalist, 217, 226, 349, 355, 391, 397, 398; pragmatist, 217, 232–36, 323, 334–35, 355; psychology, 242–43, 246, 483; reconstruction in philosophy and society, 5, 9, 22; religion, 242–44, 473, 475, 480; Rorty's use of, 155, 223, 324; value theory, 381, 386–87; writings, 245
Dialectic, 6, 28, 31, 37–39, 59, 294, 296, 309, 336, 353, 355, 416; 16th–

18th c., 78, 106, 116; Abelard, 63; Anselm, 62; Aquinas, 59; Augustine, 60; dialectical structures and interpretations, 93, 106, 112, 192, 196, 262, 276; Hegelian, 138–40, 366; in critical theory, 300; in medieval curriculum, 59, 61, 143; Kierkegaard, 265–66; late Renaissance-Reformation, 71; Marxian, Marxist, 120, 250, 254–55, 292; materialist, 126; Sartre, 259. *See also* Aristotle; Plato.
Dialogue, 28, 31, 72 (Ong), 271, 272, 274, 298
Dilthey, Wilhelm, 123, 125, 157, 272, 280, 296–97, 300, 430, 485
Dominicans, *see* Scholasticism
Donagan, Alan, 197, 395, 401
Dretske, Fred, 320–21
Dualistic thought, 25, 84, 313; critiques of, 246, 292, 350, 364
Ducasse, C. J., 414, 419
Duhem, Pierre, 418, 421
Duns Scotus, 25, 52, 61, 64–66, 143, 220; Heidegger on, 280; metaphysics, 66; Peirce on, 237, 240; Scotist studies, 66; universals, 63
Dupré, Louis, 253
Durant, Will, 9
Durkheim, Émile, 39
Dutens, Louis, 88
Dworkin, Ronald, 400, 438, 441, 442, 444, 455–58

Eastern thought, 156, 159, 310, 475
Eberhard, Johann August, 117
Ebner, Ferdinand, 271
Eckhart, 25
Economics, 44, 108, 145, 190, 252, 447
Ecumenical, 400
Edel, Abraham, 392–93, 398, 415, 446
Edgley, Roy, 171
Education, 491; 17th c. reform, 77; 19th c. reform, 147, 439; effects of rhetoric on, 60; higher, graudate, professional, 34, 497; liberal, 495; political, 442, 447, 497; progressive, 439; Renaissance, 60; schools of, 490. *See also* Education, philosophy of; Rhetoric.
Education, philosophy of, 111, 117, 128, 146, 147, 178, 190, 212, 242, 244–45, 266, 316, 375, 377, 386, 396, 402–3, 444, 490–500; administration policy, planning, 494, 496; bibliography, 503; educational research, 494;

forms of knowledge, 494–95; history of, 492–94; indoctrination, 496–97; "ism" approach, 492; liberal-social emphasis, 493, 495; pedagogy, curriculum, 491, 494–97; progressivism, 493. *See also* Education; Morality.

Edwards, Jonathan, 98, 216, 221
Ehrenfels, Christian, 380
Einstein, Albert, 105, 416, 514
Eleatics and Pluralists (Greek), 16 (Allen)
Emerson, Ralph Waldo, 221
Emmet, Dorothy, 214, 354, 357, 393
Emotion, *see* Mind
Empedocles, 14, 16
Empiricism, logical empiricism, empiricists, 25, 226, 235–36, 314–15, 316–24, 343, 475–77, 487; 18th–19th c., 102–3, 107–9, 128, 129, 143; critique of, 102–3, 147, 151, 223; rationalism and, 75, 94, 101, 108; roots in Ockham, 67
Engels, Friedrich, 126, 249–52, 254
Epicureans, 47
Epicurus, 33, 48, 248–49, 394
Epistemology, 31, 47, 51, 180, 187, 202, 209, 211, 226–28, 232–33, 236, 240, 269–70, 299, 313–27, 328, 354, 367, 497; 17th c., 75, 81, 87, 95, 313; 18th c., 97, 107–9, 113–14, 120–21; 19th c., 131, 143, 146; cognitivism, noncognitivism, 319; external world, 104, 114, 219, 237, 315–24; "the given," 314–15, 317, 321; history of, 9, 163, 166, 176, 313–21; innate ideas, 318; late scholastic, 63–67; meaning and reference, 95, 180, 315, 321–22, 343; sense data, 131, 177, 314, 319, 321; social justification of belief, 321, 324; verifiability theory, 153–54, 166, 200, 207, 322, 350, 353, 416, 418, 476, 477. *See also* Induction; Logic and language; Method; Perception; Truth; Universals.

Erasmus, Desiderius, 70, 72
Erdmann, Johann, 136, 137
Erigena, 143
Essentialist positions, 105, 157, 493
Ethics, moral philosophy, 30–31, 42–44, 59, 70, 146, 178, 187, 226, 228, 232, 243, 246, 254, 263, 265, 269, 276–77, 294, 296, 316, 331, 367, 373, 381, 385–409, 497, 506; 17th c., 84, 87, 90, 95; 18th c., 98, 105, 107–8, 110, 115, 116; abortion, 405; American,

386–88; animals, 400; British, 161, 387–89; categorical imperative, 121; commitment, 399–400; Continental European, 389; deductive method, 78; deontological approaches, 92, 393–94, 444; egoism and altruism, 399–400; environmental issues, 405; eudaemonistic, 99; future generations, 400; hedonism, 144, 394, 397; Hegelian, 140; history of, 146, 386–89; ideal observer theory, 393, 394, 397; idealist, 147–48; in Hellenistic philosophies, 47, 49; intuitionism (nonnaturalism), 387, 391, 400, 402, 404; "is" and "ought," 396–97; Kantian, 44, 117–18; law and, 456–57; "love" approaches, 394, 399; moral psychology, 244, 365, 386, 387, 401–2, 458; natural law, 65, 93, 391, 395, 452, 455; naturalism, 387, 391–93, 397, 400, 403, 404; naturalistic (definist) fallacy, 387, 392; noncognitivism (emotivism, prescriptivism), 387, 390–92, 397–98, 400, 404; objectivity and subjectivity, 393, 397–99; of belief, 316; practical uses, 404–5; responsibility, 403–4; right-based theory, 401; self-realization approaches, 265–66, 294, 309, 368, 394; situation ethics, 392; teleological approaches, 84, 116, 117, 393; theological, religious, 388, 390, 394, 399, 403, 441; utilitarian, 44, 128, 144–46, 185, 393–94, 400, 439, 444; Victorian, 388; virtues, 54, 65, 391, 402–3. *See also* Morality; Practical reasoning; Relativism; Rights; Skepticism.

Eudoxus, 13, 23
Evil, problem of, *see* God
Evolutionary views, 198, 200, 218, 220, 224, 228, 235, 240, 242, 243
Ewing, A. C., 146, 163, 170, 187
Existential thought, 85, 100, 110, 123, 137, 157–58, 196, 207, 221, 223, 259–60, 262–84, 286, 289, 291, 314, 357, 373, 493–94; bibliography, 510

Faith, *see* Morality, virtues; Religion: faith; Theology: faith seeking understanding
Farber, Marvin, 287, 289
Fate *(moira)*, 17 (Greene), 354
Feibleman, James K., 221
Feigl, Herbert, 153, 362, 364–66, 410,

411, 413–15, 417, 418, 485; bibliography, 424 (Feyerabend and Maxwell)
Feuerbach, Ludwig, 101, 123, 126, 136, 137, 249, 253, 473
Feyerabend, Paul, 202, 334, 411–14, 416–17
Fichte, Johann Gottlieb, 123, 126, 137, 147, 300
Ficino, Marsilio, 70
Findlay, J. N., 25, 28, 132, 140–41, 170, 366, 381, 388
Fisch, Max, 100, 241
Fischer, Kuno, 133, 136, 137
Fiske, John, 218, 219
Fletcher, Joseph, 392
Flew, Antony, 9, 169, 342, 363, 388, 473, 474, 476, 477
Fodor, Jerry, 341–43, 365–66
Fogelin, Robert, 208, 320
Foot, Philippa, 395, 397, 403
Franciscans, *see* Scholasticism
Frank, Philipp, 153, 414, 417
Frankena, William K., 387–90, 395–96, 399, 401–3, 436, 492, 496
Frankfurt, Harry G., 81, 82
Frankfurt School, 258, 260, 299
Frederick the Great, 99
Freedom, free will, 57, 76, 86, 87, 89, 90, 114, 252, 263, 271, 273, 274, 316, 354, 373, 471, 478; and determinism, 98, 255, 349, 361, 375–77, 419, 432; *see also* Will
Frege, Gottlob, 123, 132–33, 153, 175, 204–6, 211, 237, 289, 322, 324, 329–31, 334, 341
French Enlightenment, *see* German philosophy; Philosophy, 18th c.
French philosophy, 98, 127, 159, 258–60, 274, 275–76, 285, 292, 298, 343
French Revolution, 111
Freud, Sigmund, 6 (Kaufmann), 7 (Lazerowitz), 262, 298–300, 301 (Keat), 472, 483, 486–87; *see also* Psychoanalysis
Fries, Jacob Friedrich, 152
Fromm, Erich, 253
Fry, Roger, 185

Gadamer, Hans-Georg, 31, 140, 297–300
Galileo, Galilei, 129, 313, 414
Gans, Eduard, 136
Garaudy, Roger, 253, 259
Gassendi, Pierre, 129

Gasset, José Ortega y, 158, 439
Gauthier, David P., 404
Geach, Peter, 148, 330–31, 364, 402, 420, 474
Genova, A. C., 227
German philosophy: 19th c., 123, 128, 130–34, 243, 263; 20th c., 157, 260, 262–63, 285, 298–300; Enlightenment, 89, 99, 140; Kantian, 119; pre-Kantian, 98–99; surveys, 8. *See also* Continental European philosophy; Critical theory; Existential thought; Hegelians; Marxism; Neo-Kantians; Phenomenology.
Gettier, Edmund, 317–18
Gilson, Etienne, 51, 56, 62, 65, 80, 352
Girvetz, Harry K., 405
Glover, Willis, 93
God, theism, 13, 41–42, 53, 84, 114, 115, 218, 315, 353, 354, 472, 476–79; absoluteness, impassibility, 55; attributes of, 57, 479; evil, problem of, 478–79; existence of (arguments for), 48, 53, 58, 62, 81, 107–8, 114, 118, 473, 477–79; government of the world, 89; image and likeness of, 71; in idealist positions, 103–4; knowledge of, 59, 64, 114; providence, 478; unchangeable essence, 56. *See also* Religion; Theology.
Gödel, Kurt, 153, 332
Goethe, Johann Wolfgang, 6 (Kaufmann), 100, 123
Goldman, Alvin, 319, 374, 390
Goldmann, Lucien, 120, 258
Grabmann, Martin, 52
Gramsci, Antonio, 258
Greek culture and society, 30; Athenian education, 33; libraries, 34–35; popular morality, 30; *see also* Apollonian
Greek philosophy: analogy, uses of, 15; development of science, 11–12; Hegel and, 141; Hellenistic, 34, 47–50; history of (comprehensive), 8, 17 (Guthrie), 56; irrational themes, 11–12; many and the one, 31 (Adkins); rationalism in, 49; Schleiermacher and, 294, 296; sphere in, 11, 16; terms, 510
Green, T. H., 146–47, 168, 242, 437
Greenleaf, W. H., 93
Gregory the Great, 60
Greig, Gordon, 187
Grice, Geoffrey Russell, 404
Grice, H. P., 343

Grimsley, Ronald, 111, 113
Grosseteste, Robert, 64
Grünbaum, Adolf, 421
Gurwitsch, Aron, 286
Gutierrez, Gustavo, 441

Habermas, Jürgen, 263, 297–300
Hacking, Ian, 76, 90, 341
Hagerström, Axel, 159, 392
Hall, Everett W., 381
Hall, G. Stanley, 219, 242
Hamann, Johann Georg, 98–100
Hampshire, Stuart, 87, 100, 167, 170,
    364, 373, 376, 397, 438, 441, 453
Hanson, Norwood, 411, 418
Hardie, W. F. R., 44
Hare, R. M., 363, 389, 392, 397, 398,
    456
Harman, Gilbert, 318, 399
Harris, H. S., 138, 141
Harris, William T., 218
Hart, H. L. A., 167, 453, 455–58; bibli-
    ography, 459 (Hacker)
Hartmann, Klaus, 141
Hartmann, Nicholai, 157, 380, 388
Hartshorne, Charles, 217, 221, 272
    (Rome), 350, 355, 473, 476, 478; bib-
    liography, 482 (Reese)
Harvard University, 168, 178, 200, 210,
    217–19, 224, 226, 235, 238, 239,
    242, 246
Haverfield, F. J., 194
Hayek, Friedrich, 199, 440, 444
Haym, Rudolf, 136
Hedonism, see Ethics
Hegel, G. W. F., 4–6, 24, 25, 99, 120,
    123–27, 135–42, 147, 157, 256
    (Hyppolite), 294, 323; bibliography,
    141; dialectic, 136–40; history, 429–
    30; Kant and, 120; Kierkegaard and,
    226; later idealism and, 135–37, 146–
    48; Marx and, 248–49, 299; meta-
    physics, 350; Nietzsche and, 268; phe-
    nomenology, 130, 136–39, 141, 285;
    politics, 437; religion, 472, 473; Sartre
    and, 276; system, 136. See also Hege-
    lians; Idealism.
Hegelians, 135–37, 313, 373; American,
    218, 242–43; anti-, 128; British, 146–
    48, 162, 174; ethics, 388; idealism
    and, 137; Scandinavian, 159–60;
    young, left-wing, 123, 126, 136–37,
    139, 249
Heidegger, Martin, 6 (Kaufmann), 125,

263, 264, 278–84, 308, 439; bibliog-
    raphy, 503; biography, 279–83; "end"
    of philosophy, 282; existentialist, 157,
    263, 278, 281, 289; hermeneutic phe-
    nomenology, 278, 281, 289, 297–99;
    history, 430; Husserl and, 280–81,
    288; influence of, 258, 275–76, 289,
    297–98, 324, 351, 355, 430, 439;
    National Socialism, 281–82;
    Nietzsche, on, 268–69; nihilism, 281,
    398; ontology, 278–83, 350; Rorty's
    use of, 155, 223
Hempel, Carl, 153, 323–24, 411, 415,
    417–18, 420, 421, 431; bibliography,
    426 (Rescher)
Henry of Ghent, 66
Heraclitus, 14, 16
Herder, Johann Gottfried, 98–100, 101
    (Berlin), 428
Hermeneutical philosophy, 5, 31, 196,
    297–99, 314, 410, 494
Hermeneutics, general, 5, 48, 69, 123,
    125, 141, 223, 262, 293–99, 411,
    416, 430, 458
Hertz, Heinrich, 131
Herzel, Theodor, 272
Herzog, Frederick, 441
Heschel, Abraham, 157, 474
Hess, Moses, 249
Hesse, Mary, 414, 418, 421
Hilbert, David, 332
Hildebrand, Dietrich von, 402
Hilliard, Asa, 381
Hintikka, Jaakko, 41, 44, 82, 90, 154,
    159, 202, 209, 228, 320, 322, 330,
    333, 420, 421
Historicism, 125, 137, 157, 194, 196–
    97, 201, 398, 429–30
History, the discipline, 70, 97, 108, 118
History, philosophy of, 79, 118, 189–90,
    193–97, 293, 294, 297, 315–16, 353;
    explanation and laws, 431–32; Hege-
    lian, 140, 259; inevitability, 433;
    Marxist, 254–59; re-enactment, 432;
    religious interpretations, 428. See also
    Action; Freedom; History.
History of philosophy, 3–10, 120, 220–
    21; analytical, dialectical, and herme-
    neutical motifs, 5–6; approaches and
    types, 3–6, 7–8; Aristotelian vs. Pla-
    tonic, 52–53; conflict in, 78; contem-
    porary, 7 (Rorty), 9, 150–60; cultural
    orientation, 9; development, 4; forms
    of, 7–8; general histories, 7–10; Hege-

lian, 4–6, 8, 141, *see also* Hegel, Hegelians; intellectual history (and history of ideas), 4, 9–10, 221, 223; modern, 6 (Collins); neo-Kantian, 8, *see also* Neo-Kantians; philosophy of the, 6; psychoanalytically oriented, 5; representative thinkers, 9. *See also* Philosophy; Philosophy, 17th, 18th, 19th c.

Hobbes, Thomas, 78, 84, 91–93, 112, 341, 379, 388, 394, 399, 437; bibliography, 93 (Hinnant)
Hocking, Ernest, 219, 221
Høffding, Harald, 160
Hölderlin, Friedrich, 280–82
Hollingdale, R. J., 270
Holt, E. B., 131
Hook, Sidney, 221, 222, 234, 245, 252, 253, 341, 376, 382, 431, 437, 446, 486, 493
Hope, *see* Morality: virtues; Religion
Horkheimer, Max, 299
Huby, Pamela, 388
Hudson, W. D., 388, 397
Humanism, 69–70, 125, 236, 250, 252, 253, 255, 259, 264, 267, 276, 282, 308, 373, 463, 473; Hebrew, 271; Italian Renaissance, 70–71; radical, 123, 126
Humboldt, Wilhelm von, 294
Hume, David, 98, 107–10, 132, 362, 472, 473, 513; atomist, 174; bibliography, 108; biography, 108; causation, 101, 419; deism, 85; economics and politics, 108, 444; empiricism, 95, 107–8, 144, 203, 211, 320; ethics, 107–8, 363, 388, 394, 397, 399, 402; induction, 76, 108, 201; Kant and, 107, 114; Newtonian, 108; positivist, the first, 129; psychology, associationist, 144, 177; relations, theory of, 236; religion, 107–8, 472, 473; Russell and, 174, 177; skepticism, 76, 107–8, 114; substance metaphysics, contra, 82; value as utility, 144
Husserl, Edmund, 125, 131, 287–91, 439; bibliography, 503; biography, 280, 285, 287–90; "essence," 157, 288; influence on existentialists and others, 263, 275–76, 280–81, 289, 291–92, 297–99; "intentional" phenomena, 131; James and, 236; language, 289; mathematics, 288; phenomenology, 262, 285–92; psychology, descriptive, 288–90, 296; realism,

131; reduction, 286, 288; science, 129, 288, 290; subjectivism, 281, 286, 288–89, 299
Hyppolite, Jean, 138, 141, 253, 259

Idealism, idealists, 130, 146–48, 159, 224, 225, 274, 323, 352, 380, 431, 475; 19th–20th c., 125, 139–40, 143, 146–48, 220; Absolute, 100, 136, 138, 147, 161, 162, 225, 350; American, 218–20; British, 136, 140, 147, 148, 163, 165, 189, 197, 220; critical, 8; critiques of, 146–47, 150, 162; historical, 192; Italian, 189, 193; Moore's "refutation," 162; objective, 103, 137, 224; Platonic, 22; post-Kantian, 123, 124; pragmatic, 240; subjective, 25, 103, 106, 137, 292; transcendental, 114–15. *See also* Hegel; Hegelians; Personalism.
Identity, 349, 356, 366; logical, 328; personal, mind-body, 167, 276, 315, 349, 362, 364, 365, 367; regarding things, 320, 322; theological, 479
Ideology critique, 221, 250, 297–300, 343, 420, 445, 447
Imagination, 87, 100, 263, 364, 367, 414, 461, 466
Immortality, external life, eschatology, 114, 368, 477, 479
Individual, individuation, 69, 71, 81, 113 (Weintraub), 282, 356, 364, 367, 372; and classes, 349, 352, *see also* Nominalism; in politics, 145–46, 258; late medieval concepts, 63; subjectivity, 116
Individualist positions, 112, 121, 123, 266, 391, 429, 438, 442
Induction, 179, 201, 315, 322, 418, 420; and analogy, 15; Baconian, 78; Hume's skepticism, 76, 107–8, 201
Intentionality, 43, 362, 363, 365–67, 372, 374, 380, 465–66; toward objects, 131, 133, 376
Irwin, T. H., 37
Ishiguro, Hidé, 90
Isidore of Seville, 60
Islamic thought, 56–57, 474; Mitakallimun, 174
Italian philosophy, 79, 193. *See also* Croce; Renaissance; Ruggiero; Vico.

Jacobi, Friedrich Heinrich, 86, 99
James, William, 217–19, 221, 234 (Ayer,

Marcell, Moore, Scheffler), 235–37, 243, 306, 323; atomist, 174; bibliography, 237; biography, 236; humanism, 236; Peirce and, 238, 239, 323; pluralist metaphysics, 235; pragmatism, 232–34, 236, 247; psychology, 235–36, 243, 483; radical empiricism, 236; religion, 232, 236, 473, 475
Jansenists, 84
Jaspers, Karl, 157, 263, 264, 268, 270, 272–74, 439, 514; bibliography, 514
Jay, Martin, 299
Jessop, T. E., 104, 106
Jesuits, 84
Jesus, 53, 272; *see also* Christ; Theology
Jewish thought, Judaism, 53, 57–58, 156–57, 474; 19th–20th c., 124–25, 248–49, 271; encounters with Arabic, 57; influence on medieval Christian, 57; rationalism, 57; Spinoza and, 86; theology non-systematic, 58
Joachim, Harold H., 86, 165, 224
Joachim of Flora, 430
Johnson, J. Prescott, 380
Jones, Rufus, 475
Jordan, Elijah, 221
Joseph, H. W. B., 81, 162, 167
Judgment, 114, 131, 133, 162, 232, 496. *See also* Axiology; Mind, philosophy of: judging.
Jung, Carl, 6 (Kaufmann)
Justice, *see* Social-political philosophy
Justinian (Emperor), 23, 36, 55

Kamenka, Eugene, 7 (Passmore), 126, 253, 255, 388, 443
Kant, Immanuel, 113–22, 147, 258, 300, 472, 513; aesthetics, 114, 115, 461; analytic philosophy and, 115, 152, 167, 207–8, 228; analytic/synthetic, 115, 116; anthropology, 117, 118; antinomies, 116; Berkeley and, 121; biography, 119–20; "critiques," 113–19; dialectic, 5, 116; education, 492; Enlightenment and, 99, 428; epistemology, 105, 113–14, 120–21, 313, 320; ethics, 114–16, 121, 186, 192, 388, 394, 396, 397, 402, 496; history, 118; Hume and, 107, 114; idealism and, 126, 146, 147; judgment, 114, 133, 461; Leibnizians and, 116–17; logic, 116, 240; metaphysics, 114, 152, 165, 281; Moore's dissertation on, 162; rationalists and, 152, 342; re-

ligion and God, 114–15, 118, 473; Rousseau and, 110, 112, 117–19; Schopenhauer and, 127; science, 118, 119, 144, 414; synthetic a priori, 115, 120; teleology, 117; transcendental idealism, 115; *see also* Neo-Kantians
Kaplan, Abraham, 156, 234, 354, 363, 446
Kaplan, Mordekai, 157
Kashap, S. Paul, 87
Katz, Jerrold, 342–43
Kaufmann, Walter, 5, 125, 138, 139, 141, 267, 270
Kautsky, Karl, 252
Kemeny, John, 417
Kemp, J., 388
Kennick, W. E., 187
Kerr, Donna, 495
Keynes, John Maynard, 163, 185
Kierkegaard, Søren, 101, 125, 159, 265–67; action, 157, 373, 432; Christendom, 138; education, 266; ethics, 265; existentialism and, 262–64, 272, 274, 280; Hegel and, 137, 139, 266; religion, 262, 473–74; self-realization, stages of, 265–66
Klein, Melanie, 103, 485
Kneale, William, 90, 187, 329, 420
Knowledge, theory of, *see* Epistemology
Knox, T. M., 197
Kohlberg, Lawrence, 403, 496
Kojève, Alexandre, 259
Korsch, Karl, 257–58
Kosman, L. A., 37
Kripke, Saul, 333, 345 (Davidson)
Kropotkin, Peter, 444
Kuhn, Thomas, 201, 202, 411–13, 415–16, 418, 420
Kyberg, Henry E., 335, 414, 417

La Fleur, Laurence J., 82
Lafuma, Louis, 85
Laird, John, 381
Lakatos, Imre, 202, 335, 411, 413, 416, 418
Lamont, W. D., 381
Lange, Friedrich Albert, 133
Language and logic, *see* Logic and language
Language, philosophy of, 100, 125, 133, 150–54, 190, 227, 280, 289, 294, 299, 300, 315–16, 318, 324, 328, 339–47; bibliography, 506; commu-

nication, theory of, 300, 321; grammatology, 343; linguistic philosophy, 154, 165–71, 199, 203, 208, 221, 315, 339, 340–41, 356, 362, 363, 389, 445; picture theory, 206; private language, 343; signs, theory of (semiotics), 59, 233, 240, 289, 340, 350, 465; speech-acts, performance utterances, 168, 323, 342; transformational grammar, 342–43; *see also* Logic and language
Lao-Tzu, 272
Laslett, Peter, 94, 438, 440, 442
Latin American philosophy, 259
Law, philosophy of, 87, 145, 316, 331, 376, 386, 404, 440, 442, 452–59, 506; jurisprudence, 401, 402, 453; natural law, 452, 455, 456, *see also* Ethics; public order and justice, 452; punishment, 458; *see also* Social-political philosophy
Lazerowitz, Morris, 5, 187, 205, 207, 209, 330, 352, 486
Lees, Robert, 342
Lehmann, Paul, 441
Leibniz, Gottfried Wilhelm, 88–91, 243; analytic philosophers and, 167, 175, 176, 211; coherence theory of truth, 323; ethics, 90; freedom, 90; in 17th c. philosophy, 78, 80, 86, 88, 129, 318; in 18th c., 89, 97, 119, 121, 313; Leibnizians, 89, 116–17; logic and language, 90, 329; rationalist metaphysics, 89, 90, 101, 356; religion, 473; theodicy, 88
Lenin, Vladimir Ilyich, 129, *see also* Marxism
Lenzen, Victor, 419
Leo XIII (Pope), 61
Lesniewski, Stanislaw, 58
Lessing, Gotthold Ephraim, 99
Levi-Strauss, Claude, 298, *see also* Structuralism
Lewis, C. I., 218–19, 221, 226, 514; bibliography, 514; biography, 514; epistemology, 314, 315, 317; ethics, 232, 386–87; metaphysics, 349; naturalist, 226; phenomenalism, 315; pragmatism, 234; value theory, 381, 387
Liberal arts, medieval trivium and quadrivium, 59, 61, 63
Liberty, political freedom, *see* Social-political philosophy
Liebeschütz, H., 56

Linguistic philosophy, *see* Language, philosophy of
Linguistics, 78, 170, 294, 340, 342–44
Literature, 287 (Natanson), 294, 309, 344, *see also* Arts
Lloyd, A. C., 56
Locke, John, 75, 94–96, 362; causation, 95, 101; correspondence, 95; eclipsed by Hume, 108; education, 94, 492; empiricism, 94–95; ethics, 95, 394; in 17th c. philosophy, 75, 78, 86, 102; innate ideas, 318; mind, 363, 365; politics, 75, 91, 94–95, 112, 437; rationalism, 94, 101; religion, 84–85, 94
Loemker, Leroy, 76, 89
Logic, 38, 48, 51, 78, 237, 255, 315, 328–38, 354, 367, 497; 17th c., 77–78; 18th c., 98, 113; 19th c., 132, 143, 148; alternatives to propositional logic, 196; as foundation of mathematics, 175, 204, 209, 210, 330–31; as the study of reasoning, 331, 334, *see also* Practical reasoning; as theory of inquiry, 3, 330, 336; bibliography, 338 (Rescher), 506; categories, 29, 38, 356; computer theory, 330, 331, 335, 336; constructionist views, 335; counterfactuals, 167, 328, 333, 419; deontic, epistemic, tense logic, 329, 334; dilemmas, 329; entailment, 328, 335; Hegel's, 139–40; history of, 9, 28, 329, 331–32; inductive, 330, 335; "logical analysis," 72; material, 116; mathematicizing of, 40, 132, 331–32; medieval, 51, 58–59, 62, 65, 329; Megarian, 329; many-valued, 330, 332, 335; Mill's, 77, 128, 143, 146; modal, 89, 154, 320, 322, 329, 330, 332–34, 356, 389; ordinary language, 332; paradox, 20, 328, 329, 355, 479; philosophy of, 209, 329–30; pluralist views, 334; Port-Royal, 77, 84; possible-world semantics, 333; reference, theory of, 180, 315; Renaissance-Reformation, 69–72; statistics, 335, 336; syllogistic demonstration (Aristotelian), 38, 40, 56, 75, 240, 329; symbolic, mathematical, modern, 157, 180–81, 211, 228, 240, 255, 328–35; transcendental, 116; types, theory of, 176; vs. metaphysical order, 66. *See also* Analytic; Analytic philosophy; Aristotle; Identity; Mathematics, phi-

losophy of; Method; Presuppositions; Probability; Stoics.
Logic and language, 52, 58–60, 150–56, 314, 342; 17th c., 90, 95; 19th c., 140; artificial languages, 151, 165, 339, 340, 343, 352; descriptions, theory of, 30, 176–77, 180, 322, 335; grammar, 39, 47, 59, 62, 70, 151, 341; names, 30, 58, 67; ordinary language analysis, 163, 165, 168, 169, 208, 227, 316, 321, 332, 339, 398, 476; pragmatics, 59, 340; propositions, 38, 63, 132, 353–54, 365; protocal sentences, 164; self-predication, 28, 30; semantics, 58–59, 132, 160, 168, 317, 322, 323, 333, 340, 343, 352, 362; suppositions, 132; syntactics, 59, 151, 153, 206, 333, 340, 352; terms, 38, 63, 509; universal language, 89. See also Dialectic; Dialogue; Language, philosophy of; Logic; Presuppositions; Rhetoric.
Logical positivism, 128, 130–31, 151, 152–54, 158, 178, 180, 199, 200, 203, 220, 226, 233–34, 322, 323, 328, 350, 351, 353, 362, 380, 392, 411, 415–16, 438, 476; bibliography, 155 (Ayer, ed.); see also Positivism
Lombard, Peter, 54, 66
Lorenzer, Alfred, 298
Lotze, Rudolf Hermann, 133, 380
Louvain, University of, 61
Love, 275, 394; failure of, 21; friendly, friendship, 16, 32 (Bolotin), 34; in metaphysics, 148; of objects, 28, 29; theological virtue, 54, 65, 403; vs. hate, 134
Lovejoy, Arthur O., 4, 131, 219
Luce, A. A., 104
Lukács, Georg, 71, 120, 138, 253, 257–58
Łukasiewicz, Jan, 332
Luther, Martin, 54, 96

Mabbott, J. D., 95, 104, 106
McCabe, Herbert, 65
Mace, C. A., 163
Mach, Ernst, 105, 123, 128, 129, 131, 174, 300
Machan, Tibor, 444
Machiavelli, Niccolo, 437, 438, 441
MacIntyre, Alasdaire, 141, 388, 390, 403, 476, 477, 486
Mackey, Louis, 266
Mackie, J. L., 393, 401, 419, 420

Mackintosh, D. C., 475
McNeill, William H., 52
McTaggart, John McTaggart Ellis, 81, 148, 161, 166, 174, 182, 186
Madden, Edward H., 414, 419, 478, 485
Magic, hermetic, the occult, 11–12, 70, 71
Maimonides, 57–58
Malcolm, Norman, 155, 204, 315, 316, 319, 362, 363, 367
Malebranche, Nicolas, 80, 101, 106
Mappes, Thomas A., 405
Marcel, Gabriel, 157, 263–64, 274–75, 276, 298, 514; bibliography, 503, 514
Marcus, Ruth Barcan, 333, 341
Marcuse, Herbert, 139, 223, 253, 299
Marheineke, Philipp Karl, 136
Maritain, Jacques, 127, 350, 460, 492, 493
Mark, Thomas, 87
Markus, R. A., 56
Martin, Jane Roland, 495, 497
Marx, Karl, 125, 248–56; action, 157, 254; alienation, 252–54; biography, 248–54; dialectical materialism, 251, 252, 254; Feuerbach and, 126, 248, 253; Hegel and, 137, 139, 248, 249, 251–53, 299; history, 254, 255, 429; humanism, 250, 253, 255; individualist themes, 250, 252–55; logic, 254–55; philosophy, critique of, 251; positivism, 129; socio-economic-political views, 201, 248–55, 437; theory and practice, 39, 255; value theory, 379; see also Marxism
Marxism, Marxists, 156, 158, 199, 223, 251, 253, 256–61, 276, 292, 298, 299, 373, 442, 443, 493–94; Bolshevism, 178; critique by Popper, 202; critique of linguistic philosophy, 170; Dewey and, 245; ethics, 388; First International, 251; French existential, 258–60, 292; German, 260, 298, 299; Hegel and, 137, 139; in critical theory, 263; interpretation of Renaissance man, 71; Leninist views, 250, 251, 253; Maoist views, 250; materialism, 356, see also Materialism
Mascall, E. L., 474
Masterman, Margaret, 413
Masters, Roger, 112, 113
Materialism, 25, 87, 92, 102, 130, 178, 226, 263, 287, 321, 352, 355, 365, 366; critiques of, 127, 147, 212, 242,

243; immaterialism, 106; Marxian, Marxist, dialectical, 249, 251, 252, 254–55

Mathematics, 115, 211, 237; arithmetic, 59; early modern, 80, 83, 102, 175; geometry, 11, 13, 59, 144, 211; medieval, 59; models, 131; universal algebra, 210–11. *See also* Frege; Logic; Mathematics, philosophy of; Russell; Whitehead.

Mathematics, philosophy of, 132, 146, 153, 175, 177–78, 180–81, 204, 206, 211, 288, 329, 330, 416

Matter, 41, 102, 178; *see also* Materialism; Mind, philosophy of

Maxwell, James Clerk, 144

Mead, George Herbert, 221, 232–33, 234 (Scheffler), 246–47, 361

Medieval philosophy, 51–69; basic studies (trivium), 59; Eastern Platonist tradition, 56; emergence of, 53; ethics, 59; handmaid to theology, 55, 62–63; in the Renaissance and Reformation, 70; influence of Augustine's theory of signs, 59; "mind" of the Middle Ages, 51; natural philosophy, 59; scholastic logic, 58; science and, 68 (Moody). *See also* Christianity; Islamic thought; Jewish thought; Nominalism; Scholasticism.

Mehlberg, Henryk, 417

Meinong, Alexius, 123, 131–32, 175, 176, 288, 380, 513

Melanchthon, Philip, 71, 78

Melden, A. I., 401, 485

Memory, 316, 367; mnemonics, 43

Mendelssohn, Moses, 99

Mercier, Desiré, 61

Merlan, Philip, 49, 56

Merleau-Ponty, Maurice, 291–93; bibliography, 503; existential phenomenology, 263, 264, 291–93; influence of, 158, 292, 299, 320; Sartre and, 259, 276, 292; socio-political views, 258–59, 292–93

Mersenne, Père Marin, 84, 129

Metaphor, 16, 343, 344, 466

Metaphysics, 51, 70, 169, 188, 207, 235, 236, 240, 251, 268, 281, 289, 314–16, 318, 348–60, 367, 382, 473, 475–76, 497; 17th c., 80–81, 87, 90, 95, 102; 18th c., 100–3, 107, 114, 117; 19th c., 127, 130, 143–44, 146–48; absolute presuppositions, analysis of,

192, 196, 353, *see also* Presuppositions; analogy in, 65; appearance vs. reality, 49; as nonsense, 129, 153, 161, 207; based on logic, 89, 163, 205, 328, 416; constructivist, 130, 133, 206, 207, 352; cosmology, 269, 355; critical, 152, 200; degrees of reality, 29, 148; descriptive, 165, 169, 356; existential-phenomenologist, 351; first principles, 40, 83, 348–49; history of, 9, 348–52; in late medieval curriculum, 59; lack of, in early scholastics, 63; late scholastic, 51, 63–67, 74; logical tools for, 58–59; modal concepts, 356; "nature," 186, 189, 212; necessity, 356; nonexistent objects, 356; ontology, 132, 140, 180, 187, 221, 226–28, 276, 278, 283, 298, 332, 348–50; process cosmology, 211–14, 350, 352; relations, 148, 349; speculative, 349–52, 355; spiritual, 380; systems, 3, 166; theological, 348, 349, 351; vs. theological order, 66; world hypotheses, 349. *See also* Aristotle; Atomism; Idealism; Identity; Individual; Naturalism; Nominalism; Personalism; Realism.

Method, philosophical: 17th c., 77–79; analogy, 15, 56, 65; analytical, 71, 75, 116, 164–65, 187, *see also* Analytic philosophy; analytics, *see* Aristotle; antinomies, 116; appeal to concrete evidence, 37, 39, 70, 78, *see also* Empiricism; architechtonic, 115, 120; argument, 3, 20, 22, 37, 40, 47, 63, 164–65, 263; Aristotelian "topics," 39–40; axiomatic, 83; canonics, 60; Cartesian, 80, 89; certainty, quest for, 75, 175, 201, *see also* Certainty; clarifying commentary, 308; classification, systematic, 34; comparative analysis, 165; critique, 69–70, 97, 200–1, 221; deductive, 78; definition, 19, 20, 38, 164; disagreement, disputation, objections, 3, 21–22, 61, 102; distinction-making, 15; division, 19; doubt, 63, *see also* Skepticism; elenchus (Socratic), 19; experiment, 74; foundational critique of the disciplines, 308, 313; genetic, 288; geometric, 86, 420; hermeneutic phenomenology, 278; historical, 37, 39, 40, 166, 176, 193, 294, 353; hypotheses, 19; joint inquiry, 4–5; "lectures," 61; mathematically patterned explanation, 75, *see also* Logic; "Ockham's razor," 67; opposition to external authority, 76; polarity, 14; predicaments, investigation of, 355; problem-solving and discovery, 40, 165, 201, 216, 275, 354; psychological, 242–43; questioning, 5, 20, 40, 61, 193, 353; reading, intelligent, 375; reconstruction in (or by), 6 (Dewey), 164, 177, 211, 222, 244, 357; reductionist, 40, 75, 175, 206, 286, 288, 335; resolution and composition, 75; rhetorical, 60, 77, *see also* Rhetoric; self-reflection, 74, 268, *see also* Existential thought; systematic, holistic, 86, 93, 97, 140, 145, 306, 308; systematics, system-building, 77, 117, 192, 200, 221, 237, 239, 240, 243; transcendental argument, 114, *see also* Transcendental; use of reason to defend reason, 82, *see also* Reason. *See also* Analytic philosophy; Atomism; Critical theory; Dialectic; Dialogue; Empiricism; Hegel; Hegelians; Hermeneutical philosophy; Hermeneutics; Historicism; Humanism; Idealism; Ideology critique; Linguistic philosophy; Logic; Logical positivism; Marxism; Naturalism; Nominalism; Perennial philosophy; Personalism; Phenomenology; Positivism; Pragmatism; Rationalism; Realism; Scholasticism; Science; Skepticism; World views.

Metz, J. B., 441
Michelet, Karl, 136, 137
Mill, James, 145
Mill, John Stuart, 144–46, 162, 318; education, 146; ethics, utilitarianism, 143–46, 391, 394, 402, 437–39; Husserl's use of, 289; logic, 77, 128, 329; mind, 363; positivism, 127–29, 314; women, 145, 438
Mind, philosophy of, 81, 82, 103, 108, 162, 167–68, 188, 190, 206, 228, 296, 315, 354, 361–71, 373, 401, 458, 466, 483; affective states, emotions, 111, 131, 133–34, 364, 367, 368, 380; bibliography, 505; cybernetics, 366; desire, 383; dreaming, 367; functionalism, 365–66; general theories, 361, 364, 366, 368; Hellenistic views, 49 (Merlan); history of, 361–63; judging, 364, 380–81; mind and body, 81–82, 313, 354, 355, 361, 363, 364, 366;

motivation, 373, 375, 486; other minds, 114, 167, 168, 208, 315, 362; philosophical psychology, 163, 186, 362; physicalism, 364, 365; predicting and deciding, 364, 383; privacy, 364; representational theory, 365; self-deception, 367; thinking, 39, 364, 368; willing, 364, 368, 380. *See also* Action; Freedom; Identity: Individual; Intentionality; Judgment; Language; Materialism; Memory; Psychology; Will.
Mind (periodical), 162, 185, 186, 242
Mirecourt, Jean de, 129
Mohammed, 56
Moltmann, Jürgen, 441
Monist (periodical), 66, 87, 177, 234, 241, 311, 340, 341, 366, 388, 403, 430, 431, 440, 443, 446, 467, 478, 484, 492
Moore, G. E., 181–88, 514; analytic philosophy, 155, 161–63, 339, 362; atomism, 192; Bell and, 461–62; Berkeley, on, 104; bibliography, 514; biography, 161–63, 166–67, 181–87, 204, 206, 223, 410, 514; common sense, 164, 181, 316; epistemology, 187; ethics, 144, 183, 185–87, 387–88, 402; idealism, and critique of, 146, 148, 162, 186; judgment, 162; Meinong, on, 132, 288; Platonist, 25; realism, 131, 161–63, 181; Russell and, 161–63, 175, 182–85; skepticism, 182; synthetic a priori, 183
Morality, 385, 394–96, 436, 441; 17th c., 76; early Christian, 53; early Presocratic, 11; idealistic objects in, 30; moral education, 496; "moral point of view," 396, 401; virtues, 54, 65, 402–3; *see also* Ethics
Moravcsik, Julius, 29–30, 36–38, 41, 44, 341
More, Henry, 76
More, Paul Elmer, 45
Morgenbesser, Sidney, 245, 414
Morris, Charles W., 153, 233, 247, 340, 343, 361, 415
Morris, George Sylvester, 242
Mounce, H. O., 397
Mumford, Lewis, 179, 228
Münsterberg, Hugo, 380
Mysteries vs. problems, 355
Mysticism, mystics, 350, 475, 479; anti-mystics, 25; bibliography, 504; Plato, 28

Naess, Arne, 160, 317
Nagel, Ernest, 146, 153, 221, 225, 226, 315, 320, 330, 352, 414, 417, 420
Nagel, Thomas, 397, 399, 441
National Socialism, Nazism, 124, 189, 281
Natural law, *see* Ethics
Natural philosophy, *see* Science
Naturalism, naturalists, 126, 129, 157, 217, 218, 221, 224–26, 233, 287, 319–20, 349, 355, 431; late medieval, 63; nonnaturalism, 391, *see also* Ethics: intuitionism
Nature, 59, 63, 212, 353, *see also* Science
Necessity, 44, *see also* Truth
Nelson, Leonard, 152
Neo-Kantians, 123, 128, 133, 152, 157, 203, 280, 298, 313, 314, 410
Neoplatonism, 25, 36, 48–49; Albert the Great's use of, 64; Augustine's use of, 56; later, 56; *see also* Plotinus
Neurath, Otto, 153, 154, 323, 415, 421
Newton, Isaac (and Newtonian views), 74, 79, 105, 108, 116, 117, 119, 143, 211, 414
Nicholas of Cusa, 243, 272
Niebuhr, Barthold Georg, 430
Niebuhr, Reinhold, 390
Nietzsche, Friedrich, 6 (Kaufmann), 124, 125, 267–71; biography, 243, 267–68; ethics and politics, 269–70, 390, 394; existentialism and, 262, 263, 272, 274, 280, 300; nihilism, 269, 398; values, transvaluation of, 379–80
Nihilism, 103, 269, 281, 392, 398
Nominalism, 25, 66–67, 78, 92, 128–29, 130, 143, 330, 334, 352, 415
Northrop, F. S. C., 219, 221
Nussbaum, Martha Craven, 37, 46

Objectivity, 95, 201, 420, 431, 460; and subjectivity, 129, 174, 264, 276, 281, 288, 289, 299, 397–98, 404, 416
Ockham, William of, 25, 52, 61, 63, 65–67, 129, 143, 220
O'Connor, D. J., 9, 65, 94, 323, 376, 388, 492
Oman, John, 473
Ordinary language analysis, *see* Language, philosophy of; Logic and language
Origen, 25
Osborne, Harold, 381, 460, 461, 463

Otto, Rudolf, 473
Oxford, University of, 52, 61, 63–64, 66, 147–48, 153, 165–69, 186, 188, 195, 308–9, 339

Paley, William, 399
Palmer, George Herbert, 224
Pantheism Controversy, 86
Pap, Arthur, 315, 322, 417, 418
Paris, University of, 64, 65, 129
Parker, DeWitt H., 221, 381, 462
Parkinson, G. H. R., 87
Parmenides, 14, 16, 279
Pascal, Blaise, 78, 83–85, 101, 120, 273
Pascal, Fania, 204
Passmore, John A., 4, 6, 9, 108, 220, 308, 331, 430
Patrizi, Francesco, 70
Peano, Guiseppe, 175, 332
Pears, David, 37, 177, 180, 208, 354, 363, 364
Peckham, John, 64
Peirce, Charles Sanders, 218, 219, 221, 233, 234 (Ayer, Moore, Scheffler), 237–41, 300; action, 157, 373; bibliography, 241 (Moore); biography, 237–39; categories, 240; Duns Scotus, 65, 237, 240; epistemology, 240; James and, 235, 238, 239, 323; logic, 237–40, 242; mind, 361; pragmatist, 217, 232–34, 236, 237–41, 247, 323, 335; religion, 473; science, 239, 240; signs, theory of, 234, 240
Pennock, J. Roland, 92, 441, 443
Pepper, Stephen C., 221, 349, 381, 462
Perception and sensation, 104, 167, 168, 291, 315, 318–21, 355
Perennial philosophy, 4, 61, 105, 493
Periodicals and serials, 126, 136, 166, 171, 185, 195, 217, 218, 239, 242, 249, 287, 291, 310, 351, 441, 463, 492, 513–15; *see also* Mind; *Monist*
Perry, Ralph Barton, 219, 221, 236, 381, 386, 391, 395
Personalism, 221, 225, 475
Persons, 82, 267, 274, 294, 349, 354, 367; personality theory, 485. *See also* Existential thought; Individual; Personalism; Self.
Pessimism, 127, 145
Peters, R. S., 93, 373, 440, 485, 492–96
Petrarch, 70
Phalén, Adolf, 159

Phenomenalist thought (epistemology), 103–5, 128, 131, 285, 315, 351
Phenomenology, phenomenologists, 158, 170, 223, 259, 262, 276, 281, 285–93, 314, 351, 355, 357, 366, 376, 402, 410, 432, 465, 494; definitions, 130–31; descriptive, 131; Hegel's, 136–39; James's, 236
Phillips, D. Z., 397, 475, 476
Philo, 56
Philosophers, 5; middle-range and para-philosophers, 101. *See also* Autobiography; Biography.
Philosophes, 97–98
Philosophy: Anglo-American emphasis, 150; areas, core and bridge, 306–7; areas, sum-up of core, 385–86; as art form, 157; as psychology, 242; as science, 28, 40–41, 313–14, *see also* Science; as social expression, 7 (Levi), 232–34; as theory of education, 244, 491; becoming a speciality, 47; children, for, 311; "contemporary," 82, 157, 158–59, 305–12; cultural and biographical factors, 4; end of, 282; general, 158–59, 305–6; "isms," 22, 231, 351–52, 492–93; Marx's opposition to, 251; "modern," 67, 69, 71, 74, 75, 80, 94, 101; "movements," 231; "philosophy of life," 309; place in curricula, 60; pluralism in, 33 (Rescher); relations to other disciplines, 214, 307–10, 314; style, 309; terminology, 89, 508–11; tradition and development in, 4. *See also* African philosophy; American philosophy; British philosophy; Cambridge; Continental European philosophy; Eastern thought; French philosophy; German philosophy; Harvard; History of philosophy; Latin American philosophy; Method; Oxford; Polish philosophy; Scandinavian philosophy; Viennese philosophy; Women.
Philosophy, 17th century, 43, 74–96, 97; British, 74, 76–79; French, 74; middle-class authority, 78; rise of philosophical rhetoric, 59; scholasticism, 74; theology and religion, 75–76
Philosophy, 18th century, 97–122; French Enlightenment, 98, 110, 129
Philosophy, 19th century, 123–49
Physics, 47, 79, 102, 117, 127, 131, 144, 210–11, 334, 414, 417, 421; New-

tonian, 175, *see also* Newton; psychophysics, 131; relativity, 178, 212; vacuum, 83; vision, theory of, 105; *see also* Science
Physiologoi, 13
Piaget, Jean, 496
Pickles, William, 113
Pico della Mirandola, 70
Plantinga, Alvin, 322, 356, 473, 477–79
Plato, 21–33, 49, 105, 167, 192, 223, 228, 513; 19th–20th c. idealism and, 146; Academy, 23, 26–27, 33–34, 42, 47, 48; aesthetics, 31, 460; analogy in, 15–16; biography, 23, 26–28; cosmology, 13, 15; definition, 38–39; dialectic, 26–28, 31, 353; dialogue, 28, 31; Dionysius (kings), 27; division, method of, 15, 38; dualism, 25; education, 31; epistemology, 31; eristics, 26, 28; ethics and morality, 30–31, 399; *Euthyphro*, 23, 31 (Allen); forms, theory of, 22–30, 38, 41, 349, 356; "genesis" theme, 41; German tr., 125, 294; *Gorgias*, 23, 32 (Dilman), 452; imagery, use of, 15; law, 452; *Laws*, 23, 27, 31; *Letters*, 27; love, 28–29; *Lysis*, 23, 32 (Bolotin); mathematics, 25, 40; *Meno*, 23, 318, 320; mind, 363; Neoplatonists, on, 48; Old Testament and, 53; Olympic games, 27; opposites, 15; *Phaedo*, 23, 26; *Philebus*, 23, 30, 32 (Gosling); politics, 26, 30, 31, 201, 202, 437; religious thought, 31, 472; *Republic*, 23, 26–27, 438, 491; rhetoric, 60; Socratic dialogues, 18–21, 26, 30; *Sophist*, 15, 23, 31; *Statesman*, 23, 31; theology, 13; *Theaetetus*, 23, 31; *Timaeus*, 13, 23, 26; "unity" thesis, 28, 45; virtues, 54; women, 438; writings, chronology of, 23, 29; writings, transmission of, 34. *See also* Neoplatonism; Platonism.
Platonism, 22, 37, 207; 17th c., 76, 84; 18th c., 104; Cambridge Platonists, 76, 98; Middle Platonists, 49 (Dillon); Renaissance, 71
Plotinus, 25, 48, 49 (Armstrong), 56
Polanyi, Michael, 158, 201, 319, 320, 404, 411, 416, 418, 420
Polin, Raymond, 429
Polish philosophy, 159, 258
Politics, *see* Social-political philosophy
Pomponazzi, Pietro, 70
Popkin, Richard, 72, 87, 220, 320

Popper, Karl, 198–203, 514; Berkeley, on, 105, 106; bibliography, 203 (Levinson), 514; biography, 166, 198–200, 202, 514; historicism, 198, 201, 202, 430; logic, 201; metaphysics, 200; psychology, 199; science and logical positivism, 154, 165, 198–202, 410, 411, 413, 415–16, 418; socio-political views, 198, 202, 439
Porphyry, 62
Positivism, 123, 125, 126–30, 267, 280, 298, 299–300, 314, 350, 352, 353, 416, 418, 420, 421, 431, 453, 455; *see also* Logical positivism
Postal, Paul, 342
Potts, Timothy, 62
Practical reasoning, 375, 399, 403–5, 455
Pragmatism, 130, 155, 156–57, 196, 216, 221, 223, 227, 231–47, 268, 314, 323, 335, 343, 355, 361, 373, 391, 410, 433, 446, 475, 493
Prall, David, 381, 462
Praxis, 138, 373
Presocratics, 11–18; archaic mind, 16; cosmology, 11–14; definition, 12; development in, 13; "genesis" theme, 41; "infinity" theme, 13; methods, 14–16; "one and the many" theme, 13
Presuppositions, 4, 20, 83, 192, 196, 288, 289, 328, 335, 343, 353–54, 357
Price, H. H., 165, 318, 477, 479
Prichard, H. A., 37, 131, 162, 165, 167, 394, 397, 402–3
Probability, 76, 110 (Stove), 154, 331, 335, 418–20
Progress, idea of, 98, 118, 233, 258, 267
Protagoras, 20, 28
Psychoanalysis, 205, 207, 297–300, 343, 352, 362, 402, 416, 472, 483–87, 496; interpretation by philosophers, 5, 103, 156, 485–87; *see also* Freud
Psychology, 97, 131, 186, 199, 219, 273, 291, 295, 361, 368, 373, 374, 377, 383, 393, 401, 403, 405, 472, 496; behaviorist, 224, 264, 365, 374, 402, 494, 496; cognitive, 365, 484; descriptive, 131, 262, 288, 290, 293, 296; Gestalt, 199, 288, 292, 319, 485; humanistic, 264, 267; psychobiology, 366; psychologism, 289; psychophysics, 131. *See also* Action; Ethics: moral psychology; Mind; Psychoanalysis; Psychology, philosophy of.

Psychology, philosophy of, 194, 206, 363, 445, 483–89; explanation, 484; motivation, 98, 373, 375, 486; science of subjective spirit, 140; social aspects, 484; therapy, 484. *See also* Mind, philosophy of; Psychoanalysis; Psychology; Self.
Ptolemy, 13
Putnam, Hilary, 329, 343, 415, 418
Pyrrho of Elis, 48
Pythagoreans, 14

Questioning, *see* Method, philosophical
Quine, Willard Van Orman, 155, 223, 227–28, 415, 421, 514; bibliography, 514; biography, 332, 514; epistemology, 315, 318, 321, 322, 412; logic, 227, 329–30, 332, 352; logical positivism, 153, 166
Quinton, Anthony, 349, 355, 356, 388

Rachels, James, 405
Radhakrishnan, Sarvepalli, 157, 514
Ramsey, F. P., 323
Ramus, Peter, 71, 77, 78
Randall, John Herman, 9, 37, 221, 431
Ranke, Leopold von, 430
Rationalism, 75, 91, 97, 116, 192, 221, 263, 264, 271, 292, 294, 323, 342, 351, 355, 398, 475; and empiricism, 101, 108, 224–25
Rawls, John, 393, 401, 403, 442, 444, 457
Raz, Joseph, 405, 444, 454–55, 457
Realism, 123, 130–33, 137, 162, 174, 181, 189, 200, 217, 218–19, 221, 224–25, 288, 333, 350–52, 355, 362, 363, 418, 421, 456; late medieval, 66; Oxford, 37, 162, 165, 189; Platonic, 22, 132
Reason, rationality, modern views of, 70, 74, 97, 114, 125, 212, 225, 263–64, 323, 417, 487; history of reason, 120
Redpath, Theodore, 187
Reformation thought, 69–73; and beyond, 54; and English Renaissance, 78; criteria for knowledge, 77; scholars, types of, 70; theological inquiry, 70–72
Reichenbach, Hans, 153, 154, 411, 414, 417
Reid, Thomas, 143
Relativism, 189, 202, 255, 257, 324, 398–99, 429

Religion: 17th c., 76, 79 (Willey), 83–84, 85, 87; 18th c., 97, 111, 117–18, 472; existentialism and, 264, 265, 473; faith, 118, 272, 475, 477, 478; hope, 117, 275, 478, 479; humanist, liberal and skeptical critiques, 107, 126–27, 242–43, 249, 473, 478–79; language of, 476, 479; nature of, 118, 126, 471–72; prayer, worship, 475, 479; rational speculation and, 11–12, 76, 84, 136, 473, 479; source in moral conscience, 110, 114; toleration, 94; world religions, 479, *see also* Eastern thought. *See also* God; Mysticism; Religion, philosophy of; Theology.
Religion, philosophy of, 51, 85, 100, 107, 114, 118, 124, 157, 178–79, 188–90, 196, 212, 265, 316, 351, 471–82; bibliography, 505, 508; miracles, 479; religious experience, 473, 475, 479; toleration, 76. *See also* Christianity; Christian philosophy; Deism; God; Immortality; Islamic thought; Jewish thought; Mysticism; Religion; Scholasticism; Theology.
Renaissance thought, 69–73; education, 60; effect in Bible interpretation, 54; English, 77–79; history of interpretations of, 72 (Kristeller); Hermetics, 43; interpretation of texts, 69; Italian, 70–71
Rescher, Nicholas, 22, 57, 90, 240, 323, 332, 383, 399, 415
Rhetoric, 3, 19, 27, 34, 35, 39, 48, 52, 58, 309, 336; 17th c., 77–78; 18th c., 98; history of, 59; in medieval curriculum, 59; in the Christian East, 60; Renaissance-Reformation, 70, 71; technical, sophistic and philosophical, 59; theory of communication, 78, 300
Richard of Middleton, 64
Rickert, Heinrich, 133, 280, 380
Ricoeur, Paul, 297–99, 376, 410, 442, 486
Rights: children's, 447; human, 118, 400–1, 440, 442, 443; property, 443; student, 440
Romantic thought, 100, 110, 126, 138, 262, 294, 368, 495
Rorty, Richard, 5, 14, 154–55, 223, 308, 321, 323, 324, 340, 415, 430, 431
Rosenkranz, Karl, 163
Rosenzweig, Franz, 67 (Guttmann), 157, 271, 473

Ross, W. D., 24, 36, 387, 388, 392, 394, 397, 402
Rossi, Pietro, 429
Rousseau, Jean-Jacques, 93, 98, 110–13, 117, 432, 437, 438, 492, 495
Royce, Josiah, 147, 217–19, 221, 224, 242, 274, 308, 473, 475
Rudner, Richard, 418, 446
Ruether, Rosemary, 441
Ruge, Arnold, 126, 136, 249
Ruggiero, Guido de, 193, 194
Ruskin, John, 190–94
Russell, Bertrand, 19, 152, 153, 172–81, 199, 513, 514; analytic philosophy, 153, 161–64, 314, 339, 341; atomist metaphysics, 163–64, 174, 175, 177, 184, 192; bibliography, 181 (Roberts), 514; biography, 172–79, 514; certainty, quest for, 175; education, 178, 492; epistemology, 163, 176, 178–80, 314, 318–19; ethics, 390; history of philosophy, 8, 178; idealism, critique of, 146, 148; Leibniz, 90; linguistic philosophy, 169–70, 179, 339; logic and mathematics, 131, 132, 151, 162–63, 173, 175, 176, 180 181, 204; logical positivism, 180; Meinong, 288; mind and matter, 157, 177, 178, 363; Moore and, 161–63, 175, 182–85; Platonist, 25; realism, 131, 157, 174; religion, 178, 179, 473; science, 410; social-political thought, 176–80, 437; Whitehead and, 173, 175–76, 210–211; Wittgenstein and, 163, 175–79, 184, 204–6, 208; writings, 176–79
Ryle, Gilbert, 165–67, 169–70, 187, 453; bibliography, 172 (Wood); dilemmas, 329; linguistic philosophy, 155, 165, 167, 169, 342, 352; logical positivism, 153; Meinong, 132; mind, 167, 362–64; Plato, 26–28; Wittgenstein and, 166

Salmon, Wesley, 14, 335, 420, 421, 477
Sandkühler, Hans Jörg, 298
Santayana, George, 217–19, 221, 226–27, 242, 349, 514; bibliography, 503, 514
Sartorius, Rolf, 444
Sartre, Jean-Paul, 264, 275–77, 514; action, 157, 373; bibliography, 503, 514; ethics, 276–77, 390, 392; existentialism, 157, 263–64, 275–77; Marcel on, 274–75; Merleau-Ponty

and, 259, 276, 292; phenomenological ontology, 275–76, 283, 289; socio-political views, 258–60, 276, 292
Scandinavian philosophy, 154, 159–60, 265
Scanlon, T. M., 441
Schacht, Richard, 125, 141
Scheler, Max, 157, 380, 386, 391, 402, 439, 445; bibliography, 134 (Frings, ed.)
Schelling, Friedrich Wilhelm Joseph, 123, 137, 138, 147, 274, 350
Schenkel, Daniel, 125
Schilpp, Paul Arthur, 152, 154, 157, 163, 178, 183, 202, 211, 223, 224, 226, 227, 245, 271, 273, 276, 416, 514
Schleiermacher, Friedrich, 125–27, 262, 293–96, 471–72; bibliography, 125 (Tice); biography, 99, 125, 126, 136, 294, 296; Dewey and, 242; dialectic, 5, 125, 262, 294, 295; Dilthey and, 296–97; Hegel and, 126, 136–38, 294; hermeneutics, 5, 123, 125, 262, 293–97, 430; idealism, 125, 137; Plato, 23, 25, 125, 294; religion, 118, 125, 294, 471–72, 482; theology, 7, 58, 243, 294–95, 474, 478–79
Schlick, Moritz, 153, 155
Scholasticism, 52, 60–67; 12th–13th c., 63–65; 14th c., 65–67; 17th c., 74, 80, 88; Aristotle in, 61–62; Augustinian and Averroist, 62; definitions, 60–61; dialectic, 62; Dominicans, 61, 64; early, 55, 58, 62–63; Franciscans, 52, 61, 63–65; harvesting of, for "modern" purposes, 69–70; lectures and disputation, 61; logic, 58–59, 77; opposition to, 74; philosophy, distinct, 61; reemergence, 19th c., 61; Renaissance and Reformation, 70–71, 77; theology, 62; treatises and commentaries, 61
Schopenhauer, Arthur, 101, 123, 126–27, 130, 131, 207, 243, 473, 514
Science: 17th c., 13, 83, 105; 18th c., 100, 104–5; 19th c., 141, 212; a priori vs. a posteriori, 89; and society, 179; Aquinas, 104; Aristotle, 37–41; artificial constructs in, 103; cultural, human, 296; dioptric, 80; empirical investigation and, 41; falsifiability, 83, 200, 202, 416, 418; Hellenistic, 47–48; high and low, 76; ideological misuses of, 130; Islamic, 57; medieval, 68

(Moody); metaphysical foundations of, 74; meteors, 80; modern world and, 212; motion, 93, 105, 210; natural philosophy, 59, 70; "natural" science, 63, 97, 115, 118–19, 411, 417–18, 421, 422; Royal Society, 84; unity of, 97, 128, 129, 415, 421–22. See also Astronomy; Biology; Physics; Psychology; Science, philosophy of; Social-political philosophy: social sciences.
Science, philosophy of, 85, 119, 129, 131, 153–54, 189, 190, 201–2, 212, 224, 228, 240, 286, 300, 314, 315, 321, 330–31, 354, 364, 410–27, 497; anomalies, 420; change and revolution, 410–13, 418, 421; concept formation, 421; "covering laws," 420, 431; explanation, 417–21; history of, 414–17; holistic approaches, 415, 445–46; information and inference, 421; logical-empirical approach, 45, 410–11, 415, 417; "research programs," 416, 418; simplicity, 420. See also Epistemology; Induction; Positivism; Probability.
Scottish philosophy, 143, 144; see also Hume; Reid
Scriven, Michael, 362, 418, 485
Sedley, David, 47
Segondo, J. L., 441
Self, 114, 148, 354, 364, 367, 391, 484, 486. See also Ethics: self-realization; Identity; Individual; Persons; Psychology.
Sellars, Roy Wood, 219, 221, 224, 226, 227
Sellars, Wilfrid S., 155, 223, 227, 318, 321, 355, 415, 419
Shaftesbury, Earl of (first), 94, 399
Shapere, Dudley, 301 (Habermas), 414, 415, 418
Shaull, Richard, 441
Sheehan, Peter, 65
Sheldon-Williams, I. P., 56
Shklar, Judith, 112, 113
Sidgwick, Henry, 144, 146, 147, 161–62, 184, 388, 391, 394, 401, 402
Simmel, Georg, 272
Skepticism, skeptics, 25, 35, 47, 76–77, 167, 178, 182, 184, 197, 226, 315–17, 419, 429, 431, 464, 474, 478; 17th c., 76–77, 81, 84, 92; 18th c., 98, 101, 102, 107, 114–15; Academic, 47–48; constructive, 77; Hellenistic,

Subject Index

50 (Schofield, Stough); moral, 392, 397, 399; Pyrrhonian, 48, 77; radical doubt, 81, 316–18; Renaissance, 70, 72, 320
Smart, J. J. C., 355, 363, 366
Smith, Adam, 379, 397
Smith, J. A., 165
Smith, John, 219, 222, 227, 475
Smyth, Newman, 242
Social-political philosophy, politics, social thought, 34, 145, 188, 190, 202, 209, 227, 242, 257, 269, 272, 289, 292, 299, 309, 311, 316, 368, 377, 386, 401, 436–51, 497; 17th c., 86, 87, 91–93, 94–95, 438; 18th c., 97–98, 108–9, 110–13, 438; 19th c., 126, 128, 139, 147–48, 296, 438; citizen, the, 65; civil disobedience, 440–41, 457; classification, 400–1; conservative, 112; democracy, 112, 145, 243–44, 386, 437, 443; equality, egalitarian views, 112, 440, 443–44; explanation and prediction, 445; foreign policy, 446; formalist, 439; history of, 437–41; holistic approaches, 445–46; industrial civilization, 178; justice, 29, 110, 440–45; liberal, 94, 110, 147, 244, 250, 438; liberty, political freedom, 92,145, 177, 178, 440, 442–45; Marxian, Marxist, 248–61, 292; natural rights, 438, see also Ethics: natural law; peace, 178; planning, 447, 458; political argument, 440, 441; political violence, 441; power, 179; practical uses, 446–47; Renaissance-Reformation, 438; social sciences, sociology, 209, 246–47, 286, 292–93, 374, 382, 410, 421, 422, 431, 442, 444–46; social self, "life-world," 246, 286, 292; socialism, 128, 133, 177; sociology of knowledge, 439; theological views, 441; toleration, 76, 94; utilitarian, 144–46, 439, 440, 442, 453, see also Ethics: utilitarianism; utopian views, 112, 129; Zionism, 272. See also Anthropology; Economics; Ethics; History; Marxism; Rights; Teleological concepts.
Social sciences, sociology, see Social-political philosophy
Socrates, 18–21, 26–29, 33, 513
Soelle, Dorothee, 441
Solipcism, 103
Sophists, 19, 33, 452; sophistic tricks, 40

Soul, 363; immortality of, 55; power of thinking in, 97; psyche, 16. See also Mind, philosophy of; Psychology; Self.
Spencer, Herbert, 129, 243, 429, 444
Spengler, Oswald, 429, 438
Spinoza, Baruch, 77, 78, 80, 85–88, 101, 207, 242, 323, 397, 473; bibliography, 88 (Freeman)
Stace, W. T., 350, 473, 475
Stebbing, Susan, 153, 163
Steere, Douglas, 475
Stenius, Erik, 159, 210
Stevenson, Charles L., 381, 387, 390, 392
Stich, Stephen, 318, 366
Stirner, Max, 137
Stoics, 11, 33, 35, 47, 48; causation, 48; cosmology, 48; ethics, 394; logic, 21, 38, 58, 329; rhetoric, 60; Roman law and, 452; substance language, 42
Stout, A. K., 82
Stout, G. F., 161, 184, 186
Strauss, David Friedrich, 126, 136
Strawson, P. F., 115, 154, 165, 169, 180, 323, 332, 342, 343, 356, 364
Structuralism, 259, 298, 343
Strumpf, Carl, 285, 288
Subjectivity, see Objectivity
Substance, 35, 40–42, 103, 283, 349, 355–56; mind and extension, 82; pre-established harmony, 89; Spinoza, 86–87
Suffering, 134
Suppes, Patrick, C., 414, 415, 418
Swain, Marshall, 318, 319
Symbols, myths, 152, 212, 246, 298, 310, 344, 365, 466–67

Tarski, Alfred, 153, 322, 323, 332, 414
Taylor, A. E., 92–93
Taylor, Charles, 139, 141
Taylor, Henry Osborne, 51
Taylor, Paul W., 381
Teleological concepts, 114, 367, 374, 419, 420, 428, 446, see also Ethics
Telesio, Bernardino, 70
Temple, William, 473
Tennant, F. R., 473
Tennemann, G. W., 120
Tertullian, 58
Thales, 11, 12
Theaetetus, 23
Theology: 17th c., 75–76, 83, 95; 19th c., 124, 402; 19th–20th c. idealism

and, 102, 147, 279; 20th c., 157, 271, 402, 473–74; analogy in, 65; apologetics, 53, 84, 102, 473–74; appeal to experience, 64; biblical, 295, 297; church and ministry, 54, 66; creation, 57, 59; crisis theology, 279; deductive method, 78; divine Logos, 53; emergence of, 53–54; existentialist, 264; faith seeking understanding, 55, 62, 478; first comprehensive exposition of, 63; grace, 54, 59; heresy and disbelief, 58; human perplexity in, 84; Islamic, 56–57; Jewish, 57–58, 157, 271; law and, 452; medieval: footnotes to Augustine, 54; mutual influences: Christian, Islamic, Jewish, 57; natural theology, 64, 129, 475, 478; nature, 54; outline of study of, 7 (Schleiermacher), 294; pantheism, 86, 242; philosophical theology, 474, 479; politically oriented, 441; prayer in, 62, 475; predestination, 54, 57; process theology, 476; reason and revelation, 53–54, 58, 64, 66, 83; Renaissance and Reformation, 72; separation of philosophy from, 218, 219, 473–74; sin, 54, 478; successor to pagan philosophy, 54; syntheses, 64–67; systematic, 58; theological virtues, 54, 65, 403; trinity, 54, 62. *See also* Christianity; Deism; Eastern thought; God; Islamic thought; Jewish thought; Religion; Scholasticism.

Theophrastus, 34, 36

Thomas Aquinas, *see* Aquinas; Thomism

Thomas of York, 64

Thomism, neo-Thomism, 8, 62, 64, 65, 135 (Maritain), 157, 170, 269, 350, 351, 388, 391, 460, 478, 493

Tiedemann, Dieterich, 120

Tillich, Paul, 58, 123, 264, 272 (Rome), 350, 351, 357, 474

Time, 114, 180, 281, 354, 421

Tipton, I. C., 106

Tolstoy, Leo, 428

Tooley, Michael, 477

Toulmin, Stephen, 204, 207, 331, 334, 404, 411, 413, 415, 417, 418, 421, 422, 485

Toynbee, Arnold, 429

Transcendental, transcendence, 30, 114–15, 273, 275, 289, 292–93, 294, 349, 380

Troeltsch, Ernst, 429

Truth, 178, 315–16, 322–24, 353; a priori, 167, 177, 234, 235, 322, 333; analytic, 89, 323, 328, *see also* Analytic and synthetic; as linguistic convention, 323; coherence theory, 316, 318, 323; correspondence theory, 320, 322–24, 332, 335; degrees of, 324; necessary vs. contingent, 89, 316, 322, 335, 349, 352; pragmatic views, 232–33; synthetic, 89; synthetic a priori, 114–15, 183

Tufts, James Hayden, 246

Tugendhat, Ernst, 300

Turbayne, Colin Murray, 106, 121

Unamuno, Miguel de, 264

Unconscious, 127, 352, 353, 362, 483, 485–86; awakening from, 16; Berkeley's, 103; pre-6th c. B.C., 11

Universals, 62–63, 147, 315–16, 322, 349, 355–56; medieval controversy, 62–63, 66

Urban, Wilbur Marshall, 221, 288, 379, 475

Urmson, J. O., 37, 163, 167, 171 (Austin), 187, 344 (Austin), 392, 510

Utilitarianism, 144–46; *see also* Ethics; Social-political philosophy

Vaihinger, Hans, 128

Valla, Lorenzo, 70, 78

Value, 45, 109 (Árdal), 128, 206, 233, 263, 299, 343, 355, 379–84, 431, 445, 446, 456, 484; economic value, 252, 379, 382; feeling, 132, 133–34, 153, 380; interest, 235, 381, 382, 386, 394–95, 399, 401; preference, 134, 381, 382; utility, 144; vs. facts, 316, 374, 379–81, 396–97, 437, 446; *see also* Axiology

Vico, Giambattista, 98–100, 101, 111, 193, 428, 430

Viennese philosophy, 153–54, 164, 166, 198–200, 203–5, 415

Virtues, *see* Morality

Vlastos, Gregory, 13, 15, 19, 24, 29, 30, 220; bibliography, 18 (Lee)

Voltaire, 85

Wahl, Jean, 272 (Rome)

Waismann, Friedrich, 151, 153, 157, 167, 341

Walsh, W. H., 4, 115, 121, 140, 197, 354, 388, 431

Walzer, Richard, 56, 57, 69 (Stern)

Ward, James, 161, 182, 186
Warnock, G. J., 104, 162, 163, 323, 388, 395
Warnock, Mary, 263, 276–77, 367, 388, 466
Watkins, J. W. N., 413
Watson, John, 145
Weber, Max, 39
Weil, E., 38, 40
Weiss, Paul, 219, 221, 237, 241, 272 (Rome), 350, 351, 355
Weldon, T. D., 438
Werkmeister, W. H., 30, 115, 120, 286, 382
Westermarck, Edward A., 159, 398
Whewell, William, 145
Whichcote, Benjamin, 76
White, Morton G., 187, 221, 223, 227, 431
Whitehead, Alfred North, 210–15, 514; bibliography, 503, 514; biography, 176, 182, 210–12, 514; education, 212, 492; in America, 210, 217, 218; mathematics and logic, 132, 151, 206, 210–12, 330, 332; Moore and, 184; Platonist, 25; process metaphysics, 157, 162, 166, 192, 211–14, 242, 350–2; religion, 212, 473, 476; Russell and, 173, 175–77, 210–11; science, 212–14, 410; writings, 212–14
Wieman, Henry Nelson, 473–75
Wiener, Philip, 220, 240, 414, 511
Wild, John, 221, 272 (Rome)
Will, 127, 130, 267, 375, 380; *see also* Freedom
Williams, Bernard A., 37, 169, 364, 367, 441
Williams, L. Pearce, 413
Wilson, John, 496
Wilson, John Cook, 37, 146, 162, 167, 189

Wilson, Margaret, 81, 82
Windelband, Wilhelm, 8, 133, 380
Wisdom, John, 153, 155, 163, 362, 485
Wisdom, 41, 44, 354
Wittgenstein, Ludwig, 6 (Kaufmann), 203–10, 286, 514; analytic philosophy, 164–65; anti-positivism, 298; atomism, 151, 164, 174, 175; Augustine, 208; bibliography, 503; biography, 203–6; early philosophy, 164, 177, 204–5, 207, *see also* atomism (above); epistemology, 206, 209, 318; influence of, 43, 298, 315, 335, 341, 342, 352, 398, 402, 410, 417, 463, 475, 477; judgment, 133; later, linguistic philosophy, 165, 205–9, 341; logic and mathematics, 132, 204–6, 209, 332; Meinong, 132; mind, 362–63; non-Platonist, 25; psychology, 205, 206, 484; Rorty's use of, 223; Russell and, 163, 175–79, 184, 204–6, 208; Ryle and, 166, 168; social-political thought, 209, 440; Viennese, 131, 200, 204, 207; writings, 204–6
Wolff, Christian, 89, 97, 117
Wolfson, Harry Austryn, 56, 57, 86
Women, 311, 438
Woodbridge, Frederick J. E., 226, 229 (Delaney)
Woods, M. J., 37
World views, 126–27, 129–30, *see also* Metaphysics
Wright, Chauncey, 218, 219, 221
Wright, Georg Henrik von, 159, 204, 205, 209, 335, 374, 402, 419, 420, 484, 514; bibliography, 514

Zeller, Eduard, 133, 136, 137
Zembaty, Jane S., 405
Zeno, 14